EXPLORER
WESTERN H
1820–

The forbidding mountain complex of the Western Himalayas was second only to darkest Africa as an arena of nineteenth-century exploration. Seduced by the secrets of its lost valleys and the challenge of its ethereal peaks a procession of romantics, spies, scientists and eccentrics trailed up into the unknown. Some never returned, and those who did were discouraged from publishing their precise findings. For the mountains were also Asia's most sensitive frontier. On the whim of a cut-throat chieftain hung peace and war, on the outcome of a skirmish fought by rock climbers empires teetered.

Researching this account of the Western Himalayas was not unlike trying to cross them. No sooner was one mountain system accounted for, than another loomed up ahead; a shaft of light shed on one personality or policy merely encouraged excursions into the shadowy motivations of other protagonists. The book, in short, outgrew the author's resources and threatened the publisher's patience. Like the erstwhile raj of Kashmir with which it principally deals, it had to be partitioned.

Chronologically the first part of the story, which appeared as *When Men and Mountains Meet* (1977), dealt mainly with exploration in territories now under Indian rule while *The Gilgit Game* (1979), the second part, dealt mainly with areas now under Pakistani rule. The division, like that on the ground, was an arbitrary expedient. Happily it is more readily rectified than the UN Ceasefire Line which still bisects the mountains. This volume at last combines the two halves, and so restores the original idea of presenting what was the first, and is still the only, comprehensive narrative of European penetration into the noblest geographical region on earth.

John Keay's recent books include a history of the English East India Company, a narrative introduction to Indonesia and, with Julia Keay, the definitive *Collins Encyclopaedia of Scotland*. He lives in the West Highlands, is married and has four children. He is now writing a new history of India.

BOOKS BY THE SAME AUTHOR

Into India
India Discovered
Eccentric Travellers
Explorers Extraordinary
Highland Drove
The Honourable Company: A History of the English East India Company
Indonesia: From Sabang to Merauke

The Royal Geographical Society's History of World Exploration
(general editor)
The Robinson Book of Exploration (editor)
Collins Encyclopaedia of Scotland (co-editor with Julia Keay)

EXPLORERS OF THE WESTERN HIMALAYAS

1820–1895

JOHN KEAY

John Murray

ALBEMARLE STREET, LONDON

A catalogue record for this book is available from the British Library

ISBN 0-7195-5576 0

Printed and bound in Great Britain by
The University Press, Cambridge

For Christina, Kranti and Rahul
and in memory of
Terence Scott, late of Chitral and Peshawar

Contents

WHEN MEN AND MOUNTAINS MEET

Great things are done when men and mountains meet;
This is not done by jostling in the street.
WILLIAM BLAKE, *Gnomic Verses*

Rope bridge in the Pir Panjal from G. T. Vigne's
Travels in Kashmir, Ladak and Iskardo

Contents

Maps

Illustrations

ENGRAVINGS

ACKNOWLEDGEMENTS

Nos. 1, 17, 18, 19 and 23 are reproduced by kind permission of Christina Noble; No. 2 by courtesy of Mrs. Lee Shuttleworth and Penelope Chetwode; No. 3 from *Joseph Wolff* by H. P. Palmer, London 1935; No. 4 from *Victor Jacquemont* published by the American Philosophical Society, Philadelphia 1960; Nos. 5, 13, 14, 15, 16 and 20 by courtesy of the Royal Geographical Society; No. 6 by courtesy of H. D'O. Vigne Esq.; Nos. 7 and 8 from *Travels in Kashmir* by G. T. Vigne; No. 9 from *A Short Walk in the Hindu Kush* by Eric Newby, published by Hodder & Stoughton; Nos. 10 and 12 by courtesy of the Director of the India Office Library and Records; No. 11 from *A Personal Narrative of a Visit to Ghuzni, Kabul and Afghanistan* by G. T. Vigne, published by Whittaker; No. 21 from *Lahore to Yarkand* by George Henderson, London 1875; No. 22 by courtesy of Gerald Morgan (photo by Ney Elias) and No. 24 by courtesy of Nick Holt.

The engravings are all taken from *Travels in Ladakh* by H. D. Torrens, London 1862.

Acknowledgements

In a book based on works long out of print and on archive material the author's principal debt must be to the libraries. I should like to acknowledge the unfailing assistance and advice of the staffs of the India Office Library and Records, the Royal Geographical Society, the London Library and the National Library of Scotland. Valuable suggestions on specific queries have been made by Colonel Gerald Morgan, Dr. G. J. Alder, R. G. Searight and H. D'O. Vigne; to all of them I am most grateful.

The Scottish Arts Council helped make the project possible, numerous friends have provided encouragement and in particular Christina Noble, John Murray and Roger Hudson have read the full text and made comments both kind and helpful.

Lastly my thanks to Julia. She has done far more than just type the whole thing; but how to acknowledge the patience, assistance and encouragement of a collaborator and wife?

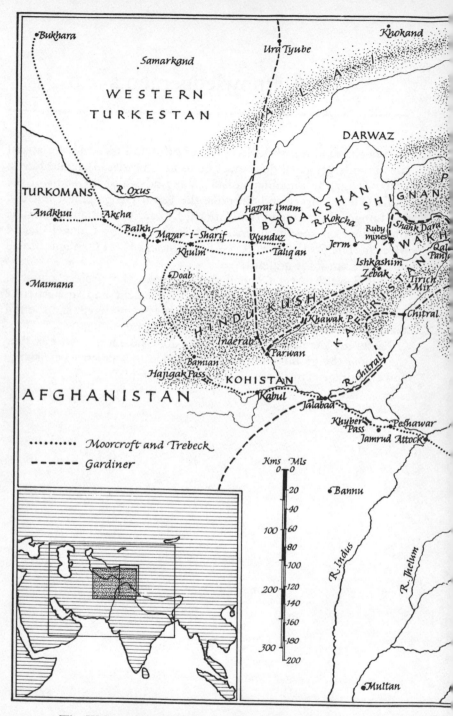

The Western Himalayas showing all the principal mountain systems
Gardiner. (To cover chapters

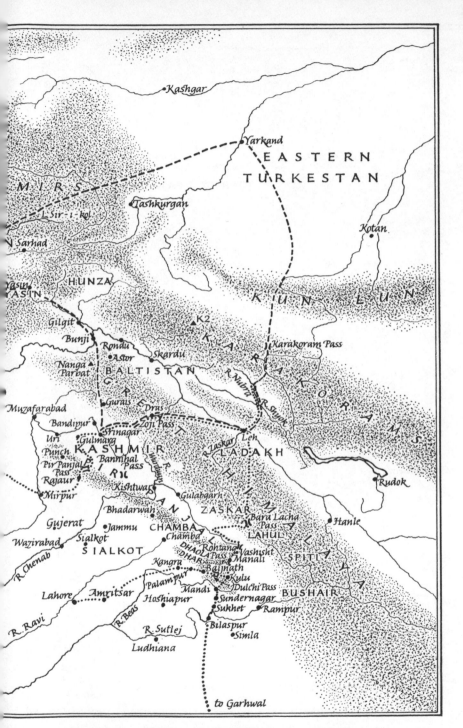

and illustrating the routes of Moorcroft and Trebeck and of Alexander
1–9 excluding part of chapter 5)

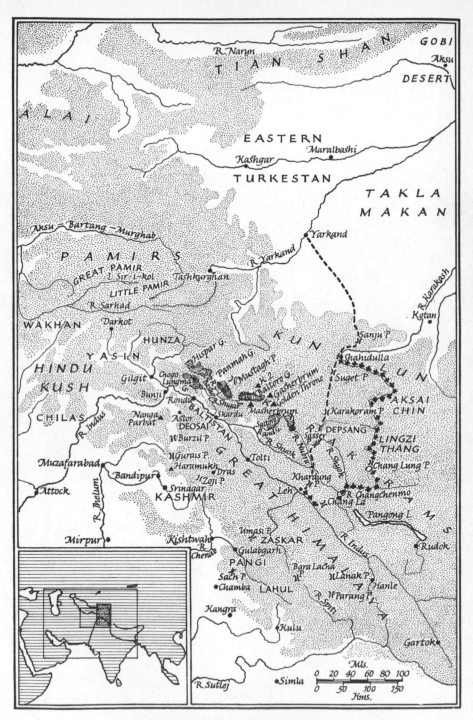

Baltistan and the Road to Yarkand showing the Karakoram and
Changchenmo routes and the main Karakoram peaks and glaciers.
(To cover chapters 10–14 and part of chapter 5)

Introduction

Arab geographers of the Middle Ages, though they knew more than most about the configuration of the world, entertained some rather fanciful notions. One of these was to regard the Eurasian landmass as a desirable woman clothed in nothing but a long chain girdle about her ample waist. The girdle was of mountains studded with snowy peaks. It stretched from the Pyrenees through the Alps, Balkans, Caucasus and Elburz to the limits of the known world in the Hindu Kush and Himalayas. This idea of an east–west mountain range encircling the earth was not new; the geographers of Greece and Rome had also subscribed to it. But it would have taken the genius of the Arabs, had they known the region, to recognise in the Western Himalayas the girdle's jewel-encrusted clasp. Nowhere on the earth's surface is there a comparable cluster of mountains. In a chaos of contours at the heart, or perhaps the navel, of Asia six major mountain systems lie locked together.

From the south-west, out of the arid hills of Afghanistan, comes the Hindu Kush. Its brown, treeless slopes grow higher and steeper as they approach the main complex. In the valleys there are no strips of continuous cultivation, just lush green oases strung together by grey, snow-fed rivers. Even below the glaciers of the 25,000 foot Tirich Mir there is still a hint of the deserts of the Middle East. The inhabitants in their small dusty villages are all, with the one exception of the Kafirs, Mohammedans. Skull cap and turban have their mountain equivalent in the rolled caps of Chitral and Gilgit, but the henna-red beard is still in evidence and *salaam aleikum* is the eternal greeting. From a miniature white-washed mosque the muezzin goes up into the thin mountain air and rouses the ragged goatherd on the hills above.

To the north the Hindu Kush is bounded by the narrow Oxus valley beyond which lie the rounded domes of the Pamirs. This is a still mysterious and almost polar region of several parallel ranges linked together, and to the other chains, by a north–south range which includes the peak of Muztagh Ata, 'the father of snowy mountains'. The Arabs called the Pamirs the *Bam-i-Dunya*, or 'Roof of the

World', a fitting name for a region where the valleys are not cosy
little clefts but open steppes as cold and windswept and almost as
high as the peaks that bound them. Here, in summer, graze the yaks,
horses and sheep of the nomadic Kirghiz, a Central Asian tribe of
squat gnarled men and smiling flat-faced women. Conditions are so
harsh that they are said to suffer from the highest incidence of still-
born babies in the world; and in winter even they forsake the mountains to shelter in the lower valleys to the north. The Pamirs are left
to their one notable resident, the Marco Polo sheep, a creature as big
as a pony with curled horns up to six feet long.

Corresponding to the Hindu Kush but joining the Pamirs from the
east is the third system, the Kun Lun. The Pamirs with their
Siberian climate are a fitting contribution from Russia, but the Kun
Lun belongs in every sense to China. Rich in jade and overlooking
the ancient silk route from Cathay, its row of blue peaks emerging
above the dust haze to the south of Kotan have always been regarded
as the rim of the Chinese empire in the south-west. The Turki
population constitutes a sort of Celtic fringe, acquiescing in the rule
of Pekin, occasionally rejecting it but never really finding a workable
alternative.

Within the angle formed by the junction of these three systems lie
the Karakorams. Mightiest of all, they radiate from an amphitheatre
of peaks that includes three of the world's six highest. This is a
treacherous and perpendicular wilderness where only the mountaineer can hope to survive. Glaciers thirty miles long and quarter
of a mile deep fill the valleys. Anything like level ground is strewn
with their moraines. Grazing, let alone cultivation, is practically non-
existent; no one lives actually in the Karakorams.

By comparison the Great Himalaya,* in its western reach, is a
modest affair. The part which falls within the Western Himalayas is
that which is drained by the Indus and its tributaries. It is more
broken than on its grand sweep through Nepal, with passes as low
as the 11,000 feet Zoji La between Kashmir and Ladakh. In Lahul and

* It is important to distinguish between Himalaya, pronounced like
'Somalia', and the Himalayas, as in 'Malaya'. The first is, strictly, the correct
pronunciation, and deriving from two Sanscrit words meaning 'the abode of
snow' should be employed in the singular only. I have used it only when
referring to a specific mountain chain as in Great Himalaya. Himalayas,
always plural, is an Anglicisation which is now more widely used than the
correct version. I have taken it in its broadest sense to imply all the mountain
systems between the Indian subcontinent and Central Asia.

had never been to Kashmir but his balmy scent-laden breezes rustling the bowers so dear to lovers somehow managed to conjure up a not unrecognisable image of the place. Kashmir was, and to some extent still is, a sensuous paradise. And if the first visitors were a little disappointed not to find more love-lighted eyes it was, as they conceded, only because the Kashmiri girls were so lovely they were more commonly met with in the zenanas of Lahore.

Moore left his heroine, Lalla Rookh, happily married to the man she loved and tripping off 'over the snowy hills to Bucharia'. Bucharia, or Lesser Bucharia, was one of the many names for Eastern Turkestan, now Sinkiang. One cannot help fearing for the safety of the delicate jewel of the East. She sets off so gaily, quite unaware that ahead lie five of the toughest passes in the Himalayas along what was later called 'the ugliest track in the whole wide world'. Moore and his contemporaries had some idea of Kashmir but none at all of the mountains beyond it. In fact it was mid-century before either their size or extent was appreciated. Cartographers of the day were still influenced by their classical counterparts. Rennel's map of 1794 shows Ptolemy's long skinny lines of peaks, the Imaus and Emodus, streaming across wide open spaces where dwell the tribes of Comedi and Byltae. Herodotus had populated the area with unicorns and gold-digging ants as big as foxes. And the prodigious wild sheep of the Pamirs, which Marco Polo reported, were still as challenging a notion as that other Himalayan speciality, the yeti.

In so far as the maps gave no real idea of the terrain, travellers were less concerned with exploring the mountains than with crossing them. Bucharia, Kashgaria, Moghulistan and Tartary were all names for the fabled lands beyond. Not much was known of their geography, but what was known was the existence there of some of the oldest and richest cities in the world. Bukhara and Samarkand, Kashgar and Yarkand, Kotan and Khokand, these were places that fired the imagination. They lay along the ancient land-locked trade routes from China to the Middle East, the routes by which the silk and the porcelain of Cathay had reached the Mediterranean. For centuries they had been shrouded in mystery, forbidden but not forgotten. About 1270 Marco Polo and others of his family found them recovered from the ravages of Genghis Khan and as prosperous as ever. Samarkand was 'a great and noble city', Kashgar famous for its estates and vineyards, Kotan for its gold and jade, and Yarkand 'where they have plenty of everything' even had a Christian bishop.

In the nineteenth century the rediscovery of these places constituted one of the greatest challenges. The unknown of darkest Africa had its appeal, but the slightly known of Central Asia was thought by many to be every bit as exciting and rewarding. It appealed not just to the missionary, the merchant and the naturalist but also to the anti-quarian, the scholar and the statesman. The explorers of the Western Himalayas, though as ill-assorted a crowd as can be imagined, have a few traits in common. They tend to be more scholarly than their counterparts elsewhere, more wide-ranging in their interests and, perhaps because of the nature of the mountains, more chastened by their experiences and more reticent about them. There are few lions amongst them but a lot of elusive and intriguing chimeras.

By way of the low Hindu Kush passes in Afghanistan, Western Turkestan with its twin cities of Bukhara and Samarkand was soon reached. Eastern Turkestan proved far more difficult. The easier route via Afghanistan and the Pamirs had to be abandoned because of political difficulties with the Afghans. The more direct approach north from Kashmir taxed the patience and credulity of a host of pioneers. No sooner was one range negotiated than another loomed up ahead. The passes grew higher and higher, the track became a nightmare. Not till the late 1860s did travellers at last return with news of Kotan, Yarkand and Kashgar. They were not exactly a disappointment but their remoteness was now at last fully appreciated. Those with a commercial or political interest in Eastern Turkestan tended to minimise the difficulties of the track, but there was no disguising the fact that the barrier between India and Central Asia was infinitely more formidable than was at first thought.

In other words the mountains were coming to overshadow the lands that lay beyond; they were now seen as in themselves constituting a legitimate field for exploration. This change is traceable from about 1860 when the survey of the whole region got under way. Earlier travellers, like Vigne and Thomson, who had gone down as Central Asian explorers who failed to get there, were resurrected as eminently successful Himalayan pioneers. People began to get some idea of the undreamt of breadth and complexity of the mountain knot. And those long skinny chains of peaks slowly gave way to something more like the vast purple bruise, riven with muddy browns and spattered with icy whites, of a modern contoured map.

The exploration of the Western Himalayas had therefore this retrospective, almost incidental character. The early travellers described modern European scholarship and is for the most part either un-authentic or obsolete.

This was written in 1840, some fifteen years after Moorcroft's great journey; its careful phrasing was partly necessitated by discoveries made in that intervening period. In 1820, when Moorcroft pioneered the exploration of the lands between India and Russia, no more was known of them than of what Wilson calls the blank between India and China. Neither, of course, was a complete blank but there was precious little that was known for sure.

NOTE: Even today knowledge of the geography of the Western Himalayas is not something that can be taken for granted. There is no handy coastline to fix their location in the mind and in most atlasses they are cut about so that the southern ranges fall within a map of the Indian subcontinent, the western ones within a map of Russia and so on. A few minutes study of the accompanying maps is recommended.

PART ONE

The Pir Panjal and The Great Himalaya

1820–1838

I'll sing thee songs of Araby
And tales of wild Cashmere,
Wild tales to cheat thee of a sigh
Or charm thee to a tear.

W. G. WILLS. *Lalla Rookh*

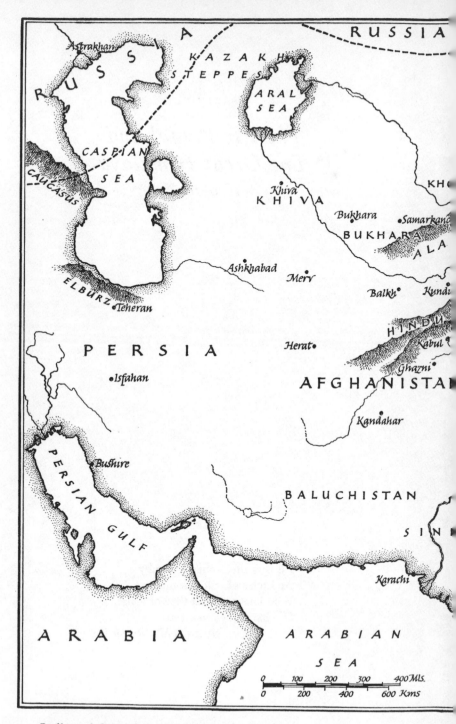

India and Central Asia showing the approximate positions of the Russian

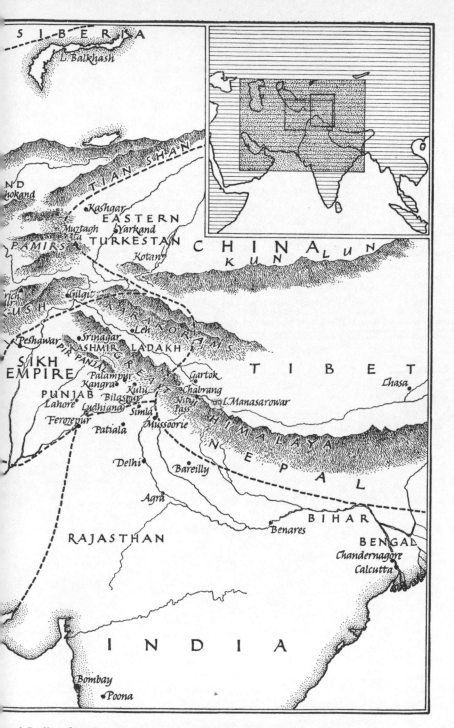

and Indian frontiers and the intervening lands in 1838

1. The Enthusiastic Moorcroft

Buffalo skins on the Sutlej

The river Sutlej, longest and most southerly of the Indus tributaries, cuts deeply into the rim of the Tibetan plateau, thunders in a dark sinuous gorge through the Great Himalaya and then slows to an unexpected standstill below the small town of Bilaspur. Its current is stayed by the towering dam of the Bhakra hydro-electric project.

Before the river was harnessed it was here about fifty yards wide and swept strongly past at five miles an hour. On the morning of March 6th 1820 William Moorcroft measured it while his party of three hundred men, sixteen horses and mules and several tons of baggage was being ferried across. The operation took an hour and a half, good going considering there were no boats. Everything had to be transported on inflated buffalo skins—or rather on the backs of the paddlers of the inflated buffalo skins. Moorcroft watched it all carefully. The skins were blown up through one of the legs. A thin rope was tied round the body and, grasping this with one hand and a paddle with the other, the ferryman flopped chest down on to the upturned carcase and awaited his load. The Englishman was impressed. Ships could be equipped with these as life rafts. A few buffalo skins could render a whole army amphibious. In a water-logged land like Bengal or in the Punjab, should they ever have to fight there, this could be of real advantage to the East India Company's forces.

It is typical of Moorcroft that in his enthusiasm for the skins he forgets to note in his diary that, crossing the Sutlej, he is bidding

farewell to the last outpost of British territory in north-west India. He is also entering the Western Himalayas. For a more romantic spirit it would have been a stirring moment. Grasping the shoulders of the half-submerged paddler and pushing off into the cold green waters was a step into the unknown, the beginning of a marathon journey which was always mysterious and ultimately tragic. It was to establish its leader as the father of modern exploration in both the Western Himalayas and Central Asia.

Considering he left behind him ten thousand sheets of manuscript scattered through Asia but now safely in London's India Office Library, we know pitifully little about William Moorcroft. Few travellers have written at greater length or on a wider variety of subjects and yet remained so personally obscure. To some extent this was convention. Marco Polo had managed to relate the story of his twenty-five years of travel without revealing more about himself than a passion for hunting. With both men one suspects a desire to be known more for their achievements than their character. But to the would-be biographer it is most discouraging and, for lack of one, Moorcroft's reputation has suffered. He still gets described as a horse-dealer, a spy or an adventurer, each of which possesses a grain of truth while sadly understating his real standing.

Not that there were any obvious signs of greatness about the man who was watching his party safely across the Sutlej. He was short and slight, red faced and fair haired, and he favoured one of those nautical peaked caps which Dr. Livingstone would invariably wear. Contemporaries speak of his 'candid manner' and 'energetic disposition' but it is by no means clear whether these are to be regarded as virtues. That Moorcroft liked to speak his mind in spite of, and usually regardless of, the consequences is self evident from his writings. And that he had an energetic disposition is not surprising; loafers make poor explorers. From one of his companions it appears that he was also dubbed 'an enthusiast', and this is important. In those days 'an enthusiast' was not a flattering description. It implied imbalance, a man with convictions as far-fetched as they were unshakable. In this light the 'energetic disposition' suggests excitability as much as wanderlust, the 'candid manner' bloody-mindedness as much as integrity.

Given his career—and it is here, as he would have wished, that his greatness lies—Moorcroft's character may best be seen as approaching that of the erratic genius. He was indeed obstinate, eccentric and

controversial, but he was also full of infectious energy and invariably ahead of the times. To anyone responsible for his activities he was an unholy terror but to his friends and followers a guiding light. He should have been safely cloistered in a progressive university rather than let loose on the Himalayas. Empires are created by men of vision but Moorcroft was a visionary.

The one thing that might have struck anyone watching this odd little Englishman as he bestrode his buffalo skin was his apparent age. From dates in his early career that can be established Moorcroft must have been born about 1765. In other words the man now starting on one of the longest and most dangerous journeys in Asian exploration was fifty-five years old. By the standards of the day that made him an old man. In terms of life expectancy amongst the British in India it was positively ancient. One stands aghast at his extraordinary courage and stamina. In the whole story of Himalayan exploration there is nothing to compare with it; almost without exception his successors were men in their twenties and thirties.

At the same time it must be remembered that this makes him very much a product of the eighteenth century. Though he was to foresee the whole course of events in the Himalayas and Central Asia and though his own travels fall well within the nineteenth century, his attitudes are those of an earlier age. His models are Marco Polo and the Tibetan traveller, George Bogle. Unlike the Victorians he never notices the Almighty's role in the wonders of nature. Nor does he subscribe to that simple equation which would make progress equal civilisation and civilisation equal Christianity. If he praises British rule it is because, compared to the lawless and extortionate administrations he encountered, it seemed fairer. Christianity he seldom mentions, but he shows a real respect for other men's religions, especially Buddhism.

The eighteenth century with its free-thinking and its commercial drive was also the founding period of the British Raj. In the last quarter of the century, under Governors-General like Warren Hastings, Cornwallis and Wellesley, the East India Company had developed from being just one of several European trading companies with a stake in the country to being the greatest power on the subcontinent and the administrator of an Empire which dwarfed the combined possessions of the British crown. By 1820 the map of peninsular India looked much as it would for the next 150 years. However this rapid growth had been achieved at great cost to the

finances of the Company. It was time to call a halt to territorial acquisition and to concentrate on more profitable activities such as revenue settlements and curbing expenditure. Like the Directors of the Honourable Company, the British Government also was cautious about expansion. They already exercised a degree of control over the Company and they were increasingly aware of their responsibilities in India. Moorcroft too probably had little sympathy with those who advocated more conquests; but he was still, at heart, a founder. Cautious retrenchment was not for him. He travels not exactly flag in hand but with many a backward glance as to its likely progress. The obsessions which filled his hungry mind and the misunderstandings which dogged his footsteps were as much a product of his unfashionable outlook as of his character.

One must also see this, his last journey, as a do or die effort. His career is virtually over, his young family is being sent back to Europe* and it is clear that if he returns he intends to resign from the East India Company's service. He continually reverts to the question of his retirement and, in the face of criticism and discouragement, he can afford a certain detachment. It also helps explain the complete lack of urgency in his movements. He is not out to make his name or his fortune. When his merchandise won't sell, his political overtures are disowned and his resources exhausted, there is still every reason for going on. It is his final fling. He stakes everything, including his life.

As a young man he had abandoned medical school in Liverpool and had gone to France to study veterinary surgery. This was in the late 1780s, when the science was virtually unknown in Britain. He returned as the first qualified vet in the country, set up practice from an address in Oxford Street in London and quickly made a small

---

* Moorcroft's family affairs are as confused as most things about him. News of his wife's death reached him in Ladakh in 1820. Her name was Mary Moorcroft and she had died in Paris. But this was evidently not the mother of his two young children. Anne, the elder, who was staying with Mary Moorcroft at the time of her death, describes her as neither as fair nor as young nor as pretty as her own mother, who was in India. One would suspect that Moorcroft had taken an Indian bride except that in that case he would hardly have sent Anne to Paris and England or have planned to send the little boy, Richard, to Harrow and medical school. Equally, from a lock of long fair hair belonging to Mary Moorcroft which is preserved amongst the Moorcroft papers, it would seem that the second Mrs. Moorcroft must have been very fair indeed.

fortune. He became joint professor of the Royal Veterinary College, founded in 1791, and wrote such esoteric pieces as 'Directions for using the Portable Horse-Medicine Chest' and 'Experiments in Animal Electricity'. A turning point came with the attempt to market his patent machine-made horseshoes. To the relief of village smithies and the eternal benefit of geographical science the venture was a flop. The small fortune was lost. Moorcroft gratefully accepted an offer from the East India Company and in 1808 set sail for India. He was to manage the Company's stud farm in Bihar, a highly responsible and lucrative appointment in those days of cavalry.

Much was expected from the supervision of such a distinguished man of science, and at first Moorcroft did not disappoint. Ever a pioneer, he introduced oats to India and by 1820 could claim that for every ten sick animals in his care when he arrived there was now scarcely one. The only thing that bothered him was the quality of his horses. He badly needed new breeding stock. Scouring India, or 'running over the country in quest of phantoms' as it seemed to his patrons, he found nothing suitable. Either a herd of English stallions would have to be shipped out to Calcutta or he would go in search of the horses of Central Asia, famed since the days of Marco Polo for their speed and endurance. The English stallions were not forthcoming. Nor were the Company enthusiastic about their stud superintendent disappearing into what was then a great void in the maps of Asia. But he was not expressly forbidden to go and for Moorcroft this was enough. He had a pretext.

That the purchase of horses, particularly the Turkoman steeds he expected to find at Balkh and Bukhara, was not to be more than the official justification for his travels is clear from an early date. Moorcroft's vision was all embracing and as much commercial and political as scientific. In 1812, on the first of his two famous journeys, he had crossed the central Himalayas into Tibet disguised as a Hindu *saddhu* and gone in search of the goats from which the fine wool of the Kashmir shawl is extracted. With Hyder Young Hearsey, an Anglo-Indian adventurer, he had scaled the Niti pass in Garhwal, just west of the present-day frontier of Nepal, and reached the Tibetan centre of Gartok and the sacred lakes of Manasarowar and Rakas Tal at the source of the Sutlej. To some geographers this journey is his greatest achievement. He was not, as has been claimed, the first European to cross the Himalayas; the Jesuit missionaries in the seventeenth century had used an adjacent pass to reach their mission centre in

Chabrang on the Upper Sutlej. Nor was he the first Englishman; George Bogle had crossed the Eastern Himalayas, admittedly an easier task, in 1774. But what he did achieve was a partial solution to the long standing puzzle of the origins of the three principal Indian river systems. He showed that the Ganges did not, as Hindu tradition and current maps had it, rise from the saċred lakes, but that the Sutlej did. And further north he correctly identified a young river flowing north-west towards Ladakh as the main branch of the Indus.

But what had the distinguished vet been doing, bargaining for goats and tracking down rivers on the Tibetan plateau? He had been absent without leave from his stud and beyond the Company's territories without its knowledge. His explanation, looking for horses, was hardly convincing. Even given the then state of geographical knowledge, striking north into Tibet can scarcely have been regarded as the shortest way of reaching Balkh and Bukhara. In Tibet the only horses he was likely to see were wild *kiangs*, impossible to catch and useless for breeding purposes.

The goats made more sense. He had actually brought back fifty, four of which eventually reached Scotland where they failed to prosper. But if shawl wool could not be produced in Britain, he argued, it could at least be tried on the Indian side of the mountains and the processing and weaving of it established on British territory. This was, after all, by far the largest and most profitable commodity in Himalayan trade. The East India Company was a trading venture and it was on schemes like this that it had grown. The whole justification for Bogle's 1774 mission to Tibet had been the purchase of these goats. Moorcroft had in fact succeeded where he had failed. There might be those who disapproved of reports, which should have dealt with the progress of the stud, being devoted to goats' wool but many sympathised with the venture. And it was to provide a channel for tapping the wool trade that, after the Gurkha war of 1814, much of the hill territory south of the Sutlej had been annexed. Weaving establishments were encouraged and at Rampur a brisk trade sprang up in the 1820s. For once Moorcroft was only slightly ahead of the times.

The shawl industry remained one of his consuming interests. It epitomised his passions for trade with Central Asia and home industries for the people of both India and Britain. To the commercial drive of an eighteenth century Englishman Moorcroft united a genuine altruism. A native of Lancashire, he fully understood the plight of the working classes and, like many of his contemporaries, believed it could best be alleviated by 'improvements'. For the people of India, too, he had a real respect. Before he had reached Bilaspur on his last and greatest journey, William Laidlaw, his geologist, had been dismissed for harsh treatment of the natives. Throughout his travels one is struck by the intense loyalty shown by all his followers. There is nothing to suggest that his ideas about colonial exploitation were particularly liberal; he was simply a good man.

Trade with Central Asia was the inspiration behind all Moorcroft's schemes. He saw the area between China and the Caspian as a vast political vacuum. British influence, in the form of a network of trading interests, could bring prosperity and order whilst making of the region an outer rampart in the landward defences of India. In 1812 he had sent Mir Izzet Ullah, his confidential Persian servant, to explore a rumoured route from Punjab via Kashmir and Ladakh to Yarkand and Bukhara. In a remarkably short time the Mir faithfully performed his mission and returned to Delhi in December 1813. The track was feasible for a heavily laden caravan and armed with this first-hand account of the current political and trading position, and flushed with the success of his own first attempt to penetrate north of the mountains, Moorcroft had started to lobby the Governor-General about the necessity of crossing the Western Himalayas.

In 1813 he recommended that Mir Izzet Ullah and Hyder Young Hearsey be despatched to Kashmir and Ladakh to explore the roads beyond the mountains and gauge their feasibility as invasion routes— precisely the mission that Sir Francis Younghusband was to get all of seventy-five years later. Moorcroft argued that rumours of a French or Russian embassy in Bukhara presaged hostile activity north of the mountains and constituted a threat to British India. It was not so far fetched. The similar pretext for Elphinstone's mission to Kabul was probably in Moorcroft's mind. But the Governor-General did not concur with his Superintendent of Stud's reading of the political situation. In 1814 Moorcroft again applied, this time on his own behalf, for an expedition co Bukhara for breeding stock. It was withheld; the complications arising out of a brush with the Nepalese on the first journey had not yet been ironed out.

As soon as the Gurkha war was over the irrepressible vet was again pining for Central Asia. He discussed his plans with Hearsey. The idea was to make a second journey into Tibet by the Niti pass,

MM—C

proceed to Lhasa and then back to Ladakh, across the mountains to Yarkand and west along the ancient route followed by the Polos to Badakshan, Balkh and Bukhara. Even for Hearsey this was a bit much. It was too difficult, too dangerous and would never be sanctioned by the government. Hearsey had a better idea. It entailed going by sea to Bushire on the Persian Gulf and thence, with the permission of the Persians, via Teheran to Bukhara and Yarkand. But to what Hearsey called 'this safe, easy and extensive plan' Moorcroft could not agree. He held out for the Himalayan route and resigned himself to doing without his friend.

An interesting point about Hearsey's plan was that they were not all to return. George Trebeck, Moorcroft's companion when he finally crossed the Sutlej at Bilaspur, was to stay at Teheran as commercial agent. Hearsey himself was to act as agent at Bukhara and, whilst there, to help the Amir organise his forces against an anticipated attack by the Russians. This was forcing the pace of history, but it gives an indication of how both men were thinking beyond purely exploratory ventures. Precisely what lay behind these schemes will never be known, but that it amounted to more than just geographical discovery and commercial exploitation seems certain. The conduct of the journey was to give still further evidence of concealed and, to some, sinister designs.

In 1819 Moorcroft at last won permission to start for Central Asia in search of stallions. The Company had apparently run out of objections. It had certainly not had a change of heart about its Superintendent of Stud nor a change of policy towards Central Asia. Its ambivalence about the whole scheme was ample evidence. Government involvement was to be a feature of exploration in the Himalayas yet only rarely was an interest in the area publicly avowed. Moorcroft's expedition was typical. Although he carried certificates under the Governor-General's seal and was provided with specialists and an armed guard from the Company's ranks, he was refused any official status. No letters of introduction were sent, not even to the most eminent potentates like the Amir of Bukhara, and Moorcroft was expected to finance the whole operation out of his own pocket. One can understand the Company's chariness about supporting an expedition like this but, having decided to do so, the refusal to accredit it was inviting trouble, particularly with a man like the erratic Moorcroft in command. He was soon signing himself 'Superintendent of the Honourable Company's Stud on deputation to Chinese and Oosbuk Toorkistan' or '... on deputation to the North Western parts of Asia', convenient titles which could be made to mean as much as he liked.

His party had left from Bareilly, one hundred and fifty miles east of Delhi, in October of the same year. Lhasa had been dropped from the itinerary and their first destination was Leh in Ladakh, a corner of Western Tibet from where, according to Mir Izzet Ullah, it should be possible to make contact with the Chinese rulers of Eastern Turkestan and plan their itinerary in Central Asia. So far as they knew no European, with the exception of the Jesuit Desideri, had ever visited Ladakh. The original plan had been to tackle the Himalayas at the Niti pass, as in 1812, and to cut across the Tibetan plateau to Ladakh. But they had reached the pass too late; it was already under snow. The untried Kulu route promised to be harder in its final stages but the first part from Garhwal to Bilaspur had involved no more than tacking through the foothills. It had been accomplished without mishap during the winter months of 1819–20.

Safely across the Sutlej Moorcroft purchased a few buffalo skins and struck north towards Kulu. A day's journey took him into the small state of Sukhet. Here the altitude is only 4,000 feet and the vegetation still typically Indian. The trees, acacia, pipal and mimosa, are the wilting varieties of the plains. Bananas and sugar cane do well and the houses, though whitewashed, are mainly of mud. The difference lies in the view. Suddenly the mountains, just a white-tipped haze from the plains of the Punjab, are upon one. To the east there are glimpses of the main Himalayan chain whilst due north, and far more impressive, rises the snowy wall of the Dhaola Dhar. This is a spur of the Pir Panjal, the outermost of the West Himalayan ranges and the first which the expedition would have to cross. In March the Dhaola Dhar is at its best. The snow lies low, not on a broken succession of peaks, but on a massive ridge which, unobscured by the dun coloured foothills, rises sheer from the plains for some 13,000 feet. It was the first rampart of Moorcroft's promised land. A week's hard travelling would see them among the mountains.

There was just one possible hitch. Between the possessions of the East India Company and the Himalayan countries (Moorcroft refers to them indiscriminately as Tibet, Tartary or Ladakh) there lay a belt of small hill states. Each had its own Raja and, until recently, had enjoyed a certain independence. But since the beginning of the century they had been first terrorised by the Gurkhas and then gradually made tributary to the rising Sikh power under Ranjit Singh, Maharaja of the Punjab. By 1820 he held the key to the whole of the Western Himalayas.

Moorcroft may have hoped that by a quick dash through Mandi and Kulu he could run the Sikh gauntlet. Certainly in Sukhet, the first of these states, there was no trouble. The villagers fled at their approach but soon flocked back to stare at the 'feringhis' and their camp style; they had never seen a European before. The night was disturbed by nothing worse than the howling of hyenas and morning saw them pressing on over the rolling countryside to Mandi. Somewhere near the new town of Sundernagar they were stopped by a tatterdemalion rabble armed with swords, matchlocks and bows and arrows. It was the Raja of Mandi's army. The Raja had no objection to their crossing his territory but some Sikhs collecting revenue in the area had. They were adamant that no one could pass without reference to the Maharaja in Lahore.

Here as elsewhere the trouble was caused by the expedition being far too big. Anything like an inconspicuous dash was out of the question. Moorcroft had with him over £3,000 worth of merchandise, most of it heavy bales of cloth necessitating scores of porters and muleteers. Partly because he believed he could make a profit for his backers, partly to sustain his assumed role as a bona fide trader and partly just to help the expedition's finances—he always had too many good reasons for a disastrous idea—he had lumbered himself with the impedimenta of a full-scale caravan. This was to be a sore temptation to the tribes in the more unsettled areas whilst here it was the hordes required to guard and carry it which caused consternation. Wild rumours began to circulate that a 'Feringhi' army had crossed the Sutlej, taken Mandi and proclaimed that the hill states were under British protection.

In the hope that contact with Ranjit Singh might be turned to good account, Moorcroft himself, along with the invaluable Mir Izzet Ullah, had set off for Lahore. But the rumours overtook him as he made his way across the baking plains and at the unlovely town of Hoshiarpur he was arrested. For the whole of April he sweated it out in a doss-house for beggars beside the town's cess pit, whilst the Mir sped on ahead to arrange his release. At last, in early May, he was sent under guard to Lahore. The heat was now so great that they could travel only at night. Much of the way the ageing vet was carried in a *jampan*, a sort of hammock slung from a pole. In his weakened state he turned vegetarian and took dinner only three times a week.

One sympathises with Moorcroft's discomforts and irritations as he grapples with the hot weather and the whims of a hypochondriac Maharaja, but at least he was doing something. Most of the party were just stuck in Mandi. This is a busy little town on the Beas river; it could be very pleasant. The riverside is strewn with small stone temples, there is a good bazaar and a fine old hill palace, like a colossal timbered barn, overlooking it. But the visitor's recollection is more often one of heat and flies and frustration. From all directions arid grey hillsides slide steeply to the river. The town nestles between them sheltered from the erring breeze and deprived of any view. At 6,000 feet it might be charming, but at 2,000 feet, for most of the year and especially during the hot season, it is hell. The air is so still that smoke and smells just hang there; the flies are so lethargic they have to be pushed away.

In charge of the main party at Mandi was George Trebeck, the son of a solicitor friend of Moorcroft's and his only European companion. (Guthrie, the party's doctor who had been lent along with Laidlaw, the intolerant geologist, by the Bengal government, was an Anglo-Indian.) Moorcroft always refers to Trebeck as 'my young friend' while the latter speaks of his leader as 'Mr. M.'. There was thirty years between them. One thinks of Trebeck as a disciple rather than a companion, a role which fits well with Moorcroft as the prophet. His letters from Ladakh will sound much like the voice of one crying in the wilderness.

For the three hottest months of the year Trebeck sat it out at Mandi. It must have been a trying time. The Sikhs would have been only too pleased to see him slip back across the Sutlej. But even with the prospect of having to tackle the journey through Kulu at the height of the monsoon he did not waver. In June, just as the rains were starting, came word from Moorcroft to proceed. The tents were struck and the porters loaded. Then once again the Sikh commandant closed in on them. The camp was invested more closely than ever and it was not till a month later that they were finally free to move out. In torrential rain they reached Kulu on July 19th.

Moorcroft joined them there two weeks later. He had been recalled to Lahore a second time and after further delays and prevarication had slipped away to the court of Sanser Chand, Raja of Kangra. Kangra had once been the largest of the hill states and Moorcroft listened with sympathy to the old Raja's tales of the Sikh perfidy which had destroyed it. His own growing dislike of the new power in the Punjab turned to an indefatigable hatred which was to colour all his subsequent dealings in the Himalayas.

Between the two men there grew up a close friendship and, when Moorcroft cured the Raja's brother of apoplexy, Sanser Chand's generosity knew no bounds. His guest was to select any tract of land in the country that might appeal to him, any horse from the royal stables and any damsel from the Raja's dancing troupes. The offer of land was one he preferred to leave until his return, though the idea of retiring to the foothills already attracted him. In the Raja's stables there was probably little to excite the Honourable Company's Superintendent of Stud but the *nach* girls, the famed dancing girls and courtesans of northern India, were not beyond his interest even at fifty-five. He always maintained that their acquaintance was worth cultivating since they were the best informed and most communicative natives of any the traveller might meet. He dallied at Kangra for a full six weeks and then sent back from Kulu 'a fine gold-embroidered muslin for Jumalo, his favourite'.

From Kangra he had crossed to Baijnath and then via the Dulchi pass descended on the Kulu valley. His spirits were high 'having now before me no further obstacles to my penetrating to Tibet [Ladakh] than the natural difficulties of the country and the weather'. Torrential rain and mud made the mountain tracks treacherous but Sanser Chand had helped out with a hundred porters and when they emerged above the clouds on the Dulchi, Moorcroft was as near poetic rapture as his scientific training would allow.

. . . vast slopes of grass declined from the summits of the mountains in a uniform direction but separated by clumps of cedar, cypress and fir; the ground was literally enamelled with asters, anemones and wild strawberries. In some places the tops of the hills near at hand were clearly defined against a rich blue sky whilst in others they were lost amidst a mass of white clouds. Some of them presented gentle aclivities covered with verdure, whilst others offered bare precipitous cliffs, over which the water was rushing in noisy cascades. In the distance right before us rose the snowy peaks, as if to bar our further progress. Vast flocks of white goats were browsing on the lower hills and every patch of tableland presented a village and cultivated fields; glittering rivulets were meandering through the valleys and a black forest of pines frowned beneath our feet.

They were soon back in the clouds and it poured throughout the four day journey through the Kulu valley. They saw little of one of the most scenic valleys in the whole of the Himalayas. The challenging peaks above the steep wooded hillsides were completely obscured, though the world down below evidenced significant changes. The people were now dressed in tweeds instead of cottons and Moorcroft marvelled at the tartan-like plaids and homespuns. The women were small and pretty; their houses substantial affairs of stone and timber with deep verandahs hung with trailing vines. Orchards were plentiful. The air was full of the noise of rushing mountain torrents and the scent of pine and cedar. Mostly they kept to the left bank of the Beas crossing to the right near the modern tourist resort of Manali and recrossing to sample the hot springs of Vashisht. Had there now been a break in the clouds they would have seen not a patch of blue sky but a craggy chunk of the Pir Panjal. They were right underneath it.

The Kulu valley ends and the Beas river begins on the Rohtang pass, a saddle at the eastern extremity of the Pir Panjal. As Himalayan passes go it is not high, a mere 13,000 feet, but for all that a killer. Sudden icy blasts still take their toll of those who cross too late in the year. Colossal snow drifts and landslides still defy all efforts to keep open the newly built road for more than six months in twelve. In the Western Himalayas the most southerly range attracts the highest precipitation while the higher peaks and plateaux behind remain comparatively dry and snowfree, though invariably colder. Thus the Pir Panjal at the Rohtang pass forms the dividing line between the lush Indian hill country and a distinctly harsher world. The magnificent forests of sycamore, oak and cedar on the southern slopes are represented to the north by a rare and stunted cypress clawing at the rocks or a few heavily pollarded willows adorning the villages. The moist green pastures and emerald rice fields of Kulu are replaced by bare boulder-strewn scarps all orange and brown. There is no handy perch for the ubiquitous Indian crow; instead there is the lighter and shyer chough, cavorting in air that looks too thin for flight. The dazzling sun strikes down, as much sharp as hot, and burns like acid. It must be one of the most dramatic physical changes on the face of the earth.

The people too are quite different. The Kuluis are Hindus of Aryan race. Lahul, the land immediately beyond the pass, has a predominantly Buddhist population of distant Mongol descent. Its square, mud-faced houses stacked one above the other up the steep hillsides are the same as those of Ladakh which would remind Moorcroft of card houses. The fluttering of prayer flags and the muttering of lamas, assisted by the ceaseless rustling of the leaves on the lofty poplars, evidence the busy piety of the Buddha's followers. In all but name Tibet starts at the Rohtang.

From this pass to Leh the party was on the move for two months. It was one of their longest spells of continuous progress. They crossed the Rohtang, pressed on through the Lahul valleys, struggled up the Bara Lacha pass over the Great Himalaya and then across the western extremity of the Tibetan plateau to the Indus and Leh. Beyond Lahul the country was bleak and uninhabited. It was bitterly cold, but the going was comparatively easy and the expedition at last settled down into a regular routine.

There was no excuse for getting lost. To the people of Lahul and Ladakh this was a well-known route and they supplied guides, porters and mules. But with most of the men on foot progress was slow and, in a land where the clarity of the atmosphere is such that one can start for a nearby ridge at dawn and be no noticeably closer to it by dusk, it must have seemed even slower. Moving in single file because of the narrowness of the track, the column stretched for at least a mile. In front would be the strings of mules, skinny beasts with many a bald scar and daily worsening sores where their heavy loads rubbed; but for all that strong, sure-footed and well acclimatised. The soft ringing of their thick brass bells, added to the tap of their shoes against the rock or the tinkle of falling stones when a hoof slipped, only intensified the oppressive silence of the mountains.

Behind stretched the straggling line of porters. In the plains heavy loads are carried on the head but in the mountains men and women will carry everything, from the lightest handful of fodder to the heaviest of tree-trunks, on their backs. Small articles are jammed in a conical basket slung from the shoulders; a sack of grain or a tree-trunk is ingeniously tied round the waist and shoulders with a single rope. The weight of each load may be as much as 80 lbs. Bent beneath it, neck sinews prominent and head straining upwards, the wiry little porter looks much like a tortoise. As the altitude increases so does the frequency of his halts. Any rock of a convenient height to support his

permission to follow were good. Through the summer and winter of 1821 he waited. A stream of messages was sent north and every trader who found his way south to Leh was collared in the long open bazaar and pumped for news. But the Chinese were traditionally suspicious of all visitors. There was no precedent; reference must needs be made to Kashgar, to Pekin. Equally the Kashmiri merchants in Leh, who held a monopoly of the existing trade, were averse to a British intrusion. An attempt on Trebeck's life was probably their doing, and it was their report to the Chinese claiming that the British party had political ambitions which finally clinched the matter.

If permission had been granted it must remain doubtful whether Moorcroft could have successfully tackled the five terrible passes that lay ahead. Though the distance was only four hundred miles he seems to have had little idea of the hazards involved or of how much more difficult was the crossing of the Karakorams and Kun Lun than that of the Pir Panjal and the Great Himalaya. Almost fifty years would elapse before an Englishman finally made it to Yarkand.

Moorcroft was very hard on the Kashmiris. He called them 'the most profligate race on the face of the earth'. But, in fairness, they had a point. For someone who professed to be a simple trader his behaviour in Ladakh was very strange. First there was the affair of Aga Mehdi, a Kashmiri Jew by birth, who was ostensibly trading between Ladakh and Russia but who, it was thought, acted as agent both commercial and political for the Tsar. This was so sinister that Moorcroft became convinced that the Russians, whose frontier at the time was all of 2,000 miles away beyond the Aral sea, had designs on British India. Did their agent not carry gifts and cash even for Ranjit Singh, the most formidable power on the Indian frontier? And were there not four hundred cossacks waiting at the frontiers of Turkestan to escort Aga Mehdi and envoys from Ladakh and Punjab back to St. Petersberg?

Letters from the agent, then on his way south, arrived in Ladakh. Unfortunately they were written in Russian and Nogai Tatar, languages unknown to anyone in Leh. Trebeck set to to make a tracing of the unfamiliar scripts and sent it off to Calcutta. Moorcroft began to see Aga Mehdi as his opposite number, 'a shrewd and able competitor', and through the long Tibetan winter of 1820–21 Russia's designs preyed on his mind. Even in his house in Leh the temperature remained for weeks below freezing. He was convinced that nothing less than the safety of India lay in his hands and, plagued by rheumatism, he prepared for the battle of wits that would come with the agent's arrival in the spring.

But Aga Mehdi never reached Ladakh. His companion and his caravan arrived in April but he himself lay dead in the mountains 'of a sudden and violent disorder'. For Moorcroft it was most disappointing. Had he only lived 'he might have produced scenes in Asia which would have astonished some of the cabinets in Europe'. Most of his papers had disappeared and Moorcroft had to be content with a letter from the Imperial court to Ranjit Singh. This, too, was in Russian, but by chance in the summer of 1822 Moorcroft met the Hungarian Csoma de Koros,* who was able to translate it. It was little more than an introduction and, though interesting evidence, did nothing to confirm Moorcroft's speculations. In spite of encouragement from the British party Aga Mehdi's companion refused to continue to Lahore and discharge the dead man's mission. He preferred to sell the rubies intended for Ranjit Singh and make off with the profits. Without the hard proof he had hoped for, Moorcroft's speculations looked like extravagant alarmism and provoked a suitably sceptical response in India.

Infinitely more serious in the eyes of his employers was the zealous but ill-advised politicking between Moorcroft and his Ladakhi hosts. At the time of his visit the political status of Ladakh was vague. Its people, language, religion and geography are Tibetan. Probably Tibet had originally been unified from Leh and there were still close ties with Lhasa involving spasmodic tribute and frequent religious contact. On the other hand it had also sought protection from the Moghuls in India and paid tribute via Kashmir to the

* The Hungarian scholar, Alexander Csoma de Koros, had armed himself with a stout walking stick and from his native Transylvania set off for China. Two years of wandering across Asia, of which no more is known than his itinerary, brought him to Kashmir. En route from there to Leh he ran into Moorcroft. The meeting changed his whole life. Moorcroft became his patron, providing money and introductions on the strength of which he devoted the rest of his life to the study of the Tibetan language and of the giant volumes locked away in the monasteries of Ladakh. After Moorcroft's death the government rather reluctantly continued his stipend. He was scarcely a financial burden; he lived off Tibetan tea, had one change of clothes and was too absorbed in his studies to notice the frost biting at his toes. He rewarded Moorcroft's kindness by eventually producing the first Tibetan dictionary and grammar; he was the leading Tibetan scholar of his day—and the only Tibetan scholar of his day. See T. Duka's *Life of Csoma de Koros*.

Emperor Aurangzeb. Moorcroft joyfully pounced on this, declaring to a correspondent, 'Ladakh is tributary to Delhi!' And Delhi in the person of the puppet Moghul was now under British protection. By the happiest of coincidences it seemed that this unknown country was already British territory.

When the Sikhs, who had taken Kashmir in 1819, demanded from Ladakh the customary tribute, Moorcroft therefore advised against it. The Ladakhis should deal only with Delhi. They were by now wholly in his confidence and he in theirs. After negotiating the commercial arrangement they were convinced that Moorcroft was an emissary of standing. What more natural than that they should take advantage of his presence to snub the Sikhs and officially proclaim their allegiance to the British? It was not the first time Moorcroft had been approached in this way; both Kangra and Kulu had also sought British protection. But it was the first time he did anything about it. With the supposed implications of Aga Mehdi's dealings in mind, he saw this chance of establishing British commercial and political authority in the Western Himalayas as heaven-sent. Moreover Leh was not only the key to the trade of Central Asia but, given access to Yarkand, also to inland China. Here was the long-sought back door into that merchant's paradise which could change the whole pattern of Sino-British relations. In the longest of longhands Moorcroft covered reams with arguments. 'Maharajah Runjeet Singh seeks the allegiance of Ladakh by invitation, intrigue and menace. Russia invites the allegiance of Ladakh by promises of commercial advantages, of titles, of Embassies of distinguished honour. To the Honourable Company Ladakh, unsolicited, tenders voluntary allegiance!!' It was irresistible. How could he do other than forward Ladakh's formal request?—he had probably drafted it too. At the same time, and this was his big mistake, he wrote to Ranjit Singh telling him of Ladakh's status vis-à-vis Delhi and advising him not to meddle further in its affairs until he heard from the British government. It was not a threat; Moorcroft was just playing for time. But it could have been read that way.

For the British authorities this was too much. The Resident in Delhi was so amazed he could not trust his own translation of the note sent by Moorcroft to Ranjit Singh. Their Superintendent of Stud had no authority whatever to meddle in the Company's external relations. Ladakh played no part in their schemes; it was too remote and too poor. Ranjit Singh, on the other hand, was a powerful and sensitive ally. It was understood that, in return for not intriguing south of the Sutlej, he should have a free hand in the west and north. An apology was swiftly forwarded to Lahore. Moorcroft was severely reprimanded and his conduct disowned. A few months later his salary was stopped and he was recalled to Calcutta. Official notification of this came in 1824, too late to catch the party before they had headed off to Afghanistan, but rumours of it reached them in Kashmir. 'It is a strange tale that Moorcroft has been recalled by the Court of Directors . . .' wrote the loyal Trebeck. 'If it were a fact they know him not who suppose he would obey the summons to return.'

Whatever the government's doubts, Moorcroft had none. It is clear that throughout he acted in the best possible faith. His reasons for accepting Ladakh's offer, though too many and too elaborate, were far-sighted rather than far fetched. But there was another reason, unexpressed. He genuinely loved the Ladakhis. They became his adopted people, and it is not without pride that he tells of a move to have him made ruler of the country. During their two years there he and Trebeck explored it perhaps more thoroughly than any subsequent visitor. They saw the comparatively verdant valley of Nubra towards the Karakoram pass, and the desert wilderness of Changthang and the Pangong Lake on the Tibetan side. They explored the Dras valley on the Kashmir frontier and the Spiti valley to where it marched with the British protected state of Bushair. And they grew to like this skeletal land where the lowest point of the warmest valley is all of 9,000 feet above sea-level.

Most of it looks like a country without a countryside, a land from which all soil and vegetation has been torn away, leaving just the bare bones of jagged rock and beetling cliff. The valleys are not the deep sheltered clefts of the Pir Panjal but open troughs along whose flat bottoms the dust-laden wind has free play. The villages are perched high up on the sides on shelves of alluvium and separated from one another by steep slopes of what look like railway clinkers. Yet Ladakh's first visitors far preferred it to Kashmir—'an odd choice' wrote Trebeck, 'but there is something fine in the dash of a torrent and the wildness of a mountain desert'.

Everywhere they were met with kindness. The people were the antithesis of their surroundings, warm, gentle and welcoming. Moorcroft's medical work brought a flood of patients who turned his house into a market place with their offerings of vegetables and livestock. In gratitude for a minor operation, a patient's old mother would come a week's march to present him with a sheep. They were as well received in the lama's cliff-top monastery as in the shepherd's stone shelter or the tall palace in Leh. There was, and still is, something wholly idyllic about this smiling and not uncivilised people in their remote and harsh surroundings. Not surprisingly Moorcroft wished to save them from the heavy yoke of the Sikhs.

Practical as ever, what impressed him most was their husbandry. Page after page of his journal and letters are devoted to their rhubarb, their barley, their minuscule sheep, their cattle fodder, bee-keeping, manuring and so on. It was the same story in Kashmir and most of the way to Bukhara. Trebeck calculated that if all Moorcroft's schemes to introduce new systems of agriculture, new crops, cattle and industries were adopted, the country would be 'gainers by a million a year'. Poring over those ill-written journals today, all of 150 years later, the reader might wonder whether any agronomist has yet sifted through them. Trebeck was exaggerating but Moorcroft's observations were seldom as crazy as they might look. He was advocating the export of Indian tea to Central Asia before it had been successfully grown in India. Yet fifty years later the man who opened trade with Yarkand would be an ambitious tea planter with surplus production.

Moorcroft was thinking increasingly of the future and one suspects that many of these observations were recorded as personal *aides memoires*. Both in Garhwal and Kangra he had looked for a suitable tract of land for his retirement. In Leh he drew up a detailed list of furniture and fittings for the house-to-be, making sure that there was nothing that could not be carried by porters; he obviously had an isolated site in mind. It was not so much a building plot that he wanted as a small territory. Surely, he asked, there must be a tract of undeveloped hill country somewhere that the government would cede to him in expectation of an increased revenue once his improvements got going? He was prepared to guarantee that the foothills of northern India could be as prosperous and productive as anywhere in the country.

*　　　*　　　*

In September 1823, four years after setting out from Bareilly and three after reaching Ladakh, Moorcroft resumed his journey. During his long stay in the mountains he had made innumerable excursions but had progressed only as far as Kashmir. He is not a good guide to the famous valley. The ten months he spent there were unusually wet, the Kashmiris, whom he cordially detested anyway, were experiencing a famine, and the oppression of their Sikh overlords again invited his contempt. The exploratory forays continued but most of his time was devoted to one of the most detailed examinations of the shawl trade ever attempted. His notes are still the most authoritative on the various production processes. Victor Jacquemont, the next European to enter Kashmir, claims that 'his chief occupation was making love and, if his friends are surprised that his travels were so unproductive, they may ascribe it to this cause'. This was before the publication of Moorcroft's travels. As will be seen, coming from Jacquemont it is a prize piece of hypocrisy. Certainly the old traveller had his troupe of *nach* girls but they scarcely seem to have interrupted the customary deluge of observations. Besides, it was to be his last chance to relax, and where better than in the balmy atmosphere of Kashmir? It was about this very time that Moore was penning his celebrated lines:

> If a woman can make the worst wilderness dear,
> Think, think what a heav'n she must make of Cashmere.

Perhaps to combat the effect of the valley's lassitude he also formed a private army. Trebeck wrote off to India for drill manuals, arms were both made in Kashmir and ordered from the British political agent on the Sutlej,* and Moorcroft had his men out in the Srinagar suburbs doing manœuvres twice a week. It was a sure way of arousing the suspicions of his Sikh hosts. Dr. Guthrie and the Mir objected strongly but Moorcroft, forbidden the cherished route via Yarkand and already in bad odour with the Sikhs, no longer worried. For the final bid to reach Bukhara he had resolved to adopt an altogether firmer line. There was to be none of the docility he had shown in Mandi in 1820. When their path was barred by Punjabi miscreants just across the Indus he drew up his thirty cavalry in battle order and unwrapped a miniature cannon which had been intended as a present for the Amir of Bukhara.

Travelling by way of the Pir Panjal pass, and avoiding the embarrassment of another rencontre with Ranjit Singh at Lahore, they made

---

* The agent in question was Captain Charles Pratt Kennedy. He had just moved into his new house, high above the river Sutlej in a village called 'Semla'. It was the founding of the future summer capital of British India.

for Peshawar and halted there a modest five months. This was the beginning of Afghan territory, then in a chronically disturbed state. If the party had roused a few suspicions in the Punjab hill states, here its motives were to be invariably misconstrued. To the Afghans it was beyond comprehension that an Englishman could venture into their troubled country simply for trade and horses. Either Moorcroft must be an official emissary like Elphinstone or possibly a soldier of fortune, or else he was a spy.

At Peshawar all went well. Moorcroft's hosts shared his dislike of the Sikhs. They also saw nothing but advantage in having a British representative in their ranks on an imminent bid for Kabul. To cement matters, Moorcroft was offered the governorship of the city and invited to tender its allegiance to the Honourable Company. This time, not surprisingly, he fought shy, but Trebeck seems to have been within an ace of assuming the governorship. Remembering how Hearsey's plan had allowed for his remaining at Teheran as commercial agent, it is possible that Moorcroft, who did not oppose the plan, envisaged a similar role for him at Peshawar. However, the offer fell through and, with their neutrality compromised, they continued to Kabul in the van of the Peshawar forces. Again they were lucky. Pitched battles were raging in the streets of the city but, for a substantial 'loan', their Peshawar allies remained firm and saw them safely on their way to the Hindu Kush. They crossed by the Hajigak pass and Bamian reaching Khulm in early September 1824. Here their luck finally ran out.

For nearly six months they were held by the chief of Kunduz, Murad Beg, compared to whose treatment Ranjit Singh's had been positively angelic. Throughout they were in daily fear for the future of the expedition, their merchandise and their lives. Reading Moorcroft's papers one gets, for the first time, a sense of impending disaster. Events, suddenly, are being telescoped. Interludes on the agriculture and curiosities of the region become scarce, while a host of new names and complex intrigues take their place. Since Peshawar the whole pace of the expedition has speeded up. Meals of a simple Indian character are taken squatting on the ground; table and chairs are no longer unpacked and Moorcroft's bed has been lost between Leh and Srinagar. There is a growing impression of disintegration. Trebeck is unwell, Guthrie becomes separated from the party and Mir Izzet Ullah, the most invaluable of all, despairs of success and, sick and dying, is sent back to Peshawar. Moorcroft, too, is a changed man. Cornered, he acts and writes with impulsive and uncharacteristic vehemence. Every rebuff from Murad Beg is a threat not just to his safety but to his cherished plans of trade with the region. In his anxiety he even loses track of the dates.

Murad Beg's object was by fair means or foul to mulct the party of everything they possessed. He knew they had valuable merchandise, a considerable sum of money and probably some political standing. The idea was to frighten them into parting with the first two and, before finally deciding how to dispose of his captives, into revealing the precise nature of the third. From Khulm to Kunduz is a seventy-mile ride over low hills and desert. Three times Moorcroft made the journey there and back. After presents, bribes and an arrangement about customs dues he would return to Khulm only to be again prevented from leaving. Gradually it became clear that they were prisoners. Moorcroft no longer minced his words. To his face he accused the Uzbek chief of hypocrisy and he threw down the letter promising safe conduct. Murad Beg exploded with rage and muttering something about infidels left the court. Only 50,000 rupees was now to save them from 'a taste of the summer at Kunduz'.

Back in Khulm Trebeck was all for fighting it out. Though hopelessly outnumbered, he reckoned that their drill in Kashmir plus surprise tactics would see them through. Whatever the outcome it would be better than this slow strangulation. But Moorcroft had another idea. He would seek sanctuary and help from the one reputedly honest man in the country, the Pirzada of Taliq-an, whom even Murad Beg respected. It involved escaping from Khulm, riding undetected for one hundred and fifty miles and chancing everything on the generosity of a man he had never met. But the risk was just his own and in the end it paid off. Heavily disguised and riding continuously for two days and two nights through heavy mud, he made it to Taliq'an. The Pirzada gave him sanctuary, listened to Moorcroft's tale of woe and, after an open disputation in which his accusers maintained he was commander-in-chief of the British forces in India, decided in his favour. He interceded with the chief and on February 3rd 1825 Moorcroft, poorer by only 2,000 rupees, left Kunduz territory. They had escaped. But the awkward fact remained that they had to return. Murad Beg's rule stretched along the south bank of the Oxus from Badakshan to Balkh. It would be almost impossible to by-pass it.

Meanwhile there was Bukhara, Bukhara the Noble, perhaps the

oldest, most revered and least known city in Central Asia. Even Marco Polo had not been there. Surprisingly Moorcroft and Trebeck were not the first Englishmen to visit it—Elizabeth I had sent an envoy—but they were the first for two hundred years. In all their schemes and wanderings it had been the ultimate goal, the hub of the land trade of Asia and the market for the horses which, if all else failed, would ensure the expedition's success. Trebeck compared their arrival to the Crusaders' first sight of Jerusalem. 'After a long and laborious journey of more than five years we had a right to hail the domes and minarets with as much pleasure as Geoffrey de Bouillon.'

Unlike later travellers they were well received. Permission was given to ride through the city, an unheard-of privilege for a non-Mohammedan, and the Amir gave them freedom to trade. They disposed of most of their merchandise and procured a hundred horses. This was not as many as they had hoped, but their performance fully lived up to expectations. The only cloud on the horizon was the prospect of another brush with Murad Beg and, unwisely, they gave vent to their feelings about him to the Bukharan chief minister. In late June they left the city heading back to India.

By November it was all over. Moorcroft, Trebeck and Guthrie were dead. So too, in Kabul, was Mir Izzet Ullah. Their horses, property and servants were dispersed through Afghanistan. Rumours of the disaster started to reach India at the end of the year, but it was not till the following May that a letter arrived from Trebeck confirming Moorcroft's death and not till 1828 that the sole survivor to reach India, Hearsey's man Ghulam Hyder Khan, found his way to British territory.

The mystery of just what happened is now almost certain to remain unsolved. For reasons that it is difficult to understand, no attempt was made at the time to establish the real facts. There seems, on the contrary, to have been a conspiracy of silence. Ghulam Hyder Khan's account of the expedition was serialised in the *Asiatic Journal* but not till ten years later and even then the final section, dealing with events after they left Kabul, was suppressed. A report from that city about the death of Trebeck in which the writer pleaded that 'a good, honest and trustworthy man' be sent immediately to retrieve the horses was ignored. The Royal Geographical Society in London, founded in 1831, published some of Moorcroft's notes from Leh and Kashmir in the first issues of their journal. But at the time they were still uncertain whether he had ever reached

Bukhara, let alone the circumstances of his death. When in 1840 Alexander Burnes discovered some revealing private letters from Trebeck, including one from Bukhara, he forwarded them to the Society for publication. Inexplicably they were neglected.

It was not till 1841 that Moorcroft's *Travels* were finally published. By then others had covered most of the ground so that they contained little that was original. Equally what was contentious in them was no longer so. This presumably was just what was intended. But who was to blame? Was it the Company who made good Moorcroft's arrears of salary in order to get possession of the papers and who were as anxious for his death to be overlooked as they had been embarrassed by his political activities? Or was it Moorcroft's successors, anxious to ensure maximum acclaim for their own achievements? Sir Alexander Burnes brought Moorcroft's papers back from India in 1832 and did much for his reputation, but only after the publication of his own *Travels to Bokhara*. In 1835, when the editor of Moorcroft's journals, H. H. Wilson, finally had the Travels ready for publication, William Fraser, a British official in Delhi, was murdered. Amongst his papers were found seven volumes of Moorcroft's journal dealing with the final stages of the expedition. How Fraser had come by these and whether he was holding them for the government or witholding them from the government is unknown. We do, however, know that he was the closest of friends with Victor Jacquemont, Moorcroft's successor in Kashmir, and had himself planned to cross the Sutlej.

It was another three years before Wilson had incorporated the new material and another two before it was published. Even then Wilson mysteriously stopped his account with Moorcroft's arrival at Bukhara. He completely ignored the last volume, 'Return from Bukhara', which had definitely been in Fraser's possession and was therefore known to Wilson.

'Return from Bukhara' shows the party setting off in a frame of mind that is still sanguine—Moorcroft's favourite adjective. In the long dissertations on the guinea worm, the raisins of Bukhara, cock-fighting and a novel way of cooking peaches we recognise vintage Moorcroft with its heavy sediment of adventitious matter. He is feeling the heat, his face is redder than ever and his lips badly blistered. But it is no worse than on the Bara Lacha. For a man of sixty who has been travelling for five years he sounds as fit and alert as ever.

They recrossed the Oxus about August 4th and at Akcha were rejoined by Askar Ali Khan, a henchman of Mir Izzet Ullah, who had been sent back to Peshawar to explore a possible return route via Badakshan and Chitral. In this he had been successful. They were thus in a position to give Kabul a wide berth, if not Kunduz. Askar Ali was now sent to feel out Murad Beg while Moorcroft, alone but for a few servants, set off across the desert, west to Maimana. In Bukhara the shortage of horses had been blamed on the disturbed state of the surrounding country. The times were too dangerous for them to be brought to market, but anyone willing to risk his neck could purchase them from their Turkoman breeders in the desert oases to the south. Moorcroft decided to do just that. He had written from Bukhara, 'Before I quit Turkestan I mean to penetrate into that tract which contains probably the best horses in Asia but with which all intercourse has been suspended during the last five years.' The experiment is full of hazard but *le jeu vaut bien la chandelle*.' The candle, as one of his later admirers puts it, had not long to burn now. At Andkhui, in the very back of beyond, he was taken ill of fever and on August 27th 1825 he died. There were rumours of poison and of 'being struck in the chest by a bullet' but the body which was brought back to Trebeck would have been beyond recognition by the time it arrived.

The next to go was Guthrie. Also suffering from fever, he was carried from Akcha to Balkh on a stretcher and there he too died. Trebeck, now alone and himself sick, was a broken man. While 'Mr. M.' lived, he was prepared to risk anything. Without Moorcroft and assailed by reports of Murad Beg's fury over their complaints against him at Bukhara, he despaired. Askar Ali Khan argued for a southerly route through the mountainous Hazara country which would avoid Kunduz. Ghulam Hyder Khan and the rest preferred to chance their luck with Murad Beg again. Trebeck seems to have taken little part in this discussion. In November, as much from despair as disease, he too died.

Moorcroft had once referred to what a later generation called 'Kunduz fever' as a fatal disease 'not exceeded by the yellow fever of America or the fever of Walcheren'. Several of his servants including Mir Izzet Ullah had suffered from it during their detention by Murad Beg. It is not inconceivable that all three men, as they once again approached the fatal area, succumbed to the same disease. On the other hand, this was one of the most lawless areas of Asia.

In the light of what happened to European travellers in the area over the next twenty years, the death of three men in such a short time, all from natural causes, stretched credulity beyond belief. It was not just that it would have been an extraordinary coincidence, but that Moorcroft's party with their considerable resources were such an obvious prey. Few native caravans emerged from the area unscathed, let alone one led by Europeans. There was also the implacable hatred of Murad Beg, who may well have had wind of the proposal to by-pass Kunduz and was quite capable of wreaking his vengeance in the petty states beyond his frontier.

Moorcroft's travels had taken him a long way from the Western Himalayas. But the mysterious circumstances of his death lent to the already puzzling character of his travels a dash of romance. He became a legendary figure. Every traveller in the mountains and deserts between India and Russia added his stone to the cairn of 'the unfortunate Moorcroft'. The old vet was dead and yet his presence for decades haunted half Asia from Tibet to the Caspian. Wolff in 1831 met one of his employees who insisted that Trebeck and Guthrie, if not Moorcroft, had definitely been poisoned. Burnes, in the same year, was the last and only traveller to find his grave. Dr. Lord in Mazar-i-Sharif in 1837 recovered some of his books and accounts, and managed to thank the incredulous Pirzada at Taliq-an. ('Is it really a fact that this is known in Feringhistan?' asked the Pirzada. 'Wulla billa,' declared Lord, 'the very children repeat the name of Syed Mohammed Khan, the friend of the Feringhis.' 'God is great', quoth the Pirzada.) Gardiner met a man north of Kunduz with a compass and a map which had belonged to Moorcroft. French missionaries in Lhasa claimed, mistakenly, that Moorcroft had lived there for twelve years and died on his way back to Ladakh. In 1835, Henderson found that Moorcroft's garden in Leh was still being tended by the faithful Ladakhis in anticipation of his return. In Kashmir and Peshawar, Bannu and Rajaur testimonials written by Moorcroft were still being proudly shown twenty-five years after his death. His signature was said to be scratched on the wall of one of the famous caves at Bamian, and there was a shepherd just over the Bara Lacha who claimed that the flock he was grazing was Moorcroft's.

As the legend grew so did his reputation. The next fifty years were to prove this extraordinary man right in even his wilder speculations. It is almost uncanny the way events fell into place as he had antici-pated. Kangra, Kulu, Lahul and the whole of the Punjab including

Peshawar became British territory. Ladakh fell to the Sikhs, as he had warned, but later came under British protection as he had hoped. Bukhara fell to the Russians, while Eastern Turkestan and the mountains beyond Ladakh became the scene of frantic Anglo-Russian rivalry. Indo-British trade with Yarkand via Leh resulted in the formation of the Central Asian Trading Company, perhaps just the venture for which he had secretly planned, though it came too late to break the near monopoly gained by the Russians. He even advocated a permanent British representative in Leh and foresaw the possibility of a Muslim rising against the Chinese in Eastern Turkestan, both of which came to pass. The story of the exploration of the Western Himalayas is to a considerable extent the story of Moorcroft's dreams and fears becoming reality. Had all his recommendations been promptly adopted, the course of exploration and political penetration might have been run by 1830. But, by the government at least, they were, for the time being, ignored.

3. My Beloved Maharaja

Of the six major cities of the Indian subcontinent Lahore is now the least important. Beneath a grand Islamic skyline, all minarets, mosques and palaces, the narrow streets are as animated as ever. The salmon sandstone and white marble of the past are obscured though not shamed by the plate glass and cast concrete of today. Yet something is missing. There is industry and there is wealth but there is no longer dominion. Lahore has become a provincial backwater. It lies too close to Pakistan's vulnerable Indian frontier to have more than regional standing. It is still the capital of Punjab but Pakistan's Punjab is just a small province. Under Ranjit Singh it was an empire.

When Moorcroft was carried there in his *jampan* through the breathless summer nights of 1820 this empire was approaching its zenith. In 1818, with the capture of Multan and Peshawar, it reached its southern and western limits. The following year saw the conquest of Kashmir, later to be followed by the subjugation of Ladakh and Baltistan. The rule of Lahore then stretched from Tibet to Afghanistan and down the Indus to the deserts of Rajasthan and Sind.

Perhaps by Indian standards it was not such a vast empire. It could hardly compare with the conquests of Akbar or the sprawling dominions of Aurangzeb. Yet it was strong, more cohesive and stable than many a larger conglomeration of lands acknowledging one rule and, militarily, more formidable than anything the British had encountered in India. The Punjabis whatever their religion were, and still are, born soldiers; their physique and history bear witness to it. Sikhism, a comparatively new and suitably military religion, had become well established in the region. It gave to the non-Muslim population a crusading zeal comparable to that of the Mohammedan *jehad*. All that was needed was a leader who could unite the leading Sikh families, harness their Punjabi militarism and promote some sort of national identity in a land where such a thing was unknown. History rose magnificently to the occasion; there appeared Maharaja Ranjit Singh.

From the time of Moorcroft's visit till the Maharaja's death in 1839, no traveller from India could reach the Western Himalayas

48

without first getting permission from Lahore. It was not the least of the obstacles the explorer faced, nor was the encounter with Ranjit Singh less revealing and colourful than the grimmer hazards of mountain travel. As a result of Moorcroft's indiscretions in Leh and his questionable activities in Srinagar, the Maharaja was highly suspicious of people professing an interest in the mountains. Kashmir was his prize possession. He guarded it jealously and had little confidence even in his own representatives there. The Honourable East India Company was equally suspicious of would-be travellers. Moorcroft had demonstrated how easily political complications could arise; the result was that the whole area was now out of bounds. Freelance travellers were strongly discouraged and officers of the Company were refused permission to cross the Sutlej as a matter of course.

For nearly ten years this situation effectively closed the Western Himalayas. No doubt the tardiness with which Moorcroft's *Travels* were brought to press was partly due to anxiety about the encouragement they might give to prospective travellers. Nevertheless, both in India and Europe, curiosity about what might lie within and beyond 'the snowy range' was growing. Three brothers from Aberdeen, James, Patrick and Alexander Gerard, made their speciality the small corner of the range which was directly accessible from British controlled territory. This lay east of Simla between Moorcroft's 1812 route over the Niti La and his 1820 route through Kulu. Any penetration into Tibet proved impossible; they were consistently turned back. But their descriptions of high altitude travel, the first of their kind, were quickly published. They reported peaks of close on 30,000 feet and themselves with the most primitive equipment reached heights of over 17,000 feet. It was under their guidance that Victor Jacquemont got his first taste of the Himalayas and was thus encouraged to present himself at Lahore in 1831 with a request for permission to visit Kashmir.

Victor Vinceslas Jacquemont was a French botanist. He had come to India to make a collection of flora and fauna for the Jardin des Plantes of Paris, a plausible story supposedly introducing a diligent and prosaic man of science. Had this been all he would have got little change out of Ranjit Singh. Nor would he have made much impression on Lord William Bentinck, the British Governor-General, whose good will he had first to solicit. But Jacquemont certainly wasn't prosaic. A dilettante and a wit, the darling of the

Paris salons and the friend of Prosper Merimée and Stendhal, he had dressed himself from head to toe in black and, armed with a bulging wallet of introductions, set foot, tall and twenty-eight, in Calcutta in 1829. Here was a very modern young man indeed. His ideas about the world were as liberal as those about himself were romantic. He is so detached from the Indian scene that he trips across it like a visitor from another planet. And so totally unexpected is he that one can understand how both Calcutta and Lahore were taken by storm.

After a turbulent but, to the would-be romantic, almost obligatory love affair with a celebrated opera singer he had sought solace and fulfilment in travel, first to America and now to India. The collection of natural history specimens was a convenient excuse. He pursued it with the sporadic enthusiasm of an eccentric's hobby; he was no mean naturalist but he found it hard to keep his eyes on the ground. Tibet, Kashmir and the Himalayas, these were already names to conjure with and, although their flora was hardly representative of India as a whole, he relished the possibility of being able to write to his Paris friends from such romantic places. Besides, the salary he received from the Jardin des Plantes was wholly inadequate. Of necessity his travels took him either to where the hospitality was warmest or else to places so remote that his frugality could pass for unavoidable hardship. He came to enjoy roughing it on milk and pillao one day and the next sitting down at the groaning board of a new British host.

This was the pattern of his journey as he sponged his way up country from Calcutta to Benares, Agra and Delhi. Probably it was the chance of more flattering attention, political gossip and square meals in Lord William's company that took him to Simla in 1830. At short notice Bentinck had to forgo his trip there that year, but Jacquemont's visit was not wasted. In Kennedy, the political agent to whom Moorcroft had first applied for arms for his private army, he found the perfect host, 'the first among artillery captains in the whole world'. Kennedy's job was to watch over a number of small hill states, which were south of the Sutlej and therefore subject to British protection. In practice he had almost unlimited authority and after an hour or two's work in the morning was free to devote himself to entertaining his guests. Simla's growth owed much to Kennedy's style. For Jacquemont the Perigord patés and truffles had to be specially ordered, but there was always a dinner lasting from seven-thirty till eleven. The visitor drank 'Rhine wine or claret or nothing but champagne, with Malmsey at desert, while under the pretext of the cold climate the others stick to port, madeira and sherry'. It was still a bachelor society in those days and after the strawberries and mocha coffee came the dancing girls. Jacquemont was reminded of Capua.

As well as the Gerard brothers here he met Dr. Murray from Ludhiana, the British listening post for Lahore. In his medical capacity Murray had been to the Sikh capital and was a good friend of General Allard, one of Ranjit Singh's French officers. News that the Sikhs employed ex-Napoleonic officers in positions of the highest authority suggested to Jacquemont a possible entrée to Lahore and thence perhaps to Kashmir and beyond. It was an opportunity not to be missed. Murray wrote to Allard, Allard invited Jacquemont and Jacquemont wrote off to Bentinck for a letter of introduction to Ranjit Singh.

This put the Governor-General in a quandary. The Frenchman was obviously a special case. He was not an employee of the Company nor was he British. To refuse him a recommendation would lead to bitterness and, possibly, embarrassing recriminations. But to give it might suggest to the Sikhs that he enjoyed some special relationship with the Company and that they supported his design to explore the mountains. Relations between the two strongest powers in India were extremely delicate. In most directions their interests were diametrically opposed. The so-called Anglo-Sikh alliance was the keystone of British India's relations with her neighbours yet, on both sides, it rested on little more than a fear of the consequences of a trial of strength disguised by extravagant and oft-repeated protestations of friendship. It was really more like a confrontation where the flicker of an eyelid on one side might send a hand flying to a gun on the other. In such an atmosphere a mishandling of Jacquemont's request could have dire consequences.

Bentinck was the soberest of Governors-General, a man dedicated to administrative and moral reform whose external ambitions were simply to maintain the status quo. He must have recalled the go-getting, empire-founding outbursts of Moorcroft with a shudder of horror. On the other hand he had a real affection for the dazzling young Frenchman, he rightly judged that he was not a political hoodlum, and he wanted to help him. He also observed that Jacquemont had a weakness for flattery. The personal letter of introduction to Ranjit Singh was, in the end, not forthcoming, but before Jacquemont could give vent to his disappointment he was introduced to the Sikh representative in Delhi in such flattering terms that he could scarcely keep a straight face. He was to continue as a freelance traveller but as 'the Socrates and Plato of the age' he could be sure of an impressive reception.

On March 2nd 1831 Jacquemont, well primed by the officers at Ludhiana, crossed the Sutlej. By contrast with Moorcroft he travelled light; just a cart, a couple of camels, three or four servants and the spirited little horse which had carried him from Calcutta. For the first few days he dispensed with the horse. For the most delicate of reasons he found the elephant provided by his Sikh escort more comfortable. 'The confidence of lofty souls meets with a poor reward at times. . . . I hope soon to have forgotten the dancing girls of Ludhiana.' ·

Often a preposterous figure, Jacquemont eventually wins one's respect. Few travellers have found their own misfortunes so amusing or been so candid about them. There had already been the celebrated episode of his stomach pump, which had made him the laughing stock of India. Like most travellers he had a vivid horror of gastric upsets and his own personal preventative. The daily clyster is by any standards a drastic precaution, but Jacquemont swore by it. So desperate was he when the vital intrument was stolen in Patiala that he confessed the loss to his blushing British friends. Descriptions and drawings were circulated to the Patiala authorities while the dispensaries of Upper India were scoured for a replacement. Eventually the original was found—no doubt the thief had mistaken it for a French hookah. The news was published in the Patiala court gazette and official notification of its recovery followed via the political department in Delhi. It was indeed the most celebrated syringe on diplomatic record.

Discomforts apart, the journey to Lahore went well. Jacquemont had been led to expect that as a guest all his expenses would be covered and that he would receive a small *nazzerana* each day. This was a cash offering which, like all such gifts, any servant of the Honourable Company had to pass on to his employers. Not so Jacquemont. And nor by his standards was the daily bag of coins so insignificant. A hundred and one rupees a day was two hundred and fifty francs. In the nine days it took to reach Lahore he would be richer by over two thousand francs, a third of his annual salary from the Jardin des Plantes. 'If Ranjit Singh feels obliged to treat his guests like this I can understand why he is not anxious to receive visitors . . . [he] has arguments that would reconcile me to the pace of a tortoise.'

Allard with a party of European officers met Jacquemont outside Lahore. They embraced with gallic fervour and in the general's four-horse barouche galloped off to the Shalimar gardens. '. . . we alighted at the gate of a delicious oasis. There was a great bed of stocks, irises and roses, with walks bordered by orange trees and jasmine beside pools in which a multitude of fountains were playing. In the middle of this beautiful garden was a little palace furnished with extreme luxury and elegance. This is my abode. Luncheon was awaiting us in my sitting room, served on solid silver.' In the evening there came presents of Kabul grapes and pomegranates and a purse containing five hundred rupees. Dinner was served by torchlight. It was 'exactly like a palace from *The Thousand and One Nights*'.

The following day Jacquemont had his first of many audiences with Ranjit Singh. Each had the highest expectations of the other; and neither was disappointed. Discarding what he imagined was a native disguise—green silk dressing gown, Indian trousers and a wide-brimmed black fur hat—Jacquemont appeared in his sober Paris suiting. He had no need of outlandish clothes. Tall and thin with cherubic countenance, vague grey eyes, a mass of chestnut curls and a new but imposing red beard, he looked every inch the romantic hero. The Maharaja liked to be surrounded by beautiful people. His most powerful courtiers, the brothers Dhian Singh and Gulab Singh, owed their elevation to their good looks; the newcomer was a decorous addition.

To live up to his billing as 'the Socrates and Plato of the age', Jacquemont tried to be as aloof and condescending as possible. But the Maharaja would not be put off. 'His conversation is a nightmare,' declared the Frenchman, 'He asked me a hundred thousand questions about India, the English, Europe, Bonaparte, this world in general and the other one, hell and paradise, the soul, God, the devil and a thousand things beside.' Jacquemont could never resist the chance to air his views and his famous charm soon thawed the frigid pose. Its combination of effortless flattery, eloquent wit and an apparently irresistible tone of voice convinced the Maharaja that here indeed was a remarkable man, a veritable demi-god. Whatever his advisers might say this was no Englishman in disguise. Nor would the

English dream of sending such a fluent and interesting young man as a spy. He could bring nothing but credit to Lahore and might go wherever he wished, even to Kashmir.

As for Jacquemont it was a case of love at first sight. 'My beloved Maharaja,' he called him. First sight of Ranjit Singh was not usually prepossessing. 'Exactly like an old mouse with grey whiskers and one eye,' was how Emily Eden described him seven years later. He was very small, almost a dwarf, and even his good eye was failing. His face was pockmarked, his speech slurred and his bearing ungainly. Yet there was no denying an impression of extraordinary energy. His solitary eye blazed with animation, his hands were alive with expression and there was no finer horseman in the whole Sikh army.

Here was a man who had moulded history, like Napoleon a self-made emperor. From obscure origins he had united the Sikh clans, repulsed the Afghans and started to build. Aged eighteen he had captured Lahore and been recognised as chief of the Sikh leaders. At twenty-one he proclaimed himself Maharaja of the Punjab and five years later was negotiating with the British on an equal footing. His courage was unquestioned; it attracted a touching loyalty from his old comrades-in-arms and the empire depended, perhaps too much, on his personal magnetism. Undoubted too were his political insight and opportunism; the British tended to call them avarice and cunning. He could neither read nor write and sometimes for days on end he would conduct no public business. Yet little escaped his attention and few were the men he misjudged.

To be flattered by such a man was praise indeed. Jacquemont revelled in it. Above all he valued the Sikh's confidences. Ranjit Singh's two greatest passions were horses and women. Moorcroft had found common ground on the former. Jacquemont was clearly better informed about the latter. A life of unremitting sexual indulgence had left the Maharaja impotent at fifty. He described his problem as a weakness of the digestion and in case his meaning was not quite clear he proceeded to demonstrate. '. . . the old roué sent for five young girls from his seraglio, ordered them to sit down in front of me and smilingly asked me what I thought of them. I said that in all sincerity I considered them very pretty, which was not a tenth of what I really thought.' The girls were then put through their paces. Even Indian singing had its appeal in such absorbing circumstances. But the Maharaja remarked sadly that he had a whole regiment of these exquisite Kashmiri girls. He would review them mounted bareback on chargers, a combination calculated to excite his deepest emotions. He would ply them with liquor till their performances became naked revels and their frolics savage cat fights. But all to no avail. His 'digestion' failed to respond. In fact the problem had become a matter for general concern. Unresponsive to the women of his own harem, he had taken to trying his jaded prowess on those of other men or even public prostitutes. The streets of Lahore witnessed scenes unprecedented as he drove through them in an enormous state carriage fitted with a verandah which accommodated twenty *nach* girls. Live performances were also given on elephant back, but it was going too far when the girl concerned was a Moslem courtesan and the particular diversion what Jacquemont calls the 'honteux pis-aller des vieux libertins'.

The Frenchman prescribed 'cantharides', evidently a species of beetle, dried. They were reputed to have aphrodisiac qualities and Elphinstone had won much acclaim with them on his mission to Kabul. Whether Ranjit Singh tried them is doubtful. He was usually too suspicious to do more than dose his courtiers and await their reaction.

Jacquemont spent two weeks in Lahore. Like Moorcroft he wanted to get away before the impossible heat of May. It was a measure of his success that instead of prevarication he received generous assistance, five hundred rupees on parting, five hundred more en route and two thousand awaiting him in Kashmir. By then his grand total would be more than two years' salary. There were other presents, Kashmir shawls, silks and jewels, camels to carry his baggage and a secretary to see that the Maharaja had a full report of his progress. Allard checked through his equipment, supplying any additions he thought necessary, and threw a grand and 'plus galante' farewell party in the Shalimar gardens. The Kashmiri girls were more lovely than ever. One in particular attracted his attention. She was beautiful by any standards, a real 'princesse d'Opera'. In the half-dark, while the servants were lighting the saloon and the rest of the party were dispersed through the garden, who should come to him but the lady herself. Allard's generosity was on a par with Kennedy's. And the ladies of Lahore did not 'betray the confidence of a lofty soul'. He left, on horseback, on March 25th.

His immediate destination was Kashmir but where Jacquemont intended to go from there is not clear. From Simla in 1830 he had attempted, like the Gerards, to cross into Tibet. In his own book he had succeeded. It is hard to follow his exact route but he claims to have crossed the frontier undetected and penetrated a day's march before being stopped by 'Chinese' guards. Thinking their reluctance to dismount was lacking in respect, he summoned one for a parley and promptly grabbed his pigtail and unhorsed him. It made an excellent story for home consumption and he had withdrawn to British territory well contented. At one time he certainly planned to continue his Tibetan campaign from Kashmir but it seems the British must have talked him out of this. The plan was now to be the more modest one of proceeding from Kashmir to Ladakh, and thence back to Simla either via Spiti and Bushair or by Moorcroft's Kulu route. In the event neither was possible. He was lucky to get as far as Kashmir safely.

Trouble started as soon as he reached the foothills at Mirpur. Ranjit Singh had promised him mules and porters to take over from the camels; neither materialised. The villagers fled before him and even his Sikh escort started to melt away. Supplies were hard to come by, the water was so muddy it looked like chocolate and when the rain was not dissolving the labels on his geological specimens the temperature soared to 93°. A man like Moorcroft would have patiently bided his time but Jacquemont was not used to fending for himself. Till now his path had been smoothed by the reassuring authority of a Bentinck, a Kennedy or a Ranjit Singh. Here it seemed that though still within the territories of Lahore it was every man for himself. Cursing, coercing and, as a last resort, considering paying his porters, he pushed on ahead with a scratch complement.

April 22nd dawned full of promise. No porters had absconded during the night, the weather was fine and cooler, and they were under way in good time. Jacquemont's horse was lame but the path was anyway too steep and rough for safe riding. He was in fact ascending an almost perpendicular mountain. The top was flat and on it stood a hill fort. After an hour's stiff haul he was over the lip and looking on a fine sward of grass with the fort in the middle. Groups of ragged soldiers armed with swords and matchlocks were dotted about and Jacquemont's party lay resting in the shade of a giant fig tree. It was very picturesque but too early for breakfast. The order to proceed was given. Nothing happened. The men weren't resting, they had been ordered to stay there. The governor of the fort turned out to be a half-starved bandit called Nihal Singh, and Jacquemont was already his prisoner.

This Nihal Singh deserves a better press than he gets from Jacquemont's biographers. He had been appointed governor of the fort by the Maharaja and right faithfully had he held it, even against the demands of Gulab Singh, the Maharaja's most powerful deputy in the mountains. Like most such governors he would have been told not to surrender his charge to anyone except Ranjit Singh himself. But Gulab Singh had seen to it that the obstinate hill man suffered for his intransigence. For three years he had received no pay. His men were starving and a prestigious hostage was just what he needed. Jacquemont had already met and liked Gulab Singh, but history has revealed him as a cruel and scheming autocrat. At the time he was busy carving out for himself a semi-independent kingdom in the mountains, the power base from which, after Ranjit Singh's death, he was to manœuvre for Kashmir. In the context of his plans this fort, commanding one of the main routes from Lahore to Srinagar, was an essential acquisition.

Cheered on by the armed rabble who now jostled and threatened, Nihal Singh explained the situation to his unsympathetic prisoner. He did not yet realise that the cruellest blow of all was to have picked on a man like Jacquemont as hostage. For the Frenchman it was to be his finest hour. The desperadoes were shaking the ash from their already lighted matchlocks. His own men were miserable with fear and closely guarded. Help, in the shape of Gulab Singh, lay many days' march away and the fort was in any case impregnable. His only weapon was bluff. He affected an arrogant, world weary and devastating unconcern; to the romantic young man it was second nature. Taking Nihal Singh firmly by the arm he sat him in the shade of the fig tree. Then he had a chair brought for himself. Undismayed Nihal Singh started again to explain; the traveller did not seem to understand that he was a prisoner. Jacquemont interrupted. He summoned his servant and ordered a drink. It was a long time coming and then he felt too hot to conduct business. His parasol was laboriously erected and another servant cooled his master with a peacock fan. At last Jacquemont turned his short sighted gaze on his captor. In the most confidential tone he pointed out the enormity of the crime contemplated and the hopelessness of Nihal Singh's position should he persist with it. Nihal Singh reconsidered. Perhaps relieved that he was not yet fully committed and a little unsure of his peculiar prey he suggested a generous compromise. He would just hang on to the party's baggage. Jacquemont exploded.

'What? Travel without my tents? Without my furniture? Without my books? Without all my clothes? I who change twice a day!'

Then carefully studying his watch he ordered breakfast. His servant explained that nothing was ready. Even milk was not to hand.

'Don't you hear?' bellowed Jacquemont at Nihal Singh, 'The lord wants some milk. Send to the neighbouring villages as quickly as possible so that it may be brought at once.'

It was his masterstroke. Nihal Singh was confused. What sort of a man was this who used not the royal 'we' but was so grand he talked of himself in the third person? He hesitated, then gave the order. A small party set off for the milk. Jacquemont waited till they were almost out of earshot before ordering them back. It must be cow's milk, not goat's or buffalo's, and they were to watch the cows being milked with their own eyes. He was just rubbing it in. The victory was his. 'They were crushed by my disdain'; it had also taken a lot of courage.

In the end Nihal Singh got just five hundred rupees and even this he would only accept on the condition it was given as a present. For now he was Jacquemont's most grateful friend and most faithful servant. He offered an escort, a doubtful security, and whispered a request for a bottle of wine. Overcome with relief, Jacquemont still had the presence of mind to give him a bottle of the Delhi arrack, which he used as a preservative, rather than any of his vintage port. Later he sent Ranjit Singh a full report of the affair and received ample compensation. Nihal Singh was captured and imprisoned at Jacquemont's pleasure. Though the Maharaja was celebrated for his leniency, this was an exceptionally humane sentence. It may have been in deference to European sensibilities. More probably it can be taken as further evidence that poor Nihal Singh had a better case than most 'brigand chiefs'.

Jacquemont pressed on for Kashmir. In Punch he collapsed spitting blood from what he took to be a chill. Sixty-five leeches fished from nearby rivers and applied to his chest and stomach seemed to cure the trouble. He crossed the Pir Panjal by the easy pass above Uri and reached Srinagar on May 8th 1831. He claimed to be the first European since Bernier to visit Kashmir undisguised. True, Forster had tried to hide his identity and de Koros, for convenience rather than necessity, had also worn native dress. But Moorcroft and Trebeck certainly stuck to their European coats.

It may be significant that Jacquemont could be wrong about this and yet surprisingly well informed about later episodes in Moorcroft's travels. In 1831 these were still unpublished. But at Kennedy's house Jacquemont had met and become close friends with William Fraser. So much so that Fraser, a renowned misanthropist, applied for permission to accompany him to Kashmir. This was the man amongst whose papers Moorcroft's last journals were found. It looks as if in 1831 these were already in his possession. Jacquemont is quite clear about Moorcroft's dying in Central Asia and the causes being 'a putrid fever, or else a dose of poison or even gunshot'. But of his doings in Kashmir, chronicled in journals which Fraser never possessed, he is poorly informed. A case in point may be discerned in his handling of approaches from Ahmed Shah, ruler of Baltistan. He seems to have imagined it was Moorcroft's overtures to this Raja, rather than to the Ladakhis, that earned him Ranjit Singh's displeasure and the Company's censure. (Moorcroft was in touch with Baltistan but it had not led to any repercussions.) Jacquemont's mistake, though it was to cost Amhed Shah dear, had the effect of bringing the existence and predicament of this remote mountain kingdom to the attention of the outside world.

Baltistan lies due north of Kashmir along a stretch of the Upper Indus and between the Great Himalaya and the Karakorams. The name derives from the people, the Baltis, who doubtless were the Byltae of the classical geographers. It is also called Skardu (Skardo or Iskardo), after the principal fort, and sometimes Little Tibet as distinct from Middle or Western Tibet (Ladakh) and Greater Tibet (the country which still bears the name). Jacquemont always calls it Little Tibet; it was the more romantic of the three. No European had ever been there and though he hoped to explore towards it, he showed no inclination to be the first. Already he had decided that Ladakh was beyond his means and was quite content making short botanical forays round the Kashmir valley.

Returning from one of these he found, instead of the expected courier with a batch of letters from France, a man claiming to be an emissary from Ahmed Shah. It was flattering to find that his fame already extended to the remotest valleys of the Western Himalayas and Jacquemont glowed at the oriental compliments of his unknown admirer. He was less happy when it transpired that Ahmed Shah had taken him for a British agent. This rather diminished the value of the compliments and threatened to prejudice his good relations with Ranjit Singh. The agent affirmed his master's attachment to the British, his dislike of the Sikhs and his expectations of what 'Jackman sahib' could achieve with a couple of British regiments. Recalling what he thought he had heard of Moorcroft's indiscretions Jacquemont made sure that Ranjit Singh had a report of the affair. The Sikhs were after all not just his hosts but his paymasters. Much as he resented the accusation, Jacquemont in Kashmir was in effect the Maharaja's spy. He returned Ahmed Shah's compliments and insisted that his interests were purely scientific.

Two months later, while botanising in the north-western corner of the Kashmir valley, he was again visited by agents from Baltistan. 'I cannot make out what these people want of the English,' he wrote. Ahmed Shah had the reputation of being a model ruler, beloved by his subjects and feared by his neighbours. His kingdom was safe enough from the Sikhs; it was too poor to attract conquerors and quite inaccessible. '. . . for all my diplomatic genius I cannot make it out'. Since there was no way the Sikhs could injure Ahmed Shah, he again sent a full report of the meeting to Lahore. But he was wrong. These reports were to have serious repercussions. The Sikhs could reach Baltistan and, armed with this evidence, were inclined to do so. The first of several attempts to invade the country was made in 1833, and for the next six years the fate of Baltistan was to be a decisive factor in the exploration of the mountains.

Jacquemont spent four months in Kashmir. He amassed a considerable collection of plants, geological specimens, stuffed birds and preserved fishes; there was even a pair of live antelopes sent by Ahmed Shah. Yet he was unhappy. It was usual for the romantic hero to carp and boredom was second nature to him, but this was something more. Earlier he had written, 'sometimes I cannot believe that it was I who did this or that or went here or there . . . at times I doubt my own identity'. No one who has been alone in strange surroundings will question such sincerity. The symptoms speak for themselves. He was lonely and very homesick. Had there been a post office he would have been hanging listlessly about outside it. He himself wrote reams, in 1831 346 substantial letters as well as his weighty journal. His regular correspondents were friends and family in France whose letters came round by the Cape to Chandernagore, the French colony near Calcutta, then up country to Wade, the British agent at Ludhiana, then to Allard at Lahore and finally across the mountains by special courier. In July he received the first news from home in twelve months. 'Now I am happy . . . my hand shakes, my ideas are in confusion.'

This euphoria was short lived. In July and August he found the heat stifling and was one of very few who have actually longed for the scorching winds of the plains. He was thinner than ever and seriously worried about his health. *Lalla Rookh* bored him, the Kashmiris depressed him and the scenery was disappointing. As for the women, they were hideous; the handsome ones were all exported to the Punjab. It was not till he received what he chose to regard as a summons from Ranjit Singh to return that his favourite aphorism reappears—'All is for the best in this best possible of worlds'.

With an escort of sixty cavalry—he was not to be at the mercy of another Nihal Singh—and some fifty porters loaded with his specimens he left Kashmir on September 19th. The route this time was via the Pir Panjal pass, the one used by Moorcroft, and thence to Jammu and Amritsar. Here he found the Maharaja who was on his way to a celebrated meeting with the Governor-General at Rupar. Jacquemont had resolved not to accompany him—'a mere Plato would be lost in the dust at the meeting of two such immortals'. Already the Sikh court was in a high state of excitement, yet Ranjit Singh found time for a protracted farewell. He tried to persuade Jacquemont to stay, offering him no less than the viceregency of Kashmir, an inducement which the Frenchman correctly judged to be purely figurative. At Hoshiarpur they finally parted.

Our last interview was long and very friendly; Ranjit lavished a thousand caresses on me; he took my hand and shook it several times at my well aimed broadsides of flattery into which I infused, spontaneously, a deal of feeling.

Moist-eyed but well pleased, both with himself and with Ranjit's parting presents, Jacquemont left the royal camp. He had understood the Maharaja better than almost any other European. They were an ill-assorted pair, the young, elegant, educated Parisian and the old, ugly and illiterate emperor. Yet as seen through the other's eyes both acquire stature. To a man from whom he correctly surmised that there was little to fear, the Maharaja displayed a genuine warmth and loyalty. Jacquemont reciprocated. He rejoiced in Ranjit's patronage but, to his credit, never abused it.

*   *   *

On the occasion of his thirtieth birthday in Kashmir Jacquemont had written, 'I think a man must be rather foolish to allow himself to die at thirty.' A year later in Poona, when ill health was getting the better of him, he claimed that 'a traveller in my line has several ways of making what the Italians term a *fiasco*, but the most complete fiasco of all is to die on the road'. A few months later he did just that. He was thirty-one.

After recouping with Kennedy at Simla and with Fraser at Delhi he had set off during the hottest months of the year for Bombay, a nightmare of a journey through the wastes of Central India. It demanded a different sort of courage to the sangfroid he had deployed against Nihal Singh, something more like grim determination. He had it in good measure; but the journey was too much. In the jungle just north of Bombay he was taken ill with fever which produced an abcess of the liver. For some weeks he suffered in appalling pain before dying peacefully in Bombay on December 7th 1832.

Much about Jacquemont is infuriating, his vanity, his posing and his selfishness. He is too glib, too determinedly witty, to be very funny. And yet one must admire him. He was no fool and no coward. He was the most unlikely of explorers, yet he was the first and by no means the least in the long tradition of Himalayan naturalists. In his death a real dignity emerges. Merimée called him 'a stoic in the real sense of the word', a man who 'took as much pains to conceal his emotions as others do to hide their evil propensities'. In his last letters the mask starts to dissolve. It does not reveal the shallow, ordinary character one suspects under all those airs and affectations. There emerges a truly courageous and generous soul. He studies the progress of his death with a calm but intense interest. He reassures his family lest they think him dying lonely and friendless. In fact he is glad they are not present; he warmly commends the Englishmen who are looking after him and fears that the grief of his father and brothers would be too much for him to bear. To the very last 'all is for the best in this best . . .' but it is impossible to read on without tears.

4. A Heathen King

In the spring of 1832, while Jacquemont was making that gruelling journey from Delhi to Bombay, another European was toiling east through Afghanistan. He had passed through Bukhara, the first visitor there since Moorcroft, and was now retracing the steps of his unfortunate predecessor towards Punjab and the court of Ranjit Singh. He, too, had his heart set on Kashmir and the lands beyond the mountains. And though as odd a character as ever set foot in the Himalayas, his chances of getting there were not to be under-rated.

But first he had safely to negotiate Afghanistan. At Khulm he escaped the attentions of Mured Beg by hiding in his room at the caravanserai and slipping out before dawn. It was altogether easier for him than it had been for Moorcroft. He had just three servants and negligible baggage. The clothes he wore were not a conscious disguise. They were just the sort of travel-stained cottons that any-one who had been wandering about the Middle East for five years might have been reduced to. Provided he kept his mouth shut, he was as safe as anyone in this lawless corner of Asia.

Four days south from Khulm, at a place called Doab, he left the lands of Murad Beg and entered the mountainous country of the Hazaras. These are a Mongol people, descendants of Genghis Khan, and every bit as wild as their Uzbek and Afghan neighbours. Something about the traveller, perhaps the tattered book which he always carried under his arm, drew their attention. They demanded to know his name.

His problem was not one of language. He could speak any number, including Persian, the *lingua franca* of the region. The difficulty was that to him it was a matter of principle not to tell a lie. He could mislead but under no circumstances would he deny his identity or his purpose. A week previously he had told the governor of Mazar-i-Sharif, a man who was sworn to kill every European and whom he believed to be personally responsible for the deaths of Moorcroft and his companions, that he came from Malta. He was not Maltese but back in 1830 it was from Malta that he had begun this particular

63

journey. The governor had never heard of Malta; he wanted to know where it was. By way of an answer he was told that there, instead of boats made of skins, they had steamships. These made a distinctive noise which the traveller imitated and in one of them you could reach Malta from Constantinople in four days. As for the Governor of Malta he was called Ponsonby Khan, son of Bessborough Khan and his wife was the daughter of Bathurst Khan. This was too much for the Mazar chief. Appalled at his ignorance of this supposed Islamic sea-power, he had beaten a speedy retreat.

At Doab the stranger was hoping to use the same tactics. They wanted to know his name. He would tell them.

'Haji Youssuf,' he replied.

Youssuf is the Arabic Joseph and a *haji* is someone who has made the pilgrimage to Mecca. The Hazaras asked for the blessing of such a holy man. But they must still have been suspicious for they now turned to one of his servants and asked if the *haji* were really a Mohammedan. The servant said yes. Haji Youssuf said no.

'Why do you take the name of *haji* if you are not a Mohammedan?'

'Even the Mohammedans in Bukhara recognise as *haji* all Jews and Christians who have been to Jerusalem.'

'This is not the custom here among us. We are *kharijee* [i.e. schismatics; they were actually Shiah]. With us many things are not allowed which are allowed by other Mohammedans.'

'I could not know your usage for I have but just arrived among you; so all you can do is not to call me *haji*; I shall tell my people not to call me *haji*.'

'The mischief is done and therefore you must either say "There is God and nothing but God and Mohammed is his prophet" or we will sew you up in a dead donkey, burn you alive and make sausages of you.'

'There is God and nothing but God and Jesus the Son of God.'

It was as good as signing his own death warrant. The Hazaras assembled with their Mullahs in a nearby cave and prepared to pass formal sentence. The traveller asked for his writing box and in great terror, for he was not a brave man, wrote the following letter.

To Lord and Lady William Bentinck.
Dear Lord and Lady William Bentinck
The moment you read this you must beware that I am no longer in the land of the living; that I have been put to death. Give to my

servants some hundred rupees for their journey and write the whole account to my wife, Lady Georgiana.
Your affectionate,
Joseph Wolff.

He confided the letter to his servants who were to travel with all haste to Ludhiana and give it to the first redcoat they saw. Then he bade them farewell and turned with the tattered Bible still under his arm towards the cave.

Joseph Wolff, that was indeed his name, was by 1832 used to persecution. Since the age of seven he had been angering people with his religious mania. And he was now thirty-eight. Born the son of a Bohemian rabbi, he had started asking awkward questions as soon as he could talk. At seven he was all for abandoning the Jewish faith in favour of Christianity. At eleven he wanted to be a Jesuit; an old aunt was so provoked she threw the poker at him. At seventeen he was baptised a Catholic, and at twenty-one he arrived in Rome to study for the priesthood. By then there was no town in Germany with the most modest academic pretensions from which he had not been expelled. Rightly he saw himself as the *enfant terrible* of the theological world, and it was just a matter of time before Rome too would reject him. In the event he was treated with great patience and retained a lifelong respect for Catholicism. But when, after eighteen turbulent months, he was still objecting to papal infallibility and flirting with protestantism, the Inquisition stepped in. He was 'rolled out of Rome' under guard and deposited in Vienna. Again he did the rounds of the German monasteries, trying even a flagellant order before he finally took up an offer of patronage from Henry Drummond, a wealthy English eccentric. He arrived in London in 1819.

It is no good looking for the modern equivalent of a man like Wolff. He was an extraordinary phenomenon and one not likely to be repeated. The twentieth century is too indifferent to religion and too sensitive about mental derangement. Such a man if not actually shut away would today be smothered by sympathy, his opinions curdling inside him. A shabby figure known to all at the public library, his greatest act of defiance would be a stream of never published letters to the newspapers. In the early nineteenth century society was less kind. Wolff was taken at his own value and made to pay for it. Instead of pity he met with ridicule. Instead of being ignored by the papers they pilloried him. And instead of being protected he was packed off to the wildest regions of Asia.

Yet he thrived on it. Wolff's life was a supremely happy one. Hardship, loneliness, exhaustion and ostracism were normal to him. Yet no man was ever further from despair. He was doing his life's work and at the age of sixty-five he could still tell the story of it with unadulterated satisfaction. Age modified some of his more outrageous ideas and caused him to regret his youthful intolerance. But he was still a little mad. He was also cantankerous, excitable and vain, a difficult man to get on with and a colossal embarrassment in public. It was, and still is, easy to be funny about him; less easy, a hundred and fifty years later, to understand how people could love him. But even Bentinck, whom Jacquemont described as an upright, simple and sincere administrator 'like a Quaker of Pennsylvania', doted on Wolff. And he was far from being alone.

The English have always had a weakness for eccentrics and Wolff liked what he saw of England and, even more, what he saw of the Church of England. Here was a Christian institution elastic enough to accommodate his unorthodoxy and rich enough to be interested in proselytising. As a converted Jew, Wolff's lifelong ambition had been to preach Christianity to the Jewish people. It was with this in mind that he had studied Hebrew, steeped himself in scripture and joined the Propaganda in Rome. Now at last he found a man, Henry Drummond, and an institution, The Society for Promoting Christianity among the Jews, both willing to support him. The latter sent him to Cambridge to continue his oriental studies and the former, two years later, packed him off to the Mediterranean on his first mission.

He was away for five eventful years. He visited almost every city of consequence between Teheran, Cairo and Constantinople, and claims to have been the first Jew since Christ to preach Christianity in Jerusalem. His diaries read rather like the daily call sheets of a conscientious salesman. 'Proclaimed Christ to so-and-so. Requests Bible in Kurdish.' He met with some rough treatment and converts were not easily won. But unlike previous Jewish missionaries from England, 'one of whom became a Mohammedan, another a thief and a third a pickpocket,' Wolff stuck to his guns.

On the day he arrived back in England he met at a dinner party Lady Georgiana Walpole, daughter of the Earl of Orford. That any woman should want to marry Wolff seems strange. In his own estimation he was a great favourite of the ladies but, even if true, this was not quite the same thing as being eligible. Besides Lady Georgiana was an altogether improbable conquest. She was passably handsome, of independent means and impeccably connected. To Wolff she became 'his darling angel in earthly shape', and six months later he married her. Neither seems ever to have regretted it. Shortly after he became a naturalised British subject. He could now count on a warm reception at any distant outpost of the Empire to which his travels might take him.

In 1827 the happy couple left England to resume Wolff's work. For three years he continued to tour the Middle East with Lady Georgiana never far behind. In Jerusalem, the scene of his earlier triumphs, he received a cold welcome and was poisoned in a coffee house. Lady Georgiana was there to nurse him, but it was galling to be an invalid and outcaste when he had expected to be the conquering hero. He was beginning to lose interest in the Jews of Jerusalem and to look further afield.

He returned to Malta in 1830. Lady Georgiana joined him there, now with their second child,* and they discussed plans to visit Timbuktu. It is not clear whether Wolff imagined he would find Jews in the Sahara but when a friend suggested Bukhara and Afghanistan, where there were not only Jews but remnants of the lost tribes, he readily agreed. 'Wolff shouted', he always writes of himself as plain 'Wolff' and he often shouts, 'Wolff shouted, "To Bukhara I shall go!"' The Society for Promoting Christianity among the Jews wanted him back in London. Wolff wrote that he was on his way—via Bukhara, Tibet and Calcutta—and on December 29th 1830 said a sad goodbye to Lady Georgiana and set off for Turkestan and the Himalayas.†

Such a journey, if successful, promised to rival that of Marco Polo. The dangers were appalling but, as he now turned to confront the Mullahs of Doab, he could reassure himself with the recollection of many an equally hopeless situation. He had already been captured

* Their first child, a daughter, lived only a few months. The second, christened Henry Drummond Wolff, was to have a distinguished diplomatic career.

† This was the 1860 account of the inspiration for the journey. In the 1835 account he says that the idea came to him while still in Jerusalem. 'I said to my wife, "Bukhara and Balkh are much in my mind for I think I shall find there the Ten Tribes." "Well," she said, "I have no objection to your going there." '

by slave dealers and dragged across the desert tied to a horse's tail. He had always escaped and he was still going strong. As a traveller his experience was unique; there was yet momentum to carry him across the Himalayas.

The mullahs of Doab were seated in the cave with the Koran open before them. Wolff himself takes up the story.

Wolff said, 'What humbug is that? You cannot dare to put me to death. You will be putting to death a guest.'

They replied, 'The Koran decides so.'

Wolff said, 'It is a lie. The Koran says on the contrary that a guest should be respected even if he is an infidel; and see here the great *firman* I have from the Khalif of the whole Mohammedan religion from Stamboul. You have no power to put me to death. You must send me to Mohammed Murad Beg at Kunduz. Have you not seen how little afraid of you I am? I have told the Afghans [with whom he had been travelling] that they should disperse and probably some of them have already gone to Kunduz.' When they heard the name of Murad Beg they actually began to tremble and asked Wolff 'Do you know him?' As Wolff could not say that he knew him he replied, 'This you must find out.' They said 'Then you must purchase your blood with all that you have.' Wolff answered 'This will I do. For I am a dervish and do not mind either money, clothing or anything.'

And thus Wolff had to surrender everything. Oh, if his friends in England could have seen him then they would have stared at him. Naked like Adam and Eve and without even an apron of leaves to dress himself in he continued his journey.

For the next six hundred miles Wolff claims that he travelled without clothes. If his friends in England could have seen him they might have looked on 'an obese and dauntless Sebastian'. That was how *Blackwoods Magazine* described him facing his critics, and it certainly corresponds with the portrait we have of him at sixty-five. On the other hand they might have seen a man 'in stature short and thin' with 'a weak frame'. This was an earlier eye-witness and one can only presume that somewhere along the line he put on weight prodigiously. He was never indifferent to food, succumbing to pizzas in Rome and plum pudding in Cairo. A profile drawing of him in 1840 already reveals a double chin. Perhaps, too, one did not normally notice his figure. The 'strange and most curious looking' visage was enough to hold the attention. It was 'very flat and deeply marked with smallpox', the complexion 'that of dough' and the 'hair flaxen'. People were reminded of Luther except that the eyes were too disquieting. They 'roll and start and fix themselves most fearfully; they have a cast in them which renders their expression still wilder'.

Such was the apparition that now flitted across the mountains of Afghanistan. The Hindu Kush here is not the majestic range it becomes in the Western Himalayas but it is still an extensive area of desolate terrain with passes of eleven and twelve thousand feet. It was only April and on the high ground the snow lay deep. Tumbling into snowdrifts and running from the icy wind, Wolff kept on for Kabul. On the first of May he emerged from the mountains and came within a few miles of the city. He was now in a state of collapse; he was also penniless and still naked. It was unthinkable to enter the city in such a condition, and anyway his servants were not going to let him. He owed them money and they wanted to be sure that his credit was good before going any further. With no great expectations Wolff wrote for help to Dost Mohammed, the ruler of Kabul, and prayed to his Saviour.

Whenever a situation like this had arisen in the past, assistance had come in the shape of 'a British soldier sent to him by God'. In 1823, when he had been sick in Jerusalem, a British colonel had appeared from nowhere and nursed him over the worst and set him on his feet again. In 1824 the same thing happened in Baghdad when he stumbled into the city after receiving a 200-lash bastinado. In 1825 it was the Caucasus. Wolff, prostrate with typhus, lay dying beside the road when a guardian angel, again in colonel's uniform, swept him into his carriage and off to the sanitorium of a nearby monastery. 1826 was a blank but in 1827 it was no less a man than General Sir Charles Napier who rescued him in Cephalonia after being washed ashore, destitute, from a shipwreck. 1828, dysentery in Cairo, and a Colonel Felix relieved Lady Georgiana of the job of nursing him. And finally 1829, when having been attacked by pirates near Salonica he had drifted ashore and wandered about barefoot for two days, it was a naval lieutenant who came to the rescue with an advance of clothing and money.

This was just the help he needed now though the chances of a British officer being anywhere near Kabul were dim. None had been sent there since Elphinstone in 1808. But Wolff had great faith and, sure enough, within two hours there appeared men with a horse and clothing for the traveller and a letter. It was addressed to him in English.

The writer turned out to be Lieutenant Burnes of the Bombay army. He had arrived in Kabul the day before along with Dr. James Gerard, one of the three Aberdonian brothers whom Jacquemont had met in Simla. At the very least it was an extraordinary coincidence. Burnes and Gerard were en route to Bukhara, a journey which was to be the making of the former and the death of the latter. Gerard was now well into his fifties and already a sick man. But he welcomed Wolff and enjoyed the diversion when their house was turned into a debating chamber for all the Jews and Armenians of the city. Burnes was less enthusiastic. Probably he was a little picqued at having been beaten to Bukhara. A year later he was to do his best to expose Wolff as both a lunatic and a liar.

Wolff did not stay long. He told Mohan Lal, Burnes's secretary, that in Bukhara he had had a vision in which Christ told him that the valley of Kashmir would be the new Jerusalem. There were also persistent rumours that Kashmir was the site of the Garden of Eden and that the population belonged to one of the lost tribes. Jacquemont particularly had remarked on the physical resemblance between the Kashmiris and the Jews. Already Wolff was convinced that the Jews of Turkestan were of the lost tribes (also, surprisingly, 'the descendents of Genghis Khan, the Nogay Tartars and those called of the tribe of Naphthali'). He was less sure about the Kafirs of the Hindu Kush, but the Kashmiris sounded very promising. He could hardly wait to get there.

He passed through Jalalabad and Peshawar and crossed the Indus at Attock. After the savagery of the Turkomans, the bigotry of the Hazaras and then the wild Pathans of the Khyber, Punjab was a welcome change. He was greeted by kind respectful people dressed in flowing white cottons. Their hands were folded as they awaited his orders. It was the sort of reception he envisaged receiving at the gates of Heaven. If only Ranjit Singh were not just 'a heathen king' but the King of Kings; 'Well done,' he would say, 'thou good and faithful servant, enter thou into the joy of the Lord.'

Ranjit Singh was not much interested in religion but he was doing his best for Wolff. Lord William Bentinck, who had been warned of the missionary's approach by the British representative in Persia, had asked the old Sikh to look after him. Instead of Jacquemont's hundred rupees a day he was getting two hundred and fifty and was free to make his own way towards Lahore. It was a striking contrast to his treatment in Afghanistan. He was entertained by Hari Singh, one of the greatest Sikh commanders, Kharak Singh, the heir apparent, and then Josiah Harlan,* an American who held the governorship of Gujerat, and Paolo Avitabile,† the Italian governor at Wazirabad. 'The kind Italian' was really a cruel libertine and the 'very interesting American' a two-faced scoundrel who played the Sikhs as false as he had the British before them. Wolff was never much of a judge of character and he was overwhelmed by these receptions. So much so that after leaving Avitabile he made what later turned out to be a fatal blunder.

Meantime, dressed in a European suit made for him in Peshawar and crisp new linen provided by the Sikhs, Wolff was carried in a palanquin to Lahore and then on to Amritsar where the Maharaja was spending the summer. On June 21st he was presented at court. An elephant was sent to fetch him and after passing through three courtyards he was ushered towards a figure which, with his feeble sight, he took to be a small boy. He was about to ask him if he was one of the Maharaja's *bachas* when he made out the long grey beard.

---

* Josiah Harlan was born in Pennsylvania, studied medicine and made his way to the Far East and thence to Burma. He served as a medical officer with the British forces in Burma and then embarked on a complex life of intrigue in the Punjab and Afghanistan. At different times, and occasionally at the same time, he served the Sikhs, the British, Dost Mohammed of Kabul and Shah Shuja, the ex-king of Kabul. He was a colourful, eccentric and clever man whose mercurial career deserves a biographer if only for the distinction he enjoys of being the only man ever to have unfurled the Stars and Stripes on the Hindu Kush.

†Avitabile's life is best summed up by the inscription on his tomb at Agerola in Italy.

Lieut.-General Paolo di Avitabile
Born October 1791. Died March 28th 1850.
Chevalier of the Legion of Honour. Of the Order of Merit of San Fernando of Naples. Of the Durrani Order of Afghanistan. Grand Cordon of the Sun and of the Two Lions and the Crown of Persia. Of the Auspicious Order of the Punjab. Naples First Lieutenant. Persia Colonel. France and the Punjab, General and Governor of Peshawar.
A man of matchless honour and glory.
Of all the Europeans in Ranjit Singh's service he was probably the most ruthless. He was also the most successful in that he alone not only amassed a large fortune but managed to get it to Europe and there to enjoy the fruits of his labours.

Ranjit Singh enquired about his travels and Wolff as usual took this as a cue to 'proclaim Christ'. The Maharaja was not even a very good Sikh; such talk bored him. He tried politics but they clearly bored Wolff and by way of distraction the dancing girls were called on. Wolff immediately objected; he 'could find no pleasure in such amusements'. The audience was turning sour. Ranjit Singh tried again and pressed Wolff to a glass of brandy. The Sikh's only tipple was concocted for him by a German doctor called Honigberger from a mixture of raw spirit, crushed pearls, musk, opium, gravy and spices. Burnes and Gerard, Scotsmen hardened on home-made whisky, were the only visitors who were able to stomach it. Later the pale lips of Emily Eden were to be severely burnt by the first sip. Wolff, finding his mouth filled with fire, was unable to swallow.

As a final gambit the Maharaja tried to pull Wolff's leg. Did he believe that nobody could die without the will of God? He did. Then why had Wolff cried out with terror when he was ferried across the Indus? This was a sore point. Few travellers were as physically handicapped as the poor Jew. Woefully short-sighted and a dismal horseman, he also had a horror of water. There had been the ship-wreck and then the brush with pirates in the Aegean and before that a lucky escape in the Black Sea. On that occasion he had requested a passage on the SS *Little* from the ship's skipper, Captain Little. But Captain Little had replied that he objected to having preachers on board and anyway his ship was too little to accommodate one. Wolff had found another vessel; the *Little* had been lost with all hands. Crossing the Oxus on the way to Bukhara he had taken the precaution of being blindfolded but, evidently failing to do the same on the Indus, his hydrophobia had been embarrassing to watch. He could only explain it by admitting that his weakness was reason to pray harder. Before he could develop this theme Ranjit Singh closed the audience and the next day Wolff was free to move on towards Ludhiana and Simla.

Nothing in this disastrous interview had been said about Kashmir. When Wolff had first arrived in the Punjab he had written to the Maharaja of his plans and there then seemed to be every prospect of permission being granted. Now his chances looked hopeless. It was a tragedy. If there was one man amongst all the early explorers who might have managed the classic journey to Kashmir, Ladakh and over the worst mountain barrier of all to Yarkand, it was Wolff. The most unorthodox of travellers he was also, to the native mind, the most convincing. It was transparently obvious that he had no political objectives. He claimed to be a *haji*, a dervish or a fakir and even the bigots of Bukhara had come to appreciate that that precisely was what he was. Moreover these religious travellers, along with a few well-known traders, were the only people who could pass freely through the mountains. Wolff had little appreciation of geography and never bothered with maps. It was another point in his favour. Travellers who enquired about distances and directions or who pored over compasses and thermometers were viewed with great suspicion. They might claim that they were travelling purely out of curiosity but no one ever believed them; it was well known that before Europeans invaded a country they sent out surveyors and scientists to record the lie of the land. Finally Wolff was obviously a little mad and this too was an advantage. Madness was thought close to godliness; it was the only qualification possessed by many fakirs and to molest such a man was fraught with dire consequences. At Doab and elsewhere Wolff probably owed his life to this widespread superstition.

For Ranjit Singh's reluctance to let him go to Kashmir, Wolff had only himself to blame. The fatal mistake he made on the way from Wazirabad to Lahore was to issue one of his famous proclamations about 'the personal rule of Christ'. His religious platform at the time had three planks, the conversion of the Jews, the discovery of the lost tribes and the Second Coming. It was the last which caused so much trouble. Having carefully combed through the scriptures, having made complicated arithmetical calculations and having observed the frequency of earthquakes, cholera epidemics and other pestilences, he was convinced that Christ would come again in 1847. If some parts of scripture were interpreted literally then all should be. He had no difficulty believing in miracles. He had heard of thousands, seen some himself and one he had actually worked, the mere casting out of a devil. Visions, too, he took for granted. Besides seeing Christ in Bukhara he had been visited by Saint Paul and the Heavenly Hosts in Malta. Saint Paul, himself a converted Jew and the first great missionary, told his protégé, 'Thou also shalt have a crown but not such a glorious one as I have.'

So why not the Second Coming? The Society for Promoting Christianity among the Jews had not liked it, and for this they had demanded his return to London. Alexander Burnes had also taken exception. He told the Calcutta newspapers that Wolff was preaching the end of the world and that soon everyone would be enjoying the rule of the New Jerusalem and walking about naked like Wolff, with nothing to eat but vegetables. When Ranjit Singh received his copy of the glad tidings he sent it off by express courier to Lord William Bentinck. Bentinck replied asking that the traveller be sent forthwith to Simla. Perhaps the journey had been too much for him; if he had now entirely taken leave of his senses it was vital to get him out of circulation.

Wolff at the time knew nothing of this but flattered by the Governor-General's anxiety to see him he pressed on for Simla. There Lord William, and more especially Lady William who was a devout Christian, decided there was nothing wrong with him. In fact they found him charming. His guileless honesty was irresistible and even about his own vanities and eccentricities he could be disarmingly candid; he was most likely to agree with anyone who called him crazy. When he realised that it was not Ranjit Singh but Bentinck who had scotched his journey through the mountains, he immediately reopened the question. Bentinck tried hard to dissuade him, but when this failed it was agreed that Lady William should make the request of Ranjit Singh. This made it less official and, if anything, more cogent. There followed a long delay, but eventually the Maharaja agreed and Wolff crossed the Sutlej at Bilaspur on September 16th 1832.

From the Governor-General's farewell letter to Wolff it is clear that he was intending not just to visit the valley but to pass through it, heading 'north of the Himalayas' for 'the countries east of Russia'. Like Moorcroft he was trying to reach the oasis cities of Chinese (Eastern) Turkestan, Yarkand, Kotan and Kashgar. Tibet, which he frequently mentions, is not Lhasa but Ladakh, which he would have to traverse on the way. Whether he intended to head from there to China or back to Europe via Russia is not known, but Lord William obviously did not expect to see him back in India. He did not realise that because of Wolff's stupidity over the fatal proclamation it was far too late in the year to reach the high passes beyond Kashmir before the winter.

It is unnecessary to follow Wolff's trip to Kashmir in detail. His route was the same as that used by Moorcroft and Jacquemont on their return from the valley. The important point is that he arrived in Srinagar on October 11th. And left, heading back to India, on the 16th. In other words what should have been an epic journey of

Himalayan travel fizzled out in a brief and pointless excursion. He made one of his rare attempts at descriptive writing when he tried to depict the famous gardens and canals of Srinagar, but failed dismally. The whole place he found a bitter disappointment. 'Instead of the splendid palaces described so enchantingly by the poets one sees only ruined and miserable cottages; instead of the far famed beauties of Kashmir one meets with the most ugly, half starved, blind and dirty looking females.' Four days was scarcely time enough to get even a general impression, but this was obviously not going to be the site of the New Jerusalem.

The only explanation given for his change of plan comes when he is writing of Little Tibet (Baltistan). 'It was much my wish to have gone there, but the snow prevented me and obliged me to return to India.' In so far as it was late to be starting the long journey to Yarkand this makes sense, but the passes into Baltistan would not normally have been closed by mid-October. Wolff is so vague in his geography that he may well have confused Little Tibet with Tibet (Ladakh); certainly the only route to Yarkand of which he knew was the one via Ladakh. On the other hand there were plenty of other reasons for heading south. From Srinagar it is impossible to see the passes to the north or to gauge their condition. Perhaps the Sikhs, not trusting even Wolff to stay aloof from political intrigues on their frontier, preferred to mislead him. Perhaps he was so alarmed by the descriptions of the Karakoram route, which he heard from Yarkandi pilgrims in Srinagar, that he thought better of it. Or perhaps, having briefly retasted the pleasures of civilisation in Simla, he realised he was not ready to return to the wilds so soon. His idea of missionary work was always more like a whistle-stop electioneering campaign than the long hard slog of those who lived amongst their flock. And even if he had wanted to, he could not see the winter out in Kashmir; the Maharaja's permit was good for only a month. With something like relief he ascertained that there were no Jews in Yarkand and quickly turned back before the passes of the Pir Panjal received their first snowfall. He followed the same route over the mountains and crossed the Punjab for Ludhiana and Delhi. This took him through Lahore. Significantly he was not given another audience by the Maharaja.

Wolff went on to make an extensive tour of India before returning to the Middle East and then, by the unusual route of Abyssinia, Bombay, St. Helena and New York, he reached London in 1838.

He made another epic journey to Bukhara in 1844, and he died, the vicar of Ile Brewers in Somerset, in 1862. In his late fifties he was still rueing that lost opportunity in 1832. He wrote to the Royal Geographical Society with a proposed itinerary: 'Bombay, Kashmir, Lhasa, Kashgar, Khokand, Kotan, Yarkand, Ili, Kamchatka, Rocky Mountains, New York, 3 Waterloo Place London and back to Ile Brewers.' It was every bit as ambitious and haphazard as usual and yet, for Wolff in his younger days, not beyond the realms of possibility.

*　　*　　*

It has to be admitted that the contributions of Jacquemont and Wolff to the geographical understanding of the Western Himalayas were minimal. Compared to Moorcroft's puzzling and painstaking odyssey, their travels have only light relief to recommend them. They were travellers and not explorers, and they wrote as much about themselves as about the lands they visited. If occasionally their observations are subordinated to the demands of good narrative one is prepared to forgive. They were both such extraordinary characters.

Yet it would be wrong, because of this, to regard them as irrelevant. They were public figures in a way that Moorcroft never was and their accounts were assured of a fame out of all proportion to their geographical significance. Before he died Jacquemont had already been officially recognised by being appointed an officer of the Legion of Honour. No time was lost in publishing his letters, and there was even an English edition by 1834. Other editions, some of them pirated, appeared in quick succession. They were immensely readable and did as much as *Lalla Rookh* to popularise the Himalayas.

Wolff's *Researches and Missionary Labours 1831–34* appeared a year later. The map which accompanied them was a disgrace. It showed the Indus rising near Kashgar, the Ganges flowing through Ladakh and a peculiar configuration of mountains; MacCartney had done better twenty years before. Yet the book ran to a second edition in the first year. Wolff was now a celebrity and when, late in life, he retold the story in his *Travels and Adventures*, a reviewer observed that 'there is scarcely a district in the country where the name of Joseph Wolff does not wake smiles and recollections, sometimes ludicrous, sometimes affectionate'. However badly depicted, the mountains beyond Kashmir were known to have defeated the indefatigable Jew. This was inspiration enough for would-be travellers.

It must also be remembered that at this time Moorcroft's journals were still mouldering in Fraser's tin trunks or stacked on Wilson's busy desk. Their very existence was known only to a handful of men. Wolff and Jacquemont thus enjoyed an open field. Excluding Foster's, theirs were the first accounts of Kashmir in over a hundred years. The excursion to the famous valley was rightly regarded as the supreme adventure of each. And if they were not explorers they were certainly pioneers.

Jacquemont, particularly, had also established something of a precedent at Lahore. He had shown that even without a letter of introduction from the British authorities it was possible to win Ranjit Singh's approval for a visit to Kashmir. The chief obstacle appeared to be not the Sikhs but the British. It was true that in 1831 Ranjit Singh had refused a request from Burnes, but Burnes's objectives were so palpably political that this was hardly surprising. Fraser's case was more typical. Despite his qualifications the Hon. Company would not consider his going even to Lahore. As long as the Maharaja lived and his empire prospered, the British were too wary of his susceptibilities to allow their own officers a free hand. The only people with a chance of reaching the mountains were likely to be independent travellers of unimpeachable reputation.

Fraser's case was a particularly sad one because of all the British representatives strung along the north-western boundary, men like Kennedy and the Gerards at Simla or Wade at Ludhiana, Fraser seems to have shown the deepest interest in the Western Himalayas. He had been to Kabul with Elphinstone, he had been in correspondence with Moorcroft and he was a host and a friend to both Jacquemont and Wolff. A strange man of satanic appearance, his character comes through strongly in the accounts of the last two. He liked to keep apart from the other British residents in Delhi. He dressed in native style, spent hours in conversation with venerable Indians and supported a notable harem outside the city. His understanding of caste and custom was profound and his children, of which there were many, were all carefully brought up in the religion and profession of their mothers' families. Yet he was also a knowledgeable administrator and a man of action. He loved to fight and would spring to arms or chase after tigers—he had killed over three hundred—whenever opportunity offered. Perhaps Jacquemont over-romanticises him, but even Wolff realised that, though a religious sceptic, he had depths of character beyond his understanding.

And of course he was the man who had the missing journals of Moorcroft. One cannot help returning to the question of why he was holding on to them. By being the first into print Jacquemont and Wolff were able to steal some of Moorcroft's thunder, but their conjectures about their predecessor were nothing if not tantalising. Probably most of Jacquemont's information came from Fraser. With Wolff this was not the case. He had never heard of Moorcroft until he reached Persia on the way out. He was the first to penetrate the region which had been Moorcroft's undoing and he found both Bukhara and northern Afghanistan still buzzing with rumour and recrimination over the affair. And in the end he was convinced that all three men, Moorcroft, Trebeck and Guthrie, had been murdered. It would have been fascinating to have eavesdropped on the conversations he had with Fraser. Fraser by then had more clues as to what had actually happened than any other man. Perhaps he was planning to write a summary and for this retained the missing journals. We shall never know. Within two years he too was dead, murdered in circumstances as obscure as those surrounding the fate of Moorcroft.

5. Three Travellers

Legend has it that the valley of Kashmir was once an inland sea lapping between the upper slopes of the Pir Panjal and the Great Himalaya. Moorcroft and Jacquemont found fossilised shells which supported this theory and geologists have since confirmed it; the water escaped by gradual erosion at the rock-bound outlet of the Jhelum. Today's traveller who first sees Kashmir from the air will, if it is spring, find the country still inundated. The lakes, left behind when the sea receded, are then indistinguishable from the flooded paddy fields. One looks down on a watery expanse where the roads are all causeways and the villages islands. Later the fields are drained, the rice is cut and the soil becomes baked and brown. Reflecting a soft blue sky the celebrated lakes of Kashmir at last stand out in all their glory. They are seen to be flanked by trees, willow, poplar, chenar* and walnut. and connected by busy canals and the graceful wanderings of the Jhelum. The acres of bright pasture turn out to be beds of lotus and water lily, swards of duckweed and floating fields of melon and cucumber.

Of these lakes the best known is the Dal on the outskirts of Srinagar. It is a fine expanse of water, possibly the loveliest in the world, and rich with romantic associations. On its shores the Moghul emperors built elaborate gardens and from the heat of the Indian summer retired to their shady lawns and graceful pavilions to enjoy a delicate paradise of poetry and love-making. For greater privacy they also constructed islands, one of which at the northern extremity of the lake, is called the Isle of Chenars. Jacquemont captured some of its departed charm when he spent a languid thirtieth birthday there musing on his chances of winning a Kashmir beauty and cooling his ardour by a plunge in the lake. Subsequent visitors were less respectful of its associations, and about 1836 a black marble stone commemorating the first Europeans to visit the valley was erected on the island. Ranjit Singh himself had given permission for the memorial but, to the Sikh governors who also patronised the place, it

* The chenar is the giant Asian plane tree, *Platanus orientalis*, for which Kashmir is rightly famous.

must have seemed like an unnecessary reminder of European interference. Doubtless it was they who turfed it into the lake, for by
1850 it was gone. No European ever saw it and we only know of the
inscription from the three travellers who erected it.

Had it survived it would have been one of the very rare reminders
of the Himalayan explorers. Leh has no Moorcroft Hotel and
Srinagar no Jacquemont Boulevard. Younghusband Glacier and
Vigne Glacier might mean something to the Karakoram mountaineer, but more prominent features like Mount Godwin-Austen and
Lake Victoria have long since disappeared from authoritative maps.
Only in the realms of natural history are the great names remembered—*Gentiana moorcroftiana, Pinus gerardiana, Parnassia jac-
quemontii, Messapia shawii* and dozens more. Otherwise there are a
very few graves, their headstones overgrown and scarcely legible,
and that is all. Unlike the other theatres of nineteenth century
exploration in Australia and Africa, the Himalayas never saw a
generation of colonists who, anxious to boost their right to be there,
would preserve the names of the pioneers.

The inscription on the marble slab on the Isle of Chenars read as
follows:

Three Travellers
Baron Carl von Hugel, from Jammu
John Henderson, from Ladakh
Godfrey Thomas Vigne, from Iskardo
who met in Srinagar on 18th November
1835
Have caused the names of those European travellers who had
previously visited the Vale of Kashmir to be hereunder engraved
Bernier 1663
Forster 1786
Moorcroft, Trebeck and Guthrie 1823
Jacquemont 1831
Wolff 1832
Of these only three lived to return to their native land.*

The first to arrive in Srinagar on that November 18th was the
Austrian, von Hugel. Three years earlier, on his way to the East
Indies, he had met Jacquemont in Poona and from him got the idea

---

* This list is far from exhaustive. It should also include Desideri, Csoma
de Koros, Lyons and no doubt others.

of visiting Kashmir on his return to India. Jacquemont didn't think much of this 'self-styled' baron. He was reputed to be a great naturalist but was floored when the Frenchman quizzed him about corvine anatomy. Actually the Baron's title was genuine, his connections—including a close friendship with Metternich—were even more distinguished than Jacquemont's, and he was a knowledgeable and systematic botanist. He had none of Jacquemont's charm, but his means and reputation were enough to ensure the co-operation of the British authorities.

Arrived in Srinagar, he set up camp in the garden where Vigne was already established, though away for the day sketching and duck shooting. Almost immediately a European was announced. Von Hugel, expecting his neighbour, called him in. There shambled through the door not the trim English sportsman he anticipated but a long skinny figure with a bony nose and matted red beard. His clothes were Tibetan but too dirty and tattered to be picturesque. His face was haggard and red, the skin torn to shreds by wind and cold. The Baron, normally a most courteous man, stared in amazement. 'Who on earth are you?' he demanded. Unabashed, with great dignity and in a strong Scottish accent which rolled the r's the stranger replied, 'You surely must have heard of Dr. Henderson?' It was a fine effort from someone who cannot have spoken a word of English for several months.

The Baron had heard of John Henderson, as indeed had most of Upper India. He was the *bête noir* of the East India Company even before he disappeared between Ludhiana and Calcutta earlier in the year. Unfortunately no record of his indiscretions has survived. Von Hugel just says that he was such an inveterate critic of the government that he was banned all access to the press. Vigne, who invariably saw only the good in men, calls him a founder of the Agra Bank and 'prominent for enterprising speculation'. He must also have had a yen for enterprising travel for, knowing that as a servant of the Honourable Company he would be severely censured, he slipped across the Sutlej and headed for Ladakh. His destination, apparently, was the source of the Indus. Kennedy at Simla was the first to sound the alarm but by then, following Moorcroft's route through Kulu, he was already in Leh.

It was the year that Ladakh was finally conquered by the Sikhs. Henderson arrived just before their army and the Ladakhis, easily penetrating his disguise as a fakir, assumed he was a British representative come in the nick of time to ratify Moorcroft's 'treaty' of fourteen years before. He was shown how the good vet's garden was still being tended and how his flocks had grown in the loyal care of the Ladakhis. But Henderson knew little of Moorcroft and nothing of any treaty. He was not a British agent, anything but, and was powerless against the invader. Dismayed, the Ladakhis put him under house arrest and hoped that the mere presence of an Englishman would be enough to stay the Sikhs. Henderson escaped. Without money or food he begged his way down the Indus to Baltistan. He lost his horses, his baggage and his two servants but the Baltis, who had just paid a fond farewell to Vigne, helped him across the Great Himalaya to Kashmir, and thus he arrived in Srinagar.

Von Hugel and Vigne, back from his duck shoot, listened to this story with interest. They warned Henderson that in British India there was a warrant out for his arrest and they clubbed together to enable him to continue his travels. His needs were simple. While he stayed with them in Kashmir he slept on the floor rolled up in blankets. The blankets, von Hugel notes, had afterwards to be destroyed; Henderson had long since foresworn soap and clean clothes. To food, too, he was entirely indifferent. The menu for their celebration dinner was 'hare soup, fresh salmon, roasted partridges, and a ham from the wild boar of the Himalaya'.* Henderson was unimpressed. But spying a jar of hot Indian chutney he emptied the lot over the salmon, exclaiming that the greatest of all his misfortunes had been when his 'chatni' reserve was exhausted.

He stayed only a few days in Srinagar and then set off down the Jhelum heading for Balkh in Afghanistan. Eight weeks later he reappeared in Lahore. Again his hosts were Vigne and von Hugel though it was nursing, not hospitality, that he needed. He was a dying man.

*   *   *

But first, 'Godfrey Thomas Vigne from Iskardo', a most important but neglected explorer whose travels take the penetration of the Western Himalayas another long stride towards Central Asia. Presumably because of his Huguenot surname, Vigne has often been taken for a Frenchman. 'Monsieur Vigne', even 'de Vigne', occur in later references to him. In fact the name was pronounced 'vine' and he

---

* Fresh salmon must mean either Mahseer or Himalayan trout. No salmon has ever reached Kashmir and brown trout were not introduced till later in the century.

was as English as could be. His family were wealthy London merchants supplying gunpowder to the East India Company and he was
born in the City of London within a stone's throw of the Bank of
England. He was educated at Harrow where his name is still scratched
on a classroom wall and was called to the bar from Lincoln's Inn.
Then in 1830, perhaps bored or just idle, he gave up the law. The
family maintained it was because he was 'too delicate', but even in
those days the law was not that rough a profession nor was Godfrey
Thomas that feeble. He played cricket for the MCC and was an
ardent sportsman.

First he paid a short visit to America and then, in 1832, set out for
what was to be an equally short tour of Persia. At the end of it,
instead of returning home, he took ship from Bushire to Bombay and
arrived in India on New Year's Day 1834.* A desert chase after wild
asses near Isfahan had laid him low with fever and perhaps he hoped
for better medical advice at a large British base. There was something
even more casual about his next move. 'As the climate and gaieties of
Bombay did not tend much to the improvement of my health I
determined, not having had the slightest intention of the kind when
I left England, to run up at once to the cool air of the Himalaya.' A
run up to the Himalaya was all very well, but there were hill retreats
nearer than Simla. One looks for a better reason for five years of
continual travel over the most gruelling terrain in the world.

But with nothing more by way of explanation Vigne set off across
India. He celebrated his arrival at Simla by trying to cross the
16,000-foot Boorendo pass into Tibet, then followed the mountains
round to Mussoorie and adjourned to the plains for the winter. It was
something of a royal progress. He had friends in most places and,
where he didn't, he soon made them. Few of the famous names in the
Upper India of the 1830s go unnoticed. He was delighted with everything and between praise for Major Everest, the Surveyor-General
then measuring his baseline for a survey of the central Himalayas,
and for Salonica, the grey arab who won the big race at Aligarh, he
lets slip a throw-away line; his permit for Kashmir has arrived. It's
as if a visit to the forbidden valley were the most natural thing in the
world and the Company's permission the merest of formalities.
Nothing could be further from the truth, of course, but this off-hand
attitude had its advantages. It relieved him of the need to offer

---

* Vigne actually says 1833 but this must be a slip of the pen since at the
beginning of 1833 he was at Trebizond en route to Persia.

explanations on such delicate points as why he wanted to go there, why the Company agreed or why Wade from Ludhiana made special representations on his behalf to Ranjit Singh. In June 1835, complete with guns, rods and easel and sporting his usual outfit of Norfolk jacket and broad-brimmed hat, he straddled a buffalo skin at Bilaspur, crossed the Sutlej and headed for Kashmir.

Inflated buffalo skins

Impulsive, entertaining and unbelievably casual G. T. Vigne is nevertheless a recognisable figure. After the enthusiasms of Moorcroft, the affectations of Jacquemont and the ravings of Wolff one shakes his outstretched hand with a sigh of relief. Here at last is a reasonable man. He takes things as they come; pragmatic common sense is his speciality. It is easy to identify with Vigne, and it would have been pleasant to travel with him. His charm is neither florid nor demanding but a quiet and genial affability. There is even a mild sense of humour, something almost unique amongst nineteenth century explorers. Away from the Himalayas he would have been happiest alone, for he was an independent character, with his gun and his dogs looking for wigeon along the Thames estuary. Surely no one who has read his books could imagine he was other than English.

Hunting to such a man was more than just a pastime. His brother Henry, who was also deemed too delicate for the bar, rejoiced in the nickname of 'Nimrod', 'mighty hunter before the Lord'. Godfrey Thomas, no less a shot and never one to be outdone, was generally known as 'Ramrod'. On his way to the Himalayas he had shot pheasant, partridge, snipe, quail, alligator, antelope, tiger, panther and 'mullet as they rose to the surface'. He had coursed with cheetahs, with hounds and with falcons and with the rod in the Elburz had 'killed six or seven dozen trout a day'. That he could find no hares in Kashmir was something that worried him deeply. It was such perfect country. On the other hand, when his terrier flushed out a fox which was 'not the little grey leading article of Hindustan but the large full brushed Meltonian', he was markedly reassured. Sport must have inspired his first interest in the mountains and he now heads the distinguished role of Kashmir sportsmen, which includes African travellers like Speke and Grant as well as most of the Himalayan pioneers.

More surprisingly, Ramrod Vigne was also a good amateur botanist and geologist and an accomplished artist. When Ranjit Singh asked what he did he replied, rather curtly for a gentleman is not usually asked such a question, 'I can draw'. He certainly could and his picture of the Maharaja looking like a satanic cyclops is probably no harsher than the reality. In 1842 he exhibited at the Royal Academy and in spite of a prolific output his work, particularly the arresting portraits, still commands a good price. His wide-angle panoramas were less successful. The eye is taken by the foreground detail, a group of figures or a dog always of sporting potential, while the faithful perspectives of the whole somehow fail to capture the peculiar character of the country; to any but a resident his view of Kabul could pass for Srinagar and vice versa.

This failure was more than retrieved by his fine prose descriptions. With Vigne we at last get a vivid impression of 'the untried and fairy wilds of Kashmir'. Over five years he came to know the valley better even than had Moorcroft. He loved it dearly and finding no fault with Tom Moore's licence declared it 'the noblest valley in the world'. He saw not just the lakes and the gardens, the trees and the mountains but the whole context of the place, something which the visitor feels but rarely analyses.

Innumerable villages were scattered over the plains in every direction, distinguishable in the extreme distance by the trees that surrounded them; all was soft and verdant even up to the snow on the mountain top; and I gazed in surprise, excited by the vast extent and admirably defined limits of the valley and the almost perfect proportions of height to distance, by which its scenery seemed to be characterised. . . . Softness mantling over the sublime—snugness generally elsewhere incompatible with extent —are the prevailing characteristics of the scenery of Kashmir; and verdure and the forest appear to have deserted the countries on the northward, in order to embellish the slopes from its snowy mountains, give additional richness to its plains and combine with its delightful climate to render it not unworthy of the rhyming epithets applied to it in the east of:

> Kashmir bi nuzir—without equal
> Kashmir junat puzir—equal to paradise.

Though much the largest of the Himalayan valleys it is perhaps the least dramatic. There is none of the savage majesty of Lahul, the Alpine clarity of Kulu or the exotic contrasts of Chitral. Its beauty is more mature and stately. It lies precisely in those 'perfect proportions of height to distance' and the 'softness mantling over the sublime'.

Vigne's descriptions of Kashmir have been raided by many a later travel writer. The country has changed little and they are now as apt as ever. The city of Srinagar is still 'an innumerable assemblage of gable-ended houses, interspersed with the pointed and metallic tops of masjids or mosques, melon grounds, sedgy inlets from the lakes and narrow canals'. A teeming but quite un-Indian city, it is both fascinating and slightly frightening. There are few streets, but there must still be many a narrow alley and smelly little canal to which no European has ever penetrated. The inhabitants too are still 'a lying and deceitful race of people'. But Vigne, and for this one must like the man, admitted what very few of his fellow countrymen would ever appreciate, namely that 'when detected in a fault their excuses are so very ready and profuse, and often so abound in humour, that it is impossible to abstain from laughing and to attempt an exhibition of anger becomes a farce'.

In all, Vigne crossed the Pir Panjal to the south five times, twice he took the western approach by the Jhelum valley, once he left by an eastern route to Muru Wurdan and Kishtwar and six times he crossed the Great Himalaya to the north. He lists twenty passes into the valley and had personal knowledge of most of them. The great revelation of his Kashmir travels lay not so much in the glories of the Dal Lake or of the Vale itself but of the surrounding mountains and valleys. Later he was criticised for the confused presentation of his material and his vagueness about dates and itineraries. It is extremely difficult to piece together his precise movements year by year. But one sympathises with his problem. Maybe he was not particularly methodical, but to have presented his travels in journal form would have been an impossible task. He covered so much ground and so often retraced his steps or recrossed a previous route that even a map of them would present a meaningless tangle.

Instead he wrote what is really a guide book and one which thirty years later was still the best of its kind. His wanderings south of the Great Himalaya extended from Chamba on the confines of Kulu to Muzafarabad, a good two hundred miles to the west. Only half of this sweep is occupied by the vale of Kashmir. The rest is extremely mountainous, but alpine rather than Tibetan, a land of fast running rocky rivers in steep gorges with fine forests above giving way to birch, rhododendron, juniper scrub and finally, between the tree-line and the snows, rich mountain grazing. Much of it was new to geography; he was the first European to plot the courses of the Ravi, Chenab and Jhelum rivers through the Pir Panjal and the first to visit Kishtwar, Chamba, Bhadarwah and Muzafarabad.

But to Vigne geography was not everything. Moorcroft and Jacquemont had both been appalled at the misgovernment of Kashmir and had reported that the extension of British rule was already earnestly desired by most of the people. Trebeck put it more forcibly. Annexation would no more constitute unwarranted interference than 'seizing the hand of a suicide or arresting the blow of a murderer'. 'And I wish to Heaven, Leeson,' he had written to his Irish friend, 'that some thousands of your own distressed countrymen and of our emigrants had a footing in the heart of Asia.' Vigne took up the cry and it was repeated by many subsequent visitors. Kashmir was not India but could and should be, as it was under the Moghuls, the brightest jewel in the imperial crown. Psychologically, strategically and economically it represented, and still does, an invaluable acquisition.

For the British it had the added attraction of a European climate. With the annexation of Kashmir, Simla would be promptly deserted and the valley would become the most popular retreat in the East. The Company's troops would have the world's finest and healthiest training ground and their officers, instead of succumbing to the heat and the bottle, would be hardened in pursuit of ibex high above the snowline. British capital and know-how combined with the skills of the Kashmiri craftsman and farmer would make the land as prosperous as it was beautiful. It would become 'the focus of Asiatic civilisation; a miniature England in the heart of Asia'. Vigne could scarcely look on the famous ruins of Martand without noting of the level ground beside them 'a nobler racecourse I have never seen'. He failed to foresee Gulmarg, then just an open saucer of turf fringed with pines and glaciers, becoming a golf course and ski resort, but he reckoned that with the addition of a herd of deer and a mansion it would make a fine English park.

It was only twelve years since Moorcroft's visit but Vigne, born in 1801, was of a totally different generation and background. Moorcroft had filled his journals with notes on how the skills and produce of the Himalayan lands could be adopted in Britain and India. Vigne conjectured on what the introduction of British skills could make of the Himalayan lands. Fresh from America and with none of the commercial priorities of a servant of the East India Company, he was thinking less of 'improvements' and trade and more of colonisation. Like Trebeck he dreamt of a little oasis of English life in the heart of Asia, a place where the rulers of India, having left the heat in the plains and having dumped the White Man's Burden on the Pir Panjal, could change into their old tweed suits and settle down before a good log fire on their own few acres.

Vigne is not as specific as this, but one can see how his mind was working. The memorial on the Isle of Chenars was meant for a future generation of English settlers in Kashmir. Three quarters of his *Travels in Kashmir, Ladakh, Iskardo etc.* is devoted solely to the valley. Thanks to him it did eventually attract a flood of Englishmen and indirectly came under British protection. But it never became a colony; in fact it was never a part of the British Raj and technically remained foreign soil to British and Indian alike until 1948.

Tucked away at the end of Vigne's work on Kashmir lies the account of his wanderings north of the Great Himalaya. It is almost an appendix and unlike the rest of the book is reticent as well as discursive. He well knew the geographical interest that would attach to this part of his travels. Some of his letters from Baltistan, waterlogged and scarcely legible, were published as soon as they reached Calcutta. The Royal Geographical Society was given an outline of his journeys directly he returned and Sir Alexander Burnes, the then authority on Asiatic travel, wrote of his anxiety to know more. But the book when it appeared in 1842 begged far too many questions. Why, when it was Kashmir that he went to see, did he make straight for Baltistan? And return there again and again? Why were the British authorities so unusually co-operative and why so Ranjit Singh, whom he did nothing to humour? And where was he really heading as he probed the mountains from east to west? One plots, rather than follows, the course of his journeyings and all the time one wonders whether it was just the man's natural vagueness masking an insatiable curiosity or whether he really had something to hide.

The route from Kashmir to Baltistan first takes the traveller over the Great Himalaya by two passes, the Gurais and the Burzil of about 12,000 and 13,000 feet respectively. This is not particularly high by Himalayan standards but, like the Rohtang and the Zoji, they attract a colossal snowfall and are impracticable for at least six months of the year. Vigne first reached Srinagar in early August 1835, and anxious to avoid being caught by a freak snowfall like that which had reputedly checked Wolff, pressed on for the mountain wall above Bandipur. On August 29th he camped below the Gurais pass. This was as far north as Jacquemont had got; from now on he was breaking new ground. The first surprise came at the top of the pass when the Balti agent sent to escort him suddenly galloped off. He was shouting something about a priceless excitement.

I quickly followed him and the stupendous peak of Diarmul or Nanga Parbat, more than forty miles distant in a straight line, but appearing to be much nearer, burst upon my sight, rising far above every other around it and entirely cased in snow excepting where its scarps were too precipitous for it to remain upon them. It was partially encircled by a broad belt of cloud and its finely pointed summit glistening in the full blaze of the morning sun, relieved by the clear blue sky beyond it, presented on account of its isolated situation an appearance of extreme altitude, equalled by few of the Himalayan range, though their actual height be greater.

Actually the appearance of extreme altitude was not an illusion. Nanga Parbat is not '18,000 or 19,000 feet' but 26,500. Vigne, ever modest with his altitudes, was, like the rest of his generation, as yet unaware that the peaks of the Western Himalayas were as high if not higher than those further east. Nanga Parbat was at the time the second highest mountain known to geography. It is not as ethereal as Kanchenjunga seen from Darjeeling nor as staggering as Rakaposhi cleaving the heavens above Hunza. It is too massive, too ponderous to be elegant. Yet it must have been a stunning discovery, this juggernaut of a mountain dwarfing the whole jagged horizon. It marks the western extremity of the Great Himalaya and lies almost at the dead centre of the mountain knot which is the Western Himalayas, a fitting climax to both.

At the village of Gurais, Vigne stocked up with provisions for the hundred miles of uninhabited wilderness that lay ahead and on September 1st with forty-five porters set off for the Burzil. With his own servants and those of the Balti agent, Nazim Khan, the party numbered about sixty. Von Hugel later complained that Vigne was far too indulgent with his men and that his personal servant, an Anglo-Indian called Mitchell, was a confirmed drunkard. Vigne certainly provided a tent for his men, a consideration not shown by the likes of Jacquemont, and was generally a sympathetic master. He was quite happy with Indian food and his only eccentricity seems to have been a concern that at any given moment on the march he should be no further from a cup of tea than the time it took to boil a kettle.

Normally the porters and kitchen servants would leave camp first and make straight for the next campsite. Vigne, having struggled into his boots and stuffed his slippers and a dry pair of socks into his pocket, would then follow by a more devious and interesting route along with his own little flying column. First came a chair, 'the indispensable accompaniment of dignity', in which were strapped thermometer, sextant, sketching materials and the vital tea-making equipment. The man underneath it was the guide. Next, puffing and blowing, came a man decked about like a Christmas tree. This was the thirsty Mitchell. In one hand he carried an umbrella and in the other a second thermometer. From his belt dangled a geological hammer, across his shoulders was slung a telescope and behind his back, wrapped in a cloth and secured goodness knows how, was a weighty plant book. Then followed Ramrod Vigne, gun in hand if there was a chance of partridge and on foot for the ascent of the Burzil. With him would be his *munshi* (secretary and interpreter), a man burdened more by responsibilities than luggage. And finally the groom, a wiry little man tugging frantically at a wiry little horse.

Four days out from Gurais they were encamped just below the pass and just above the treeline when, in the fading light, Vigne spotted a Balti scout on the rocky skyline. High passes have an eerie stillness about them. The traveller, feeling exposed and slightly edgy, stays close to the camp fire and the warmth of companionship. Suddenly out of the brooding silence came a noise like no other on earth, 'the loud, distant and discordant blasts of Tibetan music . . . the sound grew louder and louder and we were all on the tiptoe of expectation'. From the darkness emerged a band of fifes, clarinets and six-foot-long brazen trumpets. Forty soldiers, 'the wildest looking figures imaginable', with their hair hanging down in long ringlets on each side of the face, followed and with them their young commander, a son of Ahmed Shah. The Raja, it transpired, was only a few miles ahead. He had issued forth from Skardu to intercept a band of robbers and was now lying in ambush for them just over the pass. Vigne would meet him next day as soon as the action was over.

A lot depended on this meeting. Vigne was well prepared. As presents he had knives, shot-belts and powder horns, pistols and telescopes. By way of diversion there was a folio of portraits and pin-ups, some prints of racehorses and hounds and even 'portable machinery for chemical experiments'. But what he didn't have, and what Ahmed Shah was bound to look for, was any diplomatic status. Moorcroft, Jacquemont and even Wolff had all been approached by emissaries from Baltistan. In spite of Jacquemont's insistence that the Sikhs would never bother such a poor and isolated kingdom, they had the following year invaded it. Ahmed Shah had seen the fall of Kashmir and of Ladakh. In 1833 he had managed to hold them off, but he knew that they would be back and that his only hope of immunity lay in a British alliance. At last he had made contact with Wade at Ludhiana, and to him officially had renewed his request that a British officer be sent to Skardu.

This much Vigne must have already been told by Wade. Rightly, it would seem, he interpreted it as a hint that the Company, although still unwilling to send one of their own people, would support an attempt by him to reach Baltistan. Wade would manage things with Ranjit Singh and would be interested in his report. But no more. He was to remain a private traveller and would get neither help if he ran into difficulties nor acknowledgement if he returned. Though Ahmed Shah would assume that anyone from British India who reached his kingdom must have official backing, he was to disclaim it completely and to offer nothing.

Such appears to have been Vigne's understanding of the situation. The only flaw in the argument is that whatever Vigne or Wade might say, neither the Sikhs nor Ahmed Shah were likely to believe a word of it. When Wade supported Vigne's hastily written request from Kashmir that Ranjit Singh allow him to proceed at once to Skardu, the Sikhs can have had no further doubts. And Ahmed Shah was pretty sure to encourage their suspicions. The presence of a British Agent at Skardu was his surest guarantee against attack. In fact Vigne had less cause for concern over the welcome he would receive than about whether he would ever be allowed to depart.

There are four elements here: the ambivalence of the British government, the enigmatic status of the traveller, the suspicious attitude of the Kashmir authorities (Sikhs but soon Dogras) and the anxiety of some remote princeling for a British connection. Often conflicting, these were to bedevil attempts to penetrate the Western Himalayas. We have seen them in Moorcroft's story and they will recur in the travels of Johnson, Shaw and Hayward. In the light of what happened to the others, Vigne was extraordinarily successful in avoiding a combination of these factors which would prove explosive. One begins to wonder whether he was quite as casual and unsystematic as he appears. It is seldom possible to penetrate the blanket of secrecy on the British side or to untie the web of intrigue on the native side. We can only judge by how each traveller managed. Vigne had taken a high-handed stance when the Kashmir authorities had tried to impede his departure for Baltistan. He was now, with equal success, about to deploy a gentler approach to Ahmed Shah.

The two men met as soon as the robbers had been successfully annihilated. Vigne in his broad-brimmed white cotton hat and white duck-shooting jacket was approached by a tall and imposing figure who doffed his turban and frequently stopped to salaam deeply. The Englishman took his hand and wrung it vigorously, explaining through the interpreter that such was his native custom. Ahmed Shah was delighted. It was his lifelong ambition to meet a 'feringi' and now it had happened on a day when he had already fought a successful action. So far so good, thought Vigne, and after more mutual flattery he was so emboldened as to ask leave to sketch his host on the field of battle. Given the situation, the result shows a remarkably steady hand.

For the next three days they travelled together across the bleak and treeless Deosai plateau. The altitude was about 12,000 feet, and even now in early September there was a heavy frost at night. The Raja presented Vigne with a pair of warm Tibetan socks. He returned the compliment with a bottle of brandy which was sent on under escort to Skardu. They were getting on famously. The Raja had 'some excellent English ideas about him' and when Vigne exhibited his pin-ups, 'engravings of Chalon's beauties', he gazed in silent admiration. There followed a print of King William IV and his consort, and the Raja insisted on writing a personal note in the margin sending to His Britannic Majesty respectful salaams and an earnest wish for protection. Vigne declared from the start that he had no political status, but he admits that till the very last Ahmed Shah did not appear to believe him. Whether and how this prejudiced their relations it is hard to say. But regardless of it there developed between them a real and lasting friendship the like of which is not to be found between later explorers and explored.

On September 6th Vigne at last got his first glimpse of Baltistan. In the morning the Raja had pointed to a line of mountains along the rim of the Deosai from which they would descend on Skardu and the Indus valley. By sunset they had reached the foot of this ridge. Vigne could contain himself no longer and galloped on ahead. He abandoned his horse on the steep climb and finally stumbled over the upper edge of a glacier and peered into the twilit distance. '. . . through a long sloping vista formed of barren peaks, of savage shapes and various colours, in which the milky whiteness of the gypsum was contrasted with the red tint of those that contained iron—I the first European that had ever beheld them (so I believe), gazed downwards from a height of six or seven thousand feet upon the sandy plains and green orchards of the valley of the Indus at Skardu, with a sense of mingled pride and pleasure, of which no one but a traveller can form a just conception.' He could see the rock of Skardu, the Raja's stronghold, rising like a second Gibraltar out of the level bed of the Indus and beyond it the Shighar valley whose river joins the Indus at the base of the rock. Further north and 'wherever the eye could rove, arose, with surpassing grandeur, a vast assemblage of the enormous summits that compose the Tibetian Himalaya'.

Vigne usually calls the country Little Tibet, and both the people and the terrain are distinctly Tibetan in appearance. The valleys are perhaps deeper and steeper than further east and they are separated not by rolling plateaux but by lofty spurs. Yet there is the same over-all impression of rock and sand, harsh white light and biting dry wind. Natural vegetation is a rare and transitory phenomenon; cultivation just an artificial patchwork of fields suspended from a contour-clinging irrigation duct or huddled on the triangular surface of a fan of alluvial soil washed down from the mountains. The water is an icy grey mercury fresh from the glaciers and glittering with mica. Shade, the other essential, is either the dappled pallor afforded by willow and apricot tree or the deep and shivery gloom of a Balti house.

The people themselves have the narrow eyes and careworn wrinkled faces of the Tibetan. But they are not Buddhists. Long ago they were converted to Shiah Mohammedanism and represent the most easterly outpost of Islam in the Himalayas. In place of the polyandry of Buddhist Tibet, which operates as a form of population control, they adopted the polygamy of Mohammed which does quite the reverse. A Balti's needs are about as basic as any man's could be. He can sustain his habitual cheerfulness and considerable stamina on a diet consisting entirely of raw apricots and a dough made from barley flour. Both, and little else, are grown extensively, but seldom in sufficient quantity to support the ever-growing population. The Balti has been forced to seek a livelihood elsewhere, usually as a porter or coolie. Vigne was the first European to exploit this potential. Later they became the essential workhorses of every expedition towards Gilgit and beyond.

The 'vast assemblage of mountain summits' which he saw from the ridge above Skardu was the next barrier between India and Asia. At the time he called it the Tibetian Himalaya but later, and more correctly, the Mustagh or Karakoram range. For the next few weeks, for five months in 1837 (1836 he spent mostly in Afghanistan) and for a similar period in 1838, he relentlessly probed this mountain barrier. It is hard to say in which year or in what order but four major journeys are discernible. To follow each one in detail would be tedious, but they are so important to the future course of Himalayan exploration that a note of each is essential.

Working from west to east the first took him from Skardu to Astor, a fort commanding the Kashmir-Gilgit road, and thence to a vantage point called Acho overlooking Bunji on the Indus. From here he could see Gilgit, and he intended to cross the river and proceed there. His *munshi*, who had been sent on ahead, gave conflicting reports about his likely reception but Vigne reckoned all would have been well if he had been able to approach without such a large Balti escort. As it was, the Gilgitis took fright. They saw what looked more like an army approaching and promptly destroyed the bridge across the Indus. Later a similar incident nearly put paid to his visit to

Ladakh. One cannot avoid the conclusion that Vigne was a little gullible where the good faith of his Balti hosts was concerned. At that time there was in fact no bridge across the Indus at Bunji; the first was built in the 1890s. There was a ferry and this may well have been destroyed, but it seems more likely that the Baltis were jealous of their guest and simply invented the story to prevent his opening relations with their traditional enemies.

The second journey from Skardu was north up the Shighar and Basho valleys into the heart of the Karakorams. On the crossing to Astor, Vigne had negotiated some large glaciers, experienced snow blindness and made his always conservative estimate of the altitude nearly 16,000 feet. He was a brave and determined traveller, fit and to some extent acclimatised. But this is not adequate preparation for the Karakorams. The 'delicate' barrister was no mountaineer; he had neither the experience nor the equipment. Indeed it is doubtful if anyone at that time could have penetrated, let alone crossed, this appalling wilderness. Vigne tried. He attempted to cross over the Hispar glacier to Hunza, intending to proceed across the Pamirs to Khokand, all of five hundred miles away in what is now Soviet Russia. He also investigated the possibility of crossing from Shighar to Yarkand by what later became known as the Mustagh pass. But both routes were way beyond his capability. The Hispar route was not crossed until Sir Martin Conway, the greatest mountaineer of his day, did it in 1892. The other route defeated Godwin-Austen and, fifty years later, Sir Francis Younghusband only forced his way through by taking the most lunatic risks. Without much prompting this time, Vigne turned back from the Basho valley.

As a result of Moorcroft's try for Yarkand the Chinese, so Vigne was told, had executed a massive wall painting of a European so that every Yarkandi would instantly recognise and apprehend any subsequent visitor. Burnes heard similar stories on his way to Bukhara, only his version had it that anyone who recognised such a *persona non grata* was entitled to appropriate him and his possessions, forwarding to the authorities as evidence just the man's head. Vigne decided it would be best to avoid the Chinese, but having established that routes to the north and west of Skardu were impractical, he turned towards the main trans-Karakoram track from Leh hoping that once across the mountains he would be able to strike west and thus avoid Yarkand.

It was probably in 1837 that he travelled up the Indus to Leh with the professed intention of reaching a glacier lake at the head of the Nubra valley. This, he was told, was the source of the Shyok, a major tributary of the Indus and by some geographers thought to be the Indus itself. On the way he inspected the confluence of the two rivers and rightly pronounced that the one from Leh which Moorcroft had explored was the parent stream. But he was still interested in the Shyok, particularly as its supposed source lay so near the Karakoram pass on the Ladakh–Yarkand route. This was the track that Moorcroft had intended to follow. It was regularly used by merchants and so well within Vigne's capabilities. But he was reckoning without the Sikhs. They were now established in Ladakh and had no intention of letting him befriend any more of their mountain neighbours.

It was bad enough that he had been given a free hand in Baltistan. Vigne in his dealings with native authorities is usually a model of good humoured patience, but the treatment he received in Leh was too much. Under constant surveillance, forbidden contact with the Ladakhis and prevented from organising his onward journey, he levelled bitter accusations of insolence and disrespect. A complaint was lodged with Ranjit Singh and an appeal made to Wade. They were successful but the necessary directives came too late. By the time he got away from Leh winter was imminent. He reached the lower end of the Nubra valley, no further than Moorcroft, before he was driven back.

In 1838—and this date at least seems certain—he made his final attempt, again via Nubra, to reach Central Asia. To avoid another brush with the Sikhs he this time tried to cross direct from Skardu to Nubra, thus bypassing Leh. Such a route existed but for reasons that became obvious it was rarely used. Striking up the Saltoro valley the expedition encountered torrential thunderstorms. The tents must have been so soaked that they were left behind to dry, and the next night they slept in the open. By then they were well up one of the vast Karakoram glaciers. Camping on ice is never pleasant but, without cover, it must have been misery. They managed to brew a pot of tea and, thus fortified, Vigne swathed himself in blankets and stretched out on the hard ice. Again the weather deteriorated. Morning found him soaked through with sleet and buried under snow. Still, and with three more such nights ahead, he wanted to go on. His guides refused; with the glacier's crevasses hidden under new snow they were right. Bitterly disappointed, he turned back for the fourth time.

To dwell on Vigne's failures would be churlish. He had achieved too much. He was the first European to visit Baltistan and Astor and the first, from that vantage point above Bunji, to sort out the complicated topography of Gilgit, Yasin and Chitral to the west and of Chilas and the so-called Indus valley states to the south-west. He was the first to give a recognisable account of Nanga Parbat; and the whole Karakoram system was virtually his discovery. At the time it was widely believed that beyond the Great Himalaya north of Kashmir there stretched a vast plateau which extended down to the deserts of Turkestan. Vigne showed that nothing could be further from reality. It was a region of mountains every bit as high and more impenetrable than the main Himalayan chain. Whether he ever saw, rising from this sea of rock and snow, the distant giants of Masherbrum, Gasherbrum and that shyest of all peaks, K2, we don't know. But in an age when geographers were still doubtful whether glaciers could exist in any latitude warmer than that of the Alps, he brought back accounts of one of the world's greatest glacial systems. He had had no chance of ascertaining their length, but the snout of the Chogo Lungma glacier he described as a wall of ice a quarter of a mile wide and a hundred feet high. From a cavern in the clear green ice there flowed not a stream, 'no incipient brook, but a large and ready formed river'. It roared forth, shunting enormous blocks of ice against its rocky bed with a noise like distant cannon; it was the grandest spectacle that he saw on the whole of his travels.

The discovery of this massive mountain system flanking the northern banks of the Shyok and Indus from Leh to Hunza put a whole new complexion on the Western Himalayas. Geographers began to get some inkling of the depth of the mountainous country north of the Punjab and of the fact that they were dealing not with a continuation of the Great Himalaya but its conjunction with a web of other mighty systems. As for future travellers, they could now forget about reaching Central Asia by striking due north for Skardu. Baltistan was a dead end. Vigne had clearly shown that the only possible routes lay west of the Karakorams via Gilgit or east via Leh. And of these the latter was the most promising. For the first time the ranges and passes to be crossed en route to the Karakoram pass were correctly set out, and on his map Vigne even suggests that there might be a further range beyond the Karakorams.

In November 1838 he left Baltistan for good. Within a year the country had been taken by the Sikhs. Both he and Ahmed Shah, and no doubt Wade too, had foreseen this. For four years his presence there, and that of a Balti representative in Ludhiana, had stayed the onslaught.* Now, for some reason, it was no longer considered necessary to bolster Balti independence. One can only speculate, but had Vigne found a practicable route from Skardu to Central Asia would the British have been so willing to abandon Ahmed Shah? Almost certainly not. And this being the case, it is worth looking again at Vigne's status vis-à-vis the British authorities. In 1836 Wade, their representative at Ludhiana, wrote an interesting letter to the Surveyor-General. He had just received the report of a native whom he had sent to explore the country beyond Kashmir. The exercise had been a success but he still regretted that, since Moorcroft, so little had been done in this direction. To make good this deficiency he recommended that 'the best mode of all would no doubt be to employ an . . . enterprising European officer . . . without being further accredited than were Mr. Moorcroft, Lieutenants Connolly and Burnes and the late Dr. Henderson'. It seems highly probable, and for a man like Wade it would not have been out of character, if he had already made just such an arrangement with Ramrod Vigne.

But if this most plausible of sportsmen was really some sort of spy, what then was his assignment? It could have been just to woo Ahmed Shah and explore his country. More probably it was to penetrate beyond Baltistan and to assess the country's strategic importance in continental terms. Meddling with the expansion of the Sikh empire mattered less than anticipating the expansion of the Russian empire. Vigne, of course, says nothing about this. But he does talk a lot about routes to Khokand, from which direction a Russian advance would most probably be made. He does speculate on the movements of merchants between Russia and India. And he did report to the Viceroy on the presence of a Russian agent in Shighar.

The British attitude towards Russia had changed significantly since Moorcroft's day, and the late 1830s found India convulsed by one of its worst ever bouts of Russophobia. In 1838 an ill-fated army was despatched into Afghanistan with the sole idea of countering Russian designs there. Two years before, Vigne himself had spent a summer in Afghanistan exploring a little known route into that country and then trying to cross the Hindu Kush to meet

* Vigne also acknowledges Henderson's visit to Baltistan in 1835 and that of H. Falconer, Superintendent of the E.I.C.'s botanical garden at Saharanpur in 1838.

Moorcroft's old enemy, Murad Beg of Kunduz. As usual he had travelled in a private capacity but again it is difficult to believe that he would have been permitted to go simply to satisfy his own curiosity. The times were too critical; the man himself too plausible. The Great Game, which came to dictate the whole course of exploration in the Western Himalayas, was already influencing the explorers. Vigne looks like one of its least conspicuous and therefore most successful players.

After fifteen years, the voice of Moorcroft crying out of the wilderness of Ladakh was at last being heeded. There was concern that the Western Himalayas might screen some vulnerable back door into India. Hence the radical departure from previous policy over visitors to Kashmir which Vigne's travels suggest. And hence his returning to Baltistan year after year. It was still the same happy-go-lucky Vigne but he had become involved in something which, for all its excitement, had its drawbacks. He had grown to like the simple Baltis too much, he appreciated their savage scenery too keenly and he esteemed their Raja too highly. It was not in his nature to abandon them to the grasping Sikhs. If their only salvation lay in his finding a flaw in the mountain wall on which to make out a case for a permanent British interest in the region, he was determined to find it. This alone explains his endless probing of the Karakorams. It also explains his intense disgust over the prevarication he encountered at Leh and the appalling risks he was prepared to take on that last desperate bid to force a way up the Saltoro glacier.

When he failed to establish that Baltistan had any strategic value, there was no point in gainsaying the Sikhs any longer. Bentinck was gone, and with him the Company's cautious external policy of the last twenty years. But it was not the Sikhs who were to be the victims of the first new wave of British expansion. They were to be the allies. In 1838 the new Governor-General was suing for Ranjit Singh's co-operation in the invasion of Afghanistan. Part of the price paid for this was recognition of Lahore's rights to Kashmir and Ladakh and a free hand in the rest of the mountains, including Baltistan.

* * *

The famous meeting of Vigne, von Hugel and Henderson took place after Vigne's first visit to Baltistan, when he was on his way back to the Punjab. Kashmir in November, as the Baron was for ever observing, is a cold and cheerless place. Henderson soon set off on his last escapade and the other two, joining forces, headed for Lahore. Neither had as yet met the Maharaja though indebted to him for their safe conducts. Courtesy as well as curiosity dictated a visit.

The Baron had spent just three weeks in the valley and had broken no new ground. Undeterred, he later wrote a comprehensive account of the region entitled *Cachemire und das Reich der Siek*. This drew heavily on information gleaned from Vigne and Henderson but curiously ignored Moorcroft's *Travels*, then at last in print. It was rather like writing on the Later Roman Empire without consulting Gibbon. Von Hugel says that he was anxious to preserve the originality of his own impressions but, as a result, his summary of Moorcroft's achievements was absurdly and indefensibly unjust.

His own observations were not much better. He overestimated the altitude of Kashmir by 1,000 feet and denied what every other visitor had found self-evident, namely that the valley had once been a lake. It follows that as a Himalayan explorer von Hugel deserves little space. Yet, and this surpasses understanding, it was to him that the Royal Geographical Society in 1849 presented its Patron's Gold Medal. It was for this particular journey and for the book that resulted from it. Both he and Vigne contributed to the Society's journal and both had their books reviewed in it. The Society had all the facts. Yet von Hugel was honoured and Vigne overlooked. The Baron was taken seriously but Vigne was regarded as unreliable. The latter's descriptions were thought picturesque but fanciful and his maps and measurements were approached with great caution. Not until 1861, by which time there was a framework of surveys against which to measure his achievements, did a contributor to the Society's journal at last make amends. Vigne's book was now acclaimed as the best work on Kashmir and more practical and trustworthy than von Hugel's. His map was 'the mine whence others were manufactured; and when the time and circumstances under which it was compiled are considered it must be regarded as an outstanding production'. Later authorities have upheld this opinion, with Sven Hedin crediting Vigne with a clearer idea of the Karakorams than Shaw entertained thirty years later and Kenneth Mason calling his book 'a classic' and the first comprehensive account of the Western Himalayas.

To Vigne, after a taste of Baltistan, the journey to Lahore must have been child's play. But to von Hugel it was a Calvary, and this in spite of a style of travel undreamt of by his companion. Sometimes the Baron rode, more often he was carried in a sedan chair by twelve bearers; he walked only to stretch his legs. His principal tent had poles twenty-five feet high and the roof alone weighed quarter of a ton. The kitchen was stocked as for a world cruise with 'preserved meats hermetically sealed in tin boxes, wines and drinks of various kinds, preserved fruits and sweetmeats'. As stocks ran out they were replenished by convoys from Ludhiana. And still the Baron was 'worn out by indifferent food'. He felt so ill and exhausted that he cast himself down and thought it madness ever to hope to see his friends again.

He was also desperately lonely. Henderson would have had some grounds for complaining of the solitude of the traveller but not von Hugel. Sixty porters and seven mules carried his luggage while thirty-seven servants ministered to his every need. There was a secretary, an interpreter, a torch-bearer, a butler, three cooks, a water-carrier, a tailor and a man for lighting his pipe. There were plant gatherers, huntsmen and butterfly catchers and, out in front, a herald and two messengers with the baron's initials emblazoned on their breastplates. Over all there was a *sirdar* of forbidding countenance with a shield on his back and a sheathed sabre forever in his hand.

And, of course, there was Vigne. The Austrian was too correct and the Englishman too easy-going for an open quarrel. But Vigne was always 'giving way to his servants' and 'always tardy'. When it rained he stayed in bed while the baron fussed and fretted in the mud. His high spirits were incompatible with the baron's dignity and his down-to-earth common sense was poor company for an aspiring soul oppressed by world weariness. By the time they reached Lahore the baron, 'heartily tired of solitude', longed for the company of a European as if his companion no longer existed.

Ranjit Singh, though now an old and sick man who spent much of his time closeted in his zenana, realised that von Hugel was of higher rank than most of his previous visitors and determined to impress him. The court was now at its sumptuous zenith, and there were treasures galore to be paraded. The Koh-i-Noor diamond, filched from the Afghans and described by Vigne as the size of a walnut and by von Hugel as like a hen's egg, prompted the baron to ponderous reflections on the value of worldly goods. Leili, the celebrated steed which had cost the Maharaja the despatch of an army, was also pointed out, though Vigne doubted whether they were seeing the real animal. Every night the Maharaja sent over delicacies from his kitchen and dancing girls from his harem. The baron was not much interested in women nor in horses but on military matters he could hold his own with anyone. Special manœuvres were held in his honour and one gorgeous parade followed another.

Everything that belonged to the Maharaja was festooned with jewellery. The nose rings of his Kashmiri *nach* girls fell to below their narrow waists in a cascade of diamonds, pearls and emeralds. The saddlery of his horses was aglow with precious stones; there were cruppers of emeralds, reins of gold thread and saddle cloths dripping with pearls and coral. The howdahs of the elephants were of solid gold or silver and their trappings set with diamonds and turquoises. The royal tents were made of Kashmir shawls and on ceremonial occasions the troops were dressed in yellow satin with gold scarves or in cloth of gold patterned with scarlet and purple. Every sword and matchlock, shield and spear was set with gems.

It was indeed one of the world's greatest collections of treasure. Some of it was old, the accumulation of Indian, Afghan and Persian conquerors. But the visitor was struck by the fact that nothing was dull or faded. The colours were bright and the gems newly set and polished. It was not the legacy of some defunct glory but had been fought for and won by the men who displayed it. The guard of honour might look like 'a row of gaudy and gigantic tulips' but over the yellow satin flowed long grey beards and beneath the gold breastplates were scars still livid.

Before this mouth-watering display von Hugel hesitated. All along his thoughts had been focused on the Bombay sailing and his arrival back in Vienna. Now the Maharaja was offering him a share of all this if he would accept employment as one of his generals. Visions of untold glory rose before him. He saw himself leading his own army into Central Asia; 'by one man's efforts civilisation might be mightily advanced'. Then as so often, he remembered his old mother back home in Austria. Whatever the cost to civilisation it was unthinkable to desert her. He declined the offer and soon after left for Ludhiana and Europe.

Vigne in all this was just a passive observer. Military matters bored him but, so as not to prejudice his chances of returning to Kashmir, he played the role of an appreciative and obliging Boswell.

His only error was when, to him too, the Maharaja offered employment. What did he think of the governorship of Kashmir? Remembering Jacquemont and anticipating the offer, he smiled. When it came he laughed outright. Unlike the baron, he realised that this was just one of Ranjit's usual compliments. No one became a general or governor overnight. Men like Allard and Avitabile had sought and fought for their commands.

In the course of three visits to Lahore Vigne became increasingly disrespectful of the Sikh court. He began to notice the sordid as well as the sumptuous. The Maharaja never washed and his idea of a practical joke was to urinate—for reasons of delicacy Vigne tells the story in Latin—from an elephant on to the turbanned heads of his subjects. He was not given to senseless cruelty but as fast as he might exalt one man he would crush another for the pettiest of reasons. As for his courtiers they were all 'blackguards . . . to whom a disregard of principle, subtle intrigue and calm hypocrisy were alike familiar and diurnal'.

In 1837, after the rough handling in Leh, he returned to Lahore burning with indignation. It was clear to him that the man behind his troubles was not the Maharaja but Gulab Singh, the powerful courtier and Raja of Jammu. This was the man who had been persecuting Jacquemont's bandit chief and who was now well advanced with his designs on the whole mountain region. Vigne was among the first to realise that he was already virtually independent of Lahore. He and his brothers held Jammu, most of the Pir Panjal and Ladakh. The addition of Baltistan would mean the complete encirclement of Kashmir. The Raja was only biding his time until the death of Ranjit Singh, when he would grab the valley and declare his independence.

Vigne had some respect for the old Maharaja but none at all for Gulab Singh. He was a cruel and scheming tyrant who skinned his prisoners alive and was hated by his subjects from Tibet to the Punjab. More specifically, it was on his instructions that Vigne had been manhandled in Leh and the *firman* from the Maharaja thus flouted. Ranjit promised redress but the power of Gulab Singh was not curbed. To Vigne it seemed that it never would be until Ranjit was dead, the Punjab and Kashmir annexed by the British and all the hill states, including Ladakh, handed back to their traditional rulers.

By now, the late 1830s, conjecture about the future of the Sikh empire after Ranjit's death was general. It was taken for granted that it would disintegrate. There was no obvious and able successor and too many immensely powerful aspirants. It also seemed inevitable that the British would be drawn across the Sutlej. As a contemporary writer put it, 'The East India Company has swallowed too many camels to strain at this gnat.' In 1839 the Maharaja finally bowed out; his body was drawn to the pyre on a ship made of gold with cloth of gold sails to waft him off to Paradise. Ten years and two hard fought wars later—the gnat had quite a sting—Lahore was in British hands. But the mountains from Jammu to Skardu and from Tibet to Muzafarabad were united under the rule of the first Maharaja of Kashmir. Vigne at this time was in London planning an expedition to Central and South America. He died at Woodford, only a few miles from where he was born, in 1863, never having returned to India or Kashmir. It was hardly surprising. The first Maharaja of Kashmir was none other than his arch enemy, Gulab Singh.

PART TWO

The Pamirs and the Hindu Kush
1826–1841

He took the one to the mountains,
He ran through the vale of Cashmere,
He ran through the rhododendrons,
Till he came to the land of Pamir.
And there in a precipice valley,
A girl of his age he met,
Took him home to her bower
Or he might be running yet.
    ROBERT FROST. *The Bearer of Evil Tidings*

6. Running Gun

With the publication in the early 1840s of the travels of Moorcroft and of G. T. Vigne, exploration in the Western Himalayas came to be concentrated on opening a north–south route from India to Turkestan via Ladakh. When the mountains were seen as a barrier, this looked like their weakest point. Whether it could be forced from India for trading purposes, or from the outside by an invading force, became a matter of deep concern in British Indian policy.

But, seen as a knot of mountains constituting a purely geographical challenge, they could as well be tackled from other points of the compass. Tibet in the east and Chinese Turkestan in the north were out of the question, but the approach from Afghanistan in the west was still technically feasible. This was the route taken by both Marco Polo and Benedict de Goes on their way to the Pamirs, and one of the busiest trade routes from Bukhara to China followed the same axis. Moorcroft's and Wolff's experiences in Afghanistan were not exactly encouraging but here there was no Ranjit Singh holding the keys to the mountains and it was too far from the British frontier for the Hon. Company to exercise a restraining influence.

Thus, while Jacquemont, Wolff and Vigne were trying to get beyond Kashmir, two attempts were made to penetrate the mountains from this direction. They were in no way connected, but, together, they shed new light on the whole mountain complex and particularly its western ramparts, the Pamirs and the Hindu Kush. The first of these journeys, mysterious, improbable and little known, was generally reckoned the less important. Geographers for the most part could make nothing of it; politicians and strategists seldom even knew of it. Yet the wanderings of Alexander Gardiner, given their date and circumstances, are perhaps the most remarkable in the whole field of nineteenth century travel in Asia. Single-handed, without official support and without any geographical training, this man had, by 1831, already explored the Western Himalayas.

Ten years before Vigne gave up his attempt to reach Gilgit, Gardiner had been there. Twenty years before Thomson tackled the Karakoram pass, Gardiner had crossed it. Forty years before

Shaw and Hayward reached Yarkand, Gardiner had passed through the city. And fifty years before an Englishman reached Kafiristan, Gardiner had returned there a second time. He had crossed every one of the six great mountain systems before the maps even acknowledged their individual existence and he had seen more of the deserts of Turkestan than any non-Asiatic contemporary.

But to win acclaim as an explorer, to enjoy the publisher's royalties, the medals and the honours, it is not enough just to have travelled. The successful explorer must interrupt his movements to take measurements and observations. He must carefully identify physical features and place names and, at the end, he must write a convincing, coherent and consistent report. On all these counts Gardiner failed. His travels are not lacking in detail. There are names galore and there is a wealth of colour and excitement; perhaps too much, for though the appearance of authenticity is irresistible, the substance is sadly lacking. The directions, distances and dates don't seem to tally, the place names and weird peoples are either non-existent or unidentifiable and his occasional companions are almost invariably men unknown to history. The one event, the one encounter, the one concrete fact or observation which would clinch the veracity of Gardiner's story is missing.

This aura of uncertainty surrounds not only his travels but his whole life. Who Gardiner was, where he came from, how he reached Central Asia, what part he played on the political scene and what schemes he was hatching at the very end of his long and eventful life, are all questions that he himself answered with the same tantalising disregard for supporting evidence. Just as there were those who could not accept the story of his travels, there were some who doubted whether he even existed. But this at least can be proved. There is the evidence of those who met him and, above all and most unexpectedly, there is a photograph of him.

'A kenspeckle figure' is a description much beloved by Scottish obituary writers. It implies that the deceased was well known to the point of being conspicuous, and that somehow his home town will never be quite the same without him. In Srinagar in the 1860s and 1870s Alexander Gardiner was a kenspeckle figure. He was six feet tall, thin and old, but he stood very straight, stared very hard and his moustaches and whiskers curled defiantly upward. No one knew quite where, or in what style, he lived. It was somewhere deep in the bowels of the city where no European—and by then there were many in Srinagar—ever penetrated. When, to satisfy the curiosity of a British visitor, he emerged from his lair, it was obvious that he had 'gone native' many years before. His uniform consisted of a turban crowned with heron plumes which, in the armies of Punjab and Kashmir, denoted rank; Gardiner called himself a Colonel. The jacket and trousers were of European style but markedly native cut. And the whole ensemble, from toe to turban, was of tartan plaid. It was acquired, according to the cognoscenti, from the Quartermaster's Stores of the 79th Highland Infantry.

Stretched in one of those long cane chairs which were an essential piece of furniture in a British home in India, Gardiner would start on his tales. The only acceptable interruption would come when he paused for a drink. His host, in embarrassment, would then fiddle with his pipe or turn to toss another log on the fire. The old Colonel had difficulty in swallowing. His now frail body bore the marks of fourteen ghastly wounds, of which the most inconvenient was in his throat. He could only manage liquids and, to get even these down he had to clamp, with one hand, a pair of steel pincers round his gullet while, tipping his glass with the other, he gulped painfully.

At first it was not easy to follow his story. His English was rusty with disuse and his expressions distinctly archaic. He was also toothless and had what sounded like an Irish accent. But once he got going, the most critical listener would be lulled into rapt attention. The photograph 'gives but a dim idea', according to one of them, 'of the vivacity of expression, the play of feature, the humour of the mouth and the energy of character portrayed by the whole aspect of the man as he described the arduous and terrible incidents of a long life of romance and vicissitudes'. However shaky his English, he knew how to tell a good story. With those staring eyes ablaze, moustaches flailing the air and surprisingly elegant hands holding the thread of his tale, he would unravel the extraordinary jumble of far-away places and unexpected encounters that go to make up his life story.

It begins in the United States in the year 1785. To a Scottish doctor and his half-English, half-Spanish wife, a third son was born on the shores of Lake Superior not far from the source of the Mississippi. He was christened Alexander Haughton Campbell Gardiner. Five years later the doctor entered the Mexican service and the family moved to near the mouth of the Colorado river and a town called St. Xavier. There the children were educated in a Jesuit school, though the young Alexander preferred to devote his time to a book of pioneer travels amongst the North American Indians. Already 'the notion of being a traveller and adventurer and of somehow and somewhere carving out a career for myself was the maggot of my brain'.

Recalling his youth all of sixty years later, Gardiner was understandably hazy. But in locations like 'the shores of Lake Superior', 'the source of the Mississippi' and 'the mouth of the Colorado river', he gives an early indication of an infuriating inexactitude. Moreover, no map has ever marked a place called St. Xavier.

About 1809 he went to Ireland. He returned to America in 1812 but found his father dead and immediately headed back to Europe. He was ever proud of his American citizenship, but never again crossed the Atlantic. In Spain he realised the estate of his mother and then, via Cairo and the Black Sea, reached Astrakhan on the Caspian. Here his eldest brother had settled down as a mining engineer in the employ of the Russian government. The young Gardiner hoped to follow in his footsteps and spent three years immersed in mineralogy. In 1817 the brother died, the Russian authorities sequestered most of his property and Alexander was refused employment. Disgusted, he packed his bags and set sail across the Caspian. He was thirty-three.

For the next thirteen years Gardiner lived in the saddle. He wandered from Ashkhabad to Herat, then amongst the Hazaras and Turkomans to Khiva, north to the Aral Sea and back across the Caspian to Astrakhan. That was just the preliminary. In 1823 he set off again, across the steppes from the Caspian to the Aral and then up the Syr river, the Jaxartes of the ancients, to Ura Tyube near Samarkand, a distance of over 1,000 miles. By now he had decided that he 'could not rest in civilised surroundings'. He was happy only amongst wild races and unknown lands. He passed by the name of Arb Shah, wore Uzbek costume and carried a Koran into which he stuffed the scanty notes of his travels.

He had also acquired a band of faithful followers. There was no law in Central Asia. Outside the cities it was every man for himself. The distinction between the predators—robbers, slave dealers and nomads—and the prey—merchants, pilgrims and herdsmen—was a fine one indeed. But, as far as Ura Tyube, Arb Shah and his friends had moved with the circumspection of bona fide travellers. Now, after a complex three-sided engagement in which they lost and then stole back their horses and property, they became fugitives. Previously they had avoided cities for fear of Gardiner's nationality being

1 In the Pir Panjal near the Dulchi Pass

2 William Moorcroft:
supposed portrait

3 Joseph Wolff in 1840

4 Victor Jacquemont

5 Baron Carl von Hugel

6 Godfrey Thomas Vigne, the Skardu Valley
in the background

7 Srinagar: The Jhelum River. From a line drawing
by G. T. Vigne

8 The Indus in Baltistan. From a line drawing
by G. T. Vigne

9 Colonel Alexander Gardiner

10 Maharaja Ranjit Singh, from a
portrait by G. T. Vigne

11 Dost Mohammed of Kabul, from
a portrait by G. T. Vigne

12 Sir Alexander Burnes

detected. Now they had no choice in the matter. They were outlaws riding by night, hiding by day and living on what they could steal.

At Hazrat Imam they crossed the Oxus into Afghanistan and headed for Kabul. Ever since leaving Astrakhan, Gardiner had had the idea of enlisting in the forces of an Asiatic ruler. The Shah of Persia, the Khan of Khokand and Ranjit Singh had all figured in his plans. In Afghanistan his best chance lay with Dost Mohammed, now establishing himself in Kabul, and he hoped that, in return for his services, he and his followers would be granted an amnesty. There is a distinguished tradition, particularly in India, of European military adventurers, men who, departing or deserting their national colours, served in the armies of native princes. Jacquemont's friend Allard and Wolff's 'kind Italian' Avitabile, are notable examples. Much later Gardiner did join them in the Sikh service, but to compare him and his desperate little band, as they came fleeing out of Turkestan, with Napoleonic officers at the head of well-trained armies, is misleading. Better by far to remember his childhood in that mysterious town somewhere on what is now the Arizona/Mexico border. Gardiner was just a desperado, a hired gun on the run. His moral standards, which later caused such a scandal, were those of Boot Hill, not Sandhurst. If, instead of a tartan turban, the old Colonel had worn a ten-gallon hat and if, instead of Srinagar, his resting place had been St. Louis, his whole career would have been more readily understood.

To avoid detection they gunned down three of Murad Beg's men near Kunduz, and would have done the same again when stopped in the Kohistan just north of Kabul. Only this time there were fifty picked horsemen who came on them 'like a desert storm'. Gardiner drew up his men and prepared to parley. His captor was Habib Ullah Khan, the dispossessed heir to the throne of Kabul, who was now waging the nineteenth century equivalent of a guerilla war against his uncle, Dost Mohammed. History has condemned Habib Ullah as a debauchee, a drunkard and a coward. Gardiner, on the other hand, painted him in heroic shades as a born leader of dauntless courage, high-minded principles and magnanimous intentions. This was important, for it struck those who wished to discredit his story as highly significant that, in his one supposed encounter with a figure known to history, he could be so demonstrably wrong.

In fact he may not have been. Posterity's verdict on Habib Ullah was that given out by his arch enemies, Dost Mohammed and his brothers, and substantiated by the Khan's depravities after his final defeat. The only foreigner who met him in the days of his youth, apart from Gardiner, was the archaeologist, Charles Masson.* Writing in the light of what later befell Habib Ullah, he too calls him 'rash, headstrong, profuse and dissipated'; but in his youth he found him a splendid figure. He dressed in gold and scarlet and was the finest looking man in the whole of the Afghan court. His vices were 'rather those of habit than of the heart and to atone for them he possessed indomitable personal bravery and lavish generosity'.

Such qualities were no match for the scheming duplicity of his uncle, but one can understand why they appealed to a man like Gardiner. Instead of a choice between death and slavery, the generous prince offered him command of 180 horsemen in his struggle against Dost Mohammed. Gardiner accepted and, for the next two and a half years, led a life of 'active warfare and continual forays . . . for the good cause of right against wrong'. From the mountain fringes between Jalalabad and Bamian they swooped into the settled lands of the Kabul river basin or waylaid caravans crossing the Hindu Kush. According to Masson they were 'eight hundred very dissolute but resolute cavalry living at free quarters upon the country'.

It was a far from settled existence but, amid such excitements, Gardiner enjoyed his first tragic taste of domestic happiness. In an attack on a caravan of distinguished pilgrims he had glimpsed the face of a beautiful young girl. As his share of the booty he asked for and, though she was of royal blood, was given this maiden. They set up home in a fort near Parwan and 'there I was happy for about two years in the course of which time my wife made me the father of a noble boy'. This was the beginning of the most difficult part of his narrative. The tone becomes subdued. Forty years had elapsed but still the tears flowed as he recalled it. 'I must hurry over this part of my story.'

By 1826 Habib Ullah's cause was lost. He was pinned down near Parwan and Gardiner was ordered back from his forays. When he arrived, the Khan's forces had already been defeated; Habib Ullah

* The American Charles Masson was originally the Englishman James Lewis of the Bombay army. He deserted in the 1820s and wandered off into Afghanistan where he spent most of the next fifteen years. Travelling in the style of Dr. Henderson, unarmed, on foot and penniless, he gained a deeper understanding of Afghanistan than any of his contemporaries. He first won attention in India with his archaeological reports on the Buddhist topes around Kabul, and in 1835 he was appointed British informant in that city.

himself, though still fighting, was severely wounded. Gardiner hacked a path through to his side only to learn, when the enemy retired, that his own fort had already been stormed. What he found, when after a frantic ride he entered his home, is best left to the old Colonel himself.

The silence was oppressive when I rode through the gateway of the fort, and my men instinctively fell back, when an old *mullah* (who had remained faithful to our party) came out to meet me, with his left hand and arm bound up. His fingers had been cut off and his arm nearly severed at the wrist by savage blows from a scimitar while striving to protect my little child. Faint from his wounds and from the miserable recollection of the scene from which he had escaped, the sole survivor, the aged *mullah*, at first stood gazing at me in a sort of wild abstraction, and then recounted the tale of the massacre of all that I loved.

The garrison had long and gallantly held their own, though attacked on all sides by an immensely superior force. They had seen Habib Ullah approaching, fighting gallantly, and had for a moment thought themselves saved, but he had been driven back and passed from their sight. The *castello* had been stormed and all in it put to the sword, with the sole exception of the old priest.

After this brief story the *mullah* silently beckoned me to dismount and to follow him into the inner room. There lay four mangled corpses—my wife, my boy and two little eunuch youths. I had left them all thoughtless and happy but five days before. The bodies had been decently covered up by the faithful *mullah*, but the right hand of the hapless young mother could be seen, and clenched in it the reeking *katar* with which she had stabbed herself to the heart after handing over the child to the priest for protection. Her room had been broken open, and mortally self wounded as she was, the assassins nearly severed her head from her body with their long Afghan knives or sabres. The *mullah* had tried to escape with the child, but had been cut across the hand and arm as aforesaid, and the boy seized and barbarously murdered. There he lay by the side of his mother.

I sank on my knees and involutarily offered up a prayer for vengeance to the most high God. Seeing my attitude the *mullah*, in a low solemn tone, breathed the Mohammedan prayers proper to the presence of the dead, in which my *sowars*, who had silently followed with bent heads, fervently joined. Tear after tear trickled down the pallid and withered cheeks of the priest as he concluded. Rising, I forced myself and him away from the room, gave him all the money I had for the interment of the dead, and with fevered brain rode away for ever from my once happy mountain home.

It was the end of his Afghan adventure and the beginning of his journey into the Western Himalayas.

The inventory of essential equipment and provisions that travellers feel constrained to present to their readers soon become dull. Those 'double fly tents', 'artificial horizons', 'tinned' cooking pots and all the endless arguments about boots versus the native grass shoes invariably presage a second-rate narrative with little pioneering content. The great explorers tend to be more reticent and less dogmatic about their preparations. Gardiner is no exception. His party of desperate men who now struck off up into the Hindu Kush, assessed the total value of their property at just over half a rupee.

They were not, of course, consciously embarking on an expedition; they were running for their lives. Gardiner himself was wounded in the neck and the leg. Washed in salt and water and dressed with powdered charcoal and clay, it was not surprising that these wounds never really healed. His outfit consisted of a high black Uzbek hat, black sheepskin coat, hair rope girdle and Turki boots. They had guns and horses but for food depended on what they could steal. Until the first well-provided caravan passed within their grasp, they lived off 'snow mushrooms' and a half rotten, partially cooked 'hyena-like animal'.

The plan at this stage was a simple one, to put as much of Afghanistan as possible between themselves and Dost Mohammed. They climbed north into the mountains, crossing by the Khawak pass and hoping once again to escape over the Oxus at Hazrat Imam. This great river, which divides Afghanistan from Turkestan proper was regarded by Gardiner as a second Rio Grande; safety always lay on the other side. The problem was that between the Hindu Kush and the river lay a hundred miles of open ground, the domain of Murad Beg. It was only two years since Moorcroft had been waylaid there and the Uzbek chief was known to be keeping a close lookout for stragglers from Habib Ullah's forces.

The first attempt to descend from the mountains was a disaster. A group of horsemen quietly crossing the plains below them suddenly changed direction and came on at full gallop. They were fifty strong. Gardiner's force, augmented by more stragglers, numbered thirteen. The only chance of escape lay over a pass which he calls Darra Suleiman and in the best Western tradition they tore off towards it. Fast and furious was the pursuit, but Gardiner's men were stretching the gap. Then, half a mile from the pass and safety, another smaller group appeared from among the rocks and barred their path.

The fray now became general, as the main body charged us, trying to save their comrades. This fortunately prevented their using their matchlocks, and we had reached the mouth of the pass, which we held with desperation. Their overwhelming numbers, however, soon broke our ranks, and they unfortunately got mixed up with us; there was no room for orderly fighting and it was a mere cut and thrust affair.

Soon we had only seven men left out of thirteen, and we slowly retreated up the pass, keeping them off as well as we could. In the pass we lost two more men and were now reduced to five, each of us severely wounded. I myself received two wounds, one a bad one in the groin from an Afghan knife and the other a stab from a dirk in the chest.

It was now quite dark and the rain was coming down still heavier than before. However our enemies followed us no further— no doubt the plundering of the dead being their chief inducement to return. We made our way through the pass as quickly as we could in the midst of heavy rain, hail and lightning, while the roll of thunder seemed to make the very rocks around us and the ground beneath us to vibrate most sensibly. What with my two former wounds still raw, and my two fresh ones (one of which was bleeding freely) I was soon so weak as to nearly faint in my saddle.

There was no further pursuit and, after a few days' recuperation in the mountains, they headed north-east into Badakshan. They were still making for the Oxus but now planned to cross it much further east where it emerges from the Pamirs. Above Jerm they descended into the valley of the Kokcha tributary, and this time there was no attack. The country had recently been depopulated by Murad Beg. After a change of travelling companions and more rest, Gardiner finally crossed the Oxus opposite the Shakhdara and entered the valley of Shignan. He was now on the threshold of the Pamirs.

The year was still 1826. In the surviving accounts of his story the next date is spring 1830, by which time he has crossed the Himalayas from north to south and is incarcerated in a dungeon five hundred miles away in Kandahar. As far as the Pamirs his wanderings have been full of detail though not all of it credible; there has been an explanation for each change of direction and, with a good map, the gist of his itinerary can be followed. Now suddenly, at what is geographically the crucial stage, his account becomes vague and disjointed. Did he actually cross the Pamirs or skirt them by way of the foothills of the Alai, two hundred miles to the north? It is impossible to say. He was aiming for Yarkand but until he actually got there none of the places he mentions can be positively identified.

The Pamirs are a polar wilderness combining the bleakness of Tibet with the ruggedness of the Karakorams. Descriptions of them are often unsatisfactory for the simple reason that there is little to describe. In summer Kirghiz nomads go in search of the grazing, but no one actually lives there. The sum total of features recorded by the first dozen visitors is two or three crumbling tombs and a dreary muddle of lakes and rivers. It is not, therefore, altogether surprising that Gardiner was unable to substantiate his claim to have been there. On the other hand one would expect some mention of the two most obvious peculiarities of the region, the cold and the wind. Lord Dunmore, who crossed the Roof of the World in 1892, reckoned it the coldest place on earth. He should have known: he had already had a taste of Spitzbergen, the Hudson Bay and Arctic Russia. At night his thermometer registered 45° of frost, and this was inside his tent. Coupled with the debilitating effect of an altitude never less than 12,000 feet, it made life a precarious business. But the wind added a whole new dimension of discomfort. Capricious in direction, unpredictable in strength and unimpeded by anything approaching shelter, it blew day and night, summer and winter, on the mountains and in the valleys, with a vicious numbing intent. It was not a lusty gale to be ridden out, nor a steady blast that one learned to live with; but more like a nagging and insidious cancer. An unprotected face it would cut to shreds in minutes; over a period of days it ate deep into the spirit of a man. Sapping his energy and numbing his senses, it claimed its victims almost unnoticed.

Now Gardiner omits all mention of this. When sixty years later the Russians established their first post on the Pamirs they found the conditions too harsh to support a normal existence. Their poultry all died and the only crop that succeeded was a woody radish. Gardiner, on the other hand talks of Shignan as a veritable orchard, a description that could only apply to the westermost fringe of the region where it borders the Oxus. He says nothing about the altitude, the cold or the snow-clad peaks. A journey of forty miles which took them all of seven days could just as well apply to the rugged country along the banks of the Upper Oxus.

Instead, he had stories of a grizzly fight with a pack of wolves, a visit to the ruby mines on the Oxus and a lot of fraternisation with the Kirghiz herdsmen of the area. There is also some questionable information on aboriginal tribes in the Alai and a ruined city near Yarkand with 'chasms and caverns . . . encrusted with corrosive salts and pervaded with mephitic vapours'. Sometimes he can be positively faulted. No yak ever survived in the deserts of Turkestan. His description of them is convincing enough and almost certainly he would have seen them in Ladakh or on the Pamirs; it looks as if his memory has simply transposed them. Moreover no one would question the old-timer's right to embroider his stories. What was significant was that something like his description of a Kirghiz wedding could be so unexpectedly accurate.

Yarkand, the first recognisable placename, was reached on September 24th. The year is anyone's guess—it could have been 1827, '28 or '29. Here the treatment again changes. A traceable itinerary re-emerges but the colourful detail is gone. From Gardiner one expects classic descriptions and harrowing predicaments amongst the mighty peaks and glaciers. But there is nothing. Just:

21st. Along banks of river to Bolong Belook.
22nd. Ditto to where Doorg meets it on other side.
23rd. Ditto to Fitkar.
24th. Ditto to Lohoo.
28th. Arrived at Leh.
30th. Leave Ladakh for Cashmere.

And so on. From his description 'the worst trade route in the whole wide world' could just as well be a pleasant country by-way and the Karakorams no more formidable than the Hog's Back.

Gardiner's omissions are really more serious than his doubtful assertions. The austere itinerary above is taken from his 'journals'. These never seem to have constituted more than random jottings and, without the accounts of those who heard the story from the

Colonel himself, they are practically meaningless. Gardiner explained that some of the journals were being studied by Sir Alexander Burnes and perished with him in Kabul in 1841. This loss, he claimed, accounted for any inaccuracies or gaps in his story. But in this particular case the journal was not lost and, even if it had been, it is hard to believe that he could recall nothing of his crossing of the mightiest mountains in the world. Besides which, Gardiner's imagination was not usually behindhand in making good any deficiencies of detail. Was it, one wonders, that this section of his travels was one which by the late 1860s could too easily be verified? Or, more charitably, does one assume that he regarded as superfluous any elaboration on his part of a route now widely publicised?

Seven weeks after leaving Yarkand he rode into Srinagar. It was good going but, for a party travelling light during the favourable autumn months, not unreasonable. Since leaving Afghanistan Gardiner had advanced no explanation of where he was heading or why. He had in fact prescribed a massive arc, north to Shignan and perhaps the Alai, east to Yarkand, south to Leh and now west to Srinagar. Here reports that Habib Ullah was again in the field determined him to complete the full circle by returning to Afghanistan. The easiest route would have been that followed by Moorcroft via the Punjab, but for some reason Gardiner and his men stuck to the mountains. They passed through Chilas, Gilgit and Chitral, and finally entered Kafiristan. These are all names which figure prominently in a later phase of exploration in the Western Himalayas. In the 1820s neither their existence nor position was certain and, even when the old traveller was spinning his yarns fifty years later, there were still few, if any, first-hand accounts of them by Europeans.

They are also the only names in his itinerary that can be identified. The rest, and in the published extracts of his journals there are many —villages, forts, 'Cyclopean' ruins—are a mystery. A footnote by the editor of the journals explains that, where the handwriting permitted, Gardiner's spelling had been scrupulously followed. But allowing for bad writing, imperfectly heard names and an erratic system of transliterating them, the reader may take the ultimate liberties in juggling with consonants and still only a handful more can be positively identified.

On the other hand, on this final stage of his journey through the mountains, there is at least some attempt to describe the terrain. Gardiner had no idea of the structure of the mountain complex and anyone who has gazed, mapless, on the chaotic contours north and west of the Indus will sympathise with him. A high pass may be taking one over one of the great Asian watersheds and therefore the spine of one of the main ranges. Or it may be just an insignificant spur. Without the time to explore each valley and follow every stream there is no way of telling. Gardiner was still moving at speed. He clearly relied a good deal on native reports for his general observations but there is sufficient mention of snow-fed torrents, steep ascents, precipitous ledges, mountains covered with perpetual snow and avalanches to make it all sound a good deal more convincing than his oblivion about the Karakorams.

The visit to Kafiristan was, in retrospect, the crowning achievement of his travels. Even today very little is known about this mountain fastness between Chitral and Afghanistan. Gardiner was the first man to claim to have visited it, though he reports that two Europeans had been there some sixty years before. This casual observation lends much credibility to his story, since exactly the same legend was uncovered by a British mission to the area in the 1880s. It was upon their report that Kipling based his story of 'The Man Who Would Be King'.

Gardiner regarded this as his second visit. The first was when he went some way east up the Hindu Kush while fleeing from Dost Mohammed. He says that he was then offered the command of a Kafir tribe and, however this may be, he does seem to have struck up a valuable friendship with this normally hostile people. Mention of them occurs so often in his stories that one is tempted to infer a relationship similar to that between Moorcroft and the Ladakhis or Vigne and the Baltis. On the second visit he adopted the goatskin wrapping of the Kafirs and travelled alone and on foot. He penetrated much further and was probably there much longer than on the first occasion. Even without the relevant journal he was later able to give a more detailed account of the place than anywhere else on his route through the mountains.

Of all the Himalayan peoples the Kafirs are the most distinctive, the most curious and the most primitive. Travellers who met them as slaves in Afghanistan were first intrigued by their appearance. A Kafir girl noticed by Sir Henry Rawlinson in Kabul was the most beautiful oriental he had ever seen. She was the only lady he had ever met who, by loosening her tresses, 'could cover herself from head to foot as with a screen'. Gardiner, who never fails to comment on the female section of the population, describes the women as having hair 'varying from the deepest auburn to the brightest golden tints, blue eyes, lithe figures, fine white teeth, cherry lips and the loveliest peach blossom on their cheeks'. Not only did they look a bit European but they had certain European customs. Marooned in a sea of peoples who habitually squat on the ground, the Kafirs sit on chairs. They make and drink wine and their dead they put into coffins.

This was not, however, enough to convince the first European visitors, Gardiner included, that they should be acknowledged as brethren. Appearances could be deceptive. The Kafirs were fascinating but they were nearer to savages than any other people in Asia. They were appallingly dirty and immoral, their language was unpronounceable and their religion the most primitive animism. Burnes records that, when a Kafir raiding party returned from a foray against their Mohammedan neighbours, it was usual for the warriors to bring back the severed heads of their enemies. Any luckless brave who came back empty-handed was debarred from the homecoming celebrations. These commenced with a ritual hunt for walnuts, the nuts having been previously hidden by the young ladies of the tribe in their bosoms. The story sounds suspiciously like one of Gardiner's. Burnes was certainly supposed to have had the journals of Gardiner's stay in Kafiristan, and more's the pity they perished with him.

Emerging into more civilised surroundings at Jalalabad, Gardiner finally completed his tour of the Western Himalayas. So far as is known he never again visited the lands beyond Kashmir, and the rest of his story can be briefly dealt with. Habib Ullah had not reappeared. Gardiner, trying to reach Persia, was imprisoned at Kandahar, escaped and eventually applied again to enter Dost Mohammed's service in Kabul. Not surprisingly he was refused but at Peshawar he found employment with one of Dost Mohammed's brothers and from there, in 1831, gravitated to Ranjit Singh's army as an artillery officer. He was one of the few foreigners who remained in the Sikh service after Ranjit's death and he played a prominent role in the extraordinary events that followed. These, as Gardiner's biographer has it, amounted to 'a rapid succession of crimes and tragedies such as have rarely been paralleled in history save in the darkest period of the downfall of Rome or the early days of the French revolution'. Gardiner himself listed nineteen participants in the power struggle. Of these, in the five years 1839–44, sixteen were murdered or died under suspicious circumstances. Events, for once, outstripped even the Colonel's lurid imagination. The facts were more macabre than fiction and his account of them has been largely substantiated. From an historical point of view it is the most valuable part of his whole tale. Of the three surviving contenders only one succeeded in retaining any part of Ranjit's empire. This, of course, was Gulab Singh, created by the British, Maharaja of Kashmir. Gardiner disliked him as heartily as did Vigne. His character was 'one of the most repulsive it is possible to imagine', and he accused him of barbarities and atrocities perpetrated in cold blood 'for the sole purpose of investing his name with terror'. Yet, only months after this damning attack, he enlisted in Gulab Singh's service and in Srinagar, as commandant of the new Maharaja's artillery, spent the rest of his active career and then a long and honourable retirement.

7. A Most Distinguished Old Man

Such, then, was Gardiner's story. He died in his bed—after such a life, no mean achievement—in 1877 aged, by his own reckoning, ninety-one. It was the end of one saga but only the beginning of another. Already a few geographers were struggling with his journals and wondering whether they were on to the greatest journey since Marco Polo's or one of travel's most elaborate fabrications. Others, in the interests of history, were trying to piece together the accounts of his life. They at first had fewer reservations, though eventually it was an historian who published the most devastating rebuttal of all.

The first and only printed extracts of Gardiner's journal appeared in India in 1853, with an introduction by Edgeworth, a Bengal civil servant. Lord Strangford of the Royal Asiatic Society drew them to the attention of the Royal Geographical Society, and it was thus that the two great umpires of Asian travel, Sir Henry Rawlinson and Sir Henry Yule, first heard of Gardiner. They only had the journal extracts to go on and these are, as noticed, semi-literate jottings, to this day unintelligible.

'Geography,' declared Yule, 'like Divinity has its Apocrypha . . . I am sorry to include under this head the diary of Colonel Gardiner.' Every attempt to construct from it a consecutive itinerary had failed. The recognisable names, Kunduz, Badakshan, Yarkand, Gilgit etc. were too few. 'But amid the phantasmagoria of antres vast and deserts idle, of scenery weird and uncouth nomenclature, which flashes past us in the diary till our heads go round, we alight upon these familiar names as if from the clouds; they link to nothing before or behind; and the traveller's tracks remind us of that uncanny creature which is said to haunt the eternal snows of the Sikkim Himalaya and whose footsteps are found only at intervals of forty or fifty yards.' He stopped just short of denying that Gardiner had ever visited those places, but on the evidence he thought it unlikely.*

* Gardiner's travels were approached with excessive caution because their currency in the 1860s and '70s happened to coincide with a case of forged maps and fabricated itineraries also relating to the Pamir region. Known as

Rawlinson was more cautious. He regarded the journals as so mutilated and exaggerated 'that the narrative reads more like a romance than a journal of actual adventure'; their author was 'untrustworthy'. On the other hand he believed that 'Gardiner did certainly visit Badakshan' and 'actually traversed the Gilgit valley from the Indus to the Snowy Mountains and finally crossed into Chitral being in fact the only Englishman [?] up to the present time ever to have performed the journey throughout'. Whereas Yule in 1872 imagined Gardiner dead, Rawlinson, writing in 1866 and again in 1874, knew that he was still alive. He knew too that there were others working on the Colonel's verbatim accounts and he fancied that Gardiner, now an older and soberer man, would yet be vindicated.

In this he was right. In Kashmir the old soldier in the tartan uniform was winning support from everyone who met him. These included Frederick Cooper, a member of the Indian Civil Service who was deputed to Kashmir in 1864. He undertook with Gardiner's assistance to write a definitive biography. The work, corrected and therefore endorsed by the Colonel himself, had progressed only as far as the Pamirs when Cooper died in 1871. This helps explain why the account of the rest of his travels through the mountains is so unsatisfactory. Gardiner was never able to contribute directly to it for, with Cooper's death, the draft and notes promptly disappeared and were not rediscovered till after Gardiner's death.

Sir Henry Durand, Lieutenant-Governor of the Punjab, visited Srinagar in 1870 to enquire into allegations brought against the Maharaja by another Himalayan explorer, George Hayward. While there he too met Gardiner and declared him 'one of the finest

---

the Klaproth forgeries from the German geographer who was allegedly responsible for them, these had the savants of the geographical societies of London, St. Petersberg and Paris locked in heated debate. The subject is a highly complicated one and is treated ad nauseam in the Societies' journals from 1865 to 1875. The forgeries had found their way into most maps of the region and had perpetuated an error originally made by the Jesuit cartographers of the eighteenth century. The fathers had managed to twist the section of their map which dealt with the Pamirs through 90 degrees so that, when mounted in an overall map of China and its confines, the Oxus ran north–south instead of east–west. Poor Gardiner, when he tried to reconstruct his travels with the help of a map, was using one that was not just inaccurate but hopelessly falsified. In view of this it is hardly surprising that the account of his journey through or round the Pamirs is so vague. He must have been as confused about his itinerary as anyone.

specimens ever known of the soldier of fortune'. He drafted a short article for the Indian press, *Life of a Soldier of the Olden Times*, but, like Cooper, died before it could be published. (He was actually knocked off the back of an elephant by a low archway whilst on a ceremonial visit to the state of Tonk.) Fortunately his son, Sir Mortimer of Durand Line fame, rescued the article from oblivion and published it, along with the rest of his father's papers, in 1883. It prompted a writer in the *Edinburgh Review* to declare that Gardiner 'should long ago have enjoyed a world wide reputation'.

We know of others who listened to and were impressed by the Colonel's story. Lord Strathnairn when Commander-in-Chief in India, Charles Girdlestone and Le Poer Wynne, Cooper's successors in Srinagar, and perhaps Sir Richard Temple, who at one time or another occupied almost every top post in the Indian Civil Service. There was also Andrew Wilson, a globe-trotting writer for *Blackwoods Magazine*, who met him in 1873. Wilson was an urbane and accurate observer, less likely to be humbugged than most, and he had his reservations. Gardiner seemed to confuse hearsay with his own experience, 'but there is no doubt as to the general facts of his career'.

All these men dismissed the journals published by Edgeworth as garbled nonsense. They relied simply on what Gardiner told them and on their own judgement. And without exception they accepted his story. Indeed, considering the narrator's age, they were inclined to marvel that there were not more gaps and contradictions. All that was now needed to establish Gardiner's credibility once and for all was a full-length biography.

Fortuitously Cooper's draft and the notes with it were rediscovered. They were put in the hands of two 'very high authorities on Central Asia', both of whom died with the papers still in their possession. In the 1890s they reached a Major Hugh Pearse who referred them to Ney Elias, then unquestionably the greatest expert on the region and a man who had himself explored most of the Pamirs. But the jinx continued. Elias too died before completing his summary. Pearse, however, found his uncompleted notes on the manuscripts. In so far as they represent the only opinion of a nineteenth century geographer and explorer who was acquainted with the journals, Cooper's draft, Gardiner's unpublished notes and the accounts given by Durand and Wilson, they must be regarded as crucial.

Elias had written:

There appears to me to be good internal evidence that as regards the main routes he professes to have travelled, Gardiner's story is truthful. When he tells us that he visited the east coast of the Caspian, northern Persia, Herat, the Hazara country, even Khiva; that he spent some time in and about the district of Inderab, and afterwards passed through parts of Badakshan and Shignan, thence crossing the Pamirs into Eastern Turkestan, I see no reason to doubt him . . . The times were on the whole sufficiently favourable to render belief in the main features of his narrative possible; and it is in a sense the truth of the general narrative that enables us to excuse the untruth of many of the details. In other words had Gardiner not travelled over a great part of the ground he professes to describe, it would not have been possible for him to interpolate the doubtful portions of his story. He could not have known enough of the surrounding conditions or even the names of the places and tribes, nor have met with the people whose clumsy inventions he at times serves out to us. It is necessary, for instance, that a man who could never have read of the Pamir region should at least have visited that country or its neighbourhood before he could invent or repeat stories regarding Shakh Dara or the Yaman Yar, or be able to dictate the name of Shignan.

Using this verdict, Cooper's draft and all the other material, Pearse produced his standard work, *The Memoirs of Alexander Gardiner*, in 1898. It was twenty years after Gardiner's death and seventy after his journey through the Western Himalayas, far too late to create much of a stir. In the interim Turkestan and the Western Himalayas had been carved up between the great powers, there were patrols and boundary markers across the Pamirs, and in Chitral and Gilgit there were British garrisons. The authenticity, the very existence, of Alexander Gardiner was of purely academic interest. But at least his wandering spirit could now rest quietly in the little graveyard at Sialkot where he had been buried.

Not, however, for long. Pearse was wrong in thinking that only the most incredulous would now question Gardiner's story. The last blow was the cruellest of all. For in 1929 there appeared *European Adventurers of Northern India 1785–1849*, which not only reversed his verdict but damned Gardiner to perdition. 'Now', wrote the author, C. Grey, after citing the various authorities who had supported

Gardiner's tale, 'to impugn the veracity of any person is an unpleasant task, and especially so when that person was believed by men of unquestioned probity and high position to have been a worthy soldier and a truthful traveller.' It is 'only to be undertaken when one is certain of the real facts, has unimpeachable evidence to offer, no personal feeling and a conviction that by exposing an imposture he is rendering a service to posterity'. Grey knew what he was doing and enjoyed it. He had the evidence. With remorseless sarcasm and self-righteous zeal he proceeded to dissect limb by limb the Gardiner legend.

His suspicions had first been aroused by the similarity of incidents recorded by other Europeans in the Sikh service to those in Gardiner's tale. An Irishman called Rattray had also lent his diaries to Sir Alexander Burnes and lost them in the 1841 conflagration in Kabul. Leigh, a British deserter (alias Mohammed Khan) had also claimed extensive travels in Central Asia and Afghanistan, and so too had Honigberger, the German doctor who was dispenser of the Maharaja's brandy. Josiah Harlan was undoubtedly an American citizen but others, notably Charles Masson, who claimed to be Americans, were really British deserters. Gardiner, too, might be in this category. Grey was not prepared to credit him with even a fertile imagination. Every incident in his story could conceivably have been gleaned from the murky pasts of his companions at Lahore.

Suspicion became conviction when, working through the Punjab records, he came across the first of two damning pieces of evidence. This was an entry dated 15th December 1831 recording a report received in Ludhiana from the British informant at Lahore. It mentioned the arrival there of two Europeans, Messrs Khora* and Gardiner, both aged about 35. The date matches well with that given by Gardiner himself, though he never mentions a companion. Asked whence they came 'they answered that they were formerly serving in a ship of war, but not being satisfied with their position, quitted it and proceeded from Bombay to Peshawar, where Sultan Mohammed Khan [Dost Mohammed's brother] had entertained them on three rupees a day. They were with him six months, but having heard

* Khora, according to Grey, was really 'Kanara' or 'Kennedy', another Irish 'American'. He too stayed in the Sikh's service after Ranjit Singh's death and was seconded by the British in 1846. He died a hero's death at the outbreak of the second Sikh war in 1848.

of the liberality of His Highness [Ranjit Singh], they had applied
for their discharge and come to Lahore.'

In other words, like so many adventurers, Gardiner was just a
deserter from the East India Company's forces. Probably he was no
more American than Masson and had never even been to Kabul, let
alone crossed the deserts of Central Asia or the Himalayas.

Vanish [crows Grey] the highly accomplished parents of such
singularly mixed breed and curious antecedents, and the long and
tangled line of an adventurous life, 'one end commencing on the
shores of Lake Superior and the other ending on the banks of the
Indus'.

Gone are the many years of schooling in the Jesuit college, the
long years of stirring travel, the high-minded Habib Ullah Khan,
and those beautiful blue eyed, golden haired Kafir ladies, and the
maiden captive who became Gardiner's wife and whose sad fate
'always brought tears to his eyes' . . . With them disappear . . .
the companionship with princes, the command of armies and that
adventurous travel and stirring adventure in lands 'where no
European had ever set foot'.

Worse, in Grey's opinion, was to come. Gardiner was not only a liar
but a brute. The other piece of evidence gleaned from the Punjab
Records was that, during the anarchy that followed Ranjit Singh's
death, Gardiner had acted as hatchet man for one of the aspirants
to the throne. When no one else could be found for the role of
torturer, it was he who had taken up the razor 'and with his own
hands, in cold blood, without personal emnity of any sort' cut from
a Brahmin, Jodha Ram, his right thumb, ears and nose. Every man
has his price, and for this service he was accorded the equivalent
of a Colonel's rank.

It needs to be emphasised that Gardiner was under orders and
had little choice in the matter. Few survived those turbulent years
in Lahore with their dignity, not to mention their lives, intact. But
it was further recorded that, for this deed, Gardiner was expelled
from Lahore by Sir Henry Lawrence when he arrived there as
British Governor in 1846. There is no question that Gardiner did
wield the razor, and many were understandably scandalised that any
European officer could do such a thing. But the fact that expulsion merely took him to Ludhiana and safety, and that Lawrence

afterwards spoke of him in the most generous terms, suggests that there were certainly extenuating circumstances.

Durand and Temple had made out the Colonel to be a paragon of virtue and 'a splendid example to the young man of today'. That he was no such thing is really beside the point. Grey had demolished his whole story. Legends based on it, and the reputation of the man who invented it, scarcely mattered any more. The question is whether Grey was right. Surely anyone with a spark of the romantic will be forgiven for trying to salvage the old boy's achievements, however unsavoury his character.

Grey's treatment leaves several questions unanswered. In the first place why, if he was really a deserter, was no action taken against him as soon as he reached British soil? Desertion was the sort of crime for which a man would be arraigned even decades later. It appears that during the anarchy in Lahore he supplied information to the British but there is no record, as there is with Masson who performed a similar service in Kabul, of a pardon being a quid pro quo.

His nationality, too, remains a puzzle. Von Hugel, who met him in Lahore in 1835 is the only one who states categorically that though he called himself an American he was in fact Irish. Where the Baron got this information is not revealed. Gardiner had indeed a brogue, but he admitted having spent five years in Ireland when he might easily have picked it up. As shown by Harlan's career, service in India did not preclude his being an American. It was improbable, but there is insufficient evidence to disprove it.

Grey is so sure that he is dealing with an 'imposture' that he can credit nothing of Gardiner's tale. 'All the claimed adventures will be found in books in our bibliography and such as are not therein in the accounts concerning Lee, Rattray, Jan Sahib, Vieskanawitch and other adventurers who served Ranjit Singh.' Unless Grey had a lot more information about these shadowy figures than he published, this simply is not true. There is nothing very original in his bibliography and, though it is possible that Gardiner pieced together from the pasts of these men an identikit life story for himself, nothing like enough is known about them to support Grey's assertion.

Of much more significance is the possibility, which escaped Grey, that the story which Gardiner gave to Ranjit Singh in Lahore was the false one; not that with which he regaled his audiences in Kashmir. The Maharaja wanted an army as disciplined as that of the British, and for this he wanted officers trained in European warfare and familiar with artillery. A wild adventurer from Central Asia with no understanding of drill or tactics was of no use to him. Such a man, to command a higher price, would naturally try to lay claim to some European service, and a supposed career in the navy would at least suggest that he knew something of gunnery. No native informant would be able to fault such a story; Gardiner admits that, knowing little about artillery, he had to bluff his way. Grey's evidence is unimpeachable all right, but, like that of Pearse, Durand and the rest, it too is based on Gardiner's word. In 1831 he had every reason to lie; in the 1870s, with one foot in the grave, very little.

Finally what of Gardiner's travels? Grey was no geographer and he completely ignored the testimony of Ney Elias, though he quoted in full the obsolete verdict of Yule. The 1860s and '70s were the golden age of travel in the Western Himalayas and explorers of the period invariably started from Srinagar. Had they, men who had seen or were soon to see the lands supposedly travelled by Gardiner, ever sought him out? It is a fairly obvious line of enquiry but one that neither Pearse nor Grey followed.

The answer, happily, is yes. Gordon, Forsyth, Hayward and Leitner all met Gardiner. Probably Shaw and possibly surveyors like Montgomerie and Godwin-Austen also knew him. Their references to him are scattered and far from conclusive. No one actually expresses an opinion one way or the other about his travels. But they all consulted him and there is no evidence that they considered him an imposter although they were men who knew the roads to Yarkand and Gilgit or who had visited the Pamirs.

Dr. Leitner merely quotes Gardiner as a connoisseur of feminine beauty throughout the Western Himalayas, and Forsyth refers to him as an authority on the mysterious mountains of Bolor.* Far more important is the testimony of Gordon and Hayward. Gordon first met Gardiner in 1852 when he watched him lead the troops at the Maharaja's weekly parade. Twenty years later, en route to the

---

* Bolor is one of those mysterious places like Atlantis and Eldorado which, though well attested by early travellers, including in this case Marco Polo, has never been identified. The explanation given by Gardiner to Forsyth, and much later by Younghusband to Pearse, is still the most probable. This assumes that Bolor is a mishearing of 'bala' meaning 'upper', i.e. the higher regions of any valley or tract. In other words it was not a place-name at all but a descriptive term. This, at least, explains why it appears to have been used of so many different places.

Pamirs, he again met him and had a long conversation with the old Colonel. It was before he had actually seen Yarkand or the Pamirs: but writing many years later he refers the reader to Pearse's *Memoirs of Alexander Gardiner* with obvious approval. Even after his travels he evidently had no doubts about Gardiner's story.

The same goes for Hayward. After his journey to Yarkand and Kashgar, he was actually concerned in trying to get the Colonel's story published. It could be that he was one of those 'very high authorities on Central Asia' who died whilst working on it, except that his death took place at a time when, according to Pearse, the papers were still with Cooper. Not only did he have no reservations about Gardiner but there is evidence to suggest that he was inspired by the old Colonel. A passion for disguise and travelling rough, a belief that the Chitral valley represented the easiest route from India to Central Asia and that the Pamirs should be approached via Gilgit, are all strongly indicative of Gardiner's teaching. This is purely conjecture but Hayward's references to him suggest that these two not dissimilar men were more than just acquaintances.

And there is one final piece of evidence. The authority in this case is a man who had no first-hand experience of anywhere beyond the British Indian frontier. He was neither a geographer nor an historian but a dogged, loyal and rather unimaginative civil servant. He had absolutely nothing in common with Gardiner, and if anyone was likely to be sceptical it was he.

Only three years before his death Gardiner, true to type, had been at the centre of a gun-running operation involving 20,000 muskets. These were supposed to be for the Amir of Kashgar, at the time regarded as a possible British ally in the Great Game. As it was, because of Gardiner's connection with the Kashmir army, the whole thing looked 'shaky' to the British authorities. The guns might never get further than Kashmir and in the Maharaja's hands could become a serious embarrassment. The transaction was therefore stopped. The letter dealing with the question went the rounds of the India Office in London. Rawlinson, who was a member of the India Council, records his doubts about Gardiner as a traveller but as usual avoids a definite opinion. Only one man, the diligent Under-Secretary Sir Owen Tudor Burne, is outspoken. He must have come across Gardiner when personal secretary to Lord Strathnairn in the early 1860s. The very existence of a connection between Gardiner and Burne is so improbable that his verdict, even if characteristically cautious, would be worth quoting. In fact it is anything but cautious. 'I know Gardiner well,' he notes in a neat hand in the margin. 'He is the most distinguished old man and has been through the whole of Central Asia experiencing the most extraordinary vicissitudes that ever befell the lot of one man.'

8. An Extraordinary Mission

Alexander Gardiner is really the antithesis of the nineteenth century explorer, a man from travel's other side. True or false, the important thing about his story is that it survives. It may stand for the unrecorded wanderings of many another vagrant and shadowy figure who perchance ventured into the Western Himalayas. In places like Australia the explorer could be confident of being the first outsider to set foot on a piece of virgin territory. This was not the case in Asia. Here there was always the possibility that, over the centuries of European contact with the East, some obscure wanderer had once strayed unknowingly along the same path. In Kabul there was a mysterious gravestone, seen by both Vigne and Charles Masson, which recorded a certain William Hicks who 'departed this lyfe' in 1666. In Kafiristan there was that legend of the two unknown Europeans, and in Kashmir Moorcroft had found a lone British deserter called Lyons and had enrolled him briefly in his private army. There was a White Russian called Danibeg who was supposed to have crossed from Leh to Yarkand at the end of the eighteenth century and there were all those mysterious adventurers, unearthed by Grey, who ended up in Ranjit Singh's army.

If a man like Joseph Wolff is a traveller but not an explorer, a further category must be found for Gardiner and those he represents. Travel to such men was a way of life; adventure its sole justification. Gardiner himself was not quite oblivious of geography. He may have possessed a compass and von Hugel found him touting a street plan of Kandahar. But maps were not part of his normal equipment and it was only after his travelling days were over that, in the hope of discovering just where his wanderings had taken him, he consulted one. At the time he can have had no idea if, when, or where he entered *terra incognita*. One desert, one range, was much like any other to a man preoccupied with staying alive. And although, after Gardiner, no European could be sure of being the first anywhere in the Western Himalayas, he himself would, at the time, have greeted with irreverent guffaws the suggestion that his desperate decampments merited the attentions of science.

Compare with such a man Lieutenant Alexander Burnes of the Bombay army. Gardiner's travels did nothing to advance a knowledge of the mountains; he scarcely knew of Moorcroft and he had no effect on the later course of exploration. Burnes, on the other hand, is a central figure in the story; and this in spite of the fact that he never actually set foot in the mountains. His career neatly links the achievements of all the early explorers. In his lifetime he was regarded as the greatest authority on the region and, as a result of his work, a whole new impetus was given to exploration. It was also under his auspices that another attempt was made on the Pamirs.

But first the man. It was not the least of Burnes's achievements that he won a degree of fame and recognition to which all subsequent travellers would aspire. In 1832, a few weeks after meeting Wolff in Kabul, he had reached Bukhara. He returned, aged twenty-seven, to the sort of reception every schoolboy dreams of. In a sense it had been easily won. He and Gerard had travelled light and in disguise, but beneath their ponderous turbans were hidden strings of gold ducats. More were sewn into their kummerbunds and stuffed into the soles of their sandals. Letters of credit for five thousand rupees were tied round their left arms and polyglot passports round their right. They were cherished employees of the Hon. Company and they enjoyed the best of both worlds; the freedom and anonymity of unofficial travellers together with the financial and political backing of accredited officers.

The risks involved were thus considerably reduced. But Burnes knew how to make the most of his success. He was a highly determined and ambitious young man, quick and canny as an east-coast Scotsman should be. 'Mercurial' is the adjective most often used of him. If Moorcroft's life is discerned in the slow uncertain light of a guttering candle and Gardiner's picked out with all the stagecraft of a *son et lumiere*, Burnes's is lit by the short-lived brilliance of a highly charged flashbulb. Likewise his character. A great talker, a good linguist and a shrewd diplomat, he had many of the qualities that showed. But later it would be asked whether he had the strong principles and staying power needed to go with them. He was also something of a scholar and, as might be expected of a distant descendant of Robert Burns,* an expressive writer. Anything his travels lost in reality they gained in the telling.

* Burns, Burnes and Burness are all variant spellings used by Robert's descendants.

From India he was sent straight to London to report in person to the Company's Board of Directors. *Travels into Bokhara* was published soon after he arrived and overnight 'Bokhara Burnes' became a legend. His observations were extensive but carefully checked, his assessments portentous but modest and discreet, and his narrative was nothing short of inspired. There was something of the wit of a Jacquemont, the sound common sense of a Vigne and the painstaking application of a Moorcroft. Yet none of these three had so far been published in England; almost all of what Burnes had to say was new. To the general public his book opened up a whole world of strange peoples and forgotten lands. Vicariously he invited the reader to share his adventures. They could feel the little thrill of excitement he experienced when a passer-by first asked him if he was heading for Bukhara. They could relish the anticipation of Hazara hospitality which reputedly included a bath and massage at the hands of the maiden of the house. And they could experience all the discomforts of native travel and the anxieties of disguise. It was the stuff of travellers' tales but Burnes made it respectable; he was not a crank but a highly authoritative and dedicated officer.

The book appeared in three beautifully bound, gilt-edged, gold-blocked volumes. The exceptional figure of £800 had been paid for the copyright and on the day of publication it sold nine hundred copies. The critics were unstinting. 'One of the most valuable books of travel that has ever appeared', thought the *Quarterly Review*; 'indispensable to statesmen, merchants, antiquarians and philosophers' chimed in the *Foreign and Quarterly*; while the *United Service Journal* was at a loss what to praise most, the statistical, geographical, geological, commercial, military or political information. For *Travels into Bokhara* was much more than just a travelogue; nothing less in fact than a scholarly and comprehensive account of the whole of Central Asia, the Western Himalayas included. Here could be found some of the first published reports of the source and course of the Upper Indus and of the Oxus, of Baltistan, Yarkand and the Pamirs. Political and scientific circles were as impressed as the general public. The young hero was introduced at Court and received the special thanks of the king. The prestigious Royal Asiatic Society elected him a member and conferred its diploma on him. The Royal Geographical Society elected him a fellow by acclamation and promptly awarded him their Gold Medal (until 1839 only one such award was made each year). And the Athenaeum Club co-opted him over the heads of 1,130 other candidates. The book was immediately translated into French and German, and Burnes dashed off to Paris to collect the plaudits of the French Royal Asiatic Society and the Silver Medal of the Geographical Society. He was 'living fast in every sense of the word' and loving it. Every reception afforded new introductions and more powerful connections. Burnes never underrated his prospects but, with an accent 'Scottish but not unpleasantly so' and a background respectable rather than influential, these were just what he needed to secure a brilliant future in his chosen field, the Indian political service.

The geographical societies would have done better to spare a plaudit for Dr. Gerard, who, though well past his prime, had joined Burnes at the latter's insistence to superintend the survey work of the expedition. From Persia Burnes had returned to India by sea while Gerard went back via Herat. He was already a sick man and took nearly eighteen months to reach Ludhiana. 'The trip killed him,' wrote one of his brothers, but he returned to their beloved retreat near Simla and there, on his deathbed, while Burnes was reaping the rewards in London, he completed the map of their travels. At a scale of five miles to the inch it measured ten feet by three and was the first attempt to link India to Central Asia by a connected series of observations.

Meanwhile Burnes was busy angling for an opportunity to return to Central Asia. Before dealing with the last stormy years of his short life, there are two aspects of the journey to Bukhara that deserve close examination. As has been said, excluding a visit to Simla, Burnes never set foot in the Western Himalayas. But the mountains intrigued him more even than the vast deserts of Central Asia. On his first visit to Lahore he had glimpsed the snowy tops on the horizon and experienced 'a nervous sensation of joy'. On his second visit, en route to Bukhara, he had actually sought Ranjit Singh's permission to cross into Kashmir; the Maharaja knew Burnes for what he was, a political agent, and duly withheld it. Both these visits to Lahore were in 1831, the same year that Jacquemont was in and out of the city on his way to Kashmir, and the same year that Gardiner finally arrived there. Early the following year Burnes met Wolff in Kabul and, on his triumphant return from Bukhara, it was he who unearthed Moorcroft's journals in Calcutta and took them back to London for publication.

He thus had his finger on the pulse of exploration into the Himalayas.

He may not have actually met Jacquemont, nor have yet got possession of any of Gardiner's journals, but he certainly used every scrap of information he had and used it to the best advantage. All his own material was hearsay. At Kunduz, where like Moorcroft he was hauled before Murad Beg, he met a party of merchants from Badakshan who were engaged in the tea trade between Yarkand and Bukhara. They provided a wealth of detail on the Pamirs and what lay beyond. Checked against what he knew of the earlier travellers and against the standard works of Elphinstone and Marco Polo, this provided a basis for an outline of the geography of the mountain region which vastly improved on anything then in print.

There were some glaring mistakes. MacCartney had given the Upper Indus three main branches. Burnes, eliminating the southern one, correctly reduced them to two but, ignoring Moorcroft, proclaimed the Shyok, and not the Ladakh branch, the main one. It was this error that sent Henderson and Vigne (until he exposed the mistake) on a wild goose chase after the supposed source of the Indus below the Karakoram pass. He was nearer a true idea of the positions of Chitral, Gilgit and Baltistan than anyone before Vigne but, contradicting even Jacquemont's evidence, made Skardu and Baltistan separate states. On the credit side Burnes included an account not only of the crossing of the Pamirs but also of the Leh–Yarkand route and it was from his book that the world first got an inkling of the mountain horrors that lay in store there. The Karakoram pass he reported as being high enough to cause severe altitude sickness and subject to storms so wild that they might delay travellers for a whole week. Beyond was a further pass of solid ice out of which steps had to be notched. On the basis of this information he doubted if the route would ever prove of much commercial significance.

However he dangled before the prospective traveller two tempting carrots, one of which was the city of Yarkand. Burnes was the first to sense something of the peculiar reputation of the place. With the merchants of Central Asia it was highly popular. Bukhara might be the noblest city, Merv the oldest and Samarkand the finest, but Yarkand was the naughtiest; it was their Paris. Western Turkestan was oppressively Mohammedan. The womenfolk kept within their windowless houses, and the visiting merchant was expected to reside in certain areas. Non-Mohammedans had to wear a distinctive rope girdle. If there had been any fleshpots, the outsider would not have had a taste of them. In Yarkand the native population was also Mohammedan, but it was ruled by the Chinese. Along with Kashgar, the other major city of Eastern Turkestan, it was the only place in the Chinese empire to which the Central Asian merchant was admitted. The Chinese vetted their visitors carefully and, once in, watched them closely. But this was not resented. Their rule was fair enough—and so too were the ladies of Yarkand. Mohammedans they might be, but they wore no veils and they hid from no man. On the contrary, from their high-heeled boots to their elaborate medieval head-dresses—all of which Burnes described in detail—they invited the very glances for which in Bukhara a man could be summarily arrested.

Some were prostitutes. There were streets of brothels and they were well patronised. But for the visiting merchant, who might spend months assembling his caravan, there were pleasanter arrangements. He got married. Four wives was the accepted maximum even in Yarkand, but a most convenient institution, what Burnes called a *nicka* marriage, limited the conjugal rights to a fixed period. It might be a year or two, or it might be just a week. And should even this prove too long, a cheap system of divorce offered an easy way out. By the time she was thirty an attractive Yarkandi girl might have had a hundred husbands. When, much later in the century, explorers and sportsmen would put into Yarkand to refit, their servants would immediately disperse into the bazaars and be married by nightfall. Winkling them out for the departure of the party was a delicate and trying business.

Burnes's other carrot, though every bit as intriguing, was more technical. In his description of the Pamirs he corroborated a reference by Marco Polo to the existence of a large lake in the centre of this barren chunk of mountains. He reported that it was called 'Surikol' and he learnt from men who had actually seen it that it was the source of the Oxus, the Jaxartes (Syr) and of a branch of the Indus. If this was the case, here indeed was a remarkable geographical phenomenon. Asia's three great classical rivers all flowing from the same icy tarn on the windswept 'Roof of the World'; it was a moving, almost allegorical notion. Lakes with more than one effluent are rare and the streams anyway are usually part of the same river system. But a lake with three effluents, each the origin of a separate mighty river system, was unheard of. Was such a thing possible? Did they ooze from a humble pool or gush from a noble sea? And where in that arid and elevated wilderness did the lake draw its inexhaustible supply? Until someone actually visited the scene and brought back an authentic account, Sir-i-kol was likely to prove as great a mystery as the snow-capped Mountains of the Moon round the equatorial source of the Nile.

So much for the geographical impetus provided by Burnes's trip to Bukhara. The other aspect of his travels which bears on the exploration of the Western Himalayas is political. With the appearance of Alexander Burnes, the Great Game, that depreciative catchphrase for the deadly serious business of Anglo-Russian rivalry in Central Asia, may be said to begin. In the 1820s the frontier of British India in the north-west lay from Simla along the line of the Sutlej to the deserts of Rajasthan, and then roughly followed the present Indo-Pakistan border to the Arabian Sea. Beyond it lay Kashmir and Ladakh in the north, Punjab and Afghanistan in the centre, and Sind and Baluchistan in the south. In a further arc beyond these lay Eastern Turkestan, the Central Asian Khanates of Khokand, Khiva and Bukhara, and Persia. Further still were the Aral, the Caspian and the Kazakh steppes—and only beyond these lay Russia. It seems incredible that anyone at the time can have contemplated the possibility of a Russian attack on India; nearly two thousand miles of desert, mountain and sea intervened. Yet at least two Tsars were thought to have planned such a move. Moorcroft had sniffed out Russian intrigues wherever he went, and in 1829 Lord Ellenborough, then President of the Government Board of Control for India, told the Duke of Wellington that invasion via Kabul, though not imminent, was decidedly possible. Burnes agreed wholeheartedly and on the way to Bukhara found further evidence of sinister Russian intentions. Only seven years later such mindless panic would greet the presence of a few Russian nationals in Afghanistan that a whole army would be despatched.

Without India the British colonies consisted of an inglorious rag-bag of semi-savage littorals. Yet India, the cornerstone of future empire, was now to be regarded as highly vulnerable. The threat came from the landlocked heart of Asia but British sovereignty rested on control of the seas. The enemy could assemble untold legions suitably equipped and acclimatised, within its own frontiers, whilst British reinforcements must undergo a four month sea voyage and then a long trek across the hot plains of India. On foreign terrain, or against a European power, neither the loyalty nor the fighting capacity of the Indian troops, who formed the bulk of the forces in India, could be taken for granted. The Russians, on the other hand, would be merely riding on the tide of history, sweeping into north-west India like countless previous invaders and no doubt aided and abetted by the Mohammedan powers of Central Asia who tradition-ally looked on Hindustan as a pampered maiden to be periodically ravished.

To those, like Burnes, who saw the threat in these terms the vital questions were where the main advances would take place and where they should be met. His antiquarian interests centred on the identi-fication of places mentioned in the histories of Alexander the Great and Timur. These men had led armies through much of the country a Russian force would have to cross. It was vital to establish their precise routes lest they be followed again. His geographical work was concentrated on assessing the feasibility of a modern army, complete with artillery, forcing the mountains or surviving in the deserts, and his political endeavours were directed towards gauging the strength and influencing the sympathies of those who ruled the intervening lands.

But there were others who actually welcomed the prospect of a Russian advance. Not into India, for this they considered beyond the wildest dreams of St. Petersberg, but as far as India. From Kashgar to Karachi the map was, in their opinion, disfigured by a patchwork of lawless, corrupt, slave-dealing states. These intervening lands, especially the Central Asian khanates, were in the last throes of decrepitude. Their rulers were cruel, bigoted pederasts and their power was founded on intrigue and terror. The very existence of such places was a challenge to all right-thinking men, and it was their instability which constituted the most serious threat to the prospect of amicable Anglo-Russian relations. The march of civilisation, as represented by Russian interests in the region, was inexorable. Britain had neither the might nor the right to oppose it and, should the eventual proximity of Russia ever tempt her to threaten India itself, that country would more easily be defended on its own frontier than in some fearful Armageddon in the unsurveyed depths of Asia.

This argument, besides dodging the vital question of just where the frontier of British India should lie, also overlooked what eventually became the over-riding consideration. This was the fear of contiguity. A common land frontier with a major European power was something for which Britannia was ill-equipped. Realists on both sides were inclined to pooh-pooh the idea of a Russian invasion. It was not just extravagant but unnecessary. As much could be gained if the Russians simply advanced as far as India. The Indian Army would then have to be augmented beyond anything that either India or the home country could afford. At the same time the co-operation of the subject peoples of the subcontinent would become highly doubtful. Imagine the situation in 1857 if the Indian mutineers could have looked to a sympathetic Goliath just across the Indus. In fact, in the long term, contiguity could prove more debilitating than a once-and-for-all trial of strength.

Here then were three ways of looking at Russian designs on India; the first military and alarmist, the second more ethical and consoling, and the third more realistic and political. They are just three shades from a whole spectrum of opinions. More people debated the Great Game than ever played it and there was more heated argument between the spectators than there were exchanges between the protagonists. Already it must be obvious that there was some confusion about the object of the exercise. Was it to prevent the Russians winning the hegemony of Central Asia, or was it to defend British possessions in India? The two were connected but they weren't necessarily the same thing. Secondly, who was playing the Game? In London there was the Foreign Office, the Company's Board of Directors and the Government Board of Control; in India there was the Governor-General in Calcutta and another semi-independent Presidency in Bombay. The authorities in India conducted their own relations with native states, both within the subcontinent and beyond it. Hence in Persia, for instance, both London and Calcutta were simultaneously represented. The Bombay presidency was nominally subordinate to the Governor-General but, in practice, had dealings with its immediate neighbours including trans-frontier states like Kutch and Sind. Yet a third area of debate concerned the tactics of the Game. Moorcroft had seen the first moves towards thwarting Russian designs as commercial and diplomatic, and Burnes agreed. But which were the markets that mattered, and who the princes to be supported? Strategically speaking, where lay 'the keys to India' and where the most defensible frontier? Was it on the Indus, the Khyber pass, the Afghan Hindu Kush or the Oxus? Within the Himalayas or beyond them? The subject is fascinating, inexhaustible and a trifle academic.

But to return to Burnes who, more than anyone, seemed to understand what the Game was all about. *Travels into Bokhara*, though discreetly written and carefully censored, brought the Russian threat into the open. His confidential reports went much further and convinced most of the players, though not perhaps Bentinck, that some initiative must now be taken. Burnes himself naturally favoured a 'forward' policy. He believed that Russian moves in Central Asia should be met, step for step, by British moves. At the moment Russia seemed busy with diplomatic and commercial operations in Persia and Bukhara. The British should follow suit, and the obvious target, because of its political instability and strategic importance, was Afghanistan. Burnes waited, confidently, for the order to return to Kabul.

Whilst in London he was offered the post of Secretary to the British Legation in Teheran. It meant promotion but not enough; he turned it down. 'I laugh at Persia and her politics; they are a bauble . . .' he told his brother. 'What are a colonelcy and a K.L.S. to me? I look far higher and shall either die or be so.' Vain words, but Burnes was like that. He stood a bare five feet nine and was of puny build. The portrait of him sitting cross-legged in Bokharan costume he thought needed a bit of touching up. His face looked 'so' arch and cunning I shall be handed down to posterity as a real Tatar'. There is no fear of that. The wide beady eyes, the long bony nose and the smug cupid's bow mouth exude satisfaction rather than cunning. Fame at such an early age had somewhat turned his head.

He resumed his old post with the Bombay government and in 1836 his patience was rewarded. Lord Auckland took over from Bentinck as Governor-General, a more active foreign policy was adopted and Burnes, now a Captain, was duly directed to head an official mission into Afghanistan. Along with three other officers he left Bombay at midnight on the 26th November. Thus began what Charles Masson later called 'one of the most extraordinary missions ever sent forth by a government whether as to the manner in which it was conducted or as to the results'. Evidence supporting this verdict is not hard to come by. For a start the mission left by boat; a dhow took them to the mouth of the Indus and then, in a six-oared cutter, they rowed and were dragged upriver. It was not the quickest way of getting to Afghanistan; but it was essential if the mission was to retain an innocuous appearance. For these first tentative moves towards an assertion of British influence in Afghanistan were being disguised as a beneficent attempt to open a new trade route up the lower Indus.

Moorcroft had once mooted the idea of opening the Indus and Burnes, before his journey to Bukhara, had been the first European to sail up the river to the Punjab. But by 1836 he at least must have realised that here was something of a red herring. It is true that river navigation still had an important part to play in India. In fact in the short period between the arrival of the first steamship and the laying of the first railway track, it must have seemed crucial. But not surely on the Indus. In the first place the river, throughout its entire length, lay beyond the Company's frontier. All those through whose land it flowed, from the Amirs of Sind to Ranjit Singh in the Punjab, were strongly opposed to the scheme. Secondly, Burnes had already discovered that the river was not really suitable as a trade route. The shifting sandbanks made navigation of even the shallowest boats extremely hazardous, whilst the shortage of fuel on the semi-desert shores was an ill omen for the steamship. And thirdly, as Masson pointed out, it didn't need opening. It had never been closed. A certain amount of trade already passed up and down, customs duties were reasonable and there was nothing to prevent expansion if the demand were there.

Still, Burnes's mission was inaugurated as if it were a purely commercial exercise. He was to chart the river, to look for timber and coal on its shores, to select a suitable spot for an annual trade fair, and to proceed to Afghanistan simply in order to make commercial treaties with Kabul and Kandahar. It looks as if the Governor-General and his advisers had almost convinced themselves that the mission had no political objectives. It would not have done, certainly, for Ranjit Singh to have got wind of British approaches to his arch-enemy in Kabul, but it surely would have been prudent to have given Burnes some idea of how to deal with the sticky question of relations between the Sikhs and the Afghans. Or how to deal with the growing surge of rumours about Russian interest in the area. As it was, when a storm of events overtook the laden cutter in midstream, Burnes had to formulate his own.

The first rumble of thunder was distant but ominous. A Persian army was reported to be massing for an attack on Herat in western Afghanistan. Encouraged, partly financed and probably officered by Russians, it looked as if the hour of reckoning might already be nigh. Herat could not be expected to hold out for long and, as Burnes knew only too well from his strategic studies, once Herat fell the easiest of approaches to India, that via Kandahar, would lie wide open. Moreover there was every reason to fear that the rulers of Kandahar and Kabul would join the invader against their long-sworn enemy in Herat. Next, and considerably nearer to the mission, came a crash from the mouth of the Khyber pass. At Jamrud near Peshawar the Sikhs and Afghans fought a full-scale battle. Dost Mohammed of Kabul had never resigned himself to the loss of Peshawar and, though his troops failed to reach it, or indeed to win a convincing victory, he was sufficiently encouraged by the result to think that Ranjit Singh might yet give it up. Burnes had no instructions as to how to cope with this quarrel but, since both Sikhs and Afghans might prove vital allies in the trial of strength that loomed ahead, it was imperative that he help find a quick solution.

During the hot months of 1837, as the mission drew nearer to Kabul, Burnes began to sense that history was in the making, and that he alone was in a unique position to influence it. He had come to look after trade and surveys, he told his brother, to gauge the state of affairs and to see what could be done thereafter. 'But the hereafter has already arrived . . . I was ordered to pause but forward is my motto; forward to the scene of carnage where, instead of embarrassing my government, I feel myself in a situation to do good.' He was throbbing with excitement. News of Russian overtures to Kabul, he told Masson, 'convince me a stirring time for *political* action has arrived'. And when rumours of similar approaches were also reported from Kandahar, 'Why zounds, this is carrying the fire to our door with a vengeance.'

The mission reached Kabul in September 1837. Burnes was already on good terms with Dost Mohammed. In 1832 en route to Bukhara he had been offered that old and deceptive carrot, the command of his army, and had left Kabul with sincere regrets. He genuinely liked the people and was now more welcome than ever. Preceded by a friendly letter from the new Governor-General, his arrival at such an opportune moment was presumed to mean that the British were prepared to put pressure on Ranjit Singh for the restitution of Peshawar. Like most native princes, Dost Mohammed had no interest in a commercial treaty. As he understood it, this was just an odd European euphemism for a political alliance; but even an alliance he would willingly concede if it meant the return of Peshawar. Burnes pondered the situation. Herat was now under siege, Kabul and Kandahar could turn to the Persians at any moment, and it was too late to seek new instructions from Calcutta. He decided that the only way to retain control of matters was by a sympathetic consideration of the Peshawar question, and he opened the ill-fated negotiations on that basis.

9. The Source of the Oxus

While Burnes juggled with the fate of nations in Kabul, another young man, in circumstances no less unexpected, was on his way to achieving the one solid success of the whole 'extraordinary' mission. Burnes had with him three British companions, a doctor and political adviser, Percival Lord, a soldier, Lieutenant Leech of the Bombay Infantry, and a sailor, Lieutenant Wood of the Indian Navy. All possessed some knowledge of surveying and on arrival in Kabul they were sent into the Kohistan, Gardiner's old stamping ground; they were to continue the study of the Hindu Kush passes. But almost immediately they were recalled; Leech was packed off to watch the situation in Kandahar, and Lord, most unexpectedly, found himself invited to Kunduz.

From Kunduz Murad Beg still ruled his insalubrious foothills and fens along the banks of the Oxus. But, with old age, his character must have mellowed. He had a brother, Mohammed Beg, who was slowly going blind. The brother had remained a loyal and suitably cruel adherent throughout the chief's long, rapacious career. Such fraternal devotion was far from normal in the context of Afghan politics. It deserved acknowledgement, though Murad Beg in his younger days would scarcely have recognised the obligation. Now, however, he was prepared even to help solve the mystery of Moorcroft if Burnes would send the 'feringhi hakim' to treat his brother.

It was the first piece of good news the mission had had. Dr. Gerard on his return from Bukhara had been rebuffed by the old chief and so, too, had Vigne during his Afghan year of 1836. Now there was at last a chance of opening relations with Kunduz and treating with Murad Beg from a position stronger than that of a helpless captive. After exacting guarantees of safe conduct Lord left for Kunduz on November 5th 1837. It seems to have been something of an afterthought to send Wood along too. In 1835 he had been the first man to take a steamer up the lower Indus and, on a mission that was supposed to be charting the river and opening it as a trade route, there was good reason for his inclusion. But in Central Asia he must have begun to feel rather redundant; there was not much work for a marine surveyor. He had exhausted the possibilities of the Kabul river and, since the Oxus was the next river of any significance between Russia and India, Burnes decided to send him on to Kunduz.

On the previous journey Burnes had been impressed by the formidable character of the Afghan Hindu Kush. Crossing just after Wolff had performed his naked flit he had found the snow still deep, the cold intense and the track, that via Bamian which was reputedly the easiest, far from gentle.* It seemed unlikely that an invading army would attempt such a crossing and, unless there were easier passes elsewhere, he suspected that an advance must be made either south of the mountains via Herat and Kandahar or, perhaps, north along the line of the Oxus towards Chitral and Kashmir. He had already sent a man up through Chitral to assess this approach. He was convinced the Oxus was navigable as far as Kunduz, but beyond there it was an unknown quantity. If at all possible, Wood was to investigate the subject.

Nothing was said about the Pamirs or Sir-i-kol. No doubt they had discussed the mysterious lake but Burnes was currently more preoccupied with the fate of nations than with geographical oddities. Only Wood, who knew and loved his Marco Polo, had begun to discern something like the hand of destiny beckoning him towards the Pamirs. There is something so improbable about the first Briton to stand on the Roof of the World being a naval lieutenant that one can understand a certain precognition as he was sucked by circumstance further and further into the heart of Asia. A month later he recorded in his journal how 'the great object of my thoughts by day and my dreams by night had for some time past been the discovery of the sources of the Oxus'.

The first attempt to cross the Hindu Kush failed and it was not till December 4th that Lord and Wood finally reached Kunduz. The dates were now becoming crucial. If Wood actually got permission to realise his dream and ascend the Oxus, it was bound to be a wintry journey. The cold would be intense, but this was no problem beside the delays that might be caused by blizzards. Worst of all, there was the risk of being caught by the first thaw when the snow would become soft and all possibility of movement have to be abandoned for weeks.

Mohammed Beg's trouble was diagnosed as ophthalmia. One eye

---

* Dr. Gerard disagreed about the Afghan Hindu Kush. After his experience of the Great Himalaya east of Simla, he regarded the passes to Bamian as child's play and quite feasible as invasion routes.

was already blind and the other failing fast. Probably Lord realised that there was nothing he could do about it. But he wanted to stay on for the winter and to make the most of Murad Beg's goodwill. He therefore embarked on a course of treatment and, since it might take some time, suggested to his host that Wood be allowed to occupy himself with a trip up the Oxus. He may even have inferred that favourable consideration of this request would assist the success of his treatment; the Uzbeks had a high, even superstitions, regard for European medicine. But equally Murad Beg may have required little persuasion. For all his faults his idea of dominion had none of the jealous political awareness of Ranjit Singh's. Wood describes him as able and despotic but still no more than 'the head of an organised banditti'. He had little to fear from his neighbours and no comprehension of the brewing power struggle beyond. Wood's plan must have sounded like an eccentric but harmless exercise and he readily agreed.

Monday the 11th December was fortunately a market day in Kunduz; so that the articles required for our expedition were at once obtained and lest Murad Beg might recall the permission he had given, we started the same evening for Badakshan and the Oxus. We adopted the costume of the country, as a measure calculated to smooth our intercourse with a strange people, and we had little baggage to excite cupidity or suspicion. Coarse clothes to barter for food with the inhabitants of the mountains, was our stock in trade; and my chronometers and other instruments the only articles of value I took with me. Dr. Lord accompanied us for the first few miles, and parted from us with cordial wishes for the success of our expedition.

Thus with bland simplicity begins the story of John Wood's lone journey to the source of the Oxus. It was thrown together from the rough notes of his journal, 'filed at the ends and twisted into narrative form'. That was about the strength of his prose; neat and manageable but not exactly inspiring. Wood too was like that, a quiet, capable but unobtrusive man. Sir Henry Rawlinson's obituary notice of him singles out as typical 'an extremely retiring disposition, in him amounting to second nature, which often prevented his coming before the world so prominently as his friends desired'. Compared to Burnes he certainly betrayed an 'invincible modesty'. But one must beware of such epithets from other explorers. Most were in no position to recognise modesty when they saw it. Basking in the glare of publicity, they ogled acclaim and revelled in controversy to an extent that is now inconceivable. Could anything be more undignified than Wolff and Burnes, the only men alive who had visited Bukhara, slogging it out in the Calcutta newspapers over whether or not Wolff had travelled in disguise?

John Wood was not like this. He shunned publicity. Home was not mingling with the mighty in London but a quiet corner of Perthshire or Argyll. This, in the eyes of a man like Rawlinson, made him a recluse, and his career does confirm the impression of a man running away from his achievements. Yet no one who relished obscurity was likely to find himself unexpectedly projected into the heart of Asia. Ambition and vision were as essential as stamina and determination. Wood had all of these; he was also a typical sailor. Long solitary hours on the bridge of some minuscule puffer had given him an introspective frame of mind. He was a bit of a dreamer, but a practical dreamer. Rather than argue his ideas he liked to test them, and if this absented him from the halls of fame so much the better.

The preparations for the journey were meagre. An elaborate expedition was out of the question and the only chance of success lay in a wild dash before the winter started to lose its grip. No tents were taken and no food or special equipment. They would travel fast and light. There was virtually no baggage and every man—Wood had seven followers—was mounted. They relied entirely on such hospitality as the authority of Murad Beg's representatives might provide. In the best Burnes tradition Wood wore Uzbek clothes, but it was not a question of disguise. A tall thin man, he stood out like a sore thumb amongst the diminutive Mongol races of the mountains. Nor were political difficulties anticipated. It was just the most practical way to travel.

As far as Jerm, then the principal town of Badakshan, all went to plan. Riding up to forty miles a day they covered the distance in a week. The countryside was as devastated as it had been in Gardiner's day. Once upon a time Badakshan had been a land of milk and honey, famed by the Persian poets for its fruits, its jewels and its climate. Now the orchards were overgrown, the mines unworked, the villages in ruins and the terraced fields barely distinguishable. The population had been slain in their thousands and the survivors Murad Beg had deported to Kunduz, 'a place', according to Wood, 'only fit to be the residence of aquatic birds'. And of course it was mid-winter. The rain and mists of Kunduz gave way to the snows and piercing winds of the mountain districts. Approaching Jerm it was 25 degrees below freezing and they were only at 6,000 feet, a fraction of the altitude of the Pamirs.

Wood, however, was in the best of spirits, as delighted to be rid of the mud and squalor of Kunduz as of the political activities of Lord and Burnes. He preferred the simple, independent life. At night he invariably found 'a snug berth' in one of the few inhabited villages. Toasting his toes before an open fire dexterously tended by some demure Tajik housewife, he would sip a cup of thick, salted tea and enjoy that most delicious of travellers' sensations, '. . . a glow at the heart that cannot be described. A calmness of spirit, a willingness to be satisfied and pleased with everything around me, and a desire that others should be as happy as myself.' It is no ecstasy, but a quiet warm joy occasioned more by what may be simmering for supper on the stone hearth than by any lofty sense of achievement.

He reached Jerm on December 18th but not till January 30th did he resume the journey. For six weeks he was stuck. The blizzards of mid-winter had arrived sooner than usual. Ahead the road to Wakhan and the Pamirs was blocked. He was told that even a short excursion down the Oxus to the ruby mines, the same as those visited by Gardiner, was out of the question. While the snow outside accumulated to a depth of several feet Wood sat by the fire 'in a brown study' and rued the missed gaieties of Christmas and Hogmanay back home in Scotland. To stave off boredom he studied the Badakshi language and entered enthusiastically into the social life of the town. There was much to admire in the people. Rich and poor lived on terms of social equality and even children might attend the councils of state. Wood was not the man to try and impress them with 'chemical experiments' or the wonders of European technology. In his open-minded appreciation of a totally alien yet practical existence there is a hint of the dissatisfaction with society at home that came later to dictate his career.

On January 30th a party from Shignan arrived in Jerm. They had found the Oxus frozen solid and had travelled on it past the ruby mines to Wakhan and thence to Jerm. So the road was now open, and Wood could at least reach the river and explore it down to the mines, even if the onward journey to its source was still doubtful. He left for Wakhan immediately.

The temperature was now dropping to six degrees Fahrenheit, the wind worse than ever and blizzards frequent. Climbing the 10,000-

foot pass from Zebak to Ishkashim they met a solitary traveller dressed in the skin of a horse. He had come up the Oxus from Darwaz beyond Shignan. The ice, he said, was already breaking up and the steep rocky walls which contained the river were even more treacherous. In the intense cold he owed his survival entirely to his steed; no longer able to ride him, he had sadly elected to wear him. Hard on his heels came another party who had also ascended the Oxus as far as Wakhan. They confirmed the bad news that winter was too far advanced. One man had lost not just a finger but a whole arm from frostbite. But much worse was their confirmation that the river below Wakhan was now so broken up that they had had to travel by a path along the steep banks. It was treacherous enough, but a greater danger was from avalanches. In one such they had lost half their party, mules, men and baggage all swept without trace into the river.

Between the Pamirs and Kunduz the Oxus wanders from its east-west course into a long loop round Badakshan. Thus far Wood had been cutting across the open end of this loop and so had still not actually seen the river on which his hopes were pinned. Now, as he topped the pass above Ishkashim, he looked down for the first time on the Oxus valley. It was not an encouraging sight. The valley here is still inhabited, comprising the small and very poor principality of Wakhan. But from the pass there was no evidence of life, just an utterly featureless snowscape, flanked to the south by the peaks of the Hindu Kush and to the north by the swelling slopes of the Pamirs. Of the river there was no sign. Like everything else it was buried beneath the snow.

Gardiner mentions getting his horse across the Oxus by lashing blocks of ice together and covering them with straw; an unlikely tale until one compares it with Wood's experience. He crossed at Ishkashim on bridges of frozen snow and, in spite of the gruesome accounts he had heard, attempted to make an excursion downstream to the ruby mines. These mines, together with some lapis lazuli workings near Jerm which he had already visited, constituted the great attraction of the region. Badakshan had once been famous for its jewels, and the mines were one of the main reasons for Murad Beg's conquest of it; they were now boarded up, largely because of his fear of the gems being stolen. Wood's interest was simply to try and assess the value of the country's one known commodity. In the event it was impossible. The river beneath its sheet of ice and snow had risen and was now covered with vast slabs of ice which moved and tipped precariously. With the utmost reluctance he turned back to Ishkashim. This left just the final and principal object of the journey, to follow the river upstream to its source. For the fifty-odd miles through the bleak Wakhan valley, all went well. Wood was getting used to the cold and the higher they proceeded up the river, the firmer became the ice. But now new problems arose. At Qala Panja he found that the river divided into two, and he had to decide which was the main feeder. It was a difficult decision. The local people insisted that the more northerly branch was the Oxus. In summer it was by far the larger and it commenced from the lake called Sir-i-kol. This tied in well with the evidence gathered by Marco Polo and Burnes. But Wood was still unsure, and with measuring ropes and a thermometer clambered down to the confluence.

Had he, as he slithered across the ice and crouched among the boulders, had any idea of the significance that would attach to his decision or of the controversy to which it would give rise, he must still have reached the same conclusion. He admits that the southerly branch, the Sarhad, looked the larger. But then it was free of ice and flowing in one channel. The Sir-i-kol branch was split into several channels, all frozen over, so that its volume was impossible to judge. Beneath the ice its current did seem to be the faster of the two and its temperature much the lower. Wood thought this indicated a loftier source and, taking all in all, plumped for the Sir-i-kol.

There is no single criterion by which geographers resolve a quandary like this. Even the longest branch, something which, given the season, Wood could hardly be expected to investigate, is not necessarily accepted as the parent river. Volume of flow, direction of flow, speed of current, altitude of origin, and local and historical tradition are all relevant factors. Wood was wrongly informed that the Sarhad came from above Chitral, that is from the Hindu Kush, and since it was generally agreed that the Oxus rose in the Pamirs this too influenced his decision. He acknowledged that he was contradicting the evidence gathered by MacCartney, which seemed to favour this branch, and he admitted that it appeared to have more feeders than the Sir-i-kol. In fact his decision was as qualified and cautious as one would expect from a man of 'invincible modesty'. But given the circumstances and the interest attaching to the lake of 'Surikol' it is hard to see how, even if the northerly branch had obviously been the junior, he could have foregone the chance of penetrating the Pamirs and solving the mystery of their famous lake.

M M—L

The other problem was to find guides and an escort for the last fearsome haul. His Afghan and Uzbek companions were unanimously opposed to further progress and seemed to be in collusion with the already uncooperative Mir of Wakhan. Wood countered this by appealing for help to the very people whose predatory habits necessitated the escort, the Kirghiz of the Pamirs. By a lucky coincidence, a large horde of these nomadic shepherds had, for the winter of 1837–38, come down to Wakhan. Wood had already noticed their sturdy yaks, 'like giant Newfoundland dogs', and their hairy Bactrian camels; he had even stayed in one of their rounded black tents. They were scarcely as untrustworthy as the Wakhis made out, and his confidence in them was rewarded by the appearance of a party of mounted men willing to chance a winter foray up to Sir-i-kol.

Bundled up like Eskimos, they set forth in single file on the final stage. The country beyond Qala Panja was uninhabited and treeless. They carried eight days' food and some fuel but they were still without tents. On the first night, at an altitude of about 12,000 feet, the mercury fell to six degrees and disappeared into the bulb at the bottom. They sought shelter from the wind among the baggage and horses, but still three men were so badly frostbitten that they had to be sent back. All next day and the following one they plodded on up the frozen river. For fuel they used dung, dug from the sites of Kirghiz summer encampments. Their only shelter came from the walls of snow, three feet deep, resulting from these excavations.

At the second 'camp' more men and provisions were left behind and a further mutinous group abandoned at the third. They were now at 14,000 feet and thought to be only twenty miles from the lake. Wood, if needs be, was prepared to go it alone but luckily, for the worst was still to come, five of his men remained loyal. Thus far they had been following the tracks of a returning party of Kirghiz. These now abruptly ceased, and on the fourth day they slowed to a rate of five hundred yards in two hours as they fought their way through fields of deep snow. 'Each individual of the party by turns took the lead, and forced his horse to struggle onwards till exhaustion brought it down in the snow where it was allowed to lie and recruit whilst the next was urged forward.' Returning to the frozen surface of the river they made better progress but the ice soon became too brittle and weak to be trusted. A mule crashing through into the icy waters was taken as a sure sign that their goal was at last nigh.

After quitting the surface of the river we travelled about an hour along its right bank, and then ascended a low hill, which apparently bounded the valley to the eastward; on surmounting this, at five o'clock on the afternoon of the 19th February 1838, we stood, to use a native expression, upon the *Bam-i-Duniah* or Roof of the World, while before us lay stretched a noble but frozen sheet of water, from whose western end issued the infant river of the Oxus. On three sides it is bordered by swelling hills, about 500 feet high, whilst along its southern bank they rise into mountains 3,500 feet above the lake or 19,000 above the sea, and covered with perpetual snow, from which never failing source the lake is supplied . . . As I had the good fortune to be the first European who in later times had succeeded in reaching the sources of this river, and as, shortly before setting out on my journey, we had received the news of Her Gracious Majesty's accession to the throne, I was much tempted to apply the name of Victoria to this, if I may so term it, newly re-discovered lake; but on considering that by thus introducing ·a new name, however honoured, into our maps, great confusion in geography might arise, I deemed it better to retain the name of Sir-i-kol, the appellation given to it by our guides.

Wood's decision not to call the lake Victoria is typical of the man. It seems equally inevitable that his cautious reasoning was later ignored and, before Speke set eyes on Lake Nyanza, Sir-i-kol was already known as Lake Victoria. As to the other rivers which sup-posedly flowed from it, Burnes had been misled. There was only one effluent, the Oxus, which in mid-winter was just five yards wide and ankle deep.

The depth of the lake itself posed something of a problem. From Qala Panja Wood had brought a line of a hundred fathoms and with this, early next morning, he sallied forth onto the ice. They shovelled away the snow and then with pickaxes started to chip into the ice. Each man had a few strokes and then collapsed into the snow ex-hausted. The difficulty of breathing at high altitudes, what Trebeck had called 'a frequent inclination, and at the same time a sense of inability, to sigh', was painfully evident. Two and a half feet down, a final and imprudent swing of the pick produced a hole too small to take the lead and a jet of water which drenched them all. Puffing with exhaustion and festooned with icicles from the soaking, they tried again in another spot. As they approached the danger zone four men stood round the hole with a rock poised above their heads. The pick shattered the final layer, at great speed the rock followed it and at last there was a hole of serviceable size. No one was soaked and Wood was soon paying out the line in the best naval fashion. But not for long. At just nine feet he struck the oozy, weed-strewn bottom.

If the lake itself was a bit of an anticlimax, not so the Pamirs. Curiously Wood continues to describe the region as an elevated plateau although, on his own evidence, there were mountains of 19,000 feet. He confirmed Marco Polo's assertion of the ground apparently falling away in all directions, and he saw the region as the focal point in both the hydrography and orography of the continent. The Syr did not rise in Sir-i-kol but, along with a branch of the Tarim river flowing east towards China and the Chitral river flowing south to the Indus, he imagined that it drained the Pamirs. In fact he was wrong about both the Syr and the Chitral, but he was on safer ground in asserting that the mountains of Asia seemed to radiate from the Pamirs. Not only the ranges of the Western Himalayas but also the Alai and Tian Shan connect to them.

Wood makes light of the cold though, like many a polar traveller, he found the desolation unbearable.

Wherever the eye fell one dazzling sheet of snow carpeted the ground, while the sky everywhere was of a dark and angry hue. Clouds would have been a relief to the eye; but they were wanting. Not a breath moved along the surface of the lake; not a beast, not even a bird, was visible. The sound of the human voice would have been music to the ear, but no one at this inhospitable season thinks of invading these gelid domains. Silence reigned around—silence so profound that it oppressed the heart and, as I contemplated the hoary summits of the everlasting mountains, where human foot had never trod, and where lay piled the snow of ages, my own dear country and all the social blessings it contains passed across my mind with a vividness of recollection that I had never felt before. It is all very well for men in crowded cities to be disgusted with the world and to talk of the delights of solitude. Let them pass but one twenty-four hours on the banks of the Sir-i-kol and it will do more to make them contented with their lot than a thousand arguments.

Wood rarely writes from the heart like this. He was not so much interested in reassuring the 'men in crowded cities' as in recording his own love–hate feelings about isolation. He goes on to protest that man's proper place is in society but his own career scarcely lived up to this dictum. From Sir-i-kol he turned back to Qala Panja, back through Wakhan and Badakshan to Kunduz and then back with Lord to Kabul, Ludhiana and Bombay. Soon after, he left the Indian Navy and returned to Scotland. In 1841 the Royal Geographical Society awarded him their Patron's Gold Medal. Wood did not even bother to go to London to receive it, and a few weeks later he emigrated with his family to New Zealand, a place then boasting little more in the way of society than the Pamirs. It was not this, but the misrepresentations put out by the colonial developers that turned him against the place, and he was soon back in Britain. In 1849 Lord Napier, one of those British officers who had tended the disaster-prone Wolff and who was now appointed Commander-in-Chief in India, requested his services. The request was vetoed by the Company's Board of Directors. In disgust Wood emigrated again, this time to Australia. He did eventually return to India but not in the service of the government. Preferring 'rather to wear out than to rust out', he passed his last years back on the Indus and commanded a steam flotilla, that by then sailed regularly up through Sind, until his death in 1871. To discover why a career begun so brilliantly ended in comparative obscurity, we must return to Burnes and Lord and the tragic events of 1838-41 in Afghanistan.

*   *   *

Lord had spent the winter in Kunduz rounding up some of Moorcroft's scattered possessions and, under cover of this harmless occupation, organising a network of British informants along the middle Oxus. In spring, well pleased with their work, he and Wood recrossed the Afghan Hindu Kush to Kabul. There, all was confusion. Burnes had already retired. His negotiations with Dost Mohammed had collapsed and a Russian envoy had taken his place. The blame for all this, and for the subsequent hostilities, rests almost entirely on the shoulders of Lord Auckland and his advisers. Burnes's behaviour is open to criticism. Masson found him too credulous of bazaar gossip, too obsequious towards Dost Mohammed and far too alarmist. He certainly exceeded his instructions and completely misread the mood of his superiors. He also scandalised those who admired him most by maintaining a harem of 'black-eyed damsels'; in the jargon of the day, it betrayed a weakness of character.

But had he been given clearer instructions about how far he might go in accommodating Dost Mohammed, indeed had his superiors been decided on this point, all might have been well. Or had Wade in Ludhiana not conceived a jealous mistrust of his activities and wilfully misrepresented his reports to the government, his predicament might at least have been understood. Burnes argued that the Sikhs must be persuaded to accommodate Dost Mohammed's claim to Peshawar. This was the price demanded by the Dost for repudiating Russian approaches and, since these appeared to add cogency to the argument, Burnes tended to inflate them. But Wade, who was a member of the Bengal service, grew increasingly suspicious of Burnes and his Bombay men. Their schemes seemed to threaten his long-standing relationship with the Sikhs, and he insisted that Ranjit Singh could under no circumstances be induced to surrender Peshawar. The endless reports from Masson and Burnes about the likelihood · of Russian intervention in Kabul he represented to the Governor-General as reason, not for befriending Dost Mohammed, but for abandoning him and his already tainted country.

Meanwhile Herat was still under siege. To many in India it seemed that British rule in Asia hung in the balance. If Herat fell, if Kandahar, already wavering, went over to the Perso-Russian camp and if Kabul followed suit, then the gates of India would have fallen. To men like Wade and Auckland's secretary, MacNaghten, it was simply a question of whether this was the time to trust a new ally at the expense of an old one; better, surely, to consolidate the old alliance and help Ranjit Singh, or a joint protégé, on to the throne of Kabul.

On Christmas Eve 1837, while Wood was stuck in Badakshan, Lord in Kunduz and Auckland being swayed to and fro by his advisers in Calcutta, a Captain Vitkievich, with a letter three feet long offering the Dost Russian cash to attack the Sikhs, arrived in Kabul. Burnes was non-plussed. But here was evidence incontrovertible of the gravity of affairs. He sent an express back to the government and confidently awaited the adoption of his plans which to him seemed more certain and urgent than ever. It was not forthcoming. On the contrary, his negotiations with both Kabul and Kandahar were repudiated. The game, in his own words, was up. Vitkievich had an open field and Burnes, unable to wait for his companions, slunk away from what was to have been the scene of his greatest triumph.

He fell back on Peshawar and then on Lahore where MacNaghten was already planning the next move in the fatal scenario. Dost Mohammed had entertained a Russian envoy and rejected a British mission. That he had been forced into this position was ignored. All that mattered was that now he was obviously an unsuitable ally and, in the face of the supposed threat from Herat, must needs be quickly replaced by someone more amenable. Shah Shuja, an ex-king of Kabul and currently an Anglo-Sikh pensioner, was the obvious choice. A tubby little man as inoffensive as he was ineffectual, it is hard to see how he could ever have held the Afghans together. Burnes, in May 1838, wrote that he at least would never lead the ex-king against his old friend, Dost Mohammed. And he didn't; not actually lead him, that is. But before the year was out, promoted to Colonel, elevated to a knighthood, still only thirty-three and still angling for the job of Resident in Kabul, he was smoothing the way for the Army of the Indus which was to install Shah Shuja on the throne of Kabul.

Such resilience, in his own view, scarcely smacked of compromise. He claimed to have espoused Shah Shuja's cause in the interests of his country, at great personal sacrifice and simply in order to help the government out of an impasse of their own creating. It was also suggested that he only did so because Auckland's alternative, to let Ranjit Singh have Kabul, was infinitely worse. But this was protesting too much. The fact was that Burnes had performed an about face. He was now deposing the man he regarded as the ablest of rulers and the closest of friends. Not surprisingly his conscience pricked.

Lord followed Burnes's lead and only John Wood, who can hardly have had much to do with the Dost, baulked. To his mind it was a sell-out. Though at the height of his fame he refused the bitter pill and, with quiet dignity, resigned. If the Board of Directors' behaviour ten years later is anything to go by, he was never forgiven. Even on their Commander-in-Chief's recommendation they refused to have him back in their service. One wonders whether that 'retiring disposition' was not more the product of circumstance than of character.

Wood's only reward for this gesture was survival. Lord, Burnes and the Army of the Indus never returned. Though the Persians retreated from Herat and with them the Russian threat, the Army of the Indus continued its fatal progress to Kabul. In stony silence, Shah Shuja was duly installed on the throne. The army stayed on, outliving the welcome it had never had, and in late 1840, near Gardiner's old *castello* at Parwan, the first serious reverse occurred. An order was given for a British force to charge the massed ranks of Dost Mohammed and his son. Not a man stirred. Only the officers,

Lord amongst them, sallied forth and were duly massacred. The following September a tribal rising trapped another British column in Jalalabad and closed the most direct bolt hole back to India. Burnes was still in Kabul, bitterly disillusioned by the squabbles within the occupying army but biding his time till MacNaghten left him in sole command. He was trying to stay aloof and he set up home in the heart of the city, surrounded by oriental splendour and with an overflowing seraglio. 'I grew very tired of praise,' he wrote, 'but I suppose I shall get tired of censure in time.' The final censure was about to come from the least expected quarter. He thought he knew the Afghans better than anyone. Long ago, in the pages of *Travels into Bokhara*, he had declared that no race was less capable of intrigue. Now he sensed danger, but not so much for himself as for the whole invading force. He continued to live miles from the British garrison and to flaunt his adoption of the courtly ways of Kabul. On November 2nd 1841 the end came swiftly. The 'guileless' Afghans appeared before his house in strength, fired the building and knifed to death its inmates as they attempted to escape. No one survived.

Thus ended the mercurial career of Colonel Sir Alexander Burnes. For ten short and controversial years his every move had been made in the full glare of public attention. If he died with his ambition somewhat blunted by cynicism it was hardly surprising. Celebrity, censure and then honours, all had come for the wrong reasons. Even his death had its irony. Not only did he trust the Afghans, but he above all others had their best interests at heart. Yet the Afghans selected Burnes as the first scapegoat.

His death was the signal for the general uprising. From the whole Kabul garrison only one man reached Jalalabad alive. MacNaghten, Shah Shuja and all the other principals were massacred. The story has been often told, but it was indeed the worst ever defeat suffered by the British army in Asia, one not equalled till the fall of Singapore exactly a hundred years later.

In time the fragments of Anglo-Afghan policy were picked up. Honour was restored by a second expedition which secured the release of prisoners and meted out reprisals. Dost Mohammed was reinstalled and the situation left in much the same state as it might have been had Burnes's advice been followed in the first place. The only positive gain was the annexation of Sind, which fell an inevitable casualty to the strategic demands of military operations so far beyond the British frontier. This advanced British rule across the Indus, but by now the painful lesson had been learned. The Great Game was not to be played in corps boots but in carpet slippers. Diplomatic pressures, exploratory feelers and, occasionally, short punitive forays took the place of territorial grabs and the heavy tramp of armies. Throughout the rest of the century Afghanistan was treated with great circumspection, heavily subsidised but never really trusted. The post to which Burnes had aspired, that of representative at Kabul, was never filled; the Afghans would not hear of it. And, so far as the Western Himalayas were concerned, no further attempt to explore them was ever mounted from beyond the Khyber pass. Afghanistan was as much closed to the traveller as Nepal or Tibet.

The effect of this was to give added significance to Wood's journey into the Pamirs. He was the first, and for nearly forty years the only Briton to penetrate them. No one was sent to verify his observations or to check on that puzzling confluence at Qala Panja. His work stood alone and, coupled with his own elusive career, constituted something of a geographical oddity. In 1873 when the British and Russian Foreign Offices got together to delimit their areas of influence in the Pamirs, it was to Wood's map that they turned. His was still the only authoritative account of the area and to this day the Wakhan corridor, that narrow finger of Afghan territory that separates Russia from Pakistan, follows the line of Wood's journey to the source of the Oxus.

The possibility that Sir-i-kol might not be the true source of the river was never quite lost sight of. Conscientious geographers and alarmist statesmen found this a disquieting thought which the conflicting reports of native surveyors, who visited the area in the 1860s and '70s, did nothing to allay. By the end of the century there were at least three claimants to be the parent stream of the Oxus. Depending on which you espoused, the demarcation based on the line of the main river could be understood to award to the British the whole of the Pamirs or none at all. To anyone with a tidy mind, a touch of Russophobia and a taste for geographical research, it was an inviting muddle.

George Nathaniel Curzon, Fellow of All Souls, MP for Southport, indefatigable traveller, brilliant scholar, remorseless protagonist and future Viceroy of India, was just such a man. He visited the Pamirs in 1894; his concern was not so much to explore the question as to exhaust it. Wood had ventured an opinion, Curzon now pronounced. He never actually saw Sir-i-kol or the confluence at Qala Panja, but he found a glacial source for the more southerly of the two feeders and, with irresistible logic and tireless reference to all the available evidence, declared it to be the true source.*

There the question rests. Curzon's *The Pamirs and the Source of the Oxus* is unquestionably a masterpiece of geographical research. The only doubt that assails the reader has nothing to do with his conclusions. It is just that one wonders whether the subject really justifies the labour and talent brought to bear on it. Matthew Arnold writes of the Oxus as having its 'high mountain cradle in Pamere', and most would be satisfied to know that it rises in the Pamir region from a number of sources, the most interesting of which is Wood's Lake Sir-i-kol though the most remote may indeed be Curzon's Wakh-jir glacier. Which of the many rills wriggling across that bleak terrain, sprawling and contracting, flooding and freezing with the seasons, should be dubbed the real Oxus seems a point of peculiarly doubtful significance.

The mistake was in picking on Wood's journey as the basis for a political demarcation. Rivers seldom make good frontiers and the Upper Oxus perhaps least of all. Had there been any follow-up to that pioneering journey of 1838 this would surely have been realised. The frontier, as elsewhere in the Himalayas, would have been based on watersheds, and there would have been no reason to call into question the claims of Sir-i-kol. With the passage of time and the indulgence of science, Wood's discovery would have become as unassailable as many another so-called source, hallowed by little more logical than tradition.

* The only paper on the sources of the Oxus which seems to have eluded Curzon was one by Gardiner. This is one of the old Colonel's classic productions. In mind-boggling detail he describes no less than nineteen feeders. As usual the challenge is to identify them and, as usual, there are just enough recognisable names and unassailable observations to suggest that it was not simply an elaborate fabrication. Gardiner did not try to prove that any of his feeders was the one true source, but one cannot but be grateful that Curzon never stumbled on the article. One shudders to think what a nasty mess the sharp stabs of his logic would have made of the Colonel's crazy ramblings.

PART THREE

The Karakorams and the Kun Lun
1841–1875

In the trans-Indus regions of Kashmir, sterile, rugged, cold and crowned with gigantic ice-clad peaks, there is a slippery track reaching northward into the depression of Chinese Turkestan which for all time has been a recognised route connecting India with High Asia. It is called the Karakoram route. Mile upon mile a white thread of road stretches across the stone-strewn plains, bordered by the bones of the innumerable victims to the long fatigue of a burdensome and ill-fed existence—the ghastly debris of former caravans. It is perhaps the ugliest track to call a trade route in the whole wide world. Not a tree, not a shrub, exists, not even the cold, dead beauty which a snow-sheet imparts to highland scenery.

T. H. HOLDICH. *Gates of India*

10. A Man of Science

Trekking in the Himalayas has been going on for longer than the tour operators would have one believe. Combined with a bit of casual shooting it was a popular holiday with the British officer and his family as early as the 1860s. Much earlier still, the first attempt at organising treks may be discerned in the activities of those three Aberdonians: Dr. James Gerard, who accompanied Burnes to Bukhara, and Captains Alexander and Patrick Gerard, who introduced Jacquemont to the mountains. In 1822, well before Burnes and Jacquemont and when Moorcroft was still in Leh, they were taking one of the first holiday parties up into 'the snowy range'. On May 7th they pitched camp at 7,000 feet on a spur of the Great Himalaya; 'Semla' they called the site after the name of a nearby village. It was a spot they knew well, and in the small hours they roused their party with the promise of an experience not to be missed. Bleary eyed and full of misgivings the trekkers followed them up a steep, well-wooded hill called 'Juckoo'. One of the party, Major Sir William Lloyd, left this memorable description of that morning.

We reached the summit of Juckoo long before daybreak and anxiously awaited the dawn. The sky appeared an enormous dome of the richest massy sapphire, overhanging the lofty pinnacles of the Himalaya, which were of indescribably deep hues, and strangely fantastic forms. At length five vast beaming shadows sprang upwards from five high peaks as though the giant day had grasped the mighty barrier to raise himself, while in the same instant the light rolled in dense dazzling volumes through the broad snowy valleys between them, and soon the glorious orb rose with blinding splendour over the Yoosoo pass, and assumed the appearance of a god-like eye. In a moment these rising solitudes flung off their nightly garments of the purest blue and stood arrayed in robes of glowing white. The intermediate mountains cast their disjointed dark broad shadows across the swelling ranges below, and the interminable plains were illumined, all the ineffable variety of earth became distinct; it was day and the voiceless soul of the great globe seemed to rejoice smiling.

This first description of the view from Simla is probably the finest. Dawn somehow intensifies the primeval desolation and the unassailable purity of the mountain wilderness. Lloyd looked on it with the wide-eyed wonder of one seeing the hitherto unseen and, without contrived art nor yet fear of the fanciful, he penned this grand evocation. It would be harder for subsequent visitors; these things look different through a crack in the chintz curtains.

Twenty-five years later when a certain Dr. Thomas Thomson was summoned from Ferozepur, he found on the ridges and spurs round Jakko Hill a sprightly and controversial little town. Since the days of Jacquemont's visit and the riotous rule of Captain Kennedy, Simla had come a long way. It was no longer the 'Capua of India' nor was it, as today, the Bournemouth. On the contrary, its hour of glory was nigh; it was about to become the summer capital of the British Raj. The first visit by a Governor-General was in 1827. Bentinck had repaired there often enough for a nearby peak to be christened 'Billy Bentinck's Nose' and, in the newly built Auckland House, Lord Auckland had finally reached his painful and disastrous decision to despatch the Army of the Indus. The Governor-General when Dr. Thomson arrived there in 1847 was Lord Hardinge. We have a description of him pacing the verandah of the same house as he read the morning's post.

Glancing up he might have seen that view of Lloyd's and thought no more of it than if it had been the wall of his study. Equally he might have seen that other celebrated Simla prospect, dense deadening mist which reveals nothing more noble than a dark conifer dripping silently into the dank grass. But, if he was lucky and happened to look up at just the right moment, his attention might suddenly have been arrested by the one glimpse which, even to people inured to the charms of that now prosaic panorama, manages still to convey something of the improbable situation of Simla. Without rhyme or reason the mist will suddenly compose itself and settle. It doesn't lift; it falls imperceptibly into the valleys. The outline of a nearby hill appears and is gone. Above it there is a brightness. It is as if the sun is about to break through. Keep looking and, high up but no longer far away, there shines down through a window in the mist, not the sun but a chunk of the Great Himalaya. Some nameless peak, some unclimbed crag or unmapped scarp it may be, but seen like this, the sun full upon its snowy hinterland and the bare black rock of pinnacle and precipice sharp against the sky and the busiest of men, even a Governor-General, must be roused.

A sobering thought to Lord Hardinge might have been the realisation that, though he ruled the destinies of a sub-continent, he must peer from his verandah on to a sea of mountains still largely unknown. The ridge of Simla is the watershed between the basins of the Ganges and the Indus. Half the town's drains empty themselves into the Giri river and thence into the Jumna, the Ganges and the Bay of Bengal. The other half, including those of Auckland House, descend precipitately to the Sutlej, the Indus and the Arabian Sea. Just as Kabul marks the westernmost extremity of the Indus basin, and so of the Western Himalayas, Simla marks the eastern limit. It was all very well to discourage hare-brained schemes of exploration from the distant security of Calcutta; quite different to deny a certain curiosity about what lay just beyond one's doorstep in Simla. Growing involvement in the affairs of the Punjab and Kashmir was shifting the fulcrum of British rule further to the north-west. This not only afforded some justification for the popularity of Simla but it also served to intensify speculation about what lay within and beyond the mountains. And although Afghanistan was now a closed door, there was still a chink of light towards Ladakh and Yarkand in the north.

Dr. Thomson found Simla in 1847 to consist of four hundred houses. Houses, be it understood, were British residences; the bazaar, where most of the native population lived, and the shacks at the end of the garden, where crowded together the servants and their multitudinous families, were not included. To build all the fanciful cottages and lodges with their dormers, balconies and rustic porches, the forests of cedar and evergreen oak had been whittled away. Already the town had that look of being spread-eagled along the bare crest of the ridge. It was no bustling city, but then neither is it today. The roads are too steep and narrow for much traffic, and the houses, secluded in extensive grounds, too far apart.

The view, the climate and the shooting all played their part in making the place a shrine for the British in India. It became a caricature of sylvan England, all rambling roses, crazy paving and casement windows, like a New Forest village, trees and all, wrapped over the contours of the Tyrol. Even Emily Eden, Lord Auckland's ever-scathing sister, grew to like it. 'If the Himalayas were only a continuation of Primrose Hill or Penge Common I should have no objection to spend the rest of my life on them.' But what most of all made the annual pilgrimage to Simla worthwhile was the society it offered. People went there because everyone else did. In the summer there were picnics, races, fairs and gymkhanas; in the winter, carols and Christmas parties with real snow outside and not some wretched sprig of mango but a proper spruce Christmas tree. They went, if they were honest, not just because everyone else did but because someone in particular did. The endless balls, dinners, at homes and evenings at the club provided a grand forum for the ambitious. Unashamedly they lobbied. Some liked to dance, to drink, to gamble, others just to watch and be watched; but all liked to lobby. This man sought a posting, that promotion, a third a wife and a fourth just an invitation.

They used Simla. And just as in its heyday the great attraction was the society so, now that that society is gone, the attraction of the place is hard to appreciate. Today, forlorn and tatty, it conjures up no images of splendour or excitement. Still there are the tea-rooms, the Gaiety Theatre and the clubs but it is hard to relish their associations. Kipling's gossipy matrons and heady young ladies were dismally parochial, and his raciest of rakes a pretty staid fellow. In the early days when Jacquemont slavered over the Perigord patés and Kennedy dispensed the dancing girls as freely as the champagne, the traveller could be excused for lingering awhile, charmed by the improbability of it all. But eccles cakes and awkward little flirtations in the saddle seem a poor substitute.

Dr. Thomson sounds as if he might have agreed. He was a rather serious-minded young Scotsman. For two and a half months he was detained at Simla but for all the notice he took of its inhabitants it might still have been virgin forest. In fact he would have preferred it like that, for his only interest was the flora. But then he had not come of his own free will; he had been summoned, and was now only concerned about pushing on as soon as possible. The delay was caused by the late arrival of his two companions. Together they were to constitute a border commission to visit Ladakh and delineate its eastern boundary with Tibet. The Governor-General had resolved to dispel some of the uncertainty about what lay beyond his verandah by taking advantage of an opportunity for the first official initiative in the Western Himalayas.

About this time, the mid-1840s, there was an apposite story going the rounds of the Simla bazaar. Like all good stories it had enough inherent possibilities to be true. There were also enough versions of it to keep one guessing where, if at all, the basis of truth lay. As told by a loyal sepoy in the Company's service it would have been Gulab Singh who, in early 1842, requested the meeting with Henry Lawrence. The Raja had pressing news and Lawrence, having himself some sobering reports for the Raja, readily agreed. Such a meeting was full of irony in the light of subsequent events. Gulab Singh, then Raja of Jammu and *de facto* ruler of Ladakh and Baltistan, was the greatest power behind the tottering throne of Lahore. But Lawrence, then Governor-General's agent in Ferozepur, was himself soon to assume administrative responsibility in Lahore.

In due course the meeting took place. Gulab Singh, with the un-hurried confidence of a man fanning himself with a royal flush, opened proceedings with a flood of extravagant compliments. Roses bloomed in the garden of perpetual friendship when the Governor-General's agent deigned to meet a humble ignorant Raja, and the power of Lahore was but as the moon beside the blazing sun of the British army. Lawrence, an impatient man, cut him short. What was the Raja's pressing news? With feigned ingenuousness Gulab Singh asked for the latest reports from Kabul. There had been none said Lawrence.

'Then it is news [said the Raja] sad news indeed. For there will be no more reports from Kabul. Burnes is dead, murdered by the Afghans. Sale's brigade is surrounded in Jalalabad. Kabul is fallen and Ghazni too. MacNaghten, Shah Shuja and the Army of the Indus—all are gone. The sun is in eclipse.'

Lawrence's thin face registered nothing. Friends of his would be amongst the captured and the dead. The British had sustained their worst ever defeat in Asia. But not a tear, not a prayer and certainly not a curse came from the imperturbable Lawrence. A man of the deepest courage and with an overriding religious sense of mission, he received the news in respectful and unflinching silence.

'If true, as I must reluctantly accept, this, Raja Sahib, is indeed sad terrible news. I respect your motives for calling me to hear it from your own lips and I thank you sincerely.'

He paused, apparently unable to say more. Then, as if pricked by a sudden and appropriate recollection, he stared hard at the Raja and continued:

M M—M

'But will you too thank me for what I must now tell you? For I also
am the bearer of sad terrible news. Out of Tibet by way of Nepal
come the reports of the rout of another army. Six thousand strong
it was. Now there are but a handful of survivors and they so frostbitten as to be useless. The army was your army. Your general,
Zorawar Singh, is himself among the dead. And the moon too is
eclipsed.'

How Gulab Singh reacted to the news would depend on the
narrator's powers of invention. But the meeting could well have some
basis in history. The two disasters were almost simultaneous, and just
as news from Kabul might be expected via the Punjab, so the defeat in
Tibet first became known from the few survivors who straggled across
the Great Himalaya into Nepal and the British dependencies between
there and Simla.

Back in 1835, when Dr. Henderson visited Leh, Zorawar Singh—
on behalf of his master, Gulab Singh—was poised for the conquest
of Ladakh. By 1837, when Vigne tried to use Leh as his launching pad
for the Karakorams, the Jammu Raja was in undisputed control of
the country and in 1840, hard on Vigne's final departure, Zorawar
Singh had overrun Baltistan. It was early the following year that he
had invaded Tibet proper.

These conquests, though initially made in the name of Ranjit
Singh, were not really Sikh achievements. In fact there is evidence
that the Sikh governor in Kashmir actually tried to sabotage them.
Gulab Singh himself was not a Sikh but a Dogra, that is a Hindu of
the martial Rajput stock of Jammu. Even before Ranjit's death in
1839 it had seemed to Vigne that Lahore was rarely informed of his
activities beyond the Pir Panjal and certainly after 1839 he was virtually independent. These should, therefore, be seen as Dogra
conquests. Gulab Singh, no longer content to carve out of the Sikh
empire a hill state for himself, was now engaged in the creation of
his own trans-Himalayan empire. He still did not hold Kashmir but
there was already talk of taking Lhasa and even Yarkand.

The invasion of Tibet in 1841 was so completely overshadowed by
the Afghan disasters that it received scant attention. Yet as an epic of
military adventure and the first ever Indian attempt to invade the
Tibetan uplands, it is unique. It would have taken Alexander
Gardiner, who was on the Dogra payroll at the time, to have done it
justice, but sadly neither he nor any other foreigners took part in

Zorawar Singh's campaigns. Very little indeed is known about them. The attack on Tibet was probably prompted by a desire to plunder the Buddhist monasteries and to gain a monopoly of the shawl-wool production. This *pashm* was, as Moorcroft had pointed out, the most valuable commodity in the trade of the region. By a long standing arrangement most of it passed through Leh on its way from the high grazing lands of Tibet to the looms of Kashmir. But the Dogra conquest of Ladakh and the emigration south of many Kashmir weavers had diverted a small portion of the trade from Leh to Rampur, a British dependency just east of Simla. Zorawar Singh now hoped to close this outlet by adding to his control of the Ladakh carrying trade that of the Tibetan regions where the wool was actually produced.

With just six thousand men he set off from Leh up the Indus. Virtually no opposition was encountered and by the autumn of 1841 he held the whole of Western Tibet. The monasteries were systematically ransacked by Ghulam Khan, his Mohammedan lieutenant, who brought to the task all the iconoclastic fury of Islam. The flow of shawl wool to Rampur dwindled to a trickle, and Dogra rule reached to the Nepalese frontier and included the centres of Rudok, Gartok and the sacred lake of Manasarowar.

Whether Gulab Singh himself was responsible for the invasion, or whether it was simply the idea of the over-zealous Zorawar, is not clear. But the implications were far from being a domestic Dogra affair. The Chinese, whose grasp on Tibet was then rather firmer than it became at the end of the century, were unlikely to distinguish between the activities of an Indian Raja and those of the British rulers of India. The British government was then in the process of negotiating a peace with China. It was a delicate state of affairs which the Dogra moves in Tibet would surely jeopardise, Added to this there was a question mark over the attitude of the Nepalese who, whether they befriended their new Dogra neighbours or with Chinese encouragement attacked them, would greatly embarrass the British policy of keeping Nepal isolated.

Thus news of the Dogra advance elicited a strong protest from the British government. Gulab Singh replied with a cheeky proposal for a joint Anglo-Dogra attack on Western China. This was rejected and reluctantly, but with an eye to the advantages of British friendship, he agreed to withdraw from Tibet. A British officer, Lieutenant Joseph Cunningham, was despatched up the Sutlej to observe and report on the disengagement. He reached Rampur in the late autumn but failed to penetrate Tibet in time for the bloody conclusion of the campaign. With slow but impressive resolve the Chinese had finally reacted. An army of about ten thousand left Lhasa in October. In November they routed the small detachments which Zorawar Singh contemptuously sent to oppose them, and in early December they were within sight of the main Dogra force. Alexander Cunningham, the brother of Joseph, pieced together the best account of what happened.

The two armies first met on the 10th of December, and began a desultory fire at each other, which continued for three days. On the 12th Zorawar Singh was struck in the shoulder by a ball, and as he fell from his horse the Chinese made a rush, and he was surrounded and slain. His troops were soon thrown into disorder, and fled on all sides, and his reserve of 600 men gave themselves up as prisoners. All the principal officers were captured and out of the whole army, amounting with its camp-followers to 6,000 men, not more than 1,000 escaped alive, and of these some 700 were prisoners of war.

The Indian soldiers of Zorawar Singh fought under very great disadvantages. The battlefield was upwards of 15,000 feet above the sea, and the time mid-winter, when even the day temperature never rises above freezing point, and the intense cold of night can only be borne by people well covered by sheepskins and surrounded by fires. For several nights the Indian troops had been exposed to all the bitterness of the climate. Many had lost the use of their fingers and toes; and all were more or less frostbitten. The only fuel procurable was the Tibetan furze, which yields much more smoke than fire; and the more reckless soldiers had actually burnt the stocks of their muskets to obtain a little temporary warmth. On the last fatal day not one half of the men could handle their arms; and when a few fled the rush became general. But death was waiting for them all; and the Chinese gave up the pursuit to secure their prisoners and plunder the dead, knowing full well that the unrelenting frost would spare no one.

The prisoners included Vigne's old friend, Raja Ahmed Shah of Baltistan. For two years he had been held by the Dogras and now duly rejoiced at their defeat. The Chinese treated him well but, when it became clear that there was no hope of being restored to his throne, he fell to pining for his lost home in Skardu and died soon afterwards. Also captured was Ghulam Khan, the desecrator of the Buddhist monasteries. He fared less well. He was tortured with hot irons, his flesh was torn off in small pieces with pincers and the mangled remains still quivering with pain were left to experience whatever residual agonies a protracted death might offer.

The Chinese forces pressed on into Ladakh and, for a short time in early 1842, actually held Leh. Then the Dogras returned in force, and a treaty was signed between the two parties restoring the traditional boundaries and inferring that the Leh monopoly of the shawl wool trade should continue. If this trade was the chief motive for the invasion then the Dogras certainly won the peace, if not the war. From a British point of view the situation, though not as fraught as in 1841, was scarcely satisfactory. There was no telling when Gulab Singh might again interfere in Tibet and the British attempt to attract some of the wool trade had been foiled. But, as soon as affairs in Afghanistan were settled, relations with the Punjab worsened and it was not till the end of the first of the two Sikh Wars in 1846 that a further opportunity to intervene arose.

During these momentous events of the early 1840s Gulab Singh can be seen playing his cards with the utmost skill. He lacked the magnetism of his old master, Ranjit Singh; his charm inspired terror rather then affection. But there is no questioning his ability. His eye was ever for the main chance and the rule he founded, though less notable, was to last considerably longer than that of the dead Maharaja. Whether or not he actually passed on the sad news of the disasters in Afghanistan, it was to the British that he increasingly turned. He had listened to their advice about withdrawing from Tibet, and in 1842 he co-operated in the reprisal invasion of Afghanistan. In 1845 he significantly failed to assist the Sikhs, still nominally his overlords, and thus facilitated the success of the British forces. By way of reward he at last gained control of the Kashmir valley and was recognised by the British as Maharaja of Kashmir, Jammu and Ladakh.*

* It is not apparently correct to say that the British sold Kashmir to Gulab Singh. Nor to say that the British never ruled Kashmir. They did, for a week. By the Treaty of Lahore, Kashmir, Jammu and Ladakh were ceded to the British by the defeated Sikhs in lieu of an indemnity for the war. By the Treaty of Amritsar a week later Gulab Singh was rewarded by being recognised as Maharaja of these territories. Several important conditions were imposed. Payment of the indemnity was one of them, but was of little significance compared with the political and strategic implications of the others.

The treaty of Amritsar, which confirmed this arrangement, reserved to the British certain rights which have an important bearing
on the penetration of the Western Himalayas. In the first place,
though recognised as an independent sovereign, the new Maharaja
was bound to accept British arbitration in any dispute with his neighbours. In return he was promised British assistance in defending his
territories. This could be seen as reserving to the British a say in
relations between Ladakh and Tibet. Equally it could be seen as
another forward move in the Great Game. Kashmir remained
nominally independent, but the frontier which the British were now
committed to defend had thus been pushed hundreds of miles
further into the mountains.

Just exactly where it now lay was far from clear. The Treaty of
Amritsar was wonderfully imprecise. 'All the hilly or mountainous
country, with its dependencies, situated to the eastwards of the river
Indus and the westward of the river Ravi' was ceded to the Maharaja.
This oft-quoted description betrays an ignorance, inexcusable by the
1840s, of the general lie of the land. Through the mountains both
rivers pursue a predominantly east–west course so that scarcely any
place can be said to be east of one and west of the other. Areas specifically mentioned in the treaty, like Ladakh, are actually bisected by
the Indus. And the only regions clearly bounded east and west by
these two rivers are not mountainous or hilly but a dead flat wedge of
the plains.

Something would have to be done to define the limits of the new
state more accurately and, fortunately, provision for this was also
made in the treaty. The precise extent of the Kashmir state was investigated and discussed for the next fifty years and played no small
part in the exploration of the region. Moreover the vague wording of
the treaty was found to have its advantages. Once 'eastward of the
river Indus and westward of the river Ravi' was seen as nonsense,
'the hilly or mountainous country with its dependencies' could
be taken to include as much of the mountain complex, stretching
over the Karakorams to the far Pamirs and Hindu Kush, as was
convenient.

More immediately, the corner of the new state which bordered the
British dependencies and Tibet needed to be sorted out. Here a continued desire to tap the *pashm* trade had prompted the British to
retain a corner of the Sikh empire, namely the small states of Kulu,
Lahul and Spiti. In 1846 Alexander Cunningham explored the water-

shed between these new acquisitions and Ladakh, and laid down a frontier based on it.

The following year Cunningham was again deputed to Ladakh. Dr. Thomas Thomson, waiting in Simla, was to be one of his companions and the other, Lieutenant Henry Strachey. Ostensibly the object was to define the boundary between Ladakh and Tibet so that Gulab Singh might never again have the excuse of a frontier dispute for re-invading Tibet. But there were also well-founded rumours for regarding the 1847 Boundary Commission in quite another light. The Royal Geographical Society got wind of these and welcomed the project as 'an exploring expedition'. Their information was that the party was heading for Yarkand and intending to spend the winter there or in Kotan. Furthermore the members of the expedition were then by different routes to proceed east, to rendezvous in Lhasa and to regain India by following the Tsangpo till it swept round the Himalayas and emerged in Assam as the Brahmaputra. If the Society was right then this most ambitious expedition represented the first official attempt for fifty years to penetrate Tibet and the first ever to cross the Western Himalayas.

A year later the President of the Society changed his tune. He referred to the expedition as a Boundary Commission and said no more about Lhasa and Yarkand. But, in fact, the original plan had been every bit as ambitious as he had imagined. No official expedition ever had a freer hand than did Cunningham, Strachey and Thomson. Reading the instructions issued by the Governor-General it is almost as if the boundary work was to be simply a front for uninhibited exploration.

There were two stipulations. They were not to be away for more than two years, and they were on no account to cross the 'Bolor Tagh' mountains. Since this might lead to 'collision with the bigotted and jealous Mahometans of Independent [i.e. Western] Turkestan', the Bolor Tagh must mean the Pamirs. Otherwise it was up to them. Once the boundary work was completed, and the Governor-General admitted that with so little in dispute it should not take long, they were 'individually to use their best endeavours to increase the bounds of our geographical knowledge'.

Winter, it was suggested, might profitably be spent beyond the mountains in Yarkand or Kotan or, failing these, in Rudok 'on the borders of the Great Desert'. Come spring Cunningham should return to the Indus and follow its course down to Gilgit, and then continue west through the so-called Dard* countries of Yasin and Chitral. Strachey might concentrate on Tibet, heading 'as far eastwards as he can go, even to Lhasa', and return via Darjeeling or Bhutan. Only Thomson was given a prosaic task. He was to 'employ himself ascertaining the mineral resources along and within the British frontier'. He did rather more than that, but for the present it is sufficient to note that the British frontier was taken to mean not Kulu and Lahul but the supposed Kashmir frontier on the Karakorams.

With a brief like this imagine what Moorcroft or Burnes might have achieved. If the Chinese had proved obstinate, Burnes would have slipped past dressed as a half-witted lama. Moorcroft, on the other hand, would have put it about that he was the Queen's own emissary, and have swept on with flags flying. Neither the exceptionally severe winter of 1847-48 nor the outbreak of war in Gilgit would have stopped them. Here, after all, was the long-awaited official initiative for prising open the back door into China, for establishing a British interest in the existing Himalayan trade, for gaining the sort of geographical information about the lands beyond the mountains that had been found so vital in the Afghan debacle, and for bringing these places within the scope of official British policy. It appeared to be a legitimate opening and one not to be fluffed by an over-nice respect for Chinese sensibilities.

Cunningham and Strachey joined Thomson in Simla during the summer of 1847, and the Commission finally got under way on August 2nd. It was the middle of the monsoon when the mist is so thick you can hardly see across the Mall—no time for a grand send-off. Half the expected porters failed to materialise, and they were thankful that their disorganised departure went unnoticed. Their route lay up the Sutlej valley to Spiti and thence to Ladakh. It was much too late for a full season of demarcating the boundary but, if the Chinese and Dogras were ready and if the job proved as simple as Hardinge had anticipated, they might yet be able to seek winter quarters further afield.

The idea that they would be allowed into Yarkand or Lhasa was based on the assumption that the Chinese would welcome the demarcation of their Tibetan frontier. This was a serious miscalculation.

* Although the word Dard was never acknowledged by any of the peoples of the region, it was identified with Ptolemy's Deradrae and widely used during the nineteenth century to describe the peoples living west of the Indus, especially in Gilgit, Chitral, Yasin and Chilas.

The Chinese had few anxieties about Gulab Singh and never welcomed attempts to circumscribe their sphere of influence; the nebulous character of Chinese and Tibetan suzerainty scarcely lends itself to the clear-cut European notion of territorial integrity. Nor was the other inducement offered to the Chinese, the commercial advantage of diverting the shawl-wool trade through the new tariff-free corridor of British territory, particularly enticing. The trading relations of Tibet were based on tradition rather than profitability and they followed closely ancient lines of religious and political intercourse. Overtures from the barbarian newcomers in India were not likely to be allowed to prejudice the traditional connection with Buddhist Ladakh. Added to all this there was the difficulty of approaching the Lhasan authorities. The invitation to them to send their own boundary commissioners went via Gartok but whether it was actually delivered there, whether it was couched in intelligible Tibetan and whether it was ever forwarded to Lhasa, are all doubtful. Another approach was made direct to the emperor via Hong Kong, but this too probably never got further than Pekin.

However, the surprising news was that two officials had already reached Gartok and, buoyed up by this, the Commission made good speed to Spiti. There, in an attempt to take a short cut across Tibetan territory, they received their first check. The Tibetans were waiting for them and, as usual, refused entry. Thomson noted, 'I have no doubt that if we had resolutely advanced no serious opposition to our progress would have been made . . .' Trebeck and Jacquemont had both called the Tibetan bluff and had got away with it. A resolute move at this stage might have made all the difference. It would not have conjured up a party of friendly Chinese commissioners, but it would have shown they meant business and perhaps opened up direct communications with Gartok. But Cunningham was a cautious man. He had been warned by Lawrence, now Resident at Lahore, to avoid any risk of a collision and, though Hardinge had had the last word, telling him in effect to ignore this over-cautious advice, he chose to stand down. The Commission meekly withdrew and reached Hanle in Ladakh by a roundabout route over the lofty passes of Lanak and Parang.

True, they were still hoping for Chinese co-operation, but at this encounter they also learnt that the Tibetans knew nothing of any Chinese border commissioners. At Hanle this news was confirmed. The Chinese officials who had supposedly arrived at Gartok now turned out to be a solitary Tibetan revenue officer who had already set off back to Lhasa. Even the Dogra commissioners had not yet appeared. Cunningham took this as the signal to abandon the boundary question altogether and to concentrate on the more interesting part of their instructions, to 'individually use their best endeavours to increase the bounds of our geographical knowledge'.

On the march

The Chinese being so uncooperative there seemed little hope of reaching Yarkand or Rudok but, with winter pressing on—it was already mid-September—they each now went their separate ways. Strachey turned east. His interests were purely geographical and they centred on Tibet. For the next ten months he prowled along the Ladakh–Tibet frontier. His exact itinerary is lost, but he appears eventually to have crossed the south-west corner of Tibet and returned to India near Moorcroft's Niti pass. He thus connected his observations in Ladakh with those he and his brother had previously made near Lake Manasarowar. The results of his travels were embodied in a weighty and authoritative official report entitled *The Physical Geography of Western Tibet*. This was later published and for it he was awarded one of the Royal Geographical Society's Gold Medals in 1852. The strength of this almost unreadable document lay in its attempt to relate the rather poetic ideas of traditional Tibetan geography to the physical configuration of the country. Western Tibet he therefore took to include not just the Rudok and Gartok regions but Ladakh and Baltistan as well. The result, in so far as it inevitably tends to emphasise the integrity of the whole region, is a curious memorial to one who was supposed to be defining a boundary across it.

Cunningham and Thomson travelled on together as far as Leh. Thence they intended to proceed by different routes to Gilgit. Thomson was to investigate the mountains to the north, while Cunningham took an easier more southerly route skirting Kashmir. If his companions had rather narrow interests Cunningham's wide range of enquiry more than compensated. When the winter turned out to be exceptionally severe, he welcomed it as an excuse to abandon the idea of Gilgit, and to concentrate on the antiquities of Kashmir. They had been told to pursue their own interests; Cunningham took this literally. He arrived back in Simla in 1848 with a camel load of Buddhist statuary, three unknown Sanscrit dramas and 'the oldest dated inscription hitherto found in India'. It was not quite what the Governor-General had expected from the leader of his Boundary Commission. However, Cunningham made amends by producing a report on Ladakh which remains to this day the standard work on the country. The format is the usual one for an official gazette, a chapter for geography, another for history, another for communications, climate, productions—animal, vegetable and mineral—and so on. What distinguished it was the degree of scholarship, embracing anthropology, language, ritual, literature and archaeology. Taken in conjunction with Strachey's work, Ladakh could be said to be not just explored but exhausted. The 1847 Boundary Commission had failed dismally to define the boundary, or, according to the official summary, 'to accomplish any of the political purposes for which it was appointed'. But they had succeeded brilliantly within the narrow limits finally accepted.

But what of Dr. Thomson? Not much was to be expected of him as an explorer. He was there as a distinguished naturalist and the party's surgeon. If there was no opening for him like that which took Lord to Kunduz, he could always be left to potter along the frontier rooting for rocks and plants. The son of another eminent scientist, he had discovered fossilised molluscs in the Clyde at seventeen and pectic acid, the vital gelatinous constituent of fruit jellies, in carrots at nineteen. Arrived in India, he had embarked on a study of the flora of Afghanistan and only abandoned it when, as a prisoner after the siege of Ghazni, he was about to be dispatched to the Bukhara slave market. He was indeed a dedicated man of science. Nevertheless he resented being written off as an explorer. Though alarmingly susceptible to the effects of altitude and totally inexperienced as a surveyor, he willingly took on the most arduous assignment of the whole expedition, that of exploring the northern confines of Ladakh towards Yarkand and Gilgit. Where Moorcroft, Wolff and Vigne had all failed, the good doctor was to try again. Some idea of his inexperience can be gained from Cunningham having to lend him a sextant and compass and then show him how to use them.

He left Leh on October 11th, aiming to cross the Karakoram pass and advance a 'few marches on the northward towards Yarkand'. But, just like Vigne before him, he reached Nubra much too late in the year for 'exploration at great altitudes'. Turning back, he followed the Shyok and Indus down to Skardu with the idea of continuing on down the Indus to Gilgit for his expected meeting with Cunningham. Again he was thwarted. Gilgit was 'not in a fit state for scientific investigation'. There were rumours of trouble between the Dogras and the natives. On December 2nd he turned back towards Kashmir for the winter. Vigne's route over the Deosai and Burzil passes was already closed and his only exit lay back up the Indus and round via Dras and the Zoji La. He spent December 4th, his thirtieth birthday, edging along the cliffs below Tolti, the twelfth fighting through blizzards and snowdrifts into Dras and on the fourteenth, for the third time, was forced to retrace his steps. The pass was closed and he was trapped. He gave up his tent in favour of the native cowhouses, and headed back to Skardu, arriving there on Christmas Day.

He was the first European to winter in Baltistan. He kept a careful check on the weather and, while avalanches boomed all round, sorted out his collection of wild flowers and rocks. Strachey managed to send down to him from Leh some brick tea, 'not superexcellent in quality', and some sugar. Otherwise he relied on local supplies. At the end of February he made a second try for Gilgit, reaching the dread gorges below Rondu before firm reports of open warfare between Gulab Singh and the Gilgitis dissuaded him from going further. He retired again to Skardu, continued up river to Dras and finally crossed the Zoji La into Kashmir and then the Bannihal pass to Jammu.

By now one would have thought he had had enough. For nine months he had been travelling almost continually and for the last six, during the coldest of Himalayan winters, he had been entirely on his own. He was not a lover of solitude or the wide open spaces, nor was he of a particularly rugged constitution. His portrait shows a pallid man of distinctly delicate habits who would not last long without a bath and clean linen. Yet he had already requested permission of Lord Dalhousie, the new Governor-General, to continue his work in the mountains. He wanted to try a new route over the Pir Panjal and Great Himalaya to Ladakh and, what was more, he wanted to have another go at getting beyond Nubra on that daunting track to Yarkand.

Dalhousie, no doubt hoping that somewhere the Commission might yet break new ground, agreed; for the fifth time Thomson turned back on his tracks. It was May 23rd 1848. The season was young enough, the ground well enough prepared and Thomson now experienced enough for what Sven Hedin calls 'one of the most important and successful [journeys] ever undertaken against the secrets of the highest mountainland on the earth'.

The route he had chosen to pioneer into Ladakh was that via Chamba and Zaskar. It seemed as direct as Moorcroft's Kulu-Lahul route and was said to be much used by native travellers. To escape the heat in the plains, he tacked through the outer hills to Chamba and then climbed the 15,000-foot Sach pass over the Pir Panjal. The Sach pass, and the Pangi region beyond, is still mule country. These days buses trundle over the Rohtang, Bannihal and Zoji but here there are no roads, no jeeps. The traffic sounds are the resonant dinging of mule bells and the fussy tinkling of sheep bells.

For the botanist there is no better place than the Pir Panjal and no better time than early summer. The pass is approached through deep woods of oak, sometimes festooned with vines. It was summer when Thomson entered them but emerging from their shade on to the bright grassy slopes above was like stepping back into the spring. Rhododendrons are in full flower in June, especially the little yellow *campanulatum*, the pride, in Thomson's view, of the Indian mountains. The grass is dotted and finally smothered with primulas and potentillas. Once on the snow there is still a wealth of interest, for wherever a rock has thawed its way through, there, right to the edge of the soft snow, springs up the same bright carpet of Alpine flora.

In the doctor's narrative there are no bold strokes, no purple passages. Plant by plant, rock by rock, he painstakingly constructs his description. To appreciate its effect and to gauge the depths of his enthusiasm, one must stand well back. One must measure the rich and sensitive treatment of this stage of his journey against his narrative as a whole. To the naturalist it was definitely the highlight of the trip.

From the Sach pass Thomson descended to the Chandrabhaga (Chenab), and followed that river west through Pangi as far as the Gulabgarh, and then turned north towards Zaskar. The grand scenery of steep pine-clad slopes, sharp mountain profiles and well wooded valleys gave way to the higher, dryer and barer terrain of Ladakh. It is surprising how much of interest a botanist can find in such a country though, with the bones of the earth comparatively bare of vegetation, even of soil, it is the geologist who now comes to the fore. Thomson's narrative dawdles through the moraines and alluvia. He cracks open conglomerates and sandstones, puzzles over schists, slates and limestones, and pockets bits of mica, gneiss and basalt. Higher still, as he climbed the Umasi La over the Great Himalaya, the ground beneath his feet became beds of snow and glaciers contoured with fissures.

What from a distance looks like a postcard snowscape becomes something more varied and intricate to anyone crossing it. It is never just snow, but new snow or old, hard or soft, resting on ice, a glacier or more snow. It may be steeper, deeper, more crevassed and, commonly, more treacherous, than it looks. On the other hand it may be a welcome relief from the boulder-hopping of a moraine, or the slithering traverse of a loose shale slope. There is no easier going than along a smooth gently sloping glacier or over the crust of a well frozen snowfield. Thomson was becoming quite a connoisseur of these things. It provided a new field for scientific observation when rocks as well as plants were buried out of sight.

As the swirling snowflakes reduced visibility to ten yards, he crouched on the crest of the Umasi La and got his water to boil at 180 degrees. This meant an altitude of 18,000 feet. Ahead lay Zaskar, the southernmost district of Ladakh. The journey across it from the Umasi La to Leh took nearly four weeks. This was far longer than he had expected, and was entirely due to the rugged nature of the country. In Zaskar it is seldom possible to follow the rivers which drain north towards the Indus. The ground is too cut up, and the track forever deviating to scale yet another lofty pass well away from the desired line of march.

Thomson was not the first to emphasise the parallelism of all the Himalayan ranges, but he wrote of this feature with understandable feeling. Zaskar combines all the difficulties of climate and altitude common to Ladakh as a whole with the precipitous character of the mountains on its perimeter. There are no open plains as along the Indus or further east. All is mountainous and since the mountains, in so far as they have any system, trend parallel to the Great Himalaya, and since Thomson's route lay from south to north across them, he was actually tackling the stiffest of all possible routes to Leh. Occasionally he ground to a standstill and held up his hands in horror at the relentless switchback.

I find it extremely hard to describe in an adequate manner the extreme desolation . . . The prospect before me was certainly most wonderful. I had nowhere before seen a country so utterly waste . . . Directly in front across the Zanskar river a rocky precipice, worn and furrowed in every direction and broken into sharp pinnacles, rose to the height of at least two thousand feet, overhanging a steep ravine, while to the right and left mountain was heaped upon mountain in inextricable confusion, large patches of snow covering the higher parts.

In Leh he found Strachey just back from another visit to the Tibetan frontier. He rested for a week and on July 19th started on the last stage of his journey. His destination he gave as 'the mountains north of Nubra'. Beside the evidence of a modern map this sounds pretty vague, but one must remember that Thomson, and Cunningham and Strachey, had no idea of the depth of the mountains that still intervened between Leh and Yarkand. The only known accounts of the route were the brief notices submitted by Moorcroft's agent, Mir Izzet Ullah, back in 1813, and by Burnes's informant in 1832. From them Thomson knew of the Karakoram pass and knew that it was on the watershed between the Indus basin and the rivers of Turkestan. The range it crossed was assumed to be a continuation of the mountains north of Baltistan. Strachey, with cautious circumlocution, gave them no name at all, while Cunningham went to the other extreme, naming 'what we call the Bolor and Karakoram . . . which probably merges into the Kuen Luen in the east', the Trans-Tibetan chain. Thomson noticed that the range further west was called Mustagh, above Nubra it was called Karakoram and might conveniently be referred to, as a whole, as the Kun Lun. In other words he, like the others, knew of only one mountain system. That the Karakoram pass had nothing whatever to do with the Kun Lun, or that the mountains to the south of Yarkand known by that name were yet another vast separate system, is not even hinted at.

'The mountains north of Nubra' were, therefore, thought to be the same as those south of Yarkand. Thomson imagined that by scaling the Karakoram pass he would be overcoming the last barrier between India and Central Asia, and he hastened on towards it. He crossed the Ladakh range between Leh and the Shyok by the 17,500-foot pass of Khardung, the first of the five classic passes on the route to Yarkand. Not long before it had been possible to by-pass at least one of these by following the S bends of the Shyok. Now that route was blocked by glaciers which had nosed right down into the valley and pushed across the river bed into the precipices on the other side. Besides which, the river in July was in spate. It would have been impossible to follow up its bed and even crossing it proved extremely difficult. Though seldom able to ride, Thomson still had his horse. Crossing the Shyok, it took four men to support and guide the beast against the racing current.

To rejoin the river in the middle of the S, he proceeded up the Nubra valley and climbed towards the second of the great passes. This was the notorious Sasser, not the highest but probably the most impressive and dangerous. In Nubra, which by Ladakhi standards is a lush and populous spot, he stocked up with twenty days' rations for the uninhabited regions ahead. The ascent was 'exceedingly steep, almost precipitous'. The track zig-zagged back and forth and was so littered with bones and skeletons as to appear from a distance to be paved white. Mostly they were the remains of mules that had died on the journey, but there were human skulls as well. Later travellers reckoned that, providing there was not a fresh fall of snow, guides were a waste of money along this macabre trail. You simply followed the bones.

Thomson was now on ground untrod even by Moorcroft or Vigne. From the top of the first ridge he gazed towards the Sasser. '. . . I was able to see something of the road before me regarding which I had previously had little information except in accounts of its extreme difficulty. These I had inclined to consider exaggerated, but the prospect before me now was undoubtedly far from tempting.' The Sasser turned out to be a network of vast glaciers. Some he reckoned were at least five miles long and between them lay moraines several hundred feet high, composed of boulders as big as houses. One good thing about Thomson's narrative is that it is never open to doubt. When he talks of desolation he means it; the day goes by without sight of a single plant or blade of grass. The savants had their doubts about Vigne's descriptions of the Karakoram glaciers. When Thomson's experience of the Sasser confirmed them, there was an end to the matter.

The altitude of the pass was about 18,000 feet. He didn't measure it but made a rough calculation and the return of a severe headache confirmed it. On the descent it started to snow; he was lucky to have got across before the weather changed. Even in July whole caravans have perished on the Sasser in a squall. Back down to the Shyok, across it and up yet again to meet it at the top of the S. There was no pass to cross this time. After a long but gentle ascent he found instead an 'open, grassy, somewhat undulating plain'. It was a good five or six miles across and its lowest point was about 17,000 feet. A remarkable phenomenon, thought Thomson; he wondered whether it was not the highest plateau in the world. In fact it probably is. It is called the Depsang plateau and, like the Pamirs only more so, it always struck subsequent visitors as 'the veritable top of the world'. Dr. Bellew, who crossed it on the way back from Yarkand in 1874, left the following description.

All around appeared mountain ranges, none of which were less than 20,000 feet high, whilst to the west rose two peaks of much greater height; yet in the distance they seemed below us, for the land around sloped away down on all sides. In whichever direction we looked the sky appeared below us and the world slunk out of sight. In fact we felt as if we had risen above the world and were now descending to it in front of us. The Karakoram left behind us appeared like a mere crest on the undulating surface of the country and the mountain ranges in front and on all sides seemed to struggle up from below to reach our level.

Nothing so fanciful is to be expected of Thomson who was more exercised by the variety of pebbles. He was also suffering severely from the altitude with a continuous headache which grew unbearable with the slightest exertion. The next geologist to take this route, a companion of Bellew's, actually died on the Depsang from the effects of altitude. The Shyok was crossed for the last time, and on August 18th he left his horse tethered and his tent standing and set off for the crest of the Karakoram pass.

Originally he may have intended to cross it. He doesn't say much in his book, but in a letter to his brother he wrote of the danger of arrest at the first Chinese post and the probable difficulty of obtaining supplies on the other side. He also made enquiries about a possible route to Kotan, which might take him round any Chinese posts. The twenty days' food he had taken would certainly have been sufficient to see him across even the Kun Lun. It looks then as if the real reason for calling it a day was his own health. He repeatedly mentions the severe headaches, added to which altitude has a general debilitating and demoralising effect.

Just possibly he might still have gone on if what he calls 'the prospect before me' had been tempting enough. Foolish as it is to expect some new and shattering vista from the crest of every pass, the traveller always does. Scarcely daring to look up, he concentrates rock by rock on the progress of his feet. He seems to move with the absurdly slow deliberation of an astronaut. Breathing is agony, the head pounds and the calf muscles scream. The top is the reward, always exciting because it has to be. Every other reason for going on seems irrelevant, and only an immediate objective can justify the appalling exertion.

Thomson had the added incentive of knowing that this was not just any pass. He was about to be the first European to stand on the Karakoram watershed between India and China. To the best of his knowledge the ground beyond sloped gently down to the fabled cities of Yarkand and Kotan. From some of the passes over the Pir Panjal you could see the minarets of Lahore. Might there not be a comparable view to the north from the crest of the Karakoram? Might he not spy some distant speck that was one of the walled cities unseen by Europeans since the days of Marco Polo?

The ascent, though agonising, was not steep. Quite suddenly he found himself on the top. It was just a rounded ridge, swept free of snow by the wind and bounded by steep slopes on each side. No grand gateway, this, but a grim and forbidding cleft. The height he made 18,200 feet, but still it was no vantage point. 'Towards the north, much to my disappointment, there was no distant view.' He could follow the track down for just half a mile, then steep mountains higher than the pass closed the view. To a sick man it was not inviting. Nor was there any consolation for the naturalist. Not even a bold little saxifrage crowned the pass. The only signs of life seen all day were 'ravens, a bird about the size of a sparrow, a bright metallic coloured carrion fly and a small dusky butterfly'.

Thomson however was content. He had achieved more than was ever expected of him. 'I think I have determined', he told his brother, 'the points of most interest both geographically and botanically.' Spurning generalisations, exaggeration, hearsay and imaginative description, he stuck to what he saw and what he recognised. The scientific habit makes him a dull writer but a great pioneer. His observations, particularly on the part played by glaciers and lakes in moulding the structure of the mountain region, and on botany and geology in assisting the geographical interpretation of it, were accepted without question.

'The remainder', he continued, 'will be done some day from Yarkand but cannot till the Russians take it from the Chinese.' Even he was mindful of the power struggle for Central Asia, though the thought that his journey had any political significance seems scarcely to have crossed his mind at the time. There were, however, those who immediately derived some satisfaction from hearing that the Karakoram pass did not seem to be the end of the mountain barrier to the north. The ramparts of the new frontier were indeed formidable. When, in 1866, the Royal Geographical Society belatedly decided to give Thomson a Gold Medal it was as much in recognition of the increasing political significance of his journey as of its scientific achievements. But by then Thomson was ensconced in London's Kew Gardens rightly enjoying the reputation of one of the greatest botanists of his time. Others had taken up the challenge of the Karakorams and the Kun Lun.

11. Plane-Tables from the Hills

The Karakoram pass scaled by Thomson was first actually crossed by two Germans, Herman and Robert Schlagintweit, in 1856. The credit could, of course, go to Gardiner but, without quibbling over his nationality or casting any more slurs on the authenticity of his travels, the fact is that his account is so meagre that even his route is in doubt. Not so with the Schlagintweits. They followed in Thomson's tracks precisely, crossed the pass and then veered off east towards Kotan. In the history of Himalayan exploration they deserve the fullest treatment. They went on to cross the Kun Lun, the first to break through the entire mountain barrier between India and Turkestan, and the first to distinguish the Karakorams and Kun Lun as separate mountain systems. In the following year a third brother, Adolph, repeated the feat and actually reached Yarkand and Kashgar. But he never returned. He blundered into a civil war and was assassinated just outside Kashgar.

Tremendous achievements they were, yet these journeys received scant attention at the time. So much so that the next Europeans to reach Yarkand liked to imagine that they themselves were the first. It would be a pleasure to redress the situation; but sadly this is not possible. One reason is that this is a story of explorers, not a history of exploration. The most self-effacing travellers, like Wood or Thomson, may stand out clearly, revealed rather than dwarfed by their exploits. They are men, 'flesh and blood and apprehensive'. The Schlagintweits are more like some impersonal machine; the individuals are quite crushed by their achievement. The mighty volumes which record their observations reveal everything about their work. We know a very little about their careers but we learn absolutely nothing about their personalities. Gardiner could be sparing of the facts but the man himself is unmistakable. It is the other way round with the Schlagintweits. They took on the whole of India, aiming to reduce it to a gigantic table of observations. Of hot springs alone, for example, they listed and described 656. In the process they damned themselves to a regrettable obscurity.

In all honesty another reason must also be conceded. The story of their travels has never been translated into English. The six quarto tomes of truly Himalayan proportions, their pages of heavy gothic script still uncut, may conceal those pearls the biographer cherishes. Maybe there is somewhere in that deep and turgid narrative a basis for characterisation. Nearly drowning in the process, the present author has searched and searched in vain.

Back in the 1850s they had sounder reasons for ignoring the work of the Schlagintweits. For a start the servants of the Honourable Company had other things on their minds. Returning from the Karakoram pass in 1848, Dr. Thomson found himself cut off again, this time in Kashmir; the Second Sikh War had begun. It lasted only till the following year, but the annexation of the Punjab that resulted was a colossal undertaking which was carried out with single-minded zeal. It was promptly followed by the Central Provinces (now Madhya Pradesh) and Oudh (in Uttar Pradesh) also coming under direct British control; the last great wave of British expansion in India was breaking in grand style. Here was more than enough to absorb the attention and tax the energies of the restless or the inquisitive. Then, when the brothers had completed their travels and when Adolph's murder might have won them widespread attention, it was 1857 and the beginning of the Indian Mutiny. The execution of a lone German in Kashgar could scarcely compete with the wholesale massacre of men, women and children that was sweeping the British cantonments from Bihar to Lahore. In this, the most traumatic event in 200 years of British rule in India, an almost inevitable casualty was the Honourable Company itself. Over the years it had increasingly shared its responsibilities with the government in London, but now in 1858 the transition was completed and India came under the direct rule of Crown and Parliament. The Governor-General became the Queen's Viceroy, Westminster exercised direct control over the policies pursued in India and the Board of Directors was no more. The fact that in the process the Schlagintweits had lost their patron bothered no one.

There is also a hint of sour grapes about the British attitude. What, after all, were these three Teutons doing, poking around the sensitive frontiers of India? They had even managed to visit Kabul. Were there not thousands of Englishmen, skilled and brave enough, who would give their right arms for such opportunities as were afforded the Schlagintweits? It was on the recommendation of Baron Humboldt, the greatest traveller and geographer of his day, backed by the King of Prussia and the Royal Asiatic Society, that the brothers had been taken on by the Honourable Company. They were to complete a magnetic survey of India, and they arrived in Bombay in 1854. The editor of the *Bombay Times* found them well-off for instruments but none too sure of how to use them. Two of the brothers smoked so heavily he doubted if they would reach Calcutta, and he summed up the general feeling by disparaging their mission as either doomed to failure or too detailed to be completed much before the end of the century.

In London the Royal Geographical Society, who also had other preoccupations at the time—namely the squabble over the source of the Nile—paid only scant attention to their activities. And, when in 1861 the brothers offered to dedicate their great work to the Society, the offer was refused on the grounds that the Society had neither commissioned nor encouraged them. No doubt there was some resentment, too, over their recognition from an altogether unexpected quarter. For in 1859 the Tsar had conferred on Robert Schlagintweit the title of Sakunlunski—Lord of the Kun Lun. It confirmed the worst suspicions of those who had always opposed the idea of employing foreigners on such delicate missions.

The President of the Society had once described the penetration of the region north of India as a threefold process. First, and well out in front, were the reports of native travellers which shed a wide but uncertain light on the vast unknown. Behind them, piercing this gloom, came narrow shafts of clearer light representing the travels of individual European explorers. Finally, and well behind, came the zone of harsh white reality shed by the surveyors and map-makers. It was a good enough simile in the 1830s and 1840s but by the 1850s the pioneers were temporarily penned back by political and physical difficulties. The surveyors were catching up with and overtaking them.

The Schlagintweits themselves were supposedly engaged on survey work. In fact their enquiries extended to almost every branch of science and their surveying amounted to little more than not always accurate astronomical observations to fix their positions. Even this was regarded as superfluous. For in 1855 the Grand Trigonometrical Series of the Survey of India commenced operations in Kashmir. This, the Kashmir Series, was to be the crowning achievement of one of the most ambitious scientific projects undertaken in the nineteenth century.

The technicalities of map-making are daunting, but no one who has had a taste of India can fail to marvel at the magnitude of the task. How much more so is this true of the Himalayas. The ordinary traveller would usually seek out the easiest route, stick to existing tracks and climb only the unavoidable passes. The surveyor had to cover all the ground. He was after vantage points. Across empty, trackless regions he moved from one high peak to another. Mostly he travelled on foot; horses were useless. He was as much a mountaineer as a traveller, and this in the days well before aerial surveys and wireless contact when there were no light-weight rations and no oxygen. Mountaineering skills amounted to strong lungs and a cool head and climbing equipment was what you might find in the garden shed, a spade, a pick and a hefty coil of rope. No wonder Godwin-Austen, in his old age, felt bitter about the technological dodges of the twentieth-century mountaineer.

Their instruments were delicate but heavy. The fourteen-inch theodolite used in Kashmir must have weighed about a hundredweight. It had to be carried over rivers and glaciers and up the steep climbs suspended from a pole borne by two men. The slightest jar was liable to upset its accuracy. The plane-tables, too, were bulky affairs. Keeping the survey parties in supplies was in itself a major operation, and many a long vigil at a station in the clouds had to be abandoned because the food had run out.

With the reluctant blessing of Gulab Singh operations started from a base line just east of Jammu in spring 1855. The Grand Trigonometrical Survey (GTS for short) had begun fifty-five years before at Madras. Its object was to construct a highly accurate framework for a map of the whole of India. The framework was to consist of meridional (north–south) and longitudinal (east–west) chains of connected triangles observed across the length and breadth of the subcontinent. A base line would be carefully measured between two vantage points. In the south they might be *gopurams* (gateway towers) of temples or in the plains, where no handy eminence was to be found, specially constructed towers. Perched on one of these 'trig. stations'—scaffolding had to be wrapped round the *gopurams*—the surveyor with his ponderous theodolite measured the angle between his base line and the line to a third vantage point. By doing this from both ends of his base line, he could deduce the exact position of the third point and the distances to it, i.e. the lengths of the other two sides of his triangle.

One of these would then be selected as the next base line, the same

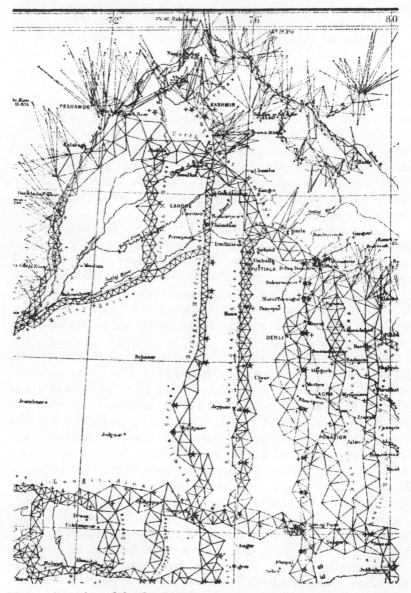

Map 4   A section of the Grand Trigonometrical Survey of India, showing
longitudinal and meridional series

process would follow and a second triangle would be constructed and so on. In practice there were many refinements and complications. Allowances had to be made for differences of altitude, the curvature of the earth and a phenomenon called refraction. Occasional checks had to be made by measuring a base line on the ground against its distance as established trigonometrically, or by tying in with another series. The accuracy was remarkable. A series carried for hundreds of miles would be found to have erred by no more than an inch or two per mile of base line.

When Vigne met the Surveyor-General, George Everest, in 1834 he was busy measuring a base line at Dehra Dun at the foot of the Central Himalayas and at the end of the principal north–south series, the Great Arc of the Meridian, which had been carried all the way from Cape Comorin. From it at Dehra Dun branched off two longitudinal series. One ran east along the base of the Himalayas into Assam. The other ran north-west through Simla and the Punjab to Peshawar. This last was finished in 1854 and, since the men employed on it had already had some mountain experience around Simla, it was they who were now deployed in Kashmir. One of the lines of their just completed series became the base line for the new series.

In the 1855 season they took their triangles across the Pir Panjal. The difficulties were appalling. Here there was no shortage of vantage points but to find a peak with a view in the desired direction, which was not blocked by another, entailed innumerable fruitless ascents. Having at last reached a suitable station, puffing and blowing from the average elevation of 15,000 feet, they had to start digging. The first job was to excavate a level platform and the best place for it was the very top. On Muli peak they dug and dug through the hard snow. What looked like the top turned out to be a cone of ice. They tried another spot and were delighted when 'only eleven feet down' they struck rock.

The advance party, whose commander was William Henry Johnson, was responsible for this selection of the stations and for the preliminary, approximate triangulation. Having dug out a platform he had to construct a masonry pillar to take the theodolite and a hut for the lampmen. They would remain there to flash their heliotropes and tend their lamps while the station was being observed from elsewhere. Lampmen would expect to be marooned for weeks, but for Johnson and his gang, living under canvas, delay was more serious. In spite of immense cold, exposure and exhaustion they had to push ahead.

They melted the snow, mixed it with lime, cemented their pillars, threw up a stone shelter for the lampmen and prayed for the clouds to lift. If they were lucky they might complete their observations in a day or so. The clouds would break. A vast array of snowclad peaks would rise from the blanket of mist in the valleys. An impossible, unearthly world of the purest beauty etched out of a deep blue sky, it seemed quite untouched by man. Then from a distant peak, indistinguishable from a hundred others, would shine out the tell-tale pinpoint of light, the 'sight never to be forgotten of a well served heliotrope'.

Alternatively the clouds might not break. Food would start to run short. The men would be suffering from headaches, snow-blindness, altitude sickness and cold. The wind would throw down their tents, the snow would make all movement dangerous and their fuel would have to be carefully conserved. Thunderstorms, which are virtually unknown in Ladakh, could be a serious hazard in the Pir Panjal. On Muli peak again, work on the platform had to be stopped when lightning set their hair and clothing crackling and great sparks leaping about. Lieutenant Montgomerie, who was in charge of the whole series and who did the final triangulation, also had trouble there. 'The small iron stove in my tent began to crackle in the most unpleasant manner . . . and the hair of my dog crackled and, in the dark, sparks were visible.' Another man had his hair set on fire and a third, who put up his umbrella to deflect the hailstones, found the thing operating as a conductor. It crackled away and 'on shutting it down it fairly hummed'.

For the winter they returned to headquarters at Dehra Dun to check their calculations and instruments, fill in the map and draw up a report. Then back again to Kashmir in the spring. In 1856 they continued up through the valley itself. One of Johnson's stations was set up on Haramukh, the presiding mountain of the Kashmir valley, and there on September 10th arrived Montgomerie with the big theodolite. The ascent had taken him four days and the altitude was over 16,000 feet. Below the station stretched a fine glacier which sloped down into the sacred, trout-filled lake of Gangabal. The view to the north was the best they had yet had.

I had the pleasure to see the various ranges of the Himalaya right up to the Karakoram. There was nothing remarkable in the first six or seven ridges . . . Beyond came the snowy points of the

Karakoram range and behind them I saw two fine peaks standing very high above the general range . . . possibly 140 miles away from me.

He managed to get bearings on both these peaks and made a quick sketch of their outlines in the margin of his angle book. The larger with its double summit he designated K1, the smaller more pointed peak he marked K2. In 1856 there were no further sightings of these giants and, without another bearing on them, no way of telling their position or their height. But in 1857 and 1858 a surveyor working across the Deosai plains to Skardu again picked them out. So did Johnson in 1859. K1 was revealed as the nearer and lower of the two, about 25,600 feet. Its local name was Masherbrum.

K2 was calculated at 28,287 feet. 'The peak', wrote Montgomerie, 'may therefore be considered as the second highest in the world.'* And he stressed that the ranges north of the Indus were proving far higher than any of the earlier travellers had imagined. There appeared to be no local name for this shyest of all giants. 'Keychu', the name elicited from their Balti porters by the earnest climbers of later years, is just a variation of those other 'local' names, 'Keytoo' and 'Kaytoo'. In 1856 Peak XV in Nepal was proclaimed Mount Everest in honour of the retired Surveyor-General. Soon after, it was proposed that K2 be called Mount Waugh after his successor or Mount Albert after the Prince Consort. Neither of these names was accepted, and in 1886 further attemps were made with Mount Montgomerie and Mount Godwin-Austen. It could be argued that Johnson was probably the first to see the mountain when he erected the station on Haramukh but it was certainly Montgomerie who first recorded it. Yet Godwin-Austen was the name which came nearest to being recognised. It was, in fact, rejected by the Royal Geographical Society but a few unofficial maps took it up and to this day the BBC, for example, calls it Mount Godwin-Austen.

This represents something of a personal triumph for, though Godwin-Austen was not the man to crave the immortality of having his name on the map, he had no love for Montgomerie. He accused him of gross unfairness in his summaries of the work done by the Kashmir series, of grabbing all the credit that should have gone to men like Johnson and himself. Montgomerie had 'got his honours and made a name for himself with as little personal hardship as any man I know

* Mount Everest had been recognised as the world's highest in 1852.

in the Indian Survey'. He had hardly ever gone beyond Srinagar and 'certainly never climbed higher than 15,000 feet'.

If this were true, then Montgomerie had never been up Haramukh or seen K2. But actually Godwin-Austen was quite wrong. In the first two years of the Survey Montgomerie spent most of his time in the field. In 1857 the outbreak of the Mutiny, closely followed by the death of Gulab Singh and the succession of his son Ranbir Singh, necessitated his keeping a closer eye on events in Srinagar. Added to which he had the job of instructing an endless succession of new recruits and initiating others, Godwin-Austen among them, who joined the Survey half way through. Both as organiser, political liaison and chief surveyor, Montgomerie deserved his honours, including the Royal Geographical Society's Gold Medal in 1865.

The Kashmir Series differed from most, in that triangulation and topographical work went ahead simultaneously. In other words, while Johnson and Montgomerie were busy laying down the framework of triangles, men with plane-tables who filled in the detail were hard on their heels. Lieutenant Henry Haversham Godwin-Austen* was one of these. He joined the Kashmir survey in 1857. In his first season he was the victim of another of the occupational hazards of surveyors. Near Jammu a band of irate villagers set about him and beat him up so badly that he was invalided out of the Survey and returned to England. No doubt he had trespassed on to some hill sacred to the local Hindu population. In 1860, lured as much by the charms of Pauline Chichele-Plowden as by the call of the mountains, he was back in India and back with the Kashmir survey.

Godwin-Austen was cut out for a distinguished career as a military surveyor. His father was a well-known geologist and his grandfather, under whom he had served as ADC, was a general and a KCB. He was educated at Sandhurst where he learnt topographical drawing from 'a master of the old French pictorial school' and received a 'certificate of superior qualifications'. Montgomerie could never quite get over the stylishness of his work. Repeatedly Godwin-Austen produced 'the most artistic board of the season', a somewhat laced compliment, one feels. He was also a keen geologist and had a feeling for both the texture and structure of savage terrain.

In 1860 he was immediately despatched to the bleak upper valleys of Baltistan where these skills could be put to advantage and where

---

* His father added the name Godwin, his mother's maiden name, in 1853. Until well into the 1860s Henry was known as plain Austen.

there was little danger of another brush with incensed villagers. He was perhaps not the most diplomatic of men. But he was strong, compact and immensely hardy, the ideal man for the mountains. The following year he married Miss Chichele-Plowden and then returned to Baltistan. His honeymoon was just over but, plagued by the difficulties of supporting his bride on a surveyor's pay, he was probably happy to see the scarred slopes of the Karakorams again. The view from his first stop, a trig. station on the edge of the Deosai overlooking Skardu, helped to put such things in perspective. 'Peak K2 appeared of an airy blue tint surrounded by the yellower peak K1, K3 and others all over 24,000 feet in height. Other minor peaks by hundreds thrust up their heads—some snow-capped, some rounded, some bare and angular, running up as sharp as needles.'

The triangulators might hop from one peak to the next, covering vast distances in a single season, but the plane-tablers moved much more slowly. They had to cover every glacier, every side valley and even for a $\frac{1}{4}$-inch map, which was reckoned good enough for a howling wilderness like the Karakorams, this meant a painful progress at ever-increasing altitudes. Godwin-Austen moved across the Indus and up the Shigar valley opposite Skardu. His first destination was the Mustagh pass. Thomson had listed three passes over the Karakorams. The middle one, and the only one about which anything was known, was the Karakoram pass. But east of there, from Rudok in Tibet to Kotan, Moorcroft had reported rumours of not just a pass but a road; while west above Skardu, amongst what were now proving the highest peaks of all, Vigne and Thomson had both heard of another route to Yarkand. This was the Mustagh pass.

The surveyors, of course, were supposed to be mapping the mountains, not crossing them. The Karakoram watershed was here regarded as the most likely and convenient frontier of the Kashmir state and officially no one was supposed to trespass beyond it. On the other hand they were asked to pay special attention to any passes and learn as much as they could about what lay beyond them. This was too much like an invitation to go as far as possible without getting caught and it is clear from Godwin-Austen's narrative that he intended, if possible, actually to cross the Mustagh. In fact, if he could get a small guard, he thought he could carry the survey 'into Yarkand country for a considerable distance'. The population there could not be great, 'nor their matchlocks much to be feared'.

Without a guard but with a party of sixty-six including assistants, porters, guides and a local liaison officer to cheer the men and smooth some of his more abrasive outbursts, he made straight for the pass. The way lay up the Shigar river over the Skoro pass and then along the great Panmah glacier. The only deviations were for what he usually dismisses as 'a steep pull' up some towering ridge from which he could do his mapping. Invariably this meant a climb of three or four thousand feet. To a neat and hard little man at the peak of fitness it was nothing. He swarmed up the rock faces and the icy slopes with the jerky ease of a spider traversing its web. And fretted, no doubt, as he waited for the heavy plane-table to arrive.

His sketching illustrates superbly the incredible perpendicularity of the central Karakorams. In the valleys the eye never pans. Always it is climbing. The neck aches from the unaccustomed action, and the sky is just a slit directly overhead. Even the side valleys offer no vistas. Minor glaciers fill them to a depth of hundreds of feet and, high above, loll over the lips of their moraines like malevolent tongues.

What no drawing can capture, but which his narrative emphasises so well, is the instability of it all. In the early hours of the morning when the frost grips everything it seems like a silent, timeless, unchangeable world. But in summer by mid-afternoon all hell may break loose. At one campsite he was taking an uncharacteristic siesta when he heard 'an unusual rumbling sound'. Someone shouted that the stream was coming and, seconds later, a black mass came bumbling out of a side ravine and bore down over the boulder-strewn bed of the valley like an express train. Rocks, ten feet tall, in a wall of mud and stones thirty yards wide and five deep, tumbled past 'like peas shot out of a bag'. It was a *shwa*, a stream which, jammed up for months by the snout of an advancing glacier, had suddenly broken through. The phenomenon is common enough in the Karakorams. The major tributaries of the Indus, indeed the Indus itself, have often been dammed in this way with fearful damage and loss of life when the offending landslip or glacier is finally broken by the lake behind it.

Four days later, at the foot of the Panmah glacier, he sat up late into the night listening to the blocks of ice and snow crashing down the terminal cliff of the glacier. As the cold increased, the intervals between each crash became longer until the glacier was finally lulled into sleep. Some of the glaciers were in retreat, their moraines of rock lying miles in advance of their present snouts. Others were still advancing. Glacial lakes had disappeared, old campsites had been overrun and he could see how the ice was mowing down all in its path, cutting through any low spurs, rooting up boulders, earth and scrub and bulldozing all before it. The devastation and mess created by a glacier surpass the wildest dreams of a construction engineer. Some appear sleek and white on the flank of a mountain but visit their vicinity, try to ascend them and you find them surrounded by an oozing morass of mud and stone, blocks of ice and shattered rock, as insecure and unpleasant to cross as the worst ice-field. This is the world as it must have been at the dawn of creation, cracking and crumbling, oozing and flowing with irresistible elemental forces. No place at all for human beings.

Godwin-Austen noted it all with calm wonder and pushed on for the Mustagh. Two days' march up the right side of the Panmah glacier the guides declared that they had reached the place to cross it. The width here was two and a half miles 'through as extraordinary a scene as the imagination could picture; it was the desolation of desolation'. The cloud hung low over the ice, occasionally revealing and magnifying the gaunt slope of a mountain, grey or ochre in colour, precipitous and savage in outline. The surface of the glacier consisted of stony ridges giving way to purer ice, frozen into waves and pitted with pools of deep green water. The air was full of the sound of invisible rocks crashing down slopes of ice and splashing into the pools below.

The last night before attempting the pass was spent on the ice. A few rocks were rolled together to make some sort of floor for the tents, but it was still bitterly cold. The tentless porters, without even the comfort of a fire, curled up three to a blanket but got no sleep. Even Godwin-Austen did not stir from his tent until the sun was full upon it. With eight picked men he started for the crest. The altitude and snow-glare made all movement painful but it was the crevasses which looked like being the worst problem.

They soon became more numerous and were ugly things to look into, much more so to cross—going down into darkness between walls garnished with magnificent green icicles from six to twenty feet long and of proportionate thickness, looking like rows of great teeth ready to devour one. I tried with our ropes to sound the depths of some of these fissures, but all of them tied together only made up 162 feet which was not enough. The snow lay up to the edges of the crevasses and travelling became so insecure that we had to take to the ropes, and so, like a long chain of criminals, we wound our way along. In this mode we moved much faster, each man taking his run and clearing even broad crevasses if they crossed the direction we were travelling.

In the heat of the sun the snow became soft. Men had to be sent on ahead to probe through it with long poles for hidden crevasses. Progress grew 'provokingly slow'. Finally, a mile from the top and just five hundred feet below it, the weather defeated them. The clouds descended and it came on to snow heavily. They were lucky to reach camp in safety as the blizzard howled about them and the glacier started emitting 'the most disagreeable noises—crunching, splitting and groaning to an awful extent'.

Godwin-Austen hoped to get another crack at the Mustagh but never did. Surprisingly, his failure had not convinced him that the pass was too difficult to be of commercial or strategic importance. On the contrary, he reckoned that the track up the Panmah glacier could be made suitable for pack ponies, considered the ascent to the pass encouragingly gradual and reported that it was in regular use. The worst part of it was not the physical difficulties but the danger of being attacked by robbers on the other side. It looks as if the government took his idea of what was practicable with a pinch of salt, for it was not till 1887 that another attempt was made to cross the Mustagh. This was by Younghusband, and largely on his own initiative. He succeeded, just, but corroborated what Vigne and Thomson had said; namely that the pass had once been much used but, early in the century, the sort of glacial movement which Godwin-Austen describes so vividly had virtually closed it to all but mountaineers.

The old pass had debouched not on to the Panmah but on to the Baltoro glacier for which Godwin-Austen now made tracks. He was not finished with the Karakorams by a long chalk and arguably his ascent of the Baltoro was a greater achievement than his attempt at the Mustagh. From it stems his association with K2.

For the meeting of the Royal Geographical Society at which his paper on 'The Glaciers of the Mustakh [Karakoram] Range' was read, his father, old Godwin-Austen the geologist, came up from Guildford. On the way he tried to translate young Henry's extraordinary discoveries into terms everyone might appreciate, and after the paper was read he rose, the proud father, to elucidate. ' If Hampstead and Highgate were presumed to be high mountains, these glaciers would descend as far south as Tunbridge and north two-thirds of the way to Cambridge.' It was a brave attempt, but no one has ever succeeded in conveying to those who have not known the Himalayas any conception of their size. To talk of mountains nearly ten times the size of Snowdon or twice the height of Mont Blanc means nothing. Homely comparisons only belittle the grandeur and no attempt at a scale can convey the effect of such mighty scenery. It is not even enough to have seen it. With head throbbing, lungs pulling fiercely at the harsh liquid air and feet burning with blisters, one must feel it. And, at the same time one must experience that very different, wholly beautiful sensation which is the peculiar reward for penetrating the greatest mountains. An unburdening of the spirit, an ennobling really, it too is indescribable; to know it, one must feel it.

If this experience intensifies with the altitude the mountaineer is to be envied. But few mountaineers can ever encounter such grandeur as awaited Godwin-Austen up the Baltoro glacier. For this is the innermost sanctum of the Western Himalayas, an amphitheatre of the greatest mountains on this planet. In the space of about fifteen miles the Baltoro holds in its icy embrace ten of the world's thirty highest peaks. They line its sides and close its easternmost end like high priests guarding the Holiest of Holies. Sir Martin Conway who, thirty years later, was the next to enter this great nave, aptly named the peak at the eastern end The Golden Throne.

Up this broad aisle of ice, mere specks on its noble extent, Godwin-Austen and his men now made their painful progress. Others might have felt self-conscious and awed into reverence by such surroundings. But not Godwin-Austen. He had his share of the calm confidence of men like Henry Lawrence plus something more. The next generation would be inclined to romanticise and to dwell on the wonders of Nature with a capital 'N'. But the men of mid-century spurned such nonsense. This was a period of technological revolution. Railways were changing the face of India, steamships had halved the time it took to get from Southampton to Bombay, and the telegraph was changing the whole character of government. Such developments had more effect on the administration within India, and on the British government's involvement in the country, than did the demise of the Honourable Company. The GTS was at the head of these advances. Their maps were essential for the planners of railways and telegraph lines; and, if this sounds fanciful in the case of the Himalayas, it should be noted that already a railway into Kashmir was being considered, and within twenty years there would be talk of a line to Kashgar. The men of mid-century, especially those involved in these

M M—O

advances, reverenced facts and figures. In the Karakorams it was the ice four or five hundred feet deep, glaciers over thirty miles long, peaks up to 28,000 feet, that mattered.

Godwin-Austen got quietly on with his job in the most practical way possible. His main problem was to discover where K2 lay in relation to the Karakoram watershed. Often the highest mountains lay not on the main watershed but on a spur from that range. It could be south of the watershed but, from Montgomerie's description, it looked as if it was north of it and therefore beyond the frontier. From the glacier he could see Gasherbrum straight ahead and Masherbrum towering to the right. To the left, where K2 should lie, intervening spurs cut off the view. In the hope of a sighting he started to scale Masherbrum. A thousand feet above the glacier there was still no sign of it. Two thousand feet up and he thought he could distinguish a more distant lump of rock and snow just nosing above the horizon. 'After another sharp push up to a point from which it was impossible to mount further there no longer remained a doubt about it. There with not a particle of cloud to hide it stood the great peak K2.' It was actually on the watershed.

So, though Godwin-Austen had not discovered it, it was he who first saw K2 at close quarters and ascertained its position in relation to the Karakoram system. If the peak itself is not strictly speaking his, there is at least a Godwin-Austen Glacier. Fittingly it is the one that seemingly pushes the watershed northwards so that it actually runs through K2.

*   *   *

Godwin-Austen had sixteen brothers and sisters, four of whom lived to be over ninety and two to be over a hundred. He himself reached eighty-nine and, when he died in 1924, he was revered as something of a grand old man of the mountains. At seventy-three he published *The Fauna of British India*, vol 1, at seventy-five he was awarded the Royal Geographical Society's Gold Medal and to the day of his death was still a forceful character with strong views on the rights and wrongs of mountaineering. He came to be regarded as the greatest of the Kashmir surveyors and the first mountaineer in the Western Himalayas.

It is an invidious business singling out a couple of men from the dozen or so who worked on the GTS in Kashmir. They all performed feats of endurance and nearly all visited hitherto unknown regions. But none more deserved a share of the acclaim given to Godwin-Austen, and none was less recompensed for his efforts than Johnson. His name rings no bells. He won no medals and he died, or more probably was murdered, in obscure and ignominious circumstances. Yet Johnson was the man who, excluding the Schlagintweits, first reached Eastern Turkestan.

In the early days of the Kashmir survey he was Montgomerie's right-hand man. His energy was prodigious, his work as a triangulator brilliant and his courage as a mountaineer unsurpassed. Year after year he broke the altitude record, 19,600 feet, 19,900 feet, 20,600 feet, and in 1862 he built a station at 21,000 feet and climbed to the, for those days, incredible height of 22,300 feet. Four of his stations were the world's highest for another sixty years. Besides doing the pioneer triangulation he was often entrusted with the principal triangulation and, in Montgomerie's absence, he took temporary charge of the whole Series.

In 1864, with the work almost finished, Montgomerie went on leave. A Lieutenant Carter was appointed to take his place. Johnson was furious. He had been with the Kashmir survey throughout; Carter had only just joined it. And he had been highly regarded by Montgomerie who repeatedly brought his services to the attention of the Surveyor-General. He protested bitterly but without success, and from this time onwards his whole attitude seems to have changed.

Johnson's trouble was that he did not quite belong. He was 'native born'; his parents were as English as anyone's, but his father was a mere Ordnance Conductor and young William Henry had been brought up in India. He had never been to England. Instead of Sandhurst he was educated at Mussoorie, a place where, in Emily Eden's patronising words, 'parents who are too poor to send their children home, send them'. He joined the Survey as a Civil Junior Sub-Assistant and, though he rose rapidly, his uncovenanted status could never compete with that of the young Sandhurst officers like Godwin-Austen. It was a rule that no civilian, however senior, could ever have charge over military officers.

With Montgomerie's departure and the winding up of the Kashmir series there was also a good deal of reorganisation. Triangulators were no longer needed, and Johnson was pressed to switch to the topographical side. He had used a plane-table before but the work did not suit him. He liked to be at the head of things, pioneering way out in front, and he refused the transfer.

Thus, embittered and with his career in crisis, Johnson had spent the last season, 1864, rounding off his work in the north-eastern corner of Ladakh. In the process he had again beaten his own world altitude record by reaching a point 23,000 feet above sea level. He had also crossed the Karakoram pass and continued for three days towards Yarkand before turning back. At the time the Maharaja of Kashmir, without apparently consulting the British, had established an advance garrison well beyond the pass at a place called Shahidulla. This excursion of Johnson's was therefore safe enough and though his survey work there was rather haphazard, he was not censured for crossing the frontier.

At the end of the season the Kashmir series was declared finished. There was no more work to do within the Maharaja's territories.* Yet Johnson was not done. It was as if he could not bear to tear himself away from the wild scenery where he had achieved so much and from the association with Montgomerie that had worked so well. As a parting present Montgomerie agreed to recommend that he return to Ladakh once again. Surprisingly the request was granted, and in July 1865 Johnson reached Leh alone, the last relic of the Kashmir survey.

In the furore that was to greet his exploits of 1865, the argument raged over whether or not he was authorised to go beyond Kashmir territory. His instructions did not specifically say so, and it could be argued that all the points that he was supposed to be fixing, though beyond the frontier, were to be observed from within it. This, however, was not the spirit of his instructions. In the direction of Rudok, which place Godwin-Austen, uncensured, had almost reached in in 1863, it was clearly understood that he would have to cross the frontier. From this, he argued, he was entitled to assume that the Superintendent of the Survey had obtained permission for him to go beyond the Maharaja's domains, though he was stretching credibility when he inferred that it amounted to 'a roving commission to explore Central Asia'.

A more difficult question that has to be decided is not whether he was authorised to cross the frontier but why he did so. Was it as a devil-take-them-all protest against being repeatedly passed over? Was

---

* Except beyond the Indus towards Gilgit. This region was still virtually unknown to Europeans. The Kashmir government was struggling to maintain its toe-hold in Gilgit itself and no amount of pressure could persuade the Maharaja to allow surveyors to visit it.

it, as he claimed, because he believed that the government would welcome such a spirited attempt to extend the boundaries of geographical knowledge and thus at last acknowledge his services? Or was the reason more political? Was he trying to force the government's hand with regard to trans-frontier policy, and perhaps even not working for the government of India at all but for the Kashmir government? A good case can be made out for each.

The bazaar, Leh

He left Leh with fifty porters, three native assistants, five mules and six horses. They headed east to the Changchenmo valley, then north across the desolate plains of Aksai Chin, and reached the Karakash river inside three weeks. This route Johnson already knew. It had the advantage of circumventing the dramatic passes of the Karakoram route but, as later travellers discovered, it was questionable whether the total absence of grazing and the continuous altitude of between 15,000 and 18,000 feet were not greater drawbacks.

The Karakash river divides the Aksai Chin plateau from the Kun Lun mountains to the north. Johnson now climbed the nearest peaks hoping to get a glimpse of Yarkand or Kotan. To have been able to triangulate their positions from the established positions of some of the Kun Lun peaks would have been a cartographical coup. But alas, there was no hope. The view from the heights of the Kun Lun was as disappointing as that which Thomson had found on the Karakoram pass. Johnson was standing not on the saddle of some simple range but on the outermost heights of another colossal mountain system. It was like the Pir Panjal; open plains lay to the south and the north was still a mass of mountains.

He should now, like Thomson, have turned back. On his own reckoning, which was extremely generous to the Kashmir government, the frontier here followed the line of the Kun Lun. To go further would mean trespassing on Chinese territory. But at this point in his narrative—and it may be significant that he leaves it till now—Johnson introduces the unexpected information that he held an open invitation to visit Kotan. The ruler of that place had heard of his travels of the previous year and had sent an emissary to Leh with the invitation. Johnson had brought the man along and now, deciding to take up the offer, sent him on ahead to ask for guides and a safe conduct. Three weeks later these were provided, he crossed the Kun Lun by an unidentified pass and reached Kotan on October 2nd.

Johnson was the first European to visit the city since Marco Polo and Benedict de Goes. Even Gardiner never claimed to have been there, and the Schlagintweits, though they reached its vicinity, never dared to enter the city. Johnson reported at length on all he saw and learnt. He was well received and, though detained longer than he wished, was allowed to depart after only sixteen days. Compared to the difficulties experienced by the next European visitors to Eastern Turkestan this says a lot for his tact as well as for the disposition of the local ruler. From Kotan he headed west towards Yarkand. If he was to get back to India before the passes were closed for the winter there was scarcely time for a visit to Yarkand as well. Yet he had good reason for trying. An offer of £3,000 had been made to him by an influential faction if he would accept the governorship of the city in the name of the British government. The city had a large Kashmiri population who could only benefit from such a development. It was probably a genuine offer, but the circumstances that prompted it, civil war within and invaders without, were enough to dissuade

Johnson from proceeding. Only thirty-six miles from the city's gates
he turned back. He knew of the Schlagintweits and of the fate of
Adolph who had blundered into a similar situation in 1857.
But though he had not been to Yarkand, he now returned to Leh
by the classic Leh–Yarkand track. His was the first account by a
European of the whole route, and he was the first to cross all five of
the great passes. Coming from the north the last three, Karakoram,
Sasser and Khardung, had all been crossed by Thomson and by himself in 1864. But the two Kun Lun passes, the Sanju and the Suget,
were new to geography. Johnson scarcely does them justice. His idea
of a difficult route is almost unthinkable. He could now claim to be
the most experienced mountain traveller of his day and anywhere
that boasted a defined track was like a bowling green to him. On the
way out in mid-summer he had noted, as a curiosity rather than as
any indication of the hardships, that the icicles in his mane-like beard
had failed to melt even in the sun. What the return journey in October
and November must have been like it would be hard to imagine
without the accounts of later travellers.

In 1889 Dr. (of Divinity) Henry Lansdell also crossed the Sanju
and Suget passes in October. The frost had its advantages. It made
the rivers fordable, the footing firm and reduced the risk of avalanches.
But the cold brought its own set of problems. Keeping a journal or,
as Johnson found, plotting a map, was impossible because the ink
froze between the heated pot and the paper. A cup of coffee not
downed at the first sip, froze solid in minutes and the apple at Lansdell's bedside was a rock by morning. On the Suget, a month earlier
than Johnson, he nearly suffocated from the need to wear his full
wardrobe.

To begin with I had put on a thick lamb's wool vest with sleeves
and drawers, then ditto of chamois leather; next a flannel shirt and
above it a chamois vest without sleeves lined with flannel; cloth
trousers and waistcoat, with jacket of kid leather, flannel lined; then
an ulster lined with fur; and above it for sleeping my Khoten coat
of sheepskin, with thick stockings and fur lined boots, together
with a woollen helmet for a nightcap. Thus I lay down on my four
trunks while Joseph covered me with shawl and lambskin. This
represented my maximum—namely five skins besides my own,
four flannels and a thick coat; yet with all this at Suget it was cold
and I never got into a perspiration, though the weight of clothing

and the effect of the *dam* [altitude sickness] proved a little too much; and I had to rise in the night feeling half suffocated . . .

It was while Johnson, less generously clad, was negotiating the Kun Lun passes that the storm broke back in India. First news of his dealings with Kotan reached the Lieutenant-Governor of the Punjab from the Maharaja of Kashmir. A letter from Johnson to the Superintendent of the GTS explaining why he was off to Kotan arrived soon after. But the first mistake had been made. As in the case of Moorcroft's dealings with the Ladakhis, it was regrettable when news of such ventures reached the government through a third party. They looked stupid not knowing the movements of their own people and were inclined to issue a harsh repudiation. In Johnson's case the GTS took the first brunt. The Superintendent was reminded that his officers had no right to cross the frontier without government's permission. He replied claiming that Johnson had acted on his own initiative, and then duly censured him. But he also entered a strong plea in his favour. No man was more conscientious in his work or more successful in his dealings with native dignitaries. He would not have gone without first assuring himself that he was welcome; the dangers he was likely to encounter were more physical than political. The government hoped the Superintendent was right, and decided to postpone all further action until Johnson returned and his report had been submitted.

This was ready by the following April. As soon as it was published the geographical world rose in Johnson's defence. In London, Sir Roderick Murchison of the Royal Geographical Society declared that he had never read a paper that better exemplified 'the character of a true, bold and scientific manager of an expedition' (and this just a few months after Sir Samuel Baker, for his explorations up the Nile, had shared with Montgomerie the Society's honours for 1865). Lord Strangford seconded him, calling it 'one of the most important papers that had ever been read before the Society'. All roundly condemned the government's treatment of Johnson and, by inference, the cautious isolationist policy of the then Viceroy. In Calcutta, Colonel Walker, the GTS Superintendent, in words that he was soon to regret, told the Asiatic Society that Johnson's paper was 'the most valuable contribution to the geography of Central Asia that has been made for several years by anybody in India'.

The government, too, were pleasantly surprised by the report.

Johnson's political and commercial findings were every bit as important as his geographical labours. For nearly ten years there had been rumours reaching Leh of momentous goings-on beyond the mountains. Johnson now confirmed them. Chinese Turkestan was no longer Chinese. The predominantly Mohammedan population had massacred their Chinese overlords and the whole country was now in a disturbed and vulnerable state. Kotan itself had reverted to the status of an independent city-state and was ruled by an ill-tempered but apparently friendly octogenarian. Fearing for his hard won and tenuous independence, he had entertained Johnson in the hope of getting British assistance and support. The danger was all too evident in the affairs of Yarkand where an invading army from Khokand waited at the gates while inside the city the recently liberated population fought amongst themselves. Johnson thought a consignment of arms and a few native sepoys to act as instructors would stabilise matters in Kotan, but neither to the octogenarian nor to the factions in Yarkand did he make any firm commitment. In the government's view this was greatly to his credit.

On the commercial front Johnson painted the picture of a populous land, rich in minerals, that had suddenly been deprived of its one, and almost its only, trading partner. The Chinese had gone and with them the market for Kotan's gold, her jade and her skins. Desperately missed too was the compressed tea which had been imported from China; any country able to make good the deficiency was sure of a warm welcome. And who better than British India? For though Johnson's outward route over the Kun Lun was unthinkable for trading purposes, he confirmed the existence of a road 'suitable for wheeled carriages' from Rudok to Kotan. This was the same that Moorcroft had heard tell of and which Thomson had listed as the third of his routes into Eastern Turkestan. There was said to be grazing and fuel at every stage and only the Tibetans to be bribed before throwing it open to Indian tea caravans.

In subsequent years many lives were risked, and some even lost, looking for this supposed highway of commerce. Johnson's optimism also seems to have ignored the little matter of Tibet still being in Chinese hands. Neither they nor the Tibetans were any more disposed towards new trading patterns than they had been in 1847. But the one note of caution that he did sound was a warning more calculated to rouse the authorities in India. In trade, as in politics, Eastern Turkestan stood wide open. And the Russians were already stepping into the vacuum. He suspected that the invaders from Khokand who were now besieging Yarkand were the precursors of direct Russian intervention. He met a Jew in Kotan who admitted to being an agent of the Russian government and he reported that Russian caravans were already regularly penetrating as far as Kotan.

Sir John Lawrence, the Viceroy and brother of Sir Henry, conceded that Johnson had made the most of his opportunity. He should not have crossed the frontier but he had already been reprimanded for this and, since he had done so, it was 'satisfactory' that he had acted so creditably. He was prepared to pay Johnson's expenses and take no further action. Another Viceroy might have offered him promotion, a reward or at least official congratulations. But not Lawrence. 'Masterly Inactivity' was how his foreign policy was usually characterised. Many questioned the 'masterly', few the 'inactivity'. He was not interested in Central Asia and would not willingly condone, let alone encourage, transfrontier exploits.

This was no good to Johnson. He was the kind of man who threw himself wholeheartedly into everything. He loved nothing more than a *tamasha*, a handy word that can mean any kind of excitement from a party to a brawl. In this case it was the latter. Johnson went to see Lawrence. Burning with righteous indignation he stressed his long record of service, cited the endless reports in which he had been commended and showed how four times he had been unfairly passed over. Next he contended that his instructions for 1865 clearly implied that he was expected to cross the frontier. Thirdly, and this was entirely new, he declared that he had not gone to Kotan of his own free will. On reaching the Karakash river he had found 200 men lying in wait for him. They had compelled him to go to Kotan. He did not claim that he went reluctantly or that he was not already flirting with the idea. But the way in which in his first narrative he withheld any mention of Kotan till this stage in his journey does suggest that there was some important development here. As we will see, the government at any rate were prepared to accept this new version.

A lot more followed. The reason he had waited till now to reveal the true nature of his visit was because previously he had been trusting to the government's voting him a substantial reward for his initiative. With this out of the question, his only hope of liquidating the heavy debts he had incurred when buying his release from the grasping officials in Kotan lay in his telling the full story and asking the government to make a compassionate settlement. The amount in question was £1,600. He reckoned the value of the surveying he had done en route at more than five times that, besides which he claimed compensation for 'the enlargement of his heart' caused by continuous exposure to the effects of high altitude. And so on.

Lawrence told him to put it all in writing. Within four days of his doing so Colonel Walker, the Superintendent of the GTS, hit back. This time there was to be no standing up for his subordinate. He had done his best for Johnson, but now the man was clearly out to make trouble and to embarrass the service. The gloves came off and the slanging match that went on well into 1867 does little credit to either party. Distasteful though it was, Walker felt bound to draw the government's attention to Johnson's having neither 'the benefit of a liberal education' nor.the ability 'to rise above the disadvantages of his position'. His report had had to be entirely rewritten, his map recast and his observations re-reduced. None in their original state was fit for publication. Johnson denied all this. The errors in his survey had crept in at the Surveyor-General's office. Walker was now trying to denigrate his journey and to disclaim all responsibility. And he did so because he now realised that it was not to be a case for congratulation. But in the beginning, hoping to cream off some of the expected credit, he had been happy enough to defend Johnson's action. Why else had he written of the journey in such glowing terms?

Two points of more substance came out. One was that Johnson, before leaving his home in Mussoorie in 1865, had raised a considerable sum of money as if in expectation of heavy expenses in the mountains. The other was that by now, 1867, he had accepted a post with the Kashmir government on three times the salary he had been receiving with the GTS. Combined, these two bits of evidence cast a sinister light over the whole affair. It looked as if he could have planned on going to Kotan as early as 1864 when he put Montgomerie up to recommending the last visit to Ladakh. Had he, all along, been in collusion with the Kashmir government? The Maharaja was known to harbour designs on the cities across the mountains. His father's expansionist policies were not forgotten. There was the advance garrison at Shahidulla which, in 1864, had led Johnson to claim that the Kashmir frontier lay some hundred miles further north than most maps showed it. And in 1865, like a runner breasting the tape, Johnson again pushed it forward, this time to the Kun Lun peaks north of the Karakash river. Even if not at the time in collusion with

the Kashmir government, he could have been angling for some sort
of subsequent recognition from them.

On the other hand, his activities could all be interpreted as a loyal,
if over-zealous and misplaced, attempt to bring the frontier of British
India nearer Eastern Turkestan and thus involve it in the affairs of
Yarkand and Kotan. His report was not uncritical of the Kashmir
authorities and his commercial recommendations were clearly of advantage only to the British. He had always been well liked by the
Kashmiris and the Ladakhis and, heaven knows, he had had ample
provocation to seek employment outside the Survey.

In 1872, after five years of obscurity, Johnson emerged as the
Maharaja's wazir, or governor, of Ladakh. His predecessor had also
been an Englishman but it was still a considerable achievement. His
rule was distinguished by 'all kinds of *nachs* and *tamashas*', but he
ruled fairly and openly and was well loved. Moorcroft would surely
have approved. He worked for the improvement of cultivation and
trade, and dispensed justice with the speed and directness that a
simple people like the Ladakhis appreciated. He also maintained
excellent relations with the British government and continued to
show a great interest in the opening of the road to Yarkand. Partly in
recognition of this, and on the commendation of his old friend Montgomerie, the Royal Geographical Society presented him with a gold
watch in 1875. In the same year he made his one and only visit to
England. Eight years later he was removed from office and died soon
after. He had probably been poisoned. It was one of the occupational
hazards of working in the intrigue-ridden atmosphere of the Kashmir
court and had no apparent bearing on the Kotan affair.

Godwin-Austen wrote a generous obituary of him. He seems to
have taken the view, which in the end is probably the right one,
that the political undertones of Johnson's journey to Kotan were
incidental. He was not, at bottom, an agent for anyone but just
a very disappointed careerist. The government too seems to have
taken this view. They accepted the later version of his story and even
agreed to refund the £1,600 spent on bribes to secure his release. As
for the money he had raised in Mussoorie, it was accepted that this
was just a security measure necessary because, in 1865, there were no
other GTS personnel in Ladakh and he could therefore not afford to
run out of funds.

This all seems to agree with what can be learnt of his character. He
was not as ill-educated or incapable as Walker tried to make out. If

anything he was too able. But to someone with as undistinguished a background as Johnson's such ability only brought frustration. If it had been Godwin-Austen who had gone to Kotan, a political motive might have to be found. But Johnson had reason enough of his own. He had been passed over too often. His career was in the doldrums and he grabbed at the one opportunity which, for better or for worse, might lift it out of them. It was a desperate gamble but, to the ever zestful Johnson, all the more appealing for that.

12. In Contradistinction

In the late 1860s and early 1870s the story of the penetration of the Western Himalayas suddenly changes character. The tempo increases. The various themes of the Moorcroft overture, developed by strategists like Burnes, scientists like Jacquemont and Thomson and doubtful 'politicals' like Vigne and Johnson, at last coalesce. The crescendo of the Kashmir Survey ushers in a grand finale of which the opening of relations with Eastern Turkestan is the object and climax. The brief heyday of exploration in the Western Himalayas has been reached. Between 1868 and 1875 no corner of the unknown aroused greater interest or was tackled with more energy. It perhaps lacked some of the popular appeal of African exploration; it was less of a free-for-all and, where possible, progress was still shrouded in secrecy. But to those in the know there was no question of its significance. 'The great mountain backbone to the north-west of our Indian Empire and Eastern Turkestan' was where, according to the president of the Royal Geographical Society, all the main geographical advances were being made. The journals of the period are thick with contributions from travellers in the region. Even mass market publications like *Macmillan's Magazine* and the *Illustrated London News* carried long stories about the bazaars of Yarkand and the jade mines of the Kun Lun. The explorers themselves reflect some of this heightened interest. They are sponsored by a geographical society, reporting to a newspaper or writing a bestseller about their travels. They are a different type of man from Moorcroft, Vigne and co., narrower in their interests, more dogmatic about their discoveries and more competitive about them. Less attractive, certainly, but also more dramatic.

An unmapped region is a great attraction to the explorer but, seemingly, a partially mapped one is even more of a draw. The Kashmir Survey produced elegant maps of Ladakh, Baltistan and all the country to the south. But to the north they showed an inviting blank. The detailed contours and shading abruptly ceased, there was a narrow limbo of Kun Lun peaks and dotted rivers, then all was white, irresistible space. The men to whom it appealed set themselves specific targets. There were to be no more of those rambling aimless journeys like the travels of Moorcroft, Gardiner and Thomson. The new explorers had their sights firmly fixed on one or more of the few remaining unknowns; there was the chance of unravelling the hydrography of the Pamirs, begun by Wood but neglected ever since, or that of uniting a survey carried up from the GTS of India with that of the Russian survey department which now reached the Tian Shan. There was the question of the extent of the Kun Lun and of how rivers, draining north from the Karakorams, broke through this further barrier. And, of course, there were the twin cities of Yarkand and Kashgar. Johnson had notched up Kotan, but Yarkand and Kashgar had yet to be visited by someone who would live to tell the tale. Now, in the late 1860s, with the Chinese gone and, with them, the policy which had kept the whole country firmly closed to foreigners, a start could be made with a determined bid to reach these fabled cities.

So at least it seemed to Robert Shaw, a tea-planter from Kangra. With a caravan of merchandise and high hopes of 'opening up Central Asia', he set off from Leh on September 20th 1868. And so too it seemed to George Hayward, a professional explorer from England, who arrived in Leh the following evening. It was pure coincidence that both men were tackling the same journey in the same season, but from now on there was to be precious little coincidence in their activities. Shaw had spent two months in Leh organising his caravan and preparing the ground ahead. Hayward, finding the trail still warm, was in and out of the place in eight days. Following hard on Shaw's heels, he was within striking distance before they reached the Karakorams.

Shaw was taking things easy. For want of carriage he had left half his goods to be sent on from Leh; a slight delay might enable them to catch up. It would also give the man he had sent ahead more time to predispose the Yarkand authorities to his visit. So far as he knew he was the only one in the field. Various attempts had been made to dissuade him from going, most notably by Douglas Forsyth, a Commissioner in the Punjab who had made Central Asian affairs his speciality. In fact Forsyth was the man who had originally given Shaw the idea of undertaking the journey. He was also his most likely rival; no one more deserved the honour of opening contacts with Yarkand. But equally, so long as the cautious Lawrence was Viceroy and so long as Forsyth remained a servant of the Crown, he had no hope of being allowed to. When, in Leh, he made a final bid to warn Shaw off, the latter paid no heed; he put it down to sour grapes. There was also a Mr. Thorp who asked if he might accompany him. He was quickly disillusioned. As for the unknown Hayward, his approach was no more than a rumour. Shaw found it hard to believe that Forsyth and the Punjab authorities could have forgotten to tell him that he had a serious rival, but, just in case, he dashed off a sharp note to the interloper. If there was any truth in the rumour, Hayward was to change his plans immediately. He, Shaw, had been preparing for this journey for years; if some bungling globetrotter were now to upset the delicate state of his negotiations with the Yarkand authorities it would foul the whole future of Indo-Turkestan relations.

Nineteen days out of Leh, Shaw was in the Changchenmo valley hunting wild yak. On the way back to camp he spotted six gigantic sheep of the Ovis Ammon variety. Fine males they were, almost as big as the Marco Polo sheep of the Pamirs and, even in those days, the rarest of Himalayan trophies. A long wait followed, then an arduous stalk. He was just getting within range when the beasts suddenly bolted. Stark against the snow, in full view of his quarry stood the culprit, a stranger. In a foul temper he bore down on the man. It was not Hayward, but it was Hayward's messenger—an unfortunate moment to arrive. Nothing in their subsequent dealings led Shaw to regret the rage in which he first learnt that he had a companion.

The two men met a few days later. They dined together crouched over Hayward's campfire. It was probably a modest meal. Hayward was travelling light, in native disguise and without even the luxury of a tent. Perhaps Shaw contributed a course from his own more elaborate commissariat. A contemporary traveller in Ladakh recommends 'cubes of soupe a l'ognon au gras from Chollet et Cie of Paris, tins of hotch-potch, tins of half boiled bacon and tins of salmon for breakfast'. Shaw might also have provided his collapsible table and chairs. Together with a cane commode, collapsible bed and a tin bath, these were regarded as essential camp furniture. There are pages of such advice in every nineteenth century account of Kashmir. Camped in a place like the Changchenmo, Shaw and Hayward must have recalled them with a bitter feeling of their irrelevance. This valley is as bleak a spot as any south of the Karakorams. The ground is stones, beyond that rock, beyond that mountains. Nothing else. The only colours are the blue of the sky and the searing yellows, browns and purples of the rocks. All that moves is the biting wind. It is as dead as the moon. Yet, for Shaw and Hayward, ahead lay worse. Here the famished ponies could tear at the few widely spaced blades of desiccated grass and the travellers could make from some carefully exhumed roots a spluttering fire such as they now crouched over. In the Aksai Chin they would remember these as luxuries.

Already, in October and at a modest 16,000 feet, it was bitterly cold. On the pass into the valley Hayward had measured twenty-nine degrees of frost. Shaw's stock of claret was freezing in the bottles and bursting them—not a total disaster; the glass could still be knocked off and the contents duly passed round, each man chipping a piece into his tumbler and quietly sucking it. Thus engaged, the two men spoke their minds, and in due course reached an understanding. First Hayward would forgo his disguise. He was dressed as a Pathan and travelling in suitably spartan style. The idea had surely come from Gardiner, now roaming the bazaars of Srinagar and far from reluctant about imparting the gems of his extraordinary life to impressionable young travellers. Times, however, had changed since his day. Adventurers of doubtful origin were now regarded with intense suspicion. Moreover Hayward's experience, though it seems to have included a spell on the Afghan frontier, was not up to the disguise. Shaw rightly felt that if the first Yarkandis they met saw through it, they would both be turned back. If it held good till they reached Yarkand, the many Pathans there would soon suspect his faltering Pushtu and then their very lives would be in danger.

Secondly, Hayward was to give Shaw ten days' start. He was to mark time in the Changchenmo while Shaw sped on to the frontier and made contact with the first Yarkandi outpost. Shaw argued that if they arrived simultaneously the Yarkandis were bound to get suspicious; assuming that his agent had done his job, they would be expecting only one Englishman. The arrival of two would be sufficient excuse for refusing entry to either. On the other hand, and this was the third point, if all went well, Shaw was to do his best to warn the Yarkandis of Hayward's approach and to persuade them that he too should be admitted.

With polite wishes for a rendezvous in the palaces of Yarkand they parted. It was their last meeting for eight months. Throughout the whole of their visit to Turkestan they would never speak again. They would be the only Europeans in a vast and strange land, often they would be in fear for their lives, sometimes they would be actually within earshot of each other, yet, other than a few bitter notes, they would hold no communication. Each advanced a different explanation for this, but the conclusion must be that basically they resented one another. It is the first and only instance of the acrimony which is so notorious a feature of African exploration showing itself in the Himalayas.

There was, of course, a great deal at stake. For years Yarkand had been reckoned the juiciest plum awaiting the Himalayan traveller. It was the largest and richest of the cities of Eastern Turkestan, it was surrounded with that aura of notoriety so vividly evoked by Burnes and, in 1868, its very position was still a matter of conjecture; estimates varied by as much as two hundred miles. How much of its glamour had survived the overthrow of the Chinese was one of the many questions to be answered but Shaw, a diligent and dedicated sort of fellow, was not much exercised by this. He preferred to restrict his vision to the commercial potential of the city. He saw it as the 'Eldorado of Asia'; his job, remember, was growing tea. At school at Marlborough he had collapsed during the entrance examination for Sandhurst. He still came out top but the long illness that followed —it was diagnosed as rheumatic fever—put paid to his military ambitions. A quiet, unexciting life free from physical and mental strain was recommended. He went up to Cambridge and then out to India where the gentle foothills climate of Kangra was expected to suit his condition. Tea is still grown in Kangra though the plantations are nothing like as neat or extensive as those in the Eastern Himalayas. For one thing, it is much too far from any Indian seaport. But it might well have turned out to be quite as big business as Darjeeling or Assam. For, as Moorcroft had conjectured and as Shaw now passionately preached, Kangra was the nearest tea-growing area to the great tea-drinking population of Central Asia. And if the caravans from China were no longer reaching the markets of Turkestan, then now was the time for the caravans from India to take over.

To this extent Johnson's report on Kotan had not gone unheeded. Lawrence and his advisers in Calcutta might not be prepared to follow up the changing state of affairs beyond the mountains but in the Punjab, now a fully fledged province of British India, they were abuzz with the possibility of opening relations with Eastern Turkestan. As early as 1861, the Lieutenant-Governor of the Punjab had commissioned a report on the trade and resources of the countries beyond the frontier. Two years later the first of several attempts was made to get the Maharaja of Kashmir to reduce the exhorbitant tariffs levied on trade to and from Yarkand through Leh. In 1866 the Lieutenant-Governor was all for sending Johnson back to Kotan to continue his good work or, failing that, to let Forsyth go. The latter was then Commissioner for an area which included Kangra, Kulu and Lahul, all of which stood to benefit greatly by the trade.

Neither then, nor in the following two years, would Lawrence hear of Forsyth's undertaking such a mission but the persistent Commissioner continued to make the running and, in 1867, scored two notable successes. On his strong recommendation, Lawrence agreed to the posting of a British representative in Leh. Another of Moorcroft's dreams was coming true. The agent's job would be to enquire further into the Maharaja's supposed stranglehold on the existing trade; to soften the pill for the Kashmir government, the man chosen was a doctor, Henry Cayley. Forsyth's other success was the inauguration of an annual trade fair at Palampur, only a few miles from Kangra, to which all those engaged in the existing trade with Yarkand were invited. Not many Yarkandis ever reached Palampur. It was too far for them to go if they wanted to return across the mountains in the same season. But it did provide a useful rallying point for the Turkestan lobby in India. There, in November 1867, Forsyth announced to the assembled company that the Leh agency was to be 'permanent, at all events for some time to come'.

This 'Delphic announcement'* was jumping the gun as far as Lawrence was concerned but, in the light of Cayley's successful first year, it was a safe prediction. Trade had increased dramatically, and the agent was convinced that, if an easier route could be found avoiding the Karakoram passes, there was no limit to its possibilities. The classic route of the five great passes was direct enough, but it was never open much before June and was too dangerous to invite exploitation. The loss of carriage beasts, evidenced by that grizzly trail of bones, was reason enough. For every laden pony the wise merchant took two spares; and this in spite of the fact that for at least three of the five passes the merchandise had to be transferred to hired yaks.

Early in 1868 Cayley reconnoitred a route further east which was roughly that followed by Johnson on his outward journey to the

* The phrase is from G. J. Alder's *British India's Northern Frontier 1865–95*, than which there is no better analysis of British policy towards Eastern Turkestan.

Karakash river. It was not a way round the mountains as its supporters later contended. The Chang La took the place of the Khardung pass, the Marsimik of the Sasser, the Changlung of the Karakoram and so on. If anything, the new passes were higher. So too,
considerably, was the intervening terrain. But it was this that made
the passes less formidable. The mountains were not being circumvented but the deep, glacier-choked bends of the Shyok were.

Cayley reported enthusiastically on this new route. It had another
advantage in that its point of departure in the Changchenmo valley
could be as easily reached from the British provinces of Kulu and
Lahul as from Leh. In fact, trade from British India could flow
through Kulu via the Changchenmo route to Yarkand, completely
by-passing the Maharaja's customs officials in Leh. This idea was
so attractive that, in 1870, a special treaty would be extracted from
the Maharaja, which would elevate this route to the status of a 'free
highway', to be dotted with supply depots and rest houses and to be
jointly supervised by a British and a Kashmir official.

In 1868 Shaw, as he thankfully drew ahead of Hayward and felt his
way forward from the Changchenmo valley, had only Cayley's first
year's reconnaissance to go by. This indicated that his next chance of
obtaining food and grazing and of seeing another human being lay
on the Karakash river, two hundred miles to the north. In between
lay the dreaded Lingzi-Thang and Aksai Chin. These plateaux with
their resounding names are usually described as deserts or plains.
Photographs of them show an utterly featureless expanse of pebbles
as flat as a dead calm sea. A group of tents and dejected horses adds
no scale. They stand without context or location; they could as well
be ten miles further back. In the hazeless atmosphere there is no
perspective. Seemingly beyond the horizon, like faint relics of an
earlier exposure on the same frame, lie low, unconvincing hills. They
serve only to emphasise the dreary flatness of the scene. Yet this is
still a part of the Western Himalayas. The hills are spurs of the Kun
Lun and Karakorams, and the plains themselves are as high as the
cruising altitude of a short-haul jet. To this day, only a handful of
Europeans have ever crossed these stony wastes. Shaw, sadly, describes them without feeling. It was too cold to write, too cold even
for his frozen fingers to pull the trigger on the rare antelope or wild
yak. Fuel was so scarce that there was not enough to thaw snow for
the thirsty ponies. And for days on end there was no grazing. Even
his yaks began to collapse with exhaustion.

It is one of the mysteries of exploration in the region how anyone can have enthusiastically recommended such a route for trading purposes. Between the Changchenmo and the Karakash river the average altitude is 17,000 feet, the cold wind indescribable and the traveller's requisites of fuel, water, shelter and grazing, non-existent. Two years later Forsyth recognised it for what it was, a death-trap. He championed the Changchenmo route only as long as he had no experience of it. But those like Shaw, Hayward, Cayley and Johnson who actually travelled it, had no such excuse. One can see their indifference to the difficulties as a measure of their personal stamina, of their enthusiasm for a direct approach from India to Eastern Turkestan and of their assessment of the dangers of the classic route. But still one would have thought that its very dreariness would have depressed their ardour.

On November 7th, ten weeks after leaving the last inhabited spot in Ladakh, Shaw scrambled over a spur in the Karakash valley and spied an encampment of Kirghiz shepherds. Smoke rose from their black dome-shaped tents and a man in a long tunic and boots was tending his yaks and horses. 'I can't describe', he wrote, 'my sensation at beholding this novel scene. Now at length my dreams of Toorks and Kirghiz were realised and I was coming into contact with tribes and nations hitherto entirely cut off from intercourse with Europeans.'

This is typical Shaw. In education he was a cut above the average tea planter, but he always wrote in a consciously popular style—one which was later adopted by his nephew, Francis Younghusband. His idea was to attract the widest possible interest in his travels and so rally support for the notion of trade with Eastern Turkestan. In the process geography suffered. He described the Indus as rising in Lake Manasarowar, an idea to which Moorcroft had put paid half a century earlier. He managed to confuse Wood's Lake Sir-i-kol with the Sarikol region just west of Yarkand, and he greatly oversimplified the whole mountain structure by referring to it as just one range.

A more pardonable aspect of his treatment was the attempt to romanticise, first about the peoples of Eastern Turkestan and then about the place. His first meeting with Yarkandi traders had taken place in Leh. Beside the cringing Indians and the buffooning Ladakh-is, he had immediately recognised in the 'Toorks' men like himself. They were tall and dignified and fair as Englishmen. They looked you straight in the face, relished a hearty joke and were above all 'good fellows'. These notions were confirmed when he at last reached Shahidulla; the fort, at the junction of the Karakash river with the main Karakoram route, had been abandoned by the Maharaja in the previous year—he had no more right to it than I do, commented Shaw—and reoccupied by the Yarkandis as their southernmost outpost. They were expecting Shaw and he was well received. He was housed in the best room and given a foretaste of the hospitality in store. The only problem was conversation. He spoke a little Persian, but even that language, the lingua franca of educated Asiatics, was rarely heard in Eastern Turkestan. Instead, communication was at first carried on by signs, amidst a lot of back-slapping and digging in the ribs. 'They are just like public schoolboys, of boisterous spirits but perfectly well-bred.' And Shaw was flattered that they continued to distinguish between him—'they call me a good fellow'—and his Indian servants whom 'they treated as animals of some sort, monkeys for instance'.

However, beneath all the camaraderie, two disquieting suspicions arose in his mind. One was that he was their prisoner. No suggestion of this was permitted to mar good relations. Shaw was anxious not to put matters to the test and so were the Yarkandis who assured him that their close attentions were simply because of the honour in which he was held. Naturally he was under observation; everything depended on making a good impression and not arousing their understandable suspicions. But then why, if he was such a distinguished visitor, was he being detained so long at Shahidulla? Daily messengers streamed back and forth across the Kun Lun to Yarkand but still there was no sign of his being allowed to proceed.

And every day mattered. 'The thorn in my flesh', 'my chief source of anxiety' and 'the incubus that constantly weighs upon me' was Hayward and his imminent arrival. Ten days they had agreed on and, sure enough, on November 19th Hayward's approach was reported. Shaw had managed to hint to his hosts that the arrival of another Englishman was possible. But he had not felt his own position strong enough to urge Hayward's case. On the contrary, he had mentioned him only to safeguard himself and then in terms that were apologetic if not defamatory. In one account he claims that Hayward's arrival upset matters just at the point when he was about to be allowed to proceed. This is demonstrably untrue. A communication from Yarkand refusing him entry had arrived a day or two before Hayward.

His plea against this order, which might have been influenced by Hayward's appearance, was actually successful.

It may be that Hayward too broke his side of that agreement made over dinner in the Changchenmo. For on arrival, he threw Shaw into a rage by announcing that he was in Shaw's employ. This seems out of character on the part of the unbending Hawyard but, if true, it would certainly have jeopardised Shaw's chances. According to the latter, the damaging statement was only suppressed by a lucky coincidence; a chain of interpreters had now been set up—it went from English to Hindustani to Tibetan and so to the Turki of the Yarkand-is—and it started with one of Shaw's servants who, in his master's interests, tactfully omitted it.

Hayward, as if in quarantine, was housed some distance from the fort. Shaw had the satisfaction of seeing most of the guard moved over there. Puzzled as to how things stood, Hayward repeatedly tried to arrange a meeting, but Shaw refused lest he compromise himself with his new friends. They could communicate secretly through their servants but the only advice Hayward got was to go away. Shaw's position was doubtful; Hayward's, he claimed, hopeless.

And so it must have seemed when a few days later Shaw, dressed in Turki style with a turban, cloak and high boots, was seen to ride out north towards Yarkand. Hayward remained stuck in Shahidulla. In despair he thought of returning to Leh but the passes thence to Kulu or Kashmir would be closed by the time he reached them and he had no wish for a dreary winter in Ladakh. Nor of giving Shaw the satisfaction of knowing he had taken his advice. Hayward was a man of controversial character, but all were agreed on his inexhaustible energy. Anything like confinement was anathema to him and, typically, the day after Shaw rode out of Shahidulla, he did too. He gave the slip to his guards and made off west into the mountains on an excursion of which, as a feat of exploration and endeavour, it would be hard to find the equal.

In regard to Eastern Turkestan, Hayward's motivation was altogether different from Shaw's. As a young subaltern lately of Her Majesty's 79th Regiment,* the Cameron Highlanders, he had presented himself to Sir Henry Rawlinson in London as being 'desirous of active employment . . . on any exploratory expedition'. The doyen of Asian geographers and Vice-President of the Royal Geographical

---

* Not, apparently, the 72nd Regiment, as Rawlinson would have it.

Society suggested the cities of Eastern Turkestan and the Pamirs, and he drew up a memorandum for Hayward's guidance. Unfortunately this is lost, but whatever it said it is clear that Hayward interpreted his mission as primarily one to the Pamirs. He was intrigued by the question, reopened more than once since Wood's day, of the source of the Oxus and of what he calls 'the lake system of the region'. No one had actually repeated Wood's feat but there were native accounts of other important Oxus tributaries and other lakes on the Pamirs. The most notable of these was the vast Lake Karakul. Hayward saw himself emulating the discoveries of Speke and Baker, and was confident that the true source of the Oxus lay in this lake. But Yarkand and Kashgar never feature more prominently in his plans than as possible springboards from which 'to bag the Bam-i-Dunya'.

The whole subject of Hayward's emergence as an explorer is puzzling. He had some experience of travel, he was a fair draughtsman and he could use survey instruments. But beyond that we hear of no other qualifications. He was anxious to set off for India immediately, yet his funds were negligible till the Royal Geographical Society sponsored him with £300. Given that in the heyday of exploration they were more casual about these things, it still seems highly improbable that an unknown adventurer could land a prize assignment as simply as Rawlinson makes out. Much more needs to be known of Hayward's previous career before the question can be answered. For instance, his experience of travel seems to have included other forays into the Himalayas. He had probably been to Baltistan and Kashmir.* He may well have already met and learnt much from Gardiner, and he certainly knew Peshawar and the foothills below Chitral. It was for Peshawar that he had made as soon as he reached India, convinced that the best route through the Himalayas lay from there up the Chitral valley to the Oxus, the Pamirs and Turkestan. This was not Rawlinson's idea; he was more excited about Johnson's route from the Changchenmo which, at the time,

* Rawlinson refers to Hayward's having crossed the Hindu Kush on sporting excursions. This is highly unlikely given the attitude of the Afghans in the 1850s and '60s. Probably Rawlinson meant the Great Himalaya north of Kashmir and not the Hindu Kush as we now understand it—the nomenclature of the various mountain systems was still very confused. This would have taken Hayward to Baltistan (Skardu), already a popular region with sportsmen.

he mistakenly imagined to be the 'royal road' via Rudok which Moorcroft had reported. The Chitral route was much closer to the thinking of Burnes and Wood and, above all, Gardiner.

So too, were Hayward's notions of disguise. He was well aware, without the reminders from Shaw, that his credentials as a traveller were likely to arouse intense suspicion in an Asiatic mind. He was not, like Shaw, a merchant nor had he any political or religious standing. Yet traders, envoys and pilgrims were the only recognised classes of traveller. Rather than disguise himself as any of these, he chose to cut the more dashing figure of a Pathan (i.e. Afghan) mercenary—exactly what Gardiner had been during his greatest journey. It is perhaps also worth a note that Gardiner's famous outfit of tartan from turban to toe was said to originate from the Quartermaster's stores in the 79th Regiment, the Cameron Highlanders. That was Hayward's old regiment. Had they exchanged clothes as well as ideas, or is this simply a coincidence?

Hayward is the only professional explorer to figure in this account. As distinct from the surveyors, the naturalists, the political agents and the men of trade, the classic explorer had a simple brief, to make a name for himself. True, he hoped to further geographical science. This was essential, but it was the means rather than the end. The successful explorer was now revered as a popular hero, in a way that would have seemed as incomprehensible in Moorcroft's day as it does today. For the most part they were difficult men. They exhibited something of the arrogance and showmanship of a screen hero. Look at the photograph of Hayward. Bearded, strung about with sword and shield and resting on a spear as if it were a shepherd's crook, he looks like some wild evangelist. Burnes was always rather self-conscious about his portrait in Bokharan costume. Vigne donned his Balti outfit for the artist with the jaunty glee of an amateur. But Hayward, brooding and indomitable, looks deadly serious.

The outfit is not his Pathan disguise but, judging by the weaponry and the corkscrew markhor horns, that of Yasin where he was to meet his tragic end. The picture was probably taken by George Henderson who in 1870 would accompany Forsyth to Yarkand. He is one of the few who got to know Hayward. They met in Srinagar and spent several nights practising their astronomical techniques together. Hayward struck Henderson as the most dedicated and indefatigable of explorers. His passion for the unknown was infectious and his impetuosity such as almost to invite danger. To give Shaw his due, it can have been no fun having such a man on his tail. When Rawlinson had decided that 'if any Englishman can reach the Pamir Mr. Hayward is the man', he was referring to his protégé's dedication. Others called it madness. Hayward flirted with danger as determinedly as most dodge it. To any companion he was a standing liability. There was a chilly aura of impending disaster about him; it caused other men to keep their distance. We know of no friends or colleagues, and, as one peers into that cluttered photograph at the bony brow knitted into a frown between deep-set eyes, it is not hard to understand why. He looks a most unsettling companion.

Given the choice of two routes, one more dangerous than the other, he naturally chose the former. So it was with the Chitral route to the Pamirs. In terms of the passes involved he and Gardiner were eventually proved right; it was the lowest of all the routes through the mountains. But, in the 1860s, it was also the most lawless. Only the direct intervention of the Lieutenant-Governor of the Punjab had prevented him from following it. Thus, as a second and distinctly soft alternative, he had turned to the Leh–Yarkand route, hoping to penetrate the Pamirs from Eastern Turkestan.

Travelling much faster than Shaw's heavily laden caravan, he had scouted a new route between the Changchenmo and Karakash rivers, and sorted out the course of the latter which Johnson had mysteriously confused with the Yarkand river. This also drained from the Karakorams through the Kun Lun into Eastern Turkestan, and it was by way of completing his survey of the hydrography of the region that he broke out of confinement in Shahidulla and set off west to find the upper reaches of this river.

He was gone for twenty days. In that time he covered on foot three hundred miles over the roughest terrain imaginable. In one continuous march of thirty-six hours he did fifty-five miles. And all this at considerable altitudes, climbing and descending spurs of two of the greatest mountain systems, fording icy rivers and in the below freezing temperatures of early December. Hunted by the soldiers who had been sent after him from Shahidulla and by the robbers who infested the region, he had to douse his camp fire as soon as a meal was cooked. Yet he was still without a tent, and at the source of the Yarkand river he recorded fifty degrees below freezing. Food sufficient for only a week had been taken. He and his porters eked it out till it was finally exhausted. This left just the yak that had carried it. There was no fuel for a fire, but the beast was killed and the famished Ladakhis fell to on the raw carcase. Hayward hesitated; later he admitted that he, too, had joined in.

Eventually, striking the main Karakoram route, he restocked from a passing caravan, met up with the soldiers from Shahidulla and, on learning from them that he had been given permission to proceed to Yarkand, made a final dash over the Suget pass, thirty-three miles in a day, back to starting point.

As a feat of endurance the journey speaks for itself. To Hayward it was a necessary baptism. He went on to Yarkand fully confident that nothing could stop him reaching the Pamirs. He had also made a considerable contribution to geography. He had discovered a new pass over the Kun Lun which, together with his new route from the Changchenmo, made a complete and, he thought, far easier crossing of the mountains. He had found the source and explored the upper reaches of the Yarkand river and he had followed it to where the route from the Mustagh pass, which Godwin-Austen had attempted, joined its banks. Until Younghusband's journey of twenty years later, Hayward was the only authority on the wild gorges and desolate valleys between the Karakorams and the Kun Lun. It was for this excursion, as much as for reaching Eastern Turkestan, that the Royal Geographical Society awarded him a Gold Medal—an indication that people were at last beginning to realise that the mountain complex was, itself, a formidable arena for exploration and not simply a barrier to the unknown lands beyond.

Meanwhile Shaw, happily rid of the thorn in his flesh, had entered Yarkand. Like all the others who had panted to the crests of the ranges between India and Central Asia, he had breasted the Sanju pass in a fever of excitement. Like them, he had peered hopefully at the northern horizon and like them he had seen nothing in particular. But he was not disappointed.

The first sight was a chaos of lower mountains while far away to the north the eye at last rested on what it sought, a level horizon indistinctly bounding what looked like a distant sea. This was the plain of Eastern Turkestan and that blue haze concealed cities and provinces which, first of my countrymen, I was about to visit.

The first glimpse of Yarkand was less exciting. A long blank mud wall stretched across the flat desert. Pagoda-like structures topped the corners and main gateway and a few leafless poplars rose above it, leaning with the prevailing wind. The only other feature was a gallows-like structure which was as high again as the walls. From a distance it was hard to appreciate the scale, but the walls were in fact forty feet high. A moat encircled them and a good size road was carried round on top. As for the scaffold-like structure, it was precisely that. Hangings were high and frequent in Yarkand.

But more than this was needed to still Shaw's excitement. He had already seen something of the land and its people, and he was convinced that it really was an Eldorado. Explorers are prone to describe their discoveries in glowing terms. As soon as they tread new ground the rose-tinted spectacles are on. The grass looks greener, the air smells sweeter and the people are more romantic. It must also be remembered that for the last three months Shaw had been in the mountains. A cultivated field, a row of shops, a warm hearth and a square meal were all joyous novelties. Added to this, he was being welcomed in no meagre style. 'A swell moghul' accompanied him over the Kun Lun. Even his servants were mounted at state expense and, on arrival at the first village, he was saluted with guns and regaled with an address of welcome from the king. The road had been specially repaired. In the villages it was lined with people and in the countryside lavish picnics awaited him at every stage. These *dasturkhans* were a distinctive feature of Turkestani hospitality. They varied from a humble spread of dried fruits and tea to a veritable cornucopia of local produce. Hayward's first comprised 'two sheep, a dozen fowls, several dozens of eggs, large dishes of grapes, pears, apples, pomegranates, raisins, almonds, melons, several pounds of dried apricots, tea, sugar, sweetmeats, basins of stewed fruit, cream, milk, bread, cakes etc., in abundance'. Shaw mentions that, by the time he reached Yarkand, he had a whole flock of uneaten sheep, his wardrobe was stuffed with gaudy robes of honour—one was given at each meeting with an official—and he had not been allowed to pay for a single thing.

Under the circumstances he looked on his surroundings with a kindly eye and was duly amazed by the fertility of the country and the prosperity of its people. It was like an Asiatic Holland, less bare than some of the French provinces and with villages that reminded him of home. In the farmyards the cocks crowed and the ducks quacked. Orchards gave way to well tended fields and ditches gushed with water beneath fine trees. The country folk were rosy cheeked and cheerful. Market day brought them thronging to the nearest village and nearly everyone rode a horse or a donkey. Compared to

India there was no poverty, no beggars and no squalor. The people 'looked respectable, brisk and intelligent'. In the cities the bazaars were orderly and well stocked. There were bakers, butchers, saddlers, goldsmiths, tailors and even restaurants. Everything, except tea, was reasonably priced and the whole population showed surprising sophistication in their shopping. Here, in short, was no backwoods country awaiting the prospector and the trapper, nor a mouldering civilisation ripe for the archaeologist, but a modern and thriving state, able to supply most of its basic needs yet commercially experienced and traditionally outward looking. It felt a bit like Europe and, as a potential market, it was of European significance.

Now this was all very well. Eastern Turkestan is certainly different from India. It belongs to the tough and restless world of the great continent and not to the gentle, fatalistic ambience of the subcontinent. The horse, not the cow or bullock, is the basis of the traditional economy. Horseflesh is a prized delicacy, horse-drawn carts ply rapidly between cities, and both men and women live all the year round in high riding boots. It gives the whole place a different feel, a sense of bracing activity, and to the people, an air of rugged independence. India lies to the south, but to the north lies Siberia. Tolstoy* was attracted to Eastern Turkestan but Tagore would have hated it.

It is not, however, an Asiatic Holland. Shaw, and to a lesser extent Hayward, was blinded by his own enthusiasm. The local name for the country was then Altyn Shahr, the Land of the Six Cities. This is a good description. Six cities, oases in fact, dotted round the Takla Makan, a great western extension of the Gobi desert. Shaw mentions sandy, uncultivated tracts as if they were narrow bands breaking the monotony of the endless villages and hamlets that he so minutely describes. It is, of course, the other way round. Nine-tenths of the country are uncultivable and the remaining tenth is at the mercy of the shifting desert sands which have buried whole cities in the past.

*　　　*　　　*

Shaw had left Shahidulla happy in the knowledge that he had seen the last of Hayward. In a letter smuggled back to Leh in a sack of flour, he told his sister 'he has not prepared his way as I have' and 'will not be allowed to come on'. He also said that in Shahidulla they

* Tolstoy told Henry Lansdell in 1887 of his interest in Eastern Turkestan, and would have liked to accompany him there.

had been prevented from meeting. This was certainly Hayward's impression, but Shaw later admitted that it was he who had rejected the idea of a meeting. As usual he feared it might compromise him. Arrived in Yarkand, he learnt that Hayward's case was not hopeless. The latter's letter seeking permission to enter the country had been written in English and was still unread. Shaw was asked to translate and noted with surprise that Hayward now claimed to have travelled the eight thousand miles from England for the purpose of trade. Where then was his caravan of merchandise? The Yarkandis were not going to believe this story for a minute. And when news came of Hayward's escape from Shahidulla, he was confident that there was an end to the matter.

He didn't realise that permission for Hayward's onward journey had now been given; he was, in fact, just starting across the Kun Lun. In due course he reached Yarkand, and for a week the two men were lodged within a hundred yards of one another. But no communication took place. In his narrative Shaw only acknowledges his rival's presence in order to take a swipe at him. Hayward had made a fool of himself by sitting before the governor with his legs stretched out 'in defiance of all oriental etiquette'. On January 4th (1869) Shaw was escorted on to the capital, Kashgar. Two months elapsed before Hayward joined him.

With both men safely into Turkestan, their main concern shifted to whether they would ever be allowed to leave. They both knew of Adolph Schlagintweit's fate, and they soon began to realise that entering the country was less than half the battle. To earlier travellers the Chinese policy that rigorously excluded all visitors had seemed unreasonable. But Moorcroft, for one, must have appreciated that it was a good deal more humane than the deceptive overtures of a Murad Beg. The time-honoured custom of the Mohammedan cities of Central Asia was to welcome all comers indiscriminately, but to show great reluctance in allowing them to leave. Not only Hindu traders and Pathan mercenaries had been ensnared in this way. A few Englishmen, Stoddart and Connolly in Bukhara and Wyburd probably in Khiva, had blundered into the trap and never been seen again.

Eastern Turkestan, now under Mohammedan rule, was every bit as dangerous a place. The exclusiveness of Pekin's rule had given way to a reign of terror and treachery which had made the land a byword for anarchy and mindless slaughter. In Kashgar, the besieged Chinese were said to have eaten the rats and the cats, then their own wives and children, before finally surrendering. In Yarkand, the Chinese governor had assembled his family and officials for a final feast, listened to their suggestions for the terms of surrender and then quietly tapped out his pipe on to a prelaid trail of gunpowder that blew the gathering, the fort and Chinese rule to kingdom come. This ushered in a decade of confused power struggles in which, even by the standards of Central Asia, life was cheap in the Land of the Six Cities. Men were of no more account than sheep—and considerably less than horses. 'Emphatically', wrote Shaw, 'every man carried his life in his hands.'

The successful contender who by 1868 was undisputed ruler of an almost reunited land was an outsider, Mohamed Yakub Beg. It was he who commanded the army from Khokand that Johnson had reported outside the walls of Yarkand in 1865. He was an invader rather than a patriot and his rule relied heavily on the Khokandi merchants and soldiers who had always figured prominently in Eastern Turkestan. But regardless of his origins and the dubious means by which he had risen to power, Yakub Beg was soon to be regarded by the British as the hero of the hour. His achievements would be compared to those of Ranjit Singh and he would be hailed as the greatest conqueror in Central Asia since Timur and Baber. For a time there was even talk of his uniting the Islamic states of Central Asia, stemming the tide of Russian advances and extending his rule as far east as the Great Wall. His ambassadors were welcomed in Calcutta, St. Petersberg, Istanbul and London.

Yet by the end of the decade he was dead, his rule was discredited, his achievements dismissed, and the Chinese were back in the cities of Eastern Turkestan for good. Far from moulding history he was now seen as a freak of circumstance, a clumsy opportunist who over-reached himself. His subjects were said to be pleased to see the alien Chinese back again and neither the British not the Russians greatly regretted his departure.

The attitudes of Shaw and Hayward towards their host anticipate this ambivalent treatment. Shaw had his first audience soon after he arrived in Kashgar. He found the king 'friendly and courteous', 'fatherly and affectionate' and 'an awfully plucky leader . . . beloved by his people'. Under his firm but wise rule the country was enjoying unheard of prosperity, the roads were as safe as in England and new public works were being undertaken. Hayward went along with this, calling him 'a man of extraordinary energy, sagacity and ability' who had already accomplished wonders. But at the same time, though enjoying lavish hospitality at the king's expense, both men had their reservations. In Kashgar, Shaw's suspicions that he was more a pampered prisoner than a respected guest were amply confirmed. Except for the occasional official visit, he was not allowed out of his quarters for three months. Night and day he was under close surveillance. His visitors were vetted and his only acquaintances were the guards and spies who attended him. If his observations on the country and its people were wide of the mark this was partly because he saw so little of them; nothing, in fact, beyond the high road to Yarkand and thence to Kashgar. If in vain one looks for news of the spirited ladies of the land, about whom Burnes had heard so much, it is because he was never allowed near the bazaars of the two main cities. For his assessment of Yakub Beg he relied heavily on information gleaned from men who owed everything to the new ruler and were mostly fellow countrymen from Khokand. His descriptions of the tall dignified 'Toorks' are not descriptions of the natives at all but of their Khokandi rulers. He had virtually no contact with the local population.

Occasionally rumours of the true state of things did reach him. His Indian and Ladakhi servants were allowed far greater freedom. They wandered into the bazaars and brought back stories of a very different kind. Yakub Beg's rule was based on a literal interpretation of Islamic law. Anyone not punctuating his day with the proscribed breaks for prayer or dodging attendance at the mosques, any woman going unveiled or man unturbanned, was summarily flogged. For a minor offence mutilation was common. For a second there were the gallows, as prominent in Kashgar as in Yarkand. The 'fatherly ruler' with his austere habits was given to fits of uncontrollable rage in which, with his own hands, he had been known to strangle a subject. One of his greatest achievements—Shaw and others honestly admired it—was the perfecting of a system of secret police. Informants were everywhere and any political divergence meant certain death. Lansdell, the man who suffered so much from the cold on the Suget pass, found in Eastern Turkestan an undreamt of refinement in the field of punishment and torture. He also claimed that the king's orthodoxy was a sham. He relished the suppression of prostitution, destroying whole streets of brothels and murdering their inmates. Yet his private life was not edifying. He had a harem of three hundred, and two of its youngest inmates, mere children, died as a result of his brutalities.

During his long detention Shaw began to give ear to such rumours. It would have been suicide to pursue them but, as the dreary days wore on full of uncertainty and gloomy forebodings, he at last conceded that 'darkness is the rule of the land'. He played along with the boisterous humour of his guards but vented his frustrations on a home-made set of dumbells and confided his worries only to the cats of Kashgar. They seemed to recognise a fellow outcast.

Hayward, still in Yarkand but under the same surveillance, was less resigned. To him, forced detention was like a lingering death. He was still unable to provide a convincing explanation for his presence in the country, and his hopes of reaching the Pamirs were fading fast. Unlike Shaw he found it hard to hide his true feelings. In February he decided once again to put matters to the test and broke out of captivity. According to rumours reaching Shaw, he drew his revolver and set off on a promenade of the bazaars. But troops were immediately deployed round the city and Hayward meekly returned to his lodging. He accepted that escape was impossible and made no further attempts. Judge of his sentiments from a caption on the back of one of his watercolours.

House in the fort, Yarkand.   22nd. Feb. 1869
The house in which they entertain their friends so hospitably in the fort of Yarkand. First enticing them into the country as guests and then confining them like prisoners. Not to destroy the peaceful harmony of the scene, a guard of eight sepoys and a Panjabashi [officer] have been judiciously omitted. This is the way they treat their guests in Turkestan.

At the end of February Hayward was summoned to Kashgar, and at about the same time another visitor from India also arrived there. This man, known as Mirza Shuja, was a native said to be in British employ. Neither Shaw nor Hayward had ever heard of him, but he soon made contact with the former, writing in English to ask if he could borrow a watch. He also asked what day of the month it was; this and the watch were vital to anyone trying to establish his exact position from the stars. Characteristically, Shaw was highly suspicious. The man must be 'a dangerous imposter' and the whole thing some deep-seated plot to implicate him as a spy. His answer was a stony silence; not even the date would he reveal. Hayward might have been a better bet but, perhaps discouraged by Shaw's cold-shouldering, the Mirza does not appear to have approached him.

The whole affair must indeed have been a bitter blow to the Indian. He was, in fact, one of a select group of native surveyors trained by Montgomerie of the GTS to carry out route surveys in the unknown beyond India. These intrepid travellers made their greatest mark in Tibet, but under code names like The Havildar and The Mullah a few operated in the Mohammedan countries further west. The Mirza had come to Kashgar from Kabul following Wood's route up the Oxus and continuing across the Pamirs. He questioned Wood's choice of the Sir-i-kol branch instead of the Sarhad as the source of the river, and furnished the first narrative of a crossing of the Pamirs since Benedict de Goes. All this had taken him well over a year, and it must have been with great excitement that, on arrival in Kashgar, he heard of the presence there of two Englishmen. It was reasonable to expect that at the very least they would smooth his relations with the Kashgar authorities.

March 1869 was, for all three men, the blackest of months. Shaw's promised second meeting with Yakub Beg had still not materialised. He was watched more closely than ever and the air was thick with disturbing rumours. The Mirza was said to be chained to a block of wood like a common criminal. Hayward had had his first audience with Yakub Beg and had been led to understand that there was absolutely no hope of being allowed on to the Pamirs. From the roof of his house he could see the range that bounded them on the east. It was only sixty miles away. To someone who had travelled half way round the world to get there, and whose 'mouth watered at the very name of the Bam-i-Dunya', it was a bitter disappointment. He gave vent to it by telling the king's representative exactly what he thought of their hospitality. At the same time he wrote to Shaw, the first letter since Shahidulla.

Now, if ever, was the moment for the two men to draw together. The cards were on the table. Shaw had no more hope of winning commercial concessions than Hayward did of being allowed to tackle the Pamirs. Their one and only objective was the same, to get out of the country alive. They were also agreed about the duplicity of their captor. Shaw makes what for him, after his extravagant praise of the king, must have been a difficult admission; that Yakub Beg was forcibly detaining them for his own purposes. As usual Hayward was more outspoken. Yakub Beg was 'the greatest rascal in Central Asia'. At their meeting the king had ominously referred to the fate of Stoddart and Connolly in Bokhara—they were confined in a pit full of snakes and scorpions and then executed—and to that of Adolph Schlagintweit who was knifed to death just a mile or two from the gates of Kashgar. Hayward believed that his life and Shaw's were also at stake and he told Shaw so in his letter.

Yakub Beg's treatment of his two captives was certainly alarming. One minute they were being lulled by promises and lavish *dastur-khans*, the next they were being neglected, reprimanded and threatened. And all the time they were a prey to the fears, fed on rumour, which mushroom in the minds of men kept in solitude. On Shaw at least this treatment worked. After three months he was feeding out of the king's hand like a turkey in early December. He had always been the more pliant and obsequious; he justified it by reasoning that therein lay his one chance of safety. Hayward, more alarmist and less receptive to the soft glove, was unimpressed. He recognised that he had no chance of allaying the king's suspicions about why he had ever come to Eastern Turkestan, and increasingly he stood on his dignity as a disinterested and independent British traveller. To Shaw's way of thinking this made him more of a liability than ever. There was no question of their pooling their efforts and the first letter went unanswered.

A second letter reached Shaw via their servants on March 24th. In it Hayward at last gave Shaw a piece of his mind. He wrote from the heart, a bitter and facetious outpouring unlike anything else in his extant correspondence. Shaw, hoping to show the sort of man he had to deal with, included an extract in his book. It is all that survives, but what an eloquent, prophetic and tragic passage.

And now I'll sketch your future for you [wrote Hayward]. You will return to be feasted and fêted, as a lion fresh from Central Asia. You will be employed on a political mission to Eastern Turkestan; you will open out my new trade route with countless caravans; you will become the great 'Soudagar' [merchant] of the age, and drink innumerable bottles of champagne in your bungalow on those charming Lingzi Thang Plains; you will write endless articles for the 'Saturday' and a work on the geology and hydrography of the Pamir plateau; you will win three Victoria Crosses and several K.C.B.s and live happily ever after. In contradistinction to all this, I shall wander about the wilds of Central Asia, still possessed with an insane desire to try the effects of cold steel across my throat; shoot numerous *ovis poli* [Marco Polo sheep] on the Pamir, swim round the Karakul Lake, and finally be sold into slavery by the Moolk-i-Aman or Khan of Chitral.

'These predictions are very singular', thought Shaw in 1870. He could have been referring to the predictions for his own future. He did return safely, he was lionised in England and his next assignment was on a political mission to Eastern Turkestan. But, in 1870, it was Hayward's prediction of his own future which struck Shaw as curious. For already Hayward had tried the effects of cold steel across his throat. His mangled corpse lay under a pile of stones beneath the glaciers of Darkot in the Hindu Kush. The supposed instigator was the 'Moolk-i-Aman or Khan of Chitral'.

13. A Bad Beginning

Reading the accounts left by Shaw and Hayward of their captivity in Kashgar, it is easy to overlook the seriousness of their plight. Their outbursts of indignation and alarm are so sandwiched between long eulogies on the country and its people that they seem out of place and unjustified. This is because both men wrote in the light of subsequent events. What, at the time, was a horrifying reality was soon remembered as no more relevant than an uncomfortable nightmare. For in April 1869 Yakub Beg suddenly changed his tune. Rumours of their impending release were nothing new to the two prisoners, but almost before they dared credit a new wave of these, they were on their way back to Yarkand. The king was not simply washing his hands of them but evincing signs of what Shaw took for genuine affection. There were apologies for the long delay, promises of commercial co-operation and fond farewells. It was even suggested that an envoy from Kashgar might accompany them to India. In Yarkand they waited for the opening of the passes back to Leh, and left on May 30th. At about the same time the Mirza was released in Kashgar.

It could be that Shaw's compliance, or Hayward's obduracy, had somehow paid off. More plausibly, Yakub Beg's change of heart had to do with *realpolitik*. The departure of the Chinese had made Eastern Turkestan, like the Khanates of Western Turkestan, fair game in the gradual Russian absorption of Central Asia. And ironically, it was to the Russians that Shaw and Hayward owed their safety.

The Great Game is usually divided into two distinct phases, the first being more or less coterminous with the mercurial career of Alexander Burnes, and the second beginning quarter of a century later in the late 1860s. After the disastrous British intervention in Afghanistan, and a simultaneous and equally abortive Russian expedition against Khiva, the Tsar's designs on Central Asia were for a time viewed by the British in India with more complacency. Men like Burnes and Moorcroft were written off as dangerous alarmists so long as Russian expansion was seen to be directed not towards Kabul but Constantinople. The Crimean War of 1854–56, far from intensifying Anglo-Russian rivalry in Turkestan, seemed to prove the point. Turkey and perhaps Persia were thought to be the Russian priorities, but not India. This was quite correct, but it did not mean that St. Petersberg had forgotten about Central Asia. On the contrary. While the Indian government was busy with the annexation of Sind and the Punjab and the implications of Kashmir's feudatory status, the Russians were pushing quietly south to the Aral Sea and then up the Jaxartes towards Khokand. Simultaneously, another line of advance was opened from Siberia south towards the Tian Shan. There was a slight lull during the Crimean War but the Indian Mutiny a year later renewed Russian interest in the subcontinent; from now on it would be a premise of all Russian thinking about India that the British Raj would be overthrown from within as soon as they were near enough to foment trouble and afford sanctuary. Under this new impetus, the advance south continued. In the early 1860s the gap between the two earlier lines of advance was filled in and a fort was erected on the Naryn river only four marches north of Kashgar. So much for the groundwork. The headline news, which heralded the second phase of the Great Game, soon followed. In 1865 they took Tashkent, in 1866 Khodzhent and in 1868 Samarkand fell. Of the three Central Asian Khanates, Bukhara and Khokand were now at the mercy of the Russians and an expedition was already being prepared to march again across the deserts to Khiva.

While the forebodings of Burnes and Moorcroft were in least favour, they were actually coming true. The British failure to take up the gauntlet of commercial competition and political influence in Central Asia had enabled the Russians, by the late 1860s, to wipe the board. Instead of two thousand miles separating the two empires, there were now barely five hundred. All that remained were the Pamirs, with Afghanistan and the Turkoman country to the west, and Eastern Turkestan to the east. From a Russian point of view, Afghanistan was too closely aligned with the British and the Pamirs were largely unknown. But Eastern Turkestan was both an obvious and attractive proposition.

No one appreciated this more than Yakub Beg. In 1853 he had himself conducted a valiant defence of one of the Khokandi fortresses against the Russians. He had then blazed a trail into Eastern Turkestan which the Russians might well follow. And in 1867 he had laboured with his own hands to throw up defences against them in the Tian Shan where there had already been frontier clashes. He had no illusions about the strength of the Russian forces and, though he prepared for defence, he also prayed for an accommodation. When, in 1868, a Russian envoy turned up in Kashgar he was therefore treated with respect. He left the city just before Shaw arrived, and he took with him to St. Petersberg a personal emissary from Yakub Beg.

According to reports gathered by Shaw, the Russians were seeking free passage for their troops through Eastern Turkestan, 'promising to turn neither right nor left but to go straight against their "brothers" the English'. Another, more realistic, version had it that they were after commercial privileges including their own premises and a permanent representative in Kashgar. Something similar had been promised in a Sino-Russian treaty of 1860 and in St. Petersberg it was hoped that the new ruler would be prepared to offer the same arrangement. Shaw says that Yakub Beg's reply was a categorical no but, more probably, he was willing to consider the idea if the Russians would guarantee his independence. Hence the despatch of the return envoy, and hence the detention of Shaw and Hayward while news was awaited from Russia.

Early in April 1869 the envoy returned. The Russians were not open to any such deal, and Yakub Beg turned with renewed interest to his two captives. At the time of their arrival it seems that the king held only the haziest notion of what lay to the south of his frontier. He was under the impression that the Maharaja of Kashmir was a great and independent sovereign. Indeed, from well-attested reports that every autumn he ejected the British from his domains, Yakub Beg was inclined to regard the Maharaja as the suzerain and the British as the feudatories. Shaw had eagerly set about disabusing him. He explained the British obsession with hill stations and summer holidays. He pointed out that no one in his right mind, the Maharaja included, spent the winter in the Kashmir valley, and he emphasised that the Maharaja was only suffered to rule for as long as his loyalty was unquestioned. Now, when Yakub Beg was at last prepared to listen, Shaw's propaganda was dramatically rammed home by the news that the Amir of Afghanistan, the most respected of Mohammedan princes, had just journeyed to India to seek arms and moral support. Under the circumstances, Yakub Beg decided that nothing could be lost by opening relations with such a bountiful power.

His envoy was not ready to accompany Shaw and Hayward from Yarkand but they left with the king's protestations of friendship for their *malika* (queen) and Lord Sahib (Viceroy) ringing in their ears. Hastily they revised their opinions of the 'greatest rascal in Central Asia' and congratulated themselves on having opened the way for further contacts. On the outskirts of Yarkand the two travellers came face to face for the first time since that dinner in the Changchenmo. Uneasily they travelled together as far as Shahidulla then, with no regrets at parting, made their separate ways to Leh.

Here more good news awaited them. Just before Yakub Beg had turned his attention towards India, the bureaucrats there had come to regard Eastern Turkestan in an altogether more favourable light. For in January 1869 the unadventurous Lawrence had been succeeded by Disraeli's unexpected nominee, Lord Mayo. A big, bold Irishman full of dash and charm, Mayo survived Gladstone's early return to power and brought to the question of British India's relations with her neighbours a mind wide open to new ideas.

Shaw, the planter, and Hayward, the explorer, had ostensibly no political interests. Lawrence would have put paid to their plans if there had been any likelihood of their engaging in diplomacy. Nevertheless, Hayward was the protégé of Rawlinson, the most vocal and best informed of the London watchdogs of Russian strategy, whilst Shaw was the friend and accomplice of Forsyth, than whom no one in India was more concerned about Central Asian affairs. Both travellers appreciated that where the explorer and the merchant might go, the envoy and the flag might follow. And both now made the most of such political and strategic information as they had gleaned. Official reports were submitted and Shaw soon had the ear of the new Viceroy.

As the Great Game entered its new phase, hegemony in Central Asia was no longer an issue; but the defence of India was. The precise nature of the threat was as ill-defined now as in the 1830s. The views of men like Rawlinson were ambivalent. In one breath they discounted any possibility of a full-scale invasion of India. Banish the thought; it was quite unworthy of any rational observer. Instead, what mattered was that Russia should be denied any further advances, and this was particularly important in the light the 1857 mutiny had shed on the loyalty of the Indian troops. But the old bogey of invasion was not so easily laughed away. In fact, it was more feasible now than ever. In the next breath Rawlinson was re-invoking it with lurid detail; '50,000 Persians, 20,000 Turkoman horse than whom there is no better irregular cavalry in the world', all officered by Russians and stiffened with formations of regular Cossacks, swarming into the Punjab. Apart from anything else this was much the best way of creating another wave of Russophobia which alone seemed to constitute a favourable condition for the formulation of a trans-frontier policy.

At the time—he had delivered this particular memorandum just as Shaw and Hayward were setting off for Yarkand—Rawlinson was more concerned about an attack from the direction of Persia. But he was also intrigued by the finger of Russian progress up the Jaxartes which seemed to be pointing ominously at Eastern Turkestan and Kashmir. The Royal Geographical Society was supposed to be strictly non-political, and it was they who sponsored Hayward. But Rawlinson, as his mentor, cannot have failed to rouse his interest in matters other than the purely scientific. Similarly, when in 1870, with Rawlinson about to be its President, the Society awarded Hayward its Gold Medal, it was not just a fair recognition of his achievements but also a good way of drawing further attention to his conclusions. For Hayward had gone still further than Shaw. He supported the reports of Russian interest in Eastern Turkestan and, from his greater knowledge of the mountains, insisted that a modern army complete with artillery could cross them; his new trade route was also a possible invasion route.

There were, then, good strategic reasons for reconsidering the role of the Karakorams as an impregnable barrier and for seeking an arrangement with Yakub Beg that would bring Eastern Turkestan into the pattern of India's defence. Mayo listened carefully to the reports of Shaw and Hayward. And he decided that Eastern Turkestan might play a role in the north equivalent to that of Afghanistan in the west, that is, be a friendly buffer state, kept strong and reasonably united on a planned diet of British support, both material and moral. To lull the suspicions of the Russians, and of the Liberals now in power at home—the party politics of Westminster were increasingly making themselves felt in India—his new policy was to be inaugurated by purely commercial overtures. This was where Forsyth and Shaw came in, for though they shared the strategic concerns of Rawlinson and Hayward, they also believed passionately in the value of the trade itself.

In late 1869 the envoy from Kashgar, who was to have accompanied

Shaw and Hayward, arrived in India. His main request was that an official representative of the government should return with him. Mayo leapt at the idea and Forsyth, assisted by Shaw and George Henderson, a doctor and naturalist in the tradition of Thomson, was deputed on the first ever official mission to Eastern Turkestan.* Shaw sped back from England where he had spent the winter enjoying the fruits of his labours and drumming up support for the opening of the Yarkand market. He hoped to join the rest of the party before they left Leh in July.

Meanwhile George Hayward too had been living out his 'singular prediction'. His goal was still the Pamirs, but denied both the Chitral and Yarkand routes he was now concentrating on yet a third, that via Gilgit and Yasin in the Hindu Kush. The Royal Geographical Society had put up another £300, and the government had paid £100 for his map and report on the journey to Eastern Turkestan. However they refused to get involved in his further plans. This time even he admitted that 'the danger is certainly great'; his new route combined all the tribal lawlessness of Chitral with the mountain difficulties of the Karakorams.

But danger was what Hayward relished. It was time to pull out all the stops. His energy during this last year of his life was prodigious. Invariably alone, pushing his luck further and further, he crashed about the mountains like a hounded stag. He had reached Leh in July 1869. In September he was writing from Murree (after a march of 300 miles), in November from Srinagar (150 miles), in January from Gilgit (150 miles), in March from Yasin (100 miles), in April from Murree (300 miles), in May from Srinagar (150 miles), in June from Gilgit (150 miles), and in July he was back again in Yasin (100 miles). It was as if he knew his days were numbered. And so, indeed, he did. He was safe from Yakub Beg, but the Maharaja of Kashmir had even better reasons for wanting him out of the way. Kashmiri agents, one of them a specially hired prostitute, had already made such determined attempts to poison him that he would accept food prepared by only one faithful servant.

All the explorers of the period, Cayley, Shaw, Forsyth and even Johnson, deeply mistrusted the Kashmir government. Kashmiri

* Mayo was at pains to emphasise that Forsyth's visit was neither official nor a mission. But since he was sent by the government specifically to discuss trade with Yakub Beg, one might ask what then the exercise was supposed to be.

traders were as bitterly opposed to British intervention in the Yarkand trade as they had been in Moorcroft's day. And the Maharaja was as sensitive about his frontiers as Vigne had found his father, Gulab Singh. But Hayward had still stronger reasons for concern. He gave it as his opinion that Russian spies were being entertained in Kashmir, and that the Maharaja had his own agents in Central Asia. Worse still, on the first visit to Yasin he had uncovered the grisly remains of a massacre of genocide proportions, by the Kashmir troops. He wrote a report on it in which, with his usual disregard for the consequences, he suggested that the British people should be made aware of what their loyal feudatory was up to. Someone took him at his word. An article, mentioning him as the authority, appeared in the press in May 1870.

At the time Hayward was in the Kashmir capital and about to set off again under the Maharaja's protection for the wildest corner of his state. It was rather like kicking the lion in the belly while he stuck his head in its mouth. His friends told him to return to India fast. Mayo sent a telegram to the Royal Geographical Society asking them to stop him from attempting the Pamirs again at all costs. He was a liability alive, but if he went ahead and got his throat cut there was no telling what the consequences might be. Hayward of course could not see it that way. He offered to sever all connections with the Society but he was not going to abandon his journey. He had put the Maharaja on the spot and believed the Kashmiris must now feel duty bound to see him safely on to the Pamirs. He left Srinagar in mid-June 1870.

A month later, on July 17th to be precise, another dinner party took place in the bleak Changchenmo valley. Hayward was absent; his route lay hundreds of miles to the west. But Shaw, along with his two companions, Forsyth and Henderson, played host. Their guests included Cayley, the Joint Commissioner for Trade from Leh, and their Yarkandi travelling companions, including the returning envoy and a cousin of Yakub Beg's. This time there was no shortage of food; the Forsyth mission was far better equipped than Shaw and Hayward had been. Given the season, the claret, too, should have flowed more easily. The only compromise that had to be made to their surroundings was that of sitting on the ground—there were not enough chairs to go round.

During the evening final arrangements were made for crossing the wilderness ahead. The baggage was reduced to a minimum. Seventy ponies were deemed unfit for the journey and some of their loads transferred to yaks. The remainder, most of it grain for the surviving ponies, was to be sent on by the Kashmiri governor of Ladakh. He was also in camp but, perhaps unwisely in view of what was to take place, he had not been invited to dinner. The evening went well. An alarm that the river was rising and flooding the camp came just after the meal was over and provided a convenient excuse for the party to break up. All retired early in preparation for a prompt start in the morning on the toughest leg of the journey.

'In contradistinction to all this', on the same night, three hundred miles to the north-west in a lonely spot at the foot of the Darkot glacier, George Hayward ate no dinner. Nor did he go to bed, but sat up through the long night writing by candlelight. In his other hand he held a pistol. On his collapsable table lay more loaded weapons.

At dawn he drank a cup of tea. All was quiet. He sniffed the morning air, then turned in for an hour or two's sleep. But the danger was not passed. He awoke to hard hands clutching at his throat. Bound and bullied he was led out on to the hillside. They took the ring from his finger, he muttered a prayer, a sword swept and his head fell from his body.

It all happened between the hours of eight and nine on the morning of July 18th. Well-breakfasted and with the self-conscious importance of men starting on a great endeavour, the members of the Forsyth mission were streaming out of camp. If Shaw looked back down the ugly Changchenmo valley it would not have been with nostalgia for his first visit. It is notable that his voice was never joined to the storm of protest and conjecture that arose over Hayward's murder. Forsyth and Cayley were loud in their accusations of the Maharaja. Others made out a strong case against the Chitral ruler, while the official line was that it was just a case of robbery with violence. Shaw kept silent. He had seen it all coming. If anyone was responsible, it was Hayward himself with that insane desire to try the effects of cold steel across his throat.*

News of Hayward's fate only reached the Forsyth mission two months later when they were on their way back from Yarkand. By then Forsyth had ample reason for holding the Kashmir government

---

* Hayward's last journeys and his murder belong to the story of the exploration of the Gilgit region. They are dealt with at greater length in *The Gilgit Game* below.

responsible. From the day the mission left the Changchenmo things started to go wrong, and within a week they too were on the verge of disaster, all thanks to the intrigues of the Kashmir authorities.

It was almost axiomatic that any expedition heading north from Leh was swindled over the hire of ponies. The beasts actually inspected and hired were never the ones that finally materialised. There was always a shortfall and the condition of the animals, as much as the terrain, was responsible for the high death toll. Hence it was not surprising Forsyth found himself so short of serviceable ponies that he was dependent on the Ladakh government for forwarding the grain needed for those that were fit. The arrangement was that the governor would immediately send the grain on by yaks and would then wait in the Changchenmo until he was informed that the mission had safely reached the first Kirghiz habitations in the Karakash valley on the other side of the Aksai Chin. In the event he did neither of these things. Knowing that his arrangements were inadequate and that the mission would probably be brought to a standstill, he quietly withdrew to Leh. It was not, and never had been, in Kashmir's interest to foster relations between Calcutta and Kashgar.

By July 21st Forsyth's position was desperate. Even Shaw, who always contrived to see Yarkand and the route thence in the best possible light, admitted in his report for *The Times* that they were in 'a critical state'. The ponies were starving. There was no question of waiting for the yaks to come up since they had run out of fuel. And there was no word from the governor as to where the yaks might be. During the next three days over a hundred ponies died. They were so desperate that they tore at the baggage in search of grain. At night, driven wild by the cold and hunger, they careered through the camp and then quietly slunk into the tents to die beside, and sometimes on top of, their tormentors.

On the 23rd the mission ground to a complete standstill. Food for the men was also getting desperately short, but it was imperative that they halt while the remaining ponies cropped what they could. The opportunity was taken for a council of war in which it was decided that, in a last desperate effort, the party should be divided into three. All hopes of survival rested on the Yarkand envoy and his followers. They were given the best horses and told to ride post haste to Shahidulla and get help. To ensure their co-operation and assist their progress they were persuaded to leave behind their baggage, their four hundred muskets purchased in India and even their womenfolk. Forsyth with his companions and the Yarkandi ladies plodded on as best he could, and a third party was left behind on the Aksai Chin to guard the abandoned baggage. A change of weather, an error of navigation or an attack of sickness and the expedition would now have been doomed. But their luck held. Forsyth reached the Karakash river on the 29th and three days later met a party of Kirghiz with laden yaks sent upstream by the Yarkandis who had safely reached Shahidulla. A few days later the abandoned loads were recovered and the mission proceeded over the Kun Lun without further mishap.

There were, however, other problems. When Forsyth eventually returned to Leh and heard the news of Hayward's death it was not just Kashmiri duplicity that he attacked. He told his brother that he also wished that he had never trusted the word of a Yarkandi. The Kashmiris were out to scare him off. They intended to give him such a horror of the Changchenmo that he would never again recommend it as a trade route. And they succeeded. The Yarkandis had a different game. They wanted the Forsyth mission to reach Eastern Turkestan at all costs, but they also knew that Forsyth's instructions were to proceed only if the country were at peace and if he could expect to conclude his business with Yakub Beg and return before winter. In fact the country was not at peace. Yakub Beg was fighting with malcontents in the furthest corner of his kingdom and there was no hope of Forsyth seeing him before the Kun Lun passes were closed by the snows of winter. But all of this the Yarkand envoy and his men kept to themselves.

At Shahidulla Forsyth started to smell a rat. The Yarkandis continued to insist that Yakub Beg was at Kashgar and the country as a whole at peace. But rumours to the contrary were rife and, once across the Kun Lun, these were amply confirmed. Forsyth determined to return immediately. He didn't like being duped. He shared something of Shaw's dedication, but unlike the diligent planter he was never accommodating. Raised in the Punjab Civil Service under men like the Lawrences, he was used to instant obedience. In matters of state he could be diplomatic enough but it was not inherent in his character. The Yarkandis protested that he couldn't return. He would need more supplies and more ponies and these could only be obtained at Yarkand. Forsyth refused to budge. Only a letter from the governor of the city assuring him that all was well, plus the fact that he was being starved into submission, persuaded him to carry on.

In Yarkand the mission paid for what was now coming to be regarded as Shaw's complacent endurance of the close imprisonment imposed during his previous visit. It was assumed that Forsyth would accept the same treatment. His first attempt to ride round the city caused as much of a furore as had Hayward's. Requests for ponies and provisions for the return journey were met with bland assurances that the king was on his way to Yarkand. It was only by a show of the utmost firmness and a refusal to pay any attention to his hosts, whatever the personal risk or the political consequences, that Forsyth eventually got away. 'I have reason to wish that I had never heard of Yarkand,' he told his brother. 'All hopes of opening out free relations with this country are at an end.' He expected to reach the Punjab by November and 'then farewell to Central Asian affairs for me'.

It was not a promising beginning for Mayo's new policy towards Eastern Turkestan. Forsyth had achieved nothing. In fact his experience of the Changchenmo route had made him doubtful of the feasibility of the whole subject whilst his behaviour in Yarkand had, if anything, made Yakub Beg more suspicious than ever. As for the Russians, they viewed the exercise with intense disapproval. The mission had done as much to precipitate their intervention as to prevent it. They moved more troops to the Kashgar frontier and invasion was only staved off by Yakub Beg agreeing to receive an impressive Russian mission in 1872 which won important commercial privileges.

Only Shaw and Henderson derived any satisfaction from the visit. Henderson secured a specimen of a magnificent falcon, bigger by far than the peregrine, which became known as *Falco Hendersonii* and Shaw, tearing a leaf from Hayward's book, at last won recognition as a genuine explorer. Geographers had been disparaging about his first journey across the mountains. He might claim to be the first Englishman to have reached Yarkand but his account of the journey was deemed far too unscientific and colloquial. Hayward was the explorer; Shaw just a popular propagandist. He encountered something of the distaste that would greet H. M. Stanley three years later. Now, however, he made amends. He had mastered the use of survey instruments and, leaving the Forsyth mission in the Karakorams, set out to make his mark on the map. His objective was the headwaters of the Shyok river. The excursion proved every bit as horrifying as Hayward's to the source of the Yarkand and he duly won his Gold

Medal from the Royal Geographical Society. But the prize cost him dear. Fording one too many ice-swollen rivers his rheumatic fever returned, and by the time he reached Leh he was a very sick man. He never fully recovered. The incredible resilience that saw him doggedly continuing to promote trade with Yarkand when the mission had so obviously failed, and that would even see him crossing the mountains yet again though his constitution was perilously frail, was purely psychological. Though neither colourful nor particularly endearing he was, unquestionably, brave.

14. Back to the Mountains

At two o'clock on a December afternoon in 1873 the citizens of Kashgar turned out in force. It was bitterly cold. They stamped their booted feet on the hard frozen ground and their breath hung in the still air. The pale sun neither coaxed the temperature above freezing nor enlivened the drabness of this brown desert city. Lining the low mud-built walls and huddling deeper into their quilted coats, the down-trodden Kashgaris waited, orderly and silent. It could as well have been another execution that they had come to see. No ripple of excitement had greeted the news that at last a grand mission had arrived from beyond the southern mountains. And there would be no appreciation of the carefully rehearsed protocol of the approaching procession. They were simply curious as, wide-eyed and stony-faced, they watched the cavalcade approach.

In front came two mounted guards, members of the Guides, a crack Indian regiment which specialised in intelligence work. They were part of a detachment seconded to the mission on escort duty. Next, in the place of honour and flanked by two orderlies in scarlet livery with silver sticks of office poised before them, came the Queen's letter. In Calcutta someone had remembered the price paid by Stoddart and Connolly in Bukhara for failing to get the Queen to address the Amir, and someone else had recalled how in the recent campaign in Abyssinia King Theodore had set great store by personal communications from Her Majesty. One could not be too careful with princes so far beyond the reach of civilisation.

Moreover the letter made a worthy centrepiece to the whole presentation. It nestled in a magnificent casket of pale yellow quartz banded with gold and bossed with onyx stones. The handles too were of gold. This rode upon a cushion of rich blue velvet borne at arm's length by the swaggering figure of one Corporal Rhind, 92nd Highlanders. In full dress uniform, silver fittings shining against a dark tartan, his kilt alone was enough to cause a sensation in Eastern Turkestan. The Governor of Yarkand, in fact, had been so taken aback that he had asked whether a mission that hustled out one of its members before he had had time to pull on his trousers was not too obsessed with punctuality.

Behind the Queen's letter came the Viceroy's. It also was in a richly worked casket all red and blue and gold and carried by a scarlet-coated Havildar, the Indian equivalent of a Corporal. Then followed His Excellency the Envoy to the Court of Kashgar and with him Yakub Beg's master of ceremonies. Behind them the members of the mission. All were mounted and in full dress uniform. Swords clanked at their sides, gold lace swayed over the blue and scarlet tunics and cocked hats rode jauntily above the peeled and weather-beaten faces.

There followed the presents, a hundred men bearing silks and cottons from India, guns and gimmicry from England. There were sewing machines, musical boxes (one was actually playing 'Come where my love lies dreaming'), working models of steam engines and steamships, lantern slides and projectors and even a small telegraph outfit; it was hoped that Yakub Beg would allow the mission to transmit messages from their quarters to the palace. Needless to say he didn't. Only the sewing machines caused a sensation; thanks to the Russians their fame had already reached Kashgar. 'The galvanic battery and the wheel of life proved as usual most popular' but the steamships, in a country two thousand miles from the nearest sea and without a navigable river, must have puzzled a few.

By the time the final cavalry escort had made its appearance, the head of the column had reached the palace. The riders dismounted and entered a gate in the unimposing flat-roofed building. They crossed two courtyards, each occupied by four hundred soldiers of the king's bodyguard seated motionless and silent along the walls. At the third gate the master of ceremonies motioned to the party to wait, peeped through and then beckoned them on. They entered another courtyard. This time there was a frozen pool and a few leafless poplars but not a soul was to be seen. The MC with bowed head, folded arms and noiseless step crept towards a raised pavilion and disappeared inside. On tiptoe the British party followed, then waited. 'We took the opportunity to whisper to each other as the tone most suited to the dreadful silence of the spot and the occasion.' It must have roused painful memories of visits to the headmaster.

The Envoy was summoned first. Forsyth—for it was he, in spite of that farewell to Central Asia—entered briskly and was half way to a blank wall on the other side of the room before his host appeared from a side door. Yakub Beg at first sight was unremarkable, middle aged, medium sized, stoutly built, plainly dressed. But once seated on the floor, the civilities over, his face commanded attention. It was full and fleshy, thick-lipped and without a wrinkle—pleasant enough except for the eyes which were cold and hard, neither trusting nor welcoming. It was not a nice expression.

One by one Forsyth introduced his companions. Lieutenant-Colonel T. E. Gordon was second-in-command. The identical twin brother of another Lieutenant-Colonel—they both eventually became generals and were knighted—Gordon was the master of discretion, a quiet, utterly reliable man, well suited to the delicate work of gathering strategic intelligence. Next came Surgeon-Major Bellew, doctor and linguist and a close personal friend of Forsyth. Then Captain Biddulph, an ADC to the Viceroy and a 'political' in the tradition of Burnes. He had already travelled extensively in the Western Himalayas and was soon to be the first British agent in Gilgit. Captain Trotter of the Royal Engineers was the party's surveyor, entrusted among other things with making a dispassionate appraisal of the Changchenmo and Karakoram routes; he had come by the former and was to return by the latter. Captain Chapman of the Quartermaster General's Department was in charge of camp and carriage arrangements. It had been up to him to guard against the sort of disasters that had struck Forsyth's first mission when crossing the Aksai Chin. He had succeeded but thanks largely to a more co-operative attitude from the Kashmiris.

Finally there was the young and gentle man of science, Dr. Ferdinand Stolicska. He was the odd man out, a mid-European civilian in a party of English officers. Forsyth had been inundated with applications to join the mission but few of them can have been from naturalists or geologists. For though Stolicska's qualifications were unimpeachable, he had an unfortunate reputation for guileless naivety. 'I am awfully glad that I have been allowed to go to Yarkand,' was his disarming but somehow improper comment on being appointed. It was ironical too, since he alone never returned to India. He died from the effects of altitude on the Depsang Plateau in 1874.*

* Not far from the bungalow built by W. H. Johnson in Leh stands an obelisk erected by the Government of India to commemorate poor Stolicska. The inscription is still clearly legible.

Under this marble lie the mortal remains of
Ferdinand Stolicska, Ph.D.
born in Moravia, 7th June 1838
died at Malgo, 19th July 1874
while returning from Yarkand with the British mission
etc.

Each man, in a curious mixture of greetings, bowed, shook hands and bid the king 'salaam', then sat on the floor alongside Forsyth. When Rhind's full figure filled the door, all except the king rose to attention. Gordon strode to the door to take the precious burden. Forsyth went half way to receive it from him, turned, advanced to the king and, with one knee bent, placed it before him. The officers closed up in two ranks behind him.

After depositing the casket Mr. Forsyth took out the Queen's letter and, presenting it to the Amir [Yakub Beg's latest title], rose and in a clear sonorous voice, addressed him as follows in Persian.

'I have the honour to present to your highness this letter from Her Most Gracious Majesty the Queen of Great Britain and Ireland and Empress of Hindustan. Since the government of Her Majesty is on terms of amity and friendship with all governments of the world it is hoped that the same relations may be established between the British government and that of Your Majesty'.

The Amir looked very pleased and brightening up said, 'God be praised, you have conferred an honour on me. I am honoured in the receipt of this letter from the Queen. I am highly gratified. God be praised.' And then bowing with the letter in his hands, unrestrainedly enquired, 'Is this box too for me?' And an affirmative reply being given, replaced the letter within it.

The Queen's presents followed and then, with the same formality, the Viceroy's letter and the Viceroy's presents. This time Forsyth's speech was a little more friendly and extravagant. Yakub Beg's countenance betrayed what almost looked like a grin of pleasure. Not, however, his eyes. They remained grim, almost melancholic. Between long silences more platitudes were exchanged till, with a great sense of relief, the procession reformed and made its way back to quarters.

Kashgar was quietly impressed. Forsyth's second mission was not only the grandest ever seen in Eastern Turkestan but the biggest of its kind sent out from India for sixty-five years—since Elphinstone's mission to Kabul in fact. Lord Northbrook, who had succeeded Mayo as Viceroy when the latter was assassinated in 1872, was taking Kashgar seriously. Pressurised by commercial interests at home where the recuperating Shaw had again been active, spurred on by news of more Russian activity in the Tian Shan and by the successful Russian mission to Kashgar in 1872, and approached once again by an envoy from Yakub Beg, he decided to take the plunge. In June he declared firmly that Kashgar was not regarded as within Russia's sphere of influence. And to show that these were not just empty words he inaugurated the sort of mission that would prove that the British considered Eastern Turkestan to be both a vital trading partner and a friendly sovereign neighbour.

To lead the mission, Forsyth was again summoned to Simla for a briefing. Sir Henry Durand once complained that no one in Asia was likely to be fooled by trade missions headed by a man like Forsyth. He was too blatantly a political firebrand. But this was now irrelevant. Northbrook continued to maintain the fiction of seeking only commercial ties beyond the mountains, but he believed in them even less than Mayo. A mission on this scale, with its soldiers and surveyors, was no more dedicated to selling tea than was Forsyth.

The debacle of 1870 had not upset Forsyth's career. He had followed instructions and in the end had managed to keep his disgust out of his official report. He was, however, in trouble. In 1872 he had been responsible for the heavy-handed suppression of a Sikh sect called the Kookas. It was one of those unpleasant incidents which seem to punctuate the normally relaxed flow of Anglo-Indian relations. Forsyth suddenly behaved as if it was the Mutiny all over again. He authorised a number of summary hangings, supported to the hilt his even more blood-thirsty subordinate, and was duly dismissed from his appointment. The Kashgar assignment came as a heaven-sent chance to redeem himself. His manner, according to a contemporary, had become 'lofty and protesting'; others saw his appointment to the mission as a way of doing penance in the wilderness. Forsyth, now in his late forties, saw it for what it was, his last chance.

The mission had formed up under the chenar trees on the edge of Dal lake outside Srinagar. Where Jacquemont had once whiled away the hours with lovelorn dreams of Kashmiri maidens, they rose to the sound of bugles, messed off trestle tables and had Rhind play the pipes after dinner. On September 3rd, they at last got under way. Besides Forsyth, Stolicska and the various army officers the mission consisted of a vast concourse of Indian subordinates. There was the Guides escort, cavalry and infantry, there were secretaries, interpreters, treasurers, medical dispensers, *shikaris* (huntsmen), taxidermists and surveyors and there were all the infinite varieties of camp servants from the cooks to the men who emptied the commodes. The envoy from Kashgar, who overtook them at Shahidulla, had a following of almost equal size including a platoon of Turks recruited in Istanbul.

In retrospect, perhaps one of the greatest achievements of the whole mission was the ease with which it crossed and recrossed the Himalayas. The man who made it possible was none other than William Henry Johnson. The old Kotan pioneer was now governor of Ladakh in place of the Kashmiri who had virtually wrecked the earlier mission. Johnson still loved a *tamasha*, and nothing quite like Forsyth's jamboree had ever hit Ladakh before. The permanent staff

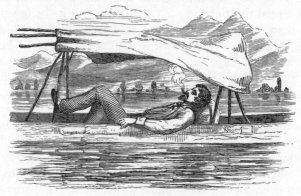

On the Dal Lake

of the mission totalled about three hundred and fifty. Their baggage animals, which were supposed to make them independent of Kashmir help if necessary, ran to some five hundred. As it turned out, they never had to carry a load the whole way to the Kashmir frontier. Johnson not only laid out supplies and fuel at every possible camp-site en route but organised carriage for the whole mission as well as for the additional food needed to feed the mission's own animals.

The economy of Ladakh is said to have taken four years to recover from the unwonted strain. During a period of two months, a grand total of 6,476 porters and 1,621 ponies and yaks plied back and forth between the different stages of the Karakoram route. The same performance was repeated for the return journey. Johnson himself went as far as Shahidulla. He felt out the ground ahead, coaxing the mission along and in places taking charge of the whole baggage train so that the envoy, unencumbered, could take a shorter and easier route. It was a magnificent effort and one that, for once in Johnson's unhappy career, did not go unacknowledged. He was congratulated by the government and, when for the first time in his life he visited England, he was awarded a gold watch by the Royal Geographical Society.

When he left the mission in Shahidulla their beasts were as fresh as they had been in Srinagar. Had they not been, Forsyth would have been pushed to cross the Kun Lun in safety. As it was there was a serious scare on the Sanju where ice and avalanches threw the whole column into confusion. Twenty ponies were killed and a number of benighted followers lost toes and fingers through frostbite. It all went to show with what skill and care they had been piloted across the far worse Sasser and Karakoram. For once no one suggested that the Leh-Yarkand road was a feasible invasion route. For trade purposes Forsyth and Trotter agreed that the Karakoram was preferable to the Changchenmo but, without the co-operation of a man like Johnson, neither was capable of supporting a modest force of infantry let alone artillery.

The size of the mission was dictated by its almost unlimited field of enquiry. Minute examination was to be given to every aspect of life in Turkestan and the final report, though considerably less readable, puts Alexander Cunningham's work on Ladakh firmly in the shade. The history, literature, antiquities, languages and ethnology of the country were explored by the two scholars, Bellew and Biddulph. To them we owe such interesting details as the easiest way to get a divorce in Eastern Turkestan—for the woman, evidence of unnatural behaviour by her husband could be delicately indicated by her placing her shoes upside down in front of the judge. Exhaustive details of the retail and wholesale trade were collected by Chapman who plunged into the bazaars and emerged with some novel descriptions of how the Kashgaris dealt with the natural incontinence of their babies. From every swaddled infant projected a skilfully designed tube procurable from shops devoted solely to the sale of this item. Gordon's job was to cast a critical eye over the rabble of Khokandi, Kirghiz and Chinese troops which composed Yakub Beg's army. He was not much impressed. Bows and arrows were still used by some contingents, and the formations of converted Chinese relied on a musket some nine feet long which it took two men to fire and another two to hold. Busiest of all was Stolicska with his native plant gatherers and bird stuffers. He witnessed the flying of eagles against foxes and wolves, which was very much a speciality of the country, and he amassed an enormous collection of rocks, plants and animals, including the wild sheep of the Tian Shan, a close relative of the Marco Polo sheep of the Pamirs.

All of which was in addition to the main task of the mission. This inevitably was commercial and political, geographic and strategic. On paper, that is in the readily understandable and comparatively uncontroversial terms of trade, the exercise was a dazzling success. A treaty was concluded with Yakub Beg which gave goods from India unrestricted entry at a low duty of two and a half per cent. Commercial agents could be appointed to places like Kotan and Yarkand, and a British representative with the status of ambassador could be installed in Kashgar. This was a lot more than the Russians had obtained in 1872. Provided he had a passport, any British subject could now enter Eastern Turkestan. Any amount of tea and cutlery and fabrics could be sent across the Himalayas and, through the ambassador in Kashgar, there was an easy avenue for developing closer political ties as the situation dictated. It looked as if British influence in Kashgar was to be even stronger than in Kabul.

When Forsyth returned to India the following year his fame was assured. He was greeted as a hero. The mission was hailed as the greatest diplomatic success for forty years. Forsyth, rebuffed for so long by Lawrence, castigated by Mayo over the Kooka affair and ridiculed by the press as late as 1873, was vindicated. He was instantly knighted and most of his companions took a step up in rank.

But in this, their hour of glory, Forsyth, Bellew and the rest had their reservations. There was room for expansion of the Yarkand trade but they could not see that it was ever likely to amount to much. Shaw, from a mixture of ignorance and over-enthusiasm, had got it all wrong. The place was largely desert, the people didn't like Indian tea, Chinese goods including the traditional tea were already finding their way into the country and, anyway, the mountains would always have the last word as a limiting factor. They had seen far more of the country than any previous visitor and it was no Eldorado.

They had also gained a far better insight into the character of Yakub Beg and his rule. This again gave cause for concern. Crime was almost unheard of, the people were orderly, the roads safe and the government secure. But by no stretch of the imagination could Yakub Beg be regarded as an enlightened ruler. He was a despot, as cruel and unprincipled as the worst of his equivalents in Western Turkestan. The country was ruled by fear and oppression. Those, including Queen Victoria, who had a sneaking admiration for this new bastion of resurgent Mohammedanism in Central Asia, would do well to revise their ideas. Here was no grafting Tudor moulding a new identity and unity for his people but a grim, unloved Cromwell. 'One of the most notable features of peasant life', wrote Bellew, 'was its eerie silence . . . we never heard the sound of music, the voice of song or the laugh of joy', and the reason was the repressive character of the government. For all its orthodoxy Yakub Beg's rule was detested by most of the people. They looked forward to the day when the Russians would intervene or the Chinese be restored. When Forsyth's mission withdrew, long faces and whispered exchanges hinted at the imminent revival of the reign of terror which had been temporarily suspended. The gigantic gallows, dismantled for the period of their stay, were about to be re-erected.

As soon as the mission returned to Kashmir, Robert Shaw, apparently recovered and now Joint Commissioner in Leh (he had given up his tea estates in favour of government employ), was packed off to Kashgar to get the treaty ratified and to establish himself as the new ambassador. He failed on both counts. Yakub Beg refused to allow him the freedom of movement enjoyed by the mission, and he found himself in much the same situation as in 1868. During a stay of six months he was never even permitted to enter the main city of Kashgar. Perhaps he had been the wrong man to send; he had always been too amenable. But Northbrook also was having second thoughts. Yakub Beg obviously did not want an ambassador, and in London there were fears that Shaw might be creating more ill-will than good. They also feared for his safety and felt that, if the Russians did eventually move in, he could only prove an embarrassment. He was duly recalled in 1875. He brought with him what he imagined to be a fully ratified copy of Forsyth's treaty. But, on examination, Yakub Beg's seal turned out to be just a complimentary note to the Viceroy. Unratified, the whole thing was worthless.

Vastly more significant was the geographical work of the mission. Forsyth planned to visit all the major cities of Eastern Turkestan, to explore the Tian Shan frontier with Russia and to return to India via the Pamirs and Afghanistan. Yakub Beg, of course, resisted. The British might, with a guide, go wherever they wanted within a day's march of their headquarters but expeditions beyond this required his specific approval. In practice, Kotan was out. So too was Aksu in the north-east, though Biddulph was allowed to visit Maralbashi, a city half way towards Aksu.

Rather surprisingly Gordon, Trotter and Stolicska were allowed into the Tian Shan. They reached one of the main passes just north of Kashgar and stood within thirty miles of the Russian fort on the Naryn river. It was as near as a British officer on duty had been to the Russian frontier for thirty years, by the rules of the Great Game a mighty move. An equivalent would have been that of a party of Russian officers surveying their way across Afghanistan and peering inquisitively down the Khyber pass. Imagine the pandemonium this would have caused; the outcry in St. Petersberg was remarkably restrained by comparison. In the process they also carried the survey from India across ground already covered by the surveyors from Russia. On the maps at least, the two empires had met.

Gordon surmised that it was his exemplary tact on this foray into the Tian Shan which finally persuaded Yakub Beg to agree to the still more ambitious scheme of crossing the Pamirs. In fact his permission was revoked; but too late. Gordon, with Biddulph, Trotter and Stolicska, had leapt at the chance and, in spite of the unfavourable season, had left on March 21st 1874. Forsyth had been warned that the Afghans would probably object to the whole mission returning via the Pamirs and Kabul, but Gordon was to verify this. He was also to enquire further into the circumstances of Hayward's murder, to clear up the question of the source of the Oxus and to explore as much of the region as possible in view of its growing strategic importance. Since Lieutenant John Wood's lonely odyssey in the winter of 1838, no European had seen the Roof of the World. Adolph Schlagintweit had probably hoped to cross it and he was murdered at Kashgar. Hayward had tried and he was killed in Yasin. A few native agents had been there, the Mirza in 1869 and a man sent by Forsyth in 1870, but the only Europeans, apart from Wood and perhaps Gardiner, were still Marco Polo and Benedict de Goes. To the geographers in Europe a first-hand account of its hydrography and mountain structure was the great 'desideratum'— their favourite word—of Asian geography.

Gordon and his companions went some way towards providing it. The story of their journey belongs to a later phase of Himalayan exploration and one in which the impetus to find a way through the mountains from India to Central Asia plays no significant part. It is sufficient here to notice just the results. They went by way of Tash-kurgan and the Little Pamir as far as Wakhan where they learnt that Afghanistan was indeed still closed to travellers and, in view of the strained state of Anglo-Afghan relations at the time, particularly so to official missions. As for Hayward's murder, the Mir of Wakhan had his own theories which, not surprisingly, implicated his old enemy Aman-ul-Mulk of Chitral. This was not exactly news.

What really mattered was that at last someone had filled in the gap between Wood's exploration up the Oxus and what was now known of Eastern Turkestan. The circuit of the northern frontier had been completed, and the expedition actually returned from Wakhan to Yarkand by way of Wood's old route up to Lake Sir-i-kol and then on across the Great Pamir. They even met an old man who remembered Wood and was delighted to meet fellow countrymen of the shy young man who had come amongst them back in 1838. Gordon agreed that Sir-i-kol, though it seemed a different shape and was not quite as high as Wood thought, was definitely one of the Oxus sources. He also reckoned it was a lot deeper than Wood's efforts with the plumb-line had indicated and, since Sir-i-kol was not really a proper name, he revived Wood's suggestion of Lake Victoria.

He left alone the question of whether it or the Sarhad was the main feeder since he had found, flowing from a lake on the Little Pamir, another entirely different Oxus tributary (the Aksu, Bartang or Murghab) which he believed to be the true parent river. If it was, then there was good cause for concern. London and St. Petersberg had just agreed on a definition of Afghan territory in the region by which the Oxus, from Wood's lake west, was to be the northern frontier. Rivers seldom make good boundaries and, as Gordon observed, most of the Oxus states, like Wakhan, stretched along both sides of the river. But, apart from this, if the Oxus did not begin anywhere near Wood's lake, then the whole agreement was meaningless.

Nor was this the worst of the expedition's discoveries. Strategi-cally the Pamirs had always been written off as too bleak and barren to appeal to the Russians and too formidable for them to cross. Wood's story suggested nightmarish conditions, which the Mirza's travels fully supported. And, in April, Gordon found the going quite as bad, the wind unbearable, the snow freezing to their faces as it fell, and fuel and provisions desperately short. But from the Wakhi people he heard a different story. In summer the grazing was, as Marco Polo had recorded, some of the best in the world. Moreover, though mountainous, it was nothing compared to the Karakorams or the Kun Lun. The Pamirs, he was told, 'have a thousand roads'. With a guide you could go anywhere and, in summer, considerable forces might cross without difficulty. The Chinese had done it in the past, the Wakhis had recently sent a contingent across to Kashgar, and the Russians might do it in the future.

Finally, and most important of all, it was discovered that the passes leading south from the Pamirs over the Hindu Kush to Chitral, Gilgit and Kashmir were insignificant. This was so disconcerting that Gordon, ever discreet, omitted all mention of it in his published account. The discovery was made by Biddulph who, while the others explored the Great Pamir, made a 'lonely journey by the Little Pamir' (a misprint in Gordon's book actually has it as a 'lovely journey'). In the process he climbed the northern slopes of the Hindu Kush and ascertained that at least two passes constituted veritable breaks in the mountain chain. One you could ride over without ever slowing from a gallop and both had had artillery transported across them. To these Gordon added yet another 'easy pass' conducting from Tashkurgan to Hunza.

In effect, Forsyth's mission had not so much thrown open Eastern Turkestan as refocused attention on the Western Himalayas. The possibility of a Russian invasion via Kashgar into Ladakh could be discounted. If the Russians did eventually take Eastern Turkestan, that country would serve not as a springboard but as a secure flank from which to support a direct thrust across the Pamirs and the Hindu Kush. In that direction there was no intelligible Afghan frontier for them to worry about, the Roof of the World was no impassable wilderness, and India's mountain wall seemed to have a gaping hole.

It was some paradox that for fifty years all eyes had been on those spine-chilling efforts to scale the Karakorams and the Kun Lun in order to reach Central Asia, when a few hundred miles to the west the traveller could, in Biddulph's words, 'go through a gate by which . . . he is practically landed in Central Asia in a single march'.

Biddulph later had cause to moderate his language. The new 'key to India' did not turn quite so easily. In the Gilgit and Chitral regions factors other than the height of the passes had slowed penetration and would continue to do so. The odd thing was that it had taken years of conquering the Western Himalayas to establish that they were not a simple barrier. The explorers themselves knew this. 'Range upon range of mountains meets the eye', 'a chaos of mountains unending', 'a sea of peaks without system or limit'. In Ladakh and Baltistan the surveyors had actually proved it. Yet, for the statesmen and strategists, the truth only now began to sink in. It was not enough to force a path through the mountains at one point and assume that the rest of the region was equally formidable. The Western Himalayas still needed to be systematically explored.

In words curiously reminiscent of those used by H. H. Wilson in his introduction to Moorcroft's *Travels* nearly forty years before, Biddulph summed up the situation.

Anyone who considers the question cannot fail to be struck by the ignorance which prevails concerning the countries immediately beyond our border. It is hardly an exaggeration to say that we know more of the geography of Central Africa than of the countries lying at our own door.

The frontier had advanced a good bit since Moorcroft's day, but Biddulph makes it plain that he is writing not of Central Asia but of Kashmir. Her boundaries were still undefined because the government only now began to realise that they were dealing not with a straightforward range but a vast, unbelievably complex mountain knot.

* * *

William Johnson died, probably of poison, in 1878. Shaw, whose delicate constitution had never fully recovered from the strain of his return journey in 1870, was soon moved to Burma and died there in 1879. Forsyth also had a brief spell in Burma and retired to England in 1876. None was therefore on the spot when the policy on which they had staked so much was suddenly and unexpectedly undermined. For in 1877 Yakub Beg was murdered, and within a year the Chinese were back in Eastern Turkestan.

This was the one eventuality that no one in India had foreseen. The country's independence had been thought vulnerable from the north, not the east; the Chinese had long ago been written off as quite incapable of mounting an offensive so far from home. Yet, against a disarrayed enemy and a far from hostile civilian population, they deployed an impressive army which reoccupied the Land of the Six Cities with scarcely a shot being fired. To emphasise the once-

and-for-all character of their reconquest they renamed the country Sinkiang, 'The New Dominion'. The Russians had always managed to hedge their bets on Yakub Beg. They had withheld recognition of him for as long as possible and they had ensured that, if the Chinese should return, they held bargaining counters with which to trade for continued links with Kashgar. Not so the British. They had backed a loser—in Chinese eyes a traitor—and the trade between Leh and Yarkand now plunged into a decline. The Russians installed a fully fledged and immensely influential consul in Kashgar, but no British official was allowed to reside there until the 1890s. It was indicative of the waning significance of the Leh–Yarkand route that, when a British consulate was finally established, its incumbents, rather than chance their luck on the Karakorams, invariably got there via Gilgit.

But a more fitting and significant postscript to a story so enriched by intrepid individuals and so full of misplaced endeavours and tragic consequences was yet to come. It happened on the 8th April 1888. That night on the very crest of the Karakoram pass, a lone Scotsman was hacked to death. His name was Andrew Dalgleish and at the time he was heading for Yarkand with a caravan of piece goods. April was no month to be crossing the mountains but he knew the track and conditions as well as anyone. In fact, for the last fourteen years his livelihood had depended on them.

The snow lay deep on the pass and, at an altitude of close on 19,000 feet, the last steep pull proved punishing. Dalgleish and his men—two servants and seven pony men—decided to halt. They were joined by a Yarkandi trader with a small caravan who was travelling by the same stages. There were also two Afghans and an itinerant fakir. All were known to Dalgleish and, in the course of the evening, he wandered over to their tent. He was offered tea but declined. However he accepted a piece of bread, sat down and they talked for a while. Then one of the Afghans slipped out. Dalgleish asked where he was going. The man said it was a call of nature and disappeared into the night.

Moments later a shot was fired. At point blank range, it passed through the tent and into Dalgleish's shoulder. He stumbled out into the dark heading for his own tent and his gun, but the Afghan was waiting for him. They were ill-matched. Daud Mohammed was a giant of a man and he wielded a massive sword. Dalgleish was short and thin, badly wounded and without so much as a knife. He tried to close on his enemy and actually grabbed the blade of his sword.

But eventually he fell. The blade at last cut through his thick sheep-skins and Daud Mohammed hacked away till he moved no more. No one came to his rescue. Only his terrier joined in the fray and soon suffered the same fate. Dog and master were left, a crumpled mess in the blood-spattered snow.*

Daud Mohammed had known Dalgleish for many years. Though an Afghan, he had been born in what was now British India and in Yarkand had been part of the expatriot Indian community to which Dalgleish also belonged. He was a braggart and a bankrupt but just why he had suddenly taken it into his head to kill Dalgleish was not clear. It could have been just a case of robbery with violence, or it could have been an outburst of religious fanaticism. More probably he was acting on instructions; but who had hired him? A commercial rival perhaps, the Chinese or even the Russians? All these were possible, but unless the murderer could be arrested the truth must remain a mystery.

In spite of protestations from the British, Daud Mohammed passed scot-free through Yarkand and Kashgar and then disappeared. In a final bid to bring him to book Hamilton Bower, a British officer who happened to be in Sinkiang combining a hunting trip with a bit of clandestine surveying, was invited to take up the trail. It was two years since the murder. Daud Mohammed was variously rumoured to have left for Mongolia, Mecca, Kabul and Bukhara. Bower under-standably thought the whole thing hopeless but, in between further hunting forays, he despatched men in all four directions. He was as amazed as anyone when, by an extraordinary coincidence, one of them came face to face with the murderer in a bazaar in Samarkand. The Russians duly arrested him and it looked as if the mystery would at last be cleared up. But Daud Mohammed thought other-wise. According to the Russians he took his own life.

Dalgleish's murder thus remains as unexplained as the deaths of Moorcroft and Trebeck or the slaughter of Hayward. But what makes it particularly relevant in the present instance is the point that Dalgleish was the last and, after Shaw, the only Briton ever to be actively engaged in the Leh–Yarkand trade. Hard on the heels of Forsyth's second mission, he had reached Yarkand in 1874 with the first consignment of goods from the Central Asian Trading Company,

---

* Dalgleish's body was recovered before it became unrecognisable from the other skeletons that strewed the Karakoram route. His grave is beside that of Stolicska in Leh.

a venture promoted by Shaw. He had stayed on in Yarkand as agent of the company then, when it failed, as liquidator, and had finally set up in business on his own. For years he was the only British resident in Sinkiang. He came to know, more intimately than any of his countrymen before or since, the horrors of what was now recognised as 'the worst trade route in the whole wide world' and the problems of what was surely the most fraught commercial venture of the century. It was with his death that the sanguine expectations of William Moorcroft and the exaggerated claims of Robert Shaw were finally laid to rest.

A small white marble pillar was erected in Dalgleish's memory. The inscription was very simple; 'Here fell A. Dalgleish, murdered by an Afghan.' It was placed on a cairn beside the crest of the Karakoram pass and there, on the grim windswept watershed between the rivers of India and Central Asia, at the gateway to which were directed the aspirations of all the early explorers of the Western Himalayas, it may still stand. So long as the present-day ceasefire lines between China, India and Pakistan all meet on that very spot, it would be hard to prove otherwise.

THE GILGIT GAME

Contents

Illustrations

ACKNOWLEDGEMENTS
Nos. 1, 2, 4, 5, 13 and 19 are reproduced by courtesy of the Royal Geographical Society; Nos. 3, 10 and 15 are from *The Making of a Frontier* by A. Durand, London 1899; Nos. 6, 7, 23, 24, 25 and 26 by courtesy of Brigadier F. R. L. Goadby; No. 8. from *Memoir of W. W. MacNair* by J. E. Howard, n.d.; Nos. 9, 11 and 20 by courtesy of the Director of the India Office Library and Records; No. 12 by courtesy of Colonel Gerald Morgan; No. 14 from *The Asiatic Quarterly Review*, vol. 2, n.s., 1892; No. 16 from *The Eastern and Western Review*, 1895; No. 17 by courtesy of Dame Eileen Younghusband; Nos. 18, 21 and 22 by courtesy of the National Army Museum.

The engravings in the text are taken from *Jummoo and Kashmir Territories* by Frederick Drew, London 1875; the engraving on the title page is from *Travels in Ladakh* by H. D. Torrens, London, 1862.

Acknowledgements

I should like to thank, first, Colonel Gerald Morgan and Dr. G. J. Alder. During the years that I have been working on the explorers of the Western Himalayas their suggestions, comments and encouragement have been invaluable; and not once has either of them made the obvious inference that I was poaching with impunity on their own chosen fields. More recently I have met with the same unselfish assistance from Dr. Schuyler Jones of the Pitt Rivers Museum, Oxford, and Mr. Graham Clarke of Lincoln College, Oxford.

My research has greatly benefited from the efficiency of the London Library, the India Office Library and Records, the Royal Geographical Society's Library and Archives (and particularly the cataloguing work of Mrs. C. Kelly), the National Library of Scotland, and the Library and Archives of the London School of Oriental and African Studies. For the patience and latitude shown by all in the face of erratic borrowings and irregular requests I am most grateful. I would also like to thank Dame Eileen Younghusband D.B.E. for allowing me to consult her father's papers, the Hon. Edward Biddulph for letting me see the journals of John Biddulph, and Brigadier F. R. L. Goadby for some helpful comments and some excellent photographs.

Janet Adam-Smith, Simon Ricketts and John Murray have kindly read through the text and made many useful comments. So, whilst typing two full drafts, has my wife, Julia; without her help, the project could never have been completed; without her encouragement and involvement it would never have been started.

Finally there are many friends in India who contributed to the mountain travels for which a book like this is the perfect excuse. Unfortunately I can't remember the names of the helpful officials and intrepid jeep drivers met in Hunza and Gilgit in 1967; but Christina Noble was then, as always, a perfect travelling companion. Geoffrey Raspin and the late Ferrier Mackay-James paved my way to Chitral where I was helped and accommodated by some of the many grandsons of Aman-ul-Mulk, notably the late Hisam-ul-Mulk, Burhan-un-din and, in Peshawar, Colonel Khushwaqt-ul-Mulk; happily I can report that their kindness utterly belied the supposed treachery of their ancestor. Also in Peshawar I received much help and encouragement from the late Terence Scott who loved the mountains dearly and to whom this book is dedicated.

Glossary
of Principal Dard chiefs

GHAZAN KHAN | Mir of Hunza, murdered by Safdar Ali in 1886.

SAFDAR ALI | Mir of Hunza 1886–91, son and murderer of Ghazan Khan.

AMAN-UL-MULK | Mehtar of Chitral, died 1892.

AFZUL-UL-MULK | Briefly Mehtar of Chitral in 1892, son of Aman-ul-Mulk, murdered by Sher Afzul's troops.

SHER AFZUL | Briefly Mehtar of Chitral in 1892, brother of Aman-ul-Mulk.

NIZAM-UL-MULK | Mehtar of Chitral 1892–5, son of Aman-ul-Mulk, murdered by Amir-ul-Mulk.

AMIR-UL-MULK | Briefly Mehtar of Chitral in 1895, son of Aman-ul-Mulk.

SHUJA-UL-MULK | Mehtar of Chitral from March 1895, son of Aman-ul-Mulk.

MULK AMAN | Ruler of Yasin until 1870, nephew of Aman-ul-Mulk.

MIR WALI | Ruler of Yasin in 1870, nephew and son-in-law of Aman-ul-Mulk and brother of Mulk Aman. Murdered by Pahlwan.

PAHLWAN BAHADUR | Ruler of Yasin 1870–76, nephew of Aman-ul-Mulk and half brother of Mulk Aman. Murdered by Mulk Aman.

JAFR KHAN | Ruler of Nagar until 1891.

UZR KHAN | Son and heir presumptive of Jafr Khan, deported in 1892.

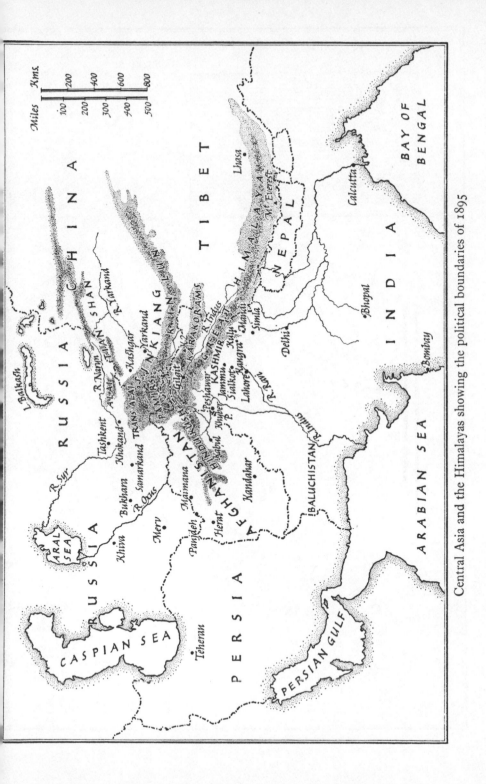

Central Asia and the Himalayas showing the political boundaries of 1895

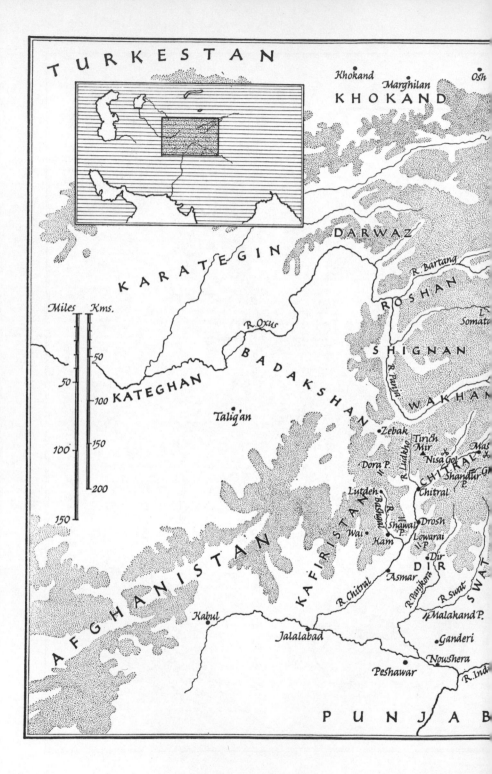

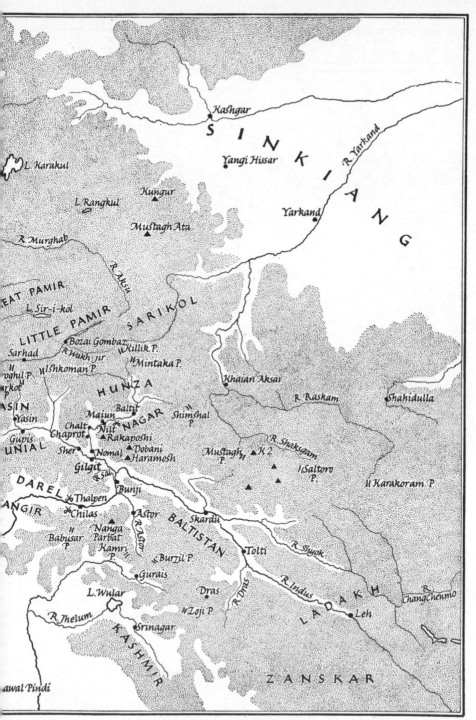

The Western Himalayas

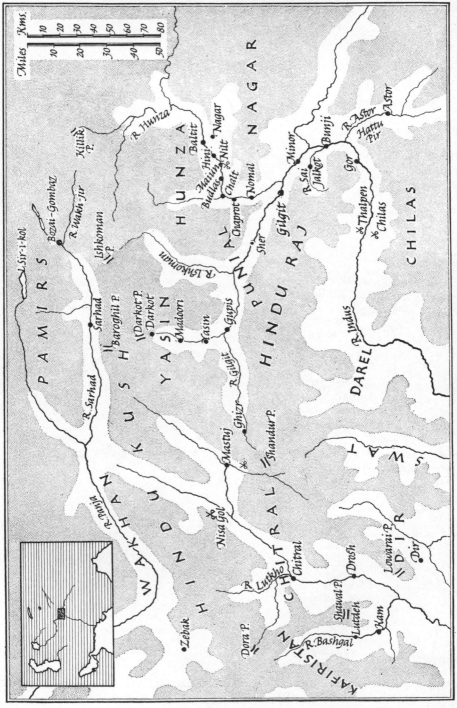

Dardistan and the Hindu Kush

Flashpoint of Asia

Gilgit is a small township in the heart of the Western Himalayas. Remote in the extreme—two hundred miles from the southern fringe of the mountains in the Punjab and a similar distance from Sinkiang on their northern flanks—the place is today the administrative centre of Pakistan's sparsely populated Northern Areas. A dusty little bazaar does a roaring trade in Chinese cottons and hardware, 'fallen' from the backs of passing jeeps. The orchards are justly renowned for their apricots, grapes and apples, and there is even an embryonic tourist industry; a couple of rest houses and a projected luxury hotel cater for the adventurous visitor come to eye the mountains.

But all this is by the way. The point of Gilgit, now as always, is strategic. High above the snowline, somewhere midst the peaks and glaciers that wall in the Gilgit valley, the long and jealously guarded frontiers of India, China, Russia, Afghanistan and Pakistan meet. It is the hub, the crow's-nest, the fulcrum of Asia.

A little over a century ago none of these frontiers came anywhere near one another. Gilgit itself was a far-flung, disaster-prone and run-down outpost of the Maharajas of Kashmir. Beyond it, and on all sides save for a vulnerable supply line back to Kashmir, there stretched virgin territory. South to the Punjab of British India, west to Badakshan in Afghanistan, north to Tashkent in Russia and east to Sinkiang in China, this rectangular sea of mountains stretched for hundreds of all but impenetrable miles. The Gilgit Game is simply the story of how and by whom such a wilderness was explored and appropriated.

It was called a game in recognition of the process being a crucial episode in the Great Game, the century-long rivalry between Russia and British India for control of Central Asia. The latter phrase had been coined back in the 1830s but came into common usage about 1870. With the popular discovery of cricket, football and tennis, suddenly everything became a game; the word was bandied about as loosely as, more recently, 'scene'. But it was also in the 1870s that the Great Game, after a mid-century lull, returned as a political feature to obsess the minds and dictate the policies of those who ruled Asia. In spite of some impossible terrain, in spite too of some of the improbable characters involved, here was one of the most desperate and portentous confrontations that the late nineteenth century had to resolve.

The Great Game has often been compared with the Cold War of the 1950s and 1960s. In both cases war as an instrument of policy was used sparingly and the global explosion that threatened never materialised. A safer outlet for imperial aggression was found in trying to secure a favourable alignment of minor powers and thus outmanœuvre the opposition. In the Great Game, China (although itself an empire), Afghanistan and Persia all provided ideal ground for such jockeying. So too, in the early days, did the khanates of Central Asia and, subsequently, the mountain states of the Western Himalayas. In retrospect the imperial rivalry looks fairly genteel and, indeed, there were those who at the time defended even Russian encroachments on the ground of Europe's civilising mission. Nevertheless, it is no exaggeration to say that, for most, the Tsarist threat in the late nineteenth century was as real and alarming as the Communist menace in the mid-twentieth.

Again like the Cold War, the Great Game was played, or fought, over a vast area and at many different levels. Any clash of British and Russian interests east of the Balkans had a bearing on the Game. The action had a way of shifting unpredictably from a concourse of statesmen in Europe to a sudden shunting of troops in the Hindu Kush; or from the activities of a lone Kiplingesque secret agent to some frantic excitement among the small-scale maps at military headquarters.

What was true of the Great Game also went for its Gilgit sector; the process of geographical and political penetration only makes sense when seen in the broadest possible context. Yet Gilgit was surely the wildest arena in which the Game was played. Diplomatic activity had to wait on the deliberations of military strategists and these in turn waited on the process of exploration. Because of the political vacuum in the area, the movements of explorers and agents could themselves constitute a valid claim to territory, and their chance friendships and difficulties could have the most far-reaching repercussions; it would be in the mountains around Gilgit that the two imperial frontiers came closest to collision. All of which, though occasionally leading to absurdities, makes the Gilgit Game vastly more exciting and romantic than most of the Great Game. From Rudyard Kipling to John Masters fiction writers have found their best material in the Gilgit story.

* * *

In *When Men and Mountains Meet* I wrote about the men who explored the Western Himalayas before 1875. They were the pioneers, and by this date the geographical outlines of what lay between India and Central Asia were established. It was now known, for instance, that the range that divided the rivers flowing south into the plains of India from those flowing west, north and east into Central Asia was a combination of the Hindu Kush and the Karakorams. In an inverted V these two systems locked together somewhere to the north of Gilgit. Their high passes could be reached only along the Chitral river up the left hand side of the V or along the Gilgit river on the right; and of these two the latter, via its several tributaries, afforded the best access to the apex. Hence the importance of Gilgit was already appreciated; of the eight or nine passes by which Central Asia could be reached direct from India, six in fact lay within a week's march from the little township. In the 1890s visitors would be so impressed with this discovery that, filled with the railway mania of the day, they would predict for Gilgit one of the world's great junctions. Here the line from India to Samarkand and Moscow would link up with the branch to Sinkiang, Mongolia and Peking.

It was also clear, though the railway enthusiasts would seem to have overlooked it, that in the Western Himalayas the greatest knot of mountains in the world had been uncovered. K2 to the east of Gilgit had just been measured and found second only to Mount Everest; there was a fair chance that a superior to both might yet be lurking somewhere to the north-west. Between Ladakh and Sinkiang the breadth of the Western Himalayas had been repeatedly crossed and all the main mountain systems had now been identified; to the south of Gilgit and parallel to the Karakorams lay the

Great Himalaya and the Pir Panjal; north of the Karakoram–Hindu Kush watershed lay the Kun Lun on one side and, due north from Gilgit, an area known as the Pamirs. This last was still very mysterious and it was far from clear whether it was really a mountain range or a vast elevated plateau. There was also confusion about just where one range ended and the next began. The threads, in other words, had been identified but the knot had yet to be unravelled. Much the same went for the rivers. The Indus and its tributaries which drained the mountains to the south were now fairly well known. Further north, though, there was still controversy over the source of the Oxus and uncertainty over the mountain reaches of the Yarkand river.

All these points could, and would, have been cleared up by 1870 if, for the past thirty years, explorers had not been rigorously excluded from Gilgit and the lands beyond. There were two reasons for this. In the first place, the tribes of the Hindu Kush around Gilgit enjoyed a reputation for unrivalled ferocity, xenophobia and treachery. Under Kashmir's rule Gilgit itself might prove safe enough for the traveller, but the valleys that radiated from it were a law unto themselves. Due north on the road to the Pamirs there was the independent kingdom of Hunza, practically inaccessible and the perfect refuge for a people addicted to caravan raiding. Yasin, at about ten o'clock from Gilgit, was less politically stable and less defensible but had nevertheless been responsible for some of the worst raids on Gilgit. At eight o'clock lay the long valley of Chitral which had close dynastic ties with Afghanistan and was deeply involved in the slave trade. And south from Gilgit lay Chilas and the Indus valley peoples who made up for their lack of numbers with a well-deserved reputation for fanatical Mohammedanism.

For convenience as much as anything, these peoples would soon all be lumped together under the title of Dards. Compared to the pliant Buddhist Ladakhis who assisted travellers across the Himalayas to the east of Kashmir, the proud Islamic Dards would evince a jealous attachment to their independence and a deep suspicion of snooping travellers. Aided by the character of their mountain defiles, and to some extent armed by the powers who sought their loyalty, they would play a part out of all proportion to their numbers. While imperial diplomats contorted themselves in an effort to avoid the dreaded Armageddon, the Dards seemed positively spoiling for a fight. It was the fate of empires apparently waiting on the word of some illiterate chieftain, or hanging on the outcome of a battle fought by rock climbers, which gave to the Game its air of baffling unreality.

The other factor which deterred explorers was the attitude of the Kashmir authorities. Then as now, Kashmir was a political anomaly. Properly speaking it was just the beautiful valley of that name around Srinagar, the capital; but with the disintegration of the Sikh empire in the 1840s all the mountain lands administered by the Sikhs were detached and designated as the new state of Kashmir under their *de facto* ruler, Gulab Singh. By the treaty of Amritsar in 1846 he was recognised by the British a Maharaja in return for his settling the war indemnity levied on the defeated Sikhs. But the treaty left to further negotiation the actual boundaries of the state as well as the exact nature of its relationship with British India. This was a situation that could be exploited by both parties; and while the Government of India at first concentrated on trying to reduce the Maharaja to the impotent status of other princely rulers within British India, the Maharaja and his successors did their utmost, particularly in the Gilgit region, to extend their territory. Freelance explorers who might publicise or censure this activity, or surveyors who might attempt to lay down a precise boundary, were therefore forbidden access.

On the other hand, as the new state of Kashmir was more firmly incorporated into British India, it became clear that the frontiers of the state could not be simply left to the energies of the Maharaja. In the north and north-west they were, after all, the frontiers of India itself, and in the event of attack the Indian government would be expected to defend them. As the Russian threat developed in the 1870s the question of finding a defensible Kashmir frontier and a reliable system of guarding it became crucial. And, just as for thirty years the jealousy of the Maharajas had kept out freelance explorers, so for the next twenty years the strategic sensitivity of the Indian government would have the same effect.

To those interested purely in the promotion of geographical knowledge it was a tragedy. The core of the Western Himalayas, the most challenging terrain in the world and the most inviting void in Asia, was being reserved solely for political agents and soldiers. Throughout the period the Royal Geographical Society in London pleaded with the government to release more information about its findings in the region; it was unsuccessful. But, conversely, one should not be surprised if some of the privileged agents and soldiers who did get to Gilgit look suspiciously like freelance explorers doing political work simply for the travel opportunities it afforded.

To the extent that the Gilgit Game takes the story of the exploration of the Western Himalayas forward in time and north-west to the extremities of the mountain complex it is a sequel to *When Men and Mountains Meet*. But with the spirit of geographical enquiry playing such a small part, it is true to say that the motivation for the Gilgit Game was entirely different. The story contains only one traveller who claimed to be a conventional explorer and his credentials are open to question. Likewise missionary and commercial incentives play no part. The object was not the usual one of finding a way through the mountains and opening it up, but of finding all possible ways through and closing them. The discovery of independent tribes and unclaimed valleys was cause for anxiety rather than celebration. A vacuum was a threat, defence was the priority, and demarcation the ultimate aim.

Compared to the earlier period of exploration, naturalists and geologists are also conspicuous by their absence. But one scientific discipline, ethnology, played an important part. Having committed itself to the idea of appropriating and defending such a remote frontier as the Hindu Kush, the Indian government was faced with the problem of how to control the tribes that lay within it. Their diversity proved as much a stumbling block as their ferocity. The study of the tribes, fascinating enough in itself, was expected to provide pointers as to how their loyalty could most readily be secured.

It did up to a point; but such recommendations were usually ignored in favour of some supposed essential of imperial strategy. And as a result, just as the Great Game often seemed to have something to do with skirmishes with the Pathans on the northwest frontier, so the Gilgit Game had a way of deteriorating from the lofty ideals of Anglo-Russian rivalry into frantic and embarrassing fracas with the mountain peoples. On what became known as India's northern, as opposed to north-western frontier, actual hostilities lasted for only four years and were never as bloody as those round the Khyber. But, because of the appalling terrain, because of the remoteness from the nearest British bases, and because of the anomalous position of Kashmir, they were both more bizarre and more critical.

PART ONE

Veni

1. Beyond the Indus

The maps mark a surveyor's trig. point above the village of Gor in the mountains of northern Pakistan. To reach it, you climb the side of the wild Sai valley, edge gingerly up a long serrated ridge of rocks and finally scramble the last few hundred feet over jagged boulders. The ascent promises nothing in particular; it could as well be that of any other spur or pass in the Western Himalayas. The altitude at the top is about 16,000 feet, enough to induce a headache, breathlessness and perhaps a slight nausea—but nothing worse; this jaunt is one for the ambitious trekker rather than the mountaineer. You flop down amidst the boulders, panting, thankful and expectant; the wind blows cold and strong. Then, cautiously, like one sampling a long cherished delicacy, you sweep the horizon.

Physical and overwhelming comes the response, a prickling of the scalp, a shudder of disbelief. But they were right; the two phlegmatic British officers who, a hundred years ago, first set eyes on this view did not exaggerate. No-one, not even the most apathetic, they wrote, could fail to be moved. Here, quite simply, is 'the most awful and the most magnificent sight to be met with in the Himalayas'.

You are standing on the extremity of a range known as the Hindu Raj which effectively blocks any view to the west of its grander parent, the Hindu Kush. But there is compensation. Eastward a chaotic sea of rugged ranges extends to the horizon. For over a hundred miles the eye roves anxiously across their grey, snow-flecked ridges. Somewhere in those deep folds should lie the villages of Baltistan and somewhere through that forbidding maze should flow the mighty Indus. But from above Gor you see just the mountains; the only relief is a hazy white where they touch the horizon. Yet even this is no soft and friendly cloud. You might just make out the black of bare windswept rock or the snow-smoke streaming off above it. It is in fact the heart of the Karakorams. K2, the second highest mountain in the world, is somewhere in that puff of white.

Turning to the left, the north, the ice bound heights draw closer. Thirty miles off, Haramosh and Dobani, the giants that guard the entrance to the Gilgit valley, are easily identified. Behind them rears the whittled point of Rakaposhi which dominates the Hunza valley and the road to the distant Pamirs. On each of these peaks you can follow the glaciers up till they finger out in ice choked gullies below the summit, or down till they tear deep into the straggling band of forest. Again, it is hard to believe that somewhere between you and Dobani there lies a green and smiling valley. Down there the orchards are laden with fruit and the streams stocked with trout. In Gilgit's bazaar the shopkeepers are sunning themselves in their open shop fronts while a clerk picks his teeth as he waits at the post office. The improbability of their situation is forgotten. It will take the distant drone of the plane from Rawal Pindi, as it weaves through the mountains and banks steeply to swing from the Indus valley into that of Gilgit, to remind them.

Before starting back down to the drowsy world of Gilgit, there is more to be seen from the cliffs above Gor; the greatest prospect of all remains. Turn back from the peaks of the Karakorams and face due south. Here lies the true horror of the Himalayas. This time there is no deep and distant perspective; the horizontal is unrepresented. You are staring at a wall; it rears from the abyss at your feet to a height for which the neck must crane back. Such is Nanga Parbat, 'the Naked Mountain'; its navel now confronts you. More a many-peaked massif than a single mountain, Nanga Parbat marks the western extremity of the Great Himalaya; it is a buttress worthy of its role. (As the plane to Gilgit works its way round it, the passenger sees nothing but snow, rocks and ice for a good ten minutes.) Beautiful is not an appropriate adjective. It is too formless; there is no slender fang like that of Rakaposhi or the Matterhorn and none of the grandiose harmony of Kanchenjunga or Mount Fuji. An uncut stone, it impresses by reason of its dimensions, not its shape.

Edge now a little nearer to the extremity of your vantage point. This mountain needs putting into some sort of proportion; it seems much too near. But move carefully; a steady hand and nerves of steel are called for. And when you are ready to look over, lie down. For between you and Nanga Parbat there is nothing.

The cliffs above Gor are sheer for three-quarters of a vertical mile from where you lie. Below that they continue down for another mile and a half of broken precipice and crag. It is probably the most frightening declivity in the world—and one rivalled only by that which faces you. Nanga Parbat too rises straight out of this trough. The top of the mountain is 26,500 feet above sea level, the bottom of the trough 3,500. At a range of ten to fifteen miles you are seeing in one uninterrupted sweep the greatest slope on the crust of the earth, 23,000 feet of elevation. That's four and a half miles from the bare black rock along the topmost ridges, down through the fields of snow and ice, down the precipices and over-hangs, down the long winding glaciers, down through the forest and scrub, and down the steep and broken slopes of gravel to the cliffs at the bottom.

What happens at the foot of these cliffs is hidden; but anyone who has driven the road from Chilas to Gilgit knows only too well. The heights above are horrifying, but the gorge of the Indus is worse. Down there one forgets about the Himalayas. It's more like the bottom of the Grand Canyon, a suffocating, rock-bound desert. Nothing grows there, no-one lives there. The rocks sizzle in temperatures around the 120 degrees mark, gravel trickles down the slopes with a dry rattle, and will o' the wisps fling sand into every parched nook and sun-cracked cranny. Through this waste land, its stern and alien ruler, the greeny-grey Indus, slides silently along. For some six hundred miles, across the Tibetan plateau, through the open valleys of Ladakh and into the tightening gorges of Baltistan, it has flowed north-west heading for the heart of Asia. But just a few miles to the north its further progress is blocked by the steep bluffs of Dobani. It careens straight into the mountain and, sinking ever deeper into its gorge, seeks for a way round, or even under, this massive obstruction. The way is barred; the buckled torrent subsides into a sulking flood, turns south and, cutting straight across the line of the Himalayas, curls down the desert canyon below.

Between the encounter with Dobani and its next collision, with Nanga Parbat, the river receives three considerable tributaries, the Gilgit and the Sai from the west and then the Astor from the east. For a moment the mountains stand back. The river, quieter but still sucking at any rock that stands in its way, emerges slightly from its gorge. Dreary lunar deserts though they are, one can speak of shores rather than cliffs. Here is the one place on its long course through the mountains that the Indus can be crossed. From above Gor you can see a stretch of the track which throughout the nineteenth century was the lifeline between Gilgit and Kashmir. Zig-zagging down the 6,000 waterless feet of the Hattu Pir spur it crosses the Astor river by the Shaitan Nare, the Devil's bridge, in those days a precarious affair of rotten rope and frayed twigs. Thence it winds up through the rocks to the settlement of Bunji and the Indus bridge.

*   *   *

A hundred years ago there was no bridge, just a ferry, and Bunji consisted of just a fort and a few mud huts. Outside one of these huts on a hot September's day in 1866 there paused a Dr. G. W. Leitner. He was not quite the first European to visit this remote corner of the then Kashmir state. In the late 1830s the explorer Godfrey Thomas Vigne had reached the Hattu Pir above the Astor river and had brought back from there the first eye-witness account of the Indus at Bunji. In 1847 two British officers had actually crossed the Indus and got some miles past Gilgit before being turned back; sadly their journey was never chronicled. By contrast there was also the oft told but seldom credited story of Alexander Gardiner who claimed to have passed clean through all the unknown lands beyond the river.* Surveyors working on the Survey of Kashmir had just completed their mapping of the whole country to the east of the Indus and sportsmen were already decimating the stocks of ibex and markhor in the mountains on that side. But few of these bothered to go down to Bunji itself; so far as Europeans were concerned it was a dead end. Whether or not the Indus ought to be the frontier of Kashmir was a debatable point. But, for a certainty, such authority as the Maharaja of Kashmir wielded in the lands beyond was of so tenuous a character that he was in no position to guarantee the safety of any traveller there.

All this country west of the Indus and as far as distant Afghanistan was usually lumped together under the title of Yaghistan,

* For Vigne, Gardiner and the Survey of Kashmir, see *When Men and Mountains Meet* above.

meaning the land of the ungovernable, of the savages. The Kashmir government's experience of it more than bore this out. In twenty-five years of trying to assert some influence there, its troops had been ambushed and besieged by each and all of the various Hindu Kush tribes. For most of the 1850s they had been forced right back across the Indus and now, in 1866, they were just reasserting their shattered rule in the Gilgit valley after another bloody uprising. Naturally the Yaghis were credited with an awesome ferocity. In Hunza captured soldiers of the Maharaja of Kashmir were used as human fireworks and in Yasin the natives were said to pluck out their hearts and eat them raw. Other tribes were supposed to be devil worshippers who offered human sacrifices. Any caravan that ventured into their valleys was immediately plundered and the only trade that could be said to flourish was the slave trade. In fact, in the absence of coin, mankind was the common currency; a hunting dog cost one male slave and a sturdy pony two females, preferably fair and fourteen.

Such at least was the reputation of the Yaghis as put about by the Kashmir troops. However, to a man like Dr. Leitner, Yaghistan had its attractions. He was not a medical doctor but an academic ('M.A., Ph.D., LL.D., D.O.L., etc.' modestly followed his name on all his gold-blocked notebooks). Particularly he was interested in ethnology, the study of races, and in how the language of a people was a reflection of its way of life. In this respect the Hindu Kush peoples sounded most promising. Discarding the term 'Yaghi' as pejorative and too political, Leitner identified them as Dards, supposed descendents of the Daradas of Sanskrit literature and the Daradae of classical geographers. This derivation was conjectural but it neatly gave to the Yaghis a distinct racial identity; it was a term of convenience yet it could be justified by what was then known of them. For example, it was clear that these Dards were neither Indian, nor Tibetan, nor of the Turkish stock of Central Asia. The miscellany of languages which they spoke, though far from being a homogeneous group, appeared totally different from any known tongue. And likewise, though most of the tribes had adopted Mohammedanism, they retained some distinctly non-Islamic cults. (The few who had rejected Islam, the Kafirs in the far west of the region, represented a still greater ethnological puzzle.) Blue eyes, fair skins and blonde or reddish hair were said to be commonplace amongst all the Dards. Vigne had been told that the people of Hunza and Nagar were so fair skinned as to be transparent; as they drank you could see the water passing down their throats. For centuries they had been shut away in their inaccessible valleys, immune from the great tides of history in Central Asia and northern India. With features that were nothing if not European, was it possible that here were the long lost descendants of the Greeks who had crossed Asia with Alexander the Great? Or, since even in Alexander's day there were reports of a similar people, were they perhaps remnants of the original Aryan race from which all the Indo-European peoples were descended? And was there perhaps substance in the myths that placed the garden of Eden somewhere in the valleys of the Hindu Kush?

Leitner must have peered across the eddying waters of the Indus at Bunji with considerable interest. In the bare hills beyond he could see the Sai valley and, high above it, that spur which ends on the cliffs above Gor. He could also make out the track that wound west up the valley towards Gilgit. Shadeless, barren and brown, it was not inviting. Nor was Leitner, at this stage, bent on following it; the idea was in the back of his mind but he had been forcibly warned of the dangers of doing so. Besides, he was more intrigued by what was going on around him. From one of Bunji's mud huts came voices. They were speaking what sounded like Chilasi, the language he had come so far to study. And like the prospector who finds a nugget in his first pan, he immediately staked out his claim; the Chilasis owned the mud hut so Leitner moved in. He unpacked and emerged, notebook at the ready.

Chilas itself is on the Indus below Bunji and below Gor. Its inhabitants had, in common with their neighbours along the river, an unusual form of government; they were republicans. Indeed each village was a self-governing entity with its own council of state to which even women might be elected. In Leitner's view this put the smallest of these republics, a village of seven houses, at a rather more advanced stage of development than the India Office in London. This peculiarity was one of the things he wanted to investigate; but there was also a rumour, which much interested the savants of the day, that Chilas might be the Kailas where dwelt the gods of Hindu mythology. Yet a third point for investigation, and in Leitner's view the most important one, was the Chilasi language. This and much else about Chilas had come to light as a result of a reprisal raid down the Indus by the Kashmir troops in 1851. Thenceforth Chilas had been nominally tributary to Kashmir sending each year a hundred goats and two ounces of gold dust. The men who accompanied this tribute in 1866—combining in a subtle way the functions of ambassadors, hostages and goatherds—had already been interviewed by Leitner in Srinagar, the Kashmir capital. There he had learnt enough to recognise their language; but, finding the Kashmir authorities reluctant to let him pursue his enquiries, he had followed the scent westward to the Indus.

Unfortunately the Kashmir governor at Bunji also had his doubts about this unexpected visitor who sat all day with his Chilasi landlord, pointing at things and scribbling in his notebook. It looked highly suspicious, considering the very questionable loyalty of the Chilasis. Accordingly Leitner was persuaded to move to a small mosque in the Bunji fort; he would have a bit more room there and, of course, he could still see his Chilasi friend. Next morning, instead of his friend, he awoke to find a guard of soldiers surrounding the building and turning away all comers. It would have tried the patience of a saint. Leitner's investigations had only just got beyond the stage where whenever he pointed at something he was told the Chilasi for finger; the work was scarcely begun and it was too bad to be baulked yet again. In a towering rage he stamped away from the fort and, like a petulant child, made the first gesture of defiance he could think of. 'I marched to the bank of the Indus, took the only boat . . . and crossed the frontier to the other side.'

Thus begins the first recorded narrative of a visit to Gilgit. It was an unconventional way to start an exploratory journey, but any other approach would almost certainly have failed. Had Leitner planned the journey in advance he would have organised porters, stores and probably a guard, all of which would have put the governor on the alert. Had he just warned his servants a few hours in advance the news would almost certainly have leaked out. As it was his move took everyone, including himself, by surprise. Faced with a *sahib* in no mood to be trifled with, and failing any orders to the contrary, the boatmen rowed him across. Within twenty minutes he landed in Yaghistan. His caravan consisted of his two servants, his guard amounted to a brace of pistols and his provisions were three jars of Bovril hastily stuffed into his pockets. If the scientific world later turned up their noses at this little foray into *terra incognita* it was hardly surprising.

But there were plenty of other reasons for raised eyebrows over the carryings on of Dr. G. W. Leitner. His career, his achievements and his personality were all, to say the least, improbable. They have the makings of a fascinating biography; yet what biographer would willingly tackle the span of countries and activities that they embrace? And, still more of a problem, how to get the measure of the man? Was he a 'self-seeking humbug' as many liked to think, or did he in fact deserve the extravagant, if prompted, praise of his admirers? There is such a wide divergence between the importance he himself attached to his every move and the derision it invariably met with in official circles, that a balanced appraisal becomes very difficult. Was he a great ethnologist and a pioneer in education, or just a glib linguist and a quack schoolmaster? Were his numerous crusades on behalf of the Dard peoples prompted by a sincere solicitude, or were they just ammunition for the inveterate sniper and sustenance to the glutton for publicity? And did he really matter? Twenty-five years after he crossed the Indus at Bunji the Viceroy of India would telegraph to London to find out who on earth Leitner was, because one of his publications was revealing classified information 'with the scarcely veiled intention of helping a possible enemy'. Lord Curzon, then a member of the India Council, replied that he knew both Leitner and the publication. 'The latter', he wrote, 'carries little weight, the former none. It would be a mistake to take any notice of him.' Yet people did take notice and this correspondence rather proved the point.

So who was Gottlieb Wilhelm Leitner? By the time he found himself on the wrong side of the upper Indus he had already crammed into his twenty-six years a remarkable career. Born in Budapest of German parents he was educated in Malta and Turkey and by the age of fifteen could speak fluent German, French, English, Arabic and Greek. With the outbreak of the Crimean War he had decided to put this knowledge to some use and was duly appointed to a first-class interpretership with the British forces, a position which apparently carried the rank of colonel. Leitner remained inordinately proud of this achievement for the rest of his life, not because he was fifteen at the time—he never mentions this—but because he had served with the British army in the Crimea and ranked as a colonel. He was surely the youngest veteran of them all.

After the war he returned to his studies in Turkey. He was now a teacher and launched the first of many educational experiments by refusing to converse with his students and colleagues in any language other than ancient Greek. He passionately believed in breathing some life into the dull business of conjugation and declension; learning languages was not just a useful discipline but the only way of getting some insight into the lifestyle and thinking of those who had spoken them. Thus, as the Government of India was soon to discover, if you asked Leitner to investigate a language, you ended up with a gazetteer of the historical, geographical and cultural environment of those who spoke it, not to mention their appearance, beliefs, diet and diseases.

In 1858 Leitner proceeded to England and enrolled at King's College, London as a postgraduate. He was soon appointed a lecturer in Arabic, Turkish and Greek and then, as dean and professor, headed the new Oriental Section of the college. As with 'The London Society of German Savants', one of his first attempts to provide a platform for his ideas, he claims to have actually founded this department. About this time he also studied law at the Middle Temple and was called to the bar. The string of initials after his name was growing.

In 1864 he answered an advertisement for the appointment of Principal at a big new government-run college in Lahore, the capital of the Punjab province of British India. If the oriental section of King's College was all that he made it out to be, it is odd that he should have wanted to leave for the East so soon. But, still more surprising, considering that he was only twenty-three and not even a British subject, was the success of his application to Lahore. The position was a highly responsible one demanding administrative capabilities as well as academic qualifications. Moreover, the newly acquired province of Punjab was the showpiece of British India and a forcing house for young administrators. Go-ahead and outward looking, its government believed in letting a young man have his head. Compared with the slowly grinding cogs of the Calcutta bureaucracy, Lahore whirred with energy and

experiment. It was just the sort of atmosphere that the educational-
ist in Leitner longed for. He took up his new responsibilities in
late 1864.

For the next twenty years India was his home. It is worth
anticipating his career during this period since, from the moment
he arrived in Lahore, it cast him in a mould that was already set
by the time he broke bounds across the Indus. Leitner found fault
with most things and the Lahore Government College, indeed the
whole educational set-up in India, was no exception. The college
was designed to turn out intelligent English-speaking clerks who
would be able to fill the lower echelons of the administration. To
Leitner this was anathema; it was not an education, just a training.
What of Sanscrit and Arabic, the classical languages of Hindu and
Muslim? These too must be taught and the pupils given some
pride in their cultural heritage. For this, what Lahore needed was
not a college but a university. Raising educational standards at the
College would be a step in the right direction but a University
should be the product of something little short of a cultural
renaissance. With an energy that the Punjab authorities could
only admire he set about mobilising public opinion. Books and
periodicals poured from his office. There were Arabic grammars,
a history of Mohammedanism, treatises on education, an Urdu
translation of *Macbeth*, a daily newspaper, two weeklies, critical
journals in Sanskrit and Arabic, and an endless stream of appeals
for funds. He aimed particularly at the rich and the culturally
influential within Indian society and they seem to have responded
nobly. His evening 'entertainments' were a real effort to bring
British and Indian society together and, though too arrogant to
win friends anywhere, he was genuinely sympathetic to native
opinion and respectful of Indian culture.

By 1870 the Lahore College had sixty undergraduates, and in
1872 the Punjab University College was founded. It was not quite
a fully fledged University but would soon become so and Leitner,
as well as being Principal of his college, became Registrar of the
University. This, however, was as far as he got in the academic
world in India. His ideas were right and his achievements considerable; but he was not admired. Amongst the men who ruled
India in the mid-Victorian period, conceit and moral superiority
were common enough vices to pass without comment. Leitner's

egotism, though, was on a totally different level. It was not an un-conscious racial presumption but a personal and belligerent bragging. Some could forgive it. After all he was a mid-European intellectual; you couldn't expect the sangfroid on which the British prided themselves. Most, though, could not. 'Leitnerian outbursts' sent shivers of horror down the good straight spines of the patriarchs of the Punjab. The man was insufferable. Exhibiting his command of languages simply to impress (he now spoke twenty odd), posing as the only European who really understood the native mind, meddling in matters, like the administration of the railways, which were none of his concern, and all with the same ungracious, garrulous, publicity-seeking impertinence, he fully merited the undying hostility of all who had dealings with him. In reality it was never quite as bad as that. Leitner's one saving grace was his predictability. Once you knew what to expect you ceased to be outraged. Subtlety or cunning did not enter into his make-up, and it was not enmity that he aroused but ridicule.

It was a case of first impressions proving right in the end. Any-one who had run the gamut of unease, distaste and horror eventu-ally came back to their first recollection of the man. Then it would have been his absurdity that registered. He stood five feet eight inches tall and, in spite of a torso that he describes as 'vigorous', weighed over fourteen stone. His eyes were small, blue and very intense, the lids narrowed with self-importance. To conserve moisture for the next outburst the mouth too was compressed. Once he warmed to his subject he spoke with a strong guttural accent. The tone grew increasingly menacing. He would switch languages for no apparent reason and, gesticulating wildly, work up to some devastating crescendo of indignation. And all the while strutting about like a bantam.

In 1865, for his first summer vacation, Leitner had gone to Kashmir. Like most Europeans he was much taken with the cool mountain climate and the grand proportions of this most famous of Himalayan valleys. In Srinagar, the capital, he got his first taste of the racial diversity of the region and this made even more of an impression. Today the Indo-Pakistan ceasefire line has severed all contact between the Kashmir valley and the Dard tribes of the Gilgit region. But there still live, in and around the bazaars of Srinagar, communities of short, slit-eyed men from Tibet and

Ladakh, tall gangling Gujars from the lower slopes of the Pir Panjal, and wizened Yarkandi refugees from across the Karakorams and Kun Lun in Sinkiang. Along with the deputations from Chilas, Gilgit and Hunza these excited the Doctor's curiosity, and in the following year he devoted his vacation to a ten-week tour of the Western Himalayas. The journey would be his making as a traveller and would provide the inspiration for his assault on Gilgit.

If Leitner was such a misfit in British India, imagine how he measured up to the ideal of the explorer. In the mid 1860s it was the African travellers who led the field; Baker had just returned from his epic journey up the Nile, Burton was still contesting the significance of Speke's discovery of Lake Victoria, and Livingstone was setting off into the interior for the last time. Glamorous and controversial, these men had won for exploration a wide and appreciative audience. People now knew what to expect of an expedition, the long columns of porters with loads on their heads, the menace of the jungle and the distant drums, the wild beasts, the lethal fevers and the naked savages. And they knew how the explorer should react as he grappled with these horrors. Against the barbarous and unchristian, the Victorian virtues should shine out in unsullied glory; deliberation, patience, fortitude and clear-sightedness must triumph in the end. An excitable German, with three jars of Bovril and a penchant for outrageous tirades, would be up against it.

2. Friend of the Dards

'At 7 a.m. on the first of May 1866 I started from Lahore on a tour through Kangra, Mandi, Lahul, Zanskar, Ladakh and Kashmir with Mr. Henry Cowie, the brother of Mr. David Cowie, then Advocate-General of Bengal.'

Thus begins the narrative of Dr. Leitner's first journey which would have as its sequel the visit to Gilgit. In spite of the precise itinerary the rest of the first paragraph makes it clear that this is to be no simple holiday hike. The previous winter had been exceptionally severe, the paths were blocked by landslides, the bridges washed away, the snow still deep. So many were the dangers and hazards encountered that Leitner reserved them for a separate book; alas it never materialised. Sufficient to say, therefore, that he and his companion succeeded in reaching Leh, the Ladakh capital, a whole month earlier than any previous traveller coming by the same route. And that, in the process, they managed to see 'a good deal that had been missed by previous travellers', to make some important archaeological discoveries, to strike up friendly relations with 'the excellent Middle and South Tibetans', and to open the way for future contact between British India and the forbidden city of Lhasa.

In a word, Leitner is off. His travelogue is much like the tirades his colleagues in Lahore so dreaded; credibility is strained, modesty discarded. The reader who knows his man may simply conclude that the two travellers, though they followed a route known to Europeans for half a century, managed to negotiate it a little earlier in the year than usual.

From Ladakh they headed west for Kashmir and further tribulations. Anyone who cried 'wolf' as often as Leitner was asking for trouble. Yet they were now on comparatively safe ground. The route from Ladakh to Kashmir was even better known than that up from Mandi. It was June; conditions were improving, native caravans were on the move and the passes were much lower. They passed Kargil where the ex-ruler, on the orders of the Maharaja of Kashmir, was 'confined in a cage in which he could neither stand, sit, nor lie down'. Then came the bridge over the Dras river. This was a notorious structure of planks, without railings, spanning a gorge about twenty-five feet deep at the bottom of which frothed a big and boisterous river. It was a place where the laden beast obviously needed to be led and where the rider automatically dismounted. Young Cowie, however, thought otherwise. According to Leitner:

> In spite of a warning, my companion insisted on crossing it on his pony, which fell into the river with its rider. I was not so fortunate as on a previous occasion [when, presumably, he had rescued his friend]; and although at one time within a yard of me, Mr. H. Cowie was swept away into the middle of the torrent, whence he was hurled into a waterfall and disappeared.

Men were dispatched downstream to try and recover the body while Leitner pressed on for the Zoji La, the pass by which the traveller from the highlands of Ladakh finally descends into the Kashmir valley. Like all the passes that debouch into Kashmir from the north, the Zoji attracts a heavier snowfall than its height, 11,500 feet, would seem to justify. It remains unpredictable well into the summer with freak blizzards, and snow bridges that become increasingly fragile. The young doctor was depressed by Cowie's death and admits that he was less careful than usual. But that hardly exonerates him from losing one man through exposure and two men and two mules through falls.

Returned to Lahore, Leitner let it be known that his colleagues were lucky to see him back alive. Not only that, but he had amassed a considerable collection of 'ethnological material' (inscriptions, utensils, clothing, etc.) which he generously displayed at one of his soirées; the fortunate few who were able to attend were also favoured with his rendering of a number of Ladakhi refrains. Somehow the idea got about that he really had done something remarkable, and his zeal and dedication caught the attention, in particular, of two of the Punjab's most respected administrators, Sir Donald MacLeod and Sir George Campbell. The latter, as a doyen of the Bengal Asiatic Society, recommended that he be sent back into the mountains to continue his researches, while the

former, as Lieutenant-Governor of the Punjab, made the invitation
official. Leitner feigned reluctance but, once assured of the
government's 'deep interest', he agreed; by the beginning of
August he was back in Srinagar.

His brief was to study the language and customs of Chilas and to
ascertain if it had any connection with Mt. Kailas. Leitner chose
to interpret this as an open invitation to investigate all the Yaghi,
or Dard, peoples. He was also warned that on no account should
he cross the Indus. In doing so he was certainly contravening the
wording of his instructions, though perhaps not the spirit in which
they were conceived. The Punjab administration was intensely
interested in the lands that lay to the north and west of Kashmir.
It had no sympathy with the then Viceroy's policy of discouraging
all trans-frontier exploration, and it attached great importance to
the commercial and political possibilities of contact with the
peoples of the mountains and beyond. Moreover Leitner did at
first try to keep his sights fixed on the Chilasis. If, in the end, he
was forced to take his enquiries elsewhere, it was not he who was
to blame but the man whom he conceived to be his arch-enemy,
Ranbir Singh, Maharaja of Kashmir.

His suspicions were aroused as soon as he returned to Srinagar.
One of the men who had been sent in search of Cowie's body had
duly reported to his *munshi* (secretary). The men had followed the
Dras river down to the Indus and eventually located the *sahib*'s
body at Tolti in Baltistan, a country now under Kashmir rule.
However, the Maharaja of Kashmir denied all knowledge of the
recovery of the body and, when Leitner asked to see the man who
had brought the news, it was found that he had disappeared. Next
an ex-ruler of Baltistan, from whom further news of Cowie was
expected, was suddenly arrested. It could all have been coincidence; but Leitner knew better. Where Cowie's battered corpse
had finally washed ashore might not seem a matter for deep concern; but to Leitner everything that concerned him was invested
with profound significance. And this being the case it was natural
enough to suspect others of dark designs to frustrate him.

Two weeks later, on the way to Bunji, he again met a man who
claimed that the body lay buried at Tolti. Time was precious now
but he recognised the call of duty; the restless spirit of his one-
time companion was crying out for a Christian burial. He turned

about and headed for Skardu, the capital of Baltistan. To keep ahead of the postal runners, whom he imagined to be converging on Skardu with news of his approach, he marched round the clock across the dreary Deosai plateau. At dead of night he descended on the little town. The Governor's *munshi* was located, dragged from his bed and ordered to produce the body forthwith. He couldn't, he said, because it wasn't there; it was buried four marches away, at Tolti.

The fort at Skardu

Perseverance had been rewarded and a triumphant Leitner dispatched his men to recover the remains.

I sent off a dozen men with instructions to take the whole block of earth in which the body was buried and to bring it to me. The men were under the charge of Mr. Cowie's bearer, Kerem Beg, who was profoundly attached to his late master and had followed me partly in the hope of recovering his body. When it was brought in we two washed away the earth with our own hands, found the skeleton, a portion of his shawl, but no vestige of his rings, watch, etc. etc. Most singular events then happened which I must not now, if ever, relate. Suffice it to say that we found and copied an entry in the Governor's official diary in which he duly reported to the Maharaja the recovery of the body, on the 22nd June 1866, of the Englishman who was drowned at Dras, whilst on 17th August following that potentate had denied to me the reception of any news on the subject. I then put the limbs into a light coffin, after wrapping them in linen, shawl wool and certain gums. An attempt was made to carry the body away, which I defeated, and against the repetition of which I guarded by keeping it under my camp bed during the remainder of my travels.

So far as is known Leitner never did reveal the nature of those 'singular events' but, really, the business is mysterious enough without his tantalising touches. Why on earth, one wonders, should the Maharaja of Kashmir have cared one way or the other about Cowie's corpse? His death had been a palpable accident and there were no secrets about Baltistan that needed to be kept from the likes of Leitner; the place was regularly visited by British sportsmen and had been thoroughly mapped by the Kashmir Survey. If it was just a question of the Maharaja hoping to rid himself of this troublesome German, then he might just as well have had the body brought to Srinagar.

That the Maharaja did, dearly, want to get rid of him was self-evident to Leitner. His enquiries were being intentionally frustrated, his servants tampered with, his supplies cut off and his very life endangered. Even if Ranbir Singh had a clear conscience about the Cowie affair, he had much to hide as regards the Yaghis or Dards. For Leitner maintained not only that the Kashmir troops had committed as many atrocities across the Indus as their enemies, but also that their presence there was in direct contravention of Kashmir's treaty arrangements with the British.

When, in 1846, Ranbir Singh's father had been created first Maharaja of Kashmir by the British, little was known of the mountain state and only a handful of Europeans had ever visited it. The Treaty of Amritsar described its extent as 'all the hilly or mountainous country, with its dependencies, to the eastward of the River Indus and the westward of the River Ravi'. Against the evidence of a map this proved meaningless and, with Kashmir's frontier being in effect the frontier of British India, two attempts had been made to define it more clearly. These established that Gilgit, though west of the Indus, did acknowledge Kashmir's rule; in 1848 the British actually urged the Maharaja to strengthen his hold on the place.

On the other hand Leitner was right in thinking that the position was suspiciously vague and that the Maharaja was taking advantage of it. Many of his contemporaries could never forgive Lord Hardinge, the Governor-General in 1846, for having failed to annex such a paradise as Kashmir; they would make a point of discrediting the Maharaja whenever opportunity offered in the hopes that the government would eventually see fit to dispossess him and take over the whole state. Leitner, however, was not impressed by the idea of Kashmir becoming 'a little England in the heart of Asia'. In fact he was in favour of all the mountain lands remaining under local rulers. His quarrel was simply with the Maharaja, 'that potentate', whose territorial encroachments, illegal and heavy handed, were threatening the independent way of life of all the Dard peoples. In 1860 Lieutenant Montgomerie, the officer in charge of the Kashmir Survey, had watched Ranbir Singh receive deputations from the Dard peoples of Chitral, Chilas, Yasin, Hunza and Nagar; it was clear to him that they were all rendering tribute and therefore might be considered as under the orders of the Maharaja. Now, Gilgit may have been tacitly acknowledged as a dependency of Kashmir, but these places certainly had not. Moreover, as Leitner continually points out, it was not simply a question of unsolicited offers of allegiance. The campaigns against Chilas in 1851, Yasin in 1860 and 1863 and Hunza in 1865 showed that the Maharaja was actively employed in coercing the trans-frontier peoples; and this was clearly contrary to the Treaty of Amritsar and to the principles on which relations with the princely states of India were founded.

It was therefore understandable that the Maharaja resented Leitner's quizzing of the Chilasis. He had no wish for the nature of his relations with any of the Dard peoples to be closely investigated or publicised. Knowing Leitner, it is also understandable how this chance of unmasking an impostor was far too good to miss. Overflowing with self-righteous indignation he tore into his task with zeal. In the process he completely overlooked the possibility that, regardless of the treaty, the government in Calcutta might be as happy as the Maharaja to see the western frontier of Kashmir left open for the time being.

*   *   *

From Skardu Leitner had made good progress to Astor, where he left Cowie's body in safe hands, and down to Bunji. Now, having taken the irrevocable step of crossing the Indus, he continued to set a breakneck pace for Gilgit. As a trespasser on the wrong side of the river, there was again a chance of his being overtaken by letters that would tell the local Kashmir officers to turn him back. Sure enough, a courier with just such instructions for the Governor of Gilgit fort, caught up with him on the first day. Leitner reports that at the time he was changing his clothes in a small stone hut beside the road. The courier approached, hurled his package through the open door and turned back; the hut was evidently a staging post. Needless to say, that missive went no further.

Though no doubt fastidious in his habits, it may seem odd that the traveller should pause to change his clothes in the middle of his first day out—if only because, given his lack of baggage, one has a right to an explanation of where the outfit came from. This is not forthcoming. Nor was the occasion one for just a simple change of breeches and shirt. Leitner had decided that the situation called for disguise; a rather tubby Mohammedan *mullah* in the turban and gown of Bukhara re-emerged into the blazing sun. What with the brace of pistols, the clattering jars of Bovril and a cork bed, 'light as a feather' strapped to his back, it must be doubtful whether the transformation was convincing.

I went on through burnt out villages and along paths here and there disfigured by hanging skeletons of people said to have been insurgents against the Maharaja's authority, but declared by the natives to be peaceful peasants hanged to support false reports of victories. . . . I crossed the bridge [over the Sai] at Jalkot where the head of the chief formed a *tête de pont* and ascended the Niludar ridge. . . . On the other side we saw the Gilgit river and the Plain of Minor.

This is the half way stage on the grim road from Bunji to Gilgit fort. Leitner and his two servants had made fourteen miles in the heat of the day over rock and sand. They were exhausted and in a cave beside the Gilgit river they hove to for the night; at last the cork bed justified its presence. But not for long. Shots rang out, the doctor tumbled out of bed, and a visitation from a man with 'a yellow moustache and cat-like eyes' was successfully repulsed. This assailant, he noted, looked just like a Russian he had met in the Crimea. It was interesting that such fair hair could belong to a Dard but also rather galling to be attacked by one of those he had come to save. Later he was much relieved to learn that the man was in the service of the Kashmiris.

Another attempt on the traveller's life, which was made next morning, also looked like the work of this renegade. Striding out in his full Bukharan canonicals Leitner 'trod on a stone trap, the effect of which is to loosen the mountainside and to hurl one into the abyss below'; the stratagem, he explains, was one often adopted by the Dards against the invading Kashmir troops. 'I was saved by accidentally falling backwards.' To him it was, of course, inconceivable that this little landslip could have been a natural phenomenon; Leitner's suspicious mind left precious little to providence. The bare lower slopes and cliffs along all the rivers in the Gilgit region are notoriously unstable. When the snows above melt they dissolve into thick avalanches of mud that spew out onto the valley floor and form the lofty fans of alluvium which are such a distinctive feature of the region. In drier weather the frost or the sun takes over, cracking and crumbling the mud and rocks and keeping up a constant fusillade of stones on the paths below. Leitner was right to cite the ingenuity of the Dards in exploiting this phenomenon; but a lot more people have been killed by natural landslips than by 'stone traps'.

Commandeering some stray ponies Leitner's party pressed on up the Gilgit river and reached the fort by early afternoon on the second day. They were not expected. The fort had just weathered another long siege and now the Kashmir garrison lay licking their wounds—literally if Leitner is to be believed. The place stank to high heaven. The sick and disabled were scarcely distinguishable from the half buried dead, and disease was rampant. Leitner was so appalled that he forgot he was supposed to be an itinerant *mullah* and, in the imperious tones of a *sahib*, demanded to see the commandant. Asked who he was, he drew himself up to his full five feet eight and said he was a European and he wanted the place cleaned up immediately. The commandant, 'rubbing his eyes from [the effects of] an opium siesta', thought it odd that he had had no instructions about receiving a *feringhi*. But, yes, he would make the place presentable and, pending news from Bunji, the visitor was welcome to stay.

Leitner spent that night in the fort but the next day moved out; the local population was proving elusive enough without his becoming identified with their dreaded oppressors. The township, indeed the whole valley, was deserted. Installed in a spacious ruin well away from the fort, he pondered the question of how to make contact with the Dards. In the recent disturbances the tribes, emboldened by the failure of a Kashmiri attack on Hunza, had poured down on the Gilgit valley and for a time only the fort had held out. But it was better provisioned than usual and when a relieving force arrived from across the Indus, the Dard confederacy had broken up, the besiegers taking to the mountains. By the time Leitner arrived on the scene the Kashmir forces had departed on a punitive raid into the hills south of Gilgit. The wounded had been left in the fort with just a token garrison since the surrounding villages had all been deserted; the only Dards were a few snipers waiting their chance on the rocky cliffs above the valley.

Leitner's solution of how to entice them down was simple and characteristic, a Gilgit soirée. Borrowing a drum from the fort he set about composing, in the few Gilgiti words he knew, a suitable proclamation. Next day, all day, one of his servants marched up and down the valley beating his drum and shouting to the deserted ruins and silent hills the glad tidings; *Doctor-Sahib* was giving a party, all Dards welcome. Amazingly, it worked. The Kashmir governor had sufficient respect for a *feringhi* not to interfere and, as darkness fell, a trickle of wild looking men with long hair curling from under their turbans descended from the heights. When the smell of roasting sheep reached their more cautious companions they too followed; that night a hundred and fifty ragged warriors enjoyed the traveller's hospitality. They gorged themselves on mutton and apricots and, when the moment seemed right, Leitner suggested a song. The musicians, usually a fife, clarinet and drums, struck up, the doctor sat back the better to appreciate his first experience of Dard culture and, obligingly, the men rose singly and in set groups to sing the sad songs and to dance the slow rhythmic dances of the Hindu Kush.

The scene was later immortalised in a drawing in the *Illustrated London News*. There sits Leitner on the verandah of his ruin,

smiling benignly and clapping his hands to the music. Before him
the dancers, ringed by their crosslegged companions, are caught in
the middle of an eightsome reel. It looks a little too vigorous. The
artist has sought to convey some idea of movement by emphasising
the swirl of the dancers' baggy clothes; cuffs, kummerbunds and
shawls trail about them as if they were whirling dervishes. But,
this apart, it rings fairly true, even to the gaunt shape of the distant
fort and the ghostly mountains behind. Some such scene may still
be met with in the valleys of Hunza, Yasin, Chitral or Gilgit. On a
moonlit night the thin strains of the flute carry far and wide in the
silent mountain air. The flare of a blazing torch glints in the wide
eyes of the frenzied drummer while the dancers, thin young boys
and gnarled old warriors, move trancelike in a slow and measured
shuffle. They seem as aloof from the music and the clapping of the
onlookers as the peaks sailing above them.

The experience is not easily forgotten. Few mountain people
blend with their surroundings as perfectly as the Dards of the high
Hindu Kush. The Balti of the Karakorams or the Inca of the
Andes seems somehow to have been defeated by his mountains,
misshapen and impoverished by the rigours of climate and terrain. But not so the man of Hunza or Chitral. He shares something of the romance of his scenery; he has kept his dignity. When
he dances he rolls his eyes and stares defiantly up at the heights.
Like the Highland shepherd on his heathered hills or the Arab
Bedouin adrift in the desert, he seems to belong.

It would be nice to think that Leitner felt something of all this.
His scholarly interests precluded a quiet enjoyment of the scene
and he was, anyway, rather unnerved by the danger of his situation; he characterises his stay in Gilgit by describing himself as
scribbling with a pencil in one hand while clutching a revolver in
the other. Yet this night with the Dards near Gilgit was one of the
highlights of his eventful life and a watershed in his career. Thirty
years later he was still telling his audiences in London of how he
braved the rigours of the Western Himalayas, the hostility of the
Kashmir authorities and the supposed savagery of the Dards, to
be the first to bring back an authentic account of their languages
and customs. Added to which he does seem to have been captivated
by more than just the sociological peculiarities of this people. He
was touched by the trust they placed in him when accepting his

invitation on that September night in 1866. And for years to come
he would crusade remorselessly for what he believed to be in the
best interests of the Hindu Kush tribes. It would be churlish to
discredit these efforts simply because of the infuriating conceit
with which he promoted them.

Next morning he left Gilgit. 'Fearing that another attempt on
my life might be successful, I rapidly moved back to Bunji, so as
to give no fixed locality or time for an assassination.' He had been
there just over thirty-six hours. Later his numerous detractors
would make much of the absurdity of his setting himself up as an
authority on the area after less than two days' residence. It is true
that for the rest of his life he wrote and lectured continuously
about the Dards. He claimed to have discovered them (which was
not true), to have invented the name Dardistan (true, though the
word Dard had been around for a long time) and to have been the
first to study their languages (also true). To be fair to Leitner he did
not claim to know everything about the geography of the country
but only everything about its people. This was something that did
not necessitate a long stay. For, though he never again visited
Dardistan, he would be surrounded by Dards for the next twenty
years.

Two of the men who would share his home in Lahore now
accompanied him back across the Indus. They headed for Astor,
where Cowie's coffin lay waiting, and then for Srinagar. Leitner
was due back in Lahore by October 20, and it was now the end of
September; there was precious little time for the usual intrigue-
filled diversions. Nevertheless, he packed in more incident than
most travellers meet with in a year of wandering. At Astor he got
into deep trouble when he discovered a cache of Dard prisoners,
girls from Yasin 'as fair as any Englishwoman', who were awaiting
distribution amongst the Maharaja's favourites. At Gurais he
survived another attempt on his life and taught the culprits 'a
lesson they will never forget'; and then, on the next day's march,
rescued 'by a timely dash' a teacher from Amritsar who had been
press-ganged by agents of the Maharaja. In Srinagar he was baulked
in an attempt to have matters out with 'that potentate', but he
contrived a blazing row with the local British representative over
the disposal of Cowie's body. The latter wanted to bury the
gruesome little box while the Doctor, still keeping it wedged under

his bed, refused; he must take it to Lahore and surrender it to Cowie's family. And so he did. With just four days for the final two hundred miles, he 'rode or walked day and night, carrying Cowie's body myself, when I could not immediately obtain coolies, and finally arrived at His Honour, the Lieutenant-Governor's house in the evening of the appointed day when I was received with great kindness in spite of my dilapidated appearance and the presence of a small party in evening dress'.

His two Gilgiti followers were soon housed in the compound of his bungalow and, taking three months leave, Leitner set about eliciting from them the secrets of their unknown tongue. Later the government procured for him two Kafirs and a Chilasi and in 1872, while inspecting schools on the frontier, he acquired representatives of the Indus valley tribes. By then the compound of his bungalow had become a standing joke amongst the British in Lahore; it was like an ethnic zoo. But it was an open zoo and many came without his prompting. There were visiting *mullahs* from Central Asia and Turkey, Baltis and Ladakhis from the Karakorams and, from beyond the mountains, natives of Yarkand and Badakshan. While his contemporaries posed for the newly invented camera with one foot on a slaughtered tiger, Leitner proudly lined up his performing Dards as if they were the school football team and sat himself in the middle. On home leave he invariably took along his prize acquisition to parade on the London scene; in 1868 it was a Yarkandi, in 1873 a Kafir and in 1887 a native of Hunza— each was the first of his race to be seen in Europe. At the same time he kept up a busy correspondence with some of the ruling families of Dardistan. The Raja of Nagar's son he had met in Gilgit in 1866 and he was still writing to him in the 1890s. A future ruler of Chitral sent him letters written on birch bark and rolled in the hollow of a twig. The Indian post office handled them reverently and the contents added substantially to the doctor's much prized collection of Dard fairy-tales.

Thus it was, by correspondence and painstaking examination of every Dard that came his way, that Leitner pieced together his dossiers on Dardistan. Unfortunately this piecemeal compilation is painfully evident in the results. A pencil-written note would first be rushed out as a pamphlet or newspaper article. It would then be included in his next published work, all of which, snowball style, would then be lumped into his next compilation, and so on. The enquiry into the Chilasi language, which had prompted the 1866 journey, blossomed in due course into *The Languages and Races of Dardistan*, published in 1877. Here the linguistic material is swamped by introductions, footnotes, appendices and digressions in the text itself. Four lists of contents covering some fifteen quarto pages still fail to keep up with the mass of accretions at the end. *The Times* would later describe his books as like the *Talmud*, so full of diverse material are they. To Leitner's way of thinking the suggestion that he was just parading his knowledge was, of course, malicious nonsense. The Druses of the Lebanon, to whom he devoted a chapter, might not, on the face of it, seem to have much relevance to the Dards of the Hindu Kush. The doctor, however, suspected there were similarities between their brand of Mohammedanism and that of the men of Hunza; and anything that bore on the life of a people was relevant to their language.

In so far as all this tended to discourage the reader, whether linguist, ethnologist or explorer, it was a tragedy. For tucked away in sub-section i of Section 22 of Part II of Volume I, one might find a really practical gem like the 'Traveller's Vade Mecum in Astor, Gilgit, Chilas and Guraiz'. Leitner berated the government for letting subsequent travellers visit Dardistan without the inestimable benefit of his scholarship; all it had to do was give him more time off to edit his material. And, sure enough, there in the Travellers' Vade Mecum lie several handy phrases which, if understood by the next visitor to the region, might have put a very different complexion on its exploration. 'We kill all infidels', 'Beat him now, kill him afterwards', are prominent amongst the Conventional Forms of Dard Greeting.

In 1886, twenty years after the visit to Gilgit and ten after the appearance of the *Languages and Races*, Leitner was summoned to Simla, summer capital of British India; the government, it transpired, wished him to undertake another linguistic enquiry. Vindication at last, thought Leitner. The enquiry was to be into the languages of Hunza and Nagar. Might this not lead to works on Chitrali, the Kafir tongues, Badakshi, Yarkandi etcetera? Visions of groaning shelves on all the languages of Central Asia swam before him. He attacked the new task with relish. Given his known antipathy to the Kashmir government and his increasingly critical attitude towards British policy, Leitner was perhaps an odd choice for the job. And there would soon be reason to regret the appointment. But in 1886 it does seem that he was not alone in regarding himself as the leading authority on the region; he was not yet dismissed by the government as a 'self-seeking humbug' whose work was 'egotistic and worthless'.

By this time Dardistan was beginning to loom very large in the anxious minds of those who directed British India's external relations. There was no question of Leitner being allowed access to Hunza; he had to be content with a visit to Srinagar. But there as usual he found Dard hostages-cum-emissaries and with their help he corrected his vocabularies and ethnographical dialogues. Then, on the grounds of ill-health, he retired to England to complete the work, taking with him a man from Hunza. After three years and a thousand pounds of government money, the *Hunza-Nagar Handbook* appeared. It is not the handiest of handbooks. Flat it makes an ample chair seat, and opened out might do as a short bed; strapped to the back would certainly be the best way to carry it. The government raised no objections to its format, and neither they nor anyone else was in a position to judge the accuracy of its grammar. But there was disappointment when by 1892 it had sold only one copy. This was heightened when in 1893 there appeared, most unexpectedly, a second and much expanded edition. Here the snowball effect of Leitner's literary output is taken to absurdity. The appendices are so numerous that they have had to be printed as a separate volume; there are no less than six introductions and rather more than three quarters of the material consists of reprints of his previous works. But the mystifying point about this new volume was that it was published not by the Government of India but by something calling itself 'The Oriental University Institute, Woking' (motto: 'Ex Oriente Lux, Ex Occidente Lex'). And it was being sold at two guineas a copy. Urgent enquiries soon revealed that about a hundred copies of the official edition were indeed missing. They had been removed by the author who apparently regarded them as an 'honorarium'. The identity of the new publisher was not hard to guess.

With the appearance of the Oriental University Institute, Leitner's career enters its final phase. Since the 1870s he had been petitioning for extensions to his home leave and, after his spell of duty in Srinagar in 1886, he relinquished his post in Lahore and retired finally to England. He even became a British citizen. Woking, then a small village with a good railway connection to London, was a far cry from the Hindu Kush; but he seems to have decided that from there he stood a better chance of influencing the fate of Dardistan than he did in India. Nowadays the place epitomises suburbia and one can't help suspecting that that grandiloquent institute may have actually operated from some dingy terraced house where the doctor would try out his latest polemic on his crusty Victorian landlady over the toast and marmalade. The scene would certainly fit with Curzon's verdict on the Institute's erratic periodical, *The Asiatic Quarterly Review*, which was 'a struggling journal' and indeed his verdict on its author, who carried even less weight than his publication.

But Leitner's career is ever full of surprises. The Oriental University Institute of Woking was not a terraced house but a massive neo-Elizabethan palace well suited to be one of the first red brick universities. It had been built to house the Royal Dramatic College, 'an asylum for decaying actors and actresses' of which Dickens had been a patron. Later the main hall would be found ideal for building aircraft in for the 1914–18 war. Leitner bought the place in 1884 and immediately stamped it with his own inimitable style. It was supposed to become the centre of oriental learning in Britain; and for a time it did. The suites of rooms, where the failing stars had passed their final days, were thrown open free of charge to visiting Hindu and Mohammedan scholars. It was affiliated to the Punjab University and its inmates could even take their degrees there. In the main hall was displayed the doctor's collection of ethnographical material, coins, sculptures and manuscripts illustrating India's past, as well as all his mementoes of Ladakh and Dardistan. As a publishing house it produced a plethora of critical journals in Sanscrit and Arabic plus *The Asiatic Quarterly Review* through whose pages Leitner kept up a steady bombardment of official policy as it was deemed to threaten his beloved Dards.

To cater for his students' religious needs there was also 'the Shah Jehan mosque'. Again unworthy suspicions are aroused. A mosque in Woking? More probably just a room in the Institute set aside for Mohammedan prayer. And again one is wrong. The Shah

Jehan mosque, complete with cupolas and minarets, was built in 1889 with money donated by the ruler of Bhopal. It was the first mosque in western Europe and it still stands today. The blue glaze on the main dome has succumbed to the weather and the mosaic courtyard with its reservoir, (about which the doctor was so particular that he had the architect wishing the thing had been built 'in Jericho or some place distant enough not to have troubled us'), has become overgrown. But there it is, the Imam still calls the faithful to prayer and it is still the headquarters of the British Muslim Society.

Leitner died of pneumonia in 1899 aged 58. *The Times*, in an obituary which gave no hint of his controversial character, generously conceded his achievements. 'As a linguist he had probably no living rival'. His was 'the first serious attempt to breathe life into the dry bones of the educational system of the [Indian] government' and he was truly 'both originator and founder of the Punjab University'. The Lahore newspaper which he had started had by then become the *Civil and Military Gazette* with which Kipling was closely associated. And the Punjab University and the Lahore Government College are still, today, going strong. By contrast his crusades for the Dard peoples and his work in England, indeed even his name in England, have now long since been forgotten. The Oriental University Institute collapsed with his death. His books are hard to come by and he is seldom mentioned in accounts of Dardistan and the Hindu Kush. He was a failure as an explorer and had little effect on the course of events in the region.

Yet, behind the cacophony of sounds to which the Gilgit Game will be played, the whispered debate of the strategists, the fanfares for the explorers and the bugles of the advancing troops, there is always this one strident voice of protest. Immoderate, eccentric and sadly ineffectual, it is at least persistent. No move will be made without Leitner taking up his pen, and his writings thus form a unique commentary on the whole story.

They make a lot more sense today than they did a hundred years ago. The young German scholar who blundered into Gilgit in 1866 passionately believed that there he had discovered a pocket of humanity which had been miraculously preserved in something approaching a state of nature. He saw it in the peculiar customs and language structure of the whole region and particularly in the Burishaski tongue of Hunza. This he believed to be 'the cradle of human thought as expressed in language'. A single consonant sound appeared to represent an idea or association of ideas, from which he concluded that he was getting to the very root of human speech, the point at which the customs and environment of the people corresponded exactly to these primitive sounds. If the Dards were really the original Indo-Aryans it followed that a study of their language and lifestyle might reveal much about how half the world still thought and spoke. For at least as long as it took to exhaust this line of enquiry it was vital that the whole area be left as undisturbed as possible.

He steered clear of the notion of the noble savage. The Dards were far from noble and not uncivilised. But he was still tempted to romanticise. Dardistan was 'a paradise', a place where men still believed in fairies and it was the ruler's job to invoke the rain. The Gilgiti for syphilis was *farangi rok*, the foreigner's disease; it, and cholera, were unknown until the arrival of Kashmiris and Europeans. Suddenly one senses familiar ground. It is the story of the Polynesians or the American Indians all over again. Leitner today is immediately recognisable as the conservationist, pleading for the preservation of a primitive and helpless people. Writing in the early 1890s he was prepared to concede defeat.

Industrial handicrafts, historical superstitions and reminiscences, national feasts, which existed in 1866, exist no longer. . . . The fairies and the prophetesses of Dardistan are silent, the Tham of Hunza no longer brings down the rain, the family axes are broken, the genealogists have been destroyed and the sacred drum is no longer heard. . . . I do not palliate the old Hunza practice of lending one's wife to a guest or of kidnapping good looking strangers in order to improve the race . . . but I do find a reproach on European and Indian morality in the fact that not a single Hunza woman showed herself to the British or Kashmir invaders. . . . It shall not be said that the races which I, so disastrously for them, discovered and named, shall suffer from any misrepresentations so far as I can help it, however much the political passions of the moment may deprive my statements of the weight that has hitherto attached to them in this speciality.

Vae victis et victoribus—for history now marches rapidly towards the common disaster. *Finis Dardarum.*

With such apocalyptic stuff the doctor inveighed against the rape of Dardistan. Nowadays he might just have scared off a development corporation. But in the late nineteenth century, a lone and immoderate polemicist defying an imperial destiny, he stood not a chance.

3. Desirous of Active Employment

From 3.30 till 4.30, weather permitting, Fellows of the Royal Geographical Society in London may still take tea on the Society's lawns. In the hallowed stone-flagged hall a grandfather clock chimes the hour; the french windows stand open. But there comes no more the stampede of thirsty explorers; instead just an uncertain shuffle punctuated by the tap of a cane. Out of the map room, past the Greenland canoe of Gino Watkins and a chunk of the tree that marked Livingstone's grave, lurches an elderly academic. A giant bust of Speke, some faded globes and a showcase of relics from some Antarctic endeavour are passed unnoticed as the professor wheels left for the fruitcake and the sunshine.

In its modern role as an august association devoted to the advance of geography the R.G.S. is, of course, a highly energetic and influential body. Yet its headquarters still retain the flavour of the last century and of an age when the explorers, not the academics, made the the running. The Society is justly proud of this past; the archives and photographic collections are being carefully catalogued and prints of most of the Society's medallists have recently been rehung in a position of prominence. Here surely is one of the finest portrait galleries of explorers. From 1839 onwards two gold medals were awarded each year and, in the nineteenth century, they invariably went to travellers. Many of the names are familiar enough; Burton, Livingstone, Baker, Sturt, Scott, Shackleton, Fawcett and Fuchs. But many are now forgotten, and none more so than the considerable number of Asian explorers. Take one of the medallists for 1870, George J. Whitaker Hayward. His frame is next to that of Samuel Baker of the Nile and it faces H. M. Stanley's. In the whole gallery there is no photograph quite so striking as Hayward's. Instead of a head and shoulders studio portrait, here we have a full-length portrayal of the romantic explorer dressed in local costume and armed to the teeth. It stands out a mile and yet, until recently, not even the Society seemed aware of its existence. This neglect is all the more remarkable when one realises that of all the medal-winning travellers in Central Asia, Hayward alone was actually sponsored by the R.G.S.

Elsewhere in the world it was not unusual for the Society to mount its own expeditions or to make substantial grants towards private ventures. Indeed it still does. But Asia was usually the exception—and an exception which the tragic and compromising fate of the Hayward expedition would seem to justify. Not that the Fellows were uninterested. Medals were showered on the pioneers of the Western Himalayas, and it was in this corner of the globe, according to the President's address in 1870, that all the main geographical advances were being made. In fact their only regret was that they could not take a more initiatory role in this exciting field. The trouble was that the Society was supposed to be purely scientific and emphatically non-political, whereas in the *terra incognita* of Asia no such thing as a purely scientific non-political expedition was possible. Here what might be regarded, geographically speaking, as an inviting slice of virgin territory was, politically speaking, no more virgin than a treacherous jezebel.

Dr. Leitner's visit to Gilgit in 1866 had drawn attention to the debatable status of Dardistan and to the highly volatile situation existing on this remote frontier of British India. That was only part of the story. Of infinitely more moment was the power struggle that was brewing over the mountains and deserts beyond and which was bringing face to face the two mightiest empires in Asia. It was this dimension that gave to the squabbles of the Kashmiris and Dards a significance out of all proportion to the size and resources of the narrow valleys and ice-bound heights of the western Himalayas. For Dardistan and the Pamirs, with Afghanistan on one side and Sinkiang on the other, was all that now separated the much coveted British-Indian empire from the steadily advancing might of Russia. It will be necessary to follow this deepening crisis closely but for the present it is sufficient to note that since the 1840s there had been ample reason for the R.G.S. to steer well clear of sponsoring expeditions to such a critical no-man's land.

Why then did they bother with Hayward? In 1868 this unknown young man waited on Sir Henry Rawlinson, vice-president of the Society, and declared himself 'desirous of active employment' on any exploratory expedition that Sir Henry might care to suggest. Within days rather than weeks he was directed towards this very region, furnished with surveying instruments, voted the sum of £300 and packed off on the first possible sailing to India. Such at least was the explanation subsequently given, though a more unlikely sequence of events it is hard to imagine. Amidst all the other mysteries that would surround Hayward's brief career as an explorer and that would bedevil every attempt to unravel the circumstances of his death, this question of why the R.G.S. adopted him in the first place is easily ignored.

Hayward's career had been as obscure as most things about him. He first appears in 1859 as an ensign commissioned in the 89th Regiment of Foot which was based in central India. There is no record of his birth in England but, since the Regiment was one of those recruited in Ireland, it seems likely that he was born there, probably about 1840. In 1863 he purchased his promotion to Lieutenant and in 1864 transferred to a Scottish Regiment, the Cameron Highlanders. The following year he terminated this short and undistinguished military record by selling his commission. The business of buying and selling commissions was about to be abolished but as yet was quite normal. Only one clear inference can be drawn from this episode; regimental life in India did not suit him. Swapping regiments and then selling out altogether were radical steps for one not obviously blessed with influential connections or a private income. Later the only aspect of military life that he recalled with pleasure was the opportunity it had afforded for sporting forays into the mountains. It could well be that the endless drill of the parade ground and the petty business of lobbying for recognition proved the despair of an independent and impulsive would-be explorer. Equally it may have been that the chronic debts, that every red-blooded young officer seemed to run up, got out of hand. Perhaps both, and then one thing more. If officers like Hayward overspent, gambled and drank it was hardly surprising. In the hill stations of British India, where alone they could hope to enjoy a normal social life, the crinoline was still in fashion and the music of the moment was the Viennese waltz. Wagner, still unperformed in England let alone India, would have been more up Hayward's street. There was an intensity about this gaunt young man, a pent-up deluge of determination and a disregard for consequences, which is irreconcilable with the shallow tenor of social life in mid-Victorian India.

Between 1865 and 1868 Hayward's movements are uncertain. Some, if not all, of this time was spent stalking the enormous wild goats, the ibex and the markhor of the Western Himalayas, for by the time he returned to England he knew Kashmir and Baltistan well. The fact that he chose to approach Rawlinson is evidence enough that the idea of returning to this part of the world was his as much as anyone's. Rawlinson, a distinguished soldier, traveller and scholar, a member of the council which advised the Secretary of State for India, and soon to be President of the R.G.S., had made Central Asia and the Himalayas his speciality. No-one in England was more conscious of the threat posed to British India by Russia's advances and no-one did more as a publicist and statesman to draw attention to this deepening crisis. In the councils of state he urged the adoption of a 'forward' policy which by trade, treaties and subsidies would bring countries like Afghanistan, Dardistan and Sinkiang within the framework of India's outer defences. At the same time, in the R.G.S., he monitored every step in the exploration of the region, badgered the Government of India to adopt a more adventurous attitude towards explorers and did all he could to wheedle from it such geographical information as its native agents in the region might obtain. It was hardly surprising if occasionally he sullied the Society's non-political stance by lapsing into the rhetoric of Whitehall. But equally, he more than anyone saw plainly that in Asia there could be no firm line between geographical discovery and political interference. Hayward's instructions emphasised the purely scientific and independent character of his expedition; in fact his being a private individual with no official connections was one of his chief recommendations. But again, geographical discoveries in such a crucial region must have a bearing on military strategy and thus on political thinking. Hayward, knowingly, was being used not just to advance science but to bring pressure to bear on the Government of India.

One other point worked in his favour; Hayward himself seemed just right and so did the timing. Since 1864 the Viceroy in India had been Sir John Lawrence whose external policy was generally characterised as 'masterly inactivity'. Now, with only six months till the end of his five-year term, this policy of non-interference in the affairs of India's neighbours was coming under strong attack. Russia's continuing advance into the Central Asian states of Khokand and Bukhara made a British policy of inactivity look anything but masterly. Reluctantly Lawrence was adopting a more friendly approach to Afghanistan and, with Disraeli in power at home (the Conservatives invariably took Anglo-Russian relations more seriously), there was good reason to expect that the man chosen to succeed Lawrence would be someone more disposed to listen to the 'forward' talk of Rawlinson. Hayward could expect to incur official disapproval and discouragement but, given this new drift of policy, there was a fair chance that if he picked his path carefully he would not be expressly forbidden to cross the British frontier.

According to the R.G.S. his destination was the Pamirs and, more specifically, the source of the Oxus. Thirty years earlier the only European since Marco Polo to have seen this remote and forbidding mountain system thought that he had solved the problem of the Oxus. Lieutenant John Wood, an endearing and improbable explorer—he was actually a naval lieutenant—had made a winter foray up the river to Lake Sir-i-Kol on the Great Pamir; the R.G.S. had awarded him a gold medal for the feat in 1841. But there was now reason to doubt whether Sir-i-Kol, or Lake Victoria as it had been renamed, was in fact the main source of the river. Native travellers had reported other and bigger lakes on what they called the Bam-i-Dunya, or Roof of the World, and other and longer tributaries winding down its open windswept valleys. Hayward, having evidently steeped himself in the travels of Burton and Speke, made much of what he christened 'the lake region of the Pamir' and was soon convinced that Lake Karakul would prove to be the real source of the Oxus and the true Victoria of Asia. This was reputedly a vast sheet of water that it took twelve days to walk round, altogether a more worthy parent than Wood's tarn, which was only nine feet deep and a mile or two across.

The Oxus was one of the great rivers of classical geography and the mystery of its source 'in high Pamere' was as old and evocative as that of the Nile. The attempt to solve it lent respectability to Hayward's venture as well as providing a focal point. But, needless to say, that was not all. The river, or its watershed to the north or south, might soon become the Anglo-Russian frontier. If a war, so terrible as to be unthinkable, was to be averted by territorial delineation, then Rawlinson for one wanted to know a good bit more about the terrain and its peoples. For instance, the idea of an Anglo-Russian agreement about the northern boundary of Afghanistan was already under active consideration. This boundary would constitute in practice a line between the accepted British and Russian spheres of influence. The problem was to define it, particularly at its eastern extremity in the Pamirs. Here even the Afghans themselves were unsure of the extent of their subject territories. In 1869 Rawlinson would be asked to supply precisely this information. He did so to the best of his ability but the agreement based on it would result in a quarter of a century's wrangling and intrigue and would give rise to at least one major war scare. All of which might have been obviated if Hayward had supplied the goods.

Not that he didn't try. Between July 1868 and July 1870 he would make four attempts to reach the Pamirs. His first idea was to follow the track from Peshawar through Dir, Chitral and Wakhan. The earlier pioneers of Central Asian travel, William Moorcroft and Alexander Burnes, had both sent native agents to investigate this route, and Colonel Gardiner, the American adventurer whom Hayward had already met in Srinagar, had himself travelled much of it. He firmly believed that it was the shortest and easiest route between India and Sinkiang. Hayward agreed and, surprisingly considering how little was known about it, they would eventually be proved right. However, the terrain was not everything and the reason that this line of approach had yet to be explored by a European had nothing to do with the height of the passes or the availability of supplies. It was shut, and would remain shut for another quarter of a century, because of its inhabitants. When the Lieutenant-Governor of the Punjab heard of Hayward's scheme to follow this route even he, who had encouraged Leitner's efforts to shed some light on Dardistan, declared it 'absolute madness'. The more favoured route to Sinkiang, that through Ladakh, passed largely across uninhabited tracts where carriage and directions were in the hands of the Ladakhis, a peaceable and smiling race of Tibetan origin. But, on the Chitral route, from Peshawar to Dir the traveller would be at the mercy first of some of the most warlike of the Pathans and then of the fanatically Islamic and anti-British Akhund of Swat. According to the Kashmir troops, the Chitralis, next in line, were quite the most treacherous and slavery-minded of all the Dards and, once out of their clutches and over the Hindu Kush, he would still have to contend with the Wakhis and the Kirghiz; the former Wood had found downright obstructionist and the latter, on whom all travel across the wastes of the Pamirs would depend, were said to owe allegiance to Khokand where the Russians were making massive inroads. Hayward's idea, also no doubt copied from Gardiner, was to travel disguised as a Pathan mercenary; he was tall and bony enough and had picked up a smattering of Pushtu in his army days. But with his breech-loading rifles, his sextants and drawing materials, he would have been pushed to convince anyone, let alone real Pathans, that he was not a snooping European. Luckily he was persuaded to give up the idea.

Discretion, in Hayward's book, was rarely the better part of valour, but in the choice of route he was also forced to bow to circumstances. What Lord Salisbury would call 'the Englishman's right to get his throat cut where and when he likes' was not generally acknowledged; had he persisted with the Chitral route he would certainly have been officially forbidden it. However, honour was partly satisfied by his discovery in the Punjab Government's records of a forgotten native account of the whole of this route; he forwarded it to Rawlinson for publication in the Society's journal. He was also pleased to report that, though his original plan had had to be abandoned, prospects of reaching the Pamirs were now better than ever. He had evolved a second plan. He would take 'the easier line' across the Western Himalayas, by way of Kashmir, Ladakh and Yarkand in Sinkiang and endeavour to return by way of Chitral. Early in September 1868 he duly set off from Kashmir to cross the Western Himalayas.

No European had yet reached Yarkand and returned to tell the tale. The 'easier line' which Hayward now followed was easier only in so far as the government were less inclined to stop him. Three of the world's highest mountain systems had to be crossed, the Great Himalaya, the Karakorams and the Kun Lun. There were five passes of over 18,000 feet, four hundred miles of uninhabited glacier and tundra, and at the end a very fair chance of being sent packing straight back to India. Moreover the precise route that Hayward selected was one which even native travellers did not use. On the other hand he did have a companion of sorts. Robert Shaw, an English tea planter, was also making an attempt to reach Yarkand and it was probably news of this venture that reconciled Hayward to the change of plan. If Shaw, who had been studying the situation and laying his plans for the past eighteen months, reckoned the journey was now feasible, then Hayward could do no better than hitch his modest caravan to Shaw's and, once across the mountain barrier, strike out on his own for the Pamirs.

* * *

The R.G.S. usually met once every two weeks from November till July with a long autumn recess. In 1868, 1869 and 1870 all three of the November inaugural meetings were taken up with developments in Central Asia. Rawlinson himself delivered a powerful paper on 'The Trade Routes between India and Turkestan' in 1868. He took the opportunity to apprise the Fellows of how the Society's Council had decided to support Hayward's venture and of how, although his plans had had to be changed, Hayward was now well on his way. Then Rawlinson was off on to forbidden ground, the trade routes being as good an excuse for launching into political matters as commerce was for pursuing expansionist policies. In a flurry of rhetorical questions he dismissed the Government of India's reluctance to countenance exploration; there was as yet no possibility of a Russian invasion of India; the government might therefore explore and trade in the lands that intervened between the two frontiers without fear of complications; India had as much right to do so as Russia and, by implication, he warned that if she failed to do so, Russia would swallow up these lands as surely as she had swallowed all the rest.

The meeting went on late into the night. Flushed by a sense of the great issues at stake Fellow after Fellow rose to add the weight of his authority or the benefit of his experience to this stirring talk. The Great Game was in play. Before roaring fires in big country house grates, or from leather armchairs in the corner of club smoking rooms, the same talk would go on into the small hours for another twenty-five years. If there wasn't a four for bridge there was always the Great Game. Hayward, slogging his way across the Karakorams, became the merest pawn; the masterminds were here by their firesides sipping their brandies. To send them amicably to bed was the only real test of diplomacy. At the R.G.S. the Chairman cleared the hall with a staggering piece of eyewash. Misapprehension, he believed, was all that kept nations apart; with men like Rawlinson so devoted to dispelling it, all would be well. The sheepskin of non-aggression, it seemed, could be draped over the most 'forward' of policies.

Nothing more was heard of Hayward or Shaw during the 1868-9 session and, when the Society went into recess in July, there were high hopes that the former might already be on the Pamirs. It was known that Shaw, at least, had been well received in Yarkand, and the fact that neither traveller had returned before the passes were closed by the snows of winter was a good sign. Compared to Dr. Livingstone, who had been missing since 1866, there was certainly no cause for alarm.

On November 8, 1869 the Society reassembled. It was another crowded meeting; even a native of Yarkand in flowing *choga* and turban, who was proudly presented to the Fellows by Dr. Leitner, failed to distract them from a rapt hearing of the President's address. The news on all counts was gratifying. Letters had arrived from Livingstone; a young man with the unlikely name of Ney Elias had just explored the changing course of the Yellow River in China; and Hayward, having returned safely from Sinkiang to British India, was about to try yet a third approach to the Pamirs. As the President put it, it seemed that all the objects which most exercised the Society's thoughts in the previous session were 'in the way of being satisfactorily carried out'.

Unfortunately he was wrong; this euphoria would be short-lived. Livingstone was soon lost again and would remain so until the famous meeting with Stanley. Elias' journey along the Yellow River would soon be eclipsed by his marathon across Asia and his travels in the Pamirs; it would be he who eventually realised Hayward's dreams. And as for Hayward himself, his new plan would soon be regarded as a decisive and fatal step.

A month later, in January 1870, Hayward's paper on the journey to Yarkand and Kashgar was read to the Society. He and Shaw, who read his own paper on the journey a few weeks later, were anxious to go down as the men who had opened up this new corner of Central Asia. Having staked everything on such a hazardous venture they could hardly be expected to underplay the significance of their discoveries. They thus went out of their way to emphasise the prosperity of the country, the ease of the routes they had followed to get there and the commercial encouragement afforded at the other end. Sinkiang, or Eastern Turkestan as it was then called, had recently broken away from the Chinese empire; both men suggested that under the firm rule of Yakub Beg it would continue as a stable and independent Muslim state of crucial importance in the power struggle between Russia and British India. The fact that they had both been held prisoner during the whole of their stay, that they had at times despaired of ever returning alive, that they had seen virtually nothing of the country and that they had suffered the most appalling hardships on the journey, was glossed over. In this respect Hayward was slightly less guilty than Shaw, but the gist of his paper was enough to send the Fellows into eulogies of congratulation. It was 'a communication of the very highest order of merit', beyond the President's wildest expectations and deserved 'the highest honour we can bestow on him'.

Hayward's geographical work during this journey had been largely confined to excursions amongst the Karakorams and Kun Lun; the production of a compass in Sinkiang would have been asking for trouble and, as for continuing on to the Pamirs, this had proved quite out of the question; when he had tried to break out of captivity in Yarkand the whole city had been ringed by troops before he reached the gate. However, that was not the point. The Fellows of the R.G.S. were now told that the Pamirs had been only one of his objectives and that the cities of Eastern Turkestan had been the other; Hayward, though he had failed on one count, had therefore succeeded brilliantly on the other, and sure enough he was awarded the Society's highest honour, the Founder's Gold Medal. His work on the hydrography of the Kun Lun was also valuable and he had displayed extraordinary stamina and determination; but this award was equally in recognition of the political and commercial importance that attached to the journey. Rawlinson, accepting the award on his behalf, was at last willing to declare himself; Eastern Turkestan and the Pamirs were of interest, he had told Hayward, 'not only geographically but commercially and politically'. The way was now open for British trade and diplomacy to compete with that of Russia in at least one of the vital areas that separated the two empires; in fact the first official British mission to Yarkand was already fitting out.

Rawlinson was also delighted that his protégé, far from being satisfied with his success—or, as Hayward saw it, discouraged by his failure—was already blazing yet another trail with the idea of 'bagging the Bam-i-Dunya' (i.e. the Roof of the World, the Pamirs). The new undertaking was 'still more hazardous' than the last but Hayward was now a giant among explorers. 'If any Englishman can reach the Pamir steppe,* and settle the geography of that mysterious region, the primeval paradise of the Aryan nations, Mr. Hayward is the man.' He had shown the necessary 'tact, temper and diplomatic skill [and now] that same indomitable will, the same fertility of expedient, the same disregard of dangers and hardships, the same iron constitution and bodily activity . . . will stand him in good stead in his present and still more hazardous undertaking'.

Many would soon be questioning Hayward's tact, temper and diplomatic skill, but of his bulldozing determination and iron physique there can be no doubt. Anything less and he would not now have been contemplating a further approach to the Pamirs which would, in effect, combine all the mountain rigours of the road to Yarkand with the lawlessness of the Chitral route. In a letter to the Society dated Srinagar, November 17, 1869, he outlined his plan.

I am leaving here for Gilgit tomorrow in the hope of being able to penetrate the Pamir steppe and the sources of the Oxus from that frontier. . . . The officials here maintain the risk to be great and give a very bad character to the tribes inhabiting the head of the Gilgit and Yasin valleys. Although not so fanatical as the Mohammedans further west they are sufficiently untrustworthy to render success very doubtful and it is quite possible that I may be a second time foiled in my attempt to penetrate to the Pamir. The danger is certainly great. . . . whether I shall be

---

* The Pamirs were still erroneously described as a steppe or plateau. See chapter 9.

able to cross the passes at the head of Gilgit before the spring of next year is doubtful.

For Hayward, who was usually incapable of recognising danger, let alone dwelling on it, this was an ominous letter. A hastily added postscript gave even greater cause for alarm. In the letter he had only praise for the co-operation and advice of the Kashmir authorities. Now, presumably in the space of a few hours, matters had changed; he begins to sound much like Leitner. 'The Kashmir government is trying to dissuade me from going via Gilgit not wishing an Englishman to see the exact state of that frontier . . . and I feel certain that every obstacle will be thrown in the way of proceeding beyond the Gilgit frontier.' Dards from Hunza had recently been mutilated and killed by Kashmir troops; reprisals seemed certain. It was as if the situation was being stirred up simply to bar his progress, and in such a climate it was impossible to say how an Englishman would be received in Dardistan. 'However I shall make the attempt; and if not allowed to go, or to enter from Gilgit, it will be a satisfaction to have tried one's best . . . I believe I shall eventually succeed in the object of my labours but it may take months, nay, years, to do so'.

This letter was read at a meeting of the Society in January 1870. In the ensuing months there came more letters from Hayward and from the Government of India, which gave further cause for alarm. But the Council of the Society kept them quiet and nothing more was made public, even to the Fellows. Hayward seemed bent on compromising the supposedly scientific character of his expedition, and the council, though most unwilling to wash their hands of him—they had actually just voted him another £300—deemed it wise to minimise their involvement. When in July the Society went into recess, all hopes once again rested on their indefatigable explorer pulling something out of the fire by the time they assembled in November.

In the event they didn't have to wait that long. First to hear the news would have been Rawlinson in his capacity as a member of the India Council. On September 9 the Secretary of State for India got a telegram from Lord Mayo, the new Viceroy. There were rumours in Kashmir that an Englishman had been murdered in Dardistan; if true, it must be Hayward. By the end of the month the news was confirmed and already Mayo sensed that this was no simple case of misadventure; there were some 'very queer stories afloat' that needed careful sifting. On October 3 the news was made public in a telegram published in *The Times*. The matter was 'yet very dark' but the foul deed had taken place somewhere beyond Yasin and the motive was said to have been robbery. Further reports during October and early November suggested that Mir Wali, the ruler of Yasin, was behind 'this saddest event', but when the Fellows of the Society reassembled the air was still thick with conjecture; they wanted to know the full circumstances. Nowhere was an Englishman's life supposed to be more sacred than in India. So how could such a thing have happened? What was the government doing about it and what of the persistent rumours that its feudatory, the Maharaja of Kashmir, was somehow involved? What had Hayward been up to during the full year that had elapsed since last they had been given any news of him and was it true that the Society was in some way compromised by the whole affair? It would be wrong to call it an angry meeting; the Fellows hadn't enough to go on. But they were distinctly uneasy and they looked to the President and to Rawlinson for a full explanation.

Meetings of the Royal Geographical Society in the 1860s and 1870s were major scientific and social occasions. An equivalent today would have to combine the tension of a vital press conference with the decorum of a royal premiere. Before the meeting, up to a hundred of the senior Fellows dined together and entertained the principal speaker and guests; the Prince of Wales, the King of the Belgians, the King of Sweden and the Emperor of Brazil all figured on the guest list during this period. Meanwhile the conference hall filled to capacity and beyond; police had to move in and prevent the crowd from rushing those places set aside for the Council of the Society. The Fellows wore evening dress and, in the absence of lantern slides, were provided with programmes which included relevant maps. Facing the terraces of stiff white shirt fronts, bristling whiskers and waving papers, was a long table at which sat the main dignitaries. A lectern for the speaker was on one side and on the other, under the steely eye of the steward and only just inside the door, was another lower table for the gentlemen of the press.

On November 15, 1870, it was Sir Roderick Murchison, the

President, who opened proceedings. He confirmed the tragedy and gave just the bare facts. Hayward had indeed been murdered, the motive was said to be robbery and the instigator Mir Wali, chief of Yasin. It was an appalling loss to geography but he was thankful that the deceased had known of his having been awarded the gold medal; in fact the award had been made so promptly, while Hayward was still in the field, because the Council had realised that he might easily lose his life.

Rawlinson was more forthcoming. He recalled that the last time he had addressed the Fellows about Hayward had been when he received the medal on the latter's behalf. Hayward was then setting out, 'a young man in the full vigour of manhood, proud of his past honours, full of high hopes for the future, starting on the daring enterprise to explore the Pamir steppe, resolved to achieve success and with every prospect of success before him'. This last statement didn't quite square with what Murchison had just said about the Council rushing to confer the medal because they half expected Hayward to come to grief. But this is carping; Rawlinson was in full flight. 'Now all is changed. Mr. Hayward lies cold in death; not on the battlefield, not in Christian or hallowed soil, but under a heap of stones on a bleak hillside near the crests of the Indian Caucasus,* the victim of a barbarous, cold-blooded murder.' It was hard to speak coolly on the subject. Hayward may have been indifferent to his personal safety; it was one of his qualifications as an explorer and, if it was a fault, it was one for which he had paid dearly. But what of his murderer? Rawlinson quoted one of the Calcutta papers with profound approval.

We have more to hear yet of this Mir Wali—Scoundrel!—more to hear yet of how poor Mr. Hayward died. The latter is certain enough gone to the great silence, and gone with his foot to the last on the path of duty. Such a death breeds heroes but such a murder should bring down penalties on the head of the murderer. We hope the Government will now do its duty as Mr. Hayward did his.

* 'The Indian Caucasus' was a general term applied to the whole mountain complex of the Himalayas including the Great Himalaya, Pir Panjal, Hindu Kush, Karakorams and Kun Lun.

More would indeed be heard of how poor Mr. Hayward died. Rawlinson set the ball rolling by giving a review of all the existing evidence. There were also the letters from Hayward written during the last year which were now made public. A few weeks later there came the report of a British subject, sent to investigate the murder, which afforded the Society opportunity for another long discussion of the affair. Later still at least two other accounts of the murder, supposedly based on eye-witness reports, came to light. And finally there was a long official correspondence dealing with both the motives for the crime and the attempts to bring the supposed murderer to justice.

Using all these it is possible to piece together a reasonably accurate account of events leading up to the crime and of its aftermath. It is hard to do so without hindsight making the whole tragedy appear inevitable but for once this involves no distortion of the facts. If ever a crime appeared all but inevitable it was the murder of George Hayward. Before he set off on his last journey he himself knew it and, in spite of those 'high hopes of success', Rawlinson knew it. Danger threatened from every conceivable quarter. The question was who, in the end, would actually be responsible for the crime and how it would be arranged. Oddly it is precisely these two points that have never been satisfactorily settled.

4. At Eight or Nine in the Morning

"It is just before dawn in the valley of Darkot. Not far from a grove of pollard willows stands a single tent. In this tent sits a solitary weary man; by his side on the table at which he is writing lie a rifle and a pistol loaded. He has been warned by one whose word he cannot doubt that Mir Wali is seeking his life that night, and he knows that from those dark trees men are eagerly watching for a moment of unwariness on his part to rush forward across that patch of light-illumined ground and seize him. All night he has been writing to keep himself from sleep, which he knows would be fatal; but as the first rays of dawn appear over the eternal snows, exhausted nature gives way and his eyes close and his head sinks—only for a moment, but in that moment his ever watchful and crafty enemies rush forward, and before he can seize his weapons and defend himself he is a prisoner and dragged forth to death."

'Ye have robbed', said he, 'ye have slaughtered and made an end.
Take your ill-got plunder, and bury the dead:
What will ye more of your guest and sometime friend?'
'Blood for our blood', they said.

"He makes one request—it is to be allowed to ascend a low mound and take one last glance at the earth and sky he will never look upon again. His prayer is granted; he is unbound and, in the words of our informant, as he stands up there, 'tall against the morning sky, with the rising sun lighting up his fair hair as a glory, he is beautiful to look upon'. He glances at the sky, at those lofty, snow-clad peaks and mighty glaciers reaching down into the very valley itself with its straggling hamlets half hidden among the willow groves, whence rises the smoke of newly kindled fires, he hears the noise of happy children, and then with a firm step he comes down, back to his savage foes and calmly says: 'I am ready'."

And now it was dawn. He rose strong on his feet,
  And strode to his ruined camp below the wood;
He drank the breath of the morning cool and sweet;
  His murderers round him stood.

"He is instantly cut down by one of Mir Wali's men, and as he falls he receives the death stroke from the sword of his treacherous friend, whose honoured guest he had so lately been."

Light on the Laspur hills was broadening fast,
  The blood-red snow-peaks chilled to a dazzling white:
He turned, and saw the golden circle at last,
  Cut by the Eastern height.

'O glorious Life, Who dwellest in earth and sun,
  I have lived, I praise and adore thee.'
                                        A sword swept.
Over the pass the voices one by one
  Faded, and the hill slept.

The verses above come from Sir Henry Newbolt's *He Fell Among Thieves*; they are inserted into the actual account of Hayward's death, on which the poem was based. This account was collected from one who claimed to be a witness of the event by Col. R. G. Woodthorpe in 1885.* With the suggestion of an almost divine transfiguration it represents the apotheosis of the Hayward legend, if not of the man himself. Such Victorian romanticising invites the historian's contempt and there is no doubt that Woodthorpe, or his informant, indulged in as much poetic license as Newbolt. It is, for instance, quite certain that Mir Wali, 'the treacherous friend whose honoured guest he had so lately been', did not deliver the death blow; he was not even present.

On the other hand there is interesting corroboration in earlier reports of many of the circumstances as here given. By all accounts Hayward knew in advance that trouble was brewing, he sat up through the night with a loaded pistol in one hand and a rifle across the table. It was only when he finally nodded off that he

* It was published in *The Gilgit Mission 1885-6* by W. S. A. Lockhart and R. G. Woodthorpe, London, 1889.

was overpowered. To judge from an account gathered by Dr. Joshua Duke, who was in Gilgit five years before Woodthorpe, there was also substance in the story of his climbing the hill for a last look at the mountains. 'He went up, knelt down, faced the rising sun and prayed'. Then he returned, resigned and serene, to his execution. Duke was told that his murderers were so impressed by his cool behaviour that, if only he had spent a little longer over his prayers, they would probably have taken fright.

The long vigil and the prayer on the hill are moving enough, but to anyone who has seen the sun rise on a mountain wilderness, more impressive by far is the notion of a brutal and bloody murder being perpetrated in that bright, disarming light. Hayward knew about killing. His taste for exploration had developed from a love of hunting. Bagging the Marco Polo sheep of the Pamirs was as important to him as bagging the Pamirs themselves. In fact his place of execution was within sight of *nullahs* (side valleys) up which he had earlier stalked. He knew how, tired and hungry at the end of the day, the sportsman was inclined to let fly at anything that moved, caring little if he frightened other unseen game. And he knew that at dawn, for the first shot of the day, it was a very different matter. Then the hunter stalks with infinite patience, checks his rifle, carefully selects his shot and aims with cold precision. Killing by the light of the rising sun is a clinical business; it is the hour for the hangman's rope. Even a Dard at such a time would need good reason to sever a stranger's head.

Amidst all the uncertainties about Hayward's death one thing is clear; it was as deliberately planned as it was ruthlessly executed. The desolate site surrounded by trees was well chosen; the success of the attack was the reward of vigilance and co-ordination; and the slaughter of Hayward's servants was surely an effort to remove all who might shed light on what lay behind the crime. As he knelt to pray, Hayward himself probably had little idea about how the attack had been engineered. But as to who might be responsible he had no doubts. Before leaving Srinagar he had made it perfectly plain that, if anything did happen to him, the man to arraign was the Maharaja of Kashmir; so far as is known nothing had subsequently occurred to make him change his mind.

For what lay behind this accusation we must retrace the events of the last year of his life. It was in November 1869 that he had written from Srinagar that letter about an imminent departure for Gilgit. Having added the ominous postscript about the attitude of the Kashmir government, he had set off. The passes over the Hindu Kush beyond Gilgit were an unknown quantity, but he had only to study conditions on the Great Himalaya passes on the Kashmir side of Gilgit to realise that the season was much too far advanced. The Kamri pass is normally closed by November 15th and sure enough this was the case in 1869; in Gilgit the long isolated winter had already begun. Hayward thought otherwise. No man in the days before mountaineering ever took more chances with the Himalayas. On the journey to Yarkand he had slept with neither tent nor fire in fifty degrees of frost. He had been saved from starvation by eating, raw, his only yak, and over the worst terrain in the world he had still managed thirty miles a day.

What horrors this winter trek to Gilgit may have held he never revealed. But the journey which usually took ten to twenty days now lasted two months. He described a massive arc, crossing the Great Himalaya by the Zoji La, following the course taken by Cowie's bloated corpse down the Dras river to the Indus, and then hugging the base of Dobani along the Indus to its junction with the Gilgit river. The total distance would be about three hundred miles and the last quarter, scrambling over spurs of the Karakorams above the cliffs on the right side of the river, had never before been attempted by a European.

In Gilgit he was expected. The Kashmir garrison had been warned of his plans and duly did their best to frustrate them. To reach Yasin or Hunza meant crossing not simply a frontier but a line of battle. The Gilgit authorities had no more wish to help him befriend their foes than the Dards had to welcome a man travelling under Kashmir's auspices. 'And in this has lain the great difficulty', wrote Hayward, 'to go through either hostile camp as it were, and still keep friends with both.'

Leitner had emphasised the distinctive languages and racial origins of the Dards; these were reasons enough for their detestation of the Kashmiri newcomers. Hayward, rightly, explained this hatred on religious grounds. The Kashmir troops were known as Dogras, that is members of the martial Rajput caste to which the Maharaja himself belonged. In practice many of the Gilgit garrison were Sikhs; but, whether Sikhs or Dogras, they were

Hindus and so was their Maharaja. The Dards, on the other hand, were Muslims to a man. To them the notion of living at peace with 'the cow-worshippers' in Gilgit was anathema. Every war was something of a *jehad*, every fallen Dard became a martyr and every defeat meant defilement. When a Dogra force pushed its way into a Dard valley no holds were barred. On both sides perfidy and atrocities were the order of the day.

For a whole month Hayward patiently tried to negotiate with the Dard chiefs. Presents and reassuring letters were laboriously smuggled into the neighbouring valleys. They were received with silent suspicion or answered with evasive excuses. The only concrete fact to emerge was confirmation that the Hindu Kush passes between Dardistan and the Oxus were, anyway, closed. They would, it was said, remain so at least until June. Hayward as usual was undismayed. Gilgit had seemed impossible yet he had made it. He had found a way through the Great Himalaya and would do the same with the Hindu Kush if given a chance.

At last, in mid-February, there came an encouraging answer; it was from Mir Wali, the ruler of Yasin. This man was one of three brothers each of whom at one time ruled Yasin. The oldest, Mulk Aman, had already been dispossessed by Mir Wali and had now thrown in his lot with the Kashmiris; the youngest, Pahlwan, at the time governor of the northern part of Chitral, would soon succeed Mir Wali. Their father had been generally acknowledged as the most bloodthirsty of all the Dard chiefs and had twice driven the Kashmir Dogras out of Gilgit. But it was Aman-ul-Mulk, the chief of Chitral and uncle of the three brothers (and also the father-in-law of Mir Wali), who now exercised the strongest influence in the area and largely dictated the turbulent careers of the three brothers.

A prodigious memory and a taste for algebra are needed to sort out the complex equations by which the ruling families of Dardistan were related; even a three-dimensional family tree would scarcely do them justice. But, in a land where dynasties rarely lasted longer than a reign and where succession was as much a matter of might as right, it will be helpful to bear in mind the three brothers who each coveted Yasin and, behind them, the cunning genius and pre-eminent authority of Aman-ul-Mulk, ruler of Chitral. All of them were to become deeply involved in the Hayward tragedy.

Though well primed on the treacherous character of all these chiefs, Hayward left Kashmir territory confident of a good reception from Mir Wali. All along he had felt that if only he could make the acquaintance of one of the Dard chiefs he would be able to allay all suspicions. In the event it seemed that, if anything, he had been too cautious. 'The courtesy and bearing of the chief was quite beyond what I expected to meet with in Yaghistan.' He found not just a co-operative raja but a real friend. Together they stalked the markhor and ibex, tested the various passes leading out of the valley, and discussed the routes beyond. The passes were all closed, so choked with snow that even Hayward had to accept the fact. But he was not discouraged. For one thing it appeared that all existing maps had the relative positions of the Chitral, Yasin and Oxus valleys wrong; the passes leading north from Yasin debouched on the Oxus itself and there was no need, as he had imagined, to trespass into Chitral and the perilous clutches of Aman-ul-Mulk; nor, on the other hand, into the Sarikol region which had just been subdued by his old adversary, Yakub Beg of Kashgar. Furthermore, Mir Wali seemed happy to assist his progress. He agreed to help with porters and supplies, and offered an armed guard to see the traveller safely across the mountains and over the Oxus. Hayward was delighted and fearing to overstay his welcome or in any way to prejudice these excellent arrangements, he returned to Gilgit to await the warmer weather.

'And did Hayward', it would soon be asked, 'give nothing in return for this attention from such a known avaricious man as Mir Wali?' He certainly gave a few presents, but of far more substance was an undertaking he made to represent Mir Wali's grievances against the Kashmir Dogras to the Government of India. Hayward, like Leitner, knew of the terms of the Treaty of Amritsar; he, too, interpreted it as outlawing the Maharaja's claims to Gilgit or anywhere else west of the Indus. On the other hand, through their father, the Yasin brothers had themselves a claim to Gilgit and it was this that Hayward agreed to urge on Lord Mayo's attention. It was a foolish move, but he had the sense to warn Mir Wali that he was not a government agent and that there was little chance of success.

He was right. Lord Mayo had no intention of antagonising the

Maharaja of Kashmir when the only gain would be the doubtful gratitude of some remote and faithless Dards and the encouragement of a meddlesome explorer. Hayward, however, had two other tricks up his sleeve, and to reveal them personally to the Viceroy he now took another lunatic risk; he tackled the direct route from Gilgit to Kashmir some six weeks before it was normally open. At Astor he waited for the weather to clear and then took a headlong rush at the Great Himalaya. Horses and baggage had been left in Gilgit. For three dazzling days and tentless nights he waded through fifty miles of waist deep snow. And again he survived; the weather held and by late April, suffering from nothing worse than temporary snow-blindness, he caught up with the Viceroy in the Punjab.

Both the revelations he had to make concerned the behaviour of the Kashmir forces in Dardistan. The first was the evidence he had seen with his own eyes of a massacre of genocide proportions perpetrated by the Dogras on the Dards of Yasin. It had happened seven years before but it was conclusive proof that the punitive raids of its feudatory exceeded in both severity and territorial reach anything that could reasonably be countenanced by the British Indian Government. His second point was that he himself had almost been the pretext for yet another Dogra attack on Yasin. On the trumped-up excuse that he had been robbed by the Yasinis, Dogra reinforcements had been summoned to Gilgit and were about to march on Yasin when he made his unexpected return. Had he not turned up in the nick of time the Dogras would have advanced, Mir Wali would have held him responsible and the Pamir expedition, not to mention its leader, would have been doomed. Which in Hayward's view, had been the purpose of the whole exercise.

Mayo listened without enthusiasm; but three days later when he met the Maharaja at Sialkot he had Hayward's written report in his pocket. Right up till the last minute he seems to have been in two minds about taking the Maharaja to task. But he didn't. A man of great charm and with all Rawlinson could wish for in the way of 'forward' thinking, Mayo, like Rawlinson, was firmly wedded to the idea of winning Kashmir's co-operation for the extension of British influence in Sinkiang; he too was concerned more with the great issues of Anglo-Russian rivalry than with the squabbles of Dard and Dogra. Moreover to have levelled Hayward's accusations would have been prejudicial not only to his own negotiations but also to Hayward himself; if the Maharaja guessed their source Hayward's game would be up. Nothing therefore was said beyond a friendly warning to the Maharaja not to lean too hard on his neighbours.

And there the matter should have ended; except that a week later, on May 9, *The Pioneer* newspaper unexpectedly came out with two and a half columns of packed print on the Yasin atrocities; Hayward's name was at the bottom. It was explosive stuff. In 1863 on the promise of a safe conduct, the beleaguered Yasinis, according to Hayward, had laid down their arms. The Dogras then corralled the women and children into the fort.

They threw the little ones in the air and cut them in two as they fell. It is said the pregnant women, after being killed, were ripped open and their unborn babes hacked to pieces. Some forty wounded women who were not yet dead were dragged to one spot, and were there burnt by the Dogra sepoys. With the exception of a few wounded men and women who ultimately recovered, every man, woman and child within the fort, and, in all, 1200 to 1400 of these unhappy villagers, were massacred by the foulest treachery and cruelty. After plundering the place Yasin was burnt and all the cattle carried off, together with some 2,000 women and men . . . most of the women are still in the zenanas of the Dogra leaders and sepoys. I have visited Madoori, the scene of the massacre, and words would be inadequate to describe the touching sight to be witnessed on this now solitary and desolate hill side. After the lapse of seven years since the tragedy, I have myself counted 147 still entire skulls, nearly all those of women and children. The ground is literally white with bleached human bones and the remains of not less than 400 human beings are now lying on this hill. The Yasin villagers returned to bury their dead after the Dogras retired, and the skulls and bones now found at Madoori are presumably only those of villagers whose whole families perished in the massacre. . . . I have written all this in the hope that the Indian public may be made aware of what our feudatory the Maharaja of Kashmir has perpetrated across the Indus. Apart from the infringement of any treaty, and putting all political motives aside, I trust that every Englishman and Englishwoman in India will join in demanding justice upon the murderers of innocent women and children. . . . The English public must not think that these innocent women were 'niggers' as they might choose to term them. They were descended from the ancestors of the true Aryan stock and had eyes and tresses of the same hue as those of their own wives and children.

The letter went on to argue that the only way to prevent a repeat of the tragedy was to insist on the withdrawal of the Dogras to their legal frontier, the Indus. Mir Wali, 'its rightful owner', should then be installed in Gilgit and a fully fledged British resident stationed in Kashmir as a further check on the Maharaja. Russian agents, it claimed, were already being welcomed in Srinagar, and Kashmiri agents, travelling by way of Gilgit and Dardistan, were intriguing in Central Asia. On the grounds of imperial defence, as well as of humanitarianism, the Maharaja's wings must be ruthlessly clipped.

Although written whilst he was in Dardistan, Hayward seems to have brought this letter back to India himself. Presumably it was therefore after his meeting with Mayo, and probably after the Sialkot conference, that he released it to the press. Publish and be damned, he must have thought; it was the blind impulse of a man who cared nothing for the consequences. Two days later, unrepentant, he was still standing firmly by it. In fact it was almost two weeks before he began to have second thoughts. 'Most unfortunate', he then told Rawlinson, was the publication of the letter; it was 'likely to interfere very much with the objects I have in view'—a classic understatement—whilst the resentment aroused amongst the Maharaja's officials was 'very great and it cannot be doubted that they will in every way *secretly* [his italics] strive to do me harm'. He also claimed that the editor of *The Pioneer* had run the story in opposition to his instructions. Certainly he had asked that his name be kept out of it, but there is no evidence of his trying to stop publication. On the contrary, the day before it appeared he was writing to a friend that he wanted not just the Indian press but the British public at home to know all about it.

And no doubt public opinion was incensed over the report. But so too was Lord Mayo at the man who had so sneakily under-mined his whole policy of soothing Kashmir. Publication of the letter he described as 'a simply wicked thing'. He had tried before to dissuade Hayward from returning to Dardistan; now he telegraphed to London to get the Royal Geographical Society to forbid it. He argued that Hayward's life was in real danger as a result of his indiscretion and, though his death would not greatly upset the Viceroy, the fact that, by it, the Maharaja was likely to be further compromised, would.

This put Rawlinson in a difficult position. Hayward was his protégé and the Pamir expedition was as important as ever; Sir Roderick Murchison had just brought all his influence to bear to get the Tsar to give Hayward a safe conduct through Russia should he decide to return that way. But Rawlinson also agreed with Mayo; the friendship of Kashmir was crucial to British interests. He must have been furious that Hayward had presumed to discredit this vital British feudatory. The idea of forcing the government's hand had completely misfired; if the goodwill of the Dards, or any other frontier people, could only be won at the price of Kashmir, it was definitely not worth it.

But how could he stop Hayward? The man was not an agent of the Society; the journey, he now conceded, had been undertaken on Hayward's initiative and at his own risk. There were no strings attached to the grants he had received and, if the Society should attempt to recall him, he was quite at liberty to disregard it. Which was precisely the point Hayward now made. He offered to sever all connection with the Society but made it quite plain that he would continue as planned. Rawlinson, powerless to interfere, therefore let the matter rest. On June 10 Mayo fired off his final warning at Hayward—'If you still resolve on prosecuting your journey it must be clearly understood that you do so on your own responsibility'—and a few days later Hayward set off from Srinagar for the last time.

He still clung to the belief that, once out of Kashmir territory and back with Mir Wali in Yasin, all would be well. But, better than any of those who warned of the dangers, he himself must have realised that his position was desperate. While the Kashmir authorities fumed over the *Pioneer* article, he had actually been in Srinagar at their mercy. Well-wishers advised him to return to

British administered territory fast. His camp was full of alarming rumours, his servants refused to accompany him because they feared foul play and Hayward himself was convinced that attempts were being made to poison him. A prostitute was apparently hired to administer the fatal dose, 'but somehow that fell through'. Outwardly the Kashmir authorities were friendly enough. In moments of optimism he interpreted this as evidence that his disclosures had put them on the spot and that, for fear of the obvious conclusions being drawn, they would not now move against him. At other times he was close to despair. Of course they would not openly or obviously waylay him. No native court enjoyed a higher reputation for intrigue and cunning; if he was to die, the one thing that was certain was that the Kashmir authorities would not appear to be responsible. In fact this outward friendliness was far more suspicious than their earlier prevarication.

Such being the case he must still have been uneasy when he reached Gilgit without mishap. But when he was allowed to proceed to Yasin and duly crossed the frontier he must have scarcely dared to acknowledge his good fortune. Sadly no records of this journey survive, but when he wrote his last note from Gilgit on July 5 there was nothing untoward to report. He seems to have left there about the 9th, reached Yasin about the 13th and Darkot at the head of the valley on the 17th. Early on the morning of the 18th, the day he expected to cross the watershed into the Oxus valley and the Pamirs, he was murdered. So too were his four servants and his *munshi*.

If bravery is obstinate, reckless, selfish and, for all that, still somehow admirable, then there died that morning a very brave man. Hayward knew the risk he was taking and he faced it with relish. But in a sense he had no choice. To have abandoned the enterprise would have been to accept that his exploring days were over; after the *Pioneer* episode no one was going to let him loose on the unknown again. It must also be suggested that to Hayward danger was attractive. He courted death as the one supreme situation left against which to test his mettle. Earlier he had written in bitter jest of 'my insane desire to try the effect of cold steel across my throat' and of the likelihood that he would 'finally be sold into slavery by the Moolk-i-Aman or Khan of Chitral'. Now, there was precious little of jest in such prognostications. The driving urge to bag the Bam-i-Dunya had become suicidal. He was beyond recall before he died.

* * *

News of the murder reached Gilgit in early August and India by the end of the month. While the government tried unsuccessfully to suppress it, secret agents of varying degrees of competence were infiltrated all along the frontier. At listening posts from Peshawar to Ladakh, Commissioners collected every available report and forwarded them to the Lieutenant-Governor of the Punjab who in turn reported to the Foreign Secretary. Thus, for nearly a year, the news continued to trickle in. But if the government really expected the facts to emerge purely by the accumulation of evidence they were disappointed. Never, surely, can a crime of this sort have been the subject of so many conflicting reports. By spring 1871 almost every man of any influence in the Western Himalayas had been implicated; the official correspondence ran to several hundred sheets; allegations and counter-allegations were doing far more harm than the original crime; the suspects were clearly beyond the reach of justice; and the truth was more obscure than ever. Not surprisingly the government opted to close the case; they accepted an explanation which, if not exactly convincing, was at least politically convenient.

The news came by two main channels and these roughly corresponded with the two most likely explanations. One was Kashmir where the Maharaja's officials reported direct to the Lieutenant-Governor of the Punjab; the other was Chitral where Aman-ul-Mulk corresponded with the British Commissioner in Peshawar. At first these two sources showed remarkable unanimity. Mir Wali had ordered the murder off his own bat and his own men had actually committed it. Aman-ul-Mulk of Chitral had promptly disowned him and had despatched Pahlwan, nicknamed 'The Wrestler', the youngest of the three Yasin brothers, to take over the country. Mir Wali had fled to Badakshan. According to information supplied to Pahlwan by the Yasinis, the immediate cause of the trouble had been an argument between Hayward and Mir Wali about the supply of porters.

Even given that in Dardistan life was cheap, this last statement sounded peculiarly unconvincing—especially in view of the supposed friendship between the two men. But in all the subsequent reports it was confirmed that there had been a quarrel; the question was whether or not it was pre-arranged.

The most thorough investigation was undoubtedly that conducted on the Maharaja's instructions by Frederick Drew, a geologist who was employed by the Maharaja to assess Kashmir's mineral deposits. He subsequently became Governor of Ladakh and later still returned to England to be a master at Eton College. It would have been better if he could have been a wholly independent investigator but his impartiality was well attested and he was at least an Englishman. He had even come to know Hayward personally. All this recommended him to the Maharaja; surely information from such a man would be sufficient for the Government of India. Drew also happened to be in Baltistan during that September of 1870 and could therefore make Gilgit at short notice. He arrived there about the end of the month.

By October 11 the first instalment of his report was ready. Based on evidence given by the Wazir, or Chief Minister, of Yasin it adduced four reasons for Mir Wali's change of heart; Hayward's failure to get the British to acknowledge his claim to Gilgit, Hayward's refusal to proceed first to Chitral as requested, the unreasonable demand for porters, and the fact that this time Hayward's presents were destined not for him but for the chiefs beyond Yasin. Hayward was said to have publicly slighted Mir Wali and then in a heated exchange to have called him 'by a hard name that he was likely to resent'. All in all there was cause enough for an unscrupulous brigand like the suspect to rob and murder. Drew had the poorest possible opinion of the Dards; the safety of a stranger in their hands would be more unaccountable than the murder of one. Mir Wali's friendship during the first visit could only be ascribed to his expectations of what Hayward might achieve in India and of what further presents he might bring back. Disappointed on both counts he reverted to character. Drew was among those who had warned Hayward not to proceed, and he was now inclined to take the line that Hayward had brought the whole thing on himself. The fellow had been amiable enough and quite frighteningly determined; but he was too hot-blooded and domineering for an explorer among such treacherous people.

He should have been sent to Australia or Africa, thought Drew, where 'a knowledge of human nature and a skill in dealing with various races of men' were not so vital.

Rather surprisingly, considering he was a servant of the Maharaja, Drew discountenanced the idea that Aman-ul-Mulk of Chitral, whom the Maharaja habitually regarded as the instigator of any Dard hostility, had anything to do with the crime. Rumours that Mir Wali sought the Chitrali's advice about Hayward had been rife for some time. It was said that Mir Wali was wholly under the influence of his uncle-cum-father-in-law and that the latter had demanded that Hayward be sent to Chitral. When Hayward refused to comply, Mir Wali was ordered to murder him. These rumours were greatly strengthened when it emerged that Mir Wali, after fleeing to Badakshan, had been permitted to recross the Hindu Kush and was now living in Chitral on the best terms with Aman-ul-Mulk. Was the whole business of Pahlwan's pursuit of the murderer and takeover of Yasin just an elaborate piece of window-dressing? It certainly looked that way when Aman-ul-Mulk first refused to surrender his guest and then, a year later, actually helped him to regain, briefly, the throne of Yasin. Drew, of course, was writing his report long before all these developments, but investigating the bare rumours at close quarters he failed to see how Mir Wali could possibly have consulted with his uncle over a hundred miles away during the few days which elapsed between his meeting with Hayward and the murder. Equally he knew that at the time, Aman-ul-Mulk had been trying to curry favour with the British authorities. This would explain the Chitrali's anxiety to see Hayward whom he regarded as a government agent. But murdering him made no sense at all.

One other observation of Drew's is worth of note. In Gilgit he learnt to his surprise that not only had Mir Wali fled but also the eldest of the Yasin brothers, Mulk Aman (not to be confused with Aman-ul-Mulk of Chitral). Mulk Aman had gone over to the Dogras some months before when he had been ousted from Yasin by Mir Wali. He had been living in Gilgit as a pensioner of the Maharaja awaiting the moment when his claim to Yasin might be put to advantage. Hayward had met him on his first visit—'an unscrupulous villain who had already murdered an uncle, a brother and the whole of that brother's family'—and so too had

Drew who reckoned him a determined fighter. That he too had now disappeared from Gilgit did not strike Drew as particularly sinister; he could see no connection between this and the Hayward business, and simply reported it as a matter of course.

Others, however, saw this piece of information in a very different light. So far the evidence examined has been mainly that presented by the Kashmir government. Against it must now be set the mounting pile of reports which, though from a variety of sources and often contradictory in substance, all evinced a profound distrust of Kashmir's role in the affair. Aman-ul-Mulk of Chitral provided some of the earliest reports of the crime, and in the second of these, which reached Peshawar as early as September 1st, he claimed that Mir Wali had acted on the instructions of Mulk Aman. Not much credence was given to this at the time—it was known that the uncle had no love for this particular nephew and that the two brothers, Mir Wali and Mulk Aman, were sworn enemies. Sir Henry Durand, the Lieutenant-Governor of the Punjab, merely asked the Maharaja to keep Mulk Aman under house arrest as a routine procedure.

It was assumed that this had been done and Durand was thus very surprised to discover, two months later, that Mulk Aman had in fact escaped. The news leaked out in a conversation with one of the Maharaja's officials. Almost immediately Drew's report holding Mir Wali solely responsible was given to Durand. The Kashmir government had been sitting on this for some weeks and now clearly felt it should be released to counteract any suspicions aroused by the escape of Mulk Aman. Luckily Durand was personally inclined towards the Maharaja's point of view. He had earlier in the year reassured the Kashmir authorities that no-one took much notice of Hayward's wild talk or placed much confidence in the *Pioneer*; never believe anything in India, went the popular adage, until you see it contradicted in the *Pioneer*. (Durand recommended the London *Times* and duly took the Maharaja's order for it.) He was thus inclined to accept Drew's report *in toto* and, though it was now clear that Mulk Aman had escaped at least a month before he got to hear of it, he also accepted the Maharaja's explanation of the affair.

There the matter rested and, with no indication of why or how Mulk Aman could have got involved in Hayward's doings, it might reasonably have been ignored, one of the many red herrings spawned in this extraordinary episode. But two weeks later, in mid-November, there came, from a totally unexpected quarter, further developments.

Following the visit of Hayward and Shaw to Sinkiang in 1868-9 a diplomatic mission had set out for Yarkand in 1870. It was led by Douglas Forsyth, a Punjab civil servant, and again included the ubiquitous Shaw. In all of its many guises as a trade commission, diplomatic feeler and scientific expedition the mission was a dismal failure. Brought to near disaster by the covert hostility of the Kashmiris and the unfathomed duplicity of the Yarkandis, the mission doggedly retraced its footsteps across the Kun Lun and Karakorams in the autumn. On October 2 Forsyth was nearing the end of the long leg across the dreary Aksai Chin plateau when he was met by a postal runner from Ladakh. Avidly he read the first news from India in months and from Mayo's private secretary learnt of the death of Hayward. Next day his party straggled down into the Changchenmo valley where a Kashmiri escort waited to conduct them into Leh. The escort confirmed the news of Hayward's murder and, in a private conversation between one of its officials and a Kashmiri member of the mission, dark deeds were hinted at. Late that night when the camp was asleep these two men crouched down over the dying embers of the fire. In whispered tones made doubly eerie by the empty silence of the bleak and inhospitable valley, one revealed to the other the blackest secret of the hour and next morning this confidence was duly betrayed to Forsyth.

The gist of the story was that the Maharaja of Kashmir had, as Hayward had always feared, been the instigator of his murder. Incensed by the *Pioneer* article, jealous of what he took to be British dealings with the Dards and anxious about the consequences if Hayward's journey was successful, it was he who had resolved to get rid of him. Instructions had been sent to his wily governor in Gilgit to arrange things in such a way that the Dogras would never be suspected. The governor had then enlisted Mulk Aman and for a fee of 10,000 rupees the latter had organised the murder. When the order subsequently came for Mulk Aman's arrest, the governor had duly warned him to flee and had escorted him into exile before reporting back that he had escaped. Drew's inquiry was instituted simply to assuage British curiosity; a trusted Kashmiri agent had been sent to Gilgit at the same time expressly to see that Drew never got near the truth.

Forsyth forwarded this account to the Punjab. Like almost every other traveller in the Western Himalayas he had the poorest opinion of the Kashmir authorities and held them responsible for all but annihilating his own expedition, a prejudice that was duly noted by Durand. But it was also clear that there was no possible way in which this story could have been fabricated by anyone on the mission. Facts like the escape of Mulk Aman, now backdated still further and thus confirming the suspicion that it had been wilfully concealed, could only have come from someone in the Kashmir government's confidence. It could still be a fabrication and Durand clearly thought so. He couldn't believe the Maharaja capable of 'so atrocious and cold-blooded a scheme of revenge'; the man was renowned, on the one hand for 'humanity and tenderness' and on the other for 'an acumen' which would have found the whole scheme far too risky.

However R. H. Davies, who succeeded Durand as Lieutenant-Governor of the Punjab when the latter died on January 31, was nothing like so sure. With spring and the opening of some of the mountain passes, there came news from Chitral that Aman-ul-Mulk now also believed the Maharaja responsible; he had it on the word of the Mir of Badakshan to whom Mir Wali had first fled. Davies made allowance for the inveterate hatred between Chitral and Kashmir but pointed out that there could be no possible collusion in the accusations levelled by Forsyth in Ladakh and those now coming from Chitral and Badakshan. While the Maharaja's credibility was in question from one end of the Himalayas to the other, little store could be set by his efforts to resolve the mystery.

By now, April 1871, it was eight months since the murder. All the main witnesses had been discredited, the scent had gone cold and there must have been few who could still follow the labyrinthine trails of evidence. To make quite sure that even they would bow out in confusion there now stepped onto the scene Dr. Dardistan himself, Gottlieb Leitner. With a truly mind-blowing deposition he virtually rung the curtain down on the whole affair. The same Yarkandi who had sat beside him at the R.G.S. when Rawlinson first rose to sing the praises of George Hayward had been supposed to accompany the Forsyth mission to Yarkand. However, he reached Leh too late and the British Joint Commissioner there had redirected him towards Yasin, probably with the idea of keeping an eye on Hayward and checking his story about the Dogra atrocities. Nine months later the Yarkandi re-emerged from the mountains and duly reported himself to Leitner's cosmopolitan compound in Lahore. Leitner had never met Hayward but he had commented favourably on the latter's attempts to make something of the Dard languages and he was of course in sympathy with the *Pioneer* article; he would reprint it in full in his next book. Already he was of the opinion that the Maharaja must be behind Hayward's murder; but the report of his Yarkandi was altogether more intriguing.

This man, on evidence given by Mir Wali's *munshi*, claimed that Aman-ul-Mulk, Mulk Aman, Mir Wali, Pahlwan, the Maharaja, the Governor of Gilgit, the Wazir of Yasin and, a new persona, the Wazir of Chitral, were all involved. Some had actually instigated the Darkot murder, others merely helped to conceal it, but since those not directly involved in the crime had organised another murder scenario just a few marches ahead, it made little difference who did what. The actual sequence of events is too tortuous to follow, but there was enough already established detail to suggest that here again was more than just wild invention. On the other hand was it possible that all the suspects, most of whom were sworn enemies, could possibly have acted together to conceal the facts? And could Hayward have marched blindly into not one murder plot but two? It stretched credibility beyond breaking point.

Holding up their hands in horror, the British authorities seem finally to have abandoned the case. Investigations came to be directed more towards discovering the whereabouts of Mir Wali. For four years he continued to flit back and forth across the Hindu Kush until run to earth by one of Pahlwan's henchmen. In a scene worthy of vintage Hollywood the two men met on a rocky precipice, locked in mortal combat and finally hurtled over the edge. Mulk Aman fared rather better. Finding sanctuary in Tangir, south of Gilgit, he continued to exercise a sinister influence in Dardistan and was still there fifteen years later, accused of attempting to snuff out another British initiative in the region.

It would be absurd at this remove to attempt a verdict on the Hayward murder. The most one can do is to present all sides of the case, particularly since no such objectivity was shown at the time. The British had a vested interest in retaining the goodwill of the Maharaja. It was therefore the Kashmiri version of events and particularly the Drew report which were officially adopted. Mir Wali was held to be the sole culprit and the motive robbery; it was conveniently ignored that to rob a man it is not necessary to kill him, even less to kill all his servants, or that the repercussions of such a murder would far outweigh the acquisition of a few guns, stores and knick-knacks. Allegations against the Maharaja were of course investigated, but under a blanket of strict secrecy; anyone giving public utterance to them was severely reprimanded. Anti-Kashmir prejudice was running high at the time. Hayward's revelations about the Dogra atrocities had been bad enough, but if the idea that the Maharaja was responsible for his murder had gained any ground, the popular outcry for his removal and the annexation of his state might have been overwhelming. Witness Rawlinson's adamant denials to the R.G.S. when Hayward's death was first confirmed. Murchison, the President, had risen waving a piece of paper in the air. 'You have entirely exonerated the Maharaja of Kashmir; but there are persons, and I hold a letter in my hand from one, who still have their doubts about it.' This was before Drew's report had been made public and Rawlinson had only the flimsiest evidence to go on. But he was positive; there was no foundation whatever for inferring Kashmir complicity and no possible connection between Hayward's indiscretion over the 'exaggerated' *Pioneer* article and his murder.

One final question needs to be answered. Why was a British officer not sent to investigate? It was said that the Maharaja had himself suggested this and had only sent Drew when the offer was refused. The reason given at the time was that it was too dangerous an undertaking and that the co-operation necessary to make the thing a success could not be counted on. But if, like Drew, the man never ventured beyond Gilgit, there was surely no risk. And, as to the lack of cooperation, a British officer would surely have stood a better chance of getting at the truth from the Dards than did Drew, an employee of the Maharaja. It is hard to resist the conclusion that the government did not want an independent British-led enquiry. Perhaps they feared that in the process more Dogra misdealings on the frontier would be uncovered. Perhaps they knew that, for all his apparent willingness to co-operate, the Maharaja would deeply resent any such intervention. Or perhaps there was a real fear that such an enquiry might reveal a Kashmir involvement too embarrassing to contemplate.

There was yet one last journey for George Hayward. His

Hayward's grave as drawn by Drew

battered remains had somehow to be recovered and given a Christian burial. Pahlwan strongly opposed the idea of anyone visiting Darkot, but eventually a lone Dogra, deputed by Drew, was allowed to visit the scene of the crime. From one of several artificial piles of stones he noticed a pair of hands protruding. They were bound together, the palms turned upwards. 'I recognised them as those of the sahib not by the colour, for that was changed [it surely must have been; this was three weeks after the murder], but by their form. Clearing the stones away I saw by the hair and beard that this was indeed the sahib's body.' The extreme dryness of the Hindu Kush climate had kept it partially intact. Along with a few personal effects—pony, tent, books, the legs of a table, a watch and sword—the corpse was carried down to Gilgit. Drew himself read the burial service and, over the newly dug earth in the corner of someone's orchard, a final salute was fired by a party of Dogra soldiers.

Hayward must have turned uneasily in the sandy soil. Here was irony run riot. To be buried by a servant of the government he mistrusted above all others, to be saluted by its soldiers, and then to be given a headstone* by its ruler was bad enough. But if Rawlinson had had his way, worse would have followed. Exactly two years after the murder, a Mrs. Fanny Fison addressed the Government of India about getting some compensation for the murder. She was an aunt of Hayward's, but her concern was for his impoverished sister and family who lived in New Zealand. Rawlinson conceded that they had no real claim on the government but he thought it a travesty that the murder was still unavenged; he suggested that the Kashmir government impose a £500 fine on the Yasinis. If this was not paid—a fairly safe prediction—it should be used as the pretext for a joint Anglo-Kashmir subjugation of all the Dard peoples. What Hayward would have regarded as a far worse crime than his own murder was actually being urged in his name. Luckily nothing came of the suggestion. The Hayward family received no compensation and the Dards were left to carry on their fight for political survival.

Besides recovering Hayward's body, the Dogra soldier also managed to get the first eye-witness account of the actual murder. It came from the village headman and has no more claim to authenticity than the later reports; the Dogra in question was soon promoted by the Maharaja and the headman would certainly have suppressed anything prejudicial to his local standing. Yet, in its simple details and stark narrative, and in the headman's anxiety to stick to his own field of observation without offering

---

*The epitaph read:
Sacred to the memory of Lieut. G. W. Hayward, Medallist of the Royal Geographical Society of London, who was cruelly murdered at Darkot, July 18th, 1870, on his journey to explore the Pamir steppe. This monument is erected to a gallant officer and accomplished traveller by His Highness the Maharaja of Kashmir at the instance of the Royal Geographical Society of London.
The headstone was still standing in the 1960s but recent enquiries have failed to discover its whereabouts.

any explanations or accusations, there is here a certain ring of truth.

That night the sahib did not eat any dinner, but only drank tea, and sat watching the whole night in his chair with guns and pistols before him and a pistol in his left hand while he wrote with the other. In the morning, after taking a cup of tea, he lay down for a hour or two's sleep. Shah Dil Iman, having sent a man to see, and found that he was sleeping, took his men by a round to the ground in the forest above where the tent was, and then himself coming asked the khansaman [cook] if he were asleep; on his being told that he was, Kukali entered the tent. One of the Pathan servants asked him what he was about, and took up a stick to stop him, but others coming round and keeping the Pathan back, Kukali went into the tent and caught the sahib by the throat, and, more at that moment coming in, put a noosed rope round his neck, and, with the same rope, tied his hands behind him. The servants were all overpowered and bound at the same time. Then they brought the sahib, thus bound, away from the village into the forest for a distance of a mile or mile and a half; and as they were going he tried to induce them to spare his life by promises, first of what was in his boxes—but that they jeeringly said was theirs already; then of a larger ransom to be obtained from the English country; and lastly, he said that he would write to the Bukshee [governor] at Gilgit for the money for them. This, however, they would not listen to. Then the sahib asked for his *munshi* to be brought, but he had been taken off in another direction, and could not quickly be found; then they took the ring off his finger, and then Shah Dil Iman drew his sword, on which the sahib repeated some words which seemed like a prayer, and Shah Dil Iman felled him with one blow. Then Kukali brought the sahib's own sword, and said he would like to try it; so he struck a blow with it on the sahib's body. It was eight or nine in the morning when the murder was committed.

PART TWO

Vidi

5. The Hunza Road

The explorers of the Western Himalayas include many unsung heroes. Although Hayward, and later Elias and Younghusband, enjoyed the recognition of the Royal Geographical Society, in the popular mind they never rivalled men like Stanley and Livingstone; they remained essentially explorer's explorers. As for the rest, they achieved not even that distinction. In an atmosphere as highly charged with political secrecy as the Gilgit Game, discretion came to be regarded as the would-be explorer's one vital attribute; not surprisingly many of the greatest pioneers thus remain the most obscure.

To make matters worse, this personal reticence is invariably coupled with a most abstemious approach to travel writing. Blow by blow accounts of the journey and graphic descriptions of the terrain are the exception rather than the rule. Where a personal journal exists, it often proves no more colourful than the official report. After all, if you may never write anything more entertaining than official reports, why bother? Younghusband, of course, would. To a commendable discretion he added a yen for popular recognition; somehow the world just had to share his excitement whenever the rising sun tipped the topmost peaks a flamingo pink. But the only way he could get away with this was by withholding so much about his actual movements that one sometimes knows neither where it is all happening nor why he is there.

More typical, both as an obscure explorer and a reluctant travel writer, is John Biddulph. By 1880 no man had seen as much of the Western Himalayas as Biddulph. Younghusband would scarcely equal his record and, in terms of the ground actually covered, he had outmarched even the indefatigable Hayward. In 1886 he had heard news of Leitner's and Cowie's fiasco at the Dras bridge while he was shooting wild yak on the uppermost Indus inside Tibet. In 1873 he had accompanied Forsyth on his second mission across the Karakorams to Sinkiang. From Kashgar he had followed the ancient caravan route to China further into the Takla Makan desert than any predecessor since Marco Polo and the Jesuit, de Goes. The following year he had made an excursion across the Pamirs to Wakhan and inspected the northern face of the Hindu Kush. And in Dardistan between 1876 and 1880 he would become the first European to visit Hunza and the first into Chitral.

Altogether a remarkable record. But if one looks for his name in the rolls of fame, one looks in vain. With the R.G.S. he made no contact at all. Some of his journeys were certainly top secret, but others could have easily been presented in such a way as not to give offence; one at least was undertaken on his own initiative and purely for the sport. The conclusion must be that here was a man who cared little for the armchair geographers and their gold medals. A certain irreverence is also detectable in his political work; and again his praises remained unsung. He pinned his reputation on an entirely new departure in British policy towards the Gilgit region; he saw it through and he saw it fail. No knighthood, not even a medal, came his way. And for the rest of his career he forswore all interest in the mountains.

His only enduring contribution to the subject was a book, *The Tribes of the Hindoo Koosh*. More organised than anything Leitner wrote, it became the standard work. Earlier writers had dropped tantalising hints about the strange Dards and their peculiar languages and customs. Here at last was a sober and authentic account by a man who had apparently lived and travelled in the Hindu Kush. It had to be a modest success and, with a bit of imagination, could have been a sensation. As it is, the only remarkable thing is how anyone with Biddulph's experience could have written such an austere account. Somewhere, surely, the traveller must slip unconsciously into a bit of narrative or toy with an evocative description. If the pioneer on virgin soil in the most dramatic terrain in the world takes no such liberties then who can? But no, Biddulph sticks to facts, to vocabularies and genealogies. He is writing a gazetteer, not a travelogue.

There is one brief but significant exception. Dealing with the northern outlet from the Gilgit valley up the Hunza river, he writes:

The river here flows between perpendicular rocks across the face of which none but the most experienced cragsman can find a path. On the occasion of my visit to Hunza in 1876 I suddenly found myself confronted with a more difficult and dangerous piece of ground than I had ever traversed in a tolerably large experience of Himalayan sport.

The statement springs off the page. What can this piece of ground have been like, to stop such a one as Biddulph dead in his tracks and to interrupt the prosaic and impersonal rhythm of his scholarship?

For nearly half a mile it was necessary to scramble over rocky ledges, sometimes letting oneself down nearly to the water's edge, then ascending 300 or 400 feet above the stream, holding on by corners of rock, working along rocky shelves 3 or 4 inches wide, and round projecting knobs and corners where no four-footed animal less agile than a wild goat could find a path.

The book is almost bursting into narrative; another paragraph, in which there is a grandiloquent description of Rakaposhi, slips past before composure is regained and it can continue on its dogged path. In his confidential report to the government and in his personal diary Biddulph uses much the same words. Clearly it made a deeper impression than anything that Ladakh, the Karakorams or the Pamirs had to offer. But to anyone who has followed in his footsteps this will come as no surprise. Biddulph was just inaugurating a tradition among travellers that lasts to this day—that of straining every literary muscle in an effort to do justice to the Hunza road.

All the Hindu Kush valleys are far narrower at their mouths than higher up. The phenomenon was first remarked by Biddulph who marvelled how valleys that supported several thousand families were accessible only by the highest of passes at the top end and the narrowest of gorges at the bottom; it seemed to explain how the Dard tribes had individually remained so distinct. According to Leitner, the men of Hunza were the most distinctive of all and, seeing the gorge by which they maintain contact with the outside world, that would seem highly probable. If ever there was a crack in the mountains up which man was not supposed to travel, this surely is it. From Gilgit to Hunza is a distance of fifty-two miles.

On a good day, travelling by jeep, it takes seven hours. Through-out, the track follows the course of the Hunza river. This river, charged with clearing the debris of glaciers, avalanches and land-slides from the Karakorams on one side and the Hindu Kush on the other, is in spate for most of the year. An analysis of its liquid would probably reveal as much solid matter as water. Rocks the size of buses trundle along in the midst of the grey flood and, whenever the volume falls, a moraine is left to mark the floodline. There are no pools for fishermen, no falls for the photographer and no grassy banks for the picnicker, just this thundering discharge of mud and rock.

It is a revolting sight, though one glimpsed only rarely. For throughout the journey up to Hunza the track runs not beside but above and over the river. At fifty feet up one can feel the rush of icy air that accompanies the flood and one must shout to be heard. Five hundred feet up and one can still hear it roaring below like some insatiable monster. At this height the place is revealed for what it is, less a valley or gorge than some gigantic quarry. The lack of any kind of vegetation is less striking than the absence of yellow excavators; one feels a distinct need for a tin helmet. A trickle of pebbles slithers down onto the track ahead. A few stones follow, bounding playfully on their way down to the river. Then a chunk of rock, in fact a whole slice of mountain, is on the move; it looks to be falling in slow motion but within seconds the track is gone and the river below is gobbling up the last of the debris. No-one travels the Hunza road without seeing a trickle of stones and wondering what may follow. The track is obliterated, on average, once a week and several hundred men are employed, permanently and perilously, in reconstructing it.

Landslides are commonest on those stretches where the loose mountain is less than vertical. The rock precipices which make up the rest of the route are absolutely sheer. Sometimes the track manages to zig-zag up and over them. The actual rise in elevation between Gilgit and Hunza is about 5,000 feet, but the road climbs and falls more like 50,000. The hairpins are so frequent that one seems to be covering more ground vertically than horizontally; so tight are they that the jeep has to reverse several times to get round. (Alternatively the passengers may be called on to bounce the rear of the jeep round; there is less danger of going off the edge but, given the gradient, a very real possibility of the vehicle turning a somersault.)

Where the sheer rock can in no way be circumvented the famous parapets or galleries conduct the track straight across the cliff face. In places engineers have managed to blast a groove wide enough for a jeep, but there are still long sections where the driver must trust to the traditional arrangement of scaffolding and trestles. The river here is glimpsed not just over the side of the road but through it. Furze, perhaps spread with a bit of mud, is the surface; the foundations are timbers, old and worn tree trunks, resting on others embedded all too loosely in any handy crevice that the cliff face offers. That is all. No sign of concrete, no cantilevers and no suspension wires. The logs creak and bounce as a jeep approaches; pedestrians cling to the rock face as much to keep their balance as to allow it to pass. To peer down on the gurgling flood four hundred feet below takes the nerves of a steeplejack.

In a way the scale of the whole thing is the most daunting feature of all. For the last few miles the opposing wall of the gorge is hewn out of the pedestal on which stands Rakaposhi, that most photogenic of mountains. Twenty five thousand feet up and yet visible from the track, its snowswept ridges wall out the day. Then slowly it grows lighter. The cliffs become slopes and, high on a sun splashed ledge, vegetation reappears. The road climbs for the last time and there, like a table spread with unbelievable colour and plenty, is Hunza.

Such was the Hunza road in the 1960s. What it must have been like in the days of pedestrians only, one can scarcely imagine. Biddulph's immediate successors speak of single logs where now there are parapets and corkscrew staircases or flimsy wooden ladders where now there are hairpins. During the winter months when the river was at its lowest a horse could just be led along it; but even then there were places where it had to be lowered by ropes and steadied by men hanging onto its tail. Laden ponies were out of the question; the only carriage was by porters. In his official report Biddulph maintained that there might be something artificial about its horrors. It hadn't actually been sabotaged but he reckoned that the Hunza people, 'intrepid cragsmen', preferred to keep it dangerous. It was their best defence against the Dogras at Gilgit and they would probably resist any attempt to improve it.

He was quite right. Hacking away at the Hunza road 'to allow of a man passing over the worst places without using his hands' contributed to his own downfall and would eventually precipitate the first Anglo-Dard campaign.

* * *

In the aftermath of the Hayward tragedy there must have seemed scant prospect of another lone Englishman being allowed to scramble with guns and dogs up into the perilous kingdoms of the Hindu Kush. But, in fact, since 1870 one or two dedicated sportsmen had annually been given a grudging permission to cross the Indus at Bunji and stalk in the immediate vicinity of Gilgit. To all appearances John Biddulph, clawing his way along the Hunza road in 1876, looked just like another of these. His passion for sport was patently sincere. In Gilgit the harrowing business of having to shoot poor Vanguard, his rabid spaniel, had upset him more than the near death of his companion or the customary prevarication of Dards and Dogras. His personal diaries read much like gamebooks, and if it hadn't been for the shy ibex and inaccessible markhor he would surely never have set foot in the Western Himalayas.

But Biddulph was also a captain in a crack regiment of the Bengal cavalry and an A.D.C. to, and close personal friend of, Lord Northbrook, Mayo's successor as Viceroy. In Dardistan he was travelling on duty. Outside of the Indian foreign department only the Maharaja of Kashmir and his deputy in Gilgit knew the facts; and they were sworn to secrecy. But this innocent-looking hunting trip was actually a front for a highly confidential and crucial piece of espionage.

That there existed tracks over the Hindu Kush between the Dard valleys and the Oxus had been public knowledge for years. Chitral boasted close ties with Badakshan and Hunza with Sinkiang; in both cases they straddled the mountain spine. Native agents working for the Government of India had brought back eye-witness accounts of some of the passes, and Hayward had personally investigated the approaches of all those that led north from the Yasin valley. But in Hayward's day no special importance attached to these tracks. They might be all right for the slave dealers goading on their pathetic caravans of Kafir children and

Dard peasants by the least frequented routes that led to the Bukhara slave-market, but they were scarcely viable as trade routes, let alone as military roads. Too lawless for the former and too difficult for the latter, they were also considered inaccessible to the Russians; the Pamirs effectively walled them off to the north.

Or so it had been thought in 1870. But by 1874 all this had changed. In that year four British officers, Biddulph being one of them, had crossed the southern Pamirs from Sinkiang to Wakhan; ostensibly they were testing the ground for the return of the second Forsyth mission to Kashgar. In the process they investigated the extent of Afghan territorial claims in the region, re-examined the supposed source of the Oxus and checked on the significance of the Pamirs as a strategic barrier. In each case they came up with devastating discoveries. First it was confirmed that Rawlinson's line for the Afghan frontier on the Pamirs, which the Russians had just accepted as a limit to their sphere of influence, was a nonsense. Without the expected benefit of Hayward's on-the-spot investigations, Rawlinson's red pencil had followed the line of what was thought to be the Oxus. Now it was discovered that all the Afghan dependencies in the region sprawled along both sides of this river. Not only, therefore, was the agreement worthless as a limitation but, in so far as the Afghans would soon choose to assert their influence beyond the river, extremely dangerous.

Perhaps by way of softening the blow the mission had reported that the river Rawlinson thought to be the Oxus actually wasn't anything of the sort. The true Oxus, they decided, flowed not west from the Great Pamir but east from the Little Pamir. Otherwise known as the Aksu, Murghab or Bartang, this river pursued its course hundreds of miles to the north of Rawlinson's Oxus and, this being the case, made a literal interpretation of the 1873 agreement meaningless. Furthermore, besides getting the geography of the Pamirs all wrong, people had also got the wrong idea about their strategic importance. Colonel Gordon, leader of the party, Trotter his surveyor and Biddulph his political advisor, all agreed that strategically the Pamirs were no barrier at all. A column of Russian artillery advancing from Khokand could reach Wakhan and the north face of the Hindu Kush considerably quicker than a British one sent up from the Punjab could reach the southern face in Yasin or Hunza—if it could get there at all. Gordon's party had lost twenty-one out of their thirty mules while crossing the Little Pamir, the wind had flayed their faces till the blood ran, and the geologist of the party would never recover from the effects of altitude and exposure. But it was April and the mountains were still in the grip of a winter exceptionally severe even by Pamir standards. With extraordinary detachment they insisted that for the other nine months of the year the Pamirs posed no obstacles. The passes were low and easy, the grazing was some of the richest in the world and the open valleys were well stocked with the herds and flocks of the nomadic Kirghiz. From Osh in Khokand to Sarhad in Wakhan only thirty miles of road needed attention.

Not only would a Russian force coming by this route have no difficulty in reaching the Hindu Kush; they would have no difficulty in crossing it either. For the last and most unexpected bombshell unearthed by the 1874 mission was the apparent ease of the Hindu Kush passes. An informant told Gordon that the Killik pass over to Hunza was 'remarkably easy' and 'open all the year round'. In Wakhan they heard tell of the Baroghil pass into Chitral and the Darkot to Yasin, the former gentle enough for field artillery of sorts to have crossed it in recent years. And the ruler of Wakhan appeared to have yet another route up his sleeve; 'Before you leave,' he told Gordon, 'I intend to tell you of a good road to India.' Gordon paid off all £45 of Wakhan's national debt, thus establishing a tradition of munificence that subsequent travellers would find hard to follow. His reward was to be told of the Ishkoman pass and the road thence to Gilgit, Chilas and on down the Indus.

Before leaving the area, John Biddulph had been sent to inspect the northern approaches to these passes. The most westerly was the Baroghil and he had tackled this first. Still, it was the wrong time of year. His horse had got stuck in a snowdrift and eventually, a mile short of the crest, so had he. The Darkot, Ishkoman and Killik passes proved still more unapproachable. But again he was not impressed. Compared to the terrible crests on what was then the only regular route across the Western Himalayas, that from Ladakh to Sinkiang, these Hindu Kush passes were child's play. The Baroghil was not much over 12,000 feet as against 17,000 and 18,000 in the Karakorams and Kun Lun. Nor could you really call it a pass; it was more like a 'break in the great mountain barrier', 'a gate' badly needing to be secured against the intruder. It was said that you could cross it without slowing from a gallop and that it was open for ten months of the year. It was a pity April happened to be one of those months when it was closed, but Biddulph was quite convinced that when it was open so too, wide open, was India.

The Government of India in the person of Lord Northbrook and his advisers had examined these various revelations in their political context. Beyond the Pamirs Russia's advance seemed at the time inexorable. In 1873 the khanate of Khiva, which for thirty years had resisted the bear's embrace, finally succumbed. Khokand and the Syr valley, nibbled away throughout the 1860s, were annexed in March 1876 and in that year Russian explorers, having already crossed the Alai ranges, first appeared on the Pamirs; a year later the Russian flag would be flown near the shores of Lake Karakul. Thanks to the Kirghiz who wintered in Khokand but in summer grazed their flocks on the Pamirs, they even inherited some sort of claim to the region. But the annexation of Khokand also had serious implications for Sinkiang. With control of the Syr valley also went access to the easiest of passes leading to Kashgar; Sinkiang was now theirs for the picking. The invasion of India direct from there through Ladakh and Kashmir could be discounted but, if a push were to be made across the Pamirs and Hindu Kush, the possession of Sinkiang, securing the flank of the advance and affording unlimited sources of supplies and carriage, had the most sinister implications.

In these circumstances any British move, however 'forward' or heavy-handed, seemed to be justified if the Hindu Kush passes could be made impregnable. But there was of course the other dimension, that of Dogra and Dard. And this, by contrast, called for extreme caution. There was nothing the Russians could do if British Indian troops were sent to hold the passes, but, in the light of what had happened when just one Englishman showed his face in Yasin, such a move was unthinkable. The murder of George Hayward had done more than any other single event to bring Dardistan to public attention. In 1874 and again now in 1876

Biddulph was commissioned to further probe the case. On the grounds of imperial prestige it was highly unsatisfactory that an Englishman's life should be forfeit within three marches of the then frontier and well within the desired one. If nothing else, the case had highlighted the impossible nature of the terrain and the volatile state of Dard–Kashmir relations. It suggested that the Maharaja had little say in the affairs of Yasin and was therefore in no position himself to undertake the defence of the Hindu Kush.

Yet this, the extension of Kashmir rule right up to the passes, and the establishment there of Dogra troops, was much the simplest answer to the problems of imperial defence as posed by all these strategic revelations. Biddulph's highly confidential assignment in 1876 was to assess the feasibility of such a scheme and to continue from the south his investigation of the passes themselves. He was thus the first official secret agent to set foot in Dardistan. Before anything much was known of the area, spies were taking precedence over such traditional pioneers as surveyors, scientists, missionaries or merchants; the region was already an official preserve. It was of necessity that Biddulph and many another political agent were shadowy, faceless figures, and it is no coincidence that we know so little of them. But if they suppressed the flamboyance of the popular explorer; if they eschewed the colourful detail and cultivated an excessively professional esprit, their status made their probings and wanderings doubly dangerous and doubly important. Clandestine reports afforded little scope for the publicity-conscious, but many a more famous traveller would willingly have traded the acclaim from an article in *Blackwoods* for the influence of a report from a roving political agent.

Hunza was not included in Biddulph's original itinerary. The principal objective of this was the Ishkoman pass, the one of which the Wakhan ruler had spoken so highly. It lay within Yasin territory and Biddulph had soon experienced the same sort of trouble that Hayward had had in trying to make contact with the Yasin chief; Pahlwan was engaged on traditional business, stalking brother Mulk Aman who was still holed up in the Hindu Raj. The invitation from the Mir of Hunza thus came as a welcome, if slightly suspect, distraction. Biddulph would ignore the question of whether already the Dards had guessed the true reason for his presence and would make a round trip, exploring up the Hunza valley to Wakhan and returning down the Ishkoman.

He had, however, taken elementary precautions. Enough was now known of the Dards for any invitation from that quarter to be treated with caution. If he was to visit Hunza, he replied, perhaps the Mir's son would like to take a short holiday in Gilgit, simultaneously; a pledge of friendship, he called it. Ghazan Khan, the Mir, could see no need for pledges between friends and asked Biddulph not to trouble himself with the matter. No trouble, replied Biddulph, but if the Mir's son were unable to get away perhaps his chief minister's son would benefit from a temporary change of scene. The negotiations dragged on through July and August. Biddulph was happy for them to take their course; Captain Grant, his ailing companion, had to be escorted back to Kashmir and there were plenty of markhor to be shot in the high forests above Gilgit. Since the idea of the visit had originated in Hunza it seemed reasonable to expect that the Mir would eventually agree. This he did and on August 13 1876 an eager Biddulph, with his escort of five sepoys and an N.C.O., headed north into the Hunza gorge.

In describing this lethal track no mention has yet been made of habitations. There were in fact half a dozen small villages dotted along the length of the gorge. Wherever a side tributary had worn back the retaining walls to create a cultivable slope, small box-like houses were stacked on a mound of steeply terraced fields no bigger than billiard tables; a fort of mud and timber crowned the position. Nomal, the first of any consequence, lay on the right hand side and though frequently attacked by Hunza forces was usually regarded as Gilgit, and therefore Dogra, territory.

Chaprot and its near neighbour Chalt, also on the right, were a very different matter. Here, after a treacherous stretch that included the worst half mile in Biddulph's 'tolerably wide experience of Himalayan travel', the track entered independent Dardistan and promptly divided. At Chalt a bridge of plaited twigs hung limply across the gorge and conducted a trail to Nagar. Hunza proper occupied only the right hand side of the river; the left was Nagar, its twin and deadly rival. And to both states the control of Chaprot and Chalt represented the difference between being besiegers and besieged. Until the previous year Hunza had been in the ascendancy but, when Biddulph passed through, the forts had just gone over to Nagar. This, as he rightly appreciated, created some interesting possibilities; Nagar, much the more peaceable of the two states, lived in dread of a counter-attack. Its only chance of maintaining its hold on the two forts lay in enlisting Kashmir support. A request to this effect had already been made and Biddulph was convinced that if the Kashmir Dogras could thus gain command of the two forts, both Nagar and Hunza would be brought to heel. At the mercy of strong garrisons commanding the approaches to both states, their co-operation in the defence of the Hindu Kush passes could be taken for granted. Or so, at least, he reasoned.

The next halt was Budlas on the new Hunza frontier. Here Biddulph dug in his heels. The Wazir's son, the hostage, was supposed to have reached Gilgit before he set off. He hadn't, nor had he been passed en route. When your only predecessor in independent Dardistan had been hacked to death, you couldn't be too careful. Biddulph refused to budge until the boy was produced, and even then moved on with the gravest misgivings. Next day these were partly dispelled. At Maiun a thin voice was heard calling from across the gorge; it was the people of Nagar sending greetings. Biddulph got out his field glasses and could just pick out a group of gesticulating figures on the walls of Nilt fort. He would have been less consoled had he known that the chasm through which the river here flows would soon figure in the military textbooks, and that the men sending their greeting swould one day take up the same positions in order to blaze away at his fellow officers. As it was, he returned the compliment; three of his men lined up along the edge of the precipice and in unison bellowed back. Then came Hini where the Mir's son, Safdar Ali, who would soon be portrayed as the worst villain on the Indian frontier, proffered a courteous welcome and escorted his guest into the incredible eyrie that is Hunza.

At over 8,000 feet above sea level, on a narrow ledge between the gloomy chasm of the river and the sheer backcloth of glacier scarred rock, Hunza is like some forbidden fairy-tale garden. Vines smother neat little houses, they wind their way up the loftiest poplars and cascade down from the topmost branches. The earth is strewn with mulberries and on every flat stone a carpet of yellow

2 The Gilgit valley photographed in 1895

1 Dr G.W. Leitner and his Dards

5 The Hunza gorge

6 Near the crest of the Baroghil Pass

7 Approaching the Ishkoman Pass in Yasin

8 William MacNair (centre) in travelling disguise
with The Syed and a Pathan

9 Officers of the Lockhart mission 1885–6:
Col. Woodthorpe, Capt. Barrow, Col. Lockhart and Capt. Giles

10 Aman-ul-Mulk, Mehtar of Chitral, with some of his many children.
Afzul-ul-Mulk is in the back row on the extreme left

11 Nizam-ul-Mulk in 1885 when Chief of Yasin. The boy
on his right is the son of Pahlwan

12 Ney Elias

13 Francis Younghusband in 1887

14 Col. Grombtchevski

15 Col. Algernon Durand

16 The famous meeting of Younghusband and Grombtchevski
at Khaian Aksai. Younghusband in bush hat,
Grombtchevski in uniform

17 Safdar Ali, Mir of Hunza, photographed when he was
an exile in Sinkiang

18 Chitral Fort

19 Baltit, home of the Mirs of Hunza

20 Uzr Khan of Nagar with attendants

21 The defenders of Chitral outside the fort: Lieut.
Gurdon, Surgeon-Capt. Whitchurch, Major Townshend,
Surgeon-Major Robertson, Lieut. Harley and Major Campbell

22 Col. James Kelly and officers of the 32nd Punjab
Pioneers inside the fort of Chitral

23 The upper Oxus (Panja) valley and the Pamirs from
the crest of the Baroghil

24 Kafir effigies of the dead

25 In the Chitral valley with Tirich Mir as backdrop

26 On the road from Mastuj to Chitral

apricots lies drying in the dazzling sunlight. To Biddulph's mind
the tiny fields were the best cultivated in the whole of the Western
Himalayas. But fruit was the staple diet and during the summer
months the people ate nothing else; to conserve fuel and precious
cereals, cooking was then forbidden. In winter there was flour
to be made from the apricot kernels, brandy to be distilled from
the mulberries and a new vintage to be sampled from the grape
pressings.

In later years, spurred on less by Biddulph's heavy prose than
by the rich copy of the glossy magazines, Hunza came to epitomise
the notion of an earthly paradise. The people were portrayed as
peaceful and industrious, living the simple life amidst idyllic
surroundings and in total isolation. There was prosperity without
money, security without taxes, no police force and no crime. In a
land where nervous tension, coronary thrombosis, obesity and
lung cancer were also unknown, it was hardly surprising that
centenarians were plentiful. Nor was the picture marred by the
more brutish aspects of primitive life. There was a delicacy about
Hunza. The menfolk were quick, intelligent and obliging, the
girls unveiled, pretty and no less obliging. Each village had its
band, every man was a dancer and the wine never ran out. Rakaposhi, towards which all houses seemed to be orientated, endowed
the scene with an irresistible serenity. Life was as full as its gently
swelling flanks and as satisfying as its honed summit.

What a contrast to the late nineteenth century's attitude to
this 'robber kingdom'. Biddulph was impressed but he had no
illusions. If the place had an air of prosperity it was thanks, not
so much to the husbandry, as to the traditional amusements of
waylaying rich caravans on the Leh–Yarkand road or of selling
neighbours into slavery. The keen expression on a Hunza face
was one of profound cunning, and that air of peaceful industry
scarcely belied the fact that here was one of the most martial of all
the Dard peoples. Ghazan Khan was a genial host, 'a short stout
man of about forty-five with coarse but not unpleasant features
and small twinkling eyes'. He betrayed a weakness for breech-loaders
and scotch; his red cabbage complexion 'betokened intemperance'.
He also had a somewhat exalted notion of his own importance;
the isolated and almost impregnable character of Hunza led him to
regard the throne of Baltit as being on a par with those of Peking

and St. Petersburg. Yet, as Biddulph soon appreciated, he was no fool. Somehow he had already discovered that Biddulph was one of the Englishmen who had been snooping round Wakhan two years before. He had no illusions about this so-called sportsman and intended to extract the maximum advantage from his visit.

The reason behind his invitation was soon apparent. Ghazan Khan wanted the restitution of Chalt and Chaprot; Biddulph might proceed to Wakhan only when this little matter had been satisfactorily settled. With ill-disguised relish he commiserated over the fate of Hayward and waited for Biddulph to act. The similarity between his own circumstances and those of Hayward was not lost on the Englishman, but still he had no intention of obliging the Mir. When Ghazan Khan demanded the return of the hostage being held in Gilgit, and when he sought to deprive his visitor of his porters, Biddulph stood firm. He pledged his own rifle (and no doubt a case of whisky) if he be allowed to proceed to Wakhan, but he refused point blank to arrange the surrender of Chaprot. Thus the matter stood for four critical days during which he was virtually a prisoner. But his firmness paid off. Ghazan Khan relented to the extent of allowing him to retreat, and Biddulph scurried back to Gilgit territory. It was an ignominious start to his dealings with the Dards; but, in the light of what happened when the next Englishman reached Hunza, Biddulph seems to have managed things exceptionally well. Faced with precisely the same situation his successor, though accompanied by three other officers, a large bodyguard and an army of followers, would capitulate within forty-eight hours.

The nature of Biddulph's recommendations for the future of Ghazan Khan and his state were not hard to guess. 'With regard to Hunza it is certainly advisable that Chaprot should be occupied by the Maharaja's troops. . . . This would effectively secure Gilgit from attack on that side. Hunza and Nagar should be openly claimed as British territory on the strength of the tribute they pay to the Maharaja and a frontier exploration of the north part of Kunjoot (the upper part of Hunza) should be insisted on.' If Biddulph had his way, Ghazan Khan was going to pay dearly for his presumption.

The 'tribute' referred to above was paid by all the Dard states not just to Kashmir but to most of their other neighbours. By the

British and the Dogras it was seen as the ideal pretext for advancing their rule, a convenient way of giving some semblance of legality to what was, more truthfully, naked aggression. The tribute consisted usually of a few ounces of gold dust, a couple of hunting dogs or a herd of sheep. Emissaries-cum-shepherds, like those Leitner had met from Chilas, accompanied it and, if the Maharaja was keen to foment trouble with the donors, these *vakils* could be detained. But in return for this so-called tribute the Maharaja paid out annual allowances of far greater value, 5,000 rupees in the case of Hunza at this time. He and the British might please to call them 'subsidies' or 'pensions' but to the Dards they were simply protection money; it was the Kashmir government's only way of buying off their neighbours' natural inclination to overrun Gilgit. Usually there was no document setting out the precedence in these arrangements and it was a gross distortion of the facts to read into them any sort of acknowledgement of Kashmir sovereignty.

The excursion to Hunza was certainly the highlight of Biddulph's 1876 travels, but his report was concerned far more with the question of Yasin and the defence of the Hindu Kush routes. The Ishkoman pass proved impossible. In recent years glaciers had plunged right across its southern approaches interposing two hundred foot walls of unscalable ice. New information had it that Darkot was also extremely difficult and that the Baroghil, though simple enough in itself, gave on to 'an easily defensible gorge of first rate importance'. Reluctantly Biddulph conceded that the alarm he had raised over the passes in 1874 might have been premature. Their insignificance as defensive obstacles was more than made up for by the fearful chasms that led down from them; evidently the Hunza gorge was typical of the whole region.

On the other hand this was no ground for complacency. At the key positions in these gorges a whole army could be kept at bay by just a handful of defenders; equally the whole position could be betrayed by just a handful of traitors. The point was that the defence must rest with men of unquestioned loyalty and in this respect the Dards were useless. Pahlwan of Yasin had treated Biddulph with effrontery tinged with outright hostility; at one point his progress towards the Ishkoman had been barred by eighty armed men. 'A dirty little man with a fierce spirit' was how a subsequent visitor described Pahlwan, adding that he fully deserved the nickname of The Wrestler. Yet this was the man who controlled not only the Yasin and Ishkoman valleys but also the upper Chitral valley with that 'easily defensible gorge of first-rate importance'. He held the keys to India and the sooner they could be transferred to safer hands the better.

Biddulph proceeded to examine how best this could be achieved. Yasin could be held without difficulty by a small force of British troops, but he was realist enough to appreciate that such a scheme was unlikely to be sanctioned. To support and supply such a force three hundred miles from its nearest base, the whole-hearted co-operation of the Maharaja of Kashmir would be essential. This could not be relied on. On the contrary the Maharaja was almost certain to oppose the scheme. Particularly since the obvious alternative was to entrust to him and his Dogra troops the defence of the passes. The Dogras had already shown themselves more than willing to take Yasin. But could they hold it? Ill-armed, ill-provisioned and permanently under strength it was as much as they could do to hold on to Gilgit.

Biddulph, however, had a better opinion of the Kashmir troops than most of his contemporaries; he thought that, with two provisos, this latter scheme might just work. But the Maharaja must first be helped with arms, cash and advice on how to strengthen his position in Gilgit and he must, secondly, accept the presence there of a British agent. In this last, of course, lay the rub. The Maharaja was to be assured that such a man would in no way interfere with his own administration and would simply operate as an intelligence channel. This needless to say was not the whole truth. As the Maharaja surmised and as Biddulph officially recommended, such a man would also be expected to act as a political liaison with the Dards, to provide the Dogras with military advice and to check on their handling of the situation. In other words, in return for being given a free hand in Yasin, the Maharaja should be asked to accept the principle of a direct British interest in Dardistan.

This would constitute a complete reversal of previous British policy and, in retrospect, may be seen as the first step towards total political control of Dardistan by the Government of India. However Biddulph was not sticking his neck out quite so far as that suggests. The idea of a British agent in Gilgit had been around for three or four years and probably originated with Forsyth who, given his way, would have had political agents in every town in Asia. Northbrook almost certainly led Biddulph to believe that some such scheme as he now proposed would have a very fair chance of acceptance. He also seems to have left Biddulph in little doubt as to who was likely to get the Gilgit job. Before taking up what would surely be one of the loneliest posts in the British Empire, such a man deserved a few months of relaxation and society. Biddulph, his report completed, therefore sailed for England and six months' leave.

6. Nearly a Big Business

Given the intense parliamentary rivalry at Westminster during the 1870s and 1880s, British policy in India shows remarkable continuity. One of the most important Cabinet posts was that of Secretary of State for India and this, of course, changed hands with the fall of governments. Yet bi-partisanship on Indian affairs was the order of the day; Indian debates were seldom controversial and were notoriously ill-attended. The only major exception to this happy state of affairs was India's frontier and foreign policy. Here there was neither consensus nor continuity. Disraeli stood for the Empire and the Monarchy; by the former he meant India as surely as by the latter he meant Victoria. To him and to the Tories the security of India was paramount and the most serious threat to it, the Russian, was taken very seriously indeed. Gladstone and the Liberals, on the other hand, put reform before Empire and Bible before Queen. In foreign affairs, policies were evaluated according to whether they were just and whether the nation could afford them; to neither of these criteria did adventures in the Himalayas and Central Asia conform. As a result the policies and personalities of the Great Game tend to come and go with the swing of votes. The first Gilgit Agency was destined to flourish under the Tories but to wither under the Liberals.

In 1874 Disraeli had been returned to power with a massive majority; as a measure of the importance he attached to India, Lord Salisbury, the brightest star in the Tory firmament, was installed as Secretary of State. As Viceroy the Conservative choice was Lord Lytton; he had arrived in India just as Biddulph set off on his first visit to Gilgit. Lytton came to India the avowed agent of Disraeli, and his two major undertakings were entirely appropriate. The first, the proclamation and celebration of the Queen as Empress of India, was effected swiftly and occasioned widespread satisfaction. The second, the attempt to bring Afghanistan firmly into the scheme of India's defences, proved quite the opposite.

Under Northbrook the Gilgit Game had been inaugurated with

an eye to events in Sinkiang. It was now to be subordinated to Afghan policy. Biddulph was wasting his time harping on the possibility of an invasion across the Pamirs should Sinkiang become a Russian supply base. The new administration's attitude towards Afghanistan had already made the adoption of his proposals for Gilgit a necessity. By New Year's Day 1878, as all India celebrated the first anniversary of the Queen-Empress's proclamation, Biddulph, back from home leave, was laying out his vegetable plot and building his bungalow in a Gilgit orchard. The loneliest and most vulnerable pawn on the entire imperial chess board was digging in.

But first this other vital factor in the Gilgit Game, the Afghan dimension. In the 1860s Afghanistan had been no more clearly defined a territorial concept than Kashmir. And, just as the Indian government was now finding it convenient to explore the possibilities of Kashmir's open frontier in Dardistan, so the same process, only on a far larger scale, was taking place in Afghanistan. The Amir of Kabul's tenuous claims to the allegiance of Badakshan, and Badakshan's even more tenuous claims to the Upper Oxus states of Roshan, Shignan and Wakhan, had been avidly championed by Rawlinson when defining the extent of Afghan territory on the Pamirs; it was a convenient way of bagging as much of the no-man's land as possible and of interposing a friendly buffer between the likely frontiers of the two great empires.

Other tenuous Afghan claims were, however, bitterly contested by the British. It is hard to say whether they were less valid but they were certainly less opportune. Those to Kafiristan and to all the Pathan states south of Chitral, for example, would have led to the near encirclement of Dardistan. And as for the oft-repeated claim to Chitral itself, this was clearly anathema; Aman-ul-Mulk traditionally exercised a commanding influence over the affairs of Yasin; acknowledging an Afghan claim to Chitral would have meant abandoning the Hindu Kush as a British frontier. But conversely, holding the passes meant coming to an understanding with Aman-ul-Mulk; it meant the designation of Dardistan as an exclusively Anglo-Dogra preserve. In the light of the Russian advance such a move might appear as purely defensive, but to the Afghans it would appear downright offensive. And this was precisely what Lytton wanted. Biddulph's plan for the defence of the

Hindu Kush had been adopted as a convenient means of breathing down the Amir's neck.

As so often, the one thing forgotten in all this Machiavellian theorising was the indigenous people. Forced to choose, the Dards would almost certainly have preferred the overlordship of a fellow Mohammedan from Kabul rather than one of the cow-worshipping Hindus from Srinagar. The Amir was highly revered as a religious leader and it was only sixty years since Afghan rule had stretched right across the region as far as Tibet. But ideally what the Dards wanted was neither Dogra nor Afghan. Aman-ul-Mulk, far and away the most able of all the chiefs, valued his ties with Kabul only as a means of off-setting Anglo-Dogra overtures. The harder he was pressed by Gilgit the more he turned to Kabul; but the moment Gilgit despaired of him, or the moment the Dogras were in real trouble, loud became his protestations of undying loyalty to Kashmir and cold his shoulder to the Afghans.

Just how cleverly he could play off one side against the other was to be amply tested. Lytton's endeavours to establish an exclusive British presence in Kabul would make of the Afghans first enemies, then friends, then enemies again, subjects briefly and finally suspicious allies. All this happened in the space of four years. The Dards, indeed Biddulph himself, could scarcely keep up with events. One minute the Gilgit agency and the Dogras were a vital part of India's defences and an ingenious way of pressuring the Afghans; the next it was being suggested that the agent be withdrawn, the Dogras penned back into Gilgit fort and the rest of Dardistan handed over to Afghan custody with a British agent based on Afghan soil. Aman-ul-Mulk, performing unheard-of feats of political gymnastics, seemed to change his allegiance daily and it was hardly surprising that Biddulph, faced with such a kaleidoscopic example of duplicity, totally misread its significance.

The first Gilgit agency really stood little chance. At the mercy of party politics and construed as a temporary expedient against Afghanistan as much as a permanent feature in India's defences, its early demise might be anticipated. What wasn't anticipated, however, was that the first Gilgit Agency was heading for something closer to annihilation. For this there would be many explanations but there was only one possible scapegoat.

In 1877 John Biddulph was thirty-six years old. He had been

eighteen years in India and was neither a prodigy nor a drudge. The appointment as A.D.C. to Lord Northbrook was probably more in recognition of his background than of his ability. Northbrook became a close friend and it was to this connection, plus his sporting activities in the mountains, that Biddulph owed his selection for political missions. The life clearly suited him and besides adequate reserves of discretion and initiative he displayed remarkable powers of endurance. All this was self-evident. But beyond it we know nothing of the man. To read into his handling of events in Gilgit serious failings of judgement, or to pounce on criticisms of his temperament made by men seeking a scapegoat for what happened, would be unfair. All the evidence points not to Biddulph being unsuitable but to the assignment being impossible.

The average time for the two hundred and twenty mile journey from Srinagar to Gilgit was three weeks. The track was impracticable for baggage ponies, subject to continual landslides and crossing the Great Himalaya by two highly unpredictable passes. Snow here closed it permanently for six months in the year and was liable to interrupt communications any time during the other six. As yet there was no telegraph, though from Srinagar telegrams could now be sent down to India.

Indian political agents were used to remote and solitary postings. But surely none was ever quite so isolated and quite so lonely as poor Biddulph in Gilgit. For ten months, he told Northbrook in September 1878, he hadn't seen a white face; in November he was still alone, but a Dr. Scully was on his way up, his first visitor in over a year. There was plenty to do, of course. He completed the bungalow, tended his garden, laid out a tennis court (though there was no-one to play with), studied the Dard languages, investigated their history and shot more markhor. It wasn't just a question of keeping sane; colleagues from Trivandrum to Kathmandu were doing much the same thing. On your own you couldn't afford to brood over the next move; you did what was expected and worked out a schedule that left no gaps for introspection. Even a letter from the dreaded Leitner was a welcome distraction. Apparently in code, Biddulph set it aside for an evening of close scrutiny. When he rumbled that it was written in Burishaski, the scriptless language of Hunza, he composed a friendly and appreciative reply. One of his main functions was to collect political intelligence. He organised a network of agents that extended well into Russian Central Asia and through the pages of the Gilgit Diary, a regular round-up of political developments, he conscientiously relayed their reports to the Indian Foreign Department. Perhaps he was a little too conscientious. It would later be suggested that he placed far too heavy a reliance on unsubstantiated rumour. But what could he do? There was no-one to discuss things with, just the diary waiting to be filled and the need, above all, to keep busy.

The immediate surroundings of Gilgit are almost as depressing as the fact of its isolation. A recent traveller describes it as like being in a cage. You feel hopelessly trapped not just by the steep-ness of the hills all around but by their terrible tawny sterility. The forests and mountain pastures up above are out of sight over the horizon. In the valley it is hot and dusty all summer, cold and muddy all winter. Every day there come stories of this road being blocked by a landslide or that washed away by the river. The distant crack of a rifle, the sudden appearance of some wild-looking stranger, or just the rustle of a cold and unexpected wind feeling its way through the orchards, sends shivers of apprehension down the spine.

For Biddulph, of course, it was far, far worse. If he felt trapped then so he was, not just by the terrain but by the people. In most of India the *sahib* could expect to meet with deference if not ser-vility from the native population; the authority of the Englishman and the sanctity of his person commanded respect in the most backward of the princely states. But this was scarcely the case in Dardistan. To the hard men who thronged the Gilgit bazaar the lone Englishman pacing his compound must have been more an object of curiosity and contempt.

In time Biddulph would learn to distinguish one gnarled, leathery hillman from another. The smiling, fickle Chitrali wore a slightly different cap from that of the quick-witted cut-throats from Hunza; the *choga*, the long buttonless dressing gown of the fanatical Chilasis, was darker and commonly dirtier than that of the indus-trious traders from lower down the Indus. But each and all had the same unkempt, piratical aspect. The open *chogas* revealed bone-barred chests. Hideous scars and missing limbs might be the work of a crop spoiling bear or an agitated neighbour; knives, swords and matchlocks, like *choga* and cap, were never removed. Big nosed men, as bony of feature as of limb, some with heads shaven, others boasting long ringlets and rat's-tails, they looked like veteran homicides from a penitentiary chain-gang. Only the eyes bespoke a fiercer pride and a nobler wit. Narrowed against the glare of rock and snow, deep-set in a web of wrinkles and jinxing with deception, they could yet deceive even such a cold fish as the solitary *feringhi*.

At the bottom of his garden Biddulph found the sculpted head-stone for Hayward's grave still lying in the grass. Over the spot where Drew had read the burial service he set it up, a reminder, if one were needed, of his own vulnerability. Yet Hayward had been just an independent traveller. Biddulph's presence was potentially far more objectionable. With his authority backed by no more than a small bodyguard and a limited exchequer, he was expected to oversee a long, undefined frontier, to arbitrate in the affairs of fiercely independent tribes and to work in conjunction with an ally of doubtful loyalty whose one object would seem to be that of getting rid of him. And all this in inconceivably difficult terrain, three weeks march from his nearest compatriot and a month from a reply to the most urgent enquiry.

The wonder really is that Biddulph retained his sanity. For the second Gilgit Agency twelve years later the road would be improved, a telegraph line would be set up, the normal complement of British officers would average out at about a dozen and they would have their own troops, artillery and supply arrangements. Yet still they would find the isolation almost unbearable. So much so that the second Gilgit Agent really does seem to have taken leave of his senses.

Biddulph did two spells of duty. The first lasted nearly two years, the second only six months. When Lytton had approached the Maharaja of Kashmir with the proposed new arrangement, the latter had been happy enough about extending his rule to Yasin and happy enough about the four guns, five thousand rifles and a million rounds of ammunition made available to help him. But he had objected strongly to the corollary of a British agent at Gilgit. It was only the nomination of Biddulph, who had reported most favourably on Dogra rule in Dardistan, that reconciled him to the idea. He was still far from enthusiastic and, as Biddulph soon discovered, this hostility was in itself enough to stultify the whole scheme.

At first it was just the Kashmir governor in Gilgit who proved so difficult. Biddulph was prepared for a bit of professional jealousy and must have expected to unearth some mild peculation. But this man appeared to be in the closest collusion with his supposed adversaries, the Dards, and to be urging them to get rid of Biddulph. From Aman-ul-Mulk he was accepting bribes in the Maharaja's name and then leaning on the Chitrali to scare off his unwelcome visitor. It also looked as if it was he who had instigated Ghazan Khan of Hunza to act so menacingly during the visit of 1876. 'It is me or him,' confided Biddulph to Northbrook. Like Hayward, and Leitner before him, he believed his life to be in real danger. But when, after strenuous objections, the man was at last replaced, it seemed to make little difference. Another plot against his life came to light. Apparently he was up against not simply the resentment of an individual governor, but the policy of the Kashmir government. He who had thought so highly of Kashmir rule reckoned by the end of his first year in Gilgit that 'no native administration under British rule can be as bad or as two-faced'. At the time he didn't hold the Maharaja personally to blame, but after another two years he had no illusions. 'The Maharaja whom for years I had looked on as a weak fool in the hands of knaves turns out to be as great a scoundrel as any in Asia and disloyal to the core.'

By then, 1879, Lytton agreed. For, early that year, it was discovered that the Maharaja had been in correspondence, if not collusion, with both Russia and Afghanistan. What made this particularly serious was that by then the latter was in a state of open warfare with the British and the former very nearly so.

These were stirring times, the late 1870s. It seemed to many, and not least to Biddulph as he desperately strove to get a disloyal ally to defend an unmapped frontier, that the Great Game was about to become the Great War. Anglo-Russian rivalry in Central Asia had always been influenced by the clash of imperial interests elsewhere, particularly in the Middle East. In 1877 the Russo-Turkish war brought Russian arms sweeping through the Balkans until in 1878 they were at the gates of Constantinople. The whole crumbling Turkish empire, and with it control of the routes from Europe to India, was in danger of falling into Russian hands. Brought thus to the brink of Armageddon even Disraeli hesitated.

But the British people were warming to what seemed the inevitable; 'We don't want to fight but by jingo if we do ...' was the hit song of the moment and accurately reflected popular sentiment. The Queen was positively horrified at the 'low tone' of her cabinet; with resignation in mind she implored them to act. At last they did. Six million pounds were voted by Parliament for military purposes, the reserves were called up, troops were summoned from India and a fleet of ironclads was sent steaming through the Dardanelles. With just the minarets and palaces of Constantinople between them, the Imperial Army faced the Royal Navy.

Russia's answer to all this was to mobilise in Central Asia. India was regarded as the most desirable and the most vulnerable of the British possessions; merely threatening it should be enough to bring Whitehall to its senses. Skobeleff, the Russian military genius, drew up a plan of invasion. Three military columns were formed and one of them in May 1878, duly set off across the Alai for the Pamirs and the Hindu Kush passes. Biddulph, if only he had known it, was within an ace of having to outshine Horatio at the bridge. But, as he could have forecast from personal knowledge, May was a bit too early to be dragging an army across the Pamirs. By the time the Russians had floundered through the snowdrifts on the Alai it was all over; far away in Berlin a congress of all the great powers had thrashed out a peace settlement.

The Russian advance on the Hindu Kush thus came to nothing, but another feature of their Central Asian offensive had far reaching repercussions. It was because of the arrival of a Russian mission in Kabul in July 1878 that Lytton had finally insisted on sending a British mission there. The Afghan refusal to receive it provided the pretext for war, and it was when the victorious General Roberts reached Kabul in early 1879 that there was unearthed the Maharaja of Kashmir's treacherous correspondence with both Afghanistan and Russia.

* * *

While all around was in turmoil, Dardistan confounded all predictions by remaining comparatively peaceful; neither belated reports of the Russian manœuvres on the Pamirs nor Afghan embarrassments at the hands of the infidel British sent the Dards scurrying to arms. On the contrary things were so quiet that at the height of the drama, in late 1878, Biddulph coolly set off on his pioneering promenade of Chitral and Yasin. This is not a journey that figures prominently in the annals of exploration; it is a little known exploit even by Biddulph's standards. Partly this was due to the extraordinary circumstances at the time, but it also has to be admitted that its results were singularly negative. The first Englishman into Chitral spent just a week there and, beyond a few strategic observations, an exaggerated estimate of Tirich Mir's altitude—'at least 27,000 feet'—and confirmation of the extent and importance of the valley, he added nothing to what was already known from native accounts.

Similarly the political results were disappointing. Aman-ul-Mulk, the chief or Mehtar, turned out to be a stocky, patriarchal character with a wedge-shaped beard and a falcon forever on his forearm, altogether rather like Henry VIII. He was also every bit as astute. 'Shrewd, avaricious, unscrupulous and deceitful to an uncommon degree', thought Biddulph. The treaty by which he was bound to Kashmir was in the process of negotiation. In return for 'Hawks . . . 2, Hunting Dogs . . . 2, Horses . . . 2', plus an acknowledgement of the Maharaja's suzerainty, he was to get 12,000 rupees a year and thus was Chitral supposed to be secured against Afghanistan and Russia. Biddulph couldn't see it. Aman-ul-Mulk candidly admitted that to realise that kind of money all he had to do was sell a few Kafirs; to make his point he pressed on his visitor a couple of doe-eyed boys dressed in nothing but their native goatskins. He also made it clear that he would much prefer an arrangement direct with the British, an offer made with an eye to another and much larger subsidy. The Mehtar's sympathies seemed to be controlled by nothing so much as the tide of battle in Afghanistan, and the moment Biddulph turned back to Gilgit, he was renewing negotiations with Kabul. Such a man could never be trusted and Biddulph recommended that he was best left out of any Anglo-Dogra defence schemes.

This seemed feasible in the light of the situation in Yasin. Pahlwan, the Wrestler, now appeared as congenial and dependable as Aman-ul-Mulk obviously wasn't; it was like Hayward's attachment to Mir Wali all over again. 'He took a great fancy to me', wrote Biddulph, and appeared 'far too outspoken and straightforward for the Kashmiris ever to understand'. To a considerable extent

Pahlwan had managed to shrug off the overlordship of Aman-ul-Mulk and he too now asked for a direct alliance with the British. Biddulph had plenty of sympathy with anyone suspicious of the Dogras and, given the strategic importance of Yasin and the good impression made by Pahlwan, enthusiastically supported the idea. Yasin at the time comprised not only the Yasin and Ishkoman valleys but also Mastuj and the upper Chitral valley. If Pahlwan's co-operation could be assured, there was no need to worry about Aman-ul-Mulk's sympathies. The Yasinis could hold the passes and, as a second line of defence, troops could always be rushed from Gilgit to Chitral by what he had found to be a comparatively easy route over the Shandur pass.

Undoubtedly Biddulph himself regarded the visit to Yasin as far from negative; only in the light of subsequent dramatic developments would it be revealed as worthless. The one remaining achievement of Biddulph's last pioneering journey—and one not to be sneezed at—was that he returned alive. From the start the Maharaja of Kashmir had strongly opposed the trip and, on previous form, might well have made it an opportunity to remove him. Aman-ul-Mulk had also objected to it and could so easily have slipped from his tightrope long enough to do Kabul the small favour of holding to ransom a British officer. Anticipating such an eventuality, the Indian foreign department had actually vetoed the trip; the news, as usual, reached Biddulph too late for him to turn back. Pahlwan would soon be revealed as having played as false as had Mir Wali before him; and in the Hindu Raj, spoiling for a chance to embarrass the Dards or to oblige the Dogras, there still lurked his brother, the dreaded Mulk Aman. Yet Biddulph sailed through. Compared to the problems encountered by both previous and subsequent travellers it was a considerable feat.

In September 1879, far from dissatisfied with his long exile in Gilgit, Biddulph returned to India. Here he found Afghanistan again in the headlines. The first British envoy to Kabul had been murdered and the troops were returning to wreak vengeance. Lytton and Disraeli faced a barrage of criticism at home; the Viceroy could scarcely be expected to give his whole-hearted attention to the far flung affairs of Gilgit. He did, however, acknowledge that the whole policy on which the Gilgit agency had been based needed rethinking. Armed with the evidence of the

Maharaja's duplicity, urged by Biddulph that the Dogras were neither capable of defending the Hindu Kush nor acceptable to the Dards, and soon freed by the fall of Afghanistan from the need to secure Chitral, he plumped for an entirely new approach. The Maharaja was 'to be relieved of all responsibilities and deprived of all powers' in Chitral and Yasin, and the agent in Gilgit would be moved to Jalalabad thence to conduct the affairs of Dardistan direct with the Dards. He was certainly right in terminating the Gilgit agency; the impossibility of Biddulph's position was conceded. But Jalalabad had yet to be detached from Afghanistan, and while serious doubts were being raised about the feasibility of this, Disraeli was defeated at the polls. The conduct of affairs in Afghanistan was the main election issue and Lytton could therefore only resign. Biddulph was left in the lurch. Failing any orders to the contrary, he returned to his post in Gilgit. He relieved Dr. Scully, his locum, in June 1880.

Though the Dards had not responded to the disturbances on the Pamirs and in Afghanistan, events were soon to show that little credit on this score could go to Biddulph and even less to the Dogra troops. Just as British schemes of defence had consistently over-rated the political and military effectiveness of the Dogras, so they had underrated the obstinacy and striking power of the Dards. In the end it was not the Afghans or the Russians, and not Lytton's new schemes nor the squeamishness of the Liberals, that put paid to the first Gilgit Agency. It was the ragged matchlockmen of Dardistan itself.

As Biddulph for the third time crossed the Indus and trotted on beneath the jagged skyline into Gilgit, he seems to have sensed that trouble was brewing. Chaprot, that fortress in the Hunza gorge garrisoned by Kashmiri Dogras against attack by Ghazan Khan, was much on his mind. With rumours of a concerted Dard attack more rife than usual, there was good cause for making Chaprot independent of supplies from Nagar and of reinforcements from Gilgit. Both Nagar and Hunza were reportedly incensed by the few improvements that had been made to the Hunza road and, if this were sufficient to push them into an alliance, then Chaprot was in real danger. Rumour also had it that Pahlwan was aligning himself with Hunza. His letters to Biddulph were certainly colder than of old but, if there were any truth in his mobilising his forces, Biddulph could only conclude that he was again going to take the field against his brother Mulk Aman. Either that or possibly his paranoia about the Dogras, to whom he had ceased sending *vakils*, had put him on the defensive.

Through the long dusty summer in Gilgit tension continued to mount. Darel and Chilas were also thought to be involved in some sort of Dard confederacy and, with Gilgit under threat of complete encirclement, Dogra reinforcements were ordered up from Kashmir. Biddulph now regarded Nagar and Chitral as the real troublemakers, though he continued to see Chaprot as the likely point of attack. He himself visited the fort in July. Both the Maharaja and the Foreign Department warned against any move that might precipitate attack; Biddulph was to understand—as if he didn't already—that he was on his own. Reinforcing Chaprot was in itself provocative, but he believed its weakness was what had inspired all the trouble; it had to be done.

In early October the air was still full of rumour. Pahlwan was on the move, apparently off to visit Aman-ul-Mulk in Chitral, and the reinforcements had still not arrived. But winter was approaching and the traditional campaigning season almost over. Then, on the night of October 27th, the crash came. Pahlwan changed direction. With a force of seven hundred he swept down the Gilgit valley, overran the whole of Punial and laid siege to the fort of Sher only twenty-four miles from Gilgit. From Darel and Tangir tribesmen flocked to join him. Ghazan Khan of Hunza sent men to Sher and himself started an action outside Chaprot. Any moment the Chilasis were expected to cut the supply line at Bunji; it was highly doubtful whether postal runners carrying the desperate pleas for help would ever get through.

Biddulph assumed command of the Gilgit garrison. Without the promised reinforcements he could raise barely five hundred combat worthy troops; the rest of the garrison consisted of invalids, adolescents and dotards. When he sallied forth to raise the siege of Sher, even the chosen few melted away. He gave up the idea of taking the offensive and, abandoning his bungalow and his precious garden, he retired within the fort of Gilgit. A long siege now seemed inevitable.

As it happened the Chilasis had not fallen on Bunji. They were waiting to see if Pahlwan would take Sher or, perhaps, they were

Gilgit fort in the 1870s

Stanford's Geogr. Estab. London.

just apprehensive about the approach of the Kashmir reinforcements. The postal runners got through; carrying the news relay style over the Great Himalaya, they delivered the first grim tidings on November 6th. 'Precedence', 'Clear the line', began the telegrams that now started to fly round India and back to London. 'Biddulph's situation may be serious', ventured the new Viceroy, reporting to the Secretary of State. Gilgit was under siege. Each report from there might be the last and, given the ten days it took them to reach India, there was no telling how grave the situation might already be. The Maharaja was to send more troops immediately, but it was unlikely that they would make it over the passes before they were closed by the first snows; the original reinforcements, to which two British officers were now rushed, had already been delayed by the weather. As Hayward had once discovered, mid-November was the usual closing date for the Burzil and the Kamri. It was a grim thought, but Biddulph and the relief of Gilgit might have to wait till the spring.

As Biddulph himself would later put it, it was 'nearly a big business'. That it was not was no thanks to the Dogra garrison, no thanks to the reinforcements, nor to the solicitude of the government. Of all people, it was to Mehtar Aman-ul-Mulk of Chitral. When Pahlwan had unleashed his forces down the Gilgit valley, a Chitrali contingent had simultaneously set off via Mastuj. It was assumed that they were coming to join the other Dards, and the timing was of course no coincidence. But what did come as a surprise, and most of all to Pahlwan, was that this force, far from advancing to join him, was out to dispossess him. Two days after news of the first attack had reached India, the scare was in fact over. Pahlwan had retreated to defend Yasin and within a week he, like his brother, was a lone fugitive in the mountains. Aman-ul-Mulk's forces held Yasin.

Having sampled the complexity of local intrigue when examining the Hayward case, the reader may be spared a second post-mortem on Biddulph's moment of tribulation. What lay behind it was every bit as mysterious. Why Pahlwan attacked in the first place, why he was unopposed all the way to Sher, and why Aman-ul-Mulk decided to get Gilgit off the hook, are all questions that have never been fully answered. Biddulph was inclined to blame the only parties who would obviously gain from the affair—Aman-ul-

Mulk who had re-established his supremacy over Yasin and would get his subsidy doubled, and the Maharaja who would now have the satisfaction of seeing the Gilgit Agency withdrawn.

But no-one now paid much attention to Biddulph. Northbrook had admired him. Lytton had merely tolerated him, but Lord Ripon, the new Liberal Viceroy, was positively horrified by him. Biddulph had got everything wrong; Pahlwan, his friend, had proved to be the rogue while Chitral and Nagar, whom he distrusted most, proved his staunchest allies. When he threatened to organise punitive raids, Ripon shuddered and ordered the agent back to Simla. There it was decided to close the Agency down. The Maharaja was to understand that the government reserved the right to re-open it if ever the situation demanded; but in 1881, with the experiment having proved such an unmitigated disaster, it was hard to envisage any circumstances that might justify such a move.

7. Out in the Cold

The failure of the first Gilgit Agency did not signify a dwindling of British interest in Dardistan. The years 1881–89, during which the Agency was in abeyance, witness further exploratory activity, though of a more covert nature. It is interesting that these years also coincide almost exactly with the brief period during which Rudyard Kipling worked in India. No-one did more than Kipling to popularise the notion of the Great Game; in *Kim* he created an underworld of spies and travellers engaged on momentous and mysterious assignments that was all vastly more exciting than strategic theory and diplomatic manœuvrings. Whether, in reality, there existed such a sophisticated espionage network is still open to debate; but certainly, during the 1880s, there was enough clandestine trans-frontier travel, enough anxiety about Russian intentions and enough concern with intelligence work to suggest such an operation.

Kim was not written till long after Kipling had left India; only two or three of the characters can be tentatively identified and the events are entirely fictional. But it is worth noting that not only do Kipling's dates coincide with what would prove to be the most undercover phase of the Gilgit Game, but also that Kipling's India, i.e. the Punjab, was that of the frontier and the mountains. The newspaper for which he worked, *The Civil and Military Gazette* of Lahore, was the descendant of that founded by Leitner; and the journal to which Kim's Bengali colleague submitted his scholarly monographs was Leitner's *Asiatic Quarterly Review*; almost certainly Leitner and Kipling were acquainted. When not in Lahore, Kipling was chronicling the official and social life in Simla; here the policies and attitudes to be adopted during the final phase of the Gilgit Game were being formulated, and the men involved were being trained. It is no coincidence that suddenly the Gilgit story is full of Kipling associations.

The mysterious journey of William Watts MacNair and the Syed (note the overtones of Kim and the Lama) begins, fittingly, on the Grand Trunk Road at Nowshera, a staging post between Rawal Pindi and Peshawar. In March 1883 MacNair, a surveyor who had been mapping in Afghanistan in the wake of the second British occupation, had applied for a year's leave; it was granted. On the night of April 9 he rode into Nowshera—and promptly disappeared.

No-one noticed. The survey of India was dominated by English officers; MacNair, though, was a civilian and 'country bred', that is born and educated in India; he had never been to England. Thirty-three years old and still only a surveyor third grade, he was not the sort to occasion much attention. He was unmarried and on leave; it was up to him how he spent his spare time. Nor was there any reason for his superiors to be suspicious of his wanting a whole year off. The most conscientious of employees, he had shown wayward tendencies only in his relations with women; no doubt a few delicate enquiries as to any young widows being in station would reveal his whereabouts. As for political interests he had none. The Game, to him, meant not the undercover world of *Kim* but the equally topical obsession of cricket. It was said a scratch XI would materialise and disperse to fielding positions at the sound of his voice; MacNair was a slow bowler, tricky and devastating in the best Indian tradition.

His only other passion was his work. He had joined the Survey of India when he was eighteen and would remain with it till his death. He loved the precision of maps and he loved the travel though not, as some, for the solitude it offered but for the society. Merchants and pilgrims met along the road, peasants across whose fields he carried his survey, and village greybeards who volunteered the names for his maps—these were the men who intrigued him. MacNair had a genuine affection for Asiatics. A *sahib* credited with an understanding of the native mind was usually one who could get a single Indian to do the work of ten; rare indeed were those who really relished the native way of life. The idea of Hayward, for instance, or Leitner successfully carrying off a disguise is preposterous; both were far too overbearing. But MacNair was different.

At Nowshera on the night of April 9 he set about proving it. First he packed his two compasses—magnetic and prismatic—into a *gooda*, a sheepskin sewn up to form a bag with the wool inside;

for a planetable he butchered a large tome on Islamic physic, retaining just the cover and a few pages of prescriptions, and devoting the rest of the book to paper holders and rulers. Then, leaving his beard to grow, he carefully shaved his whole head; skin colouring was achieved with 'a weak solution of caustic and walnut juice applied to face and hands'. By 3 a.m., dressed in the heavy turban and loose robes of a Kaka Khel Pathan, he was ready. As Hakim (doctor) Mir Mohammed he headed north for the mountains.

His rendezvous was for the 13th at Ganderi just beyond the British frontier. He arrived undetected on the appointed day; waiting for him were two genuine Kaka Khel Pathans who traded regularly between Peshawar and Chitral, a Kafir lately converted to Islam, and the Syed, the originator of the whole scheme. Syed Shah had been MacNair's assistant during the recent operations in Afghanistan. Probably he actually was a *syed* or Mohammedan holy man; such a profession, entailing a good deal of travel, would have particularly recommended him to the Indian Survey; he was in fact being trained with a view to joining that most select corps of native travellers known to history as The Pundits. Since the 1860s these men, under the auspices of the Indian Survey, had been making secret route surveys beyond the northern and north-western frontiers; much of what was now known of the routes through the Western Himalayas and into Central Asia—and nearly all of what was known of Tibet—was the result of their work. Operating under code names or initials—the Mullah, the Havildar, A.K., etc —they included Buddhists and Hindus as well as Mohammedans; C23, otherwise the horse-dealer Mahbub Ali in *Kim*, was inspired by what Kipling could glean of their activities.

In attempting now to make a route survey from the Punjab to Chitral and Kafiristan, the Syed was doing just what he had been trained for. The trouble was that this particular assignment had not been officially commissioned and that, anyway, Pundits were not supposed to be accompanied by their British colleagues. Under the cautious Lord Ripon, Dardistan was strictly out of bounds to all government servants; as for an Englishman going there, the visits of Hayward and Biddulph furnished eloquent testimony of both the dangers and political embarrassments that could result. Both men were therefore risking not only their lives but their careers. MacNair makes it clear that the original idea was the Syed's; no doubt this can be ascribed to the over-enthusiasm of a new recruit. But no such excuse can be made for MacNair himself. He admitted joining the Syed on his own insistence, but is mysteriously silent about what prompted him to take such a dangerous and uncharacteristic step.

From Ganderi the party crossed the Malakand pass into Swat and headed for the Lowarai pass into Chitral. This was the route that Hayward had originally hoped to follow, the most direct line between British India and Dardistan. MacNair was the first European to see it. Diligently he observed the height of the passes and the width of the rivers. He had no experience of the higher ranges of the Western Himalayas but, by any standards, this was not a difficult route. The Malakand was open throughout the year and mules could cross without having to be unloaded. By pretending to wander off in search of roots and herbs for his patent medicines, MacNair was able to continue his mapping. Once he was all but surprised; four armed men caught him poring over his planetable; just in time he shot the ruler up his sleeve and heaved shut the book of remedies. On the whole the disguise was working well. He had grown proficient at eating with his hands and could crouch for hours native style. His companions, of course, knew his true identity but in Dir, where he treated a stream of patients, no-one else seems to have guessed that he was other than a respected *hakim*.

It was thus extremely unfortunate that he was given away not by any slip on his own part but by a malicious, and probably purely speculative, rumour. Floated by a bitter rival of the two Pathan merchants, this rumour had it that both the *hakim* and the Syed were British officers in disguise. With an outright denial, the Khan of Dir sprang to their defence; it was sufficient to secure their immediate immunity. But the rumour surged ahead of them over the Lowarai into Chitral and Kafiristan. The latter, their original destination, could only be reached by passing through a belt of fanatically suspicious Mohammedans. Letters arrived from this quarter warning them to steer well clear, and below the snow-choked Lowarai, the southern gateway to Dardistan, MacNair hesitated.

If he had turned back now, he might well have made it back to

British territory without trouble. The Government need never have known of his transgression and his career would not have been compromised. But of MacNair's many endearing traits, a lack of professional ambition is one of the most notable. To him, as to Kim, the game was far more important than the prize. When credit was due elsewhere he paid it, regardless of how his own reputation might suffer. Few public servants, and certainly no other explorer, ever presented an account of his achievement that both began and ended by awarding the full credit for the whole enterprise to his native companions. A senior of the R.G.S. would call it 'one of the most adventurous journeys that has ever been described before the Society'. Yet, when all he got for his pains was an official reprimand, MacNair would show no resentment; he simply 'never troubled his head about promotion or preferment'. So it was at the foot of Lowarai. Having got this far he was certainly not going to play safe. If they couldn't make direct for Kafiristan, they could still press on for Chitral and there trust to Aman-ul-Mulk's good services.

The Lowarai, over 11,000 feet high, proved very different from the Malakand. Though rugged and steep the latter is essentially a desert pass like the not so distant Khyber. It can prove formidable enough when defended, as the next British party to tackle it would discover; but it is rarely affected by snow and too low to pose altitude problems. The Lowarai, on the other hand, is a true, if modest, Himalayan pass. The winding approach leads up through fine stands of conifers, haunt of the marauding bear; from boulders on the grassy banks of mountain torrents redstarts bob and flutter. Higher up, the trees give way to close cropped mountain pasture which for half the year is buried beneath the snow. For a comparatively dry area, the Lowarai boasts an impressive snowfall; telegraph poles get buried to within a foot or two of the wires and the avalanches are some of the most lethal in the Himalayas. In April, as MacNair discovered, the snow still lies for several miles on each side of the saddle; all his party's baggage had to be transferred to porters and much of the track consisted of snow slides or steps cut in the ice. It was truly a gateway into the mountains and, if he and the Syed now felt safe from the interference of government, they were also beyond its assistance.

To Aman-ul-Mulk, MacNair made no secret of his real identity;

if they were to enter Kafiristan from Chitral it was essential to have his co-operation. The Chitrali responded favourably enough; 'Mr. William', as he called him, could go wherever he wished, even into Kafiristan; but what he must not do was take his companions with him. Relishing the role of the righteous, Aman-ul-Mulk refused to believe that MacNair was anything but an official British emissary or that the Syed was any more than his guide. He insisted that since the Syed did not know Kafiristan, the *sahib* would be better served by one of his own trusted agents who did. Moreover, he also secretly wrote to the Indian Government to apprise them of the safe arrival of their man.

Pondering their next move, MacNair and the Syed made an excursion up the Ludkho valley to view the Dora pass leading into Badakshan. It seems that they didn't actually climb the pass, but MacNair had no doubt about its significance. 'I can safely pronounce it to be the easiest of all routes leading north from Chitral.' Here was news for the Indian foreign department; it was almost as much of a bombshell as the 1874 discovery of the Baroghil and Ishkoman. And whilst these latter had proved to be less vulnerable than was at first thought, the Dora was destined to remain a source of concern until the end of the century; this was the pass used by Kim's colleagues to penetrate into Central Asia.

Meanwhile, what to do about Kafiristan? MacNair was loth indeed to go anywhere without the Syed. Yet duty as much as inclination demanded that no opportunity of getting a man into Kafiristan should be passed over. This strange land lying between Chitral and Afghanistan was the only sizable slice of territory south of the Hindu Kush watershed that remained totally unexplored. On the maps it was not quite a blank. Peaks up to 16,000 feet gave some idea of the ruggedness of the place, and a number of unconvincingly dotted rivers suggested habitable valleys. There were also a few outlandish place-names—Kam, Wai, Shu—contributed by the likes of MacNair's Pathan companions. But as yet no European had ever managed to enter the country.

The people were even more of a mystery than the geography. In the racial jigsaw of the Western Himalayas, Kafiristan was a piece that simply did not fit, and the Kafirs had been an enigma to just about every branch of the social sciences for half a century. Reputedly as primitive and unapproachable as the Bushmen, they were Asia's greatest ethnological mystery. Leitner, with uncharacteristic candour, admitted that in calling them Dards he was doing so simply out of convenience; in fact their languages, religion and customs appeared to have nothing whatsoever in common with any of the Dard peoples. Surrounded by tribes once influenced by Buddhism but long ago converted to Islam, the Kafirs seemed to have been bypassed by every religious and cultural development since the stone age. They worshipped spirits, wore goatskins, and hunted with axes or bows and arrows. To look at they were almost as fair and fine featured as Europeans; Sir Henry Rawlinson had seen a Kafir girl whose long blonde hair formed a veil that reached to the ground; she was the loveliest oriental he had ever come across. But they were also said to smell quite abominable and to indulge in orgies of unspeakable obscenity. Sir Henry Yule, who with Rawlinson umpired the exploration of Asia, summed up the situation: once Kafiristan had been explored the R.G.S might close its doors; it was the last big mystery. MacNair could scarcely shy off just because he felt the prize not rightfully his.

Accordingly, on April 23 he parted from his companions and headed west in the company of a lone Kafir. Two guides, he later concluded, would have been a better arrangement, one to find the way, the other to help him along it. The paths were terrifying. They ascended one of the valleys that opens onto the Chitral river and were soon among faces 'pink rather than blond'; blue eyes were occasionally encountered and golden hair was quite common. These, however, were the Kalash Kafirs, a rather debased variant of the true Kafirs and subservient to Chitral. Independent Kafiristan began over the Shawal pass. MacNair pushed ahead and two days later breasted the pass after seven hours' toil in the snow.

The view on the *kotal* as the sun was rising was a sight never to be forgotten; near and around us the hills clad in white with different tinges of red showing, and clouds rising in fantastic shapes, and disclosing to view the blue and purple of the distant and lower ranges.

For the surveyor this was a chance not to be missed; rapturously he sketched in the features of this hitherto unseen land. 'Pictur-

esque, densely wooded and wild in the extreme', it had all that
the romantic pioneer could wish for. At the first villages in the
Lutdeh valley he was well received, and, when the weather deteriorated, happily settled down to observe Kafir life. Observation, for
MacNair, meant participation. He was soon joining in the Kafir
dances, sampling their wines and cheeses and visiting their shrines.
His hosts looked pretty wild. For one thing they shaved the whole
of their heads except for a small patch on the crown whence
streamed a long, never-cut rat's-tail. The women wore an elaborate
cap from which two, sometimes four, long horns of hair protruded.
But 'all were exceedingly well disposed towards the British';
MacNair 'might venture further and state that they would not
hesitate to place their services, should occasion require, at our
disposal'.

What a thing it would have been to present the government with
the unsolicited and unconditional allegiance of the whole of
Kafiristan. In a short story entitled *The Man who would be King*
Kipling chose Kafiristan as the primitive mountain kingdom where
two British 'loafers' were deified by a credulous and savage people.
That the Kafirs looked on the British as long lost brethren who
would deliver them from the oppression of their Islamic neighbours, even that the Kafirs were anxious to adopt Christianity
as a first step, were more than rumours in the Punjab cantonments.
But it did not fall to MacNair to exploit this situation. In fact his
visit was about as short as it could be; within a day or two of crossing the Shawal, Aman-ul-Mulk summoned him back to Chitral;
fearing for the safety of his colleagues, he obliged. Meanwhile,
showing a different face to the Government of India, the Mehtar
boasted of the special favours he was showing to the government's
representative; a case of breechloaders, he hinted, would do very
nicely as a mark of gratitude. (Instead, there eventually arrived
three antique brass mule guns.)

So short, in fact, had MacNair's visit been that neither of the
two British travellers who followed him to Kafiristan before the
country's tragic demise would concede that he had really been
there. Sir George Robertson, who admittedly acquired a deeper
knowledge of Kafiristan than anyone, insisted that though MacNair
travelled among the Kalash Kafirs he could not have crossed the
Shawal pass into the Lutdeh valley; he had heard from a Chitrali

who claimed to have accompanied MacNair that he did not cross the pass, and all the customs described by MacNair related only to the Kalash.

In the light of the later dismemberment of the Kafir country, much importance was attached to the distinction between the Kalash, who came under the administration of Chitral, and the true Kati Kafirs of what had been independent Kafiristan. In MacNair's day the distinction was less noteworthy, and he might well have crossed the Shawal without appreciating the extent to which it was a political and ethnological watershed. Equally, since he makes no mention of him, it seems unlikely that he had a Chitrali companion. But MacNair, unfortunately, was dead by the time these accusations were made public; in seeking to deprive such a modest character of his one outstanding achievement, Robertson was probably displaying as much professional pique as sound judgement.

After his recall to Chitral, MacNair must have been close to despairing of the whole expedition. There was no chance of returning to Kafiristan, and there would have been little consolation in knowing that only two years would elapse before another expedition, spurred on by his own partial success, would complete his work. The most that could be salvaged from the trip was to complete the circuit of Dardistan and return to India via Gilgit and Kashmir. This, after acrimonious exchanges with Aman-ul-Mulk, MacNair and his companions achieved. They reached Srinagar at the end of June. A journey for which they had allowed a whole year was over in three months.

As soon as he had scrubbed off the walnut juice and confessed to the name of William Watts MacNair there came a summons from Simla and the stiffest possible reprimand. It was lucky he couldn't care less. Unsubdued and with nine months leave to squander, he promptly set off on another journey of discovery; he sailed for England. There the R.G.S. sprang to his defence. He was a guest of honour at their anniversary dinner and received the coveted Murchison Award. His brief and modest account of the journey was shown to great advantage by the discussion that followed. First Leitner launched himself from his chair with a long and ungracious outburst about the presumption of anyone visiting Dardistan without inviting along the foremost exponent of its languages or at least devoting some attention to them. This was a bit unfair; he hadn't seen MacNair's confidential report in which the traveller had made a very creditable attempt to follow the doctor's example. He had collected a useful little vocabulary—the Kafir for salt was 'o' and for water 'w'—and had illustrated it with ethnographical dialogues and a delightful section on Kafir recipes.

Next came Rawlinson with the absurd pronouncement that the route which for twenty years he, in his wisdom, had recognised as the 'great natural high-road' from India to Central Asia had at last been opened up. Great natural high roads were one of his specialities; ten years before he had been saying the same thing about the so-called Changchenmo route from Ladakh to Sinkiang. As to how a man travelling in disguise and in fear of his life could be said to have opened it up one doesn't ask. MacNair, anyway, didn't bother. Perhaps after a consolatory visit to Lords Cricket Ground, he returned to India and there, still a surveyor 3rd Grade, he died of fever while planetabling in Baluchistan in 1889.

* * *

Like Kafiristan, MacNair doesn't really fit. Amidst the collection of rabid careerists and brooding romantics who dominate the Gilgit story, his sheer normality amounts to a delightful distinction. One wonders how on earth such a man ever got involved. Why did he, in fact, take that fateful step in Nowshera on the night of April 9, 1885? The reader of *Kim* will naturally suspect a secret motive; and he will not be surprised that till his dying day MacNair refused to reveal it. But it is more significant that Mac-Nair's contemporaries also found his explanations somewhat lame. They suspected that there was more to this improbable journey than met the eye; and the Indian papers in particular thought they could detect the influence of none other than the Quarter Master General of the Indian Army, Sir Charles Metcalfe MacGregor. MacNair staunchly refused to acknowledge any dealings with 'old Mac'; to have done so would obviously have compromised the Q.M.G. who would soon be in dire enough trouble anyway. But opinion at the time was in no doubt that, if MacGregor hadn't actually urged MacNair to go, he had certainly known in advance what was planned and had indicated approval. Moreover he alone is on record as welcoming back the disgraced surveyor 'with open arms'. The visit to Kafiristan thus looks like the first of many exploits in Dardistan that would be inspired by the thinking of this most controversial exponent of the Great Game.

Though founder of the Indian army's Intelligence Department, MacGregor was scarcely the mastermind of an espionage network. A soldier, simple and brave, 'a big bluff gruff man' according to Younghusband, he was also a far cry from the shady and devious Lurgan Sahib of *Kim*. If indeed he served Kipling as a model at all it was more probably for one of those self-seeking government servants satirised in *Departmental Ditties*. So much has now been written to eulogise and glamorise the everyday work of the men who ruled India that it is easy to forget more objectionable details like the system, if one can call it that, of promoting one's career. To anyone with an ambitious streak, the normal channels of advancement proved far too sluggish. The ladder was there not so much to be climbed as to be by-passed. For soldier and civilian alike this meant getting onto someone's personal staff, joining the political service or being co-opted for a special assignment. The way to set about it was by cultivating one's connections. Cut-throat lobbying and manœuvring were as universal as the obsession with rank and the craving for honours that prompted them. Biddulph had owed everything to his Northbrook connection, and many another would never have seen the Western Himalayas but for the workings of patronage; similarly, but for the prospect of medals and promotion, many another would never have wanted to.

MacNair, far from ordinary in this respect, was the exception that proved the rule; MacGregor was the classic example. As a subaltern his zeal to catch the eye of his superiors had been legendary. He drilled his men to distraction and then turned to his horse, perfecting parade-ground feats straight from the circus ring.

> He clubbed his wretched company a dozen times a day;
> He used to quit his charger in a parabolic way;
> His method of saluting was a joy to all beholders
> But Ahasuerus Jenkins had a head upon his shoulders.

Kipling's man chose the easiest way up; he wooed Cornelia

Agrippina 'who was musical and fat' but who 'controlled a humble husband who, in turn, controlled a Dept.' MacGregor just kept on trying. He bombarded the press with letters, invented a new type of saddle and, at the despairing suggestion of his colleagues, bought his own trumpet and learnt to blow it—anything, in fact, to bring his name to notice. As a matter of course he volunteered for every expedition under the sun, including Forsyth's to Sinkiang. But better by far was a military expedition; a V.C. would mean a degree of recognition by no means beyond the dreams of his ambition. Friends were the first to concede that he was not an easy man to get on with. He was too grim and self-absorbed; only in the heat of battle did he become relaxed and good company. True to the traditions of Rob Roy, a supposed ancestor, he faced the bullets with a tartan plaid over his shoulder and a massive claymore in his hand. 'One of the most fearless men in the Indian Army', it was thought, but he was also one of the most blood-thirsty—and one of the most ambitious. 'Oh for a campaign', he cried, 'a long one and a fierce one. One that would put me in my grave or place me above injustice.' Injustice, of course, meant simply a lull in his promotion prospects. In the conduct of India's external relations every official attempt to negotiate rather than fight was viewed as an unkind thrust in the path of his career.

Another favourite ploy of the ambitious was the writing of anonymous and unsolicited reports. MacGregor had been a great one for this, tackling subjects that ranged from *On Clandestine Prostitution* to *On The Storing of Supplies in Abyssinia*. The idea was that the moment one was known to have been read with approval by someone in authority, forward would step the none-too-bashful author to acknowledge his work. Nauseating it may have been, but that was the way to get ahead. And for MacGregor it had at last worked. As Quarter Master General from 1880–85, he had already been knighted. He was only a step away from a generalship and he had a good chance of realising his ultimate ambition – Commander-in-Chief of the Indian Army.

But MacGregor, in the end, wrote one report too many. His longing for a campaign led him to take a passionate interest in the Great Game. Whilst his contemporaries were inclined to argue the Central Asian question as if it were some kind of academic discipline, he took the view that the Russian menace was not a question but a fact. The army as a whole were naturally more 'forward' in their views than their civil equivalents; but even by their standards MacGregor was way out ahead. In all these articles and reports alarm-mongering had been his speciality and, while under Lord Ripon the Russian threat was officially played down, MacGregor conceived it as his personal mission in life to keep the flame burning. He cared little if he was more often ridiculed as a fire-eating prophet of doom; somehow the administration just had to be brought to a true realisation of India's imminent peril.

In his youth he had travelled widely in Afghanistan and Persia and there formed his views on India's vulnerability. But it was not as a traveller that he impinged on Gilgit; nor as a military reformer, in which role some claim he deserves recognition as the father of modern India's army. Rather, and more modestly, it was as the man who selected and coached the Gilgit Game's most distinguished players. His was the thinking that guided them and his the personality that influenced them. Within the Q.M.G's department he devoted his considerable energies to the creation of an Intelligence Branch for collating and analysing reports from across the frontier; MacNair's was one of its prize exhibits, Younghusband one of its most distinguished graduates. On the question of Afghanistan he badgered the Commander-in-Chief to get the troops sent back there a third time with the object of establishing a permanent hold on Herat and the middle Oxus. He also, with more success, urged on Ripon and the British Foreign Office the necessity of demarcating the northern boundary of Afghanistan. In his case it was not so much a question of showing the Russians just where they must draw the line in their advance through Central Asia, as of getting the despised 'politicals', and the equally contemptible Viceroy, to commit themselves to a line which, if encroached on, would mean war. Simultaneously information was amassed about the likely strengths and deployment of both Russian and Indian troops in the event of war breaking out. The results of this last were embodied in the fatal report, *The Defence of India*, published secretly in 1883, soon after MacNair's return.

In his blunt military way MacGregor set down, by numbers, the troops that would be available to both sides and the objectives they could reasonably attain during the first ninety days of hostilities. The Russians would probably launch a five-pronged attack, three columns being aimed at Kabul and Herat, one at Chitral and one at Gilgit and Kashmir. Without advance warning he thought it doubtful whether, in the present state of India's defences, any of these places could be saved. To occupy them in advance of hostilities was therefore a basic precaution. But this in itself was not enough. The expected assault would for the first time embroil British troops in a major continental struggle along a landlocked frontier. British resources in terms of manpower were not up to such a challenge; but India's were. The Indian army should be reorganised and expanded to constitute a major fighting force of continental proportions.

Lord Ripon was a great admirer of Sir John Lawrence, the originator of the policy of 'masterly inactivity'. In the light of recent Russian behaviour which included the capture of Merv just beyond the Afghan frontier and another spate of activity on the Pamirs, this policy could scarcely look less appropriate. Moreover MacGregor didn't hide the fact that his paper was not just an academic exercise; it was a polemic designed to arouse the administration or, failing that, to create such a wave of Russophobia that the administration would be discredited.

'I solemnly assert my belief', he concluded, 'that there can never be a real settlement of the Russo-Indian question till Russia is driven out of the Caucasus and Turkistan.' This was going too far. Turkistan was virtually the whole of Central Asia. Russia's advance, it seemed, was not to be held up but to be reversed, war not shunned but invited and the frontiers of India pitched deep into the heart of the continent. Such intemperate rantings did his cause no good at all. But it was not this that caused all the trouble; MacGregor was entitled to his own views. Where he went wrong was in promulgating them while Quarter Master General and in allowing the press to see a paper that was supposed to be strictly confidential. Such indiscretion looked too much like the attempt it obviously was to pressurise the government. Gladstone regarded it as a direct criticism of Liberal policy and demanded an explanation. The Q.M.G. was allowed to retain his post but the suppression of *The Defence of India* and the reprimand that followed spelt death to his future prospects.

In disgrace he saw out his term of office as Q.M.G. and in 1886, a sick and embittered man, accepted a vastly inferior posting. The following year he was gazetted a Major-General on compassionate grounds; he was a dying man. Sadly the news of his promotion arrived a fortnight too late. The irony of such an intensely ambitious man realising one of his greatest dreams two weeks after being laid in the grave is rivalled only by his disgrace coinciding with a period during which all that he stood for was coming back into favour.

In December 1884 Ripon resigned as Viceroy and was succeeded by Lord Dufferin. Again this was Gladstone's choice; but Dufferin was altogether a more flexible and outward looking statesman. He had once been a Tory, his background was diplomatic including a spell as Ambassador in St. Petersburg, and, in India, foreign affairs would remain his speciality. Which was just as well; for, three months after taking office, he was faced with a major war scare as grave as that of 1876. MacGregor had urged the idea of demarcating the north-western section of the Afghan frontier as a way of getting a timid administration to commit itself to a line that it would be bound to defend. Ripon went ahead with the scheme confident that a well defined frontier would reduce the risk of war. In the event it all but precipitated it. Staking out a prior claim to the Panjdeh oasis, Russian troops coolly routed an Afghan detachment. Immediately British troops in India were put on the alert, Gladstone secured a vote of credit for £11 million and Dufferin began seriously to consider sending the army to hold Herat. Had the Amir taken the matter to heart as much as the British, these preparations would have been more than justified. But probably he had never heard of Panjdeh and it was his total indifference to the affair which more than anything cooled the atmosphere. Nevertheless MacGregor's grim forebodings appeared to have been partially vindicated; clearly it was high time that the merits of a 'forward' policy were reconsidered.

When a great man's career was in eclipse, or when the policy for which he stood was out of favour, the long appendage of subordinates who had pinned their colours to his standard lay low in the regimental lines, biding their time. Then, the moment the climate seemed to change, out they all came brandishing their connections and clamouring for promotion and appointments. In 1885 MacGregor himself was out of the running, disgraced beyond redemption; and the change of government that usually heralded such a move actually followed it. Otherwise the signs were unmistakable. General Frederick Sleigh Roberts, the go-getting 'our Bobs' of Kipling and a comrade and admirer of MacGregor's, was appointed Commander-in-Chief. About the same time, April 1885, Dufferin chose as his Foreign Secretary the young Mortimer Durand. In his 'forward' outlook Durand was altogether more subtle and realistic than MacGregor, but he was still MacGregor's man; he had once shared a house with him and was now his brother-in-law. Then in June 1885 Gladstone resigned and Lord Salisbury, Disraeli's successor as Tory Leader, formed his first ministry. It was pure coincidence, though not one without significance, that on the very day that he did so the first ever major British mission to Dardistan marched out in a long column from Srinagar. It was headed by Colonel William Lockhart, MacGregor's closest friend and his deputy in the Intelligence Branch.

The Lockhart Mission was conceived primarily as an expression of this new climate of opinion; its roving character, its varied objectives and the whole conduct of the exercise will bear this out. However it had to have some specific points of reference and this was where MacNair came in. His modest little journey had raised four intriguing questions; could the direct route from Peshawar— or Nowshera—to Chitral be opened for British use; could the 'well-disposed' Kafirs be incorporated into the scheme of India's defences; was the Dora pass really another of those alarming backdoors into India; and had Aman-ul-Mulk of Chitral changed his tune since the days when Biddulph had virtually written him off? In *The Defence of India* MacGregor had emphasised the importance of Chitral by awarding it the attention of a whole Russian column. MacNair had no good opinion of Aman-ul-Mulk but he did report that the old chief was seriously exercised about Russian activities on the Pamirs; in 1883 one group of Russian explorers had reached Shignan and another, surveying, had touched Wakhan. The latter had given it out that they were hoping to reach Chitral and Kafiristan. In fact Aman-ul-Mulk understood that they were empowered to make him an offer for the Ludkho valley leading down from the Dora or the Darkot valley where Hayward had been killed. 'Shall I kill them or make prisoners of them or send them to Your Excellency?' he had asked Lord Ripon.

Lockhart was to advise him; indeed the need to secure Chitral was now considered so great that terms of friendship were to be established regardless of the Mehtar's known duplicity. No longer was this all just a reflection of British anxieties about Afghan dealings with Chitral; rather it was a straightforward attempt to thwart Russian ambitions. Lockhart and his men were cautioned about leaking news of the expedition to the press; 'the less the public hears of it the better'. It was recognised that news of a British visit to Kafiristan would bring a protest from the Amir and perhaps even an attack on the Kafirs. But the reason for designating the rest of the mission's itinerary as top secret was simply to steal a march on what Kipling called 'the power to the North'.

Since the closure of the Gilgit Agency four years earlier, the Dards and the Dogras had been left to themselves; Biddulph's bungalow stood empty, goats grazing the garden. This was not because Ripon had evolved some new policy for guarding the Hindu Kush routes. On the contrary he had still relied on the Dogras doing the job for him, and this in spite of the fact that they were clearly incapable of exercising any influence beyond Gilgit and were scarcely more trustworthy than the perfidious Dards. However, the country had remained at peace. The Maharaja, now an old man, knew from bitter experience just how far he could go. Sensibly he refrained from pushing the likes of Ghazan Khan or Aman-ul-Mulk. The subsidies were paid out, the *vakils*, with their scrawny sheep and their little bags of gold dust, trooped in, and high in the Hindu Raj, well out of harm's way, the final act in the saga of the Yasin brothers was played out; Pahlwan was gunned down by his equally outlawed brother, the dreaded Mulk Aman.

Life in Dardistan was hardly idyllic but it was as settled as it had ever been. So much so that Leitner would soon look back on this period, the lull before the storm, as a sort of golden age. Dogra rule, compared with what was to follow, did not seem such an unmitigated disaster as he had once thought. Its sheer ineffectiveness meant that the Dards at least maintained their independence and their unique way of life. Increasingly it seemed that the real irritant was the arrival of a British officer. Like a wasps' nest the Hindu Kush was quiet enough until stirred into frenzy by the meddlings of a Biddulph or a Hayward. Or indeed a Lockhart.

8. The Lost Brethren

From Srinagar the new mission followed the usual route over the Great Himalaya. Losing two weeks waiting for the Kamri pass to open and several days ferrying their baggage across the Indus at Bunji, they reached Gilgit in late July 1885. Biddulph's bungalow was commandeered by the officers—'a capital house' thought Lockhart—and Dr. Giles, the mission's surgeon and geologist, set up his dispensary. If the presence of the mission was not immediately resented it was largely thanks to the doctor's dexterity in the matter of restoring noses; plastic surgery had a great future in a place where the normal punishment for the pettiest of crimes was mutilation.

Meanwhile Lockhart took stock of his party. Undoubtedly there had been a good case for getting away from the clandestine one-man-shows that had previously represented British attempts to explore Dardistan. The Lockhart mission, however, went to the other extreme. There were four British officers—Lockhart, Giles, Colonel Woodthorpe in charge of surveying, and Captain Barrow also of the Intelligence—each with two ponies and three or four servants. Then there were five native surveyors, a military escort of Sikhs and a baggage train of 300 mules laden with beads for the natives that included an arsenal of breech-loaders. Mortimer Durand, the new Foreign Secretary, almost certainly wanted it this way; the unspecified object of the mission was to give the Dards some inkling of the true prestige and might of British India.

Lockhart, too, doubtless relished the kudos such a mighty force conferred on its leader. But already he was becoming aware of its drawbacks. In the recent hostilities in Afghanistan he had been Q.M.G. to General Roberts' force and had thus played an important part in the famous Kabul–Kandahar march. He seems, however, to have had no previous experience of the Himalayas. Nor had he apparently sought Biddulph's advice. For he, surely, would have stressed the idiocy of taking a mule train into Dardistan; in fact his own solution to the problem of mountain carriage had been a flock of pack-bearing sheep as used in Tibet (they didn't need feeding and, when you had eaten their loads, you could always eat their mutton). Other travellers had equally imaginative solutions; Hayward was a yak man—it was the only beast that could match his own powers of endurance; and Younghusband, introducing the idea of supply dumps along his proposed trail, plumped for the high load factor of the Bactrian camel. Lockhart presumably thought that in adopting the mules that had performed so well in Afghanistan he was playing safe. But the parapets and rock staircases of Dardistan were not built for quadrupeds that could not be carried; and hauling several hundreds of them up and down on ropes was a slow process. Accordingly, at Gilgit, he took on two hundred porters and reduced the mules to sixty. Or rather, fifty-nine. For on the first day's march out of Gilgit a significant portion of the mission's exchequer, 4,000 rupees in silver, plus the mule to which it was tied, plummeted down a sheer cliff face into the river. A day was wasted, fishing fruitlessly, and for the whole year that the mission would remain in the field Lockhart would be desperately scrounging cash from anyone willing to advance it. It was a bad start.

From Gilgit he headed west for Chitral via the direct route over the Shandur pass. Woodthorpe and Barrow, meanwhile, were sent round via Yasin to study the Darkot and Baroghil; in the process they recorded that transfiguration version of the Hayward martyrdom. The passes, or rather the approaches to them, were less impressive. The Baroghil was all that Biddulph had said; it presented 'the most curious and startling feature in this part of the world; the mighty range suddenly sinks down abruptly into absolute insignificance'. But how deceptive this was. For an invading force, once across the pass, had either to climb up the Darkot into Yasin or down the glaciers into Chitral. Woodthorpe tried both. In each case his men were severely frost-bitten and the party all but benighted; and this was in August, supposedly one of the best months for travel in the Hindu Kush. A platoon of marines might get through but an army with artillery was out of the question. Without extensive road building the danger was one of infiltration, not invasion.

Oddly, the only pass in the region that would ever see the passage of artillery was that which Lockhart was negotiating with the baggage. The Shandur is neither very high nor steep and its position between transverse valleys well south of the Hindu Kush watershed relegated its importance purely to that of internal communications. Lockhart preferred to call it a plateau rather than a pass. He got his party across without mishap and agreed with Biddulph in regarding it as an excellent corridor by which the route down the Chitral valley could be commanded from Gilgit. But ten years later an ageing Irish colonel with a desperate band of followers would beg to differ. In mid-January with the snow shoulder deep and the temperature well below freezing, the Shandur was a nightmare. Guns could neither be dragged over nor ponies manage to carry them across. To the men who finally shouldered the heavy steel-rimmed wheels, the icy barrels and the boxes of ammunition, Lockhart's name would be one best not mentioned.

On September 2 Woodthorpe and Barrow rejoined the main party at Mastuj and the mission started down the Chitral valley to the capital. The road was execrable. Then as now, each little group of hamlets in its green oasis was cut off from the next by miles of sizzling rock. The foaming river monopolises the narrow valley floor forcing the track to switch-back relentlessly up and down the steep and dusty bluffs. Here the only thing that grows is artemisia, a desert shrub that fills the air with an astringent, thirst provoking aroma. The colours too are desert colours, brown rock, pale sand, white sky. In the higher side valleys there is timber and grazing but along the channel gouged by the Chitral river the aspect of parched austerity is more Afghan than Alpine; lizards cock their horny heads just out of reach, while tumbleweed and will-o-the-wisps make fair play on the gentler slopes.

The contrasts, too, are typically those of desert lands. An irrigation channel crossing the face of a hill draws a straight line between Sahara and garden. In one stride you pass from glare and dust into the rich green of rice fields and the scent of wild roses. On one side not a tree, not a blade of grass; on the other chenars, poplars and acacias, and below them a tangle of fruit trees, apple, pear, peach and pomegranate. Golden orioles flash through the branches and asparagus, introduced by a grandson of Aman-ul-Mulk, grows wild in the grass.

Lockhart and his men took eight days over a journey of sixty odd miles. In spite of Biddulph and MacNair no-one had really explored Chitral; the new mission now made good the deficiency. Giles was a geologist and something of a naturalist. With his help and that of Woodthorpe and his surveyors, Barrow was able to compile the first gazetteer for the whole valley. Tirich Mir, 'looking like a mass of frosted silver' according to the poetically inclined Lockhart, turned out to be rather lower than Biddulph had estimated, about 25,000 feet, and no other serious rivals to Everest or K2 were spied. But the oases were every bit as populous and prosperous as Biddulph had hinted. Chitral was at last revealed as much the largest and most important of all the Hindu Kush valleys—as well as being the most vulnerable.

As the mission approached the largest oasis, which even today hardly justifies the name of Chitral town, Aman-ul-Mulk's letters became increasingly frequent. This was presumably a good sign though, as they were written in rhyme, it was hard to tell; even the versifying Lockhart could make nothing of them. Four miles from his fort, where the valley opens out, the Mehtar was waiting for them. Extending a fist like a prizefighter's he grasped the colonel's fingers and, 'according to the very disagreeable custom of the country', continued to fondle them as they rode side by side. Across the river, Chitrali irregulars were drumming and shouting for all they were worth, horsemen in garish robes swept back and forth blazing away with their matchlocks while from the fort an artillery salute, 'most irregularly fired', boomed across the valley; 'the effect was good'.

As a centrepiece, the Mehtar and the colonel hand in hand could hardly have been bettered. Lockhart was cut out to be an imperial figure. Hooded eyes and droopy moustaches gave him a St. Bernard's look of noble imperturbability tinged with a hint of disdain. Big by any standards he stood patrician head and mighty shoulders above the tallest Dard and required six strong men to hoist him onto his pony. (In Chitral it was not customary for the mighty to mount unaided.) But the Mehtar was also a six man proposition. Not so tall, he was broad almost to squareness. Lockhart guessed 'the old fox' was knocking 70; he was also toothless which made it hard to follow his mumbled Persian. But there was no denying the nobility of bearing. Nor the 'determined cast of countenance' characterised by a scimitar of a nose, fair skinned and bony, cleaving the face between turban and henna-red beard.

Eleven o'clock next day official exchanges began. The officers
swopped their battered tweeds for dress uniforms and their walking
sticks for swords. Tents were so arranged that a long street ran
through the lines to a flagpost before a brightly coloured awning.
The Union Jack was raised, the Chitralis were welcomed by a
guard of honour, a salute was fired and official introductions
were performed with due ceremony. It might have been the
beginning of some grand durbar, except that there then followed a
sticky snack of 'tea, coffee, cake, chocolate and toffee'. Just why
Lockhart should bother to report to Durand, the Foreign Secretary,
in such detail about a minor matter of decorum is not explained.
But it's good to know that the Mehtar then 'filled his mouth with
snuff, slowly chewed it and spat the result into the turban of one
of his officers'. Lockhart should have been warned. The veneer of
propriety and cordiality was both thin and deceptive.

More probably the colonel was simply amused. The son of a
landed Scots minister, he would eventually realise MacGregor's
ambition of becoming Commander-in-Chief in India; he was a
good, even a great soldier whose manipulation of the strings of
patronage won him remarkably few enemies and many intensely
loyal friends. 'His heart was as sound as his head' according to an
obituarist, and for once this wasn't just an epigraphic platitude.
But hard-headedness to the point of insensitivity and stalwart determination to the point of obstinacy were not what was required
of a political officer negotiating with the treacherous Dards. Nor
were geniality, inoffensiveness and the best will in the world much
better. It is impossible to avoid the impression that Lockhart, and
the rest of his staff, handled the Chitral situation with incredible
naïvety. What they wanted was some sort of guarantee that,
in the event of a Russian move from the north, Aman-ul-Mulk
would hold all the key gorges into Chitral and allow free passage
for British troops. Given the now acknowledged difficulty of the
Hindu Kush routes, such an attack could only be small scale. The
Chitralis, whom Lockhart reckoned 'perhaps the best men anywhere up or down a precipice', should be well capable of with-
standing it until British troops could storm up by MacNair's route
from Peshawar and finish the enemy off. Imagine, then, Lockhart's
delight when the Mehtar unasked, offered to do just that. All he
wanted in return was the willingly given guarantee that Chitral

territory should descend intact to his heirs. Barrow could hardly draw up the treaty quick enough.

But then 'the old grasper' raised the question of his subsidy. From Kashmir, in return for a few hawks and greyhounds, he was now getting 16,500 rupees a year. How much more might he expect in anticipation of these new services? Lockhart had already presented his own little trousseau of Sniders, revolvers, broadcloth and 'a miscellaneous assortment of tools, combs, looking glasses, knives, scissors, thread, buttons, braids and toys' valued at 5,000 rupees, not to mention much of his camp furniture (some of it is still to be found about the valley today). He was not empowered to offer more, and the fact of the matter was that Aman-ul-Mulk would defend the whole of India on these sort of terms; he was also happy to sign treaties to that effect. But it didn't mean that 'we now have a hold of Chitral' as Lockhart triumphantly announced to Durand.

The question of the subsidy was left to be sorted out by one of Aman-ul-Mulk's sons who would visit India for the approaching winter. Lockhart noticed no obvious decline in the Mehtar, but the next visitor to Chitral would find him semi-senile. At all events he couldn't last much longer and it was vital to sow the seeds of future friendship with his heir. For this, six months of V.I.P. treatment in India was reckoned the best possible grounding. The only problem was to decide who should receive it, and again Lockhart made a hideous blunder.

Aman-ul-Mulk was reputed to have sixty sons of whom three or four were regarded as serious contenders for the throne. There was Amir-ul-Mulk, an unpredictable youth of psychopathic tendencies who had already objected to his share of the mission's bounty. Then there was a child of five whom the mission had passed on the road from Mastuj riding on a white pony. This was Shuja-ul-Mulk, a very long shot indeed for the succession though, in the end, the only one to survive the impending bloodbath. Much better known to Lockhart were the two most serious contenders, Nizam-ul-Mulk, the playboy chief who had been installed in Yasin, and his deadly rival Afzul-ul-Mulk, the quiet athletic chief of Mastuj. It seems pretty clear that already Nizam was considered the senior in precedence. There was no simple rule of primogeniture but he was the older and both as ruler of Yasin, the more important dependency, and as the companion of his father during the official welcome given to the mission, he looked to be the favourite. Lockhart chose to ignore this. Afzul was the better man so Afzul should be the British candidate. Nizam was all that he couldn't stand, 'a greedy beast' who exhausted the mission's supply of sugar, tried to make off with their mess-tent and pestered Giles for his Arab and his retriever. He was also a homosexual and his rowdy parties with a troupe of dancing boys kept the mission awake half the night. If Afzul should 'deprive him some fine day of his sleek, curly head', Lockhart for one would have no objections. 'Dear Afzul', he was altogether different; strong, manly, generous and without a sweet tooth in his head. His comrades adored him and so did Lockhart. 'Will you please be very civil to young Afzul'. he told Durand. 'I mean exceptionally civil. He is worth it.'

Durand, however, had scarcely heard of Afzul. Nizam was the heir presumptive and it was to Nizam that he had just sent the official invitation. Informed of this, Lockhart was all for sending both men to India; the government could then judge for themselves. But their father thought otherwise; Lockhart might choose, but only one son might go. 'Of course Nizam must go,' he replied, furious at having been made to look such a fool. Worse was to come; the following winter in Gilgit he found himself having to act as the gay young chief's chaperone. With his usual gang of musicians, dancers and hooligans Nizam descended on Kashmir territory, determined to whoop it up all the way to Simla. 'The young barbarian' set fire to the hospital, smashed up the telegraph office (there was an office but no line back to Kashmir as yet) and demanded 'the fattest sheep, the finest flour and [inevitably] the most expensive sugar'. He was petulant in the extreme when Lockhart had to explain that the Dogra troops were not willing to dance for him; and he left in a huff, with the boys still pirouetting and the bands still playing, on New Year's Eve.

Aman-ul-Mulk's main interest in the whole affair had been to leave as open as possible the selection of his heir. Patricide was the first thought of any Dard crown prince and the Mehtar's best chance of dying a natural death therefore lay in seeing that none of his sons acquired pre-eminence in his lifetime. Lockhart's adoption of Afzul must have seemed a heaven-sent opportunity of redressing the senior status enjoyed by Nizam. Although the trip to India would seem to have given Nizam another advantage, Lockhart would see to it that Afzul was not forgotten; in 1887 he too received the V.I.P. tour. The result was that, when the crisis finally broke, the Indian government would be in the embarrassing position of having two rival candidates.

Lockhart had been invited to choose who should go to India and so he had done so. He had been offered assurances about the defence of Chitral and he had accepted them. Gullibility wasn't in it. He had also been told that Chitral was his; he might go wherever he pleased, even east into Dir or west into Kafiristan. He determined to do both. To Durand he wrote that 'it would be a great thing to get hold of Dir as we now have hold of Chitral'. Except for a narrow belt of Pathan country between there and Peshawar, this would effectively open up MacNair's route from British territory. However Aman-ul-Mulk knew this too; he had no intention of seeing it opened up, nor of incurring the hostility of his Pathan neighbours by doing so. Every political initiative in this direction, including Lockhart's, came to nothing and it would eventually take a corps of fifteen thousand to force the Malakand and open the Lowarai. The nearest Lockhart's mission got was to Drosh on the Chitral side of the latter.

As regards letting the mission cross into Kafiristan, the Mehtar also had second thoughts. He made much of the difficulties of the country and of the savagery of its people. And he insisted that, if the British party went ahead, he be relieved of all responsibility for their safety. Lockhart agreed, giving him a signed paper to that effect. This was extremely dangerous; 'the old fox', armed with such a carte blanche, could dispose of the mission whenever he felt so inclined. But the Dora pass had to be visited and it was essential to explore further the political sympathies of the Kafirs who lived in its vicinity. On September 19, abandoning the last of the ill-fated mules, the mission headed west up the Ludkho valley.

* * *

When, before the R.G.S., Leitner had savaged MacNair for entering Kafiristan with neither a linguist nor an ethnologist, he had actually made a good point. The great interest of the country was, after all, its people. Kafirs reaching the slave markets of Bukhara invariably caused a sensation. One Russian authority had actually claimed that they were Slavs—which might sound absurd but, given the tempo of pan-Slavism in the Balkans at this time, had ominous implications. The Russians had noted not only that Kafiristan was a racial anomaly but also that it was the one place along the whole mountain frontier that had had no diplomatic dealings with either the British or their feudatories; it just might be the long sought chink in India's defences.

Lockhart, though he too lacked the services of an ethnologist, was immediately impressed by the Kafirs' willingness to accept the British as long lost brethren. To their Mohammedan neighbours both races were *Kafirs*, i.e. infidels, and to them it was a source of malicious glee that the savages of Kafiristan honestly believed that they shared a racial heritage with the mighty *sahibs*. When the ever co-operative Afzul had procured a few Kafirs for Lockhart's inspection, their first reaction had been 'to give out quite proudly that they are of the same race as the English and expect to be treated as such'. Like some rare pedigree of dog encountering one of its own species for the first time, the Kafirs were consumed with a curiosity that far exceeded that of their visitors. The tweed of the Norfolk jackets was closely examined, the heavy boots sniffed and weighed and, to make sure that the newcomers really were white all over, the Kafirs craned their necks to view down a shirt front and jerked at a passing trouser leg. Lockhart endured the scrutiny with his usual strained geniality. He certainly appreciated that in encouraging this supposed relationship lay the simplest means of winning the Kafirs' loyalty. One wonders, though, whether he appreciated its corollary; that if the Kafirs regarded the British as brethren because they were white and non-Islamic, they might think exactly the same about the Russians.

The importance of such a consideration was heightened by what the mission discovered about the Dora pass. 'Could rapidly be made fit for wheels', wrote Lockhart. Some of the party had ridden to the top without dismounting and the approach from the Badakshan side looked just as easy. Having now inspected most of the other passes into Dardistan they were confident that this was much the most vulnerable. It was higher than the Baroghil and, where the track skirted a lake (now renamed Lake Dufferin), could easily be barred. So could its approaches near the mouth of the Ludkho valley where the path wound through a mountain crack four hundred feet deep and no wider than a country lane. But Lockhart's point was that if the natives co-operated with the aggressor this route, and this route alone, posed no serious obstacles to the passage of artillery and substantial numbers of troops. There were no glaciers, little snow and therefore predictable river crossings. The Dora to Lockhart would become what the Baroghil had been to Biddulph, the reason for, and focus of, a scheme for the defence of the whole of Dardistan.

But first the Kafirs. From the Dora the mission struck southwest into the bewildering mountain network to which this strange race owed its survival. All seemed to go well. The high valleys offered a wonderful contrast to the heat and dust of Chitral. Woods of evergreen oak, cedar and pine, sparkling streams at the foot of grassy slopes and the cool bracing air from the snowfields above reminded Lockhart of the Alps. Though still accompanied by a party of Chitralis, pressed on them by Aman-ul-Mulk, they had no difficulty finding Kafir guides and at the first village were again welcomed like long-lost prodigals. To the village shrine they were taken to be reconciled with Imbra, the great spirit supposedly common to all white peoples. Lockhart emptied his pockets of small change, the priest addressed a large boulder and Imbra was reported to be gratified.

'The Kafir religion', according to a later visitor, 'is a somewhat low form of idolatry with an admixture of ancestor worship and some traces of fire-worship.' Lockhart missed the fire-worship but the ancestors were everywhere; he was introduced to a fresh clump at each village. The Kafirs' greatest artistic endeavours were lavished on the carving of these effigies of the dead. Some were as much as fifteen feet tall. Seated, standing or mounted on horseback the ancestors were positioned in sociable groups; there, time and the prevailing wind would gradually loosen their foundations till they keeled over like drunken sailors. But the hard cedar wood and the dry atmosphere militated against decay. They remained straight-backed and beetle-browed like pieces of a giant's chess set, even when flat on the grass. Lockhart was making the acquaintance of the accumulation of centuries, much of which is now dispersed through the world's museums. Along with some low straight-backed chairs, a few carved timbers, some weapons and implements, they represent the pathetic legacy of a now defunct people.

As the mission penetrated deeper into the country they, like MacNair, were gradually initiated into the local specialities, the wine, the cakes that tasted like plum pudding and, above all, the dancing.

It was a mixture of country dance and Highland Schottishe. Advancing and retiring in lines, intermingling in couples, they kept excellent time to the music of reed pipes and two small drums, and marked points in the dance by ear-piercing whistles on their fingers and by brandishing their axes. The red firelight, the savage figures, and their fierce but perfectly timed gestures, presented a weird spectacle, which it would be difficult for the on-looker ever to forget.

No women took part because, as the menfolk explained, it would be degrading in the presence of outsiders like the accompanying Chitralis. Lockhart and company were relieved; the women were proving a sore trial. 'To judge from their manners their morals cannot be very high. To put it in the mildest language they cannot have much modesty.' Precisely what Lockhart was trying to imply is not clear. Was it just their lewd gestures that so upset him or was he being importuned in more direct ways? The only subsequent European visitor to Kafiristan was invited to consummate the reunion of the races by taking a Kafir maiden to bed. But it looks as if the colonel and his men had to resist more than just an invitation.

Lockhart might draw the line at seduction, but nevertheless he acquired a son. Gumara was a man about the colonel's own age. He was also 'strong and had a reputation for bravery (having killed twenty-nine Mussulmans), so it seemed that his adoption as a son might be of use to the party and the proposal was agreed to'. The suggestion had come from the Kafirs; Lockhart had no idea what was involved other than that he would acquire a useful ally and oblige his possessive hosts without betraying Mrs. Lockhart. In the event he may well have regretted such solicitude for his spouse. The adoption ceremony started reasonably enough. A sheep was sacrificed, its kidneys removed, lightly toasted and passed to the two principals on the point of a knife. Between mouthfuls father and son stood a foot apart and blew kisses at one another. Then the surprise. Lockhart's coat and shirt were torn open, butter was rubbed on his left nipple and the Kafir hastily applied his lips. Gumara sucked like a vampire, the colonel winced in pain and the reunion of the races was at last achieved; the long lost Kafirs of Gish, the great war god who was supposed to have deserted Kafiristan for London, were reconciled with their Kafir brethren, the children of Imbra.

Gumara proved to be a model son. He carried his father across every stream and generally tried to be of use about the camp. But back in Chitral his anxiety to be never more than kiss-blowing distance from the colonel grew wearisome. Communication was impossible after they had parted from their bilingual guides and the poor Kafir had to be abruptly orphaned. It was a pity Lockhart didn't remember Leitner's Lahore home for the strayed and unwanted of the Hindu Kush.

Gradually the mission's policy of humouring their hosts seemed to pay off. The Kafir chiefs were eating out of Lockhart's hands and Barrow was instructed to draw up what must surely be one of the British Empire's most bizarre defensive treaties.

> Covenant made between Colonel W. S. A. Lockhart on the part of the British Government, and the following chiefs of the Bashgal tribe:
>   1. Mara
>   2. Malik
>   3. Gulmer
>   4. Chandlu, son of Mara
>   5. Merig, son of Malik
>   6. Shtaluk, son of Gulmer
> In the event of an enemy of Great Britain approaching the frontiers of Kafiristan, the above-named will send all available men of their own to the threatened quarter, to hinder or repel the invader. In return I agree, on the part of the British Government, to pay the several chiefs mentioned the sum of ten rupees per mensem per man placed in the field, and to provide arms for them; the chiefs on their part agreeing to receive one British officer per 500 men so raised, as instructors and leaders. This agreement has been sealed by the ceremony of sharing a goat's heart between myself and the above-mentioned chiefs.
>   W. S. A. Lockhart. Colonel.

The treaty was dated 1st October 1885. Lockhart, like an eager Monopoly player collecting his set, was confident that he had now got hold of Kafiristan too. Before passing on the good tidings to Durand, however, he had cause for second thoughts. At 9 a.m. the following day the mission's path was barred by a crowd of excited Kafirs brandishing their axes. A Chitrali sent forward to parley was pitched over a cliff and a Kafir who remained loyal to Lockhart was hit on the neck with an axe handle. The situation looked extremely nasty. The Sikh escort were instructed to loosen cartridges and the Chitralis were ordered back out of the line of fire. This last move, however, abruptly cooled matters; it was clear that it was the Chitralis whom the Kafirs found so objectionable.

'Go away now by the Shawal pass,' the Kafir spokesman commanded. 'Don't be angry; we are your friends but are determined not to let the Chitralis remain another day in the valley. Come back in the spring but come without the Chitralis and you can go wherever you like.'

Lockhart replied that he would do just that; he might try to engineer an approach from Badakshan in which case he would not be travelling under the auspices of Chitral. The Kafirs were satisfied. They kissed his hands and again begged him not to be angry.

Peeved rather than angry, Lockhart headed back to Chitral along the route taken by MacNair. On the Shawal pass he found a couple of tarns by which to commemorate his old friend—they became the MacGregor Lakes—and reached Chitral on October 7. Aman-ul-Mulk's reception of the mission was less enthusiastic than in the previous month; his one ambition was to send them packing before they devoured the valley's entire supply of winter fodder. Lockhart took the point, sending the baggage straight on to Gilgit and himself following as soon as all outstanding business had been completed. In early December he reached winter quarters in Biddulph's bungalow.

Here two interesting bits of news awaited him. The first was that he had just narrowly escaped being waylaid by the dreaded Mulk Aman, last of the three Yasin brothers. As in the past, rumour had it that the Kashmir governor in Gilgit had paid Mulk Aman to stir up trouble for the mission. So reminiscent of Biddulph's and Hayward's vicissitudes was this that Lockhart too conceded that the Dogras were just a liability; they should be sent back to Bunji and the east bank of the Indus. During the long Gilgit winter he brooded over a new scheme for the defence of the Hindu Kush which, for the first time, excluded Kashmir completely. He recommended not so much the reopening of the Gilgit Agency as 'the acquisition of Gilgit'. He might disguise it simply as a reinstatement of the arrangement that had led to Biddulph's appointment; but the nineteen British officers he wanted at Gilgit were to have administrative and revenue duties as well as the purely military. The mountain battery and the twelve companies of infantry were to consist of Dard levies and men recruited from 'a good man-producing part of the Punjab'; their diet was to include huge quantities of beef, anathema to the Hindu Dogras. To Lockhart's way of thinking, the beauty of the scheme was that by doing away with the Dogras the main source of friction in the area would have been removed; all his predecessors in Dardistan would have agreed. However they would surely have had reservations about his corollary; that Dard treaties and Dard troops were infinitely more trustworthy. The cornerstones of Lockhart's scheme were his new alliance with Chitral and his conviction that the Dards, helped by British officers and arms, could defend their own passes.

The other bit of news that awaited him in Gilgit would eventually result in a second and rather different conclusion being drawn about how best to defend the Hindu Kush. A lone *farangi*, it was said, had arrived in Shignan on the upper Oxus, having crossed the Pamirs. 'An Englishman from Yarkand', apparently, 'a middle-sized man, clean-shaven, with his following and baggage all on ponies'. Who is he, asked Lockhart in a letter to Durand? And what is he doing here? The description gave nothing away except that the stranger must be a trifle eccentric; baring one's chin to the razor in the below-freezing temperatures of the Pamirs could better be described as masochistic. No British traveller had been that way since Gordon and Biddulph in 1874. And since Lockhart himself was toying with the idea of heading for the Pamirs as soon as conditions permitted, he was sorely troubled by the identity of this unfortunate interloper.

His mind was hardly put at rest when the answer finally came. It took the form of a letter not from India but from Zebak in

Badakshan; and on the face of it was a matter-of-fact request for news and medicine. But to men who had just spent six hard months establishing for themselves a reputation as travellers and explorers the signature at the end was the ultimate put-down; they must have felt like venturesome seagulls sighting their first albatross. It was signed, in an infuriatingly neat hand, 'Ney Elias'.

9. Too Old and Too Broken

The dedicated scientific explorer is a notoriously difficult beast to interpret; but surely none was ever more dedicated or more baffling than Elias. The problem is not a lack of evidence, as with Biddulph, nor of credibility, as with Leitner. Neither is Elias merely unexciting like Lockhart. Quite the contrary. In his lifetime he was both legend and enigma. To all who followed him into the heart of Asia his very name was an inspiration. Yet few knew his precise itineraries, fewer had actually seen him and scarcely any, had they done so, would have recognised him. Younghusband was an exception. He found himself sitting next to the slight and self-effacing hero on a train to Simla in 1889; he also had access to the secret itineraries. Not a man to diminish the pioneering content of his own work, he would later concede, in a remote corner of the Pamirs, that 'Mr. Ney Elias has travelled in this, as he has in almost every other, part of Asia'. In fact Younghusband did as much as anyone for the Elias myth; who, his wide public would wonder, was this elusive figure with the peculiar name to whom even the great Younghusband was anxious to bend a knee? And why, if he was such a giant among explorers, was he a plain 'Mr.' with neither rank nor honours? Nowadays the legend is badly in need of rehabilitation, but the enigma is as puzzling as ever. In an exhaustive and faithful study his recent biographer finds him still mysterious, still riddled with contradictions.

Wintering in Gilgit in 1886 Lockhart simply wanted to know what this celebrity was up to, trespassing on his sector of the frontier. In no mood to make allowances, he interpreted the short note from Zebak as a personal challenge; it was just what one might expect from another intensely ambitious explorer. One of the perks of travel was that of impressing lesser mortals by date-lining one's letters from the back of beyond; and the business of emerging, unannounced and ever so casually, from the unknown was a cherished vanity. Younghusband would be as bad as Leitner at bursting in, travel stained, weather scarred and all but forgotten, on unsuspecting dinner parties. Stanley erupting from the Dark Continent, Burke crawling in from the Outback or Philby looming out of the Empty Quarter, this was the stuff of travel, moments to be carefully managed by the explorer and long treasured by his fans.

But Elias, announcing himself from the wrong side of the Roof of the World? One can't be sure. It could have been the grand gesture; he certainly had plenty to crow about. While Lockhart and his battalion had been slogging laboriously from Srinagar to Kafiristan and back to Gilgit, a distance of about seven hundred miles, Elias with just four servants had whizzed right round him like an orbiting comet. Starting almost simultaneously, but from Simla, he had covered more like two thousand miles and had crossed in the process five of the world's grandest mountain systems (the Pir Panjal, Great Himalaya, Karakorams, Kun Lun and Pamirs). He had also found time to clarify that vexed question of the source of the Oxus, he had come up with some new and constructive observations on checking the Russian advance to the Hindu Kush, and he was now evidently blazing a trail round Badakshan. Lockhart, in spite of Woodthorpe's surveys and Barrow's political work, could scarcely compete; his mission had been eclipsed.

The whole thing was made much worse from Lockhart's point of view by the fact that no-one had ever bothered to tell him that Elias was in the field. It was one thing to be shown up as an amateur, quite another as a fool; to have had to wait for the 'clean-shaven Englishman' to reveal his identity had added insult to injury. For once he reacted with energy. No civilian explorer, albeit one working as a government agent, could be allowed to run rings round a highly organised military mission. His instructions had made no mention of the Pamirs or the Afghan provinces and, as for that idea of reaching Kafiristan from the Afghan side, it had been little more than a pipe-dream; the Afghans were not even supposed to know of his dealings with the Kafirs let alone provide him with access to them. But now, under the impetus of Elias' letter, the dream became a pressing resolve. With or without official sanction, Lockhart determined to force a path through Hunza, muscle in on Elias' achievements on the Pamirs and continue through Badakshan into the Kafir country. Showing all the do or die competitiveness of the last phase of the Gilgit Game he was out to get his own back.

But was this being fair to Elias? If Lockhart had been less preoccupied with the reputation of his own mission he would surely have conceded that Elias was not a man for gestures of one-upmanship. The letter could simply have been written to warn him of the other's whereabouts and thus forestall any conflict of operations. Elias shows none of the dismissive conceit of the great explorer. 'That mute inglorious Milton', was how a contemporary described him; 'invincible modesty alone prevented his being known as one of the greatest English travellers'. His obituarists would all agree; he was morbidly sensitive about self-advertisement; none did so much and talked so little about it; and 'his true distinction was to die undistinguished'. Not, surely, the sort to cock a snook at anyone.

That Elias was one of the greatest of English travellers ought to be beyond question. In 1868 he had surveyed the mouth of the Yellow River in northern China. In 1872, making one of the most adventurous solo journeys of the century, he had crossed the Gobi desert, the Mongolian steppes and most of Asiatic Russia en route from Peking to Moscow. For this marathon he was awarded a gold medal by the R.G.S. in 1873; the other, that year, went to H. M. Stanley for his discovery of Dr. Livingstone. Early in 1875 he had taken part in a mission from Burma into western China. In 1876 he had been appointed as British Representative at Leh, the capital of Ladakh, and from there had made two journeys across the breadth of the Western Himalayas into Sinkiang. He still pined for a chance to explore Tibet proper, but he was already regarded as the greatest Asian traveller of his day. At forty-one years old he might reasonably have settled for the Pamirs as the crowning achievement of an outstanding active career.

However, besides the modest retiring nature, Elias had another much commented on trait; he was never satisfied. A degree of restlessness is essential to the make-up of any traveller; but this was something much more intriguing. His portrait gives a hint of the trouble. The fashionably lush moustache successfully hides the tell-tale line of the mouth; yet the eyes are arresting, a little too wide and intense, the eyebrows ever so slightly raised. A man of discernment, one feels, high-principled, aspiring. In fact he was all that and more; he was a perfectionist. His goals and his standards were ever the most ambitious conceivable. Yet, travel and government service being what they were, his achievements consistently fell short of them. A report from Elias on one of his journeys always begins with a catalogue of failures; even the great crossing of Asia is portrayed as a saga of frustrated plans and missed opportunities. Colleagues, when he has any, prove incompetent and irksome, his official instructions either incomplete or misdirected. And always there is some vital line of enquiry, some unmeasured peak, some unseen ruin or some untrodden path, that he has failed to pursue. A gratifying discovery is no consolation; it just serves to remind him of all the others he has missed. Perhaps it can be explained by the perfectionist's anxiety to anticipate every possible criticism. But the suggestion has been made that this determination to denigrate was the product of some far deeper psychological exigency bordering on masochism. One certainly wonders whether that famous modesty was not something far more complex. The man who acknowledges only his own standards can afford a certain detachment about his public image; but what others take for humility is really the outcome of an impossible vanity.

As a traveller he was the most professional and exacting imaginable. Observations for latitude and longitude, for altitude and temperature, distances and bearings were as essential to his progress as the availability of carriage and supplies. As a schoolboy, his diary had amounted to little more than a careful daily log of the weather and, now as then, his journals rigorously excluded all personal detail. In blizzard or sandstorm, on a mountain pass or in a Simla office his handwriting remained impossibly neat, his prose concise, his calculations meticulous. And always—proof surely of a relentless professionalism—written in indelible pencil on the flimsiest of paper. Other travellers might indulge in the odd luxury; Leitner found pocket space for his Bovril and Younghusband was wont to squeeze in a bottle of sherry; missions like Lockhart's boasted tinned foods from Fortnums and a veritable cellar of claret and madeira. Not so Elias. If there was room for a bottle of sherry he would have filled it with a spare sextant.

Not surprisingly he was also a loner. His passionate belief in small unencumbered expeditions looked sensible in the context of deserts and mountains where supplies were hard to come by; and in the Pamirs it would be dramatically vindicated. In fact Lockhart's extravaganza would be the only one of its kind to enter Dardistan; Younghusband would revert to the one-man show of earlier days. But in Elias' case the belief was also prompted by personal predilection. He found it extremely hard to work with others, a feeling that was no doubt reciprocated. Durand, the Foreign Secretary, later described him as 'a very difficult kind of creature'. Any companion would not only have to work to his impossible standards but also put up with a highly irritable temper and rough it to an extent that only Hayward would have appreciated.

How the unusual name of Ney came into his family is not known. As a boy it must have taken some living down, but if he had now come to terms with it and even perhaps relished its distinction, this was certainly not true of the Elias. His parents had actually given up the Jewish faith and young Ney was brought up a Christian. But they didn't change their name and nor did Ney. Instead he suffered agonies of embarrassment; to be dubbed 'the wandering Jew' would have filled him with horror. That a man with such a name and so acutely sensitive could have failed to come to terms with his ancestry is another of his baffling contradictions. Again it hints at some psychological chastisement, some need to punish his spirit in the same way that his travels punished his physique. Allied to the more predictable traits of the outsider, domineering mother and eccentric overseas education, it resulted in an inability to confide and a horror of sentiment. A classic introvert, he remained a bachelor, shunned society and knew neither friends nor loved ones.

For such a man travel in empty places had much to be said for it, and had he possessed the wealth and influence of contemporary aristocratic travellers he might, in time, have come to terms with his own personality. As it was, the Eliases were Bristol merchants; their second son started his travels with a posting to the Shanghai branch of the family firm. His expeditions to the mouth of the Yellow River, though of considerable scientific merit and conducted with true professionalism, were in the nature of holiday excursions. The marathon across Asia, made in his early thirties, was also on his own initiative and at his own expense. To the extent that he was at last recognised as one of the most scientific and determined explorers, the investment paid off; he attracted the patronage of Sir Henry Rawlinson. But it didn't ensure a succession of geographical assignments such as Elias had hoped for. Rawlinson, no doubt recalling the Hayward fiasco, played safe. He recommended him not to the R.G.S. but to the foreign department of the Government of India. If Elias wanted to go on travelling he was going to have to operate as an official government agent.

This he accepted. He never enjoyed political work and continued to regard it as less important than geographical and scientific discovery. Yet he proved one of the ablest and most dedicated of India's select band of trouble-shooting emissaries. His grasp of the political and strategic requirements of the country's defence was second to none and, perhaps a little surprising in a man so different from the rest, his views were fully in tune with those of MacGregor's 'forward' disciples. On the other hand, where he failed was in refusing to fall in with the prevailing esprit of the political service. Durand complained that he would not learn the work of the department and was thus a bad political officer. All the evidence suggests that he just failed to conform to the way in which the department operated. To a man like Elias the system of patronage and promotion that nurtured MacGregor, Lockhart and Durand himself must have been horrifying indeed. He would remain in government service for most of his career, always the most perceptive and dependable of agents, yet he still refused to identify with the service. He stood apart, aloof, his recommendations either ignored or appropriated by others, his reputation as much above censure as commendation, and his career uniquely static. When he later heard of Lockhart's scheme for the re-opening of the Gilgit Agency he ventured to Durand, 'Would I do for it or it for me?' No heavy lobbying, no long-winded report on the subject, no mustering of qualifications and years of service—just this quiet diffident little hint. Needless to say it cut no ice with the Foreign and Political Department.

A sad man, lonely and ultra-sensitive, disgruntled in his professional life and disturbed within himself, he was also, by 1885, a sick man. He probably never knew precisely what was wrong, but it can be taken that that request from Zebak for medicine was genuine enough. Dyspepsia and anaemia figured on the medical report which had invalided him home in the previous year. A liver condition had also been diagnosed and it was this, exacerbated by

dysentery—both the lightning bacillus and the nagging amoeba—
that was undermining his constitution. Throughout the Pamirs
expedition his health would continue to deteriorate. Worry no
doubt contributed to his physical decline but it was also intensified
by it. To a man such as Elias nothing can have been more upsetting
than the slow realisation that this was likely to be his last major
expedition.

When he had returned from sick leave in 1885 he had immediately
volunteered to return to Leh, 'if not a mountaineer a man for the
mountains' according to his biographer. Dufferin and Durand had,
however, a far more attractive proposition; and with Elias in
Simla and available at just the right moment, for once the most
qualified and able of the usual herd of applicants got the job. He
headed north across the mountains on May 29. He had been
offered the services of a doctor but, preferring as usual to be the
sole European, had opted for just a native medical assistant. A
touch of 'the gravel' in Kashmir and one of his 'attacks' in Ladakh
were ominous send-offs.

* * *

Not even a fire-eater like Charles MacGregor could complain that
Dufferin was not making the most of a Tory ministry at home. In
spite of the Panjdeh crisis the Afghan boundary commission, now
under Colonel Sir West Ridgeway with 35 British officers and over
1,300 native assistants, was still inching its way east towards the
middle Oxus. In Dardistan Lockhart and his men seemed to be
securing the country piecemeal and, though no-one would have
mentioned his name in the same breath, it was about now that the
government commissioned Dr. Leitner to compile his Hunza–
Nagar Handbook. That took care of half the crescent of buffer
lands between the Indian and Russian Empires; it left Sinkiang
and the Pamirs for Elias.

The Viceroy and his Foreign Secretary might have preferred
something a little more imposing than the solitary explorer and his
meagre following; but the uninhabited character of the Pamirs
and the sensitivity of the Chinese ruled it out. In fact, at the last
moment, Peking withheld the official accreditation for the mission.
Elias thus found himself in the extraordinary position of leader of

an official mission which, the moment it crossed into Chinese territory, was downgraded to the status of 'a party travelling for pleasure and instruction'. This was precisely the sort of mix-up that the perfectionist found intolerable. Of the four written objectives of the mission the first two, to do with improving political and trading relations with the Chinese authorities in Sinkiang, depended entirely on his being able to negotiate from a position of authority; nowhere did rank and face count for so much as in the Chinese empire. Moreover, even if the Chinese did show willing to treat, they could be expected to come under strong pressure from a fully accredited and immensely influential Russian consul already installed in Kashgar. He had just succeeded in running Andrew Dalgleish, the only British subject in Sinkiang, out of the country and was sure to try the same again with the newcomer.

Yet here was Elias, expected to take on the indifference of the Chinese and the hostility of the Russian consul with no more authority than that of a tourist. With justifiable indignation he pounced on the absurdity of the situation and, one feels, was almost gratified to find the Chinese not only unwilling to negotiate but refusing to admit that there was even common ground to discuss. Algernon Durand, the Foreign Secretary's younger brother and a man with a big part to play in what he christened the Gilgit Game, would later maintain that Elias was the 'only Englishman that the Chinese funked'; 'they sh-t when they think of him' was how one of his spies put it and there can be no doubt that in 1885 Elias pushed matters as hard as he knew how; the mission would entail enough reverses without his needing to invent any. Nevertheless, having started with a resounding failure, having vented his disgust at the way the mission had been despatched and having emphasised the utter hopelessness of his situation, Elias could turn to his other objectives with an altogether freer hand.

These were less specific and therefore more intriguing. He was to take up George Hayward's mantle and explore the Pamirs and Upper Oxus with particular reference to the territorial status of the region. He was also to monitor Russian movements in and around it. One thing his Chinese passport did specify was that he was to be allowed to leave Sinkiang by way of the Pamirs. The Afghans had been told to expect him from this direction and had agreed to assist him. He was further armed with a letter of introduction from the Aga Khan which was evidently Leitner's idea; the doctor had long ago noted that many of the peoples of Dardistan and the Upper Oxus were Ismaili Mohammedans; with their spiritual leader happily settled in Bombay it was only common sense to enlist his support. Elias found no fault with these arrangements and resumed his journey heading west from Sinkiang on September 30, the day Lockhart was negotiating his treaty with the Kafirs.

British geographers of the day laboured under a misapprehension about what they called 'The Pamir'. They imagined it was a steppe or plateau, elevated but not especially mountainous. It was rectangular in shape which was unusual for a mountain system, and it was boxed in on all but one side by true ranges with peaks up to 25,000 feet. They also knew that the Arabs had designated it 'the Roof of the World' and a roof, to an Arab, would have been something flat. Finally, according to every authority since Marco Polo, a Pamir was a strath of high-altitude grazing. Lord Curzon, later Viceroy of India, who made a determined effort to clear up the misapprehension, reckoned that there were in fact eight true Pamirs. He also emphasised that though they were wide, level and, in summer, well grassed, they were not plains nor even plateaux; they were valleys. Furthermore, although the most distinctive feature of the region, they were hardly typical. The Pamirs as a region was a mountain maze. In fact here was a true mountain system as formidable as any of its neighbours. Geologically speaking it was far older, which accounted for the filling up of some of the valleys and the rounding of the peaks. But geographically it was as much part of the West Himalayan mountain knot as the Hindu Kush or the Karakorams.

The Russians appreciated its character rather better than their British rivals. Indeed, by the time Elias set foot in the area, they had already explored it. Since 1870 botanists, surveyors and military spies had been pushing south from Khokand over the Alai and Trans Alai ranges or east from Bukhara through Karategin and Darwaz. In 1883 a party of Russian army mapmakers reached the northern slopes of the Hindu Kush and were all for crossing into Chitral and Kafiristan; it was rumours of this that had so alarmed Aman-ul-Mulk at the time of MacNair's visit. The same group had also carried their survey to points that the Survey of India had already plotted, thus rendering the Pamirs no longer a geographical void. The whole story, though a minor one compared to the penetration of the Western Himalayas to the south, would no doubt repay research. Here it is sufficient to note that in 1886 Elias was not embarking on *terra incognita*. The Russian authorities were altogether less secretive about the work of their explorers. The R.G.S., for instance, had a correspondent in Paris who kept them posted month by month on the movements of Russian travellers; reports presented to the St. Petersburg geographical society were quickly translated and printed in the Society's journal. Elias owed a great deal to his rivals and would derive much satisfaction from magisterial corrections or commendations of their work. But, if not a pioneer, he was the first to cross the area from east to west. He was also the first to put it into the context of the Western Himalayas and of India's defence.

The journey from Yangi-Hissar in Sinkiang to Zebak in Badakshan took just over two months. In that time Elias crossed or reconnoitred more than a dozen passes of over 13,000 feet and discovered a peak of over 24,000 which even the Russians appeared to have missed; he named it Mount Dufferin.* The valleys were indeed as bleak, empty and featureless as the high plains of Western Tibet, the passes never as difficult as those he had crossed in the Karakorams and Kun Lun. But still these were definitely not steppes. True to his ideal of the scientific explorer, he suppressed any mention of the difficulties of the journey. The intense cold and appalling wind of a Pamir winter have to be inferred from a chance remark about four consecutive nights of heavy snow, or the exquisite comfort of finding shelter behind a cliff face, or the joy of descending to an altitude where the temperature at midday was above freezing. (The contrasts between shade and sun were equally dramatic; the following year a traveller recorded simultaneous readings of 100° F in the sun and 35° of frost in the shade.) In the summer the thermometer could fall forty degrees in as many minutes, and during the course of a day might show a variation of

---

*The name did not stick; the peak is usually known as Mustagh Ata. A discussion of its nomenclature and of its confusion with the neighbouring mountain of Tagharma or Kungur can be found in Gerald Morgan's *Ney Elias*, London, 1971.

ninety degrees. In winter it was less volatile; if the mercury didn't freeze solid, it was distinctly sluggish. Elias says nothing about his own precautions, but on Lake Rangul he noted how the geese had to keep flying round all night to avoid being frozen in.

The only other wildlife on the Pamirs were the packs of wolves and the herds of Marco Polo sheep. These sheep, almost legendary beasts, stood five feet high and their curled horns, to judge by skeletons strewn about the slopes, grew up to six feet in length. Biddulph, who in 1874 had vowed to bag the first, never got within range of one. Elias was slightly luckier; he had one shot. But his aim, though good, was not quite good enough and the wounded beast made off. Pursuit was hopeless—another failure to add to the record. Whether his disappointment was on humane grounds or whether because of the loss to science is not clear; he was certainly no trophy hunter. Nor was he yet so gloomy as to read any personal significance into the incident. But could there be a better analogy of his own circumstances than this crippled specimen of an elusive and incongruous beast limping off into the mountains?

Actually, Elias had long been of the opinion that high altitudes were good for his condition; it was partly on health grounds that he had volunteered to return to Leh, 11,000 feet above sea level. Descending from the Karakorams and Kun Lun into Sinkiang his irritability had returned with a vengeance. But now, up in the Pamirs at an average of 12,000 feet, he regained peace of mind and body; total absorption in his work was the surest sign that Elias was in good heart. The strain, nevertheless, began to tell. Anyone who shaved every day in those sort of conditions must have had a truly spartan regimen. For hours he would stand braced against the icy blast while he took his readings; then sit up half the night to observe his position from the stars. And there could be no delay. Winter was about to close the high passes, rendering any movement between the various Pamirs impossible. If he was sustained by the altitude he was also fascinated by the emptiness, the wilderness; to the scientific explorer as much as to the tortured introvert it was an inspiration. Ahead, the low lying and populous regions of Badakshan and Kateghan presaged nothing if not the severest reaction.

Just as he was leaving the upper Oxus the first mail since Sinkiang caught up with him; it had taken two and a half months from Simla. Long-awaited instructions from Durand as to what he should do next were not included, but there must have been mention of Lockhart's winter quarters for immediately, on December 6, Elias penned his note to Gilgit. By the 26th, before the letter had even arrived, he was fretting about having had no reply.

He was also sinking fast. It shows clearly in his journal which suddenly becomes uncharacteristically personal; scientific enquiry gives way to morbid vitriol, the people are loathsome, the country depressing, the expedition a disaster. 'How sick and tired', he writes on entering Badakshan, 'one gets of everlasting hills, brown, rocky, barren and snow-topped, and of deep, narrow valleys.' It was no better when the hills gave way to the plains of Kateghan, 'a dreary, gloomy land and one that depresses the spirit more than any place I know of'. The native Uzbegs were 'like savage curs muzzled by their Afghan rulers . . . surly and sullen . . . . an ill-favoured, coarse, Chinese race with bad features and bad characteristics stamped upon their faces'. Here it was wet as well as cold. 'Civilised domestic animals would not be able to live in this climate unless better cared for than an Uzbeg.'

Far from blazing a trail, as Lockhart imagined, he was limping along on his last legs. At Taliq'an on January 8 he felt 'very unwell' and had to rest up. 'It has been the most dreary and uninteresting journey I have ever made.' He wrote to Ridgeway of the Boundary Commission asking for a doctor to be sent to his aid. He was still waiting for Lockhart's reply, and the next letter from India, only twenty-nine days out from Sinkiang, again failed to include Durand's promised instructions. In his reply he asked for the doctor who had been offered when the mission first set off. Ridgeway had now told him that he could not detach his own doctor and that if Elias wanted treatment he had better come and get it. That meant crossing the breadth of northern Afghanistan. It also meant the indignity of throwing himself on Ridgeway's mercy and, worse still, it was likely to jeopardise the continued existence of his mission. Elias knew nothing of Lockhart's plan to take him in the rear, but he did know that Ridgeway was anxious to lead all or part of his Commission to the upper Oxus. Needless to say, he strongly advised against it. With no further instructions from Durand, it looked suspiciously as if there were some scheme afoot to put his own party at Ridgeway's disposal. His best chance of continuing on his own therefore lay in remaining in the field and as far from the big battalions as possible. Always assuming, of course, that his health bore up.

Sadly it didn't. On January 28, after a brief recovery he was again struck down. 'The cutting wind or some other cause has made me unwell again.' The weather had indeed deteriorated. It was as bad as anything he had experienced on the Pamirs. Finally, on January 31, the day his letter actually reached Lockhart, enfeebled and desperate, he threw in the sponge. Whatever the price to his dignity as an explorer, to his independent survival as a political mission and to his ebbing state of health, he must cross Afghanistan and seek out the Boundary Commission.

Illness will not allow me to go any further without medical aid. I must try and reach there [the Commission was near Maimana] or not at all. This is a sad end to all my labours and upsets all my plans for the future. The expedition has been a bad business from the beginning . . . and no doubt I was too old and too broken ever to have undertaken it . . . To have broken down after all and to have to leave the work unfinished and plans upset is a bad business.

His mind was rambling, and when he finally succumbed to a stretcher he felt it was 'the beginning of the end'. Four weeks later, in late February, his sorry little party fell in with a survey group from the Commission.

One can scarcely expect Elias to have relished being back among his own—mortified would have been nearer the mark—but one good thing about contact with Ridgeway, and at last news from Lockhart, was that he could afford to take a less gloomy view of his own achievements. In terms of the ground covered he had, of course, outmarched and outsurveyed everyone. The first Englishman to cross the Pamirs, he was also the first actually to visit the Afghan dependencies of Shignan and Roshan about which there had been so much political heartache, and he was the first to inspect, in Roshan, the vital confluence of the two principal upper Oxus tributaries. Geographically, this last was the most significant achievement; for after careful measurement of the flow of the two rivers and after exhaustive enquiries, he felt confident in reversing the 1874 verdict of Gordon and Biddulph. There was precious little in it but in terms of annual volume of water the Panja, and not the Bartang-Murghab-Aksu made the greater contribution and was therefore the true Oxus. Up to a point, and quite fortuitously, Sir Henry Rawlinson had been proved right after all. Although there still remained the vexed question of which of the Panja's feeders was the principal one, Elias had at last disposed of the thorniest problem.

On the political front his main contribution arose from an unexpected discovery concerning the territorial status of the Pamirs. There was no new Russian advance to report and, according to an informant in Sinkiang, the Russians were more exercised about his movements than he about theirs. If this were true they must have wondered over Elias spending as much time quizzing the Kirghiz nomads as he did assessing the military capabilities of the passes. But unlike Biddulph or Lockhart, Elias was a civilian. He was less concerned about how the Russians might overrun the Pamirs, more concerned about whether they had any right to.

In the squabble for this inhospitable core of the continent, the Great Game is revealed in its most fatuous aspect. If the Pamirs had to be parcelled out, surely the only logical way to do it was along the parallels of latitude. For here, excluding more favoured districts along the encircling arms of the upper Oxus, was the proverbial howling wilderness, a mountain tundra fashioned and governed by the cruellest wind outside the polar circles. Its dominant race consisted of wolves; in vast packs they tore across the frozen wastes snapping at the heels of some prodigious ram. Man scarcely counted. In 40,000 square miles there was one indecipherable inscription, a couple of derelict mausolea and a few makeshift sheep-pens. If a Kirghiz family elected to see out the winter with their yaks in the mountains they still lived in tents—scarcely a settled population. The history of the region was just as sparse, amounting to some Chinese legends about dragon infested lakes, a dubious account of the flight and pursuit of some luckless rebels and two pages of wide-eyed wonderment in Marco Polo. Nothing here to assist the diligent Elias trying to establish a traditional carve-up. Nor was the geography any more helpful. The headwaters of the Oxus tributaries trickled from icy tarns or gushed from cavernous glaciers to wander in easily forded rills that in winter disappeared beneath a foot or two of ice. Their very direction of flow was sometimes hard to ascertain. As Rawlinson now admitted, they were not much good as frontiers. But then neither were the mountains. Ill-defined ranges with comparatively gentle passes they posed no barrier to the indiscriminate grazing of the Kirghiz herds and marked no major watersheds. In desperation Elias at one point toyed with the idea of a 'bazaar-shed', a line based on the shopping habits of the nomads, as the only logical solution.

Dr. Leitner, as usual, had a better one. 'Left as a huge happy hunting ground for sportsmen, or as pasturage for nomads from whatever quarter, the Pamirs form the most perfect neutral zone imaginable.' The problem of their status, 'created by the conjectural treaties of diplomatists and the ambition of military emissaries' would attain the heights of absurdity if territorial claims were to be based on the wandering propensities of nomads; 'neutralisation' was the ideal solution. Unwisely he prefaced his comments with a reference to the neglected wisdom of all his earlier prognostications and duly committed this one to oblivion; 'whoever does not belong to the regular military or civil service has no right to know or to suggest'.

In fairness, it was also too late for such a Utopian solution. The Indian government had sponsored the Afghan claim to Shignan, Roshan and Wakhan and now accepted that these states extended across Rawlinson's Oxus frontier and onto the Pamirs. In fact Elias' investigations were regarded as a necessary preliminary to the Boundary Commission continuing its demarcation of the Afghan frontier as far east as it could be made to run. It was in this connection that he had made his most important discovery. The Afghan frontier, he reported, could be continued right across the Pamirs till it touched territory claimed by the Chinese on the north-east bank of the Murghab-Aksu tributary. This would create a belt of neutral buffer territory right across the region and thus effectively screen the whole of the Hindu Kush and Dardistan from direct contact with Russia.

Elias' authority for this highly satisfactory discovery was the word of the nomadic Kirghiz. Although few and far between in the heart of the Pamirs, their black domed *yurts* were comparatively plentiful around Rangkul and the Murghab. The gnarled little men Elias found 'vain and fickle like all nomadic races'; they tended to offer allegiance to whichever power was likely to trouble them least. But even around Lake Karakul, which his map designated as Russian territory, they welcomed Afghan suzerainty. This was in marked contrast to the settled populations of Shignan and Wakhan who heartily detested the Amir and his deputies. No doubt the Kirghiz too might change their minds when they had a better idea of Afghan dominion; but in Elias' view this should not discourage the government from urging the Amir to establish garrisoned outposts right across the region.

One can imagine how the Russians felt about this. In 1873 they had agreed to an Afghan frontier that stopped at what Rawlinson had designated as the Oxus. Subsequently the Indian government had discovered that the states awarded to Afghanistan on the basis of this agreement stretched at least thirty miles across the river; they had asked the Russians for a new definition taking this into account. Now Elias, finding Kirghiz nomads on the other side of the Pamirs who professed some shadowy allegiance to Shignan—and hence to Badakshan and thus to Kabul—urged that this elastic Afghan arm be extended a further hundred miles to the east. At this rate St. Petersburg might reasonably have looked to the day when a British agent, making confidential enquiries in the Kun Lun, would make out a good case to wrench an Afghan finger to the threshold of Tibet. It might all be done in the spirit of defence but to an outsider it looked scarcely less acquisitive than Russian claims to the whole of the Pamirs; deriving from traditional Kirghiz links with Khokand, they too were 'based on the wandering propensities of nomads'.

The significance of Elias' new discovery was, as usual, not immediately appreciated. In 1886 Durand was increasingly preoccupied with an Amir who had suddenly become hostile to the whole concept of frontier demarcation. It was only after Elias had retired from the field that his discovery was suddenly pounced on and elevated to a cardinal feature of British policy towards the Pamirs. The Wakhan corridor, though narrower than he would have liked, exists to this day and is Elias' peculiar legacy.

In the spring of 1886 there was also the possibility that all his recommendations would at any moment be superseded. His mission was, after all, a reconnaissance; a more detailed and thorough appraisal was expected from the Boundary Commission. With Ridgeway about to move in on the whole upper Oxus region, with Lockhart about to extend his operations to Wakhan and with Elias himself anxious to get back to the Pamirs, it seemed sense to wait on events. If all went to plan the Pamirs would be overrun with surveyors, a satisfactory boundary would emerge, the Marco Polo sheep would be decimated, and the whole country be reduced to a weighty gazetteer and a large scale map.

Oddly none of this came to pass. Throughout 1886 not a single British boot left its mark on the virgin Pamir snows. What amounted to the best ever chance of gaining the topographical knowledge vital to a settlement of the Pamir question was passed up. Afghan hostility was partly to blame and so too was the disinterest and bungling of the Foreign Department. But what finally put paid to this golden opportunity was the intense personal rivalry of the three principals, Lockhart, Ridgeway and Elias.

*   *   *

Surprisingly it was Colonel Lockhart and his companions who alone in 1886 broke new ground. Emerging from winter quarters in Gilgit on April 16 they made straight for Hunza. 'It is doubtful whether I am not guilty of disobedience,' wrote Lockhart in his diary. A frantic exchange of letters between Gilgit, Simla and Kabul had still not elicited permission for the party to enter Afghan territory; in fact Durand had just ordered him not to start until the position had been clarified. Lockhart wouldn't wait. Every day the Hunza river was rising with newly melted snow; if he delayed he would miss the opportunity of by-passing the worst of the parapets by taking to the river bed.

As it was, the road proved 'the worst in our experience this trip'. But, after an exact repeat of Biddulph's difficulties over eliciting hostages from Ghazan Khan, he successfully negotiated the gorge and, dodging past the avalanches thundering down the flanks of Rakaposhi, reached the Mir's eyrie. En route he received news that his plans had finally been accepted by the Amir and sanctioned by Durand. The gods were on his side and Lockhart beamed on Hunza with a warm and wondrous eye.

Only one slight doubt ruffled his calm self-confidence. Durand had taken the opportunity to request that he make supply arrangements for the Boundary Commission's movement through Wakhan or Chitral. A more acute mind than Lockhart's might have already guessed that the new itinerary had only been approved because it might serve the interests of the more important Commission. Always more sensitive in matters of seniority, he did however realise that he, like Elias, was in danger of being placed under Ridgeway's orders. His protest to Durand produced an assurance that no such move was intended but that Ridgeway's work took precedence and he must co-operate. Then, and throughout the next two months, Lockhart's reaction was to keep the Commission at arm's length. He could cope with Elias, but not with the favoured Ridgeway. Every request from the latter regarding supplies or routes was met with dire warnings about the difficulties and shortages likely to be experienced if the Commission came anywhere near Dardistan or the upper Oxus. He might also have mentioned that such supplies and goodwill as did exist would be more than exhausted by the passage of his own party.

Encamped amidst the apricot blossom on the ledge of Hunza, the mission continued with a virtual re-run of Biddulph's trials of ten years before. Ghazan Khan, 'sixty, fat, blackish, ugly but with rather a merry eye' welcomed them effusively. Well he might; four British hostages afforded even better prospects of realising his long-cherished dream for the restitution of Chalt and Chaprot. These two strategic forts in the Hunza gorge were still held jointly by the Dogras and by the Mir of Nagar, his deadly rival. Lockhart, learning nothing from his predecessor's experience, had walked into precisely the same trap.

'A hitch', he called it when first wind of Chalt and Chaprot being the price of the mission's further progress reached him. Next day he was calling it 'a facer', and the day after he was in despair; it was 'the collapse of all our fine plans'. He could do one of three things: retreat, fight or capitulate. The first would involve an unacceptable loss of prestige, not to mention the personal ignominy. The second, though he reckoned that they could give a good account of themselves, was appallingly risky and might involve the government in a rescue operation beside which the one that had recently failed to save Gordon in Khartoum would look like child's play. That left capitulation. 'Give me Chaprot and my people shall carry you through the Killik snows [the Killik was the pass he intended to follow from Hunza to the Pamirs] as if you were women', declared the Mir. With the merry eye there went a colourful turn of phrase. He proceeded to emphasise the strategic importance of the forts; they were 'as dear to him as the strings which secured his wives' pyjamas'. Sadly, though, the forts were not Lockhart's to give. They belonged to Nagar and the garrison arrangement with the Dogras was considered vital to Gilgit's security.

In the end two things happened. First Ghazan Khan modified his demands. According to later information gleaned by Elias, he had recently strengthened his ties with the Chinese in Sinkiang to the extent that Hunza was now regarded as 'an outlying district of the Chinese empire'. On hearing of Lockhart's proposed visit, the Mir's new suzerains had despatched an officer with two cannon to help him keep the British out. It was the news that the guns had just been abandoned in the snows of the Hindu Kush that now dramatically weakened the Mir's bargaining position.

The other development was that Lockhart had second thoughts about capitulation. He slept on the problem, then sat for a long time gazing forlornly across the Hunza valley. On all sides the avalanches boomed like distant artillery; the vista was one 'which cannot, I think, be beaten in the whole world'. But, far from subscribing to the usual reaction of an overwhelming sense of insignificance, Lockhart emerged from his reverie more determined than ever that, regardless of consequences, the mission must succeed. He couldn't transfer the two forts, neither could he bid the Dogras relinquish them; but he might just risk an official wigging to the extent of dispossessing the chief of Nagar. This temporarily satisfied the chastened Mir and was most acceptable to the Dogras who would undertake the expulsion. He also committed the British government to the extent of seeing that Nagar received some financial compensation.

It was not a good idea to give in to a man like Ghazan Khan, nor was this a nice way to treat Nagar, the most loyal of all the Dard states. In fact for a British officer who prided himself on his sense of justice, it was downright shameless. But Lockhart looked on the bright side. No force was to be used against the Nagaris and

Durand was to understand that the forts would still be held by Kashmir. 'I don't think I have sinned . . . I don't think I could do anything else than what I am doing.' Face had been saved and, 'in spite of many predictions to the contrary', a British mission was about to traverse the whole of Hunza. 'No one will ever want to come up this way again,' he wrote, the inference being that it scarcely mattered if he had trodden on a few toes. From someone who two months before had been recommending the virtual subjugation of Hunza and Nagar as part of his scheme for the new Gilgit Agency, it was an odd remark. Predictably, from now on, Nagar would resist as staunchly as Hunza any overtures from Gilgit. The next party to enter the country would have to fight every inch of the way.

Lockhart pushed on to further tribulations. Whatever else one can say about the man he was certainly resilient; he was on new ground now and nothing was going to stop him. Not even the Killik pass which proved a nightmare. Two porters died from exposure, nearly all the party suffered from snow blindness, frostbite or both, and Lockhart's pony had to be abandoned in a snow drift. When they struggled into the first outpost in Wakhan they had been without food for two days. They congratulated themselves not, as they might, on being the first Europeans ever to cross the watershed of the high Hindu Kush, but on their luckiest of escapes. Had the pass been tackled a day earlier or a day later, they would have perished in one of the heavy snowfalls. Had they taken a day longer, they would have starved.

As the mission settled down to a cauldron of boiled mutton provided by their new Afghan hosts, Lockhart was again convinced that their troubles were at an end. Woodthorpe's men had continued their survey right across the watershed and would soon be swarming along the sides of the Wakhan valley. Besides satisfactorily puncturing Elias' monopoly of the upper Oxus they would also be forestalling the Boundary Commission. No need now for you to visit Wakhan, Lockhart wrote to Ridgeway; the surveying would be done by Woodthorpe and he couldn't recommend the place for 'sight-seeing or pleasure-making'.

Nor, much longer, for hospitality. The Afghan reception proved cordial indeed compared with Hunza's; but it was short-lived. For one thing it transpired that the mission was expected to pay cash, on the nail, for all supplies. Ever since losing the treasure chest nearly a year before, Lockhart had been short of funds. He had managed to borrow from the Kashmir governor in Gilgit but this money was now exhausted and the next cache was not till Badakshan. Thither it was his intention to proceed as rapidly as possible but it also now transpired that the Afghans had no intention of allowing him to do so. The Amir had in fact withdrawn the permission to enter his territory within days of granting it. Lockhart was therefore trespassing. He should retrace his steps and, if he couldn't afford to pay for his supplies, he would do well to move off immediately or again suffer the pangs of hunger.

For two weeks he stalled. Fuming over this 'most monstrous piece of impertinence', he waved the telegram from Durand that had given him the all-clear. He accused his immediate adversary, the governor of Badakshan, of disobeying the Amir's instructions, and he finally sent him a copy of a fabricated letter that logged all the governor's misdeeds and advocated his removal. He also complained that his mail was being withheld and his funds sequestered —Elias had written that there were indeed 14,000 rupees awaiting him in Badakshan. It cut no ice with the governor. 'I cannot allow you to either advance or remain on the border without His Highness' permission'. What made it still worse was that the wretched governor kept quoting Elias at him. Elias had come with the requisite permission and Elias had been treated with due honour. 'Had you been similarly authorised, I should have treated you with the same distinction.' Lockhart had been told by Durand how well the great explorer had hit it off with the governor. He also knew that Elias was then in Badakshan. Why wasn't he doing something?

On June 4, after a third ultimatum, Lockhart formed up the mission and set off—forward. With his Sikh escort primed for action he expected trouble at every bend of the road. So did the Dards just across the watershed. According to news received by Leitner, Nizam-ul-Mulk, the gay young chief of Yasin had a force waiting on the Baroghil to whisk Lockhart back to safety. Whether the Afghans even knew of this is doubtful, but the people of Wakhan itself were sufficiently disenchanted with Afghan rule to see that Lockhart was not starved or waylaid in their valley.

By the time he reached Badakshan, where he was potentially

more vulnerable, the dust seemed to be settling. Elias, only a day's
journey away, excused his inability to help by explaining that no-
one in the country would admit to knowing the mission's whereabouts or intentions. From this it appeared that Lockhart was to
be allowed to slip quietly through. There came also a note in cipher
from Durand which confirmed that Anglo-Afghan relations were
under strain and advised Lockhart to repay Afghan restraint by
slipping quickly away. Above all he must abide by their demand
that he refrain from revisiting Kafiristan. It was now clear that
the Amir's suspicions centred on his dealings with the Kafirs. If
not exactly Afghan subjects, they were traditional Afghan prey
and the Amir was highly resentful of direct British dealings with
them.

Thus Lockhart now had every reason to retire with good grace.
To the chorus of those demanding such a move were added the
voices of Ridgeway and Aman-ul-Mulk of Chitral. The former
claimed that the advance of the mission had forfeited the goodwill
of his hosts and brought the whole Commission to a standstill;
the latter begged him to retire simply for his own safety. Lockhart,
congratulating himself on being able to take a hint and glowing
with a sense of having done the magnanimous thing by Ridgeway,
withdrew.

Before he did so, on June 11 at 12.00 noon, and at, of all places,
Zebak, 'Mr Ney Elias appeared'. That's all Lockhart records of the
meeting and, indeed, it is his last mention of the explorer. Elias for
his part is equally reticent; when it was decided that he should
travel back to Chitral with Lockhart he significantly opted to follow
in his wake rather than march at his side. Two more dissimilar
characters it would be hard to imagine; the one a transparent
careerist, hearty, well-met, insensitive and unstoppable, an extravagant traveller, a gullible political agent and an overbearing
soldier; the other a slight, tight, prickly introvert, racked with self-
doubt, obsessive and impossible; yet a shrewd and unshakeable
negotiator, a scrupulous explorer and a man to whom travel was life.
Only in their work might they have found common ground but
of that the one was too jealous, the other too embittered, to speak.

Lockhart plodded over the Dora pass dutifully averting his
gaze as he skirted the inviting passes into Kafiristan; even to the
entreaties of Gumara—his adopted son, who had reappeared—he

turned a deaf ear. Mild disappointment, but no more, was his only reaction to being denied what was supposedly the goal of the whole contentious journey. In the last six months he had stirred up more trouble than any previous visitor to the region—and that was saying something. Nagar was alienated, Hunza encouraged, the Afghans antagonised and the Kafirs disappointed. To this tale of woe Aman-ul-Mulk added a postscript by irritably hustling the mission from the one state in which they felt they had really gained ground. Lockhart found the Mehtar much aged and wondered how long this pillar of his whole defensive scheme for Dardistan could survive. Yet failure he would never concede, remorse he wouldn't have recognised. He had confounded the sceptics by entering Kafiristan and by passing through Hunza; he had thus completed the exploration of Dardistan. He had also inspected both sides of all the main Hindu Kush passes and had arrived at the reassuring conclusion that, with the exception of the Dora, none would admit anything more formidable than a small exploratory party.

Simla evidently concurred with this highly favourable summary of his work; before the mission left Chitral on the road back to Kashmir, Lockhart received an urgent summons to drop everything and hasten home to take over from MacGregor's successor as Quarter-Master-General. The mission had served its purpose; Lockhart's future looked rosy. Ten years later as General Sir William Lockhart he was appointed Commander-in-Chief in India.

'Too old and too broken', the tired melancholic explorer who followed him back to Simla went unnoticed. Six weeks' winter convalescence with the Boundary Commission had restored Elias' strength only temporarily. He was still a sick man and, if possible, an even more embittered one. Exhaustion and hypochondria had been all the Commission's medical officer had made of his condition; after such a diagnosis it was hardly surprising that the patient proved a difficult one. Equally predictable had been Ridgeway's reaction to his presence; he sought instructions that would place Elias under his command. Whether Durand agreed to this is not clear; Ridgeway thought he had, Elias that he hadn't. But in the end it made no difference. The official go-ahead for the Commission to continue its work into Badakshan and the upper Oxus region rendered Elias' role superfluous. He had intended to complete his work in Badakshan and then return to the Pamirs. If the only way he could do this was by accepting the invitation to join one of Ridgeway's survey parties he rightly preferred to decline. To a gold medallist of the R.G.S. and the greatest Asiatic explorer of his day such an offer was positively insulting.

In May he had headed slowly back across northern Afghanistan. Though surprised not to be overtaken by the advance party of the Commission, he was so confident that they were hard on his heels that he did not recommence his survey. In Badakshan, where the governor still treated him with kindness, he was bombarded with requests from Ridgeway, as well as from Lockhart, about supply arrangements and itineraries. The Commission's daily requirements included half a ton of fire wood, five hundredweight of flour, a ton of grain and two tons of hay. 'There will not be much of Badakshan left uneaten,' he complained and he emphasised the appalling strain of such a vast procurement and the near impossibility of getting the stuff carried up into the Pamirs. It was no wonder the Afghans were having second thoughts about the whole business of boundary demarcation.

It also looked as if Lockhart's battalion from the east and Ridgeway's from the west were set on a collision course. Neither man would back down and Elias, like a nettled policeman in the middle, desperately tried to fend them off. If Lockhart was really storming through Wakhan then Ridgeway had better forget Wakhan and the Baroghil and send his forces round via the Dora and Chitral. 'It will have a bad political effect on Chitral and Badakshan if the *Sahibs* are seen to be opposing each other. You could make much better *bandobast** that way and if you had to come face to face with Lockhart you would not be so much at his mercy as if you left him uncontrolled on your flank.'

Meanwhile his own remaining ambition was, as he put it to Durand, 'to try to elbow my way through the crowd of commissioners and surveyors and get back by Kabul or Chitral (or wherever famine has not set in) and hand myself over to you for disposal'. He had already approached Aman-ul-Mulk about passing through Chitral and, although Lockhart's decision to take the same route

Bandobast is a word with wide connotations; the nearest English equivalent is something like 'organisation' or 'arrangement'.

almost dissuaded him, he was still anxious to see the Dora and to form some idea of Dardistan. No doubt he was also anxious to be the first traveller to complete the circuit of the Western Himalayas by adding the Hindu Kush to his tally of ranges. He succeeded, but as he squelched to the top through the mud and snow churned up by Lockhart's men, triumph can seldom have tasted so bitter.

The pass itself he reckoned far too defensible to warrant Lockhart's alarm. Similarly his verdict on Aman-ul-Mulk was one in the eye for the colonel. 'No guarantee given by an irresponsible barbarian of this kind could ever be effective, and no semblance of a reasonable or continuous policy could ever be hoped for.' He approved wholeheartedly of Biddulph's appraisal of the Mehtar, 'avaricious, unscrupulous and deceitful to an uncommon degree'. adding only that he was now also senile and thus still more unpredictable; he was 'best left out of the account altogether'. As if bent on a thorough demolition of Lockhart's work he went on to recommend that the way to secure Chitral was not by subsidies and treaties but by intimidation. With remarkable foresight he suggested that Chitral would not be safe until it could be controlled not from Gilgit but by way of MacNair's route from the Punjab.

On this combative note the official report of his 1885–86 journey ends. It was not however the end of his disappointments; the last were in many ways the cruellest. In the first place, unbeknown to him until he reached Gilgit, Ridgeway had abandoned his attempt to survey the upper Oxus. In other words Elias could after all have completed his work there; indeed the Commission's withdrawal would have made his further work doubly valuable. It seems unlikely that the objections raised by the Amir to Ridgeway would have applied to Elias and, with the prospect of another sojourn in the wastes of the Pamirs, even his health might have improved.

But it wasn't to be; and the reason, quite simply, was that no-one had told him. Ridgeway's problems had begun in May but, for what one can only assume to have been reasons of personal jealousy, he failed to tell Elias. Likewise Durand; he capped his long history of neglecting Elias by failing to pass on the information. When word did reach him, he was halfway back to India and desperately longing for a rest. He naturally assumed that the failure in communications reflected the government's lack of interest in the matter; they had shown little appreciation of what he had done already, so it was no surprise that they should have no desire for him to continue.

Such pessimism seemed fully warranted when in October, after seventeen months and three thousand miles, he finally reached Simla. Ridgeway had got his knighthood while still in the field, Lockhart's came soon after his return, Elias' never came. Nor was there even the customary letter of thanks from the Viceroy. An invalid again, he sailed for England wanting only to forget the whole business. In this there should have been no problem. His report was so secret that only thirty copies were printed. He was forbidden to lecture or publish anything about the journey, and only the barest of itineraries ever became public knowledge. To those who knew anything about the region his feat seemed improbable; though it fuelled the Elias legend, it brought little acclaim.

And so it should have ended. But if Elias was obsessed by his failures it was partly because others would never allow him to forget them. A year later there came a devastating reminder; he was gazetted a Commander of the Indian Empire. Then, as now, there were honours and honours. A C.I.E. to one of the greatest English travellers for his last marathon was, as the papers put it, like 'throwing a bone at him'. Mischievously, or possibly mistakenly, Ridgeway had once given him the initials when they were communicating about the supply of a doctor. Making his feelings plain enough, Elias had then inveighed against the whole honours system and described the C.I.E. in particular as 'that damning mark of faint praise'. True to his principles he now took the unprecedented and highly controversial step of returning the medal. The newspapers drew in their breath and officialdom frowned in disapproval; Mr. Ney Elias could now be pretty certain of remaining a plain Mr. however long and distinguished his subsequent career.

In fact he had only ten relatively unremarkable years ahead. But the really interesting aspect of this *cause célèbre* is the light it throws on his personality. He was more than justified in returning the medal, but was this the action of an excessively modest and retiring nature? It won for him a notoriety that almost overshadowed his reputation as a traveller. Modesty would surely have dictated a more supine reaction. Again one suspects that he fought shy of recognition not from modesty but either because he scorned all opinion other than his own or because he knew too well how honours were customarily acquired; probably both.

10. The Exploring Spirit Was Upon Me

On one point Lockhart and Elias had been in rough agreement; MacGregor had got it wrong when he predicted that the Russians would send part of any invasion force across the Pamirs and over the Hindu Kush. The thing was impossible. Devoid of supplies, unbearably cold and mountainous throughout, the Pamirs could be crossed only by small reconnaissance parties operating between July and December. As for the Hindu Kush, just one route was still canvassed as suitable for troops, that via the Dora, and to reach this an invader would first have to wrest Badakshan from the Amir. The notion that the Gilgit Game had to do with holding the northern gates of India against invasion would be a long time dying; too many statesmen continued to ignore the geographical realities, too many soldiers could think only in the broadest strategic terms and too many political officers had a stake in seeing that the region retained its priority. But it is true to say that as a rationale for a British interest in Gilgit the defence of the passes would no longer do.

However, as the Russians had protested when justifying earlier advances, 'in the East it is impossible always to stop when one wishes'. Translated into a British context this might have read, 'it is impossible always to withdraw when one ought'. Leitner, not without justification, put it more crudely, 'the devil finds work for idle hands'. New 'forward' policies had a way of emerging before the old ones had been dismantled, and once a new threat had been identified, proof of its plausibility was soon to hand. Invasion could be discounted; but what about infiltration and subversion? Kipling certainly saw the Russian threat in these terms; in *Kim* pseudo-sportsmen from across the frontier slip through the Hindu Kush passes to woo 'the five kings' who are clearly the Dard chiefs. The reality in the 1880s differed only to the extent that the Dard chiefs appeared to need little wooing. A Russian reconnaissance party had, it was argued, only to cross the Hindu

Kush for the whole of Dardistan to explode like a keg of gun powder. Disaffection in Hunza and the near certainty of a disputed succession in Chitral, plus the traditional weakness of Kashmir's hold on Gilgit, amounted to an open invitation. In 1883 Russians had reached Wakhan; it was only a matter of time before some Tsarist agent with a pocket full of roubles and a caravan of breech-loaders would come glissading down the glaciers on the wrong side of the frontier.

Sure enough, in May 1888, less than two years after Elias, Lockhart and Ridgeway had fled the field, the first party arrived. Preceded by wild rumours of a whole Russian detachment, it materialised as three dazed and desperate intruders straggling down from the Baroghil pass. At Mastuj, Nizam-ul-Mulk was waiting for them. Displaying considerably more sense than Lockhart had ever credited him with, he promptly arrested them and wrote to Simla for instructions.

It was a false alarm. Nizam reported that his captives admitted to coming from Russia but he was surprised that they brought neither presents nor promises; indeed they appeared to be totally destitute. They also claimed to be not Russian but French. So they were. Telegrams in cipher from Simla to London elicited from the Russian ambassador that they were 'bona fide French geographers'. To Gabriel Bonvalot and his two companions thus falls the honour of first bridging the Pamirs gap between the British and Russian empires. Though an experienced traveller who had already traversed most of Central Asia, Bonvalot tackled the Pamirs on the spur of the moment. He was no Anglophile and found much to criticise in the excessive liberality of previous British visitors to the region. But he was also no Russian agent. The most in the way of political significance that could be extracted from his achievement was that the journey from Russian to British territory was tougher still than had been anticipated. Lord Dufferin, who got Nizam to send his prisoners on to Simla, listened with sympathy to their tale of suffering and deprivation; they had been benighted on the Alai, snowed in on the Pamirs and robbed in the Hindu Kush, they had lost the whole of their baggage train and were lucky to get away with their lives. But, to Dufferin's mind, this was 'excellent news'. It confirmed that for at least six months the frontier was firmly closed.

It was in the following year, 1889, that the real thing came; a Russian political officer with a Cossack escort entered Hunza. Dardistan did not exactly explode but the welcome accorded this Captain Grombtchevski was in marked contrast to the treatment meted out to Biddulph and Lockhart. Offers of money and arms appear to have been accepted. In return the new Mir of Hunza, Safdar Ali, son and murderer of Ghazan Khan, gave permission for a Russian post to be set up on his territory and agreed to seek Russian aid in repelling any further aggression from Gilgit. These arrangements for long remained a matter of speculation in Simla, but the mere fact of a Russian entering Hunza, when seen in the light of recent developments, had the most sinister implications.

For one thing it could hardly be a coincidence that in the same year Safdar Ali assumed the offensive. He recaptured Chaprot and Chalt, and Hunza forces got to within striking distance of Gilgit. Again the Kashmir troops proved incompetent and badly officered; defeat was staved off by suing for peace; it was an ignominious and all too familiar predicament. But what made it worse from a British point of view was an untimely reminder from the Chinese. As Elias had reported, they were taking an unusually lively interest in 'their outlying dependency' and, when Safdar Ali was pressured into surrendering his recent gains, they demanded an explanation from the British representative in Peking. Dufferin provided it. In categorically repudiating all Chinese claims on Hunza, he insisted that the place was a vital dependency of Kashmir. As he explained to the Secretary of State, whatever the legality of China's claim, it was totally inadmissible on the grounds that if, as still seemed likely, Russia should annex Sinkiang, then she would inherit the claim.

The whole question of the Hunza–China connection was also highlighted by Safdar Ali's other move. He reinitiated the traditional Hunza pastime of raiding caravans on the Ladakh–Sinkiang road. The 1888 attack took place between the Karakorams and Kun Lun on what was supposed to be Sinkiang territory. Amongst those who were captured and ransomed were some Kirghiz of the region. They appealed to the Chinese but, receiving neither redress nor sympathy, turned to the British agent in Ladakh. It could be argued that if the Chinese failed to restrain one lot of doubtful subjects and failed to protect another they could scarcely aspire to sovereignty over either. But more intriguing from a British point of view was how the Hunza highwaymen had managed to get undetected from one end of the Western Himalayas to the other. Lockhart had explored only the Killik pass out of Hunza; there were evidently others both to the north and the east, plus a corridor of unexplored territory that ran the length of the Karakorams. As so often, unexplored meant unappropriated. This corridor started from that part of the Pamirs which neither Chinese nor Afghans effectively controlled. If the Russians grabbed the one they would grab the other, and a wedge of Russian territory might suddenly be driven not just south to the Hindu Kush but east between Kashmir and Sinkiang.

Lord Dufferin's Viceroyalty terminated in December 1888. In the previous year Mortimer Durand had argued strongly for the reopening of the Gilgit Agency; he paid little attention to Lockhart's grandiose scheme for 'the acquisition of Gilgit' but he believed firmly that, with the western sector of Afghanistan's frontier now defined, Russian pressure would move east to the undefined Pamirs. Grombtchevski's appearance in Hunza convinced Dufferin that his foreign secretary was right. Accordingly Captain Algernon Durand, younger brother of 'Morty', was despatched to Gilgit to draw up recommendations for the reopening of the Agency. These were ready just before Dufferin left India, but the decision on whether to implement them was left to his successor, Lord Lansdowne. It was a mere formality. The new man, as nominee of Lord Salisbury and the Tories, was as much obsessed with the needs of imperial defence as his Tory predecessor, Lord Lytton; within two months of his arrival in India he was talking of 'the necessity of assimilating the frontier tribes', and within six months Algy Durand was on his way back to Gilgit as agent. His first job was to beard the lion in his den; he was to visit Hunza and get Safdar Ali to abandon his raids and forswear all dealing with Russia and China. As an incentive he was to offer a greatly increased subsidy.

So much for the diplomatic response. The other obvious need was for military intelligence. Someone must explore the country behind the Karakorams and around the perimeter of Hunza; and in the process he must stand by to counter any further Russian or Chinese overtures towards Hunza. This mission, even by the standards of the Gilgit Game, called for quite exceptional talents. Hayward, who back in 1868 had made a short foray west of the Karakoram pass, had reported on the appallingly difficult nature of the country. Rock-choked rivers swirling through beetling ravines formed the valley gutters between the Karakorams and Kun Lun. One either scrabbled and waded through their icy depths or climbed to the moraines and glaciers that spewed chaotically from the greatest cluster of peaks in the world. To negotiate such terrain called for the skills of a mountaineer. The desolation of the country and the duration of the enterprise demanded a traveller fitted by both temperament and experience to survive long spells of hardship and solitude. And the delicate political eventualities necessitated someone utterly dependable but more tactful and resourceful than many of his predecessors. The man chosen was barely twenty-six years old, a captain in the 1st King's Dragoon Guards, by name Francis Edward Younghusband.

For the next five critical years Algy Durand, the Gilgit Agent, and Frank Younghusband, the roving explorer, would epitomise the Gilgit Game. In character they were almost as wildly dissimilar as Lockhart and Elias. Yet they worked tolerably well together, kept their suspicions of one another out of official correspondence and, coincidentally, shared two points in common. In the first place both had ties with the same part of England, Northumberland. Durand had spent much of his childhood at the ancestral home of the Dukes of the county and Younghusband could trace his ancestry through eleven generations of Northumbrians. They regarded themselves not as British but as English and Durand, at least, rejoiced in traditions of repelling Scottish incursions; as Gilgit Agent he liked nothing better than to be described as the warden of India's northern marches. Younghusband, for his part, always pointedly excluded the Scots from his eulogies on English rule and civilisation. Each thus saw himself as continuing a family tradition in an imperial setting. It imparted a depth of dedication to their work which few of their contemporaries can have shared.

They were, on the other hand, nothing if not typical in both being intensely and unashamedly careerist. The carrot of a medal and the plum of promotion were sustenance to all, and it made little difference that Durand chose to disguise his ambition as a desire to live up to the expectations of his distinguished brother; or that Younghusband sublimated his pursuit of personal recognition in some wider civilising crusade. Yet the odd thing is that five years of distinguished service on the Gilgit frontier brought to neither the conventional success he sought. Younghusband unlike his father, two uncles and two brothers, never attained the rank of general; when he left Dardistan he determined to resign from active service altogether. Durand, unlike his father and two brothers, failed to get a knighthood and he, too, resigned from government service soon after leaving Gilgit. The explanation for this lack of recognition has nothing to do, as well it might, with some official sense of remorse for the politics pursued in Dardistan. Nor is it any reflection on the conduct of the two men; both, in fact, were popularly regarded as heroes. But what happened is that the experience changed them; in the mountains Durand discovered his limitations, Younghusband found a new vocation.

* * *

As he rode out of Leh for Hunza and the Karakorams in July 1889, Younghusband's reputation stood high but precarious. Recently elected the youngest Fellow of the R.G.S. he was better known than Elias. Yet his fame rested on just one great journey; addressing the R.G.S. he had been conscious of his lack of geographical training, and in government circles he was still handicapped by having had no political experience. The new mission struck him as a perfect chance to flesh out his reputation. It also accorded exactly with his personal inclinations; as he later put it, 'the exploring spirit was upon me'.

'I wonder', he had told his sister four years before, 'if I shall ever really settle down in any place for more than a few months at a time.' He had been reading through the papers of his uncle, Robert Shaw, the man who with Hayward had made the first successful journey to Sinkiang. He had also just had his first taste of the mountains, making a brief trek to Kulu and Lahul. Travel, and particularly mountain travel, had suddenly become his one passion in life. But with his enthusiasm so often doused by 'pig-headed red-tape men', he was seriously considering resigning his commission and travelling freelance.

It was Lockhart who changed this. He claims to have been the first to have spotted Younghusband's talents as a political officer; 'I picked him out in '85 as just the man required for the Intelligence Branch explorations.' He got him transferred to the Q.M.C's department, but then refused to take him on the mission to Dardistan. Instead it was MacGregor who gave him his first break. 'Damned rum name that,' MacGregor had commented on first being introduced to Younghusband and, though the new recruit had since learnt the whole of *The Defence of India* by heart, he still held the Q.M.G. in great awe. With trepidation, therefore, in 1886 he proposed that he should undertake a mission to the mountains of Manchuria. 'If the Indian Empire is to be saved,' he tried to convince MacGregor, 'I must at once be sent on duty to Manchuria.'

Manchuria lies between Mongolia and Korea. It was not self-evident even to MacGregor that India's security was endangered by any developments in that quarter. But he had to admire the boldness of Younghusband's thinking. The government could hardly be expected to pay for such a trip, nor could it possibly warrant eighteen months' absence from duty. Six months, though, he could arrange; Younghusband was launched.

The Manchurian journey afforded experience of travel in the remote parts of China; but as an expedition it paled into insignificance beside its sequel. For instead of returning to India by sea, Younghusband grasped the opportunity of an overland journey across the breadth of the Chinese empire and through the Western Himalayas. Elias, rather than Shaw, was his inspiration as for weeks on end he urged his camels across the Gobi and on to the oasis cities of Sinkiang. A lone European travelling by night through the star-filled immensity of the Central Asian deserts, he felt the stirrings of a spiritual curiosity that would transform his travels into a symbol of a more vital journey, that of inner exploration. It all began with little more than a naïve sense of wonder. He experienced a sense of deep humility in the awareness of a man's insignificance beside the silent immeasurable vastness of Nature (always with a capital N); at the same time, and seemingly in complete contradiction, he was filled with a fierce pride in the authority and stamina that enabled him, a stranger and a youth, to prevail over men of other races and over terrain as hostile as could be imagined.

What was the lesson of Nature's perfection and what the secret of human ascendancy?

The onward journey from Sinkiang to India provided a still sterner test and hinted at some of the answers. His commanding officer in the Intelligence Branch had suggested that the greatest value would accrue from his expedition if, instead of following the usual trade route from Sinkiang to Ladakh, he were to strike out for the central Karakorams and investigate a pass called the Mustagh; Colonel Henry Godwin-Austin had attempted it in 1861 and, though unsuccessful, had reported it as being in regular use.

Younghusband was compelled to differ. The challenge of the unknown route was irresistible but the pass proved a death-trap. The glacier ascent defeated his baggage ponies and the crest, at 19,000 feet, gave onto an almost sheer ice face; only a well equipped mountaineer could hope to get down it. Younghusband knew nothing of climbing; he couldn't even assess the degree of danger. But by now he was committed to the mountains. His initiation was over; it was time for the baptism of fear.

This quasi-religious language may sound fanciful, but that undoubtedly was how Younghusband saw the Himalayas. Not for him the *sangfroid* of Elias, the stern detachment of Biddulph or the genial exasperation of Lockhart. The Hindus regarded the mountains as the abode of the gods and no-one of average sensitivity could deny that this was an appropriate and inspiring notion; it was high time someone treated the world to a taste of their majesty and mystique. After all, the traveller for sport could have done better in Africa, an ethnologist like Leitner might have been happy in the Levant, and those like Elias for whom travel was some kind of personal exorcism might have satisfactorily wrestled with their problems in a desert. Only for the explorer who sought not man, not beast, but God, were the mountains unique; or, put another way, the traveller who would love the mountains and understand their allure must also be a seeker. Younghusband, earnest and impressionable and already dissatisfied with the narrow credo of an evangelical upbringing, responded to the Himalayas with a long sigh of recognition.

I lay down on the ground and gazed and gazed upon the scene, muttering to myself deep thankfulness that to me it had been [given] to see such glory. Here was no disappointment—no trace of disillusionment. What I had so ardently longed to see was now spread out before me. Where I had reached no white man had ever reached before. And there before me were peaks of 26,000 feet, and in one case 28,000 feet, in height, rising above a valley bottom only 12,000 feet above sea level. For mountain majesty and sheer sublimity that scene could hardly be excelled. And austere though it was it did not repel—it just enthralled me. This world was more wonderful by far than I had ever known before. And I seemed to grow greater myself from the mere fact of having seen it. Having once seen that, how could I ever be little again.

A wiry but slight five feet six, he was here inviting ridicule. But cynicism, whether directed at his competitive outlook, his intellectual naïvety or his biblical prose, was something to which he was all but impervious. In earlier days, happily and proudly, he had risen to the bait of every test of stamina his schoolfellows and regimental colleagues could devise. No man ever cared less about making a fool of himself; the important thing was to welcome each challenge, to forge ahead and to excel, regardless.

So it was with the Mustagh pass. The thing was impossible, therefore he would do it. Knotting turbans and reins for ropes, hacking steps in the ice with a pickaxe and trusting to a grip from frozen, bootless feet, he managed what the great Swedish explorer, Sven Hedin, would call 'the most difficult and dangerous achievement in these mountains so far'; it was hardly surprising that at the time he believed Providence guided his every step and was preserving him for some still greater feat.

Not only Providence but the eyes of the world seemed to be forever on Frank Younghusband. Embarking now on the new mission to Hunza he marvelled at the trust bestowed on him and was overwhelmed by the need to do well by his country. No pious claptrap this; Younghusband was too direct, too honest. He lived in the awareness that men hung on his every deed and that civilisation waited with bated breath for his revelations. The rapt attention of family, superiors and country made every trial a Herculean challenge and every achievement an occasion for profound analysis. Moreover, in the glare of the footlights, there was no place for self-doubt. His judgements must be unassailable, his courage inexhaustible. Supreme self-possession became the Younghusband hallmark. It might rile his colleagues and amuse his superiors, but to his juniors and more particularly, to his native followers, it amounted to charisma.

An instructive comparison might be made with Lawrence of Arabia; each in his day captured the popular imagination and was hedged about with romance, each was controversial and each mystical. Yet where Lawrence was cold, tortured, tragic, Younghusband was all warmth, simplicity and good cheer. The man from the deserts stood aloof and impossible; the man from the mountains was down to earth, almost endearing. In fact they were about as different as could be, and nowhere does this show better than in their charismatic appeal. Lawrence secured the loyalty of his Arabs by becoming one; Younghusband won the devotion of his guides and porters by doing exactly the opposite. He remained obtusely English. He baulked at native dress and could speak no Asian languages other than the obligatory Hindustani. Faced with someone who clearly understood not a word he was saying, he was most likely to repeat himself in English, slowly and ever so distinctly, rather than lend his tongue to some foreign inflection. Yet, through a barrage of interpreters, his self-assurance, his transparent honesty and his genuine solicitude for others somehow shone through. For all his Englishness and his sense of superiority, he was fascinated by the small hardy men of the mountains. He admired their courage, he valued their companionship and, to an extent that only the mountaineer can appreciate, he trusted them. The *sahib* of his day might have offered rupees to the man who could find a way down from Mustagh—or have berated the man who had led him to such an impasse. Younghusband had done neither; he had held his tongue and waited; with a sidelong glance at their imperturbable leader, the men had set about risking their lives for him. Whether Balti porters, Ladakhi guides, Gurkha soldiers or Yarkandi ponymen they became very much a part of the whole mountain experience that so thrilled and troubled him.

Even the Kirghiz, about whom he was even less complimentary than Elias, were roused from their spineless stupor by his confidence and determination. The first object of the 1889 mission was to rendezvous with the men who had fallen foul of the Hunza raiders. He was to reassure them about the government's efforts to protect them and thus secure their co-operation in exploring the route by which the raiders had come. After 185 miles travelled in six days including three passes of around 18,000 feet, Younghusband reached the Kirghiz camping grounds at Shahidulla. His offer of money to repair the abandoned fort there and of a small Kashmir garrison to hold it, together with his irresistible air of authority produced a dramatic effect. The cowed nomads forgot their fear of Hunza's retribution and agreed to betray the unknown route. In fact they were so taken with their obliging visitor that they were all for tendering allegiance to Kashmir and thus to British India.

What made Younghusband's performance particularly impressive was the awkward fact, which gradually dawned on him, that Shahidulla and its Kirghiz residents were none of India's or Kashmir's business. His uncle, Shaw, had been the first to make the point when he had observed that 'the Maharaja [of Kashmir] has no more right to Shahidulla than I do'. The frontier lay several marches south on the crest of the Karakorams. If the official justification for claiming Hunza was that it lay on the Indian side of the main watershed, then, by the same coin, Shahidulla, north of it, must be Chinese. Younghusband was poaching; yet awareness of his weak ground cramped his style not a bit.

For someone with such a deep respect for the local peoples, his insensitivity about the rights of other administrations is surprising. For most of the next two years he would be roving about beyond the British frontier; yet in marked contrast to Elias he never approached an understanding of the motives and fears of the two principal authorities, the Afghans and the Chinese. He saw things exclusively in terms of the great imperial struggle and is not without blame for the upheavals that occurred in his wake, most notably on the Pamirs. His temporary adoption of the Kirghiz of the Kun Lun had typically disastrous consequences. The Kashmir soldiers were in due course withdrawn; the Hunza raiders relieved the Kirghiz of the rupees before they could rebuild the fort; the Chinese demolished the rest of the old fort and built a new one much closer to the frontier; and three years later the Kirghiz leader, with whom Younghusband had hit it off so well, was still paying for his pro-British sympathies in a Chinese prison.

Younghusband, however, was content to have secured the immediate objective, the co-operation of the Kirghiz; 'the real excitement of the expedition was now to begin'. On September 3 accompanied by his escort of six Gurkhas, a Pathan surveyor—he was still weak in this department—two Ladakhis, two Baltis and five Kirghiz, he headed west for Hunza. The pass by which the Hunza raiders crossed the main range was reputedly called the Shimshal and lay on the eastern edge of Hunza territory. Between there and Shahidulla the nimble-footed Dards threaded trackless defiles and cluttered gorges for some two hundred miles. The Shaksgam and Raskam rivers that drained these gloomy gutters had to be forded five and ten times a day. From their waist-deep waters Younghusband's ponies now emerged festooned with icicles; the men clung to their tails to avoid being swept under by the current or knocked down by the icebergs that bobbed along in it.

It was hard, cold and unrewarding work. A spare figure at the best of times, Younghusband lost weight so dramatically that his signet ring slipped from an emaciated finger. A later traveller would be constrained to wonder whether 'such an inhuman mass of snow, lifeless mountain and ravine was not meant to be denied to mankind'; even the view was 'frustrated on all sides by stark black mountains imprisoning the stone-filled valleys'. Younghusband felt much the same; but after a hard day's march he would make a point of shinning three or four thousand feet up the nearest precipice just to glimpse the view. The sight of those peaks and glaciers refreshed his spirit. All that white untrodden snow and those curling swelling glaciers hypnotised him; they were a challenge and something more, a message perhaps, a mystery.

Twice he found a pretext for breaking the monotony of the grim battle in the gorges and again exploring the snows. The first was the rumour of another pass which, like the Mustagh, debouched into Baltistan; a traveller in the 1830s had called it the Saltoro and had made an unsuccessful attempt on it, the mapmakers later dutifully recorded it and Algy Durand, a few months before, had tried to get a look at it from the south. The second was purely wishful thinking on his own part; approaching Hunza and fearing that the Shimshal would prove a disappointment he chose to ignore his guide's advice and explore the conjectural position assigned to it on the map. On both attempts he forced a path up the glacial moraines, crossed onto the main glacier and made good progress over the ice till brought up short by impassable crevasses—'great staring rents in the ice fifty or sixty feet deep'. Though a mountaineer at heart and now with as much Himalayan experience as any contemporary climber, he still had neither the equipment nor the occasion for a serious mountaineering enterprise that might keep him amongst the snows for weeks rather than days.

If this was a disappointment the two excursions were not altogether fruitless. Officially he could justify them as affording conclusive proof that the central Karakorams were watertight; barring mountaineers, no expedition from the north could hope to reach India that way. 'The fact is that from the Karakoram pass to the real Shimshal there is an immense glacier region equalled in extent by no other glacier region in the world; the mountains are of most stupendous height and rugged in the extreme; and between the two passes mentioned above the range . . . for practical military purposes is impassable.'

But it was on a personal level that these new tussles with the mountains made their greatest mark. If the Mustagh pass in 1887 had been his baptism, the Karakorams in 1889 were his first communion. At last he could feel the mystery, he could read the message. The same factors as in 1887 worked to heighten his spiritual perception. On the Saltoro pass he again looked death in the face and came away unscathed. Dawn on September 16 had found his small party blundering through a heavy snowstorm just below what they took to be the pass. They seemed to be beyond the worst of the crevasses and were cutting their way up an ice slope before descending into the ravine that led to the pass.

. . . suddenly we heard a report like thunder, and then a rushing sound. We knew at once that it was an avalanche; it was coming from straight above us, and I felt in that moment greater fear than I have ever yet done, for we could see nothing, but only heard this tremendous rushing sound coming straight down upon us. One of the men called out to run, but we could not for we were on an ice slope, up which we were hewing our way with an axe. The sound came nearer and nearer and then came a cloud of snow-dust, and the avalanche rushed past us in the ravine by our side. Had it happened a quarter of an hour later, or had we started a quarter of an hour earlier, we should have been in the ravine and buried by the avalanche.

As if this were not enough, a second avalanche promptly thundered across the path they had just cut, obliterating all trace of it. 'We have to trust to something higher than man to lead us through everything safely,' he had written in his diary. Now he had the desired proof that Providence was still on his side.

On what he designated the Crevasse Glacier it was not the danger but the spectacle that impressed him.

When I can free my mind from the overpowering sense of grandeur which the mountains produce, and from the thoughts of the stern hard work we had to go through in those parts, I think of the beauty of that glacier scenery, the delicate transparency of the walls of ice, the exquisite tinting of the blues and greens upon it, the fairy caverns, the deep crevasses and the pinnacles of ice, as forming a spectacle unsurpassed in its purity of loveliness. Other scenes are beautiful and yet others are impressive by their grandeur. . . . But it is high up among the loftiest mountain summits, where all is shrouded in unsullied whiteness, where nothing polished dares pollute, that the very essence of sublimity must be sought for. It is there indeed that the grand and beautiful unite to form the sublime.

The searing whiteness of those snowy realms, the hard dazzling purity of ice, the unsullied unpolluted virginity of it all, these are what impressed him most and the same themes occur again and again in all his mountain descriptions. Not the savagery of wind or the brute force of avalanche or even the eerie silence which makes man feel an impostor. On the contrary, Younghusband felt at home; he was being vouchsafed a foretaste of heaven and a vision of how the world should be; he was being commissioned to go forth and make it so.

Each excursion was followed by a period of rest during which he retired to his tent for a couple of days to read. His library was small but amidst such awesome scenery and following such traumatic experiences, each word took on a heightened and personal meaning.

'As I read the thoughts of men on the deepest meanings of it all, I was unwontedly elated. I seemed to be on the brink of discovering a new religion. All the inessentials were fading away. And before me was appearing a religion so clear, so true, so convincing that when men saw it they would surely leap to seize it.' It was like K2 with the clouds suddenly being torn from its summit. A work on Buddhism caused him to reflect on his followers, not just on their performance but on their innermost aspirations. Whether Buddhist, Mohammedan or Hindu they too believed in living the good life and, when under great stress, they too turned to their gods. This common ground impressed him to the extent that he found conventional Christianity too exclusive; the innermost meaning of all things, the eternal truths of which his new religion would consist, must be readily acceptable to all creeds.

On the other hand he couldn't but be struck by the superiority of Christianity over all rivals. This, it seemed to him, explained the ascendancy of the white man in India. On a personal level it accounted for his own success in getting his men to follow him to the ends of the earth. Applying Darwinian theories of evolution to religion and ethics he saw the races of mankind at different stages of development on the ladder of moral awareness. The Hindu and the Chinese might be intellectually smarter, the Sikh and Mohammedan braver, but the English Christian occupied the top rung in moral ascendancy. The teachings of his religion imbued him with a greater resolution, a greater self-denial and a deeper sympathy. And this, moreover, was the way ahead, not bigger brains or tougher skins but warmer hearts.

Elitism is no virtue; Younghusband was later ashamed of presuming that Providence had singled him out. He must also have been relieved that he had not drawn the obvious parallel between moral superiority and the attainment of great physical altitudes, or that he had not suggested that his personal single-mindedness was somehow being rewarded by a glimpse of Nature's purity. Yet, at th time, he was not innocent of such vanities. He would look back on this spell in the Karakorams as the turning point in his life and, as if afraid to pursue the logic of his awakening, would prefer to regard the whole thing as a mystical experience. One would shudder were it not for his disarming naïvety and for the unquestioned sincerity of his subsequent retraction.

About October 12, brimming with new found resolve, Young-husband ascended the real Shimshal pass and came face to face with the dreaded Hunza raiders. Throughout the previous weeks he had set a watch day and night in case of attack. Now news reached him that Algy Durand, although not actually manhandled, had found Safdar Ali in a truculent and unpredictable mood; the Mir had been warned of Younghusband's approach and the new subsidy was not to be paid out till he was safely through Hunza territory. It was not, however, clear whether the chief would co-operate or whether he had agreed to Durand's stipulation about no more caravan raids. If he hadn't then resistance might well be offered to any British officer snooping at the vital pass by which the raiders went; the Dards were not unnaturally jealous of the few geographical secrets that remained to them.

After two hundred miles of uninhabited wilderness the first evidence of human endeavour was predictably grim. A square stone tower, windowless and forbidding, hove into sight. It stood on the end of a bluff that formed the farther wall of a deep ravine cutting clean across the valley floor. At the other end of this wall, where the ravine tucked itself into the sheer mountain side, there was another tower with a large gaping door; between the two towers ran a high stone rampart. With the unfordable river on one side and the mountains on the other, the only possible access was down the ravine and up the zigzag path under the rampart to the open doorway. All was peaceful; just a thin plume of smoke betrayed that the position was held.

With a couple of men to interpret, Younghusband plunged into the ravine; he left the Gurkhas to offer covering fire if needed. Half way up the other side the silence was suddenly shattered by a loud report; the door in the tower had been slammed shut. Then waving figures, brandishing matchlocks and shouting, appeared along the rampart just fifty feet above him; at that range stones, let alone bullets, could have annihilated his party. With the cool of a man who felt himself indestructible, Young-husband halted and quietly signalled for someone to come out and parley. His serenity was infectious; the shouting died away, the door opened a crack and two wild looking Dards obeyed his summons.

Though jittery and as uncertain of their chief's intentions as they were of their visitor's, the garrison lapped up his self-confidence. By nightfall the long haired and heavily armed raiders were sharing a fire with their timid Kirghiz prey. The grave Pathan surveyor, the sturdy Gurkhas and the long suffering Baltis and Ladakhis stood amongst them. And the solitary Englishman could not but again marvel at 'the extraordinary influence of the European in Asia'.

Next day it transpired that Safdar Ali had indeed acceded to Durand's demand in the matter of arranging for Younghusband to continue to the Hunza valley; he therefore proceeded on up the Shimshal pass. He still hoped for another glacier-bound wilderness like the Saltoro or a knife edge like the Mustagh but, from native report, was not altogether surprised to find a gentle snow-free ascent and a crest as open and level as a pamir. It was so easy that, like Biddulph with the Baroghil or Lockhart with the Dora, he was inclined to draw the wildest conclusions about the vulnerability of Dardistan. Study of the reports of his predecessors should have warned him that the difficulties were to be expected not on the pass but amongst the gorges and glaciers beyond it.

These he did not explore. Having reached the top of the pass he surprised his Hunza escort by promptly turning about and heading back the way he had come. While Safdar Ali was on his best behaviour pending receipt of the subsidy, Younghusband would take the opportunity of visiting the other passes between the Shimshal and Lockhart's Killik. Both debouched onto the Pamirs and therefore he would continue round the Hunza perimeter along the Raskam river.

There was however another considerably more pressing reason for delaying his entry into Hunza proper. At least four other parties of Europeans were taking advantage of the favourable autumn conditions of 1889 to explore neighbouring valleys on the Pamirs and Kun Lun. One consisted of two English sportsmen combining a bit of surreptitious surveying with the pursuit of the Marco Polo sheep; from them Younghusband had just learnt that Grombtchevski, the Russian agent who had reached Hunza in the previous year, was again in the field and was now lurking somewhere in the Raskam valley.

To what extent the movement of Russian travellers dictated his own is not clear, but in retrospect Younghusband liked to look back on the whole 1889 mission as an elaborate game of hide and seek. 'The game was on', he wrote when, soon after leaving Ladakh, he had learnt that a large Russian expedition was refitting in the northern foothills of the Kun Lun. At Shahidulla he had kept an anxious eye on their activities and at one point thought that they were stockpiling supplies for some sort of invasion. They also had 'road-making equipment' (spades?) and had enlisted the services of a Frenchman with wide experience of the Kashmir side of the passes. One is reminded strongly of the climax in *Kim*; the players and the setting of the 'game' are enough to establish that Kipling knew his Younghusband. The plot, however is quite different. This Russian expedition had no designs on India. Too big for espionage and too small for an invasion force it was actually a scientific and military undertaking commanded by a disciple of Przhevalski, the greatest of Russian travellers, and was continuing his work along the Sino–Tibetan frontier. As for the Frenchman, this was M. Dauvergne, an expert on carpet manufacture who was under contract to the Kashmir government. Also a sportsman and an inveterate traveller, he soon parted from the Russians, continued on to the Pamirs and thence crossed into Dardistan. He was probably no more in the espionage business than Gabriel Bonvalot.

Younghusband's suspicions were however justified in the case of Grombtchevski. Lord Curzon would soon identify him as the 'stormy petrel of Russian frontier advance', and there can be no question that his travels were politically motivated. With regard to Hunza he had been actively engaged in intrigue and he had also tried to enter Chitral and Kafiristan undetected. Even Dr. Leitner, who from the Oriental University Institute, Woking, took up Grombtchevski's case with some vigour, seems to have concluded that a bona fide representative of the Imperial Geographical Society had no business to be crossing frontiers in uniform and with a military escort.

Anxious to get further news of this notorious figure, Younghusband chased after the two English sportsmen. A week after leaving Shimshal he received a letter written in Turki from the man himself; he was waiting at the next camping ground. Thus, at a spot called Khaian Aksai, British and Russian agents for the first time came face to face. It was almost as if the place had been chosen. One march to the north the Raskam river disappeared into a gorge that divided the Kun Lun from the Pamirs; a similar distance to the west the Karakorams merged into the Hindu Kush. Inacessible it was, yet strategically valuable and surprisingly fertile—in Younghusband's view alarmingly so; for the waving grass and grey willows, so inviting beside the brown desolation of rock and scree, were a true no-man's land, unknown and unclaimed. The Russian had as much right to hoist his flag there as the Englishman.

Considering the veil of secrecy that would be drawn over all Younghusband's activities in 1889 not the least improbable feature of the occasion was that it was recorded on film. Grombtchevski had a camera and the following year he obligingly sent Younghusband, then in Kashmir, a print; this was reproduced only twice before being lost to posterity. It was never a great picture and on the one occasion that it appeared in a British publication the rough handling across Asia, as well as the loss of detail in reproduction, did not improve it. Yet as a remarkable record of a celebrated and desolate encounter it can scarcely be equalled; imagine the excitement if a photograph of Stanley's meeting with Livingstone ever came to light.

Instead of the conventional studio portrait, here we see the explorer in action. Bearded and in a battered bush hat, with one hand on hip and the other on his gun, Younghusband at last looks convincing. The jaunty air bespeaks a dauntless physique and one can sense the assurance that so impressed his followers (here ranged on his right). No doubt that pile of sticks and tree trunks in the foreground was their doing. The Gurkhas were uncomfortably aware of their lack of stature beside the burly Cossacks and had already begged their leader to explain that they were in no way typical of their regiment; he was to tell the Russians that most Gurkhas were a good six foot six. Aware too that their commander was somewhat undersized they appear to have got him to climb on top of something and then to have concealed the object behind the unlit bonfire. Younghusband thus stands shoulder to shoulder with the massive Grombtchevski, a man of six foot two with a frame to match.

Though now a Lieutenant-Colonel in the Imperial army—and

wearing a uniform to prove it—Grombtchevski was a Pole by birth. He was ten years older than Younghusband and had served with distinction in the Imperial Bodyguard and under the vaunted Skobeleff in Turkestan; he was now designated a Special Frontier Commissioner for the province of Ferghana, previously Khokand. As one of Russia's most experienced travellers he had attracted the patronage of the Tsar and was regarded as the natural successor to the famous Przhevalski. Besides the journeys of 1888 and 1889 he had been the first, in 1885, systematically to explore Sinkiang and in 1886 to work up the Naryn river into the Tian Shan.

In the present year he had left his Russian base on June 1, and accompanied by seven Cossacks (standing behind him in the photo) and Dr. Conrad, a German entomologist (seated on his left) had again set off for Kafiristan. In Roshan and again in Shignan the Afghans had performed with zeal the role envisaged for them by Elias; they refused to let him pass. Hunza would therefore have been the next logical step and it seems that Safdar Ali did invite him back. But for some reason he declined. Even to a would-be protector the Hunza chief could be a sore trial, but more probably Grombtchevski, still with no more than promises, hesitated to compete with both Durand and Younghusband. He had therefore turned to the exploration of the Raskam valley and the chance of a battle of wits with a British agent on neutral ground.

Actually the meeting turned out to be a most dignified and amicable affair. Younghusband inspected the Cossacks and Grombtchevski the Gurkhas; they exchanged invitations to dinner and the Russian officer plied his guest with vodka; doing his best to reciprocate, Younghusband broached his one bottle of brandy. The Englishman was impressed and delighted to find his opposite number such 'a very good sort of fellow'; though rivals and soon perhaps enemies they yet, as individuals, had much in common. Grombtchevski was equally gratified; here was a young man who truly appreciated the extent of his travels— something no-one seemed to understand in Russia—and the hardships they involved. He had expected a challenger and he had found a disciple. As icy gusts felt their way down from the Pamirs to tug fiercely at the guy ropes, the affable Pole and the irrepressible Englishman clinked glasses, huddled deeper into their sheepskins and mulled over the future of Asia. Combining the incongruous, the momentous and the romantic in equal measure, it is perhaps the most representative and memorable vignette in the whole of the Great Game.

Two days later they parted. The Gurkhas presented arms and the Cossacks drew swords. Grombtchevski pressed on Younghusband a fine sheep and made a little speech about how he hoped they would meet again 'either in peace in St. Petersburg or in war on the Indian frontier'. Younghusband repaid the courtesy by presenting the Russian with his book on Buddhism—he had finished it anyway—and left him with what he would have regarded as a magnanimous parting thought; 'we are both playing at a big game and we should be not one jot better off for trying to conceal the fact'.

They actually met again rather sooner than anticipated—in Yarkand the following summer (1890). By then they had every reason to distrust one another but again they got on famously. After going his separate way from Khaian Aksai, Grombtchevski had sought permission from the British Resident in Kashmir to spend the winter in Ladakh. The predictable refusal of such an unprecedented request was a long time coming and while the Russian cooled his heels in Shahidulla, the Kirghiz suggested an exploratory foray east towards the Tibetan frontier. Younghusband claims to have put them up to this, the idea being to cause the Russian 'extreme hardship and loss'. If such a plot existed, it worked. Grombtchevski leapt at the idea of seeing the eastern extremity of the Kashmir frontier, and the Tibetan plateau did the rest. At an average height of 18,000 feet, without water, fuel or grass, the party was soon in trouble. Tears caused by the icy wind got no further than their eyelashes before freezing solid. The baggage ponies went down one by one and the Cossacks became too weak to carry their rifles. They all suffered severely from frostbite; a year later Grombtchevski was still on crutches. When they made it back to Shahidulla they had lost all their ponies and all their belongings.

Grombtchevski never suspected Younghusband of such a wretched prank; he held the Kashmir Resident responsible, by his refusal to allow him across the frontier. In a sense, though, he got his own back. For when Hunza raiders returned to relieve the

Kirghiz of the money given them by Younghusband in the previous year, he was on hand to point out the lesson of his rival's empty promises. So much so that the Kirghiz agreed to betray to him, too, the route by which the raiders came.

But at Khaian Aksai some sort of gentleman's agreement seems to have been reached whereby Grombtchevski would in future steer clear of Hunza and Dardistan in return for a free hand north of the watershed. Safdar Ali's affairs were therefore of less interest and, besides, the expedition was in no fit state to take up the Kirghiz offer. When the two men met in Yarkand in 1890 Grombtchevski thus had a clear conscience. Younghusband kept quiet about his own role in the Russian disaster and they again parted the best of friends. Two years later it was reported that Grombtchevski kept a photo of Younghusband on his bedside table and nearly thirty years later, in 1925, Younghusband received a letter from his old rival. But by then the genial Pole was a decrepit and dying man. He had risen to the rank of Lieutenant-General, had been imprisoned in Siberia by the Bolsheviks and was now bedridden and destitute in Warsaw; he died the following year. With the letter there was an account in Russian of his travels. It included the only other known reproduction of that remarkable photograph.*

* This account of Grombtchevski's travels has now been traced and is available in an Italian translation by Lionello Fogliano.

PART THREE

Vici

11. Looking for a Pretext

To Dr. Leitner, now setting up home in Woking, the re-establishment of the Gilgit Agency was, of course, a hideous mistake. But worse still was the assumption that for the Agency to be effective it was necessary for the Dards to be subdued. In Leitner's view the military roads that would open up the Dard valleys amounted to crude provocation, the engagements that would ruthlessly suppress Dard independence amounted to atrocities, and the promotion-crazed soldiers who would run the country were no better than vandals. Instead, Dardistan should have been left as a kind of nature reserve in which the Dards could roam at will, living in their traditional style, speaking their ancient tongues, and visited only by scientists observing them from a discreet distance. This was not only the most morally acceptable solution but also the most politically expedient. It would cost nothing; the Dards, uncowed, would continue to defend their independence as fiercely as ever, and would naturally favour whichever power was most willing to respect it; their country, undisturbed by road and bridge builders, would remain as impenetrable as ever; and together these two factors would make of the region a far more effective barrier against the Russians than the most ambitious network of outposts and supply lines. Grombtchevski had confided to Younghusband that he had seen enough of Hunza and Safdar Ali not to risk his neck there again; the Dards could be trusted to see off any subsequent agents and, if the Pamirs could be made a neutral zone thus doubling the line of defence, so much the better.

By the 1890s Leitner was no longer alone; Younghusband, for one, also had his reservations, though of a more moderate nature. The Russian menace was as real for him as for anyone and he accepted that Dardistan must be more effectively controlled. But he doubted whether force need be used; instead of Algy Durand's policy of inviting confrontation, more effort should be made to work with the Dards. He was a great believer in having a man on

471

the spot; it was no good exchanging letters and trading ultimata for insults. What was needed was a good political officer in Hunza and another in Chitral; and if this policy had been pursued from the start the co-operation of the Dards could have been won without a shot being fired.

Support for such views was also growing in official circles. Lord Lansdowne and Morty Durand faced increasingly stiff opposition both within the Government of India and at Westminster. Apart from the rights and wrongs of the policy, there was the little matter of expense. Lockhart's scheme for the reopening of the Gilgit Agency had been greeted with horror because it entailed the services of nineteen British officers and a sizeable nucleus of British Indian troops. Algy Durand, in 1888, had been sent to draw up an economy version of the same scheme that would cost half as much. Four British officers, he concluded, would be enough, plus a small bodyguard of British Indian troops; the rest of the necessary troops, as well as finance for an elaborate system of roads and telegraph lines, was to be provided by the Kashmir government. This looked fine on paper but it soon proved the thin end of an extremely thick wedge. Two years after its re-opening there were eighteen British officers attached to the Agency, two hundred British Indian troops and a mountain battery. By 1892 the number of officers had risen to twenty-three, and still Durand cried out for more. And in 1895 Chitral alone claimed the attention of close on fifteen thousand troops. Not surprisingly people wondered if it was all worthwhile. Questions were asked in Parliament and a long debate on the whole future of Chitral and Gilgit resulted.

Durand and his men in Biddulph's now much extended and handsomely furnished bungalow had no time for such criticisms. If Younghusband ever dared voice his doubts there, no-one paid much attention; a good fighting man, thought Algy, but 'not overburdened with brains'. As for Leitner he was 'a liar and a traitor to boot'. There were just so many imperatives for extending British control to all the Dard states that the methods employed were almost irrelevant and criticisms hardly worth answering. But if pushed, the one stock answer, which even those unacquainted with the day-to-day exigencies of frontier relations must acknowledge, was the Russian threat.

Algy Durand honestly believed that as matters stood in 1889 'there was absolutely nothing to stop a Russian officer with a thousand Cossacks from reaching Astor in ten days after crossing the passes of the Hindu Kush, and from watering his horses in the Wular Lake [in the Kashmir Valley] four days later'. Imagine, he went on, the repercussions. Out of Kashmir in a wild stampede would come tumbling the British Resident, the Maharaja and a gaggle of holidaying *memsahibs*; the Indian Army, straining its eyes in search of Russian columns advancing across the Afghan deserts, would find its flank already turned and its lines of communication across the Punjab exposed. Regardless of expense such a calamity must be forestalled; 'the Gilgit Game was well worth the candle'.

Durand had joined the Intelligence Branch of the Q.M.G.'s department just after MacGregor's departure, but 'old Mac' would surely have approved of this lurid deduction. His disciple knew every inch of the Gilgit road and spoke with the greatest authority. So alarming was his prognosis that had it been leaked, like *The Defence of India*, it would have caused a furore. Perhaps for that reason it was never examined as closely as it might have been. For Durand, letting the cat out of the bag many years later, failed to note that such a manœuvre by the Russians would only have been possible during four months of the year and then always assuming that the weather had been favourable. Furthermore the Dards would have had to show unprecedented forbearance if a small army was to be allowed to pass unscathed through their valleys, whilst the Dogra troops, incompetent as they were, could hardly have failed to take such an elementary precaution as withdrawing their Indus ferry. But assuming favourable conditions and assuming that, for reasons inconceivable, both Dard and Dogra welcomed the Russians, they would have first had to get across the Pamirs undetected and intact; Durand had no experience of this part of their route. Nor had he of the glaciers and gorges into which the Hindu Kush passes immediately debouched; but every traveller who had, from Biddulph onwards, had declared them totally unfit for the passage of troops. Finally, on the Gilgit–Kashmir section of the route, his experience indeed illustrated the possibility of moving large bodies of troops. Conveniently, though, he seems to have forgotten the appalling headaches and losses this occasioned, and that success was only achieved after two years of road building.

However interesting it would have been to put these points to the new Gilgit Agent, it would scarcely have altered the course of history. Durand would simply have changed his ground; how to stop the Hunza raids and counter Chinese claims? Or how to guard against a conflagration throughout Dardistan as a result of a disputed succession in Chitral? Or perhaps he would have held to the still more questionable view of maintaining that the Dards were the aggressors; that he was somehow forced into invading not only Hunza but states like Nagar and Chilas who had long since thrown in their lot with Kashmir. Doubtful, indeed, is it that he would have confessed the obvious, that given the role envisaged for the new Gilgit Agency, given its constitution and given the men sent to staff it, Dardistan was doomed and war of some sort inevitable.

The new scheme had been approved as if it was merely the re-establishment of Biddulph's Agency in the light of changing circumstances. In fact it was nothing of the sort; Durand's position was radically different. For one thing he had companions, only four to start with but all his closest friends, and soon many more. Secondly and far more important, though he had only a small bodyguard of British Indian troops, he was in command of the entire Dogra force in Dardistan. The change had been achieved as a result of the creation of the Imperial Service Corps in 1888. One can only assume that Dufferin and Morty Durand had Gilgit much in mind when they launched this scheme whereby troops employed by the native states of India were to be trained by British officers and were to serve alongside troops of the regular Indian army. It was projected as a useful way of augmenting the standing army and also of restoring some dignity to those feudal battalions of martial Sikhs, Rajputs and Dogras who previously had no obvious role other than as playthings of their Maharajas. In effect it neatly solved the whole problem of entrusting the defence of Dardistan to the dispirited Kashmir forces. It maintained the fiction of Kashmir's role without all its drawbacks, and it obviated the need for British Indian troops by providing a force that would soon, under British tutelage, be just as effective.

Durand held not only the military reins at Gilgit but also the political reins. Unlike Biddulph he was entrusted with sole responsibility for all dealings with the Dards. Kashmiri officials continued to exercise powers of internal administration but even here his precedence in matters of supply and communications gave him a commanding say. Like his predecessor he would still find the Kashmiris highly obstructive, but at least his efforts were not habitually sabotaged; and he was never the object of an assassination plot. Subsidies, like that dangled before Safdar Ali in return for abandoning his raids, were now to be offered not on behalf of Kashmir but of British India. One of his first assignments was to tour Nagar, Hunza and Chitral and explain just how different the new Agency was; the chiefs were to be convinced that a new era in Anglo–Dard relations was beginning.

Immediately, all this authority was to be deployed in curbing the independence of Hunza. Safdar Ali had precipitated the re-establishment of the Agency and he was to be the first to receive its attentions. In mid-August 1889, just as Younghusband was settting out from Ladakh, Durand, accompanied by his trusty comrade, Surgeon-Major George Robertson, had edged his way up the Hunza gorge. Already anticipating the day when they would have to fight their way through it, they sketched the main defensive positions and pondered the engineering problems of making the track fit for supply trains.

At Chalt they diverged from the route followed by Biddulph and Lockhart and crossed the river on the long swaying bridge of plaited brushwood to the Nagar side. Durand claimed they were the first Europeans to set foot in Nagar; he conveniently forgot that, by his predecessors, Chalt and Chaprot had both been regarded as part of the state. The chief was an octogenarian, 'wise and amiable' according to Leitner, 'a patriarch with a large family and preserving the keenness of youth in his old age'. Durand found him just 'a paralytic debauchee' with a persecution mania. His audience chamber was reached through a trapdoor in the floor to which the only access from below was by a single long tree trunk. As the Gilgit Agent heaved himself through the hole, spiked helmet first, then frock coat, dangling sword, high boots and spurs, he noted that this arrangement must be the Dard equivalent of a portcullis and moat. He was not surprised that the Dard chiefs had a reputation for longevity. Nor, in this case, did he regret it. The chief was remarkably co-operative, 'Raja Jafr Khan and his son Uzr Khan are undoubtedly desirous of being on friendly terms with the British government', he reported.

He might profitably have recalled the difficulties Biddulph had had in reconciling his early friendships with later developments; he would soon regret ever having said a good word about the ruling family of Nagar. Before he had met him he had pigeon-holed Uzr Khan, the heir apparent, as a 'rascal of the first water'; much later he would become 'the Nagar cur'. But now he found him simply 'boorish'. The photographs suggest a rather fine figure, a trifle jowly but bewildered rather than mischievous. They correspond better with the man's history than Durand's erratic judgements; it was he whom Lockhart, three years before, had dispossessed of Chalt and it was he who, two years hence, would be made the pretext for armed intervention.

Durand and Robertson were more exercised by their reception from Safdar Ali of Hunza. On another perilously frayed rope bridge they crossed the chasm, three hundred feet deep and about the same across, that divides the two states, and climbed through the neatly terraced fields. The reception was on a more lavish scale than at Nagar; amidst the Bukhara carpets and the silks of the courtiers Durand felt less conspicuous. But the chief was a sad looking figure, twenty-two years old and delicate, 'with shifty Mongolian eyes' and a foxy little red beard. When some of the Agent's bodyguard were prevented from crowding into the audience chamber, Durand found him 'showing a tendency to insolence'. And when he 'funked' taking a dose prescribed for him by Robertson it was clear that he was also a coward; 'this sounded bad for a rank coward is a dangerous man to deal with'.

So it proved. Safdar Ali, true to Hunza tradition, was out to extract the maximum benefit from his visitors. In return for promises of no caravan raids and of entertaining no Russians, he was being offered a subsidy of 20,000 rupees. He would make no bones about the promises—he had no intention of keeping them anyway—but he would insist on a larger subsidy. Durand refused, whereupon the Mir flew into a rage. The British presentation—a breech-loader or two (but very little ammunition) plus the usual collection of knicknacks—was hurled about the room. Back in camp Durand ordered his escort to arms and broke open the cartridge boxes. As night fell pickets of Hunza sharpshooters were seen to command the camp on all sides; to the two Englishmen it seemed like 'the beginning of the end'.

It was, of course, no such thing. Safdar Ali was just piling on the pressure—successfully too, for he did eventually get the extra 5,000 rupees he sought. At the time, though, Durand stood firm; before day broke, the pickets had vanished and the mission was free to scuttle back along the cliffs towards Gilgit. As they dropped with a sigh of relief from the Hunza ledge into the gloomy gorge, they heard a farewell salute booming away from the country's only cannon. Soon after, the Mir's chief minister panted up with his master's best wishes and a few anxious questions about when the subsidy might be expected. 'After Younghusband is safely in Gilgit,' replied Durand. He himself intended to continue straight on to Chitral but he made a mental note to be back in time to march to Younghusband's aid if required.

Durand was now convinced that there must needs be a day of reckoning with 'young Saffy'. Younghusband's visit would not, however, be made the occasion for it. 'That intrepid and never to be denied traveller has arrived [in Gilgit] safely,' reported the Indian Foreign Department in December 1889. He had not only arrived safely but he was the first British officer to pass through without even being threatened. He may have been 'too soft' by Durand's standards but at least he made some attempt to understand Safdar Ali's predicament. One wonders whether they are writing of the same man. Far from being shifty and Mongolian, Younghusband's Safdar Ali was 'almost European in appearance and could have passed for a Greek or an Italian'. He had a good sense of humour and, though rebuked for his importunate behaviour, bore no ill will. When the shortage of cultivable land was given as the reason for the caravan raids, Younghusband was all sympathy for the desperate straits to which the providers of Hunza were reduced; the raids were just a repetition of the survival tactics of highlanders throughout the world. Safdar Ali was more to be pitied than anything. Immured in his mountain fastness, his intransigence was simply the product of ignorance. When asked if he had ever been to India he replied that great kings like himself and Alexander the Great, from whom he claimed descent, never left their kingdoms. The traditional nature of

Hunza's external relations was that of extracting blackmail from their richer but more vulnerable neighbours. He honestly believed that the British and Russians feared him as much as did the Kirghiz and Dogras; and when they sent representatives to treat for his friendship he treated them accordingly.

Younghusband's more sympathetic report did less to win Safdar Ali a reprieve than the fact that Durand was not yet ready for hostilities; having seen the Hunza road he now knew better than to attempt it with no more than 'a corporal's guard'. The new policy of buying Hunza's co-operation thus got a trial, albeit a short one. Six months later Algy wrote to brother Morty, 'all my savages have been going wrong', and cited in particular the news that Safdar Ali had again been after the Sinkiang caravans; it was on this raid that Hunza men relieved Younghusband's Kirghiz friends of their defence fund. The raiders also killed one of Grombtchevski's servants, but Durand was giving no credit for this. The prospect of 'a row with Hunza and Nagar' was again in the forefront of his mind and feverish attempts were made to build new barracks at Gilgit, to improve the supply line back to Kashmir and to construct the first stage of a mule road to Hunza.

All should have been ready for pursuing a more active policy by the end of the year; more troops arrived from Kashmir as did the Agency doctor and a team of engineering contractors. Durand however had retired on leave to India and thence to England. By the time he got back to Gilgit it was November and his new troops were still a long way from being battle ready. As usual, nothing like enough grain had been brought over the Great Himalaya during the short season of open passes and, though the engineers had arrived, their workforce was stranded on the Kashmir side of the passes. Safdar Ali had won another reprieve.

Younghusband's complaint was that for all this time, in fact for two years after his own visit, no British officer went near Hunza or Nagar. In view of the otherwise adventurous character of British policy at the time, one can only assume that this was deliberate. As will be seen, Younghusband himself spent most of the period prowling about the Pamirs and badgering the Chinese authorities in Sinkiang. With an equally fine disregard for possible consequences, Surgeon-Major Robertson was sent by Durand to the other side of Dardistan to re-open dealings with the Kafirs. He paid them a brief visit in late 1889 and the following September returned to spend over a year in the country, assessing 'the exact value of Kafiristan as a factor in the general problem of how best to secure the safety of the North West frontier of India'. Often sick and invariably in danger, he somehow survived this grim exile amongst the most primitive people in Asia and, in the process, achieved the distinction of being one of the first field-workers in social anthropology. It would, however, be naïve to explain his long stay on the grounds of scientific curiosity. 'It seems to me a great pity', he wrote in 1889, 'that a fine vigorous race such as the Kafirs should ever come under the yoke of the Afghans.' Instead he searched diligently for a pretext, strategic or political, to bring them within the sphere of Gilgit's authority. This quest proved self-defeating. The Kafirs showed themselves too disunited ever to be a political asset, whilst his own activity amongst them was actually intensifying Afghan jealousy. In the end, all he could hope to achieve was a holding operation. To stave off the evil day of an Afghan invasion he let it be thought that the British were still interested in the country, first by staying on as long as possible, then by leading a deputation of Kafirs back to India.

All this was to have disastrous consequences for the Kafirs; but the solicitude shown them at the time was in marked contrast to the cold shoulder turned on Hunza. While Robertson was in Kafiristan, Durand's other political assistant was kept firmly at Gilgit. Even when a man had to be sent up to the Pamirs he was routed via Yasin rather than Hunza. As early as 1889 Durand had been committed to the idea of a Hunza campaign; he did nothing to make the subsidy arrangement work and merely awaited the completion of his preparations and a pretext to attack.

This might have come in May 1891. A report reached the Agent that Uzr Khan of Nagar had murdered one of his brothers and was about to attack the Dogra troops at Chalt. There is no doubt about the murder. The brother appears to have been Durand's rival candidate for the succession; he had been living at Gilgit and, whatever the reason for his return to Nagar, the moment he set foot outside Kashmir territory he was asking for trouble. Fratricide, to a Dard prince, was the must normal behaviour and Durand had no right to be so indignant about it. Whether Uzr Khan also decided that this was the moment to reassert his claim to Chalt is less certain. But Durand needed an excuse to strengthen the Chalt garrison and to push his mule road forward another stage. The opportunity afforded by the rumour of Nagar's supposed mobilisation was too good to miss; he was in Chalt with four hundred men and a mountain battery, and had cut the 'rope' bridge across the river, before Uzr Khan had made a move. Taken in conjunction with two other minor incidents, the kidnapping of a Kashmiri and the disruption of mail passing through Hunza to Younghusband on the Pamirs, this affair also strengthened his case for more troops and bore out his predictions of imminent hostilities. As a down payment he received the services of another two British officers and in the autumn he set off for Simla to bargain for more officers and more troops.

According to one of those who served on the Gilgit staff at this period there were three reasons for a man being posted to the Hindu Kush. The first was debt, the second the Intelligence Branch and the third 'the chance of a scrap'. He should have added a fourth, the right connection. Algy Durand would never have been given the Agent's job if he hadn't been Morty's brother—the eldest brother, as Resident in Nepal, had not been forgotten either—and few of those who followed him to Gilgit would have done so if they hadn't been Algy's friends. It is no coincidence that those not straight from the Intelligence Branch were largely from his old regiment, the Central India Horse.

In spite of the notion of banishment to the outposts of the Empire, Gilgit was a much sought-after posting. The men who in 1891 received telegrams—'Colonel Durand applies urgently for the services of . . .'—were overjoyed. It was the big break, the reward for years of regimental slogging and patient lobbying. A scrap must be in prospect; if not, in Gilgit of all places surely, one could be engineered. The heading on the Agency's notepaper read '*Telegrams:* Gilgit via Srinagar, *Railway Station*: Rawal Pindi'. None of the new recruits imagined they could climb into a cab at Pindi station and be whisked off to the Gilgit Agency for dinner. But with the Indus, the Great Himalaya and a few hundred miles between Gilgit and the nearest telegraph office or railhead, and with the encircling mountains reputedly teeming with promenading Russians and brigand chiefs, what better chance could be hoped for; C.B., C.S.I., C.I.E., a campaign medal at least, must be in the offing and always there was an outside chance of the real thing, a V.C.. Promotion too; everyone in Gilgit, including Durand, who in eighteen months had risen from Captain to Lieutenant-Colonel, seemed to hold an acting rank above that to which they were entitled. Nor was this just wishful thinking. Over the next four years six British officers would win the V.C. in Dardistan and many more be recommended for it. Durand succeeded in mentioning in despatches so many of his fellow officers that he would be singled out in Parliament as having brought the whole system into disrepute.

Arrived in the hard dry air of the Hindu Kush the young officers soon caught the sweet scent of distinction; it made them keen to the point of incitement, brave to the point of folly. One or two had served in the Sudan under Wolseley and Kitchener; with Egypt peaceful, they had transferred to India and now chased appointments to wherever there was the best chance of action. Their lack of interest in the Dards as people or the mountains as scenery was shared by most of their colleagues. It was a measure of their professionalism. The fact that many of them were also deeply in debt in no way contradicts this; Durand's cronies just happened to be a trifle racy and high-spirited. From time to time Algy himself had found it necessary to reassure Morty that he was living within his means. Lieutenants 'Charlie' Townshend and 'Curly' Stewart, the two men who joined him after the Chalt business, were outspoken devotees of riotous living and were more at home backstage with the ladies of the Alhambra; while Algy grimly chronicled his manic forebodings to brother Morty, Townshend and Stewart would rattle off love letters to their favourite actresses. Another type was exemplified by the meticulous Manners Smith and the languid Bruce, both of whom were athletes so reckless they might have qualified as stunt men. One looks in vain for the introvert or the man of even average sensitivity.

Only Younghusband was an obvious misfit; he must have felt it just as he had amongst his hard-drinking fellow subalterns in the King's Dragoon Guards; and no doubt it heightened his sense of somehow being set apart. But if Durand's pals ridiculed this odd little officer with the wide credulous blue eyes and heavy conversation, they paid a grudging respect to his achievements. They also had cause to be grateful for them; for it was Younghusband, of all people, who eventually precipitated the first campaign.

* * *

On September 29, 1891 a cable reached *The Times* from their Bombay correspondent. 'In spite of repeated contradictions it is persistently rumoured here that Captain Younghusband has been killed by the Russians in the Pamir country'; an officer from Gilgit had recently been sent up to the Pamirs and no confirmation or denial could be expected until his return. Not surprisingly this was too much for the victim's father who promptly got the Foreign Office to wire the Indian government. Young Frank, it transpired, was alive all right, but the incident which had given rise to the rumours, though still obscure, was of such an explosive character that nothing more could as yet be revealed.

The Prime Minister had in fact just sent a letter of protest to the Russian Foreign Minister; its tone was such that the latter thought war was about to be declared. So did another *Times* correspondent who happened to be in Kashmir at the time; he regarded the incident itself as equivalent to a declaration of war. General Roberts, Commander-in-Chief in India, agreed; he promptly mobilised a whole division with the idea of grabbing Afghanistan before the Russians got under way. Weeks later when Younghusband got back to India, Roberts was still of this opinion and, with a friendly squeeze of the arm, assured the explorer that 'Now's the time to go for the Russians'. Younghusband, for his part, needed reassurance. He was so shaken by the whole affair that he told his father he would resign unless full satisfaction were exacted from the Russians. Anything less and he must assume that he no longer enjoyed that full support of the government which meant so much to him.

What had actually happened was that, at last, the genteel jockeying for control of the Pamirs had become a muscle-testing brawl. In June 1890, less than six months after his return from Hunza, Younghusband had been sent back to the Pamirs to continue the work of Ney Elias; the latter's report had finally won recognition as the most constructive contribution on meeting the threat of Russian territorial advancement to the Hindu Kush. Younghusband was to take up the question of where the Afghan and Chinese boundaries should be made to meet. Contrary to Elias' recommendations though, he was to champion the Chinese cause and, having made his award, he was to press on the Sinkiang authorities the need to make their occupation effective right up to the new frontier. Elias had found the Afghans infinitely more co-operative, and militarily more formidable, than the Chinese. Now, however, it was rightly felt that for political reasons the Russians were more likely to respect Peking's sovereignty than they were Kabul's.

In his published account of the journey, Younghusband, like every other visitor to the Pamirs, found precious little to comment on. It was a mountain wilderness certainly, but the grandeur and the glory of the Karakorams were sadly lacking, nothing here to rouse a man's spirit, no 'essence of sublimity'. The perils were not the sudden sweep of an avalanche or the treacherous grin of a crevasse but something more abstract and insinuating, a relentless physical deterioration occasioned by the ceaseless wind, sustained cold and excessive altitude. At a spot called Somatash, well west of Elias' proposed Sino-Afghan boundary, he found a sheltered rock inscribed in Chinese to record some forgotten foray; it provided a useful salient round which to construct his new boundary. He also visited the great Lake Karakul in the extreme north of the region which was the one Hayward had hoped to establish as the source of the Oxus. Younghusband was now a gold medallist of the R.G.S.; it was not inappropriate that he was the first Englishman actually to see it. A fine stretch of water, wind-tossed beneath scudding snow clouds, the barrenness of its black beaches was set off by the snow clad slopes of the Alai, But as Elias had learned, precious little water flowed into it and none at all out of it.

With the temperature inside his tent falling to below zero Fahrenheit, Younghusband adjourned to Kashgar, the Sinkiang capital, for the winter. One may ridicule Elias presenting a carefully shaven cheek to the cruellest wind known to man, but Younghusband had taken his spartan habits one further. He continued to indulge his passion for an early morning dip. It became less of an indulgence, he records, when the water, thawed for the purpose and poured steaming into his rubber tub, had acquired a coating of ice before he had had time to undress.

Six months of patient negotiations with the Chinese authorities
in Kashgar and he felt that he had made his point about the new
frontier. A Chinese general was on his way to Somatash to establish
an outpost. The gap had been closed and the Russians could now
only advance towards the Hindu Kush by 'committing an act of
very open aggression'. Unfortunately Petrovski, the Russian consul
in Kashgar, and Grombtchevski, now governor of the Russian
frontier post at Marghilan, thought otherwise. The former with
his 'trumpery kind of cleverness' ran rings round the straightforward Younghusband and was able to report every move of the
negotiations back to Russia. Grombtchevski duly despatched a
force of close on two hundred to stake out a prior claim, and when
the Chinese general finally came up against them at Somatash he
opted for discretion. What should have been the occasion for
establishing 'an act of very open aggression' turned into a harmon-
ious Sino-Russian rendezvous; the Chinese general, according to
his superiors, had made the excursion simply to offer felicitations.

Younghusband knew nothing of this about-face, but just before
his recall to India he got wind of the Russian manœuvre. To
investigate it he decided to return home via the Pamirs. He took
with him a companion, a young lieutenant called Davison who,
fired by his own example, had recently set out to scale the Mustagh pass; unable even to find it, he had fetched up without passport, money, baggage or friends in Sinkiang. As they climbed west
into the mountains the scent grew strong. There appeared to be
two Russian detachments in the field and their object was nothing
less than to annex the whole of the Pamirs. One was at Somatash
whither Davison was promptly despatched. Like a character
straight out of G. A. Henty, the spirited young subaltern cantered
off to witness the expected Sino-Russian clash. Only he was
disappointed; there was no clash and instead of becoming the
hero of the hour he was promptly arrested by the Russians and
marched off to Marghilan.

Meanwhile Younghusband went after the other party that had
made straight for the Hindu Kush. He found their base camp on
the Little Pamir beside a crumbling tomb known as Bozai Gombaz
in what was thought to be Afghan territory. There he awaited them.
On August 13, six Russian officers with thirty Cossacks, and the
Russian flag carried before, them rode into camp. Younghusband

offered tea and demanded the facts. Was it true that they were annexing the Pamirs? It was. Marked in green on their map the whole of the Pamirs, excluding the inhabited parts of Wakhan, were now Russian territory; they had a frontage on the Hindu Kush fifty miles long and direct access to nearly all the passes into Yasin and Hunza. Indeed, that was where the Cossacks had just been. They had crossed, not without difficulty, into the Ishkoman valley of Yasin and thence, hugging the watershed, had crossed the Darkot and Baroghil passes back to Wakhan and the Little Pamir. Younghusband must have been starting out of his camp-chair. Whatever the status of the Pamirs, this latter foray was unquestionably a provocative infringement of British territorial sovereignty.

On the other hand, there was nothing he could immediately do about it; on the present expedition he didn't even have a Gurkha escort. The Russians were pleasant enough and Colonel Ianov, their commander, wore the coveted Cross of St. George, equivalent to a V.C. An invitation to dine was therefore accepted and that night, to Ianov's proposing the health of Queen Victoria, Younghusband dutifully replied with the health of the Tsar, Alexander III.

Next morning the Russians departed north. Younghusband stayed put, waiting for Davison and waiting to make sure that the Russian exit was not a feint. At 11 p.m. on the night of the third day as he lay in bed, there came again the clattering of hooves on the stony ground and the jingle of swords and spurs. Peeping out. he saw in the moonlit wastes the Cossacks returning with the flag in their midst. Hastily pulling on a greatcoat, he again greeted Ianov and invited him in for a meal. The Russian was grim faced. He had come, he explained, on an unpleasant mission; Younghusband was trespassing and he had now received orders to escort him from Russian territory back to Chinese; he must leave in the morning or face arrest.

Ianov was as courteous and apologetic as the situation permitted. Next day he presented Younghusband with a haunch of Marco Polo sheep and volunteered to trust him to make his own way back without the embarrassment of an escort. But the insult remained and it was the indignity of the whole affair that rankled most of all. British prestige had suffered a body blow. A British officer on Afghan soil and within sight of his own frontier had been hauled out of bed in the dead of night by a Russian patrol and told to scram. The political implications of the annexation of the Pamirs and the trespassing across the Hindu Kush were horrifying, but this picture of the solitary Englishman shivering in his pyjamas while some officious Russian colonel gave him his marching orders was somehow worse. It was no wonder that the victim demanded satisfaction nor that, within the incredibly short time of two weeks, the strongest possible protest had been lodged in St. Petersburg. Nor was it surprising that a projected adventure in the Hindu Kush that promised to restore British prestige suddenly found unexpected favour; Younghusband had made the Hunza–Nagar expedition an urgent necessity.

First, though, a summary of subsequent events on the Pamirs. Faced with such a storm of protest the Russian foreign office backed down. Younghusband had been threatened with arrest, it was claimed, not because he was trespassing at Bozai Gombaz but because he had trespassed on Russian territory near Lake Karakul. This he did not dispute. As for Bozai Gombaz it was not and never had been, according to the Russians, part of Afghan Wakhan. The Indian government first contested this, then conceded it, while Younghusband tried to argue that if it wasn't Afghan then it must be Chinese; what else could it be in view of his having established that the two frontiers met further north at Somatash?

He had actually done rather more than join the two frontiers, he had made them overlap. To award Somatash to the Chinese he had had to get the Afghans to withdraw. Inevitably the Amir took exception to his troops being thus shunted around. He protested to an embarrassed Indian government which duly apologised and retracted. As a result, when the Chinese after Ianov's departure deigned to take up their option on the place, they found it again in foreign hands. Quarrels broke out between the two garrisons and more protests, this time from both Peking and Kabul, rained down on the Indian government. Eventually the Chinese decided they had had enough of trying to co-operate with British schemes on the Pamirs and, withdrawing completely, urged the Leitnerian idea of neutralisation.

The Russian foreign office also disowned Ianov's action in declaring the Pamirs to be Russian territory. This did not mean that they disclaimed all rights to the region, merely that they felt annexation was premature and that their objects might be better gained by negotiation. With this the Russian military command and, in particular the military governor of Turkestan, did not agree; better to move in first and talk about it afterwards. In May 1892 the military party won the ear of the Tsar and Ianov was despatched on a repeat performance. This time the unfortunate Afghans took the brunt of it. In a bloody little affray at Somatash all but one of their garrison was killed. The Russians then removed the inscribed stone by which Younghusband had set such store and, for good measure, continued south destroying a Chinese fort and again scaling the Hindu Kush. Before returning they installed a permanent garrison on the Murghab where for the first time Europeans got a taste of living on the Pamirs. It was not a success; their hens perished, the only crop to thrive was a woody radish and their greatest excitement was when a passing British sportsman taught them the secrets of ludo.

More serious were the consequences of the Russo-Afghan clash at Somatash. Like the Chinese, the Amir was now having serious doubts about defending such an unremunerative chunk of tundra. As he threatened to withdraw towards the Oxus, the gap which Elias and Younghusband had endeavoured to plug yawned a hundred miles wide. The Indian government recoiled from the idea of trying to match Ianov's promenades and now pinned all their hopes on reaching an agreement on a frontier delimitation direct with the Russians. The diplomatic negotiations that followed were long and complex. The Chinese would take no part in them. The Amir vacillated between wanting as much territory as he could get and wanting none at all. The Viceroy and his council were also uncertain about their priorities and caused the Foreign Office in London almost as much heartache as did the equally contradictory Russians. The ebb of concessions and the flow of revived apprehensions continued to have an influence on the course of policy in Dardistan but by 1893 the Tsar was listening to more moderate councils and all sides were committed to delimitation. The British priority of a strip of Afghan territory between the Hindu Kush frontier and the Russian was accepted in principle; in return the Russians got most of the Pamirs; the Amir, who stood to lose by this arrangement, was mollified by British concessions elsewhere on their joint frontier (most notably, as will be seen, in Kafiristan). Thus was created that anomalous strip of Afghan territory known as the Wakhan corridor. In 1895 a joint Anglo-Russian boundary commission marked out its eastern extremities and, separating Pakistan from the Tadjik S.S.R., it survives virtually untouched to this day.

12. Precipice Warfare

News of Younghusband's expulsion from Bozai Gombaz reached India in early September, 1891. For Algy Durand, just arrived in Simla, it could not have been better timed. He had expected a tough wrangle to get the authorisation and troops necessary for a strike up the Hunza gorge; now his path was made smooth. Another fifteen British officers, two hundred Gurkhas of the regular Indian army, two more mountain batteries and a much cherished Gatling gun were placed at his disposal. He was also given carte blanche to handle the affair as he thought fit. If anyone still had doubts about the need for a campaign it was explained that all these precautions were purely defensive; with the passes about to close for the winter it was the only way of ensuring that Durand would be able to forestall another Dard attack such as that supposedly intended against Chalt in the previous May.

But if these same preparations, and the terms Durand was empowered to offer Hunza and Nagar, were not also intended to goad the Dards into defiance one wonders what would. In May the fort at Chalt had been reinforced, its garrison augmented, an old fortification that commanded it demolished, and the road thither from Gilgit had been improved. Now it was intended to go further. The road which, battered by landslips, had a way of reverting to its previous condition, was to be again taken in hand. The fort, the strategic importance of which Ghazan Khan had likened to that of his wives' pyjama strings, was to be demolished altogether, and new military roads were to be driven into the heart of Nagar and right through Hunza. Sadly Ghazan Khan was no longer around to give his metaphor the obvious twist; but this was the rape of Dardistan with a vengeance. With the new roads was to go the right to move troops to any part of Nagar and Hunza; it meant the end of their isolation and so of their independence.

Durand's terms allowed of no compromise. Had Safdar Ali's flagrant disregard of those accepted in 1889 been made the pretext for interference he might have wriggled off the hook; certainly

Nagar would have been in the clear. As it was, no mention was to be made of past misconduct. The two chiefs were to be told that the roads were vital for the defence of India against Russia. If they objected they were to understand that the roads would be built regardless, but that troops would first clear the way. Should they wish to retain their freedom they must therefore fight; it was as simple, and as brutal, as that.

The British case was based on the premise that neither state had much to lose since they were already tributary to Kashmir. In the case of Hunza this was a distortion of the facts. Like many other Dard states, the Mir had reciprocal tributary arrangements with all his neighbours. The subsidies received were regarded as protection money; the token tributes paid out were simply pledges of good conduct. As Elias had pointed out, there was no difference between Hunza's tributary arrangements with Sinkiang and those with Kashmir. Younghusband agreed and was even now urging that the Chinese must at least be consulted.

Nagar's position was different to the extent that her tributary arrangement appears to have been exclusively with the Kashmiris at Gilgit. The reason was geographical; Nagar's only feasible outlet lay over the Chalt bridge and down the road to Gilgit. The place, in other words, was a dead end. But, by the same token, one wonders how its subjugation could be justified in strategic terms. None of the Hindu Kush passes debouched into the state and, to judge by their maps, the Russians were not even aware of its existence. Aside from the vexed question of Chalt, the only reason Nagar was being drawn into the conflict was because Durand had decided that much the easiest way to invade Hunza was to move up the Nagar side of the river. Ever since Biddulph's day the Nagaris had been regarded as less militarily formidable than their Hunza neighbours. Furthermore, with Nagar conquered, the flank of Hunza, in the elementary strategic language of the day, would have been turned. In winter there should be no difficulty in fording the Hunza river at any number of places and the whole country would thus be exposed.

Durand, marshalling his troops and arranging extra rations and clothing for them with the overstrained Kashmir commissariat, left his departure for Gilgit to the last moment. He arrived there on the very day that the final detachment of his precious Gurkhas was overwhelmed by the first blizzard of winter on the Great Himalaya. Significantly the casualties almost equalled those that would be sustained during the whole of the forthcoming campaign; a hundred men were frostbitten, many lost hands and feet, and twenty died. The weather and, above all, the mountains could be as formidable as the firepower of the Dards.

As the passes were slammed shut behind him Durand, like a breathless traveller who has hurled himself aboard a moving train, settled down to the counting and disposition of his possessions. The greatest worry concerned supplies and transport. One of his officers reckoned that to keep a single regiment supplied for a week required nine hundred and twenty porter loads. At Gilgit there were two Kashmir Imperial Service Regiments—not to mention the Gurkhas, Agency bodyguard, engineers, etc.—and they were about to be marooned for six months. Gilgit produced barely enough for its own inhabitants, so that everything had to be brought in from Kashmir. Wending over the Great Himalaya passes to Astor, down the Hattu Pir descent to the Shaitan Nare, then across the Indus in a flimsy ferry boat and on to Gilgit, there had plied all summer a never-ending stream of Balti porters and mules. To be pressed into service on the Gilgit road, according to one observer, was the equivalent of being sent to a Siberian salt mine. Men and mules died like flies and the track became a grizzly two-hundred-mile-long knackers' yard. The guideless traveller followed the bones; a blind man could have followed his nose.

The situation by the end of October was that most of the supplies had crossed the high passes but were stuck at Astor. To bring them on down the worst stretch of the whole road from Astor to the Indus required the services of every man and beast available. But these thousands of extra mouths could not possibly be fed through the winter. Somehow they had to shift the supplies during the next three or four weeks and then be got out of Dardistan to Kashmir or Baltistan. This massive operation was still in progress when the guns finally opened fire up the Hunza gorge. A combination of superhuman effort and a favourable turn in the weather saw its successful conclusion, but those who described the war as 'one of the most brilliant little campaigns in military history' were thinking as much of the logistical achievement as of the heroics at the front.

Matters were made somewhat easier thanks to teams of Pathan road-builders and Kashmiri boat-builders. Captain Aylmer, Durand's only military engineer and a key figure in the campaign, threw a new bridge across the Astor river and, with the help of a roll of telegraph wire awaiting erection at Bunji, constructed a rope ferry across the Indus. In the previous year Robertson, en route for Kafiristan, had lost all his baggage and most of his followers when the current had swept away one of the ferries. Now, with new boats and with Aylmer's wires to attach them to, the crossing was both quicker and safer. The improvement of the Kashmir–Gilgit road had been entrusted to private contractors who were working round the clock. With road-building envisaged as the rationale for the whole campaign, these contractors were now needed at the front. The Pathan navvies, to their huge delight, were formed into a paramilitary force and issued with guns. So were their English overseers, who were enrolled as officers in the Volunteer Reserve. A couple of globe-trotting sportsmen who had got caught up in the mêlée were similarly pressed into service as was Mr.E. F. Knight, special correspondent of. *The Times*; he found himself commanding a platoon of Pathan navvies.

Including a few local levies this gave Durand a total force of about two thousand men. Half of these, however, had to be kept in reserve to organise and guard the supply line. The possibility of the Chitralis exploiting the situation or of the Chilasis descending on Bunji was as real to Durand as it had been to Biddulph. In fact, in the case of the Chilasis, Durand rather hoped that they would rise; already he was thinking ahead and looking for a pretext to occupy Chilas and open direct communications from there to the Punjab.

It was thus with just on a thousand men that in late November the Hunza Nagar Field Force moved up to Chalt. On the 29th the ultimata about extending the road to Nagar and Hunza were sent off. The replies were a mere formality; Durand had already jumped the gun to the extent of building a new bridge across the Hunza river. Uzr Khan of Nagar deprived the envoy of his horse and sent him packing. Safdar Ali was so abusive that his actual words were deemed too unpleasant for publication. 'We will cut off your head, Colonel Durand, and then report you to the

Government of India' had been one of his more recent threats. On December 1 the British force duly crossed the river and entered Nagar territory. By nightfall they occupied the first ridge and were within sight of the fortress of Nilt. No opposition had been encountered but it was known that Nilt was held in strength.

Just what the enemy's strength amounted to was an open question. Estimates at the time put the combined forces of Hunza and Nagar at five thousand men. But given the total population of thirteen thousand this is certainly too high. Four thousand might be nearer the mark but of these half were stationed on the Hunza bank and appear to have taken little part in the action. In the main their arms were matchlocks, long cumbersome weapons that had to be loaded by ramming the charge down the barrel and ignited with a smouldering fuse. A few, indeed, had breech-loaders left by the likes of Lockhart and Grombtchevski, and much was made of this fact by those anxious to prove that it was a fair fight. It seems unlikely, however, that there can have been more than a hundred modern weapons and the ammunition for them was almost exclusively home-made. The British force, on the other hand, was equipped throughout with breech-loaders and also had the Gatling—a machine gun—and two seven-pounder mountain guns.

These last were expected to make short work of the Nilt fortifications. On December 2 they came into action at the unprecedentedly short range of two hundred and fifty yards and had no effect. The Dards, howling their derision and firing from the narrowest of peepholes, plugged away at anyone foolish enough to provide a target. Casualties mounted, while the defenders went practically unscathed. 'It was a terrible task to set any man', but the only way Durand could see of gaining the advantage was to send Aylmer with fifty Gurkhas to blow up the main gate. As the latter scurried forward to lay their charge, Durand, giving a display of heroics out of keeping with his position, stood in full view and a comfortable hundred and eighty yards range of the enemy; he was promptly bowled over. The bullet, a homemade one consisting of a garnet encased in lead, had hit him in the most delicate part of the body variously described as the upper leg, the pelvis and the groin.

Meanwhile Aylmer had reached the main gate and was laying his gunpowder. According to the man from *The Times*, who seems to have deserted his post in order to get a good view of the action, this was 'one of the most gallant things recorded in Indian warfare'. The sappers were being fired into at such short range that when Aylmer was hit in the leg his uniform was scorched by the gunpowder and his skin singed. At the first attempt the fuse went out. Again he had to brave what looked to Mr. Knight like certain death. A rock, hurled from the wall, crushed his hand but, at the third go, he struck a match and re-ignited the fuse. 'This time a terrific explosion followed'. Before the debris had settled three British officers and six Gurkhas, their revolvers blazing and *kukris* flashing, tore into the breech. In a desperate scuffle in which all but one was wounded they held the position and prayed for reinforcements. Unfortunately though, in their frantic pursuit of glory, they had forgotten to sound the advance or to tell the rest of the storming party what had happened. The breech was enveloped in dust and smoke, and to all but the nine sappers it looked as if the explosion had come from a powder magazine inside the fort. The storming party therefore stayed put, the guns continued to pound the walls and the sharpshooters to fire at the peepholes. Not till Lieutenant Boisragon, the only one of the nine still unwounded, retraced his steps through the fire of his own side to look for reinforcements, was it realised what had happened. The news was greeted with lusty cheers that echoed across the valley. Within minutes a steady stream of men was pouring into the fort whilst on the far side the Dards poured out into the ravine of the Nilt tributary. 'The boys had behaved like heroes', thought Durand, and for Aylmer and Boisragon V.C.s were waiting.

'And now', according to Durand who wrote a fraught letter on the engagement to brother Morty, 'came the mistake of the day.' Instead of pursuing the Dards down into the Nilt ravine as he had ordered, the whole force entered the fort and stayed there, 'collecting flags' and generally ransacking the place. This gave the Dards time to occupy a network of prepared defences on the far side of the precipitous ravine; by morning they were in a defensive position stronger than that provided by the walls of Nilt. Captain Bradshaw, the luckless individual on whom command devolved when Durand was hit, maintained that the Kashmiri regiment had let success go to their heads and were out of control. No such excuse was made by their commanding officer, the flamboyant

Townshend. He seems to have been in complete ignorance of Durand's masterplan.

However this may be, by next morning Durand's fears had been justified. As the Pathan navvies moved forward to repair the zigzag track down the ravine they were met by a devastating fusillade from the other side. Three men were killed and five wounded, including the British officer in charge of artillery. This was half as many casualties as during the whole of the previous day's action, and it brought the number of British officers seriously wounded up to four. Bradshaw hastily withdrew and Knight was in no doubt that the skirmish must count as a victory to the Dards. Worse though was to follow. For there was no way round the enemy's new position; the guns made no impression on their stone breastworks and reconnaissances along the bed of the Hunza river and across to the other side of the valley revealed no chinks in the defensive position. The advance was halted, the officers scratched their heads at what seemed to be a position more formidable than any dreamt of in the military text books; and for nearly three weeks the affair hung in the balance.

Durand, tossing on his sick bed, was frantic. What the devil had Bradshaw been doing? 'The game was in our hands . . . or rather we had won all but the last trick and my partner threw that away and the rubber.' He was in despair and for the first time the cracks began to show in his deadpan, devil-may-care outlook. The failure of the expedition and the incompetence of Bradshaw became obsessions. 'There was nothing to stop us, nothing that evening, and if I had been on my legs we should have had another fort by nightfall.' He was tempted, he later admitted, to blow his brains out. His nerves were so shattered that, instead, he ordered himself back to Gilgit, 'for here I cannot worry'. But worry he did and most of all for the blow to his reputation and for the effect this reverse would have on the future of the Agency. Lansdowne and Morty would stand by him but 'the fools at home may funk'.

'I am wonderfully well, no pain in the day and only discomfort at night and bad rest,' he wrote on December 11. Had the bullet been fired from a rifle he would have been dead. As it was, half-spent, it had 'threaded half a dozen important passages without injuring one'; as a curiosity the lead-encased garnet would have been better in a museum than in his groin, but he would now present it to his sister as a keepsake; Morty was to get the cane he was carrying at the fatal moment.

This levity soon faded when it was discovered that an abscess had developed inside the wound. The scar had to be reopened and it was months before he was on his feet, and a year before he could walk without a stick. As an explanation for his wildly erratic state of mind throughout 1892 the constant pain and frustration go a long way. Durand was nothing if not a man of action. Fortuitous though his appointment to Gilgit may have been, he had soon acquired a taste for the mountains and longed to come to terms with them. A little surprisingly it was he who wrote most convincingly of the lure of mountain travel.

It was the existence of the nomad, the charm of which, once tasted, works like madness in the blood and suddenly fills the sufferer, when mewed up within the four walls of a house, with a wild longing to be away, wandering it matters not where.

For the next three months he would have his fill of being mewed up within four walls and the experience did not please him. Gilgit became hateful, the steep drab slopes seemed to imprison him and the distant snow-capped peaks to mock him. He must live vicariously, through the heroics of his boys and above all through the exploits of his closest friend, George Robertson. If there is another explanation for his state of mind it is the comings and goings of the Surgeon-Major. Robertson was two years his senior but looked more. He was tall, bald and stern faced, a man 'whose determination was matched only by his tact'. The less stable Durand didn't just trust his judgement implicitly; he hung on his strength and maturity; Robertson was reassurance. When he was about, everything was possible but when he left the world fell apart; there was no-one to talk to, no-one to encourage him.

All had been worry and uncertainty before the departure of the Hunza Nagar Field Force. Then in the nick of time Robertson had arrived back from his long exile in Kafiristan; it was almost as if the expedition had been delayed specially for him. Along with the Kafir chiefs he was piloting back to India, he had been redirected up the Hunza road to serve as Durand's assistant for the duration of the campaign. It was knowing that Robertson was still there at the Nilt ravine that kept Algy sane during the anxious days after his disablement. In spite of Bradshaw, George would pull something out of the bag.

George, acting as Agent in Durand's absence, was doing his best; but the news was not good. 'Still at Nilt,' he cabled on December 3; 'desultory firing; weather fine; troops in good health', on the 4th; 'force remains at Nilt, everything satisfactory', did for the 6th. But by the 8th something more by way of an explanation was obviously called for; 'the position to be taken is practically a precipice unturnable at both ends. The seven-pounder gun has no effect on rebel's defence.' On the 9th the troops were still healthy and in good spirits and everything satisfactory, but by the 15th there was again no progress to report; 'all our reconnaissances have failed to find a way of forcing rebels' position so far. It is of immense strength while they multiply their *sangars* [breastworks] daily. There is nothing for it but patience.'

This was all very well, but the spectacle of the first British offensive in Dardistan being brought to a standstill was not doing much for imperial prestige; the wonder was that all the other Dard tribes had not already risen. There was also a very real threat that if the stalemate lasted through the winter Safdar Ali would have either Chinese or Russian allies by the spring. By now, too, news of the expedition had broken in the London press. The traditional way of disarming Westminster's chariness about such escapades was to announce that the action was already over, the frontier readjusted, British arms triumphant and the natives garlanding those who had delivered them from oppression. This time there was only the storming of Nilt to report. All the evidence suggested that the enemy was offering staunch and united support. By Robertson they might be labelled as rebels, but to the few who had ever heard of Hunza it was not at all clear that the state lay within India's traditional frontiers nor that any good would come of its conquest. On the 13th a Reuters' correspondent, in search of background, filed a long report from the Oriental University Institute, Woking, in which Leitner castigated the whole Gilgit policy. 'I cannot conceive anything more wanton or suicidal than the present advance'. The doctor had just had a letter from Jafr Khan of Nagar and was confident that, if only the government of India had asked him, he could personally have settled the whole

business without a shot being fired. Next day he addressed a
public meeting in the Westminster Town Hall and again went over
the same ground. The metaphors might get mixed and the grammar
muddled—the government was 'troubling waters in order to fish
in them', and Hunza-Nagar had been 'mismanaged owing to the
incompetent manner in which my information has been misused'
—but the meaning was clear enough. The Gilgit Agency must be
withdrawn, the Dards left alone and, in particular, the policy
of opening up the place with military roads—which could only
assist any Russian advance—must be abandoned.

By now the unfortunate Bradshaw might have been tempted to
agree. He was doing his best—full scale attacks were mounted on
the 8th and 12th—but the Dards were better entrenched than they
had been two weeks ago. The position looked hopeless and, with the
cold at night becoming intolerable, he was all for blowing up Nilt
and withdrawing to Chalt. Supplies were also running short and
first the Pathan navvies were ordered to the rear and then Bradshaw himself was recalled by Durand. It looked as if the game
was over.

The Dards, inferior in every department save a doubtful
numerical advantage, had played their one trump and it was
unbeatable. What every traveller in the region had noted about
the incredible strength of some of the natural defensive positions
was being dramatically demonstrated. The largest and best
equipped force that could reasonably operate in such terrain had
been halted less by men than by mountains. How instructive it
would have been to have watched the action from the glistening
terraces of Rakaposhi immediately above. And how sobering.
Tearing one's gaze from the majesty of rocky summits sailing
above a sea of billowing snow, one would dutifully peer down the
spine of some lolling glacier to the dark ledge where the Dards sat
huddled round their cooking fires. From a pile of stones on the
extremity of the ledge would come a puff of smoke; the thin
report would arrive minutes later. Across the chasm that divided
this ledge from the next the reply would be a loud sharp crack or
the thump of a seven-pounder. A reconnaissance party crawling
down the cliffs to the bed of the Hunza river would appear as
absurd and unworthy of the setting as Mr. Knight out practising
with his golf clubs, or the Gurkhas chasing a football. There is

something not just ridiculous but profane about organised war-mongering in such wild and mighty surroundings.

Come December 20 the watcher on Rakaposhi might have noticed that the firing was brisker and that, today, in the very bottom of the chasm, there was a small force of a hundred or so British and Gurkhas; they had crept down there during the night. Now, with ropes and pickaxes, they started to climb the two thousand feet of sheer precipice directly below four of the Dard breastworks. The defenders craned over their *sangars* to see what was happening and were greeted by a hail of bullets from across the chasm. The climbers continued to inch their way upwards; an avalanche of boulders toppled down by the Dards narrowly missed them. By mid morning they were near their destination. A flash of bayonets and a few fleeing figures were all that could be seen of the first encounter. But as the attackers issued from the captured breastworks and worked their way to the next and the next, a pattern emerged, the sudden rush, the flurry, the bolting figures, the dynamiting of the *sangar*. As the defenders fled they provided an easy target for the guns across the ravine; 'it was like potting rabbits'. The answering fire faltered, Dards no longer waited to be attacked, and a mass exodus gathered momentum. Not only from the Nilt ravine but from all the forts further up the Nagar ledge and from their equivalents on the Hunza side, the men streamed out, discarding their guns, heading home.

Insignificant as it would have looked from Rakaposhi, it meant a lot to the men who had spent three weeks on the Nilt ridge. Imperial and regimental honour had been satisfied, another legend added to the many, a handful of reputations made, another V.C. won. The 'unassailable position' had been turned, 'the rebels' routed, and the British Indian frontier established, at last, on the Hindu Kush. If one looks at the Nilt ravine today and one ponders the problem as it then presented itself, one cannot but marvel at the bravery and ingenuity that led to its capture. The trouble is that as one looks on the setting as a whole, from the dark and terrible river gorge to the stacked grandeur of precipice and peak, the thin strata to which human endeavour is limited is almost lost to sight.

'Brilliant achievement on the 20th', began Robertson's telegram. 'Shall be in Nagar tonight. Jafr Khan has made complete submission. Uzr Khan fled.' On the 22nd an advance party crossed the

Hunza river and occupied the Mir's palace. Safdar Ali had also fled and resistance was at an end. 'If you only knew how happy and relieved I am,' wrote Durand from Gilgit. 'I was heartbroken at the thing failing that should have been a success and now luckily owing to George Robertson and Colin Mackenzie [who had succeeded Bradshaw as military commander] it is again a brilliant success. Morty is not landed in a hole and my reputation is saved.'

Safdar Ali was pursued up towards the Killik pass but he escaped to Sinkiang with his wives. Uzr Khan, having no such bolt hole, was eventually captured and deported. The Hunza palace was ransacked and its contents, including what Leitner called the archives of the Hunza state, were auctioned in Gilgit. As military governor of Hunza, Durand appointed Charlie Townshend—'I didn't know how to thank him'—and his pal, Curly Stewart, as political officer. The Mir's zenana was soon decorated with pin-ups of the Alhambra starlets; and as Stewart, gazing forlornly across the moonlit valley at Rakaposhi, bemoaned the absence of 'mashing' in the Hindu Kush, Townshend shattered the serenity of the loveliest view in the whole world with a rousing chorus to the accompaniment of his beloved banjo.

A proclamation was issued declaring that Hunza 'now belongs to the British government and so long as the inhabitants obey the British officer at Hunza all will go well with them'. It was clearly Townshend's impression, and Durand's intention, that annexation and the post of military governor would be permanent. This was a far cry from earlier protestations that the demands of imperial defence need not interfere with the independence of the state, or that the British quarrel was not with the people of Hunza but with their ruler. Durand himself was still suspicious of the Dards and would continue to regard the smallest incident as evidence of treachery. But fortunately wiser counsels prevailed. Townshend was quickly withdrawn and his post abolished. Stewart soldiered on as political officer until the summer when Younghusband came up from Kashmir to relieve him. By then a half-brother of Safdar Ali had been installed as Mir and the Chinese were laboriously moving towards an acceptance of the loss of their 'outlying dependency'. Younghusband's position was further helped by the presence of a small garrison of Kashmir Imperial Service Troops. But he still found evidence that his earlier diagnosis had been correct; that the war had been unnecessary and that the right sort of officers could have won the co-operation of the people without a shot being fired. Far from resenting their conquerors, the men of Hunza showed a ready loyalty and rather proved Younghusband's point when in 1892 and again in 1895 they voluntarily furnished a force of irregulars to serve under Gilgit's orders in Chitral.

But an even more damning indictment of the 1891 war was revealed by the map-making activity that followed. The Russian Foreign Minister of the day is supposed to have said, on hearing news of Hunza's defeat, 'ils ont fermé la porte au nez'. In fact the door had been closed for a very long time. When the Killik, Mintaka, Shimshal and all the other passes that led down into Hunza had been mapped and assessed, the officer in charge of the survey reported that 'we have no reason to fear a Russian advance through the passes'. This was borne out by the officers of the Pamir Boundary Commission in 1893. An invasion force half the size of that feared by Algernon Durand could never have reached Hunza, let alone Kashmir.

13. A Stroll Down the Indus

'One down and two to go' would have been an apposite toast for the Gilgit officers as they ushered in the new year of 1892. Durand himself was feeling a new man. The wound seemed better, the papers were hailing the Hunza expedition as 'brilliant' and his precious reputation was restored. He had just written to Morty apologising for recent gloom, and he was putting a brave face on the imminent departure to India of George Robertson. It was to be business as usual. The success of the Hunza–Nagar affair vindicated his hard-line approach to the Dard problem; he was emboldened to proceed further. Of the two other centres of Dard intransigence, Chitral might have to wait; Aman-ul-Mulk still clutched the reins of power and no pretext for direct intervention could be expected till he died. But Chilas, which it would anyway be preferable to secure first, was a different story. The Chilasis had held back during the Nagar fighting but now they were showing more spirit; in January they ejected a man who was said to be the Kashmiri agent in the place. 'I am of course going to make something out of this', Algy wrote to Morty. A few weeks later he had worked out a scheme; 'I think it could be done without fighting, or with hardly any, this winter if we manage it properly.'

Chilas, lying south of Gilgit in the sweltering canyon of the Indus, was a long way from the Hindu Kush watershed and had no obvious relevance to the Russian threat. Since Leitner had brought its existence to notice quarter of a century before, it had been neglected and probably no European had ever entered the town itself; the people had a reputation for fanaticism and were best left alone. True, they could in theory cut Gilgit's vital supply line by falling on Bunji whenever they felt like it. But, since defeat at the hands of the Dogras forty years before, they had been a peaceable if not punctilious feudatory of Kashmir; the recent expulsion of one Kashmiri was no reason to suppose that all this had changed.

What had changed, though, was the relative importance of the place. For, far from the Indus valley being a dead end of impenetrable gorges and savage tribes, Durand now believed that through Chilas and south from there over a pass called the Babusar lay the most direct route between Gilgit and British India. He might make a lot of the vulnerability of his supply line at Bunji but the fact of the matter was that Chilas was less a threat than a temptation. If he could open the Babusar route he might in time be freed from his dependence on Kashmir. No more pleading with devious Kashmir officials and no more heartache over the inefficiencies of the Srinagar commissariat. When reinforcements were needed, instead of waiting for months for another ill-equipped batch of half-trained Dogras, he could whistle up a battalion of regular Sikhs straight from their barracks in the Punjab. Except for the Babusar pass, 14,000 feet, the route was comparatively low lying and supposedly in use for nine months of the year; it cut the distance from Gilgit to the railhead at Rawal Pindi by almost a third. Once opened, the government would soon realise the absurdity not just of trying to service Gilgit via Kashmir but of trying to control Dardistan through the Maharaja. The agent would soon be reporting, not as at present to the Resident in Kashmir, but to the Lieutenant-Governor of the Punjab. And once that was established as more logical and expeditious, Kashmir must soon be relieved of all responsibilities in Gilgit and Dardistan.

That was Algy Durand's dream—it had been Lockhart's too—and one that Morty probably shared. It was not, however, the policy of the Government of India. 'Rumours as to the prevalence of excitement amongst the Chilasi tribes', which was all they would concede to Algy's repeated warnings of trouble, were not to be used as a pretext for a move down the Indus. No action was to be taken 'that might lead to a collision with the Chilasi tribes', and there was no intention of opening the new road. All this was made as plain as could be during the summer of 1892. At the time Algy was unable to heed it, later he was simply unwilling to.

The flash of new year sunshine which had bathed all his schemes in a bright and possible light had been followed by black despondency. Gilgit, a far from beautiful place at the best of times, is dreary beyond credence in winter. The riot of pasture and blossom that in summer marks out the little oasis from river sand and mountain rock is gone; the town is indistinguishable from the scarred sterility of its surroundings. The dust turns to mud, the snow is more often slush, and firewood is at a premium. The noblest of Dards looks less than picturesque as, pinched and snivelling, he coughs away the hours in some dripping, smoke-filled *chai* shop.

By February Durand still couldn't walk and remained confined to the Agency. The absence of Robertson began to tell. Manners Smith, his other political assistant and the man who had won the V.C. at Nilt, was no comfort; he presumed to have serious misgivings about the Chilas scheme. Stewart was in Hunza and the irrepressible Townshend had been sent to Baltistan; in Gilgit his Kashmir regiment could not be fed through the winter. With the exception of Mackenzie, 'the only man I can talk to', his heroes were getting on his nerves. Once again, brooding gave way to an unreasoned sense of danger; disaster, imminent and disgraceful, stalked his day-dreams and filled the long wakeful nights. He must have more officers, more troops, more encouragement.

As February gave way to a long and dismal March, his letters to Morty plumbed the depths of a despair that was now close to manic depression.

I can see nothing but defeat unless we are reinforced and you cannot do that before June. It is a nightmare to me that we should be beaten here, and it will in the end ruin my head and my heart. I have had three years of anxieties and worries which no-one who has not been here can conceive—folly, ignorance and lies in Kashmir have driven me to the utmost limits of my endurance over and over again. We have no roads, no bridges, no food, consequently not enough troops. I can see nothing but disaster every night and try to think things are brighter in the morning, but this is no condition for a man to be in. My wound is not yet healed up and I am weak and useless. It is not right to leave me here for the country's sake. I had rather die in obscurity than fail and bring defeat on the first force to meet the Russians. . . . How can one do any good with such depression? If you can get me away from this place with honour by April 1, for God's sake do so.

And a few days later.

I must get away and trust you have sent for me. I cannot stand this place much longer. .... I am beginning to hate the whole thing and to loathe the sight of my table. .... I feel that if you do not send for me at once on duty, I must leave or resign my appointment.

There was no need to read between the lines; Algy was cracking up and the sooner he was out of Gilgit the better. Morty sent Robertson to take over as Acting Agent and Algy was recalled to India. He was to take six months' home leave. But as soon as the pressure was off, he regained his equilibrium. He spent three months in Simla showing no anxiety to see England; then, when occasion offered, he gave up the whole idea of rest and dashed back to Gilgit. Morty, who alone had the evidence of his erratic state of mind, should have stopped him. He didn't and by October Algy was back in the Agency bungalow, still badly crippled, still far from stable and about to face the worst crisis in his career.

The occasion that had offered itself was certainly tempting. On August 20 Aman-ul-Mulk of Chitral at last died; the long foreseen struggle for the Mehtarship began immediately. Afzul-ul-Mulk, Lockhart's manly favourite and Durand's too, chanced to be in the vicinity of Chitral fort and promptly seized power. From a British point of view it was most satisfactory. There was therefore no great outcry when he proceeded to liquidate every conceivable rival; only Nizam-ul-Mulk, Lockhart's *bête noir*, and a half brother, Amir-ul-Mulk, managed to escape. Nizam sought asylum in Gilgit, which was something of an embarrassment; better that, though, thought Durand, than that he should turn to the Russians. The half-brother, who survived the holocaust because he was thought mentally defective, fled south to his uncle, an agressive Pathan prince called Umra Khan who was observing the situation in Chitral with as much interest as Robertson. The latter swiftly congratulated Afzul on his succession and waited on the Government's permission to visit Chitral, there to dictate terms for recognition of the new Mehtar and for the continuation of the subsidy paid to his father.

It was just as well that for once Gilgit did wait. For, in November, almost simultaneously with the go-ahead from Simla, there came news that Afzul was dead. He had been murdered, and succeeded, by an uncle with the confusingly similar name of Sher Afzul.* This was truly a bolt from the blue. It was known that Umra Khan had been intriguing with both Nizam and Amir-ul Mulk, but this Sher Afzul was a complete outsider. He had in fact been lurking in Badakshan for most of his brother's thirty-five year reign. A pensioner of the Amir of Kabul, he was presumably the Afghan candidate—which was distinctly bad news for Gilgit. Anglo–Afghan relations were going through another uncomfortable phase; and with Ianov showing scant respect for Afghan territory on the Pamirs, Chitral too could soon be the venue for Cossack manœuvres. Suddenly the presence of young Nizam in Gilgit took on a new significance. From being the liability of Lockhart's day and the embarrassment of Afzul's short reign, he emerged as the great white hope. Was he not, argued Robertson and Durand, the rightful successor? And for all his faults was he not uncharacteristically humane, well disposed towards the British and, above all, totally dependant upon them?

Lord Lansdowne was not so sure; he was all for waiting to see how Sher Afzul behaved. But Algy Durand could not let the opportunity pass. Dispensing, this time, with the obligation of referring his plan of action to India, he simply launched the new candidate from the top of the Shandur pass into the choppy waters of Chitral. Officially he pleaded that the idea was Nizam's, that he had no right to detain him in Gilgit, and that if Nizam succeeded it could only be in the best of British interests. In fact, he almost certainly instigated the move; he definitely encouraged it and he took every possible precaution against its failure. This included massing troops and artillery in Nizam's rear and sending the local levies, that is the Hunza volunteers proudly sent by Younghusband, to march with him. If the boat was somewhat frail it had been launched with enough push to send it clean across the pond.

While Durand, having limped to the confines of Chitral, gazed approvingly on Nizam's progress, Robertson, showing even less respect for Dard feelings, was burning down Chilas. Durand would soon concede that it was a big mistake to tackle Chilas at the

---

*The Dards were not the only ones with a confusing similarity of names. Amongst less than fifty British officers who would serve in Gilgit between 1890 and 1895 there were two Stewarts, two Bruces, a Dr. Roberts as well as a Dr. Robertson, and a Gorton, a Gordon and a Gurdon.

same time as Chitral. It would strain his staff, his troops and his transport, not to mention his peace of mind, beyond breaking point. But, on the other hand, why not strike while the occasion offered? Arriving back in Gilgit in October he had found the place so well stocked with grain and supplies that he could afford to keep all his troops in Dardistan throughout the winter. Chilas had furnished further provocation; another Kashmir agent had just been ejected, this time with a bullet in his back. And finally, for this winter, he had the services of Robertson. He had just wangled another six British officers out of the Viceroy bringing his total to twenty-four, but George was worth more than the whole lot together. Moreover George shared his dream about the Chilas–Babusar route. If he himself had been impressed by the official warnings against interference in the Indus valley, Robertson had soon chafed away his anxieties. The thing had to be done and, if Algy was a trifle chary, the Surgeon-Major was quite happy to shoulder the responsibility. At the beginning of November, just as the Chitral crisis was exploding, he had marshalled a small force and set off for Bunji and a stroll down the Indus valley.

Unlike the Hunza–Nagar expedition, or the later siege of Chitral, the Chilas affair would be ignored by contemporary chroniclers of British bravado. It scarcely made the newspapers, let alone stiff covers. No V.C.s were awarded and no congratulations telegraphed. Inglorious, even a little shaming, it was hushed up and then speedily forgotten. 'It had no pretentions to being war,' explained one of those involved; 'it was just a thoroughly important and sporting move which included fighting'. For Lieutenant C. G. Bruce, the man who wrote this, it was quite true. He shot the Indus rapids with a couple of convicted assassins and, in the absence of supplies, provided for his troops by stalking partridges; the troops covered him while he did so. It all looked very casual and if things didn't go according to plan it could be maintained that there wasn't a plan and that the various actions were just impromptu skirmishes. A plan there was, however, as witnessed by Durand's letters of the previous winter. He regarded it as the boldest stroke of all and characterised the whole business as 'l'audace, toujours l'audace'. The two principal engagements were serious and hotly contested battles in which casualties were heavy. And if the paraphernalia of full scale war was missing, if there was no ultimatum or declaration, if the troops involved were comparatively few, and if supply and communications arrangements were negligible, this was not because they were thought unnecessary; rather because there was no opportunity to arrange them. It was a rough and ready affair which clearly revealed the Agency's tactics towards the Dards as the stark combination of recklessness and provocation that Leitner had always suspected.

Robertson's proclaimed destination was Gor, the small semi-independent settlement above the Indus between Bunji and Chilas. According to Durand's published account the move had been sanctioned by the government and was made in response to a request from the local people for closer ties with Gilgit. The first part of this was quite untrue. The government knew nothing of the move, would have stopped it if they had, and had anyway forbidden interference in this direction. The pretext, too, sounds unconvincing. The people of Gor proved less than enthusiastic about their visitors. Moreover, had they really sought closer ties, it should not have been necessary to send two senior officers—Robertson had with him a Major Twigg—to such a remote cluster of villages. Nor, if it was meant to be a peaceful mission, should they have needed three hundred troops.

Durand's account is also very insistent that no advance beyond Gor was originally envisaged; for what followed he laid the credit —or as others saw it, the blame—on Robertson. Perhaps this time he was being honest, though Bruce didn't think so; he baldly states that it was Durand who 'found it necessary to move into Chilas with troops'. Certainly Durand can't have overlooked the unsettling effect of sending such a force into a hitherto untouched area. The possibility of a hostile reaction from Chilas was something he probably counted on; as he told Morty, it certainly was not cause for alarm. 'All promises to go without a hitch,' he wrote, 'we shall make a good business of it in time.' His only real anxiety was that the government might get alarmed.

In Gor, Robertson left instructions with Twigg to push forward more troops and supplies as soon as carriage could be arranged and then, with as many men as he could feed, promptly 'disappeared into space'. This colloquialism of Bruce's is a fair description of the Indus valley; there is something distinctly other-worldly about its horrifying emptiness. Save for the dramatic changes in temperature, the seasons pass unnoticed; rainfall is negligible, vegetation non-existent. The scenery, if one can call it that, is a testimony less to the gentle forces of nature than to sudden primordial upheavals. Seismic rumbles set the crags oscillating; cataclysms scour out the defiles. When earlier in the century, a chunk of Nanga Parbat fell across the river, it dammed it to a depth of a hundred fathoms and the lake tailed back almost to Gilgit; when it broke, a Sikh army camped two hundred miles away in the Punjab had been wiped out.

Undeterred by this 'abomination of desolation', Robertson led his little force along precipitous tracks on the right bank of the river from Gor to a village called Thalpen. It was the only defensible place within his reach, he explained; it was also well beyond Gor territory and immediately opposite the town of Chilas on the left bank. The attack, for fear of which he had sought shelter, now obligingly materialised. Twigg was ambushed in Gor, relief detachments from Bunji had to fight their way through and, before Thalpen, the enraged Dards surrounded the invader in their hundreds. In a move that would soon be repeated in Chitral, Robertson tried to cross to Chilas and seize that first. The enemy anticipated him, his rafts were fired on and for a time the situation looked extremely grave. Because of the troops concentrated on the Chitral frontier in support of Nizam, there were insufficient at Gilgit to provide a relief force. It was too late in the year to call for reinforcements from Kashmir and the most that could be done was to try and keep open the communications line down the river.

But ultimately it was the patent weakness of Robertson's position that saved him. Instead of starving him out, the Dards decided to rush in for the kill. Outnumbered by ten to one Robertson still had the important advantages of superior arms and a well entrenched position. The attack spent itself and, as the enemy turned, out rushed the defenders. In the rout that followed, the Kashmiri soldiers pulled off their trousers the better to give chase; the Dard losses were considerable. Robertson immediately crossed the river, burned Chilas and began construction of a fortified position just above it. No doubt the Chilasis would be back, but for the time being the place was in his hands. Predictably Durand decided to retain it and throughout the winter of 1892–93 all efforts were directed to improving communications back to Bunji.

As in the previous year, Christmas again brought plenty to celebrate. Sher Afzul had fled back to Afghanistan and Nizam was safely installed in Chitral; true to his promises, he was now requesting the visit of a British mission to confer recognition of his title and the establishment of a permanent British agent in Chitral. Durand, again without waiting for government approval, acceded to the first request and Robertson was withdrawn from Chilas to head the new mission. 'He is everything to me,' Algy told his sister-in-law; 'no one has any brains to compare with his or knows anything of the management of natives.' As for Chilas, 'I knew I was right and that though the game was bold it was the only one worth playing.' If Robertson could now 'keep his head for a week in Chitral', the Gilgit Game would be won.

By the new year Algy's optimism had risen to a wild euphoria. 'It's a lovely game we have on this frontier', and if any of 'those dogs in [the Viceroy's] council' presumed to question his recent moves, 'God smite their souls to the depths of Hell'. Would that Morty could come up and look over 'this place that I have made'; how good he would find it. With the whole of Dardistan about to fall into his lap he was planning for the future—a political agent in each of the Dard states and, of course, more troops to provide a garrison for each of the passes. Robertson should get at least a C.B. and he himself should be made a full colonel and an A.D.C. to the Queen. 'Then I do not despair of being Commander-in-Chief some day, but I must get on *now*.' Brother Edward had just been knighted and Morty had been Sir Mortimer for some time; surely it was now his turn.

Morty should have taken the hint, not about the knighthood but about his brother's frame of mind. Algy was again embarking on that vicious psychological see-saw; the higher the high the lower the low. By February he was betraying a sense of unease. A hundred miles away Robertson, finding Nizam both unpopular and unnerved, was getting dangerously embroiled in Chitrali politics. Worse still, seventy miles in the opposite direction, the Chilasis, with their warlike neighbours from further down the Indus valley, were reportedly massing for a counter-attack. With troops already committed to Yasin in support of Nizam and others needed to keep an eye on Nagar and Hunza, Durand had few men to spare and no idea which way to send them.

In the event it was Chilas which exploded first. The Indus Valley Rising, which had been anticipated for three months, nevertheless took the garrison in their makeshift fort above Chilas completely by surprise. The town was re-occupied under cover of darkness. When an attempt was made to clear it, a third of the garrison was either killed or wounded and all but one of the officers, including Major Daniell in command, fell. It was probably the most disastrous battle yet fought in Dardistan; had the Chilasis continued to press their attack nothing could have saved the rest of the garrison. But when Robertson had burned the town in November he had also burned the year's grain supply. 'Nice move that', thought Charlie Townshend who was now on his way back to Gilgit. Without food the attackers dispersed to their villages after twenty-four hours.

News of the disaster reached Durand while he was playing polo on the Gilgit *maidan*—the leg was at last better. He immediately sent a small detachment to relieve the Chilas garrison and, calculating that the Chilasis would allow a forty days mourning period for the slain, set early May as the deadline for reinforcements. Then came news from Robertson in Chitral; from a man who was normally impervious to panic it was serious indeed. 'We seem to be on a volcano here,' he announced. The Pathan, Umra Khan, had already grabbed a corner of the state and was threatening to chase Nizam all the way back to Gilgit. He was also threatening to attack the Kafirs. Supposedly to frustrate any such move but more probably to grab Kafiristan first, the Afghan Commander-in-Chief with three thousand troops was poised at Asmar just south of Chitral territory. From Dir in the east a fanatical mullah with a wide following was sending hired assassins against the infidel British emissaries; and, in Chitral itself, popular contempt for Nizam and his revelling was rapidly curdling into an active resentment of his foreign backers. So accustomed was the mission to threats of imminent extinction that when one of their few supporters was shot during the night on their threshold, Robertson scarcely woke to register the news. Nevertheless he was alarmed and urgently requested Durand for more troops and for the Agent himself to come to his rescue.

'It is too much,' cried Algy. 'I have had some anxious times in
my life but "upon me God", as Curly Stewart says, this about
takes the lead.' He had just paid a visit to Chilas, and the vulnerability of his Indus valley conquests had suddenly dawned on
him. Chilas itself was being properly fortified but, should the next
wave of attackers decide to mask Chilas and concentrate on its
supply line, there was no way he could see of keeping communications open. There was still no news of reinforcements from Kashmir and he had barely two hundred men left to play with. If every
one of them was moved into the Indus valley, it was unlikely that
the outposts dotted down that now simmering gorge could be
protected. 'I am anxious about Chilas but Chitral is *what I am
afraid of.*' Not only were there no more troops to send to Robertson but the Shandur pass was closed; snowblindness and frostbite
had got the last consignment. For the next month at least Robertson
would be cut off.

All this was written on April 16. Exactly a week later he again
wrote to Morty. Now mysteriously, his reserve force numbered
three hundred and he was keeping them for Chitral regardless,
apparently, of the state of the Shandur. As for Chilas, that was now
acknowledged as a hideous mistake; the Indus valley was a death
trap and troops should never have been allowed to stay there. In
fact the whole game had gone sour at the last throw. His contradictory judgements were symptomatic of a deep disillusionment.
Had even Morty deserted him? Not a word, not a line about the
desperately needed reinforcements.

I have wished myself dead over this business. . . . If I can live
through this fortnight or month I must come down to India and
go home. I cannot stand this sort of thing any longer and I will
never return to Gilgit again . . . but I don't think I shall get out
of it and I see nothing but smash and despair before me, though
I try to look at the best light but it is black. . . . Oh how I wish
I had never come to this place.

On each frantically scrawled sheet of paper he was mocked by that
fatuous direction, *Railway Station: Rawal Pindi*. Would he ever
see civilisation again? He thought not and ended with the ominous
news that he had just drawn up his will.

Whatever the wild imaginings of his tortured mind, it is pretty clear that the danger was less of defeat than of despair. Gilgit itself was in no immediate peril and his own position was less vulnerable than that of any of his predecessors. The letter was not the composition of one going forth to die for his country but of one in a state of mental collapse. It was a suicide note and probably he was only saved by the arrival of instructions recalling him to India. This time they were not issued on compassionate grounds. Within the Viceroy's Council the outcry over his unauthorised attack on Chilas and support for Nizam had become irresistible. Robertson was again to take over as Agent and Durand would never more sit at the table he so loathed nor walk through the orchard where Hayward lay buried—and where he had so nearly joined him.

14. Finis Dardarum

In the event, none of Algy Durand's gloomy forebodings of April 1893 materialised. The Chilasis did not renew the attack and the Indus Valley remained peaceful; Robertson extricated himself from Chitral; and Nizam-ul-Mulk, though still menaced by Umra Khan, managed to dig in as Mehtar. Furthermore, in November 1893, Mortimer Durand negotiated an agreement with the Amir which, while clearing the air as a prerequisite to the solution of the Pamirs' problem, included the question of Kafiristan. In effect the Kafirs were partitioned; the southern valleys, which Robertson and Lockhart had scarcely travelled, went to Afghanistan, but the northern ones, notably the Bashgal river and its tributaries, were declared outside the Amir's sphere of influence. If the stability of Dardistan could not as yet be guaranteed, the threat of Russian or Afghan intervention was visibly receding and, under the steadier hand of George Robertson, the Gilgit Agency could afford to open its doors a little. In 1893 a stream of privileged sportsmen passed through on their way to stalk on the Pamirs and the first mountaineering expeditions began to explore the glaciers and reconnoitre the peaks of the Karakorams.

Hard on their heels came the first politician 'to see for himself', a Tory who was then Member for Southport. Globe-trotting M.P.s were a standing joke in British India and the butt of many a Kipling tale; but the one who descended on Gilgit in the autumn of 1894 was no ordinary student of the East. He was, in fact, 'that most superior person', George Nathaniel Curzon. With a typical mixture of determination, scholarship and arrogance he was doing his homework for the position he most coveted, and would so young achieve, that of Viceroy of India.

Travelling from Kashmir along the new road constructed during the hectic days of 1891, he marvelled as much at the telegraph line that now ran all the way to Gilgit as at the scenery—'more impressive than beautiful, more sullen than joyous, more rugged than picturesque'. On a lintel at Bunji he carved his initials beside those of all the other sportsmen and soldiers who had ventured beyond the Indus, and then crossed 'that Tartarean trough' on the suspension bridge just completed by Captain Aylmer, V.C. Robertson was on leave at the time but the Agency afforded a warm welcome; he was particularly impressed by Biddulph's bungalow. In addition to a tennis court there was now a golf links where the wise player took a gun as well as clubs, the object being not self-defence but snipe. The whole place seemed to be booming. Besides the still numerous complement of political and military officers there was also, at last, a regiment of British Indian infantry; Algy Durand, though censured, had managed to make his point about more troops. A less acceptable sign of the times was the presence of the first British woman in Gilgit. The wife of 'some fellow in the transport corps', she was not exactly a *pukka memsahib* and it was an occasion for shudders of horror when lines of 'dubious looking lingerie' were spied in an orchard.

From Gilgit Curzon strode and rode up the new Hunza road to the Pamirs. Rakaposhi inspired a purple passage—'In that remote empyrean we visualise an age beyond the boundaries of human thought, a silence as from the dawn of time', etc.—the ruins of Nilt furnished an excuse for a rerun of the events of December 1891, and the Hunza road, still 'one of the worst tracks in the world', accounted for 'the personal physical accretions of an entire London season'. Thence over the Killik pass to the Pamirs. Like a conscientious sightseer, he quickly bagged his Marco Polo sheep and set about the sources of the Oxus. The famous paper on the subject which he later delivered to the R.G.S. lists eight Pamirs, of which he visited three, and four contending streams. Built upon the reports of every traveller and geographer who had ever hazarded a guess on the subject, buttressed with a wealth of classical allusions, and crowned with his own magisterial pronouncement, this monograph on the Oxus is a truly monumental work. But with the draft of the Anglo-Russian Pamirs agreement in its final stages, the important point was that political significance no longer attached to the subject. Elias had shown that the Panja tributary was the main feeder, Curzon decided that the Sarhad was the main feeder of the Panja, and the Wakh-jir of the Sarhad; thus the Wakh-jir glacier was the source of the Oxus. With no-one having a vested interest in disputing the matter, his verdict still stands.

Returning by way of Wakhan and Chitral, the M.P. was welcomed back to British territory at the foot of the Baroghil with a glass of cold beer and a vigorous handshake from Frank Younghusband. Younghusband, five years older and a good deal more reserved than in the days of his Karakoram travels, was now the British representative in Chitral. He had gone there with Robertson in the early days of 1893 and had stayed on when the latter was recalled to take over from Durand at Gilgit. The position should have suited him well. In Nizam-ul-Mulk, as in Safdar Ali, he was able to see the good as well as the bad; he made a real attempt both to understand and enlighten the Chitralis and he relished the responsibility of being the sole political officer in the country. He had always believed that personal contact was the best way of handling the Dards; during his stay, Nizam had strengthened his position and the country had remained at peace. His only reservation was that he wasn't actually in Chitral. He was based at Mastuj, three days' hard travelling from the capital.

The swing of the political pendulum accounted for this. In London the Liberals were back in power (which was why Curzon was at a loose end), in India Lord Lansdowne had been succeeded by Lord Elgin and on the frontier 'forward' policies were again out of favour. While Younghusband, supported by Robertson, urged that he must be permanently established in Chitral town, the most the government would concede was that he might remain temporarily at Mastuj. The Afghans had agreed to keep Sher Afzul out of the country and, if Umra Khan could also be coaxed into leaving, then Younghusband was to be withdrawn altogether as soon as the Anglo-Russian Pamir agreement was signed. The object, in other words, was not to establish an influence in Chitral—just to make sure no-one else did.

Younghusband had taken the rejection of his plans much to heart. 'Government gave the impression that they could get on perfectly well without me', and they showed it by promoting officers of half his experience over his head; it seemed that examinations counted for everything, his missions for nothing. As soon as his term in Chitral was over he would therefore resign from the service. But the man with whom Curzon rode down to Chitral was not exactly bitter. For one thing he had now finally decided 'to make religion the first interest of my life'. During the lonely months spent amidst the magnificent mountain scenery of upper Chitral 'the exploring spirit' had again come upon him. Reading and meditating, he longed to be free of government service and to devote his life to 'showing men the way across the spiritual unknown'. His mission was still vague, his belief in Providence still naïve and his motivation somewhat arrogant. But, over the years that led up to his founding of the World Congress of Faiths in 1936, he would become the first to recognise these faults.

Another consoling influence was Curzon himself. Cerebral, incisive, polished, frigid, the guest was everything the host was not. Discussing frontier policy Curzon seemed totally to discount his companion's experience and to enjoy ridiculing his opinions. Yet this was just the parliamentary habit; for to judge by his later reports in *The Times* he was lapping up every word Younghusband let fall. Unable to compete, but recognising in one another something each respected, they became the staunchest of friends. Moreover, they found common ground in a deep sense of England's imperial destiny and an equally deep mistrust of Russia. The sort of frontier bullying typified by Algernon Durand they both rejected; but their ideas were no less 'forward' and provocative for that. It was to Younghusband that Curzon, as Viceroy, would turn ten years later; and it was while doing Curzon's work as political officer to the Lhasa expedition, that Younghusband would become the scapegoat for a national sense of outrage over the handling of the Tibetans which far exceeded any doubts that were ever voiced over British policy in Dardistan.

Finding all well with Chitral and its Mehtar, Curzon returned to Gilgit over the Shandur pass. At Gupis, the first fort of any importance on the Gilgit side of the pass, Charlie Townshend, his 'somewhat unusual host', posed a rich contrast to Younghusband's austerities. His house was decorated with 'daring coloured illustrations from Parisian journals of the lighter type; and he regaled us through the evening with French songs to the accompaniment of a banjo'. A few miles upstream his 'mucker', Curly Stewart, was the political officer in Yasin and together they were again lending a distinctive style to frontier life through itching for another 'scrap'. Gupis fort was 'The Garrick' and Stewart's new house 'The Adelphi'. Of an evening they foregathered to plan their next assault on the West End. Cheap cigarettes and whisky were a poor

substitute for cigars and brandy, but there was no denying a
certain innocent pleasure in writing to the ladies about the pri-
vations and dangers of frontier life.

'I don't see how we shall get through this winter without a
pantomime rally of sorts up here,' confided Townshend to one of
his girlfriends at the beginning of November. But Curzon passed
on, primed with firsc-hand impressions; then came Younghusband,
muttering a farewell to the mountains but with the inner light
burning bright. And still all was quiet in Chitral. At the end of the
month Robertson, just back from leave, arrived on an inspection
tour of his domain; he brought with him Captain Campbell, his
senior military officer and Lieutenant Gurdon who was to resume
Younghusband's duties at Mastuj. These four men, Townshend,
Campbell, Gurdon and Robertson, would soon be seeing more of
one another than was conducive to mutual respect. During the
siege of Chitral, Robertson would blame Townshend for never
having taught his Dogras to shoot straight. At the time, though,
Townshend has him approvingly exclaiming 'Those are the men
for us.'

December passed without incident, but on January 4, 1895, the
Gupis 'Garrick' exploded into activity. According to news frantically relayed to Gilgit by Townshend, Nizam-ul-Mulk had just been
shot in the back by the half-witted Amir-ul-Mulk. The murderer
had assumed the Mehtarship, and Gurdon, who had gone to pay
his respects to Nizam, was still in Chitral town and, with an escort
of only eight men, surely in the gravest peril. Townshend immediately moved troops up to the Shandur and waited for Robertson's
authorisation to speed to the rescue.

For the Agent, as for Townshend, this was the long-awaited pretext. At last it was to be Chitral's turn. But if they were spoiling
for a fight, it is also true that events played into their hands in
such a way that the whole manœuvre appeared unavoidable.
Gurdon wrote that he was in no immediate danger and that though
Amir-ul-Mulk was the candidate of Umra Khan, he was now seeking British support. Here was justification for a political mission.
On the other hand Gurdon felt that if he attempted to withdraw
he might well be attacked—obviously cause for a hefty military
escort. Accordingly Robertson, with Campbell, Townshend and
three other officers plus some five hundred troops, embarked on

the fatal mission of 1895. In intense cold they crossed the Shandur pass and reached Mastuj on January 25. If it was just a question of observing developments and standing by to rescue Gurdon, here they should have stopped. But again events played into their hands. News now came that Umra Khan had crossed the Lowarai pass and invaded Chitral proper. Gurdon was in imminent danger again and the whole mission must press on to Chitral town. It was altogether too much like a repeat of the Chilas affair. Robertson still believed in the bold dash; communications, supplies, artillery would take care of themselves so long as one retained the initiative. The essence of dealing with the Dards was to dodge through the mountains before they could stop you, dig in and then invite attack.

On January 31 the mission reached Chitral and Robertson immediately began angling to get his force installed in the Mehtar's fortress. The situation now developed with alarming speed and unforeseeable complexity. Umra Khan's forces advanced on the important base of Drosh. Amir-ul-Mulk, who had supposedly called in the Pathans, now opposed them and begged Robertson to send his troops to stiffen the Chitrali resistance. Robertson was highly suspicious of any move that would divide his force and refused. On February 10 came news that Drosh had been betrayed. Robertson used this as grounds for taking over the fort and, once safely installed behind its twenty-five foot walls, agreed to send a token force to help against Umra Khan.

The fort was unquestionably the largest and most defensible building in the country, if not in Dardistan as a whole. Each of the four walls was about eighty yards long and the four corner towers rose to sixty feet. If there was to be fighting, its occupation was essential. On the other hand, no single move contributed more to the inevitability of conflict. For this was not just a fort; it was the *Noghor*, the ancestral home of the Mehtars of Chitral, their armoury, their treasury, their palace and, to a Mohammedan most important of all, the zenana of their womenfolk. No man had been acknowledged as Mehtar unless he held the *Noghor*, and to Chitralis of every class it represented the independence of the kingdom. Amir-ul-Mulk, for perhaps the only time in his unhappy reign, spoke for the whole of his people when he declared to Robertson that no such shame had ever come to Chitral before.

Eighty years later, it is this move that the Chitralis still regard as the most shameful and provocative of the whole siege.

Robertson realised this. 'Not one argument, plausible or ridiculous, was left unuttered to stop us making this move.' Chitralis who genuinely favoured British intervention were as incensed as the rest, and all considered it 'tantamount to annexation'. Not a single man could be pressed into moving the mission's baggage and, had not all the Chitrali troops been engaged in the hostilities with Umra Khan, there would certainly have been armed opposition. After such an outrage Robertson's belated offer to assist in the defence of the country was politically worthless.

As it was, some Chitralis were already fighting not against Umra Khan but for him; the supposed explanation was that they had no faith in Amir-ul-Mulk. Desertions now increased and, about February 20, reached landslide proportions. For it was then that Sher Afzul, the Afghan candidate, again taking everyone by surprise, reappeared on the scene. Robertson was flabbergasted. The man was supposed to be in Afghan custody four hundred miles away. Yet here he was, still the most popular claimant to the Mehtarship and now apparently inclined to side with Umra Khan. Robertson tried to negotiate and was even prepared to accept Sher Afzul as Mehtar. The government had specifically ordered him not to recognise anyone till it had been consulted; but the Agent was now down to his last card. When Sher Afzul refused to co-operate unless the *Noghor* was evacuated, Robertson promptly turned again to Amir-ul-Mulk. In a last bid to secure the loyalty of at least a few Chitralis, he recognised Amir as Mehtar. The combined forces of Umra Khan and Sher Afzul then advanced up the valley, and the British and Dogras withdrew into the fort. The order of battle was all but established—except that at the eleventh hour Robertson dramatically changed his mind about Amir-ul-Mulk. A brother of Amir, a boy of twelve whose extreme youth had alone saved him from liquidation, was suddenly preferred. After only three days as the British candidate, Amir was ceremoniously deposed in full durbar and, leading young Shuja-ul-Mulk to the biggest armchair in the fort, Robertson proclaimed him the Mehtar of Chitral.

Thus was installed the fifth Mehtar in three years. The odd thing is that throughout this period of instability there is absolutely

no evidence of Russian intrigue. Fear of it had provided the rationale for the policies that Robertson was now following to their
logical conclusion. Yet the Russians were apparently not interested.
As in the days of Lytton and Biddulph, the real complication was
provided by the Afghans. There could be little doubt that Kabul
had connived at Sher Afzul's escape from custody: it was later
established that some Afghans were actually fighting at his side.
Robertson himself was firmly convinced that there was some
massive plot uniting all the various opposition forces and it was for
this reason that he had finally turned to the youthful Shuja. Just
how formal the plot was he could only conjecture; but he could see
how all four parties stood to gain by it. In return for providing the
fighting muscle Umra Khan would get territorial concessions; by
virtue of his being the Afghan candidate, and in return for later
acknowledging Afghan suzerainty, Sher Afzul would get the
Mehtarship; Amir-ul-Mulk, as a reward for his co-operation,
would be recognised as Sher Afzul's successor; and Abdurrahman,
Amir of Kabul, who alone was capable of masterminding such an
abstruse intrigue, would have thwarted British designs on Chitral.

Looking at the thing from the outside, the Government of India
reached much the same conclusion. As the plight of the besieged
Chitral mission slowly dawned on British India, the foreign department concentrated its diplomatic offensive on neutralising the
Afghans. Up to a point it succeeded; the large Afghan force still
lurking around Asmar on the confines of Chitral stayed on the
sidelines, the Amir was mollified and Umra Khan's jealousy
of the Afghans was re-aroused. But the price for all this was
high—no less, in fact, than the surrender of the remaining half of
Kafiristan.

It was not exactly a betrayal. To the bureaucrats in Simla,
Kafiristan appeared a dead loss; they were not even certain that
under the terms of the 1893 Durand treaty, the Bashgal river, the
northern part of the country, was rightfully theirs. No-one had yet
made out a good case on strategic grounds for a British interest,
the Kafirs were too disorganised even to treat with, and, by all
accounts, Afghan influence in the shape of Islamic proselytising
was already eroding their independence. To meet the Russian
threat British policy had long favoured a strong and united Afghanistan; and it had always been accepted that the modern weapons so

readily supplied to Kabul might be used for subjugating any pockets of internal resistance.

But the irony of the whole business was that the Kafirs were being sacrificed to save the one man who might successfully have pleaded their cause. For George Robertson, the surrender of Kafiristan *was* a betrayal. Long ago he had observed that the equilibrium which had permitted the Kafirs to survive into the nineteenth century had been irreversibly upset by the arming of the Afghans; against modern breech-loaders the mountains and defiles of Kafiristan no longer compensated the Kafir archers; unless protected and patiently nursed to political maturity, the Kafirs were doomed. More than any man he had studied their way of life. He had experienced some rough handling and he had voiced some stern condemnations. Yet he had found much to admire—their blind courage, their feral grace of movement, their stamina and agility, their gaiety and, above all, their uniqueness as an ethnic curiosity. His first book, which would surely have aroused enough interest in the Kafirs to bring their imminent plight to public attention, was, in 1895, already in manuscript. But by the time it appeared, and by the time the dust settled over Chitral, it was all over; precious few independent pagan Kafirs still defied the Afghan troops; and they, like their brothers, would soon be sold down the Bashgal river—literally, if the Anti-Slavery League was to be believed.

*   *   *

Nothing military captures the imagination of the man in the street like a long and desperate siege. 'What is Gilgit?' was apparently not an unusual reaction in the early 1890s; but by the summer of 1895 most people knew about Gilgit and everyone about Chitral. In the press, from small beginnings as a telegram, the story blossomed into whole page reports and spilt over into the leader and correspondence columns; every traveller with experience of Dardistan or the frontier rushed into print. More stirring news came from the main relief expedition as it fought its way relentlessly into the mountains. But would it reach Chitral in time? The plight of Robertson and his men lifted the whole thing above the level of an ordinary frontier affair. For seven weeks not a word was heard from the beleagured *Noghor*. If they were still holding out, what was it like in there; had they enough food and water and ammunition; and if they were forced to capitulate what would be the fate of Robertson and the rest? Mrs. Robertson, a bride of only a few months, was on the high seas en route to join her husband; what news would await her in Bombay? And what price now a love-letter from Charlie Townshend?

The story of the siege has been told often enough, though never so well as by Robertson himself. It lasted for forty-eight days and included three serious engagements. The first, on March 3, the day after Shuja-ul-Mulk's installation, resulted in the defeat of a major reconnaissance effort by the garrison. One British officer, two Kashmiri officers and twenty-three other ranks were killed while the thirty men seriously wounded included Campbell, the military commander. The Kashmiri forces were reduced to a state of demoralisation from which they never really recovered, whilst the enemy were given just the encouragement necessary to press the siege with vigour.

The next potentially disastrous situation arose a month later in the early hours of April 7. A major assault on one side of the fort was used as a cover for setting fire to the other. One of the main towers went up in flames and, during frenzied attempts to extinguish it, Robertson himself fell a casualty, badly wounded in the arm. But the fort was nearest to falling on April 16. That night the sound of digging was heard in the bowels of the building. Connected with a lot of recent activity round a summer house just outside the walls, it could only mean that the place was about to be mined and that the shaft had already reached its destination. Next day the cream of the garrison's troops stormed the summer house, found the mouth of the mine, bayonetted thirty-five men who were working in it and blew the whole thing open. It was not a moment too soon; the Chitralis evidently intended to fire the mine that night and, had they been able to do so, it would not only have breached the wall but have brought most of the fort down on top of its defenders.

Fortunately the Chitralis and Pathans, though well-off for breech-loaders, were entirely without artillery; hence the attempts to mine and fire the place. The other, very real, possibility was that the garrison might have to capitulate. Arrangements were successfully made for bringing water along a covered way from the

river, but food was short; by the end all were reduced to quarter
rations and the officers had eaten their way through their horses.
Small deprivations caused disproportionate distress; the cigarettes
ran out, tea was rationed to a quarter of an ounce per man every
day and, for want of a grinding stone, the only flour was dangerously impregnated with grit. Worst of all, though, was the stench.
Four hundred troops, plus another hundred and fifty servants and
'loyal' Chitralis, were cooped up for seven weeks in a space not
much bigger than a football pitch. The old stables were designated
as the latrines, but there was a limit to the number of trenches
that could be dug and refilled; because of incessant rain in the
middle of March this limit was speedily reached. The men
sloshed through the mud in search of relief and came out retching.
The sick list grew till nearly a quarter were out of action. Even the
exuberant Townshend, who, with Campbell incapacitated, was in
military command, grew to hate the life and, in spite of the prospect of glory, to wish himself elsewhere.

Between him and Robertson there arose something more than
the inevitable friction occasioned by anxiety and close living.
Robertson preferred to think less in terms of being relieved than of
being reinforced. The last letter smuggled out of Chitral asked
for more troops to be rushed down from Mastuj. From the top of
one of the towers Robertson would daily scan the hills. There was
no question of peering up a long open valley; two miles upstream a
wall of rock made one wonder where the river came from. Behind
and above it ridge upon ridge of mountains paled away till the eye
rested on that other world of cloud and snow that was Tirich Mir.
Compared to the scarps on either side, it was at least a view,
though not one to inspire hope. Robertson knew the *paris* and
gols, the cliff faces and chasms, of the Mastuj road and he knew
how difficult it would be to force a way through them. But he
didn't despair easily. This was how it had been at Chilas. The
important thing was to be ready so that, when reinforcements
did show, they could immediately assume the offensive.

Townshend, on the other hand, was more realistic. After the
disastrous engagement of March 3 he refused to countenance
the idea of any more forays and prepared for a long siege. He had
no great hopes of seeing anything of the small detachments that
were supposed to be marching from Mastuj, and he agreed with

Algy Durand's criticism that Robertson was 'inclined to bluff about troops and get away with less than necessary'. In short, unconcerned about the questions that must one day be asked of the Agent—like what was he doing in Chitral in the first place, and how come he had assumed the role of the country's kingmaker— Townshend accepted the situation as a purely military problem and reached the obvious answer; their only chance was to sit tight. Twenty years later he would use exactly the same tactics when besieged in the fortress of Kut during the Mesopotamian campaign of the Great War; only then it would be for one hundred and fifty days. Imperturbable, patient and, so long as he had the banjo, endlessly exuberant, he was discovering in long sieges his vocation.

The last note to come out of Chitral was dated March 1 and warned that future communications might be interrupted. Ten days therefore slipped by before the horror of the situation began to dawn on the government. When it did, frantic calculations were called for. It was estimated that the besieged could not hold out beyond the end of April. But could a relief force large enough to cope with the expected resistance also make good speed over the snows of the high passes when they were just beginning to soften and when the weather was at its most unpredictable; spring is the worst possible season for mountain travel. A force sent via Kashmir—or even via the Babusar pass and Chilas—had little chance of reaching Gilgit in time, let alone Chitral. Yet the only other way into the place was the route through Dir pioneered by MacNair in 1883. MacNair was still the only European ever to have tried it. Meantime the xenophobia and fanaticism of the Pathan tribes who lived along it had not diminished. Umra Khan was one of their leaders; as the main objective of any advance, he would see to it that every inch of the route was bitterly contested.

If there were a few in the councils of state who, at first, resisted the general panic and were more concerned about how on earth Robertson, the shrewdest of Agents, had managed to get himself into such a mess, they too changed their tune about the middle of March. For it then became clear that Mastuj, too, was under siege and the whole of Chitral therefore disaffected. Worse still was the soon-confirmed rumour that both the detachments of reinforcements sent from Mastuj to Robertson's aid had been ambushed on the way; the Agent was wasting his time scanning the foothills of Tirich Mir. Half of the first batch of sixty men had been killed and the rest taken prisoner including their two British officers; in addition to such eminently ransomable material, the enemy had also acquired the forty thousand rounds of ammunition they were convoying. The second batch, also about sixty strong, was virtually annihilated. Only ten men straggled back into Mastuj having left their commanding officer, Captain Ross, and the rest of their comrades-in-arms strewn among the rocks of a treacherous defile and bobbing thence down the river towards Chitral. No doubt, at the time, none of the officers concerned fully appreciated the gravity of the situation. But equally they took not the most elementary precautions. Ross, in particular, scorned the idea of reconnaissance and accused anyone who suggested it of cowardice. Ever contemptuous of the Dards, and tortured by the possibility that they might miss out on the anticipated heroics before the walls of Chitral, they paid the price of the Gilgit conceit.

'An undertaking of great magnitude', was how the Viceroy described the relief force that was now clearly imperative. He was not exaggerating. A whole division, fourteen thousand strong, under Major-General Sir R. C. Low, was assembled at Nowshera; it included both British and British Indian troops amongst which were such prestigious regiments as the Gordon Highlanders, the Buffs and the Bengal Lancers. To Umra Khan was sent a formal ultimatum telling him to get out of Chitral, whilst to all the intervening tribes a proclamation was issued in the hopes of winning their acquiescence. Both were ignored. On March 14 the Division was formally mobilised and two weeks later the first troops crossed the frontier and headed for the hills; assured of fighting most of the way, they would not be disappointed. 'We have before us a single issue', declared the Viceroy, 'the claim of brave men, British and Indian, who have not flinched in the performance of their duty, to the support of their countrymen in their hour of need.' According to the Commander-in-Chief, this lent a degree of sanctity to the expedition. It was unnecessary for either to draw the obvious parallel; the memory of Khartoum, the spectre of Gordon hacked to death on the steps of the beleaguered palace, and the tragedy of the relief force arriving only a couple of days later, were engraved on every heart.

Meanwhile, two hundred miles away in Gilgit, the situation was regarded with less solemnity though plenty of fervour. Curly Stewart, acting as British Agent in Robertson's absence, had summoned all his available troops and was looking forward to leading them to poor Charlie Townshend's aid. So, far away in Calcutta, was Algy Durand, now military secretary to the new Viceroy. (He had just married the Viceroy's niece.) Durand had lost confidence in Curly Stewart; he was good for nothing but sending the 'most infernal stupid telegrams'; in fact the whole Agency seemed to have become terribly casual. Should he not personally return to sort out the Northern Marches? And was this his 'chance of getting level with those devils, the Dards'?

It wasn't. The government turned to neither Durand nor Stewart for the very good reason that they had just discovered a fully fledged lieutenant-colonel lurking in the Indus canyon near Chilas. A small, fragile-looking Irishman, now in the evening of an undistinguished career, Colonel James Kelly was ordered to take over command of the Gilgit troops and make whatever arrangements he could to co-operate with the main relief force. For Kelly, belatedly—he was nearing sixty and sported a beard that had been out of fashion since the Mutiny—the trumpet of destiny had sounded; Kelly's March has been well acclaimed 'one of the most remarkable in history'.

Frankly the government didn't give much for his chances; 'relief from that side [i.e. Gilgit] was felt impossible' according to Lord Elgin. It was made still more so by the fact that Kelly could have no reinforcements and that he was ordered, at all costs, to avoid taking risks; there had been too much in the way of disastrous heroics already. In this respect Kelly looked a safe bet; he was simply to do his best with whatever troops the already depleted garrison of Gilgit could spare. Foremost amongst these were the men of his own regiment, the only British Indian one in Gilgit, the 32nd Punjab Pioneers. The pioneer regiments were a peculiarly Indian phenomenon. Recruited from the lowest castes and Untouchables, their speciality was digging. They could perform other tasks, carpentry and the like, but essentially they were the army's road-builders. A pickaxe was as vital a piece of each man's kit as a rifle. When the alarm sounded in Chitral they had been hacking a track round the base of Nanga Parbat. They were not strangers to action and they enjoyed a reputation for stubborn bravery; but they were probably not the one regiment the authorities would have selected for the stirring challenge ahead.

Kelly duly made his arrangements. Four hundred of the Pioneers and four of their officers would be the core of his expedition. Then there were a hundred Hunza–Nagar irregulars, invaluable for reconnaissance and precipice work, plus Lieutenant Beynon of Intelligence, the only man around who had actually been to Chitral, and Lieutenant Cosmo Stewart with a Kashmir mountain battery. This last choice was either a stroke of genius or a colossal blunder. If just one or two guns could somehow be lugged into Chitral it would have as salutary an effect as a thousand troops. Yet the Chitralis were confident that it was quite impossible and so too, presumably, was the Indian government; it would be hard enough to get men across the Shandur pass in April, never mind artillery. Kelly, however, thought it worth a try; and in Cosmo Stewart, another Irishman, 'the most bloodthirsty man I have ever met' according to Beynon, and one who loved his guns as if they were his children, he had found just the man to pull it off.

The force marched out of Gilgit on March 23. It crossed the snowline at Ghizr, twenty-five miles short of the Shandur and ran into difficulties soon after. Porters absconded and the mules carrying the guns ground to a standstill in snow that reached to their girths. Reluctantly Kelly turned back to Ghizr. Next day the blizzard, which had been blowing for five days prior to their arrival, returned. An advance guard which had been pushed to one march short of the pass was marooned. Neither they nor anyone else had tents and, since they depended on the country for both supplies and carriage, the plight of the expedition looked desperate.

Cosmo Stewart thought otherwise and spent the day experimenting. As a preliminary, the Kashmir troops who were based at Ghizr were told to commandeer what spades they could and dig a track for the guns over the pass. This was clearly a long term solution; even a snow plough would have taken weeks to do the job. Meanwhile he considered yaks. There were not enough to carry the guns but he thought that by driving them in front a usable track might result. Unfortunately he knew nothing about the dainty footwork of the yak. Each beast trod exactly in the footsteps of the leader; the result was a neat but useless line of holes. As a final throw, someone suggested sledges. This, surely, was the answer. Using tree trunks for runners and with eighteen men pulling, the prototype carried nearly a ton. A few trial runs round the camp were successful and the regimental carpenters were soon busy knocking up a whole fleet.

Next day, April 3, the snow stopped. At dawn the guns were sent forward to join the advance guard. On mules they were lugged up to the earlier point of return and then transferred to the sledges. Disaster. The track beaten by the advance guard was too narrow for the runners while the frozen crust of the virgin snow was not strong enough for the weight. There was nothing for it; they must be abandoned. But by now the whole force had become infected with Stewart's determination. The guns were everything, a talisman, a symbol of the expedition's corporate esprit, and a challenge as great as the relief of Chitral itself. Simultaneously an officer of the Pioneers and an N.C.O of the Kashmir gunners stepped forward to volunteer to carry the precious pieces. The rest soon followed suit. Each box of ammunition weighed over a hundredweight, the barrels and carriages more like a quarter of a ton. Strung from poles, and with four men to each pole, fifty yards could be gained before the men collapsed and another team took over. It was not just the weight. In places the snow was shoulder deep; when a man lost his balance añd slipped from the narrow track he disappeared. There were also the problems of altitude exhaustion—they were now approaching 12,000 feet—intense snow glare and a wind so cold that no thermometer went low enough to record it. That night they struggled on till long after dark making scarcely five hundred yards an hour. Then they slept in the snow, every six men huddled together beneath their pooled blankets and sheepskins. At dawn they started again. So it went on for three days, till on the night of April 5 they were cheered into camp on the far side of the pass.

Nothing, [recorded Beynon] can be said too highly in praise of this splendid achievement. Here were some 250 men, Hindus and Mussulmans, who, working shoulder to shoulder, had brought two mountain guns, with their carriages and supply of ammunition, across some twenty miles of deep soft snow, across a pass 12,320 feet high, at the beginning of April, the worst time of the year. These men were also carrying their own rifles, greatcoats and 80 rounds of ammunition and wearing heavy sheepskin coats; they had slept for two nights in the snow and struggled from dawn to dark, sinking at every step to their waists. . . . Their officers took turns with the men in carrying the guns and gave their snow glasses to sepoys who were suffering from the glare.

In the wake of such an achievement the rest of the expedition crossed with confidence. Amongst the troops there were a few bad cases of frostbite; the officers found their faces shredded by the wind till the blood ran and some suffered slightly from altitude sickness; the only one totally immune seemed to be the bearded Kelly who, belying his years, 'trudged along without a halt all day'. But, really, it was the gunners and their companions who assured the march of immortality. As they started off down the valley towards Mastuj, Stewart and his men had to be led by the hand; their heads swathed in bandages, they were still blinded from the snow glare. Yet they had achieved the impossible and Kelly, with the immense advantages of surprise and of possessing the only artillery in Chitral, was in with a real chance of becoming the saviour of Chitral.

First, though, there was Mastuj. The siege there had never really been pressed. The fort, with three British officers and a small garrison, was well placed for defence and the enemy had been happy to isolate it. The Pathans, who constituted the most formidable opposition, seem never to have penetrated much north of Chitral town and the whole of the upper part of the valley was held by Chitralis under the command of Sher Afzul's foster brother. Had they anticipated an attack from Gilgit the logical place to have stopped it would have been between the pass and Mastuj. Short of supplies, short of carriage and with only the snows to turn back to, Kelly could have been in real trouble. And indeed there was opposition. At one point the way ahead was blocked by a well planned net of breastworks. But they were manned by only an estimated four hundred. Stewart got the longed for chance of showing off his seven-pounders and the Chitralis duly panicked after the first few shells. There were no fatalities amongst the Pioneers and by April 9 they were in Mastuj.

Seventy miles to go and by now the prospect of beating a path to glory ahead of Low's so-called 'Chitral Relief Expedition' was in the back of every mind. Beynon's 'first man in Chitral gets a C. B.' was funny because it was exactly what they were all thinking. They didn't know it but Low had almost exactly the same distance to go. After a stiff fight up the Malakand pass he had crossed the Swat river and Aylmer, of Nilt fame, was throwing a bridge across the Panjkora. Militarily they were repeatedly getting the better of the tribesmen, but between them and Chitral there still loomed the Lowarai pass; and as Kelly could vouch, the physical difficulties were likely to be every bit as formidable as the human.

Besides playing David to Low's Goliath, the Gilgit column sought the added satisfaction of demonstrating that the Agency could look after its own. Given a choice, Robertson would surely prefer to be relieved by his own men; it would go some way towards vindicating his handling of the Chitralis and, in the last analysis, would show that the idea of controlling Chitral from Gilgit was not impracticable. However, the game wasn't over. The enemy were reported gathering in strength at a notorious black spot a couple of miles below Mastuj. On April 10 and 11 Kelly cast about for supplies and porters, on the the 12th he sent out a reconnaissance and on the 13th he moved out to the attack.

The place to be attacked was known as the Nisa Gol. By the Chitralis it was believed impregnable and with a force of fifteen hundred, over double that of Kelly's, plus the immense advantage of prepared positions, they had good reason for confidence. In configuration it was a bit like the Nilt ravine. A sloping ledge, shut in by the mountain wall on one side and the river on the other, was sliced in two by a cleft three hundred feet deep. The sides of this ravine were perpendicular and the enemy's position consisted of a line of bunkers and breastworks along the far side. High up in the mountains more men were stationed with the object of panicking the exposed attackers with landslides, while across the river, from a staircase of breastworks that reached well above the snowline, sharpshooters commanded the whole ledge across which the advance would have to be made.

The Chitrali breastworks were concentrated at the one spot where it was feasible to get down into the ravine and up the other side. Kelly's only chance was to find another crossing place, and with this in mind he had made some elaborate preparations. But first the Hunza irregulars were told off to scale the mountains and work round towards the landslide men. Meanwhile Stewart's guns got to work silencing the *sangar* that controlled the longest reach of unscaleable ravine. Under cover of this heavy fire Beynon crept up to the lip of the chasm, selected a spot and gave the signal. On trotted the secret weapon, a troupe of men brandishing ladders and ropes. It must have been a bit like the Royal Tournament. Over the edge in a flurry of belays went the storming party, the guns were limbered up to fire on the main concentration of breastworks, and as the first heads started to appear out of the cleft on the far side, down from the heights with bloodcurdling screams came the Hunza levies; the position was turned. The Chitralis started to bolt and the main force advanced in good order by way of the proper track. Bar the fact that the guns were not then slung across the ravine on pulleys, it was a show worthy of a command performance. Six of Kelly's men had been killed for nearly sixty of the enemy and the prestige of British arms had been restored in Chitral. It was too cheap, too quick a victory to rate as a classic; but it was a very creditable example of how careful reconnaissance, intelligent thinking and complete co-ordination could take care of the most impossible terrain.

Much the same could be said of the whole of Kelly's March. One looks in vain for brilliant strategy or personal heroics. His moves were always deliberate, his innovations simple and his successes corporate. In the heat of battle he himself, unlike Durand or Robertson, stayed well under cover and out of the limelight. Instead of inflaming the enthusiasms of his young officers he threw cold water on them. In Mastuj he wouldn't be panicked into a dash for Chitral but spent three days reorganising. And in the earlier action he had had occasion to remonstrate with Stewart for coming into action at too close a range and thus causing unnecessary bloodshed; after neither engagement was any attempt made at pursuit or a punitive demonstration. Nor were there any acts of conspicuous bravery or any obvious candidates for a V.C. This was not the Gilgit way and it won Kelly neither the adulation of his subordinates nor the unqualified approval of his superiors; he was duly recommended for both a knighthood and a generalship but got neither. On the other hand it resulted in the most successful and most humane campaign ever fought in Dardistan.

It was also the last. The Nisa Gol battle would in fact be the last set engagement between the Gilgit forces and the Dards. Steadily, keeping his men together, refusing to countenance a flying column and moving all at the speed of the cumbersome guns, Kelly closed on Chitral. By the night of the 17th he was within three marches of the town. Low was still on the wrong side of the Lowarai and, though there was still the prospect of the Chitralis making a final stand, the prize was surely his. And so it proved, though not quite in the classic style most would have wished.

There was as yet no news from Robertson and, beyond the fact that the *Noghor* was still holding out, Kelly had no idea what to expect. His officers looked forward to a grand fight beneath the walls but, as they did so, the whole business was being decided in that summer house by the shaft of the mine. The besiegers seemed to have staked everything on this last ploy and when, on the 16th, it was foiled, the game was up. Umra Khan's Pathans had already drifted south to oppose Low's remorseless advance and, alone, Sher Afzul now recognised that he had no chance of taking the *Noghor*.

Leitner quotes an apt Chitrali aphorism of the day; 'a sparrow who tried to kick a mountain himself toppled over'. Deserted by his allies and demoralised by Kelly's eruption and the disaster of Nisa Gol, Sher Afzul threw in the sponge. On the 18th the garrison awoke to find the besiegers gone and on the same day, instead of another line of *sangars*, Kelly was greeted by a messenger from the fort with the news that the siege was over.

On the 20th, dressed in their best, with the buglers to the fore and the guns still in their midst, Kelly's men crossed the Chitral river and approached the battle-scarred fort. From one of the towers a home-made Union Jack fluttered in the spring breeze; the whole place was strangely quiet. Outside the main gate five wan officers were assembled in line. Kelly, from the back of his diminutive Chitrali pony, gave a wave of his walking stick, the officers replied with a salute, hands were shaken. Robertson had his arm in a sling and his expression was as stern as ever; later, though, he admitted that he had been near to tears. A skirl of the pipes from Low's Highlanders would have made for a more romantic conclusion and there were many, particularly Stewart, who were bitterly disappointed that the Chitralis hadn't made a final stand. But if there was a sense of anti-climax it was not so much because of the let down as from utter exhaustion.

A week after Kelly's arrival a harbinger of Low's brigade galloped up in the shape of Frank Younghusband. As special correspondent of *The Times* he had accompanied Low's troops from Nowshera and had now dashed ahead to be the first man from the south into Chitral. After awarding full credit to Townshend, though not to Robertson for whom he had never had much time, he selected Kelly and his men as the heroes of the hour. 'This famous march', he cabled, 'will ever be remembered as a unique exploit of the Indian Army.' The Commander-in-Chief agreed, citing in particular the crossing of the Shandur, and from the Queen herself came 'gracious approbation of this remarkable exploit'. Robertson too was deeply impressed; but what struck him most was the unusual reserve and mutual solicitude shown by this bunch of heroes. 'They were the most singularly generous and modest men I have ever met'; it just wasn't in the Gilgit tradition.

Hard on Younghusband's heels came the Buffs, the first of Low's battalions. It wasn't easy for true British troops to doff their hats to the low-bred Pioneers; but as soon as the serious business of ceremonial manœuvres got under way, first Kelly's men, then Robertson's, were given a sort of benefit parade and each man was awarded an extra six months' pay.

As the celebrations wore on, the garrison must have begun to wonder whether they were still under siege; Townshend, in particular, was hankering to get back to civilisation and the promotion of his now promising career. Robertson just felt weary. The siege had been more of a strain than he had realised; and now that it was all over he was still the senior political officer and there were still a lot of questions to be answered. But deliverance was on its way; last on the scene came 'my long time friend and former chief, Colonel Algernon Durand'. Durand had watched the whole siege with mounting horror, he had postponed a visit to England and pestered Lord Elgin to let him return to the aid of the man 'who once pulled me out of my mess'. With the crisis over, the

Viceroy relented and Durand was allowed to make one last visit to Dardistan. There was talk of writing a report on the siege and of delivering some Viceregal paean, but really he had come to conduct Robertson back to Simla. In an ending worthy of the wide screen, they galloped off over the Lowarai pass together; significantly they forwent the Shandur and a sentimental visit to Gilgit.

* * *

'I should be less than human if I did not break a last lance for the tribes that befriended me,' began Dr. Leitner in July 1895. The siege of Chitral had occasioned the sort of public discussion, including a parliamentary debate, for which he had always canvassed. The point at issue was whether Chitral should be retained and garrisoned as part of India's frontier; this involved discussion of the whole Gilgit policy in relation to the Dards. Ranged against the extension of British territory into such a hostile wilderness there were now many big guns; and with the Afghan and Russian frontiers in the area finally defined, they had a convincing case. But none was so strident and indiscriminate in his rhetoric as the now ageing doctor.

For thirty years he had been pleading for the independence of the Dards and the preservation of their way of life. He had watched the peace-loving Nagaris and Chilasis being gunned down with Gatlings, he had noted the desecration of Hunza—'that cradle of human thought as expressed in language', and now it was the turn of the affectionate and submissive Chitralis. 'I have no hesitation in stating that one and all of the complications with these places have solely arisen from the personal ambition of our officers under the influence of the K.C.S.I. or K.G.B. mania.' Excluding Biddulph, not one man, not even Robertson ('that ambitious medico'), who had lived amongst the Kafirs, had bothered to learn one of the local languages. Yet 'long before journalistic knights met three empires in all safety [Knight, the *Times* man, wrote of the Hunza campaign in *Where Three Empires Meet*], or travelling MPs rediscovered the friendship of an old ally [Curzon and Nizam-ul-Mulk]', Leitner had elicited the linguistic secrets of the Dard peoples and made them readily available to all. Having uncovered this unique ethnological treasure-chest he had consistently raged against its exploitation. Yet, in Hunza and Nagar the Dard tongues were already being corrupted, the prophetesses were silent, etc.; in Kafiristan the Afghans, using breech-loaders supplied by the British government and as a result of an agreement with the same government, were forcibly converting and dispersing the wild and wonderful Kafirs. Chitral was all that was left of Dardistan as he knew it and Chitral must, and could, be saved.

For once it looked as if he might just get his way. Convinced that there was no longer a strategic imperative for a British interest in Chitral, the Liberal government opted for a complete withdrawal. In June 1895 they declared that the Nowshera–Chitral road would not be kept open and that, as planned in 1893, there would be no permanent political agent in the valley. The debate, however, raged on and, a matter of days after reaching this decision, the Liberal government fell. By the end of the month Lord Salisbury's Tories were back in power and by August they had reversed the decision. Chitral was to have not only its own agent but a bigger garrison than Gilgit; the Nowshera road was to be kept open and another garrison was to be posted on the Malakand pass to police it. In effect Chitral was to be more closely integrated into British India than Gilgit itself.

By 1896 Leitner was forced to concede defeat. In a letter to *The Times* prompted by the publication of George, now Sir George, Robertson's second book on the Kafirs, he started with the usual recitation of his past dealings with the Dards. But then, instead of some explosive indictment, there came a quiet, diffident and rather sad surrender.

All in vain. No one perhaps has struggled more on behalf of the Dards and Kafirs than myself during thirty years, but the cause is lost and now their only chance of survival is a complete and loyal acquiescence in the new order of things.

The new order of things eventually led to the detachment of Chitral from its Dard neighbours in the Gilgit Agency and its incorporation in the North-West Frontier Province of British India, and now Pakistan. Greatly outnumbered in this predominantly Pathan province the Chitralis have nevertheless retained something of their identity. Political unrest is still a feature of the valley and the Afghans, as part of their policy to support self-determination for all the peoples of Pakistan's frontier province, continue to take an interest in the place; the tribal frontier agreed in 1893 and now known as the Durand Line is totally repudiated. Yet, if Leitner would not be entirely disappointed by Chitral today, it is more thanks to geographical facts than political ones. The Lowarai pass is still closed by snow and avalanches for months on end; whole busloads of travellers get robbed and ransomed in Swat and Dir, and no vehicle larger than a jeep can negotiate the rocky bluffs of the valley itself. Gun-runners and miscreants still dodge undetected across the Dora pass and the tourists who are flown into Chitral's miniscule airport have less of an impact on the country as a whole than the far-ranging sportsman-administrators of the British Raj.

The same might be said for the rest of the old Gilgit Agency. Until 1947 it continued as an anomalous and much sought after posting in British India. Retired Indian officers often maintained that the Great Game was still being played in the 1930s, but in Gilgit, with the Pamirs frontier finally settled and with Chitral no longer its responsibility, anxieties over the proximity of Russia were purely theoretical if not imaginary. Compared to the excitements of the 1890s all was peace and quiet in this remote look-out post of the declining Empire. Individual officers were free to concentrate their energies on an all out assault on the markhor and ibex or a further study of the tribes.

With Independence and the partition of the subcontinent in 1947, the Maharaja of Kashmir, after much vacillation, elected to incorporate his state in the Indian Union; he was after all a Dogra Hindu. His Mohammedan subjects resented this; the peaceable people of the Kashmir valley pinned their hopes of altering his decision on a plebiscite to be held under United Nations auspices; the Dards simply took up arms. The successors of those Hunza and Gilgit levies who had fought with Robertson and Kelly in 1895 were known as the Gilgit Scouts, a crack mountain unit which had been armed, trained and uniformed under British officers. With the help of Pathan co-religionists they bundled the Maharaja's representatives out of Gilgit and pushed the Dogras back to Astor and up the Indus to beyond Baltistan. Leitner

would surely have applauded this evidence of the unbroken spirit
of the Dards; and by a curious coincidence the Kashmir ceasefire
line of today is not very different from what he and Hayward
believed the Kashmir frontier always should have been.

Bibliography

When Men and Mountains Meet

I CHAPTER NOTES

Chapters 1 and 2

It is a brave man who sits down to reconstruct Moorcroft's travels from the India Office Library's collection of Moorcroft Manuscripts. I have referred to them only where H. H. Wilson's edition of *The Travels of William Moorcroft and George Trebeck* (London 1841) seems to raise doubts, or in order to pursue specific lines of enquiry. Other unpublished sources to which reference has been made include Trebeck's letters to George Leeson and Stirling's account of the fate of the expedition as given by Askar Ali Khan ('Luskeree Khan') both in the Royal Geographical Society's archives and relevant volumes of Bengal Political Consultations in the India Office Records. John Murray has also kindly supplied copies of correspondence with H. H. Wilson.

Moorcroft's 1812 journey is described in Asiatic Researches vol XXI (Calcutta 1816). Francis Watson's article in the Geographical Magazine (vol XXXIII 1959) also deals with this journey.

The Asiatic Journal (vols XIX old series to XXI new series, 1825–36) has frequent references to Moorcroft's last journey, including a letter from Bukhara and Ghulam Hyder Khan's account of the journey as far as Peshawar.

The Journal of the Royal Geographical Society (vols I and II 1831 and 1832) carries Moorcroft's notes on Kotan and Kashmir.

Of more recent works the following have been particularly useful:

H. W. C. Davis' *The Great Game in Asia 1800–44*, London 1926
G. J. Alder's *British India's Northern Frontier 1865–95*, London 1963
A. Lamb's *British and Chinese Central Asia 1767–1903*, London 1960
K. Mason's *Abode of Snow*, London 1955
S. Hedin's *Southern Tibet* vol VII, Stockholm 1922.
and the introduction to the Moorcroft MSS in the *Catalogue of the India Office Library* (Manuscripts in European Languages vol II).

Chapter 3

The standard biography of Jacquemont is by Pierre Maes, *Victor Jacquemont*,

Paris 1934. David Stacton's *A Ride on a Tiger*, London 1954, gives an entertaining account of his period in India.

His journal was published in six volumes entitled *Voyage dans l'Inde pendant les années 1828–32*, Paris 1835–44, but more entertaining are the letters. These, as Prosper Mérimée says, tell the tale better than anyone could. There are several collections. I have used:

1. *Correspondance de Victor Jacquemont avec sa famille et ses amis pendant son voyage dans l'Inde 1828–32*, New Edition, Paris 1869.
2. *Letters from India*, translated from the French, London 1834.
3. *Letters from India 1829–32*, translated and with an introduction by C. A. Phillips, London 1936.

In this and subsequent chapters, descriptions of Ranjit Singh and his court have been taken at random from the accounts of travellers like Burnes, Vigne and von Hugel and from those of a motley collection of other visitors and residents. These include:

Up the Country, The Hon. Emily Eden, London 1866.
The Court and Camp of Runjeet Singh, The Hon. W. G. Osborne, London 1840.
Events at the Court of Ranjit Singh, Punjab Govt. Record Office, Lahore 1935.
Travels in India, L. von Orlich, London 1845.
Five Years in India, H. E. Fane, London 1842.
The Punjaub, Lt. Col. Steinbach, London 1845.
Journal of a March from Delhi to Peshawar and Kabul, W. Barr, London 1844.
Thirty-Five Years in the East, J. M. Honigberger, London 1852.

Chapter 4
Wolff's autobiography, *Travels and Adventures*, London 1860, sometimes contradicts and invariably elaborates on his journals. The relevant journal is *Researches and Missionary Labours among the Jews, Mohammedans and other sects*, London 1835.

He apparently dictated the autobiography to relays of secretaries with little or no reference to the journals. This suggests a prodigious memory and it is remarkable that there are not more inconsistencies.

There is a biography of Wolff—*Joseph Wolff, His Romantic Life and Travels*, by H. Palmer, London 1935. It is compiled almost exclusively from the *Travels and Adventures* and, considering the subject, is surprisingly dull.

His 1844 journey to Bukhara to discover the fate of two British officers,

Stoddart and Connolly, has been well told by Fitzroy MacLean in *A Person from England and other Travellers*, London 1958. The journal for this expedition has recently been reprinted as *A Mission to Bokhara*, edited and with introduction by Guy Wint, London 1969.

In the Royal Geographical Society Archives there are a few letters from Wolff. They are chiefly concerned with his being unable to afford the subscription; he needed the money to buy coal for his poor parishioners.

Chapter 5

Professor H. W. C. Davies in his Raleigh Lecture to the British Academy in 1926, *The Great Game in Asia, 1800–1844*, also implies that Vigne's travels had reference to Anglo-Russian relations. He claims, however, that Vigne met Henderson in Ladakh and that part of his mission was to convince Ahmed Shah that 'not Russia but Great Britain . . . would be the truer friend'. Vigne had met Henderson before but in Ludhiana, not Ladakh, and I have found nothing to suggest that Ahmed Shah needed any convincing about where his best chance of salvation lay. But that Vigne went to Baltistan 'to spy out the land' seems highly probable. Vol IV of R. H. Phillimore's *Historical Records of the Survey of India* (1945–65) has been useful in this connection.

Henderson was again robbed of everything, including his diary, on his last journey and died before he was able to write even a summary of his travels. The relevant works of G. T. Vigne are *Travels in Kashmir, Ladakh, Iskardo etc.*, 1842, and *A Personal Narrative of a Visit to Ghazni, Kabul and Afghanistan*, 1840.

Von Hugel's work was translated into English as *Travels in Kashmir and the Punjab*, 1845. The Journal of the Asiatic Society of Bengal (JASB) vol V 1836 and vol VI, part II, 1837, The Asiatic Journal vol XXI (New Series) Sept–Dec 1836 and the Journal of the Royal Geographical Society (JRGS) vol IX 1839 contain letters and notes by Vigne. The latter (JRGS) vol VI 1836 includes a contribution from von Hugel. Their books are reviewed in vols XI 1841, XII 1842 and XXXI 1861, presentation of von Hugel's medal is in vol XIX 1849 and his obituary in Proceedings of the RGS (PRGS) vol XV 1870–71.

For biographical information on Vigne I am indebted to Mr. H. D'O. Vigne and to the entry in the *Dictionary of National Biography*.

Sven Hedin's *Southern Tibet* vol VII and Kenneth Mason's *Abode of Snow* along with JRGS vol XXXI 1861 have the best assessments of Vigne's geographical work.

Chapters 6 and 7
So many have succumbed while working on Gardiner's story that one moves on with a sigh of relief. Since Major H. Pearse edited his *Memoirs of Alexander Gardiner*, London 1898, the lethal Gardiner papers, including Cooper's draft, have again disappeared. Should they ever come to light, it will be a brave man who undertakes to re-examine them. I doubt too whether they will help to solve the mystery.

For Gardiner's spell in the Sikh service Pearse used them hardly at all, but it is on evidence from this period that C. Grey in *European Adventurers of Northern India 1785–1849*, edited by H. L. O. Garrett, Lahore 1929, bases his demolition of the case for Gardiner.

Sir H. M. Durand's *Life of a Soldier of the Olden Time* will be found in *Life of Sir H. M. Durand*, by H. M. Durand, vol II, London 1883. Edited extracts from Gardiner's journals are in Journal of the Asiatic Society of Bengal (JASB) vol XXII, 1853 and information derived from his employment at Lahore in *A History of the Reigning Family of Lahore*, edited by G. Carmichael Smyth, Calcutta 1849.

The minute dealing with Gardiner's gun-running operation is dated June 30th 1874 and is in Secret Home Correspondence, vol 79 in the India Office Records.

Other works referred to in this chapter are as follows:

C. Masson's *Narrative of Various Journeys in Balochistan, Afghanistan and the Punjab*, London 1842.

T. E. Gordon's *A Varied Life*, London 1906.

G. W. Leitner's *Languages and Races of Dardistan*, Lahore 1877.

A. Wilson's *Abode of Snow*, Edinburgh 1875.

G. Hayward's letters in Proceedings of the RGS (PRGS) vol XV 1870–71.

Edinburgh Review, January 1872.

Journal of the RGS vol XLII 1872.

Chapters 8 and 9
Besides *Travels into Bokhara*, London 1834, Sir Alexander Burnes wrote *Cabool, A Personal Narrative of a Journey to and Residence in that City, 1836, 7 and 8*, which was published posthumously in 1842. The Bukhara journey is also dealt with in *Travels in the Punjab etc.*, London 1846, by Mohan Lal, Burnes's interpreter, and in the letters of Dr. Gerard published in JASB vol II 1833. Charles Masson's *Narrative of Various Journeys in Balochistan, Afghanistan and the Punjab etc.*, London 1842, gives a valuable insight into the events of 1836–38 in Kabul and Vigne's summary in *Travels in Kashmir etc.* also provides a useful, because impartial, assess-

ment. Burnes's letters were published as Parliamentary Papers and are quoted in more digestible form in an article by George Buist of the *Bombay Times* which may be found in a little book entitled *Notes on his Name and Family*, by James Burnes, Edinburgh 1851. James Lunt in his recent biography, *Bokhara Burnes* (edited by George Woodcock), London 1969, has also used the Buist article extensively.

Burnes's role in the Great Game is discussed by H. W. C. Davies in *The Great Game in Asia*, J. L. Morison in *From Alexander Burnes to Frederick Roberts* and T. H. Holdich in *The Gates of India*.

The only unpublished papers to which I have had recourse are the Reports of the Burnes Mission to Kabul, 1837-8, in the India Office Library and some letters of Burnes to John Murray.

Wood is an altogether more elusive subject. His *Journey to the Source of the River Oxus* was published in 1841. A second edition, with a preface by his son and a long introduction by Sir Henry Yule, appeared in 1872. The description of the journey in JRGS vol X 1840 adds nothing to the book. His only other published work seems to have been a pamphlet accusing the New Zealand Company of misrepresenting the delights of their islands. PRGS vol XVI 1871-2 contains Rawlinson's obituary notice and from this, together with his son's preface as above and the entries in *DNB* and in vol IV of R. H. Phillimore's *Historical Records of the Survey of India*, I have ventured to reconstruct something of his character and career. There are a few unrevealing letters from him in the RGS archives but sadly no portrait.

Chapter 10

The quotation from Sir William Lloyd comes from *Narrative of a Journey from Caunpoor to the Boorendo Pass*, Major Sir William Lloyd, London 1840. He also has a magnificent description of sunset over the mountains seen from Kotgarh. For the history of Simla see *Simla, Past and Present*, by E. J. Buck, Bombay 1925.

The Tibetan Campaign of Zorawar Singh is described in Cunningham's *Ladakh* and is discussed in K. M. Pannikar's *The Founding of the Kashmir State; a Biography of Gulab Singh*, London 1953, and in *Britain and Chinese Central Asia, The Road to Lhasa*, by Alistair Lamb, London 1960. I have also used the latter for its lucid presentation of the background to the 1847 Boundary Commission.

The official instructions to the Commission are in vol III no. 48 of Enclosures to Secret Letters in the India Office Records. The reports of the Commission are in Board's Collections vol 2461 no. 136806, 1851.

JRGS vols XVIII and XIX 1848 and 1849, contain the first mentions of the 'expedition' and vols XIX and XXIII contain the abbreviated accounts of Thomson and Strachey. Letters from Cunningham and Thomson were published in JASB vol XVII 1848. The three great productions of the Commission are *Ladak, Physical, Statistical and Historical*, by Alexander Cunningham, London 1854, *The Physical Geography of Western Tibet*, by Henry Strachey, London 1853, and *Western Himalaya and Tibet*, by Thomas Thomson, London 1853.

Sven Hedin's *Southern Tibet* vol VII and Kenneth Mason's *Abode of Snow* contain geographical appraisals of the Commission's work.

Chapter 11

For a recent publication R. H. Phillimore's *Historical Records of the Survey of India*, 1945–1965, Dehra Dun, is hard to come by. It is a mine of information on the Kashmir survey and well worth tracking down. Shorter accounts may be found in *A Memoir of the Indian Surveys*, by Clements R. Markham, London 1871, and in Kenneth Mason's *Abode of Snow*; longer ones in the annual *General Reports of the G.T.S.*, in the *Records of the Survey of India* and in the synoptical volumes of the same.

Godwin-Austen's report *On the Glaciers of the Mustakh Range* was published in JRGS vol XXXIV 1864 and Johnson's *Report of his journey to Ilchi, the capital of Khoten* in JRGS vol XXXVII 1867. Discussion of the first will be found in PRGS vol VII 1863–4 and of the second in PRGS vol XI, 1866–7. Johnson's obituary is in PRGS vol V 1883.

Godwin-Austen's comments on Montgomerie are to be found in a letter to Bates of the RGS in the RGS archives. For the other side of the story see Everest's letter to Norton Shaw of May 11th 1861 also in the RGS archives. The story of K2 comes principally from Phillimore as above.

The repercussions of Johnson's visit to Kotan can be followed at length in vol 91 no. 93 of Collections to Political dispatches to India in the India Office Records. They are discussed by Alistair Lamb in *The China–India Border*, London 1964.

Gluttons for punishment may reconstruct the travels of the Schlagintweit brothers from *Results of a Scientific Mission to India and High Asia*, London 1861–5, *Reisen in Indien und Hoch Asien*, Jena 1880, PRGS vol I 1857 and JRGS vols XXVII 1857 and XXVIII 1858. Sven Hedin in *Southern Tibet* vol VII summarises their work and the British attitude to them may be gathered from the delightful *Travels in Ladakh, Tartary and Kashmir*, by H. D. Torrens, London 1862, and from

letters in the RGS archives from George Buist (14 Nov. 1854) and George
Everest (Nov. 1861).

Chapters 12, 13 and 14

Accounts of the first British journeys into Eastern Turkestan are by
Robert Shaw, *Visits to High Tartary, Yarkand and Kashgar*, London 1871,
George Henderson and Allan Octavian Hume (ornithologist and founder
of the Indian Congress Party), *Lahore to Yarkand*, London 1873, H. W.
Bellew, *Kashmir and Kashgar*, London 1875, T. E. Gordon, *The Roof of
the World*, Edinburgh 1876, and *Sir Douglas Forsyth*, an autobiography
edited by Lady Forsyth, London 1887.

These together with the official *Report of a Mission to Yarkand and
Kashgar in 1873* were raided by several writers who cashed in on the
Eastern Turkestan fad during the 1870s. They included D. C. Boulger
(*Yakoob Beg*, London 1878) and G. R. Alberigh-Mackay (*Notes on Western
Turkestan*, Calcutta 1875).

Hayward's activities are chronicled in the Journal and Proceedings of
the Royal Geographical Society 1868–71. His report on the journey to the
source of the Yarkand river and to Eastern Turkestan is in JRGS vol XV
1870; vol XVI 1871 contains Montgomerie's report on the Mirza's
journey. The Society's publications give much additional information on
the Forsyth missions and on Shaw's journey down the Shyok in 1870.
Reading these one gets a good idea of the excitement which attached to the
whole subject of exploration in the Western Himalayas. Only Dr. Livingstone's disappearance and death are allowed to share the limelight.

There are a few political memoirs which bear on the subject, notably
O. T. Burne's *Memories*, London 1907, G. R. Elsmie's *Thirty-five Years
in the Punjab*, Edinburgh 1908, the *Life and Letters of H. M. Durand*, by his
son Sir H. M. Durand, London 1883, and *A Varied Life*, by T. E. Gordon,
London 1906.

An exhaustive study of the political background to the various journeys
will be found in G. J. Alder's *British India's Northern Frontier 1865–95*.
This makes light work of an extremely complicated subject and I owe Dr.
Alder a great debt of thanks. His article on Hayward's murder in Journal
of Royal Central Asian Society, 1965, has also been consulted.

Letters from Shaw and Hayward in the RGS archives have proved
useful in tracing their changing attitudes towards Yakub Beg and their
relationship with one another. Some of Hayward's watercolours are filed
with them. Hayward's murder is the subject of endless reports and correspondence in the India Office Records. These shed little light on the man

himself but a lot on the attitudes of Forsyth, Cayley and others towards the Maharaja of Kashmir. Reports by Gordon and Biddulph on the Pamirs expedition of 1874 are also in the India Office Library.

The account of Dalgleish's murder has been taken chiefly from H. Bower's *A Trip to Turkestan* in the Geographical Journal vol V 1875 and H. Lansdell's *Chinese Central Asia*, London 1893.

II GENERAL BIBLIOGRAPHY

For the most part this list is supplementary to the works mentioned in the Chapter Sources and consists of recent publications or those relevant to the subject as a whole.

ALDER, G. J. *British India's Northern Frontier 1865–95*, London 1963.

CURZON, G. N. *The Pamirs and The Source of the Oxus*, London 1896.

—— *Russia in Central Asia*, London 1889.

DABBS, J. A. *Discovery of Chinese Turkestan*, The Hague 1963.

DAINELLI, G. *La Esplorazione della Regione fra L'Himalaja Occidentale e il Caracorum*, Bologna 1934.

DAVIS, H. W. C. *The Great Game in Asia 1800–44*, London 1926.

DREW, F. *Jummoo and Kashmir*, London 1875.

EDWARDES, M. *Playing the Great Game*, London 1975.

FAIRLEY, J. *The Lion River; The Indus*, London 1975.

HEDIN, S. *Southern Tibet*, Stockholm 1922.

HOLDICH, T. H. *Indian Borderland*, London 1901.

—— *Gates of India*, London 1910.

LAMB, A. *British and Chinese Central Asia*, London 1960.

MASON, K. *Abode of Snow*, London 1955.

MORRISON, J. L. *From Burnes to Roberts*, London 1936.

PHILLIMORE, R. H. *Historical Records of the Survey of India*, Dehra Dun 1945.

RAWLINSON, H. *England and Russia in the East*, London 1875.

SEVERIN, T. *The Oriental Adventures: Explorers of the East*, London 1976.

WILSON, A. *Abode of Snow*, London 1876.

The Gilgit Game

I CHAPTER NOTES

Chapters 1 and 2

Dr. G. W. Leitner's principal works are *The Results of a Tour in Dardistan*, Lahore 1877, *The Languages and Races of Dardistan*, Lahore 1877, *The Hunza–Nagyr Handbook*, Lahore 1889 (second edition, Woking 1893) and *Dardistan in 1866, 1886 and 1893*, Woking 1893. These include most of his pamphlets up till 1893; after that his views can be traced in *The Asiatic Quarterly Review* published sporadically from Woking. A review of the *Life and Labours of Dr. G. W. Leitner* by J. H. Stocqueler, Brighton 1872, provides some biographical detail but with the subject still in his early thirties and the author one of his staunchest admirers, it is neither exhaustive nor balanced. His reputation in Lahore can be surmised from *Thirty-five Years in the Punjab* by G. R. Elsmie, Edinburgh 1908, and his standing as a traveller and savant from the *Journal of the Royal Geographical Society* (*J.R.G.S.*) (vol. XLIII, 1873, contains some of the many scattered references to him). His brush with the Government of India can be followed in the India Office Records (Political and Secret Home Correspondence, vol. 128, and Political and Secret Letters from India, vol. 65). His work with the Oriental University Institute is described in *Victorian Woking* by J. R. and S. E. Whitemen, Guildford, 1970. His obituary is in *The Times* for March 25, 1899.

The view from the cliffs above Gor was first seen by Col. H. C. B. Tanner and Major J. Biddulph and is described in *Proceedings of the Royal Geographical Society* (*P.R.G.S.*), vol XIII, New Series, 1891.

Chapters 3 and 4

George Hayward wrote no books and there are no books about him. The only published work seems to be the article by Dr. G. J. Alder in the *Journal of the Royal Central Asian Society* for January 1965. To Dr. Alder and, for biographical information, to Brigadier R. A. Gardiner of the R.G.S. I am deeply indebted. Hayward's career as an explorer is best

549

followed through the Journals and Proceedings of the R.G.S. (*J.R.G.S.*, vols XL and XLI, and *P.R.G.S.*, vols. XIII, XIV and XV) and in unpublished material in the R.G.S. archives. The Society's publications also include a full account of the murder but reference should also be made to extensive reports on the affair in the India Office Records (India Foreign and Political Proceedings, 766; Secret Home Correspondence, 71, Political and Secret Letters from India, 14, and the Argyll Papers on microfilm, reel 312). Further accounts of the murder occur in F. Drew's *The Jummoo and Kashmir Territories*, London 1875; J. Duke's *Kashmir and Jammu, A Guide for Visitors*, second edition, 1910; A. Wilson's *Abode of Snow*, Edinburgh 1875; W. S. A. Lockhart and R. G. Woodthorpe's *The Gilgit Mission*, London 1889; and the *Edinburgh Review*, January 1892.

Chapters 5 and 6
The Tribes of the Hindoo Koosh by John Biddulph, Calcutta, 1890, gives no indication of the author's work in Gilgit. Fot this one must go to unpublished sources. I am indebted to Dr. Alder, again, for putting me on the track of Biddulph's journals, and to the Hereford County Record Office and the Hon. Edward Biddulph for letting me see them. They do not, however, afford a short cut as against a scrutiny of the official records in the India Office. (Political and Secret Letters from India, vols. 14, 18, 21, 23, 25 and 26; Political and Secret Memo, A18 1878 and 1881; the Lytton Papers and the Northbrook Papers, 1878–80). *The Journal of the Asiatic Society of Bengal* has an interesting description of a trip to the Gilgit valley by Captain H. C. Marsh in vol. LXV, 1876. For the Forsyth missions to Sinkiang see the bibliography in my *When Men and Mountains Meet*, London 1977.

Chapter 7
The starting point for a study of Kafiristan should be Dr. Schuyler Jones' two-part *Bibliography of Nuristan (Kafiristan) and the Kalash Kafirs of Chitral*, Copenhagen, 1969. It is far more than a mere record of sources and I am deeply indebted to Dr. Jones, in spite of failing to consult his work until this book was almost finished.

MacNair's paper on his *Visit to Kafiristan* is in *P.R.G.S.*, vol. VI, New Series, 1884, and is reproduced in the interesting pamphlet, *Memoir of William Watts MacNair*, by J. E. Howard, published in India but undated. Political and Secret Letters from India, vol. 39, gives the official attitude towards the journey and MacNair's detailed report is entitled *Confidential Report on the Explorations in part of Eastern Afghanistan and in Kafiristan during 1883*, Dehra Dun 1885. MacGregor is far better documented and I have used only published sources. His personality and the whole system of advancement come over strongly in *The Life and Opinions of Sir C. M. MacGregor*, edited by Lady MacGregor, London 1888. He is noticed in a number of contemporary memoirs and biographies, including A. V. Lyall's *Life of the Marquis of Dufferin and Ava*, London 1905, and P. M. Sykes' *The Right Hon. Sir Mortimer Durand*, London 1905. The fatal report, *The Defence of India*, was published in Simla, 1884. For a recent appraisal of MacGregor's work I have also consulted the article by Adrian Preston in the *Historical Journal*, vol. XII, 1969.

Chapters 8 and 9

The published account of the Lockhart Mission is a book to cherish. Entitled *The Gilgit Mission 1885-6* by W. S. A. Lockhart and R. G. Woodthorpe, 1889 it is extremely hard to come by, immensely long, thoroughly entertaining and illustrated with delightful photographs. I am indebted to the India Office Library for processing a photocopying order that far exceeded their regulations. Lockhart himself is referred to in many standard biographies of the period and has an entry in the *Dictionary of National Biography* and the *Dictionary of Indian Biography*, ed. C. E. Buckland 1906. His obituary is in the *Geographical Journal* (*G.J.*), vol. XV, 1900. Where MacNair and Lockhart left off in Kafiristan Sir George S. Robertson took over. For more information on some of the customs referred to by Lockhart I have used his *The Kafirs of the Hindu Kush*, 1896, also R. C. F. Schomberg's *Kafirs and Glaciers*, 1938.

The Elias biography referred to at the beginning of Chapter 9 is *Ney Elias, Explorer and Envoy Extraordinary in High Asia* by Gerald Morgan, London 1971. This is based on the voluminous Elias papers in the R. G. S. Archives. I have referred to these only for the journal of the Pamir journey 1885-6 and letter drafts, etc., of that period. Colonel Morgan has kindly made available the fruits of subsequent research including references to Elias in the Dufferin Papers. He has also provided a copy of Elias' *Official Report of a Mission to Chinese Turkestan and Badakshan in 1885-6* and the note by Sir S. Bayley *On the Pamir Question and the North East Frontier of Afghanistan*, London 1891.

Chapters 10, 11 and 12

There is a wealth of sources on the last years of the Gilgit Game. Recorded here are only those I have found particularly useful.

Sir Francis Younghusband badly needs a new biography; the existing one by George Seaver, 1952, scarcely does him justice. Nor do Younghusband's own works on the period, *The Heart of a Continent*, 1896, *The Light of Experience*, 1927, and *Wonders of the Himalaya*, 1924; the last was written for the young reader but the same popular and rather patronising style characterises all of them. The best appreciation of the man is probably that by Peter Fleming in *Bayonets to Lhasa*, 1961. One volume of his journal for the 1889 journey is in the R.G.S. archives but the others are missing. Instead there are his letters in Demi-Official Correspondence, vol. 3, in the India Office Records, his *Reports of a Mission to the Northern Frontier of Kashmir in 1889*, Calcutta 1890, and a report in *P.R.G.S.*,vol. XII, N.S. 1890. For the Pamirs journeys of 1890–91 there is an interesting letter to his father, dated August 20, 1891, amongst the papers in the possession of Dame Eileen Younghusband to whom I am most grateful. Reference has also been made to *P.R.G.S.*, vol. XIV, N.S., 1892 *G.J.*, vol. II, 1893, and the note by Sir S. Bayley referred to above; also to *Macartney in Kashgar* by C. P. Skrine and P. Nightingale, 1973. Useful sidelights on his travels of this period are shed by R. P. Cobbold in *Innermost Asia*, 1900, C. S. Cumberland in *Sport on the Pamirs and Turkestan Steppes*, London 1895, the Earl of Dunmore in *The Pamirs*, London 1893, and R. C. F. Schomberg in *Unknown Karakoram*, London 1936. The photograph of the Younghusband–Grombtchevski meeting was traced to the *Eastern and Western Review* of 1895. Leitner's *Asiatic Quarterly Review* is a good source for Grombtchevski's travels, especially vols. 2 and 3, N. S. His journey of 1889–90 was translated from the Russian by E. F. H. MacSwiney, Simla 1892. There are scattered references to his movements in *P.R.G.S.*, vol. IX, 1887, vol. XII, 1890, and vol. XIII, 1891, N. S., and in *G.J.*, vol. III, 1894. *High Road to Hunza* by B. Mons, 1958, sheds some light on his negotiations with Safdar Ali.

The thinking behind the re-establishment of the Gilgit Agency can be followed in Political and Secret Letters from India, vols. 57, 58 and 59. The account of the Hunza–Nagar campaign has been put together from five contemporary sources: *Where Three Empires Meet* by E. F. Knight, London 1894, *The Making of a Frontier* by A. Durand, London 1899 (and the comprehensive introduction to same by Dr. G. J. Alder in the recent Graz reprint), *Townshend of Kut and Chitral*, by E. Sherson, London 1928. Parliamentary Papers, Command No. 6621, *Correspondence relating to Operations in Hunza–Nagar* and last, but by no means least, the very personal letters of A. Durand amongst the papers of Sir H. M. Durand in the archives of the School of Oriental and African Studies, London. Dr. Alder directed my attention to them and again I am in his debt.

Chapters 13 and 14
In addition to the sources listed above for A. Durand, C. G. Bruce's *Twenty Years in the Himalayas*, London 1910, has been creamed for details of the poorly documented Chilas campaign. Chitral, bibliographically, is a very different matter. The fullest and most readable account of the siege is Robertson's own, *Chitral, the Story of a Minor Siege*, by Sir G. S. Robertson, 1898. Sherson's *Townshend of Kut and Chitral* as above, includes long extracts from the papers and letters of Townshend, while *With Kelly to Chitral* by W. G. L. Beynon, London 1896, was compiled from the letters of the author written to his mother at the time. There is also an account by Cosmo Stewart of the artillery's part in Kelly's March; it first appeared in *Blackwood's Magazine*, Nov. 1926, and has recently been included in *Tales of the Mountain Gunners* by C. H. T. MacFetridge and J. P. Warren. Edinburgh 1974. Both of the two Younghusbands who collaborated for *The Relief of Chitral*, London 1895, accompanied Low's division but it was Frank, who knew the Shandur route as well as anyone, who wrote the chapters on Kelly's March. Another contemporary account is H. C. Thomson's *The Chitral Campaign*, London 1895. More recently the story has been retold briefly by P. G. Fredericks in *The Sepoy and the Cossack*, London 1971, and with great spirit in *Much Sounding of Bugles* by John Harris, London 1975. Brigadier F. R. L. Goadby has kindly lent me a *Regimental History of 32nd Sikh Pioneers*, Calcutta, n.d.

For facts and figures I have relied on the *Official Account of the Chitral Expedition* by W. R. Robertson (no relation), Calcutta, 1898, and for official correspondence on that reproduced in Parliamentary Papers, Command no. 7864, relating to *Chitral, 1895*, and Command no. 8037, relating to the occupation of Chitral, 1896.

The last also includes correspondence relating to Afghan proceedings in Kafiristan. *The Pamirs and the Source of the Oxus*, 1896, was Curzon's great work but for the story of his travels in Dardistan it is necessary to turn the *Leaves from a Viceroy's Notebook and Other Papers*, 1926. An article by G. H. Bretherton in the *Contemporary Review*, vol. 74, 1898, gives an interesting picture of Gilgit towards the end of the century. Sources for Younghusband and Leitner are as given above, with the addition of Leitner's letter to *The Times* of Dec. 26, 1896.

II GENERAL BIBLIOGRAPHY

The bible for anyone interested in the Western Himalayas in the second half of the nineteenth century must be G. J. Alder's *British India's Northern Frontier 1865–95*, London 1963. Without it, this book could scarcely have been written. Dr. Alder's forty page bibliography renders any further attempt at a comprehensive list of sources redundant. The works listed below are merely those of general or peripheral interest which have not been mentioned in the Chapter Notes but which have provided facts or ideas.

BARKER, A. J. *Townshend of Kut*, London 1967.

BELLEW, H. W. *Kashmir and Kashgar*, London 1875.

BLACK, C. E. D. *Memoir of the Indian Surveys 1875–90*, London 1891.

BONVALOT, G. *Through the Heart of Asia*, London 1889.

CONWAY, W. M. *Climbing in the Karakoram Himalayas*, London 1894.

CURZON, G. N. *Russia in Central Asia*, London 1889.

DANIELLI, G. *La Esplorazione della Regione fra L' Himalaja Occidentale e il Caracorum*, Bologna 1934.

EDWARDES, M. *Playing the Great Game*, London 1975.

FAIRLEY, J. *The Lion River, The Indus*, London 1975.

GILLARD, D. *The Struggle for Asia 1828–1914*, London 1977.

GORDON, T. E. *The Roof of the World*, Edinburgh 1876.

HEDIN, S. *Southern Tibet*, Stockholm 1922.

HOLDICH, T. H. *The Indian Borderland 1880–1900*, London 1901.

—— *Gates of India*, London 1910.

KIPLING, R. *Kim*, London 1901.

—— *Departmental Ditties*, 18th edition, London 1904.

LANSDELL, H. *Chinese Central Asia*, London 1893.

MARAINI, F. *Where Four Worlds Meet*, London 1964.

MARVIN, C. *Russia's Advance towards India*, London 1882.

MASON, K. *Abode of Snow*, London 1955.

MASON, P. *A Matter of Honour*, London 1974.

SEVERIN, T. *The Oriental Adventure; Explorers of the East*, London 1976.

SHAW, R. *Visits to High Tartary, Yarkand and Kashgar*, London 1871.

STONE, S. J. *In and Beyond the Himalayas*, London 1896.

WOOD, J. *Journey to the Source of the Oxus*, Second Edition, London 1872.

See also p. 556 for an additional list of titles published since the text of this book was written.

Additional Note

ADDITIONAL NOTE

Much of relevance to the Western Himalayas has been published since the text of this book was written. The list of titles below is by no means exhaustive. Outstanding new biographies of William Moorcroft and Francis Younghusband merit particular attention. Unless stated otherwise, the place of publication is London.

ALDER, G. J. *Beyond Bokhara; The Life of William Moorcroft*, 1985.
ALLEN, CHARLES *A Mountain in Tibet; The Search for Mount Kailas etc.*, 1982.
AMAR KAUR JASBIR SINGH *Himalayan Triangle; A Historical Survey of British India's Relations with Tibet etc., 1765–1950*, 1988.
FRENCH, PATRICK *Younghusband; The Last Great Imperial Adventurer.* 1994.
HOPKINS, H. E. *Sublime Vagabond; The Life of Joseph Wolff – Missionary Extraordinary*, Worthing 1984.
HOPKIRK, PETER *Trespassers on the Roof of the World; The Road to Lhasa*, 1982.
——*The Great Game: On Secret Service in High Asia*, 1990.
INGRAM, EDWARD *The Beginning of the Great Game in Asia, 1828–34*, Oxford 1979.
KEAY, JOHN *The Honourable Company; A History of the English East India Company*, 1991.
MORGAN, GERALD *Anglo-Russian Rivalry in Central Asia 1810–95*, 1981
SHAHID HAMID, S. *Karakuram Hunza*, Karachi 1979.
SNELLING, JOHN *The Sacred Mountain*, 1983.
WALLER, DEREK *The Pundits; British Exploration of Tibet and Central Asia*, Kentucky 1990.

Index

Index